The Complete Rigger's Apprentice

SECOND EDITION

The Complete

RIGGER'S

APPRENTICE

SECOND EDITION

*Tools and Techniques for
Modern and Traditional Rigging*

BRION TOSS

Illustrated by Robert Shetterly

Incorporating *The Rigger's Apprentice* and *The Rigger's Locker*

McGraw-Hill Education

New York • Chicago • San Francisco • Athens • London • Madrid • Mexico City •
Milan • New Delhi • Singapore • Sydney • Toronto

8 9 LCR 23 22

ISBN: 978-0-07-184978-4

MHID: 0-07-184978-5

e-ISBN: 978-0-07-184977-7

e-MHID: 0-07-184977-7

Library of Congress Cataloging in Publication Data

Toss, Brion.

    The complete rigger's apprentice: tools and techniques

for modern and traditional rigging / Brion Toss; illustrated

by Robert Shetterly.

    p. cm.

    Includes bibliographical references and index.

      ISBN 978-0-07-184978-4

    1. Marlingspike seamanship. 2. Knots and splices.

    3. Masts and rigging.   I. Title

    VM531.T66 1997

    623.8'62–dc21.   97-20479

                                    CIP

McGraw-Hill Education books are available at special quantity discounts to use as premiums and sales promotions, or for use in corporate training programs. To contact a representative, please visit the Contact Us page at www.mhprofessional.com.

*This book is dedicated
to the memory of Nick Benton, Master Rigger*

Contents

Preface

30 years ago, with an old cable spool as a chair, and my workbench as a desk, I began to write the first version of this book. I wrote longhand, on a yellow legal tablet, slowly filling page after page with what I hoped and meant would become a primer on sailing vessel rigging. I wrote as much to refine and clarify my own meager understanding of the subject as to inform anyone else; even then I had an inkling of the vast scale of what there was to know about rigging, and how incomplete my own comprehension was. But I was also filled with an evangelical zeal. I wanted the world to know about this beautiful art.

In the years since, I have worked on hundreds (thousands?) of rigs. On some days, I seem to have acquired some level of competence. On other days, the learning curve is unbearably steep. On those days, to paraphrase Clifford Ashley, I feel that if I can just keep improving at this rate, and if my health holds out, I might someday manage to get a grasp of the fundamentals. Therefore, gentle reader, consider this new edition to be a work in progress. It is certainly an improvement on the previous edition —almost every page of my copy is marked with red ink—and in addition to corrections and evolutions you will find new ways of thinking about and working with rigging.

Some general bits of advice:

CROSS-POLLINATE

In the course of my career it has been my privilege to work with theater riggers, industrial riggers, arborists, timber framers, circus riggers, mountain climbers, etc., in addition to riggers of all types of sailing vessels. The particulars of each branch of the art vary widely, and not all of the insights in one field are applicable in another, but we all have a lot to learn from one another.

DO THE MATH

Many of my clients have been engineers or architects, and they have been unfailingly generous and patient in expanding my understanding of the design aspects of the art. Rueful admission: when I was in high school, there was only one class about which I said, "I'll never use this crap." That class was trigonometry. It turns out that you cannot be a competent rigger without some understanding of trigonometry.

TRUST/VERIFY

Whether you get your information from a professional, or someone down the dock, or YouTube, be sure of its validity before you put it into practice. Math can be a big help here, but so can discussion, direct experiment, and common sense. This advice (I pause here to wince) goes for some of the recommendations found in previous editions of this book. The current one as well, for all I know. You can be wrong about things you sincerely believe in. It is overwhelmingly likely that you are wrong about many things, right now. This can have a paralyzing effect, partly because it can be embarrassing, but mostly because, in rigging, people's lives are at stake; your beliefs translate directly to safety. Or not. That's why we have civilization, which at its best functions as a non-genetic means of preserving and transmitting aids to survival. Test results, engineering standards, theories, and algorithms are the left-brain means to this end. But don't underestimate the power of story, of anecdote. For instance: some electricians were rewiring a house. Their client, observing their work, saw that they were, um, selectively disregarding certain portions of the electrical code, specifically those sections that the city inspector was unlikely to check. When the client called them on this, the job boss said, "Come on, when was the last time you heard about someone being electrocuted by their *house*?" He just didn't understand that every line of that code was written in blood, that the reason that our houses are unlikely to electrocute us is that we have made formal note of things that have killed people, and seek to avoid them, with a further subtext being that the logic behind every line of construction code is not always immediately apparent to the casual observer.

Attend, then, to standards, to tradition. And do your best to work out the reasons behind the standards, to keep them alive, and to make them easier to pass on effectively. Which brings us to:

TEACH

I have traded in my legal pad for a laptop, but I still want to keep this gift moving. Teaching is a way to express a basic human need: helping to take care of others. Some people teach as a way of showing off, others because they actually can't do anything else, but the best teaching is an *aspect* of doing, and it benefits the teacher as well as the student; you simply cannot transmit a complex body of knowledge without organizing it, and you cannot organize it unless you understand its components to some degree, as well as the part each component plays in the whole, and even then you cannot teach it unless you can figure out an effective way to present it to someone who doesn't understand what you understand, and you can't do any of that unless you work harder at mastering your subject than you ever would if you weren't trying to teach it.

LEARN

We crave competence. The feeling of being good at something, of doing it well, is tremendously reward-ing. But *getting* good at something requires failure, sometimes a lot of failure, and that doesn't feel good at all. As if that weren't enough, our fellows are sometimes all too ready to offer a sarcastic "way to go" if we perform poorly. And even worse, it is so easy to delude ourselves with a comfortingly competent self-image, and it is painful when our actual abilities don't live up to that image.

But the sweet beauty of learning is too valuable to allow these obstacles to stand in our way. Did you know that "failure" derives from a Latin word that means "to deceive"? When we fail, we aren't lesser-than; we are on the wrong track, and we need to expend some effort to get on the right one. Setting goals is all very well, but it is only through practice—maybe arduous and lengthy—that we get on track. In the words of Archilocus, "We do not rise to the level of our expectations. We fall to the level of our training."

We likewise can learn to recognize sarcasm as rooted in insecurity, and to recognize that self-image is a placeholder by which we mark our progress, and which therefore needs to be as objective as we can manage. We can learn, in short, to detoxify the process of learning.

One of my students, a Coast Guard inspector, really had the hang of this. After taking a rig survey class, he had a charter boat taken out of service for what he now recognized as grievous safety issues. The owner said, "Wait a minute. Just last year you passed me with flying colors. My boat couldn't have gone downhill that far in just one year!" To which the inspector replied, "It's not about your boat, it's about me. And I reserve the right to be smarter than I used to be. And not as smart as I'm going to be."

As riggers, we do things that people trust their lives to. None of us is incapable of error. None of us can rest on our laurels. It is only through continuous learning that we can continue to approach our ideals. My hope is that this book is now a better tool, an aid in approaching those ideals.

BRION TOSS
Port Townsend, Washington

Forewords

LARRY PARDEY

I first met Brion Toss at the Port Townsend Wooden Boat Festival in 1979, where he and Nick Benton were giving a hands-on lesson in Liverpool splicing to a large group of enthusiastic sailors. As I watched them I could see the joy they derived from passing on the information and skills they'd learned from other, older riggers. And so goes the haphazard way of passing down practical skills, which is why these skills are so often lost unless some dedicated person will take the time and effort to commit his inherited knowledge to paper. When I learned that Brion was going to do just that I became impatient. His writing has always been scientific but humorous, the accompanying illustrations clear and concise. So I knew his book would allow many sailors, including myself, the creative satisfaction of making gear such as a new headstay, lazyjacks, or a jibnet from wire, rope, and a few thimbles. This handmade gear is a joy to the sailor's eye—strong, simple, and best of all, repairable—right on the deck of a sailing vessel. This means no traveling to find a hydraulic swaging machine operator, no running around hoping to find the perfect end fitting for the millimeter wire you bought in Tahiti when you have sailed to another country that uses fittings measured in inches.

Even more interesting to most of us is that if you rig your own boat you will save cruising funds. The cost of the wire and thimbles used for the standing rigging on our 30-foot, 17,500-pound cutter was only $350. If I hadn't spliced this wire myself I'd have had to pay an average of $21 to $25 for each 5/16-inch swage in addition to the cost of the wire. Readers of this book who have nimble fingers and slim pocketbooks will find they can outfit an efficient sailboat at a savings of several thousand dollars.

Beyond recording what the old-timers have taught him, Brion Toss keeps looking for new methods and materials that will combine the best of the old with the practicalities of the new. He has tested the strengths of different wire splices and swages and used this information to develop a smooth-entry Liverpool splice that averages 99 percent of the manufacturers' rated wire strength, a vast improvement over the 85 percent figure we used to use for hand-spliced eyes. When I heard about this fair-entry, high-strength splice, I had to learn how to do it before I made up the standing rigging for our new cruising boat, *Taleisin*. Fortunately, Brion published that section of this new book in *SAIL* magazine just when I needed it most.

Now, as I read the final manuscript for this book, I feel confident that most of the practical riggers' tricks will remain available to exercise and delight the fingers and eyes of the next generation of sailors.

September 1984

PETER H. SPECTRE

I first met Brion Toss a dozen or so years ago. He was demonstrating traditional rigging techniques at a wooden boat revivalist encampment down by the shores of Lake Union in Seattle, Washington.

He had a long length of rope stretched between two posts set in the ground, and he was worming, parceling, and serving, which is to say he was up to his elbows in pine tar and enjoying every drop of it.

Brion was also lecturing the crowd about his belief that the word "marlinspike" was an unfortunate corruption of "marlingspike" and must therefore be rooted out of the American nautical lexicon, now and forevermore. He was introducing his rigging posts as Emily and Wiley ("Post!" he shouted to the bewildered audience, "Now do you get it?") and his rigging vises as Old Shep and his sister Edna St. Vincent Belay. His act, which was half carefully constructed and half anarchistic, was a cross between Popeye dancing the hornpipe and a street mime imitating Zsa Zsa Gabor. It is my favorite memory of the man.

My favorite piece of memorabilia from Brion is a leather jacket he gave me a few years ago. It's a tad out of date—a garment with a past—but I love it nevertheless. For one thing, it smells of boatyards and rigging lofts, as it kept Brion warm while he learned the rigger's trade. For another, it has been customized with varnished star knots in place of the original buttons, a touch that reminds me of the work of Clifford Ashley, Cyrus Lawrence Day, Hervey Garrett Smith, and other writer-riggers of an earlier generation.

Writer-rigger. Now there's an interesting combination. Marlingspikes and manuscripts; pine tar and the pen. Who would ever imagine it? Yet within the broad nautical field there has always been a tradition of writing about rigging and a subgenre that could loosely be described as literature about the art of rigging.

No, I'm not talking about knot books. Those are a dime a dozen, and they are usually written by people who discovered how to tie a bowline yesterday and are trying, unsuccessfully, to describe the process in print today. Lots of drawings with bights and frayed ends, and arrows pointing this way and that, and not enough text to make them understandable to a maritime savant. "Insert A in B, loop it around C, and pull" is about as literary as the run-of-the-mill knot book will ever get.

Yet there is art in rigging, and there is art in describing what rigging is all about. No wonder that, among the classics in the genre, there are titles such as *The Arts of the Sailor* by Hervey Garrett Smith and *The Art of Knotting and Splicing* by Cyrus Lawrence Day. (Clifford Ashley was an artist, too, though not quite as highfalutin; his monumental work, superior to all others, was titled simply *The Ashley Book of Knots.*)

Smith, Day, Ashley—they were traditionalists who saw the understanding of rope and rigging as a continuum involving the drag of knowledge from the past into the present. Their additional responsibility, as they saw it, was to push that knowledge into the future, and in most respects, they were successful at it. But our times are different from their times. We have rope, of course, and they had rope, but ours is vastly different from theirs in both composition and manufacture, and therefore working with it is different. So, too, is describing how to work with it. The straight transfer of knowledge from the past to the present is not enough; with it must come an appreciation of the evolutionary, developmental nature of modern ropework and rigging. That is where Brion Toss, a traditionalist who can talk about the pluses and minuses of swaged terminals with the best of them, comes into the picture.

Brion Toss doesn't write knot books. Oh, sure, he has his diagrams and his arrows, and he will go on about shoving this rope end through that loop, but this is just the beginning, the jumping-off point for discussions about where this knowledge all came from and where it might be leading. Brion is a true writer-rigger, a legatee of the gentlemen of the past who saw the art of rigging as part history, part scholarship, part mythical anecdote, and part down-and-dirty grunt work, complete with rope burns in the palms, wire cuts on the fingers, and leather jackets permeated with pine tar and bear grease. His, like that of his predecessors, is the layered approach, with the concept of the knot or splice or rigging element at the top of discussion and the meaning of it all at the bottom. In between is all manner of relevant (and sometimes entertainingly irrelevant) material on purposes, origins, and applications. In some ways, Brion Toss's pitch is charming; in others it is profound. In no way is it boring.

April 1992

DES PAWSON

Once every few generations a writer comes along who adds to the real body of knowledge available to the ropeworking world, and here indeed is a first-class practical book on rigging. When I first read articles by Brion Toss in the American magazine *WoodenBoat*, I was excited by the prospect of a promised book. When it came, *The Rigger's Apprentice*, I was not disappointed. Eight years later when it was followed by *The Rigger's Locker*, I learnt even more. Brion is not a man to stand idle, for in combining these two books in the volume you now hold, he has continued to refine and add further information as he has discovered it.

The strength of Brion's writing is that he is a rigger who can and wants to write. He wields the marlingspike he speaks about, gets tar on his hands, and has to solve the problems that are given to him. He is also aware of the wide body of knowledge nearly lost, of innovators and innovations, and wishes to pass on to the world all those tips, tricks, and techniques that he has learnt from others. He is himself an innovator who is steeped in the past, taking from that past and adding to the future. He thinks through everything he writes about, analysing each twist of a wrist, each turn or hitch, so showing that he understands it, as well as the implications of why and how he can pass on this knowledge. All this is done with great joy, aided by the fine illustrations of Robert Shetterly, making a valuable aid to anyone who wishes to work on and understand their rigging. How lucky we are to be able to read this book and gain so much from it.

March 1997

Acknowledgments

The trouble with writing about a traditional art is that there are millions of people to thank. The list would fill pages even if I limited it to the riggers, sailors, boatbuilders, shopkeepers, truckers, and others from whom I received instruction in the course of my own apprenticeship.

So to pare the list down to those who have had a hand in the production of this book, many thanks to: Jim Bauer, Kathy Brandes, Maynard Bray, Ted Brewer, Nancy Caudle, Jane Crosen, Jon Eaton, Robin Lincoln, Tom McCarthy, Carl Meinzinger, Freeman Pittman, Peter Spectre, Roger Taylor, Emiliano Marino, and Jon Wilson. In the current edition, Janet Robbins and Molly Mulhern were extraordinarily patient, efficient editors. Special, loving thanks to my spouse, Christian Gruyè. Several thanks to the staffs of *SAIL* and *WoodenBoat* magazines, wherein portions of this book first appeared. Millions of thanks to all the rest.

Introduction

Rigging is the art of using knots and lines, either to move things or to keep them from moving. It can be put to such mundane tasks as guying telephone poles or raising the flag at city hall. But it is expressed in such monuments to engineering as an ocean racer's minimalist rod spiderweb or the awesome hoisting gear of a 300-ton shipyard crane. Somewhere between, there is a branch of the art, best expressed in classic and contemporary cruising vessels, that seeks to combine technological achievement, human scale, and a minimum of tools and expense. Knowledge of it enables one to sail more efficiently, with the help of fewer experts and fewer costly manufactured contrivances, and with the confidence and peace of mind that result from personal resourcefulness. It is called traditional rigging, and it is the subject of this book.

At the beginning I would like to emphasize the distinction between the terms "traditional" and "archaic." No amount of reverence for our maritime heritage will lead us to put tarred-hemp standing rigging on modern craft; time, engineering, and newer materials have rendered that practice obsolete for all but historical reproductions. On the other hand, many procedures and materials from the 19th century and earlier are still in use today, unchanged or only modified to meet new demands. Basic knots such as the Bowline, Anchor Hitch, and Figure-Eight are good examples, as are blocks, winches, seizings, lashings—well, the list is continued in the following pages. These items have survived because long, hard experience has shown that they can be counted on to do their jobs with minimum fuss and maximum

effect. It is up to the individual sailor to decide how much of the old to mix with the new; there is always some mixing, for even an ultramodern vessel carries elements of the past in its design and gear.

Because contemporary rigging is machine-made and technology-intensive, it tends by its very nature to exclude sailors from participation. If we find it difficult to be involved, it's a short step to assuming that we *can't* be involved. I once took some yacht club members on a tour of the *Elizabeth II*, a working replica of a 16th-century British trading ship. The huge, heavy masts and yards of such vessels are held up by little bits of string— the carefully made marline seizings that secure the lower ends of the shrouds. The yacht club members had all seen old ships before, but they'd never looked closely at the details of the rig. When they understood what these seizings were doing, they were literally open-mouthed in astonishment. It had never really occurred to them that a human being, with nothing more than a stick, a piece of marline, and a little skill, could make something just as structurally significant as a modern swaged terminal.

What a contrast this makes with the days of the original *Elizabeth*. Because rig materials were so fragile and degraded so quickly, the crew's daily activities were intimately involved with the life of the vessel, so much so as to blur the distinction between the two. Modern rig materials require far less of our time for maintenance, but precisely because they are so evolved, so inaccessible to simple manual skills, they can require far more of our intelligence and resourcefulness. We can still be the life of our boats, albeit at an intellectual remove.

Of course intelligence and resourcefulness are no guarantee of success. I once heard of a highly intelligent individual, a structural engineer, who was the skipper of a Great Lakes C-scow. Unlike some skippers, he liked to handle both the tiller and the mainsheet, instead of having another crewmember trim the main. But at 3:1, the sheet's mechanical advantage wasn't quite enough to work one-handed. But he was an engineer; it was easy for him to figure out that inverting the sheet tackle and adding a turning block would give him a 4:1 mechanical advantage, disregarding the slight extra friction from the extra block. Just to be sure, he had his mate, who was also a highly intelligent engineer, check his figures. No problem, his mate said, confirming his skipper's 33 percent increase in advantage.

They did the work—it took only a few minutes— and shortly thereafter started a race. On the way to the first mark, the skipper was able to prove empirically what the calculations had predicted. No surprise: He was an engineer. But when they rounded the mark and let the sheet out for a run, they suddenly realized that when you increase a tackle's advantage by 33 percent, you also have to make the line 33 percent longer to span the same distance. They hadn't. The Figure-Eight knot in the end of the sheet fetched up in the turning block with the boom half out, and the scow went over so hard it sheared the windvane off when the mast hit the water.

That's the trouble with intelligence: It doesn't always see far enough into the future. That's why technological fixes tend to spawn technological problems, which require more fixes, and so on.

Nor is resourcefulness always enough, even when it's coupled with intelligence. I once heard of a sailor whose mast folded in half at the spreaders when the backstay parted. The top half didn't break completely off, but hung above the deck, connected to the lower half by a thin strip of aluminum. It would have been suicide to climb up there and cut it away. Pulling it down from deck level didn't seem any safer. So the skipper sent the crew below and got out the assault rifle he had on board (he was cruising off Ethiopia and felt it prudent to borrow the gun from a friend). Reclining in the cockpit, he set the rifle on single shot and proceeded to blow his mast away.

And it worked.

Certainly the skipper gets points for resourcefulness—it takes a flexible mind to see a Kaloshnikov as a potential rigging tool. But this success masks a failure: The skipper had recently replaced the jibstay after finding broken wires in it. He had not replaced any other standing rigging—even though it was all the same age and had endured the same relative loads—because nothing was breaking yet. But prudence indicates that the failure of the jibstay should be considered an indicator of the state of the rest of the gang.

That's the trouble with resourcefulness. It doesn't address what might have been. That's why it can easily degenerate into innovative-Band-Aids-as-a-way-of-life.

Successful innovation, in rigging or anything else, starts with understanding that a given question or problem is always part of a greater, more complex system. An appropriately context-based approach will automatically help weed out dysfunctional responses and encourage useful ones. Three steps I like to follow are:

1. Adapt the Traditional

Old rigging procedures tend to stick around, even in the face of radical changes in design and materials. They survive because they are effective and adaptive, even in circumstances completely alien to their origins. Consider, for example, bungee cord. Remarkable, handy stuff, with no precedent in the history of rigging. Like all other cordage, it can only be put to work once you attach it to something. Unfortunately it is so intractably slippery that old standby knots, like the Bowline, crawl right out of it. Hence the variety of clunky mechanical terminals and the corresponding lack of versatility—you can't readily adjust length or eye size as you can with a knot.

Enter the Angler's Loop (Figure 3-19), a simple old knot developed in the days of presynthetic fishing line. It was perfect for gut, and it turned out to be equally well-suited to extremely springy modern monofilaments. This is a rare thing for an old knot, but this one goes ones step further, and is happy with bungee, too.

If you're going to adapt the old, you have to know it. This can mean devoting yourself to the study of what might seem hopelessly outdated ideas. But think of this study as building a database, one that will reward you with maximum versatility. It's no coincidence that sailors well-steeped in traditional skills are the most valuable ones to have aboard in a modern boat emergency.

2. Invent the New

If you explore the old and come up dry, at least you'll know that you'll be inventing, not *re*-inventing. Now you can go to work with an informed resourcefulness, free to find the truly new, and, with your tradition-bred prudence, the truly workable.

People have been innovating for a long time, so genuine novelties are rare. But there are still some doozies coming out. One of my favorites is an item in Chapter 12 that also involves bungee cord. It's called Tom Cook's Internal Bungee Snubber (Figure 12-6), and it's the kind of item that is so good it has no competition. So new materials can be opportunities as well as challenges.

It's always good to assume that any solution to a problem—whether new, old, or a combination of the two—will require some effort on your part to:

3. Work Out the Bugs

Continuing the bungee theme, there was once a sailor, sailing in choppy waters, who'd hung a kerosene-filled anchor lamp from his topping lift. He'd secured it from swinging with a long piece of bungee cord, attached to the lamp at one end and the stern of the boat with the other. This involves less tension than a piece of rope would have generated, and was less likely to jar the lamp. Unfortunately it also let the lamp move around enough to loosen the bottom shackle on the topping lift. When the pin popped out, the lamp came zinging to deck, striking the sailor and spewing flaming kerosene all over the cockpit. With great presence of mind, the sailor picked up what was left of the lamp and threw it as hard as he could astern, neglecting, however, to detach the bungee cord. The fire-trailing lamp roared into the night, hung suspended for a moment against the stars, and then roared back to the cockpit, there to spew still more flaming kerosene. Fortunately, both sailor and boat escaped without serious damage, leaving us all with the lesson that a little novelty can be a dangerous thing.

An old saying has it that there's "a short splice for every sailor, a long splice for every ship"; I trust the reader will understand that my personal rigging style is reflected in the following pages. Given time and experience, riggers can—indeed, properly ought to—establish their own variations and preferences, making their own unique contributions to the context of tradition. Toward that end, I hope to provide enough procedures, principles, and knowledge of the standard materials to let the reader deduce the *sense* of rigging. That half-intuitive sense, once gained, can guide one's own innovations.

I am writing this Introduction some 13 years after the first publication of *The Rigger's Apprentice*. In the course of those years I've run a bit of cordage and wire through my loft, hung from a lot of masts, and waved good-bye from a lot of docks and decks. All those experiences changed and expanded my perspective. So when it came time to rewrite *The Apprentice*, it changed and expanded, too.

Much of the new material comes from folding in the contents of my second book, *The Rigger's Locker*. But much of it, like the section on "exotic" braided-rope splicing, is truly new, added because its absence would have too seriously compromised the apprenticeship.

Much of the old material, though polished a bit for this edition, is the same unapologetically outdated stuff it has always been. Like a good martial art, it is still breathtakingly effective, still demands skill, discipline, and intelligence on the part of its practitioners, and will still get you through tight spots when more modern concepts jam and fail.

Because this is only a book, and not five years with a master, one will find a limited sort of apprenticeship here. It may propel you to work up a new gang of rigging for your boat; it will improve your handling of rope, wire, and rig; and if you ever have to improvise a jury rig, it will stand you in good stead. If you like what you see here and want to continue, then *find a rigger* to teach you more. Watch, badger, cajole, do scut work, even pay for lessons: Learn.

If your marlingspike expertise is past the apprentice stage already, consider this a collection of variations on old themes, many little-known, that you might find useful. Tradition involves constant upgrading.

While writing this book, I have tried always to keep in mind the virtues of resourcefulness, simplicity, and enduring strength; they are conducive to good rigs, and to happiness. So I trust that what follows will be not only a collection of procedures, but an enjoyable way of proceeding.

The Good Luck Knot (front view): elegant, graceful, useful.
See page 344 for an explanation.

CHAPTER 1

A Rigging Primer

Welcome. This apprenticeship begins with a few of the basic artifacts, principles, and procedures that define and make possible the art of rigging. They're simple, but using them to good effect requires thought and care.

ROPE

Rope is elegant, ubiquitous, ancient. A creature of tension, it exists to be stretched between opposing forces. It is a highly evolved tool which, in its myriad sizes, materials, and constructions, can meet every sort of rigging need. Limitations are likely to be on the part of the user; it is for us to develop skill appropriate to the tool.

Start simply by observing rope at work. In shipyards, farmyards, and construction sites it transmits power and performs its many jobs. Look at the size

of the rope used, how it is made, how it looks when new and worn, how it is handled by the people who make a living with it.

Before continuing with this chapter, go to a chandlery and get a roll of nylon twine (36-48 thread), 50 feet of ⅜-inch-diameter, double-braid Dacron rope, and 50 feet of ⅜-inch, three-strand spun Dacron rope. Each strand of the latter is made up of short polyester fibers that have been spun together into yarns, much as wool or cotton is. The

clerk will measure off 50 feet of rope from a coil or spool, but by cutting it, she or he will transform it into a 50-foot *line*; usually, *rope* is a general term and a description of the raw material, while a *line* is what you make from rope. Thus a halyard is a line that raises sails, and a sheet is a line that trims them. There are exceptions to this terminology, so you can ignore the oft-repeated pedantry that "there are no ropes aboard a vessel." Anyone who says that isn't familiar with a tiller rope, manrope, footrope, bell-rope, or the roping on sails.

Rope as Battery: Coiling and Stowing

Rope in use is in clean, linear tension—an exercise in geometry. Rope that's not in use is a perverse creature, an incipient tangle, a rat's nest waiting to happen. If you let it have its way—and too many people do—you're liable to find yourself in situations that are at best annoying and at worst dangerous. Think of each unused portion of rope as a battery, upon which you might need to draw at an instant's notice.

When you go to build your battery, it helps to understand the material it's made of. Three-strand rope, for example, is usually right-laid—its strands spiral to the right—and is made with just enough twist to hold the three strands together without rendering the rope too stiff to use. These structural details prove significant when making a coil.

As the chapter opening illustration shows, the turns of a coil should be regular and even, to dis-

Figure 1-1. *The turns of a coil will not lie fair without a slight twist put into each*

courage the loops from intermingling. When coiling onto your hand, develop rhythm and a sweeping motion for minimum effort, smoothness, and a style conducive to contemplation. Heavy lines are coiled on deck, then either hung up or turned over so they're ready to run. Leave the ends hanging below the coil so they won't become entangled in the turns. Now notice that as you coil you must impart a slight twist to each loop to lay it neatly against the others (Figure 1-1); no twist means independent-minded loops. This is the reason for that ancient, seldom-explained admonition to "always coil clockwise." When the coil runs out, all those little twists have to go somewhere, and if you coil clockwise (Figure 1-2A), right-laid three-strand rope can unlay a bit to absorb them. A counterclockwise coil in right-laid rope can look just as neat, but when it's stretched out, the twists you put in will only tighten an already pretty firm lay, and you're liable to end up with kinks and hockles (Figure 1-2B). Conversely, in the unlikely event that you come up against left-laid rope, be sure to coil counter-clockwise.

In any rope, make the largest loops you conveniently can, or the largest ones that won't drag on the deck if height is limited, so that there will be the fewest total turns and fewer twists to absorb.

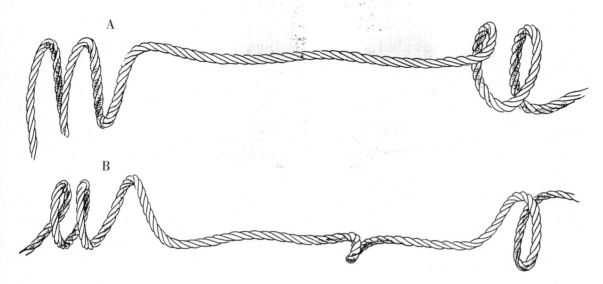

A

B

Figure 1-2A–B. *Coil right-laid rope clockwise (A) . . . because if you coil it counterclockwise, the lay tightens further when the line is uncoiled, resulting in kinks (B).*

Alternate Hitch Coiling   Braided rope presents a special problem: its "lay" runs in both directions, so the twists have nowhere to go no matter which way you coil. This problem has been the source of so many crises that some sailors, finding that a heap on the deck is less liable to foul, don't coil at all. But this approach is not satisfactory either, as a stray wave or stumbling crewmember can reveal. The best solution is Alternate Hitch Coiling, in which regular turns that impart twists in one direction are alternated with hitches that impart twists in the other direction (Figure 1-3). The twists cancel each other out, resulting in a kink-free line. Alternate Hitch Coiling is also the method to use for wire rope, garden hoses, electrical cable, and other lay-less lines. But beware: If an end gets accidentally passed

Figure 1-3. *Alternate Hitch Coiling, the best method for braided rope, alternates regular clockwise turns with Half Hitches. To make the latter, grasp the rope with the back of your hand toward you and turn palm toward you as you bring your hands together.*

through the coil, a string of overhand knots—not just the usual tangle—results (see the end of Chapter 11, "The Lovers").

On belayed lines, another important way to avoid hockles is always to coil away from the pin or cleat. That way, any twists you do impose will be worked out as you move toward the end.

Securing a Coil   Once all the turns are neat and pretty, you need to take steps to keep them that way. On a vessel, this usually means hanging them on a pin or cleat, either directly or, more likely, by reach

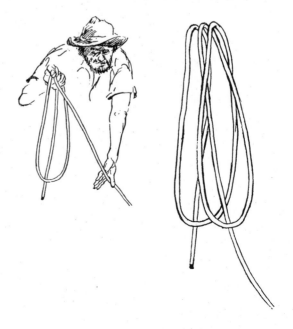

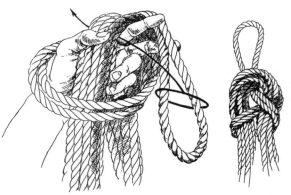

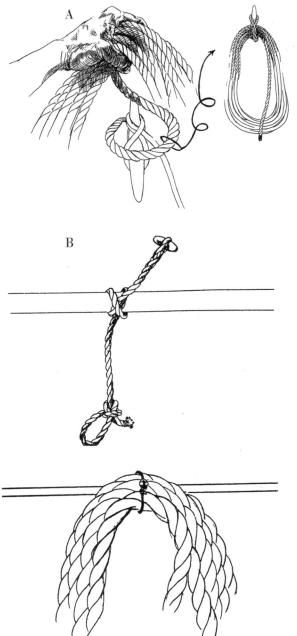

Figure 1-5. *The Bight Coil Hitch. Bring the last turn up to form a long bight. Pass the bight down, and wrap it around the coil, then over its own turn, and finally through the coil. Note that the wrap is made from right to left, to form a clockwise loop at the start. This makes for a fairer start.*

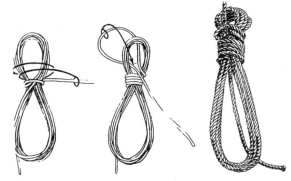

Figure 1-6. *The Gasket Coil Hitch. Using a long working end, make several wraps around the head of the coil, each wrap lying atop the one previous. Always start the wraps as with the Bight Coil Hitch, above, so that the turns have a fair start. Finish by passing a bight through the coil, then dropping it over the top.*

When using this coil for a belayed line, always make the wraps with the standing part; if you make them with the end, it is easier, but the turns of the coil will deform from the weight of the rope when it is hanging.

Figure 1-4A–B. *Securing a coil on a pin (A). To secure a large coil, hang it from a separate, toggled bit of line that is hitched or seized to a sheer pole (B).*

Figure 1-7. *To secure large lines and wire rope for long-term storage, coil them and bind with small stuff at regular intervals.*

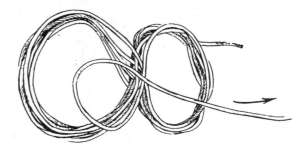

Figure 1-8. *A figure-eight coil will run clear even at high speed. It is always made on deck rather than in hand. Believe it or not it was only coincidence that made Figure 1-8 a figure eight.*

ing through the coil, twisting a bight near the belay, then putting that bight over the coil and jamming it down on the pin or cleat (Figure 1-4A), or by making a round turn with the (untwisted) bight. This is the best method for braided rope, or for very stiff twisted rope. When there's a great large amount of line to deal with, as on the halyards of a gaff-rigged vessel, it's best to toggle the coil to a sheer pole with a separate piece of line (Figure 1-4B).

Spare lines can be coiled and hung up out of the way with a Bight Coil Hitch (Figure 1-5), a very quick and tidy method. More security can be obtained with a Gasket Coil Hitch (Figure 1-6), which is good for working lines as well as for spare ones, either hung up or stowed below. Note that the coil is finished using turns of the standing part, not the end. That way the weight of the hanging coil doesn't deform the turns. To stow very large lines and wire rope below, the best method is to tie small stuff at regular intervals around the circumference of the coil (Figure 1-7).

Letting It Run   When it's time to put a coil to use, lay it face down on deck—that is, with standing part uppermost. When you cast off and let the line run, guide it by letting it run through your hand above the coil. This minimizes the whipping-around of the turns as they come out, and gives you some control should a tangle appear. For those gaff halyards or other long lines, it's a good idea to prepare for run-

ning by converting the regular coil, which can be hung up but might run foul, into a figure-eight coil (Figure 1-8), which can't readily be hung up but will run clear even at high speed. In every instance, even when the line is apparently securely belayed, keep your extremities out of the coil; getting yourself jammed upside-down into a halyard block is a nuisance and an annoyance.

TWO MORE TOOLS

There are many tools associated with ropework, but only three are truly indispensable: rope, the marlingspike, and the rigging knife. The latter two in use reveal characteristics and properties of rope in much the same way that hammer and saw teach a carpenter to understand wood.

Snap-On Spikes

Snap-On, makers of seriously high-quality tools, is under the delusion that they produce three sizes of scratch awls. What they actually make are three sizes of small marlingspikes with a taper very similar to the classic Drew pattern. The steel in these alleged awls is very hard and highly finished; all a sailor has to do is file the point into an acceptable, rounded, not-too-sharp "duckbill taper" and drill a lanyard hole in the plastic handle. Not as classy as having the real thing machined up, but an excellent tool nonetheless. The middle or large sizes are good for the average yacht.

The late Nick Benton, master rigger of extraordinary talent, turned his mind to every aspect of rigging. Appalled by the blunt clubs sold as marlingspikes these days, Nick analyzed the proportions of classic Drew spikes, and came up with the accompanying diagram. "X" refers to the diameter of wire you'll be working with. A spike for ⅜-inch (9.5 mm) wire, for example, would be 9 inches (229 mm) long, with a diameter of ⁹/₆₄ inch (3.6 mm) at the widest part of the "duck taper" at the tip.

This design is suited to more than splicing; it will let you get the point into shackles of a size you're likely to use with ⅜-inch (9.5 mm) wire. There'll be enough meat that you won't have to worry so much about bending or breaking the spike. For most yachts, a spike scaled to ⁵/₁₆-inch (8 mm) wire—7½ inches (191 mm) long—is appropriate.

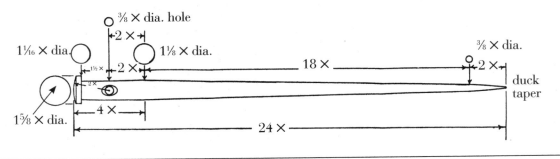

The Marlingspike

All of rigging—right up through its most abstract engineering complications—is based on principles and procedures relating to this tool. It is used for pulling seizings and lashings tight, making splices, loosening jammed knots, and tightening shackles. It's also called on to function as a crowbar, wrench, hammer, weapon, and musical instrument (ting!), so it pays to have a good one. By "good" I mean that it:

• Is made of smooth, hard steel, either carbon or stainless;

• Has a long taper and small flattened point for easier splicing, prying, and such; and

• Has a lanyard hole for tying the tool to your belt or rigging bag so that when you are working aloft, it does not accidentally become a weapon (thud) or a musical instrument (ting! splash!).

Length depends on the job and individual taste; 6 to 10 inches is a good range for shipboard use. Many people like the folding rigger's knife-spike combination, but I don't; a spike is too often needed in a hurry when you don't have both hands free.

Fishery supply stores are the source for conventional spikes, but the ones available today are usually stubby things. If you want to make your own, see the accompanying sidebar "Universal Marlingspike Proportions."

Note that, in a shop near Port Townsend, a very talented smith named Richard Soine is now producing Drew-style spikes. You can get them through our shop (see Sources and Resources).

The Rigging Knife

This is the spike's complement, a specially designed blade that is equally suited to cutting heavy rope

---

Figure 1-9. *The marlingspike, rigging's most essential tool.*

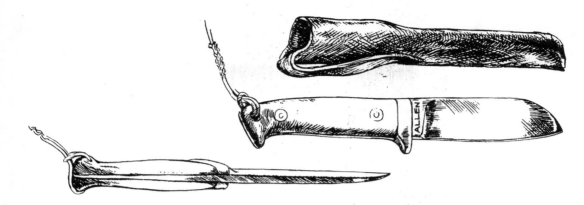

Figure 1-10. *The rigging knife is a specialized blade intended for rough use. A sturdy, molded sheath keeps it safe and secure.*

or trimming light seizings. The one shown above is of near-ideal design, incorporating some important features:

- A heavy, broad-backed blade. The neatest, quickest way to cut rope with a knife is to use a mallet to pound the knife through. Ordinary knives don't stand up well to this treatment, or to heavy shipboard or loft use in general. Serrated knives are popular these days, because they are so good at cutting rope. Trouble is, they're only good at cutting rope; a rigging knife is just as likely to be called upon for shaving, chipping, or prying on everything from plastic to lead. The back of the blade can be used as a seam-rubbing tool for canvas work and can be rubbed back and forth over the surface of wire rope to remove meathooks. You may need to round the edges of the back of the blade a bit, if they're too sharp for this work. Use a fine file, followed by fine sandpaper.
- The point is fine enough to reach into tight spots or for delicate work, but blunt enough so you're not liable to poke yourself accidentally some dark and stormy night.
- The blade is slightly curved. Most rigger's knives are flat-bladed, but a little "belly" makes for easier sharpening and slicing, and it lets you cut rope on a flat surface, since the tangent point is

aft of the tip, even with the presence of a finger guard.

- Like the spike, a good knife needs a lanyard hole. And again, avoid folding models; they're all right in the shop, but afloat, and especially aloft, you often need a knife one-handed, and now. A good knife and spike combination comes from the Myerchin company. You'll find their products at many chandleries. Pricier-but-worth-every-penny knives can be gotten from custom makers.

SMALL STUFF—SPIKE KNOTS, SERVICE, SEIZINGS, AND CONSTRICTORS

You'll find a multitude of uses for the following Knots, Service, Seizings, and Constrictors.

Marlingspike Hitch

It is difficult—even painful—to put much tension on twine or small-diameter rope using only bare hands. But cordage necessarily relies on tension, both for holding things in place and for making knots secure. The handiest solution to this problem is to attach to the twine some other, more comfortable-to-grip object, and then haul on that.

The traditional knot for this purpose is called the Marlingspike Hitch. It isn't much, just a Slip-knot made around a spike, but consider this: The Viking longboats of roughly 300 B.C. to 800 A.D., vessels capable of navigating the open ocean, were held together, partially or entirely, by linen twine

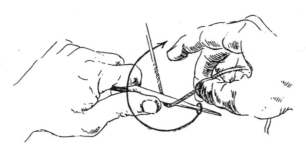

Figure 1-11A. *The Marlingspike Hitch. Hold line between thumb and middle fingers of one hand. With other hand, lay spike across line and pivot it in a full circle, ending with the point behind the standing part.*

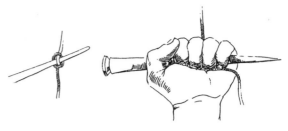

Figure 1-11C. *The completed knot.*

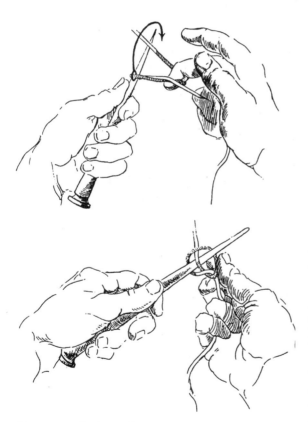

Figure 1-11B. *In mid-pivot, snag the standing part close to the spike with the tip of your middle finger. This makes it easy to grab (with thumb and forefinger) the bight of line on top of the spike and to pass it over the end of the spike.*

lashings. Each lashing was hove taut with this stick-in-hitch procedure, which the Vikings called "marling"—hence "marlingspike" (commonly but with less regard for linguistic antecedents spelled without the "g"), "marline (n)," and incidentally, "mooring." Rivets, nails, glue, and bolts eventually replaced lashings as hull fastenings, but the point remains that flimsy, inexpensive bits of twine can be made structurally significant with tension. With the advent of materials like Spectra, we have seen a sharp resurgence in the use of this and other hitches, because very high loads can now be put onto extremely small, slick line.

The amount one can save in chrome-plated fittings alone can make spike knots worthwhile, and in an emergency they might be a sailor's only recourse. Good knots to know, even if you're not planning to raid the coast of England.

The single version of this knot has been all that anyone needed for a few thousand years, but today we sometimes need a double version for dealing with very small, very strong synthetic line. When in doubt, use a double. To tie it, start as though for a single Marlingspike Hitch, but pass the standing part around the tip of the spike twice, before completing the knot as usual.

The Marlingspike Hitch is used to draw up a variety of knots. Some of these knots are marvels of intricacy, but we'll start with a simple one. Snub the end of some twine under two or three turns of its own standing part, around a piece of rope or wire rope (Figure 1-12). Make your hitch, and, exerting even tension, wind on a series of tight, tangent turns. That's "service," a means of protecting sails and rigging from chafe. Service is frequently seen over splices; on shrouds, especially where headsails come into contact with them; on mooring lines where they pass through chocks; and on grommets that go around rope-stropped blocks. When sealed with tar, service prevents rot and corrosion in the steel rigging it covers. Made over Spectra, it protects that material from ultraviolet as well as chafe. Served Spectra is basically immortal.

Service

Service is properly applied, as shown in Figure 1-12A, B, over a bed of twine "worming" and tarred canvas "parceling," usually with a specialized tensioning device called a serving mallet (see Chapter 6),

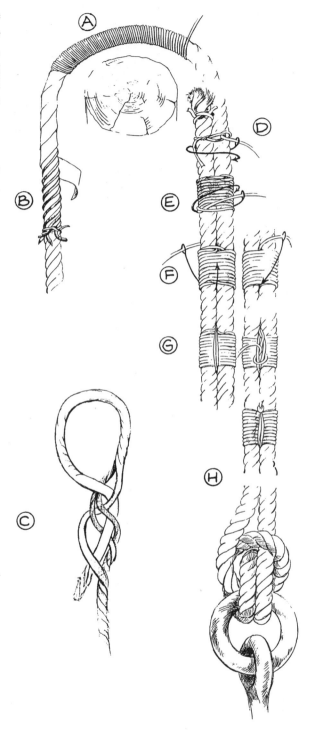

Figure 1-12A. *Service applied tightly, with the aid of a Marlingspike Hitch, provides waterproofing and protects rope from chafe.*

Figure 1-12B. *Worming is set tightly, filling the spaces where moisture could gather. Parceling of tarred canvas or friction tape provides waterproofing and smooth bedding for service. Worming, parceling, and serving are treated more fully in Chapter 6.*

Figure 1-12C. *Structure of rope-yarn splice needed to start Round Seizing.*

Figure 1-12D. *Make splice and pass end through eye, forming Slipknot around legs of line to be seized.*

Figure 1-12E. *Wind on tight turns, as with service, binding legs together. When seizing is roughly square, half-hitch at bottom and proceed to make riding turns over first layer.*

Figure 1-12F. *Back at the top, pass the end through the eye of the rope-yarn splice and make two snug crossing or frapping turns.*

Figure 1-12G. *Finish with a Flat Knot on the back side of the seizing. Haul the knot tight and cut the end off close.*

Figure 1-12H. *A Round Seizing is used here to supplement an Anchor Hitch.*

but a marlingspike will do in a pinch. One might say it is used with absence of mallet. For more on service, see Chapter 6.

As turns of service are taken, the hauling part shortens. When it becomes too short, the hitch is capsized back into a straight length that in a few more turns becomes part of the service itself. This capsizing calls to notice a hidden characteristic of the Marlingspike Hitch. Notice that the direction from which strain comes on the knot minimizes any tendency for it to jam. To prove this for yourself, make the knot and anchor both ends. When it is pulled on from the wrong direction, it tends to slip around to one side of the spike and jam there. But if pulled the other way, it will remain stable, and disappear without any fuss once the spike is removed. Be careful, then, to make the hitch as shown.

Seizings

Now consider seizings, a more sophisticated variety of binding knots than service. Seizing is defined in *Steel's Elements of Mastmaking, Sailmaking, and Rigging* (see Bibliography) as "joining two ropes, or the ends of one rope together, etc., by taking several close turns of small rope, line, or spun yarn around them."

That's right: A seizing is basically service made around two or more parts. But the function is different, since a seizing does not just sit on a line—it must hold separate lines together against lengthwise or lateral strain. There are dozens of specialized seizings, but for general use the preferred knot is the Round Seizing. It starts with a layer of "round turns," on top of which is laid a protective layer of "riding turns," and finally a tightening finish of "crossing" or "frapping turns" (Figure 1-12E, F). The rigger's way to secure the end is with a Flat Knot (Figure 1-12G).

As with service, each turn of a seizing is hauled tight with the aid of a marlingspike, but with a seizing one pulls harder across the face than around the corner. This keeps the rope from twisting as much from the force of the turns. The riding turns should be tight, but not be so tight that they displace the round turns. The importance of strong, consistent tension will soon become apparent; nothing looks or works worse than a slack or lumpy seizing.

The Round Seizing is ideal for ditty bag, water bucket, bosun's chair, deadeye, and many other lanyards, as well as for joining grommet, shell, sheave, and thimble together for a rope-stropped block (see Figure 2-22). What's more, it can be used in combination with other knots for added security. As an example of the latter, consider the Anchor Hitch (see Chapter 3) with the end seized to the standing part. This is neat, strong, and easily cast off to stow the anchor or to shorten the rode if it becomes chafed. When made on wire rope (see Round Seizing, Chapter 6), seizings can provide strength and security to rival any other terminal. But when made on rope, no matter how tightly and how well, they will slip under heavy lengthwise loads. This is because, unlike wire rope, fiber rope shrinks significantly in diameter in a heavy load. Spectra is even worse, because it is also very slick. Use seizings on rope with caution, and only for lateral loads.

No maintenance is needed for temporary seizings, but it's an important consideration when you want your work to last. Rope rots, but as with wood or wire, regular inspection and maintenance will prolong its working life. If a stretch of service receives excessive chafe, replace it, then double-serve (two layers) or leather that spot to ease the problem. Seizings, too, can suffer from chafe or accidental cuts, but most often they and service are most affected by water, sun, and wind. See Chapter 6 for preservative mixes to apply to seizings and service.

Materials Tarred nylon seine twine makes excellent seizings, but extra care must be taken to pull hard enough to remove initial elasticity. Used as service, it holds up well but is vulnerable to sunlight, so regular slushing with a preservative mix is extra important.

Marline is the traditional material for seizings, but has given way almost entirely to the much more durable tarred nylon. If nylon isn't available, look for marline made from hemp or linen. Avoid jute or sisal.

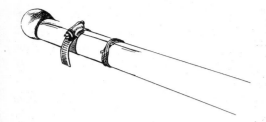

Figure 1-13. *The old and the new side by side on a sprung tiller: John Henry versus the steam hammer, the Constrictor versus the hose clamp.*

Constrictors

There are times when you'll want to make a more temporary seizing. For this, nothing beats the Constrictor Knot, a convenient, relentlessly secure way to bind parcels, to keep rope ends from unlaying, or to hold things in place for the application of permanent seizings. To know the knot is to constantly find uses for it (Ashley recommends it for everything from flour sacks to atomizer bulbs). When drawn up sufficiently tight it is an amazing thing, at least as valuable as the kingly Bowline. It is by no means a new knot, just a neglected one. But then, old knots never die; they just wait for us to come to our senses. For example, hose clamps seem to be the emergency recourse of choice for binding cracked tillers, spars, boathooks, etc. Once I even saw one on the end of a raveling line. The prevailing attitude about them is that though they are expensive, time-consuming to apply, snag on everything, and look awful, they're better than anything else for temporary repairs, right?

Wrong. For all the above jobs, and for hundreds of others besides, hose clamps can do little that Constrictor Knots can't—including clamping hoses. A Single or Double Constrictor made with a piece of job-scaled nylon or polyester twine is a quick, easy, unobtrusive, durable, and essentially free way to bind things together. If the Bowline is the King of Knots, surely the Constrictor is the Queen.

In recent years, sailors and landspeople alike have been coming to their senses in sufficient numbers that a Single Constrictor Knot is no longer a rarity. But the Double Constrictor still is. The

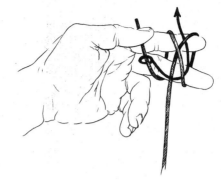

Figure 1-14A. *To tie a Single Constrictor with the end, make a crossed round turn, crossing from right to left. Bring the end up on the left side of the standing part, then lead it over to the right and under the crossing point, away from you.*

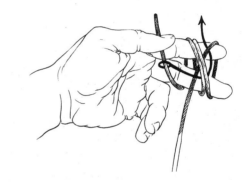

Figure 1-14B. *The Double Constrictor gets an extra crossing turn, parallel with and to the left of the first. The end goes under three parts as it passes under the crossing point.*

Double is for those situations where extra strength and security is a must, as for semi-permanent lashings, whippings, or for large gluing jobs where a hose, "C," or other kind of clamp might be unavailable or too bulky. The double is also more secure in slick twine, especially when it's waxed.

Either the Single or Double Constrictor can be tied with the end (Figure 1-14A,B) when you need to fasten it around a ring, stanchion, spoke, etc.

But whenever possible—whenever you can make the knot and then drop it over the

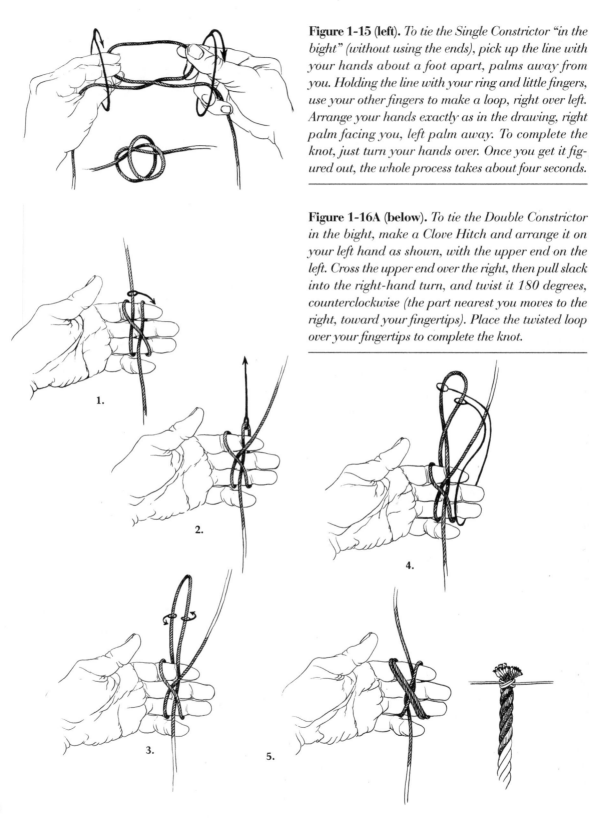

Figure 1-15 (left). *To tie the Single Constrictor "in the bight" (without using the ends), pick up the line with your hands about a foot apart, palms away from you. Holding the line with your ring and little fingers, use your other fingers to make a loop, right over left. Arrange your hands exactly as in the drawing, right palm facing you, left palm away. To complete the knot, just turn your hands over. Once you get it figured out, the whole process takes about four seconds.*

Figure 1-16A (below). *To tie the Double Constrictor in the bight, make a Clove Hitch and arrange it on your left hand as shown, with the upper end on the left. Cross the upper end over the right, then pull slack into the right-hand turn, and twist it 180 degrees, counterclockwise (the part nearest you moves to the right, toward your fingertips). Place the twisted loop over your fingertips to complete the knot.*

1.

2.

3.

4.

5.

constrictee—tie Constrictors in the bight (Figures 1-15 and 1-16), a faster method.

Bear in mind that the Double does not draw up as easily as the single; work out as much slack as you can before pulling on the ends. And be sure none of the turns are twisted. The best way to tighten a Constrictor is to hitch a spike, stick, or the like to each end. Pull. With heavy nylon twine you can exert even more force by bracing one stick between your feet and holding the other with your hands (Figure 1-17). Make a wish. For extremely tight Constrictors made with rope for large jobs (splinting a broken boom, for instance), position the constrictee between two sheet winches and crank away. No matter what the scale or tension, always arrange the knot so that its Overhand Knot portion lies over a convex surface, or on a corner of a flat-surfaced item.

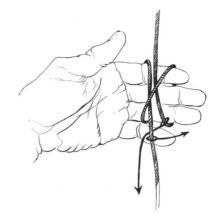

Figure 1-16B. *Tying the Double Constrictor using a Clove Hitch with the lower end on the inside.*

Turk's Head from Single Constrictor

Moving aside from strict utility for the moment, try making the circular braid known as a Turk's Head from a Single Constrictor. When doubled or tripled, this knot makes a decorative ring for ditty bags, bellropes, bottles, wrists, oars, etc.

To turn a Single Constrictor into a Turk's Head, arrange the knot around your left-hand fingers and open it up as shown. Pass the upper end down behind your fingers, up on the left side of the standing part, then pass it under, over, and under as shown, tucking up and to the right. Double and triple the knot by leading the end back into the knot, parallel with the standing part. A four-lead, three-bight knot results.

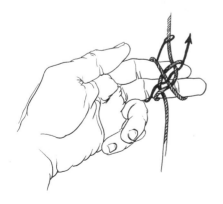

Figure 1-17. *For very tight Constrictors, seat yourself on deck and hitch a spike (or functional substitute) onto each end of the twine. Brace one spike between your feet and hold the other in your hands. Pull.*

LASHING

Viking raiders lashed together seagoing dragonships, but their skill was almost trifling compared to that of their victims in Europe. At that time and through the Renaissance, cathedral builders were lashing whole trees together steeple-high for scaffolding. Smaller buildings, carts, furniture, tools, and many other items of daily life also relied on rope for their construction. And it's not as if things have changed so much, even here in the technical vastness of the future. Lashings are still used for scaffolds in Asian shipyards, in the backs of computer cabinets where they keep bundles of wire together and out of the works, for the outriggers that anchor suspended scaffoldings for window washers and masons, and at the docks of the most modern superferries, where electronically aided pilots still dock by caroming off a bunch of pilings lashed together with wire rope. In recent years, high-tech racing sailors have rediscovered low-tech deadeyes and lanyards to lash their shrouds to chainplates. And every morning you lash your shoes to your feet.

Far from being archaic, lashings still exist in enough profusion to fill a volume of descriptions. No doubt some compulsive cataloger will eventually do just that, but for the practical knotter it's more important to understand the varying demands placed on lashings, and the basic techniques used in response. With these "elements of lashing," one can tie confidently in a wide variety of circumstances.

Pulley, Frap, and Wedge

Lashings rely on tension to do their work. A few tight turns put on with the aid of a marlingspike will sometimes suffice, but often the object to be lashed is heavy enough that some form of mechanical advantage must be used to provide adequate security. When something is to be lashed down to a deck, car roof, truck bed, or the like, lines are generally anchored on one side, passed over the cargo, and cinched down on the other side with one form of advantage—the pulley. (No, not a sheave turning on a pin, but the principle is the same.) Disregarding friction, the two arrangements on the left in Figure 1-18 provide a three-fold purchase. That is, the load is shared by three parts so that the part you haul on gets only one third of the load. Put another way, your efforts are multiplied three times; a 100-pound downward pull locks your cargo in place with, in theory, about 300 pounds of force. I say "about" because we can only disregard friction in theory.

The line on the left in Figure 1-18 is made into a pulley with the aid of a knot called a Trucker's Hitch, of which there are many forms. This one is

Figure 1-18. *Trucker's Hitches.*

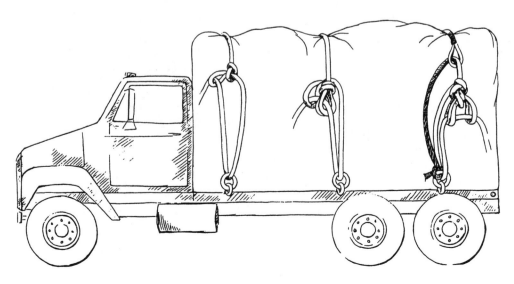

Figure 1-19A-C. *Basic Trucker's Hitch—a Slipknot made with one hand. End is led through ring, then through loop. Very handy but has tendency to jam.*

Figure 1-19D, E. *An improved Trucker's Hitch, the Biegner Hitch—a Slipknot made with a bight. Less liable to jam, wider radius for rope to pass over*

very fast and easy to tie (Figure 1-19A–C) and is a good knot for light-duty use and emergencies. Unfortunately, it and most other Trucker's Hitches either jam under heavy tension or can spill if tension is removed. What's more, the single loop makes a hard bend for the hauling part to go around, resulting in lower breaking strength and shorter rope life.

The knot used in the middle of Figure 1-18 offers some improvement. (It was introduced by Norman Biegner in the August 1980 issue of *Cruising World*.) As the illustration shows, the Biegner Hitch is a Slipknot made with a bight (Figure 1-19D, E), and the hauling part is rove through all three of the resulting loops. This knot resists jamming and presents a broad bearing surface; use it for medium-to-heavy loads or for any situation when you can take a little time. The most secure and slowest-to-tie loops are the nonslipping variety, detailed in the "Six in the Bight" section of Chapter 3. Use them for permanent lashings.

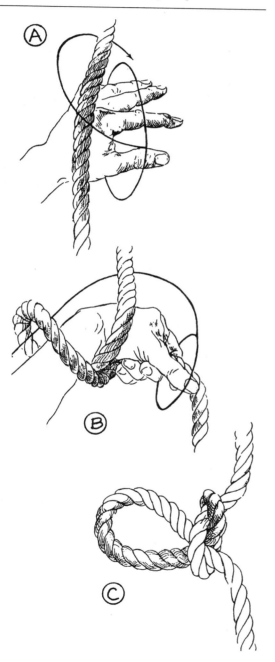

The right-most lashup in Figure 1-18 is a configuration that is about as involved a Trucker's Hitch as you can get before friction defeats mechanical advantage. Here the line passed over the cargo is cut to an appropriate length and has a thimble spliced in its end. A separate lanyard is anchored by one end below, a bight is passed through the thimble, a Biegner Hitch is made in that bight, and the other end is rove through the hitch. This creates a six-part purchase. If that doesn't do the trick, you need a come-along or some chain binders.

Frapping

To compound the tension on a lashing, apply "frapping" turns. These are made at right angles to the basic lashing to snug it still more; these turns can be so effective as to rip ringbolts out, so use them with discretion. In Figure 1-20, frapping turns are taken on the head-tensioning strings of a drum, and they tighten the round turns made to finish the "mousing" of a hook (see the sidebar on page 17), to keep the load from hopping off the hook when things are slack. These two far-removed examples should help illustrate frapping's extraordinary

Dragging with a Hook

When dragging an item with a hook, make sure the hook goes in with the bill pointing down, so it won't fall out if the load is released.

handiness and adaptability. Swaying or sweating up on a halyard is another application of the same principle.

Wedging

When you can't frap, wedge. Figure 1-21 shows an impromptu clamp made for gluing up some stock. Round turns are made tightly around the work, but there's no place to put frapping turns, so smooth, hard wedges, whose tips are under the lashing to start, are driven in to tighten as well as any clamp. For wide work, like a cutting board, it may be necessary to weight or clamp the work to keep it flat.

Before large bar clamps were generally available, wedged chains were used to hold deadwood assemblies in place for boring. It's still an inexpensive alternative.

Figure 1-20. *Frapping can be put to such widely divergent uses as lashing drumheads and mousing hooks.*

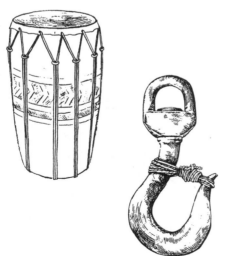

Figure 1-21. *Wedging. Make a series of tight turns around the tip of a wedge whose corners have been rounded. Drive the wedge down to tighten the lashing.*

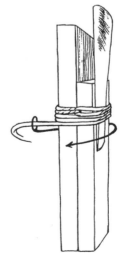 

Mousing a hook prevents the load from hopping out. But make certain before you apply the load that the load is on the hook, not on the mousing.

load coming
on mousing   mousing

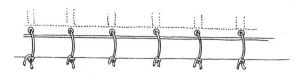

Figure 1-22A. *Boom lacing. Short lines square-knotted around boom; uses the least line and is fairly snug.*

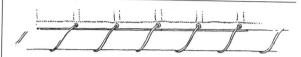

Figure 1-22B. *Spiral lacing—quick and easy, but loose.*

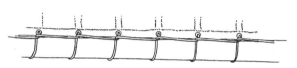

Figure 1-22C. *Half Hitches—more time-consuming, but more snug.*

The Subjects

Consider the things you want to lash. What shapes are they? What materials? How heavy? Under what conditions are they expected to remain together? Is the lashing permanent or temporary? The answers to these questions will determine the configuration, degree of tension, and the kind and size of cordage used for the lashing. Remember that with mechanical advantage, you can often afford to be gentle. Don't crush a light, fragile load. To preserve the rope, pad corners and contain the load just to the extent the situation demands. On the other hand, don't be afraid to snug right down on a heavy subject; loose deck or freeway loads can be murderous.

The Long and Short of It

Use a minimum of material, especially for heavy work. This promotes economy. Take the shortest distance between points, to minimize stretch. Avoid figure-eight turns unless nothing else will do—they use more line than round turns and so can generate more slack. Use several short pieces in preference to one long one for optimum fit, minimum slack, and insurance (if one parts, the others might hold). On

the other hand, long pieces are sometimes appropriate when the idea is more to contain than to bind, or where only moderate tension is needed.

Sometimes, whether to use long or short lengths of cordage is a matter of judgment, as on the boom in Figure 1-22 where several techniques for lacing the foot of the sail are shown. The ideal technique would be strong, adjustable, unobtrusive, easy to remove, and would simultaneously snug the foot down and pull it aft. One method (Figure 1-22A) is to have a short line through each eyelet, the ends square-knotted around the boom. This uses a minimum of line and is stout and adjustable. Next comes a simple spiral through successive eyelets, a method employed on the Gloucester fishing schooners. While easy to apply, and remove, it can't be adjusted along its length for changing sail shape. Half Hitches (Figure 1-22C) are less convenient but more snug. They are made in small line, one at a time, and tightened with the aid of a marlingspike. Make the hitch up close to the eyelet so that as it tightens it pulls the sail down

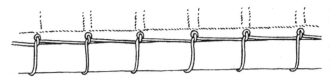

Figure 1-22D. *Marling Hitches—still more time-consuming, but still more snug.*

and aft (the pulley principle). Better still, "marl" the sail on. The Marling Hitch (Figure 1-22D) is a form of overhand knot with the ends led at right angles to the turn. It is less likely to slip and pass slack along the boom than Half Hitches. Compare these two knots, the Marling Hitch and the Half-Hitch, until you are sure of the distinction between them.

Marling is an excellent general-purpose lashing for bundles of wood, pipe, etc., and especially for tarp-covered cartop loads, where it keeps the tarp from blowing to noisy shreds as you drive.

Swedish Furling

Moving forward from the main boom, we come to a doused headsail. It only needs to be held in place temporarily. We'll want to break it out with a minimum of fuss, so marling is too time-consuming to use here.

The usual procedure is to tie "stops"—short lengths of rope or webbing—along the sail's bun-

dled length. This works well and uses little material, but short pieces aren't really necessary, since a little slack matters less here than on the mainsail. And the oceans of the world are littered with dropped, blown, or washed overboard sail stops. So, take an old halyard instead (or use the sail's downhaul), and get into "Swedish Furling." No, this is not an ethnic joke like "Irish Pennant" or "Spanish Reel." It's a series of slipped hitches, again worked aft (Figure 1-23).

Start with a Bowline, bring the standing part around the sail, and pass a bight of it through the eye of the Bowline. Pull the bight through until it is 12 to 18 inches long or so, depending on the size of the sail. Now bring the standing part around again, in the opposite direction, and pull another bight through the eye of the first one. Repeat this maneuver, making a zigzag of interlocking bights down the length of the sail. At the end, make a longer bight and half-hitch it around the sail, or belay it to a convenient cleat, post, or crewmember. To undo, cast off the last bight and haul on the standing part. Zip, zip, zip! Ready to hoist. This technique also works on boomed sails, though care must be taken to keep blocks and cleats from snagging the bights.

A Marline Lashing

Moving aft, we come to a life-preserver bracket lashed to a lifeline stanchion. This is a permanent seizing of small twine made around a relatively light

Figure 1-23. *Swedish Furling. Easy to tie, a pleasure to untie.*

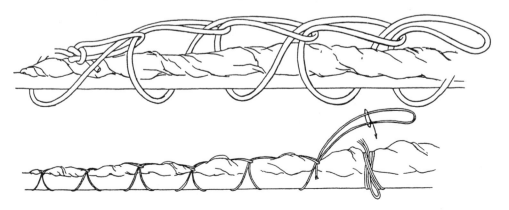

object. A sufficient number of turns taken in almost any pattern will hold it in place. But it might be nice if it didn't break away when you grabbed it to keep from falling overboard, or at the very least if it didn't shift under your weight when you leaned on it. When considering how strong to make a lashing, it is well to consider more than one intended use. Neatness is no small matter, either, nor is economy of time and materials. Even this quick job is worth doing well.

Start with parallel turns around the two pieces, as shown in Figure 1-24. Haul on each turn with your spike. Make four or five circuits, being sure that none of them rides over the others, as this would prevent an even distribution of strain. Next, make a not-quite-as-snug layer of riding turns (optional, not shown). These provide extra strength and protect the first layer from chafe. Finally, make three or four frapping turns very tightly. Secure with a Clove Hitch, tying a Figure-Eight Knot in the end as close to the hitch as possible. This is insurance against the end pulling free.

If the bracket is shaped to fit the rail, leaving no room for frapping turns, use wedges. Round their outer corners so they don't cut the twine. Even a sprung tiller can be temporarily repaired by lashing and wedging battens, screwdrivers, driftwood, or what-have-you in place for some distance on either side of the crack.

Escape Artist

Say you want to secure your dinghy for an extended passage. It's not hard to work up a lashing that looks secure, but once at sea with the forces of wind, water, and its own weight to help it, that innocent little boat will be transformed into a master of escape—Houdinghy, if you will—out to defeat your attempts to contain it. As challenger, your first inclination might be to cover the hull with a rat's nest of turns and hitches—the more-is-better school of knots. But this type of job is tedious to tie, difficult to remove, and just plain ugly. Worse still, it provides the escape artist with his greatest ally—slack. Extra turns mean more rope to stretch. Before you know it, things have worked loose and Houdinghy

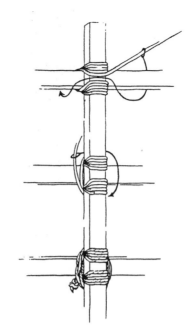

Figure 1-24. *A marline lashing.*

has stepped free, to the amazement of the wildly cheering crowd.

So instead, go with the less-is-more lashing in Figure 1-25 (see next page). Lay two or three lines from side to side, padding any sharp turns, and snug them down with Trucker's Hitches to chock padeyes, as in Figure 1-18. By taking the shortest distance across the hull, you simultaneously minimize potential slack and create opposing forces, bracing the lines against each other. Bind everything together with frapping turns of smaller line, hauling the remaining initial elasticity from the larger pieces. For extra security, lead the painter forward and lash it tight, too. There you have it, a handsome, escape-proof setup that is as easy to make, adjust, or remove as it is to describe.

Extemporaneous Work

No matter how carefully you study the above techniques, the odds are strong that you will eventually come up against a situation that seems to defy solution and for which neither this nor any other set of instructions has prepared you. It's like the

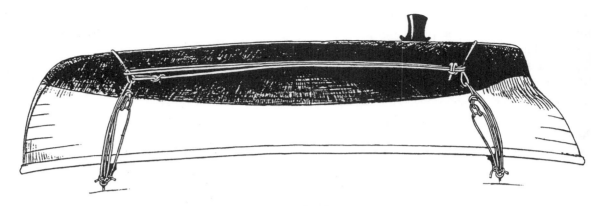

Figure 1-25. *A lashing that will restrain the great Houdinghy.*

old Bob Newhart routine about the carefully trained rookie security guard. His first night on the job is in the Empire State Building, and King Kong shows up. ("There's nothing about this in my manual.")

As it happens, most lashings are extemporaneous. Some things are just too big, but success is usually a matter of simple adaptability. Relax, take an inventory of your materials, and mentally arrange them in different configurations. Invent.

CHAPTER 2

Creating and Managing Tension

If you can serve, seize, lash, and coil, and if you understand the materials involved, you're well on your way to becoming a rigger; everything from here on is a matter of elaborating on what you already know. You can do much to elaborate on your rigging know-how simply by mastering the concept of "tension." A rig accomplishes its main purpose if it creates, contains, and directs tension efficiently.

Tension is not always as readily apparent as it is in the bar-taut weather shrouds of a sailboat on a hard beat. Riggers learn to recognize its many more subtle manifestations. In the "Lashing" section of Chapter 1 we examined several methods of increasing tension to hold an object securely in place. Here we will look at ways of creating greater tension than can be supplied by wedging, frapping, or Trucker's Hitches.

When it's puny you against big, heavy, ornery them, you need an advantage. A mechanical advantage, that is, for all the heavy-duty hoisting, dragging, stretching, and tightening jobs that rigging and sailing entail. For a lot of tension, advantage is usually provided by some form of either lever or inclined plane, or by both of these fundamental tension-gaining tools in combination. Which ones you use for a given situation depend on how fast you want something how tight, with what degree of control, over what distance, and at what expense. Safety and efficiency are determined by the appropriateness of your choices and by the size and health of the gear, so experience and a healthy respect for the forces you are dealing with are important. Choosing the proper pulling gear is a form of design.

Rope is the running part of running rigging. It comes in so many forms, and is made from so many materials, that it's understandable that the majority of vessels sport less-than-ideal running rigging. The rigger's first job here is to get the right rope for every job, and that can come only with a thorough understanding of the options.

ROPE CONSTRUCTION AND MATERIALS

Always choose the highest-quality, appropriately elastic (or inelastic), longest-lived running rigging that suits your vessel.

Running rigging is subject to the same considerations that standing rigging is (including economic ones); and inelasticity and longevity come dear. Ground tackle is different only in that you want it to stretch as well as to be strong.

Weight and windage matter as much with running rigging as with standing rigging; rope is relatively light, but there is a lot of it up there, and

<table>
<tr><td colspan="5">*Table 1.* **Recommended Sizes for Nylon Docklines and Anchor Lines (With permission, courtesy of Miriam Holbrook, Inc.)**</td></tr>
</table>

Docklines

Boat Length	Diameter	Bow Line Length	Stern Line Length	Spring Line Length
up to 20'	⅜"	20'	10'	15'
20–30'	½"	25'	15'	20'
30–40'	½"	30'	20'	25'
40–70'	⅝"	35'	25'	30'

Anchor Lines

Boat Length	Power Line Length	Power Line Size	Sail Line Length	Sail Line Size
up to 20'	75'	⅜"	100'	⅜"
20–25'	150'	⅜"	150'	⅜"
25–30'	200'	½"	200'	½"
30–40'	200'	½"	200'	½"
40–50'	250'	⅝"	300'	⅝"
50–70'	300'	¾"	350'	¾"

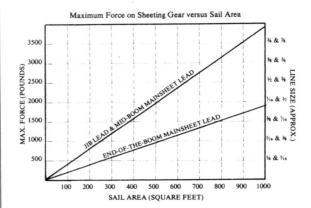

Figure 2-1. *Maximum force on sheeting gear versus sail area, and recommended Dacron sheet sizes:*

the pounds accumulate. Windage, too, even if you run halyards inside the mast. And because synthetic rope is so strong, you'll be tempted to scale its size for a comfortable grip as much as for structural requirements, and this can lead to oversizing. The accompanying sidebars will help you select appropriate sizes and materials for sheets and halyards, docklines, and anchor rodes for vessels up to 70 feet. (For more information on loading, see the formulas and graphs on page 386-387 in the Appendix.)

Constructions/Materials

There are three basic constructions to choose from: three-strand, single-braid, and double-braid. Three-strand is the least expensive, easy to splice, and generally ranges from very elastic to fairly inelastic. I like three-strand, but wouldn't recommend it for halyards or headsail sheets that go to a winch; the heavy loads for which winches are designed imply a need for the strongest, least elastic rope you can wrap around them, which is to say some form of braid, either Dacron or an exotic like Spectra. Use, or at least try, three-strand wherever high-tech and high-strain aren't big issues. Three-strand or single-braid is often preferable for mainsail sheets, boomed

forestaysail sheets, staysail halyards, dock lines, and anchor lines.

Single-braid costs a bit more than three-strand in a given material and size, but is stronger for its size, usually even easier to splice than three-strand, tends to be far more supple—and to remain so over time—resists hockling, and can be had in a wonderful variety of materials, so some form of it will suit almost every job. When made of Spectra for a halyard it can be amazingly inelastic. When made of nylon for a mooring line it will absorb energy better than three-strand or double braid. In any application it is a handsome, hand-friendly rope. Yes, I have a thing for single-braid.

Double-braid is the most costly of the three constructions, and the hardest to splice. It is, in fact, a bizarre and often difficult-to-understand splice. Double-braid comes in fairly elastic to very inelastic materials. In conventional synthetics like Dacron and nylon it is the strongest and least elastic construction for a given size. This is a plus in Dacron, which is generally used for halyards and sheets, which should be inelastic, but not a great thing for mooring lines and rodes, where elasticity/energy absorption is of paramount importance. As near as I can tell, the only reason that people use double-braided rope for these applications is that it looks more modern. Some double-braid ropes have a high-modulus (HM) core—basically they are single-braid ropes with a coat of armor.

For running rigging, you could say that manila,

I used to say that Sta-Set-X (see page 25) was the best halyard for the money. Its core is a bundle of parallel filaments, so it can have more of them per cross-section than if they were braided. The resulting extra mass means greater core strength. It's so much greater that just the core of Sta-Set-X is stronger than the combined strength of core and cover of conventional double-braid, like Sta-Set. Parallel fibers, plus lack of twist to those fibers, also means the elimination of the constructional elasticity that is unavoidable with braided cores. The result is a rope that costs almost exactly the same as double-braid, but is stronger, and stretches about 40 percent less (1.95 percent vs. 3.2 percent). Sounds impressive, and it is; over a typical 50-foot run, at 20 percent of breaking strength, that means less than 1 foot of stretch for the -X, versus over 1.5 feet for Sta-Set. This difference is so dramatic that I typically only use Sta-Set or similar ropes where inelasticity is not very important, like on drifter halyards, sheets, vang tackles, etc.

Sta-Set-X also tends to be more durable than regular braid, because, as with HM ropes, all of the strength is in the core, so the cover can suffer UV or chafe, with no loss of rope performance.

One downside of -X is that it is heavy, with each halyard adding a half-pound or so of weight aloft over that same run when the sail is hoisted, and a pound when both ends of the halyard are on deck (assuming $7/16$" rope). Not a deal-killer, but it undoes some of the benefits of the inelasticity. The rope is also quite stiff, owing to the double wrapping of gauze that keeps the core fibers tightly packed; handling can be difficult. Some people, including many professionals, say it is difficult to splice, but frankly I think they are just using the wrong tools; a Wand makes short work of it.

On the whole, -X is a great rope, but can we do better? Yes, as it happens, we can. For instance, you can have a rope that is even stronger, weighs about $1/3$ as much, and, with the same load in pounds, stretches much less than Sta-Set-X (.7 percent vs 1.95 percent). Total stretch over that 50-foot run is now just over 4". Wow. The catch? We've just described a $1/4$" Spectra single-braid which will be too small to hold onto comfortably, and too small and slick for stoppers. To make it work, we'd have to come up with a skill-intensive rope-to-rope splice, so we could put a fat Dacron tail on, for handling. We could also start with a covered rope with a Spectra core, and use a different splice to connect it to that Dacron tail.

Those splices are outside the scope of this book, but they are precisely what racers and performance cruisers use. They probably aren't worth going through for most boats, though. We need a compromise.

Enter VPC, a rope that takes a standard core-to-core splice. (Sta-Set uses a standard double-braid splice, and Sta-Set-X has its very own sort-of-core-to-core splice.) VPC has a core that is part Vectran, part polyolefin filler. That's right, filler; the Vectran provides all of the strength of the rope, just enough to be about the same strength as Sta-Set or X, but with much less stretch than either of them (1.4 percent at 20 percent of break), resulting in a bit over 8" of stretch over that 50-foot run, at a cost somewhat higher than $7/16$" Sta-Set. And the difference varies, with the price for VPC being almost the same as Sta-Set, from some suppliers. Take a breath. We are juggling prices, splices, and elasticities, and now we are also embarking on market pressures. But that is what one needs to do, I think, when deciding what rope to buy, for a given boat, for a given application. To help decide what to buy, let's take a look at those elasticity numbers. I said that Sta-Set stretches about 1.5ft. over a 50-foot run. That doesn't mean that you will be watching the head of your sail yo-yo-ing up and down by that amount while you are under way; it means that, going from no tension to going-to-weather-in-a-breeze-tight, you'll stretch the rope that much with the winch. When you stop winching, the length will stabilize, ideally at a tension that balances the force of a given amount of wind. If the wind adds any additional load, the rope will stretch fractionally more. What we want to do is to make that fraction as small as practicable, to maintain sail shape. Sta-Set-X will move a fraction that is 40 percent smaller than Sta-Set, and VPC's fraction will be about 30 percent less than that. At some point we will get to an elasticity where the luff and leech of the sail just doesn't notice the difference, where there will be no point in reducing the elasticity further. For most contemporary sailboats, excluding extreme racers, I think that point comes at about what VPC provides.

Add to that the rope's superior flexibility and toughness, and you can see why it is my favorite halyard these days.

Note that other manufacturers provide blended-core ropes; Samson has XLS Extra, and Yale features Vizzion. Both are excellent ropes, comparable in every way. I just prefer New England's products.

made from the leaves of the abaca tree, is the traditional material. But given the low, low quality in which it is generally available today, I would not recommend it. Besides, Dacron, the standard contemporary choice for either three-strand or braided rope, is far stronger, lasts much longer, is more chafe-resistant, and doesn't stiffen or shrink when the weather turns wet.

"Spun" three-strand Dacron, in which the yarns are spun from a series of short fibers, is relatively weak, but is sometimes a preferred construction because of its comfortable feel. "Filament" Dacron, with the yarns made up of continuous fibers or filaments, is slicker but significantly stronger and less elastic.

One other running-rigging choice, especially appropriate for traditional craft, is ultraviolet-stabilized split-fiber polypropylene—a multisyllabic way of saying that it won't break down in sunlight or chafe to pieces as fast as ordinary polypropylene does. Roblon and Navy Flex are two of the better-known brands of this kind of rope. You still need to be very conscious of chafe with the stuff, using large blocks and making sure all leads are fair, but it is inexpensive, has a delightful feel to it, holds its lay, is easily spliced, and even floats. That's a blitz of things to choose from, but the process need not be confusing. Again, evaluate your craft and sailing style, then choose accordingly.

For example, think of the variables involved in choosing rope to control the sails. There are so many different jobs to be done, each with its own variables of magnitude, handling, and compatibility with things like cleats, winches, and stoppers. You could practically have a different rope for every line aboard. That would be silly, of course. But considering the spectrum of running rigging requirements, it is equally silly to have just *one* type of rope aboard, and you see that a lot.

As a compromise between specialization and simplicity, it's sensible to divide the rig into general requirements, and install rope to suit (see chart, page 25). For example, halyards would be one category. In that category you'd first scale for load, using catalog recommendations or sail area/boat speed formulas. Then you might ask yourself how much performance matters to you. If you planned to race, you'd start shopping for a rope of the needed strength that was maximally inelastic. If you were planning to cruise, you might wander off in search of any old rope because "it's only for cruising," but don't—mediocre rigging will cripple your boat.

For cruising or racing, you might subdivide the halyard category, dedicating the most extreme rope to the most extreme loads. So there'd be a little less size and a little more stretch in the drifter halyard than in the jib halyard, for instance.

But then you might match your ideal requirements with the rope that meets your specs, look at the price per foot, and decide to take up powerboating. If that's the case, it's time to go back over your ideals and see if you can get what you want, or something like it, for less. And you probably can; ropemakers know that some of their high-tech stuff is absurdly high-priced, so they do what they can to get comparable performance out of lower-tech. The best example of this is New England Rope's VPC, (see below), a product with a blended HM core that stretches half as much as double-braid Dacron, and costs half as much as rope with an all-HM core.

You can also save a lot by playing with size. Nine-sixteenths-inch might look right, but if you look at the actual loads you might find that $3/8$-inch is way plenty strong, and still feels fine in your hands. Pay attention to diameter even if you do have money to burn; extra diameter means extra weight and windage.

One more useful useful distinction: with most running rigging at the deck, the loads are usually highest when the runs are shortest, whereas with most running rigging aloft, the loads are usually hightest when the runs are longest. So with the mainsheet, for example, you don't get high loads until the boom is strapped in tight and you are going to weather, while the halyard for the mains'l, in the same circumstance, has to run all the way up the mast, and partway back down, to get to the head of the sail. Because elasticity is a function of length, the sheet won't stretch much no matter how high the load, but that halyard will. So it makes sense to invest in low-stretch material for the halyard, but the same material would be wasted on the sheet.

In addition, you handle the sheet all the time, while the halyard is infrequently adjusted. So stiffness is not a big issue in a halyard rope, while suppleness and a good grip are very important for a sheet. So ergonomic needs are well-served, too.

We have such a wide variety of ropes because there are so many jobs for rope to do, because each of us—and each of our boats—sets differing priorities, and because each of us is willing to spend more or less money to effect those priorities. Accordingly, the accompanying chart is meant to illustrate rope characteristics, not to recommend selection; the ideal rope for a given job is largely a matter of who you are.

For example, let's say you're a sailor on a limited budget, with a low-tech daysailer. You might make all your halyards and sheets out of a single-braid rope such as Regatta Braid. As the chart shows, it is very supple, stronger and less elastic than three-strand, fairly durable, and low-priced.

If you were a sailor who put a higher premium on performance but didn't want to pay for it, you might stay with Regatta Braid for your sheets, vang, and traveler lines, but go with VPC or Sta-Set-X (see sidebar, page 23) for your halyards. The chart shows that these

are much less elastic than a single-braid, cost just pennies more per foot, and are more durable. Sta-Set-X is stiff, but this is not objectionable for halyards since you're not constantly handling them.

A sailor with a performance cruiser and a less-constrained budget would do well to go with one of the exotics such as Spectra for halyards (teensy stretch, long life), double-braid for jibsheets (low stretch, strong for its size, supple), and single-braid for multipart purchases (stretch isn't an issue, but handling is).

And so on. In every instance, the nature of the boat, and of those who sail it, will determine what the running rig inventory will look like. And the options above cover only a few variables; you might also throw in color coding, stripping the Dacron cover off an exotic to save weight and windage, or any number of other customization wrinkles. But it all starts with knowing the characteristics of the stuff you're dealing with.

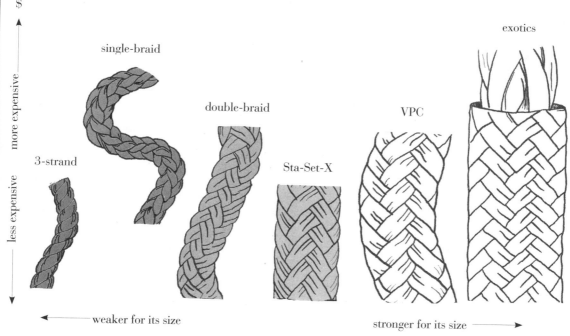

KEY
Height = Expense
Width = Performance (inelasticity)
Distance to right = Strength per diameter
Curviness = Handling (more curvaceous, better handling)
Dark shading = Least durable
Light shading = More durable
No shading = Most durable

Performance and cost numbers based on lines of approximately equal strength, not size.

With sheets and halyards, "durability" means UV resistance, as well as resistance to chafe. Three-strand and single-braid expose all yarns to sun; double-braid, half; Stay-Set-X and exotics, none. Exotics have toughest covers.

Selecting mooring, dock, and anchor lines is quite different than it is for sail-control lines: There are fewer constructions to choose from, and only one material—nylon—in general use. This is because the job requirements are simpler, involving only adequate strength and adequate stretch.

As the chart below shows, three-strand has the advantage of being the cheapest.

A single-braid rope, such as New England Rope's Mega-Braid, has the advantage of being more flexible than three-strand, especially in the long run. This could be a deciding factor if you have to stuff the rope into a tiny stowage locker, or if ease of handling is an issue. As it happens, storage lockers are generally tiny, and ease of handling is a fundamental virtue for rope. Other than that, the big appeal of single braid is appearance—it looks so sleek that many people buy it on that basis alone. And this is not a bad thing; why have an anchor line you can't stand the sight of? This appearance appeal is even true for double-braid nylon. The chart gives it lowest marks for performance, but it handles well, and is stronger for its size than the other constructions. These hardly

seem like compelling qualities, particularly considering its cost, but it is hard to talk people out of using it for mooring or anchor lines.

Regardless of which construction of line you select, it is a good idea to incorporate a snubber into anchor lines. I like to use Dacron, as it-is far more chafe-resistant than nylon (see End-of Bowsprit Anchoring, page 92).

Another nice option for mooring lines: end-to-end splice a short length of Dacron braid to the inboard end of each mooring line. The Dacron section goes to the cleat or bitts, and is just long enough to reach from the belay to well outboard of the chock or hawsehole. By far the greatest chafe point is where the line exits the boat.

One could also join the sections with two eye-splices, but these are more liable to hang up on fixtures while you're handling the lines. Bear in mind that end-end splice is only 80 percent or so of the line's strength. So oversize the line accordingly, or look for a rope manufacturer's instruction pamphlet showing the more involved 100 percent end-end splice.

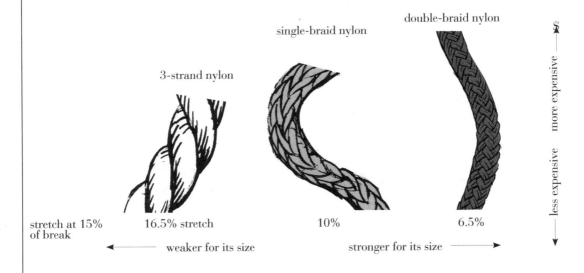

double-braid nylon

single-braid nylon

3-strand nylon

more expensive →

less expensive →

stretch at 15% of break

16.5% stretch   10%   6.5%

← weaker for its size   stronger for its size →

KEY
Height = Expense
Width = Performance (elasticity)
Distance to right = Strength per diameter
Curviness = Handling (more curvaceous, better handling)
Dark shading = Least durable
Light shading = More durable

No shading = Most durable
Performance and cost numbers based on lines of approximately equal strength, not size.

On this chart, mooring line "durability" means resistance to chafe. In the world, UV is a strong degrader of nylon, as well as other rope materials.

BLOCK AND TACKLE

In Figure 2-2, a line is led up from the load, through a block, and down to the hauler (force). The only advantage here is convenience—the force is equal to the load, and you can haul something light up over your head.

In Figure 2-3, the line comes down from an overhead support, through the block, which is attached to the load, and thence to the hauler. Now the hauler shares the load with the overhead support, so the load is halved; you can pick up a much heavier load than before with no more effort, but you can't pick it up far unless you add another block, as in Figure 2-4. This one, like that first single block, adds no advantage. As we keep adding parts, it will become difficult to figure out when we've added advantage and when the lead is just being redirected. The basic rule is that you count the number of parts coming out of the moving block(s). In Figure 2-4, the block that is attached to the load moves as the load is raised. There are two parts coming out of that block, so there is a two-part purchase. The other block doesn't move, so it adds no advantage.

Important detail: We show the upper blocks separated here for clarity, but in the real world this would cause a loss of power; the angle formed on

Cunninghams

A Cunningham is a block and tackle on the luff of the mainsail that adjusts sail shape. Originally used by racers as a way to get untaxed luff length, it is of great benefit to cruisers, since it allows for adjusting the luff without having to mess with the halyard, and especially without tightening the leech. Because a Cunningham pulls from the bottom of the sail, where the greatest area is, it is more effective at moving draft around, and with less effort than the halyard.

Cunninghams are also a great idea for the genoa, for the same reasons as for the main. They are particularly useful for roller-furling headsails, since a properly located halyard swivel limits the range of halyard adjustment.

the moving block means that you are devoting some of your effort to pulling sideways, leaving less to pull up. The wider this angle is, the more effort is siphoned off.

In Figure 2-5, a small type of block and tackle called a handy-billy is set up to the load. The lower block shows us that there is a three-part purchase here. Figure 2-6A, B shows the same gear inverted—resulting in a four-part purchase. Again, we have gained height by adding a block aloft, as in Figure 2-4. We could use two fiddles to the same effect (Figure 2-6B), or we could make up a purchase as in Figure 2-7, simultaneously changing the lead and

Figure 2-2.

Figure 2-3.

Figure 2-4.

Figure 2-5.

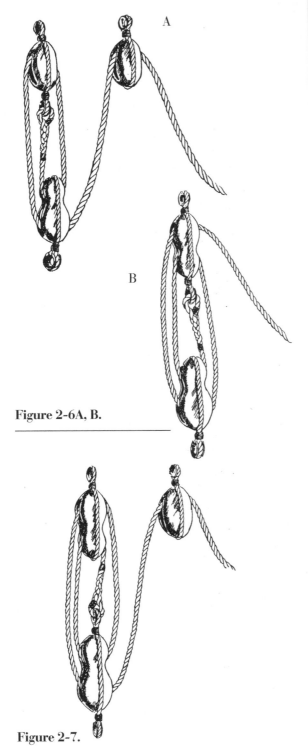

Figure 2-6A, B.

Figure 2-7.

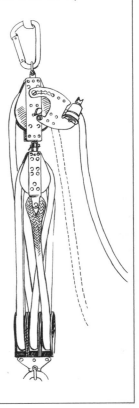
adding another part to the moving block for a five-part purchase. In both cases, the arrangement with the greater power is said to be "rove to advantage," and the one with the lesser power is "rove to disadvantage."

Compound Purchase

It's rare to find a sailboat these days that has any blocks aboard with more than two sheaves. This is because the winch (see "Choosing Winch Power" below) has largely taken over the high-tension running rigging jobs. But this doesn't mean that you are limited to only a five-part purchase with your tackle collection; the power of any configuration can be not just added to, but literally multiplied by hooking up another configuration to it (Figure 2-8). Figure 2-9 shows how combining sets of single and double

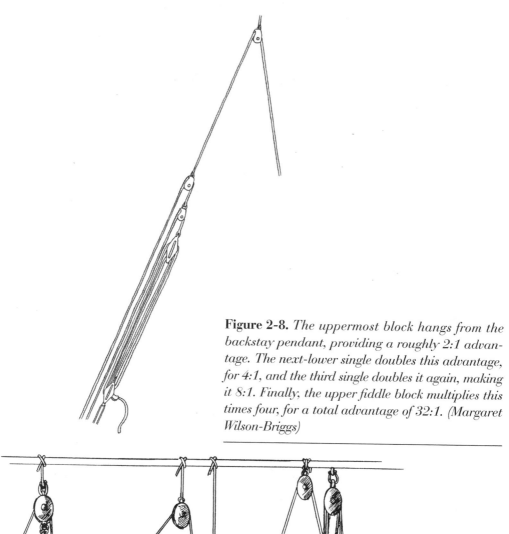

Figure 2-8. *The uppermost block hangs from the backstay pendant, providing a roughly 2:1 advantage. The next-lower single doubles this advantage, for 4:1, and the third single doubles it again, making it 8:1. Finally, the upper fiddle block multiplies this times four, for a total advantage of 32:1. (Margaret Wilson-Briggs)*

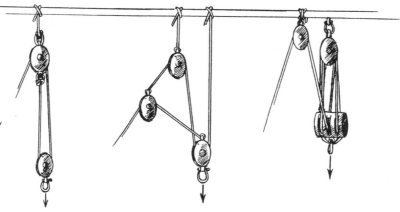

Figure 2-9. *Purchases used in combination multiply each other's force. Thus the four-part handy-billy at left, when combined with the two-part purchase, results in an eight-part purchase (4 × 2). Together with the Spanish burton (third from left), the handy-billy makes a 20-part purchase, and with the seven-part purchase at right it gives an advantage of 28. Note that the blocks have been separated laterally for clarity; in practice, lateral separation reduces effective purchase (see Fig. 2-18).*

blocks can produce from 8 to 28 parts of purchase. On modern boats, you'll find compound purchases on outhauls, vangs, and even on the backstay—that's right, we make running rigging part of the standing rigging.

Right-Angle Reeving

With blocks that have their sheaves mounted side by side—most often the case—the manner in which the rope passes from sheave to sheave can make a great difference in hauling efficiency. Figure 2-10 shows two double blocks reeved in the usual manner, called Lacing. The line travels in a spiral from one side to the other as it passes through the sheaves. This method is simple and easy to remember, but when the blocks are hauled close to one another—"two-blocked"—the rope bears strongly against the cheeks of the blocks, causing undue friction just when you need it the least.

The alternative is Right-Angle Reeving (Figure 2-11), sometimes known as Boat-Fall Reeving, the latter name deriving from its frequent appearance on lifeboat davit gear, which is usually two-blocked

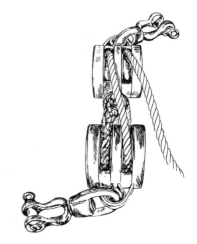

Figure 2-10. *"Laced" double blocks, in which the line proceeds in a spiral course through the sheaves.*

when the boat is hoisted. This method requires a little thought at reeving time, but if you've ever had to lift a heavy load the full range of your tackle and felt your power agonizingly diminish as you neared the top, you know that Right-Angle Reeving is worth the effort. Less friction means the rope lasts longer, too.

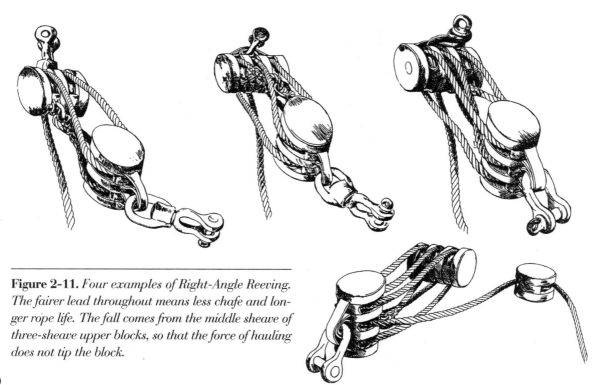

Figure 2-11. *Four examples of Right-Angle Reeving. The fairer lead throughout means less chafe and longer rope life. The fall comes from the middle sheave of three-sheave upper blocks, so that the force of hauling does not tip the block.*

BLOCK CONSTRUCTION

Blocks, those ancient, indispensable sail-control tools, have been high-tech'd. For so many years they were simple, stolid assemblies of wood, bronze, and steel. But nowadays they're likely to evidence Spielbergian gee-whiz design and obsessively close-tolerance engineering of multisyllabic plastics.

And more has changed besides materials and appearance; old-time blocks were mostly variations on a simple theme, but modern ones are specialized as to function, load, and (often novel) rig detail. On a typical production boat today you'll find standup blocks, two-line turning blocks, ratchet-sheave blocks, flip-flop (I am not making this up) blocks, over-the-top blocks, etc. And old-style blocks, adapted and updated, are still very much in the picture. Far from being outdated, they add to the rich variety of hardware that today's sailor has to choose from. What follows is information about the details of blocks, old and new, to help you pick the gear that best suits you and your boat.

The Body of the Block

There are two components to every block: the body, or shell, and the sheave. It is helpful to consider these separately.

The body is a combination of sheave housing, load bearer, and rope protector. In a traditional block, all of the load is borne by a metal strap that runs down the inside of the block, on either side of the sheave. Wooden "cheeks," there to protect the rope, are set outside this strap, and are fastened together with spacers, called "swallows," in between.

Modern blocks are aluminum- or steel-cheeked to save weight and bulk. On some models the cheeks are the weight-bearing structure, but that job might also be done, as with traditional blocks, by a metal strap (Figure 2-13). The strap is preferably of type 316 stainless steel, a particularly corrosion-resistant alloy. Bronze straps are also excellent, since they are both corrosion- and fatigue-resistant, but many sailors just like the look of shiny steel.

When choosing between wood and metal bodies, the first consideration for many sailors is weight—will the cumulative mass of a lot of blocks make the boat top-heavy, compromising sailing efficiency? I used to think that this was only an issue for very high-performance boats. And while light rigs are more significant for racers than for cruisers, it is generally a good idea, on any sailing vessel, to reduce weight aloft. It is possible to go too far, reducing the roll moment to the point where every little wavelet and puff of wind makes the boat lurch. The motion resulting from an underweight rig, especially when exacerbated by a stiff modern hull, is hard on the crew, and shortens rig life, too. But you have to take a *lot* of weight out of a rig to get that kind of unfortunate result. It is far more common to find that the rig is overweight; doing what you can to reduce weight aloft will help the boat sail upright, so crew comfort is improved, helm balance improved, and reefing frequency reduce. So, to get

Figure 2-12. *Examples of two modern blocks. Blocks like the air block (left). Here a piece of bungy cord has been threaded through the hole where the axle used to be. The block can now be suspended from an adjacent lower lifeline, so it won't bang on the deck. On other airblocks, this space can be used as the deadend of a purchase system. A Harken "flip-flop" block (right) is another recent development in block design. The line enters the block through the hollow axle, turns on the sheave, and exits at the cam cleat. The block can pivot, so can be tended from either side. The cam can also be adjusted for lead. (Margaret Wilson-Briggs)*

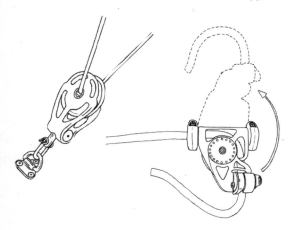

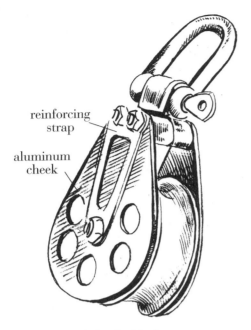

reinforcing strap

aluminum cheek

Figure 2-13. *A Schaefer block.*

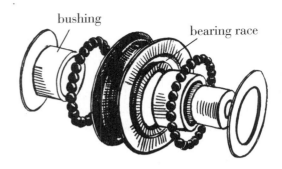

bushing

bearing race

Figure 2-14. *A Schaefer block with N.T.E. bushing and thrust-load ball bearings..*

back to blocks, get the lightest ones that are consistent with your safety factor, your quality-control analysis, and your wallet.

The Heart of the Block

The sheave, that little grooved wheel, that axle-transfixed puck, is the heart of the block. It exists to direct and share the load on a line. But every time a line runs over it, friction siphons off some of the force that the line is trying to deliver. The amount of friction at design load level can vary from 2 to 10 percent per sheave, depending on bearing efficiency. For a 100-pound load, this translates into 8 to 40 pounds of extra force you must exert to overcome friction in a typical four-sheave mainsheet. Technology has proven most useful in the effort to minimize friction.

Sheave friction is generated at four bearing points: where the rope passes over the grooved edge; the two sides of the sheave where they rub against the side of the block, and where the hub of the sheave bears against the block's axle. Given a fair lead and an adequate-diameter sheave (see below), it is the axle bearing that usually generates the most friction (Table 2, page 34).

Bearings The simplest axle bearing, called a "bushing" or "plain bearing," is essentially a reinforced hole. It is closely matched to axle size to assure the broadest distribution of load on the pin, and thus less friction and wear, as in Figure 2-14. Today's slickest (3 to 5 percent), most expensive bushings are made from an epoxy-coated carbon fiber–reinforced blend of Nomex and Teflon (N.T.E.). This exotic mix is durable, stable under load, and actually gets slicker with use, as bits of it are smeared onto the axle. A nylon bushing is too soft and sticky for all but the lightest loads. A fiberglass bushing is harder, but not nearly as hard or as distortion-resistant as N.T.E. Delrin, an acetal resin, makes a good, inexpensive, medium-duty bushing. And bushings made from oil-impregnated bronze are another good, low-tech option. They're not as slick as the plastics (5 percent), but hold their shape well under static loads.

More Elaborate Bearings Ball, pin, or roller bearings reduce friction by reducing the surface area of contact with the axle and/or block sides, and by rolling instead of sliding under the load (Figures 2-12 and 2-13). Bronze roller bearings, still available on some traditional blocks, are simple and bulletproof enough for prolonged deep-water use, yet slick enough (3 to 5 percent) for the performance-minded. But these days you are more likely to find roller bearings made of Torlon, a hard, slick, durable plastic. Maintenance aside: to keep your plastic ball bearings running free, rinse them occasionally with fresh water, and then apply one drop of "One Drop," from the McLube company, to the bearing race.

Racing gear, and even the light-air gear on a cruiser, demands the absolute minimum of weight as well as friction for maximum ease, speed, and smoothness of adjustment. Sheavologists have come up with some exquisite variations on bearing themes for these applications. Nowadays most use bearings made from Torlon. You'll find blocks with roller bearings on the axle, and ball bearing races on the sidewalls, for thrust loads. Resistance under moderate loads can get down around 2 percent. Schaefer's Circuit Sheave uses an NTE bushing for the axle and keeps the thrust-load ball bearings, making for a simpler, less expensive sheave with comparable friction characteristics.

Plastic ball, needle, and roller bearings are extremely light and easy to maintain (just keep them away from solvents and grit, and rinse them regularly with fresh water), but they will distort under heavy, static loads. This is most often a problem with halyard sheaves for mainsails and jibs, a good spot for metal roller bearings or perhaps an NTE bushing if weight is an anorexic issue.

The "Air Block," pioneered by Harken, is the biggest innovation in rigging since the invention of sheaves. If I'm exaggerating, it's only slightly. In this type of block, the axle hole has been expanded beyond all belief, leaving a big hole in the middle. There is no axle at all; the sheave rests on a bed of bearings, which in turn rest on a rim. Because this rim is so wide, there are a lot more bearings under the load than with a standard block, so the load is distributed over a greater surface. This means that a higher load can be sustained with less friction, and with less distortion to plastic bearings. Many other manufacturers now make similar blocks, and competition is driving the development of simpler, cheaper designs. The improvement is so great, even without taking weight savings into account, this has become *the* standard block type.

Sheave Material   Loads on the sheave itself are not so concentrated as those on the bearing, but sheave material can be important relative to cost, weight,

and stability under load. Nylon, for instance, is very cheap and light but can distort under heavy load. Worse, it swells when wet, increasing sidewall friction. Delrin sheaves are more stable and nearly as cheap, making a good medium-duty sheave. Bronze, stainless, and aluminum sheaves are heavy and expensive but will stand up to extremes.

Sheave Shape   A consideration peculiar to modern blocks is that of sheave score profile (Figure 2-15). It used to be that all sheaves had a semicircular profile, and this shape is still appropriate for three-strand and standard braided lines.

With wire-to-rope halyards, the long-accepted standard was a semicircular profile with a notch cut out of the bottom. The semicircle was for the rope, the notch for the wire. Because serious loads only come onto these halyards after the rope part is clear of the sheave, the little notch doesn't tear up the fibers. All-wire halyards simply used a very skinny sheave with a semicircular profile. But for all-wire or part-wire halyards the modern V-groove sheave supports the wire much more completely, reducing fatigue and the onset of "meathooks," sharp stubs of broken wire yarns. And it's also easy on fiber rope.

Most sheave-related problems occur when sailors change halyard materials or diameters without changing sheaves. Running an all-rope halyard over an old-style wire-and-rope sheave with a sharp edged notch is asking for trouble (when the sail is fully hoisted, the rope will chafe away in the notch). A different problem can occur if you do replace a sheave to match halyard type, but the new sheave doesn't fit snugly in the block or mast mortise. The halyard can chafe on entrance and exit points or the top of the mortise, or can jump out of the sheave groove and jam between the sheave and the mortise wall, an eventuality that can be prevented with "keeper bars" (Figure 2-16).

Sheave Size   Related to the question of sheave score profile is sheave size relative to rope diameter; different materials are more or less susceptible to fatigue, and increased sheave diameter reduces fatigue by reducing the sharpness of the bend the

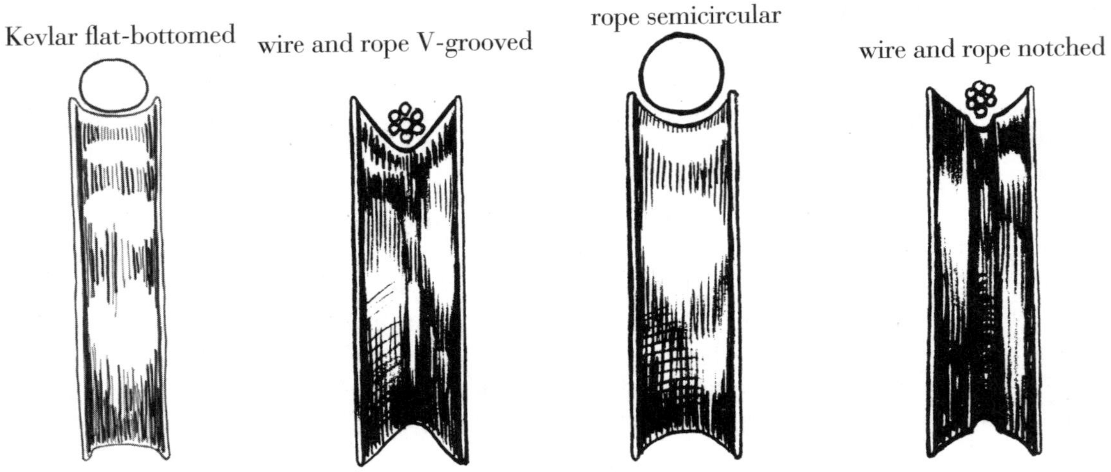

Kevlar flat-bottomed

wire and rope V-grooved

rope semicircular

wire and rope notched

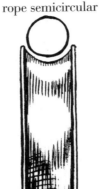

Figure 2-15. *Sheave score profiles.*

Figure 2-16. *Keeper bars can be welded on across a halyard sheave opening to prevent the wire halyard from jumping out and jamming between the sheave and mortise walls.*

Table 2. Recommended Minimum Sheave Diameters and Block Sizes

The "standard" tread diameters shown in this table are sizes that will guarantee the longest wire rope life and highest strength. But if it is not practicable to put a sheave that size into your mast, be aware that as you approach the "critical" diameter the wire's strength and longevity are severely compromised. The accompanying diagram illustrates tread diameter. Block length rather than sheave diameter is the desired standard when working with fiber rope. *(Source of minimum tread diameter: MacWhyte Wire Rope Co.)*

Rope or wire rope diam. (inches)	Sheave tread diameters for 7x19 wire (inches) Std.	Critical	Inches of block length for fiber rope
⅛	5 ¼	2 ¼	1
⁵⁄₃₂	6 ⁹⁄₁₆	2 ⅞	1
³⁄₁₆	7 ⅞	3 ⅜	1 – 1½
⁷⁄₃₂	9 ³⁄₁₆	4	1½
¼	10 ½	4 ½	2
⁵⁄₁₆	13 ⅛	5 ⅝	2½
⅜	15 ¾	6 ¾	3
⁷⁄₁₆	18 ⅜	7 ⅞	3½
½	21	9	4
⅝			5
¾			6
⅞			7
3" circ.			8

rope takes in passing over a sheave. Standard three-strand and braided rope is happy on a sheave four to six times the rope's diameter—i.e., a ½-inch (13 mm) line needs a sheave 2 to 3 inches (52 mm to 78 mm) in diameter. Wire rope should have a sheave at the very least 20 times the wire diameter.

To get an idea of how much difference this ratio can make, take a look at Figure 2-17, which shows the effect of sheave diameter on wire-rope life (graph courtesy of the MacWhyte Wire Rope Co.). Wire life is almost doubled in going from a ratio of 15:1 to a ratio of 20:1, and more than tripled between 15:1 and 25:1. Friction enters into it, too. The resistance of each sheave turning on its axle robs from 2 to 10 percent of the tackle's power at typical working loads. In addition, too small a sheave for the rope size used causes excessive resistance, especially, of course, if the rope rubs against the walls of the block mortise. A larger sheave, because of its gentler curve, produces less surface friction as the rope passes over it. Furthermore, axle and thrust-bearing friction is relative to the ultimate strength of the

Figure 2-17. *The effect of sheave diameter on wire-rope life. Fiber rope is generally less sensitive to diameter, but it is recommended that the sheave be six to eight times rope diameter. (Source: MacWhyte Wire Rope Company handbook)*

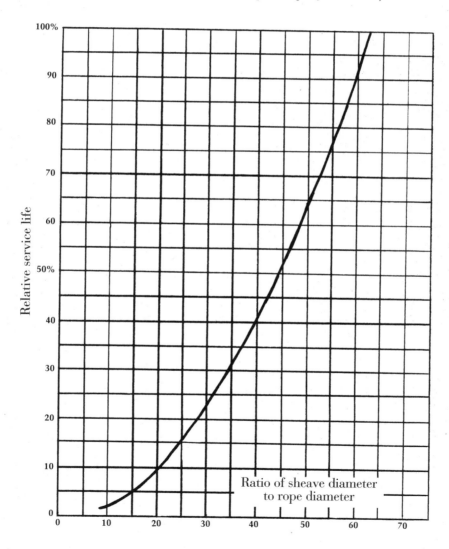

Relative service life

Ratio of sheave diameter to rope diameter

sheave; by using an oversize sheave you reduce the relative load, and thus further reduce friction. (This is the source of that old rigger's blessing, "Big blocks and small lines to you.")

Considering all the above, it obviously makes sense to use the biggest sheave you can, no matter what your halyard material. But there are practical limitations. For one thing, bigger blocks cost a lot more than smaller ones. For another, an oversize block might just plain not fit in a tight space, especially at the masthead, trapped between mast and stays. And of course, big means heavy. Altogether, we're left with the compromise of using the biggest sheave that will fit, is light enough, and won't bankrupt us.

Block and Rope Strength

One more consideration: block strength relative to rope strength. In the days of manila and hemp, blocks were built to match the strength of the rope that fit them. But since synthetics are at least twice as strong as natural fibers and can be used safely at a lower safety factor (they are less prone to rot),

this is no longer practicable. For example, take a modern block with a 2-inch (50-mm)-diameter sheave and a breaking strength of 2,500 pounds (1,136 kg), designed for ½-inch (13-mm) line. That line has a breaking strength of 6,300 pounds (2,864 kg). Apply just one-third of that line's breaking strength, and you'll have a load of 4,200 pounds (1,909 kg) on the block, 2,100 pounds (955 kg) on each side. You'd have to go down to an uncomfortable-to-grip ⁵⁄₁₆-inch (8-mm) rope before block strength would be in scale with rope strength. But nowadays rope size is scaled for lowest stretch range, ease of handling, and fitting into cam stoppers and winch-tailer caps. You might never put even a 1,000-pound (455-kg) load on that ½-inch (13-mm) line. So instead of trying to match block and rope strength, the procedure is to match block sizes to design loads—the actual loads they'll bear.

Figure 2-18A. *The effect of turning angle on block loading.*

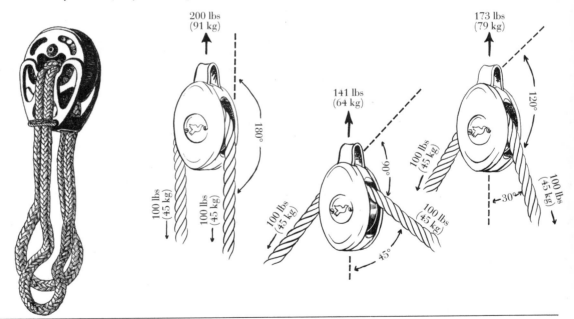

Figure 2-18B. *Airblock Spectra grommet. Blocks like this one use rope instead of hardware as the means of attachment. The result is a block that is considerably stronger, as well as lighter and more versatile than shackled blocks. (Left illustration by Margaret Wilson-Briggs)*

Also note in Figure 2-18 that as the angle of incidence of a line to its block widens, the load on the block lessens. So fairlead blocks can be considerably smaller than blocks through which the rope takes a 180-degree turn.

Miscellaneous Practicalities

Cruisers, for whom a broken block can be more than a simple inconvenience, should always use generously sized blocks, for a high safety factor. Reduced friction and prolonged rope life are other consequences of prudent oversizing.

All sailors should bear in mind that swivel blocks fail most frequently; unfortunately, manufacturing efficiencies have dictated that most of the blocks being made today are of a type that can be either swiveling or non-swiveling; the conversion is usually made with a couple of set-screws. So if you don't need a swivel, get solid bail blocks if you can, and get high-quality, heavy-duty locking swivels if you must.

Poor lead is a major cause of block failure; be sure that all lines lead fairly to and from all blocks,

for even strain, low fatigue, and low friction. Make sure, in particular, that the block can articulate adequately for a fair lead coming into and out of the block. If block angle changes depending on point of sail (a mainsheet deck block, for example), check the lead at all possible angles.

Snatch blocks (Figure 2-19) can be stupendously handy for impromptu fairleads and hoisting, but they do have their limitations. Avoid using them on a line that is subject to violent flogging—like Genoa sheets—as this can cause them to spring open. There are many snatch block designs, so read the maker's literature closely for other limitations.

Holding a snatch block up with a short bungee cord will help hold it still while you open and close it, will keep it from clattering on the deck when the load is off, and will help to dampen motion from a flogging line.

Nearly all snatch blocks available today come with a snapshackle attachment. So flogging or inattentive closing can result in not only the block but also its snapshackle coming open. One form of snatch block, developed for mountain rescue, is positive-locking (Figure 2-20). It's a little slower to open and close, but you can trust it with your life. It's perfect for use as a turning block when hauling someone aloft (see "Living Aloft," Chapter 7).

Figure 2-19. *Snatch blocks. The center illustration is a soft shackle incorporated into one of Colligo's sheaveless snatch blocks. Spectra slides readily through this block. (Middle drawing by Margaret Wilson-Briggs)*

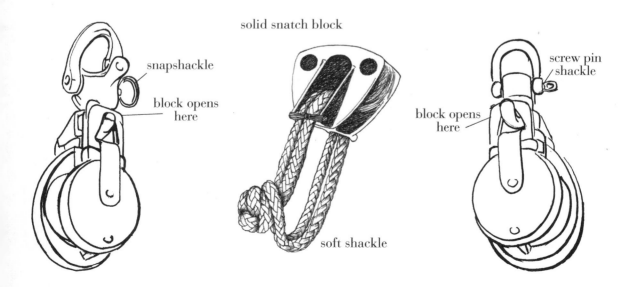

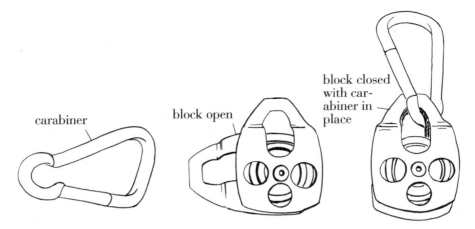

carabiner

block open

block closed
with car-
abiner in
place

Figure 2-20. *Mountain climber's block, for use as a turning block on a halyard that is taking someone aloft or in other mustn't-fail situations. A screw pin shackle, soft shackle, or locking carabiner will hold the block closed, and connect it to its attachment point. Available at climbing and camping supply stores, in aluminum with a plastic sheave or stainless with stainless sheave.*

With that advice, I'm edging away from changeable technology and toward a timeless, personal responsibility: that each sailor assess and make skillful use of the available gear. One can, for example, combine light, free-running plastic sheaves with tough, lovely, wooden blocks if that's what's needed or preferred. No matter how high-, low-, or middle-tech the gear is, it must be mated with given jobs on a given boat, and it is the sailor who plays the matchmaker.

TACKLE APPLICATIONS

Tackles provide low to moderate tension, quickly, at prices that range from very low to very high, depending on complexity and refinement. Used by themselves, they're all you need for small-craft halyards (one-part) and sheets (two- or three-part). Given sufficient crew and numbers of sheaves, they can also serve for gaff- and square-rigged vessels of any size. For peak and throat halyards on medium to large gaffers, a "jigger" on one end of

a double-ended halyard compounds the primary purchase for a maximum of luff tension with a minimum of effort and cordage (see the "Jiggers" sidebar). Block-and-tackle boomed-sail sheets of sufficient purchase are all that most craft require, gaff or Bermudian. It's also easy to rig a two-part purchase for boomless staysail sheets, using either bullet blocks or hardwood "lizards" spliced into the ends of sheet pendants (Figure 2-21). Nowadays, for many application, the lizard has been reborn as a machined aluminum ring. These combine slickness, toughness, and lightness. Highly recommended for vangs, outhauls, runner deck blocks, and many other uses where ultimate slickness isn't the top priority.

Also to be considered are boat falls, downhauls, gantlines, lazyjacks, topping lifts, and flag halyards. Scale these to the job, checking out other vessels if you're unsure of proportions. Once again, the catalogs of block and rope manufacturers are a good guide to selection, but only if you first familiarize yourself with conditions on actual boats.

Deciding

Take a good, hard look at your boat and at yourself. What kind of sailing do you want to do? In what climate? For how long? Will you often be far from land, or will there always be a boatyard nearby? List as many rig considerations as you can think of, and rate them in order of their importance to you. Compare cost benefits of different rigging materials. Keep in mind that, with any form of mechanical

Load on a halyard varies over its hoist; at first you're only picking up the weight of the sail, and perhaps a gaff or square yard, and the going is relatively easy. But at the end, when you want to tighten the sail up for an efficient shape, the going is decidedly difficult.

With most contemporary boats, it's the winch that applies the final, heavy load. But on gaffers and square-riggers, it's done with a jigger: The halyard is double-ended; one end leads down to deck on one side of the mast and is pulled on by hand as far as possible, then belayed; the other end leads down to deck on the other side of the mast and has a three-, four-, or five-part block-and-tackle hanging from it. This purchase compounds the primary purchase aloft. That is, if your throat halyard has a four-part purchase, a jigger of three parts will give you a $3 \times 4 = 12$-part purchase at the end of the hoist for easy luff tensioning. You could, of course, make up a 12-part primary purchase, but then you'd need a halyard three times as long, and there's already enough string to deal with on a gaffer.

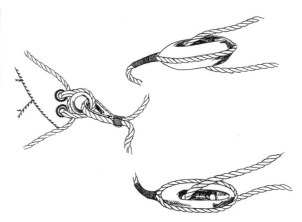

Figure 2-21A. *Bullet blocks spliced into the ends of sheet pendants provide a two-part purchase, an alternative to winching on traditional craft. The blocks are shaped to prevent snagging on the stay during tacks. The pendants are sometimes called "lizards."*

Figure 2-21B. *A hardwood "lizard" is a sheaveless alternative to a single block for small craft or for smaller sails on large craft.*

advantage, you can have either power or speed, but not both. If, for example, your mainsheet has a 2:1 advantage, it may bring the boom in very fast, but only in light airs. If you change up to a 5:1 advantage, it'll be easier on your arms, but a slow, slow experience. What will be the ideal compromise, for you, between ease and speed? One solution might be to combine a fast, low-power purchase with a winch. The powerful, slow winch would sheet things in in heavy airs, while the block and tackle would stand alone in light airs. But do you want to invest in another winch? Will it work in your cockpit?

Most sailors just go with whatever the boat comes with, and may not even realize that there are alternatives. But rigging materials are specialized in order to suit any sailing style; you might as well get what suits you.

Racing craft feature blocks that are extraordinarily light, strong, low-friction, and high-cost. This is appropriate. But racing considerations pervade the sailing craft marketplace to a ridiculous degree, so that the gear of most craft is not appropriate. If you're more interested in a solid, repairable block

than a SORC ambience, look for ones that look the part. Read technical data about them. Ask around about the reputation of the brand or brands you're considering; there are some good-looking lemons out there.

Rope-Stropped Blocks

As the diagrams in Figure 2-22 show, I have a thing for rope-stropped blocks. Not exactly an off-the-

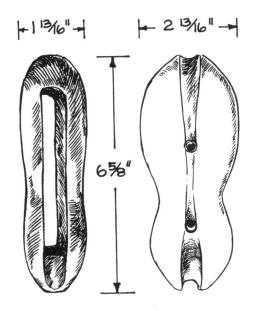

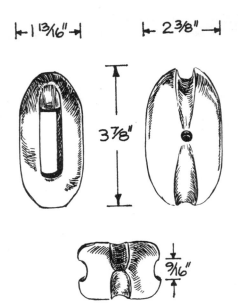

Figure 2-22A. *Two views of a fiddle (without sheaves) and three views of a single block. Note faired-in strop grooves. The dimensions, which are those of the fiddle and block in the author's handy-billy, are ideal for use with ⁷⁄₁₆-inch line.*

SINGLE BLOCK

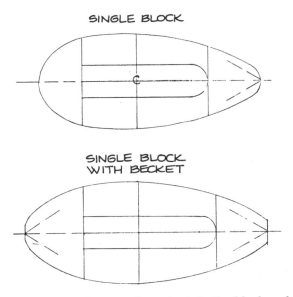

SINGLE BLOCK WITH BECKET

Figure 2-22B. *Patterns for a single bullet block and a single bullet block with becket. Scale the sizes to the line.*

shelf item these days, but they're fairly easy to make; they're less inclined to bang up brightwork; they're dirt cheap and undeniably attractive; and they really, really work. There are two elements to stropping a block: the grommet that encircles the block and its thimble (see Chapter 6), and the Round Seizing that is applied between block and thimble to hold them in the grommet (see "Seizings," Chapter 1). And note that HM rope has brought about a resurgence of rope stropping, with Spectra loops replacing steel shackles for block attachment. The result is stronger and much lighter, and the loops can be made from scraps.

CHOOSING WINCH POWER

Figure 2-23 illustrates the principle of that magnificent rotating lever, the winch. The winch handle is the lever arm, the barrel axis is the fulcrum, and the load is applied at the barrel face. Divide the distance between fulcrum and face into the length of the handle, and the result, in an ungeared winch, is the amount of your advantage. Internal gearing in two- and three-speed winches in effect lengthens or shortens the lever arm so you can take up slack quickly when the load is light, then switch gears for greater leverage as the load increases.

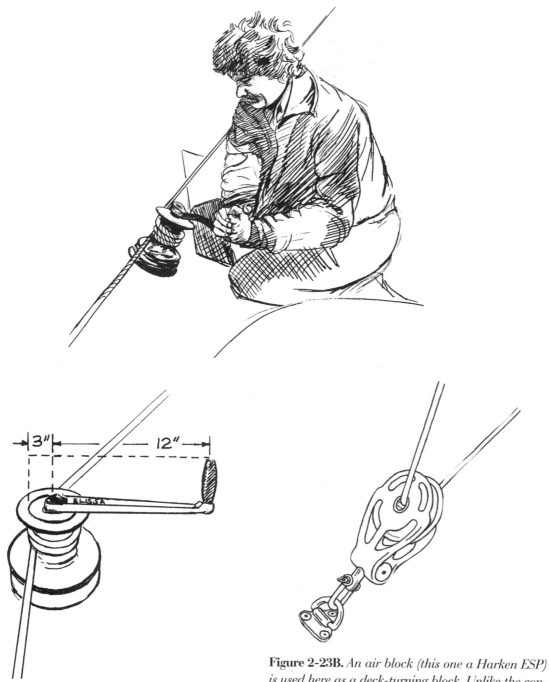

Figure 2-23A. *The winch is a rotating lever with the fulcrum at the winch face and force applied by the handle. Internal gearing compounds the leverage. In this case, the advantage is four to one.*

Figure 2-23B. *An air block (this one a Harken ESP) is used here as a deck-turning block. Unlike the conventional block shown in Figure 2-24a, this one has no bail to attach the bungee cord to. Instead the cord is rove through the hole in the middle of the block. (Margaret Wilson-Briggs)*

Winches take various forms, depending on the load and application they are designed for, but they all have two requirements in common:

1. *Good lead.* Several turns with the hauling line around the barrel is the winch equivalent of reeving; the grip of the turns allows force to be applied. The hauling part should form a 95- to 100-degree angle with the winch drum, or a "wrap" (override) may result. Very bad news, especially if you need to get the line off the winch in a hurry. When the hauling part's lead isn't fair, or when the lead might interfere with crew traffic or other hardware, a turning block is added between the load and the winch (Figure 2-24). The tailing part is, well, tailed, either by a crewmember or a self-tailing attachment on the top of the winch (Figure 2-25).

2. *Efficiently applied force.* These things are expensive, so you might as well get some performance out of them. To begin hoisting or sheeting-in a sail, leave the handle off for the moment, make your turns (three or four), and begin taking up slack by hand. Pull with your palms away from you to get a full range of motion as you work your arms in alternation (Figure 2-26). Keep your hands well away from the winch in case a sudden load slips the turns. When the slack is out, the person with the handle plugs it in and begins cranking while you tail, or you can do both jobs yourself, slowly and carefully with a normal winch, slick as you please with a self-tailing model. For maximum cranking efficiency, get your weight over the handle and keep it there. Use both hands when possible. When you're running a capstan use a straight-arm, palms-on-handle technique to take up slack, then switch to the low and slow crooked-arm technique as you take a strain.

Winch Size
Winches, unmatched in their combination of speed and power, predominate aboard today's short-

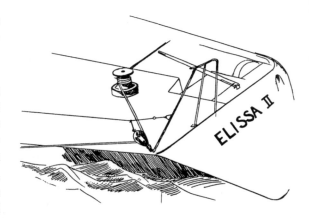

Figure 2-24A. *The turning block next to the stanchion feeds the line to the winch at a good fair angle. Note the shock cord running from the turning block's becket to the lifeline; this arrangement keeps the block from falling down and fouling when the line is slack.*

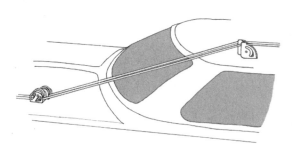

Figure 2-24B. *These are "over-and-under" blocks, doing what their name says, taking the lead between levels. With these blocks, the lead can be taken vertically past a house, or other obstruction. (Margaret Wilson-Briggs)*

handed high-tension vessels. But winches are also unmatched in their combination of high price and maintenance needs, so use as few of them as you can, and lighten their loads whenever possible by working them in tandem with tackles. As noted above, sheets can be controlled by blocks alone or by blocks compounded by a winch, depending on how much strain the weather is giving. Running backstays and the halyards for full batten or gaff sails

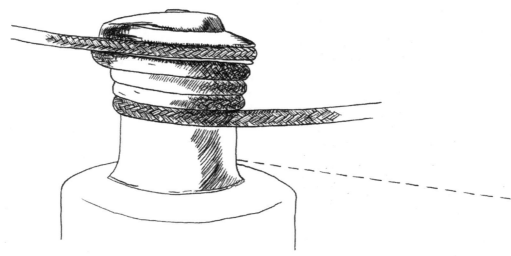

Figure 2-25. *A self-tailing winch ingeniously eliminates the need for a human tailer. Since they're not fail-safe, don't trust yourself to a self-tailer when going aloft. Note that if the winch is worked with the standing part at the angle shown, an override will result; the standing part should lead slightly downward (dotted line). (Margaret Wilson-Briggs)*

Figure 2-26. *Human tailer.*

are two more candidates for block-and-winch teamwork. An extra part or two on a purchase means you can go with a smaller winch that will receive less strain than a larger one doing the job all by itself.

A modern sail plan comprises a few large, very powerful sails. The intent is to produce greater efficiency and less complexity than the traditional approach of more and smaller sails. But the modern sail plan concentrates forces to such an extent that a large, expensive machine—the winch—is the only practicable way to make things work. Largely because of market pressures, boat manufacturers tend to fit winches that are smaller (and thus cheaper) than you and I might consider ideal. Smaller winches are less powerful, so the price we pay for lower cost is increased physical effort. What is more, every winch suffers some loss of efficiency due to internal friction, even when it is exquisitely maintained.

How big, then, does a winch have to be to overcome both the pull of the sails and its own drag? The answer starts with how much effort is acceptable for you. For most people, 35 pounds (15.9 kg) is a comfortable maximum sustained load. An undersized and/or badly-maintained winch makes you work harder. That's why it's so hard to sheet that Genoa in.

Bear in mind that we're talking about loads that you'll only encounter going to weather in a stiff breeze—a relatively infrequently encountered situation, but one in which boat motion, fatigue, and discomfort all conspire to render you least capable of concerted physical effort. It's a situation in which you're most appreciative of adequate mechanical advantage, and hang the extra cost. By investing in a worst-case-scenario power level, you also get extra-easy sail handling in lighter airs. A final bonus is that the larger drum size means more surface area, and thus more gripping friction on the rope for every turn you make around the drum. So, fewer turns to put on and remove, and better control when easing slack around the drum.

Workload Formula

Mechanical efficiency aside, winch load is determined by sail area and apparent wind speed. You will find details on this on page 371, but here is an example: You have a 700-square-foot Genoa, and the apparent wind speed is 25 knots. Since wind force varies directly with sail area, but with the square of wind speed, we multiply 700×25^2, which equals 437,500. That's the foot-pounds of force on the sail. Now we have to isolate the load on just the clew of the sail, because the other two corners don't load the sheet. This involves some fairly complicated number-juggling, which Wallace Ross (author of the wonderful book *Sail Power*) mercifully compressed into a constant: .00431. Multiply our number by this, and we get a clew load of nearly 1,900 pounds. Divide this by our desired handle load of 35, and we need a winch with a low gear rating of at least 50:1.

Note that if we reduce the wind speed by just five knots, we get a significantly lower load of 1,200 pounds, while going up just five knots results in a load of 2,700 pounds. This is because of that square function of wind speed. So when you are choosing winches, be sure of the conditions it will actually be handling. And note that it is apparent wind speed, so a faster boat will have higher loads, and thus need bigger winches, than a slower one.

Efficiency Alternatives

If the cost of a big enough winch is too high, or if you're driving a race boat and the extra weight is a consideration, there are five other ways to get more from your winches:

1. *Brawn.* Keep a very large, muscular, and willing individual around to do your winching. This is the traditional option for racing craft.

2. *Handle Leverage.* A winch is a form of lever, with leverage from internal gearing compounded by leverage from the handle. A 12-inch (305-mm) handle will provide 20 percent more leverage than the 10-inch (254-mm) handle your winch is probably fitted with now. This advantage is somewhat qualified by the slowness and awkwardness of swinging the handle through a wider arc, but many people hardly notice the difference, and love the ease. Also consider getting a two-hand handle, either 10 (254 mm) or 12 inches (305 mm) long, so you can make better use of the leverage you have, getting the strength of both arms completely into the effort.

3. *Compound Advantage.* By combining a winch with a block and tackle, you compound your mechanical advantage. So a 40:1 winch hooked to a 4:1 block and tackle yields 160:1, minus friction. For quick, coarse take-up at low loads, you can use the block and tackle alone, hooking up the winch for power and refinement. This setup is the rule for mainsheets, but it's not generally a good idea for staysails; blocks hanging from sail clews can be real crew-killing deck floggers. On large traditional boats, with clews well above deck, it's still the viable option that it's always been.

Another old practice is to put a block on the head of a sail, for a 2:1 advantage, to be compounded by the halyard winch. With a 50-percent-lower load on the winch, you can use a much smaller, cheaper winch. This generates savings that offset even the long-term costs of the 50-percent-longer halyard. These days 2:1 halyards are popular on boats with full-batten mains. The extra power means you can get the sail up faster and with less effort, before putting the halyard on the winch. Mast compression is also reduced by 25 percent.

4. *Fairleads, Big Blocks, and Lubrication.* By using a minimum number of large, high-quality, strategically placed turning blocks, you reduce friction. By being one of the minuscule minority of sailors who strip down and lubricate their winches on a regular basis (at least once a year), you reduce friction by a lot more.

5. *Design.* Staysails are any boat's most significant edge to weather, but their size and significance have been greatly exaggerated by some racing rules. So if you are daunted by the prospect of shelling out the bucks for a comfortably powerful winch, consider making your sails smaller instead of making your winches bigger. This can mean getting smaller, more efficient staysails, or reefing or changing down more deeply and sooner than you currently do, or increasing the size and power of your main, particularly with full-length battens, among other options. Skillful trimming of skillfully made sails can compensate for the loss in headsail area. So if your sails are wearing out now anyway, consider a design change.

Whether your winches have help or work by themselves, protect your investment with regular, careful inspection and maintenance; it's amazing how many people just crank 'em till they freeze up, treating them like convenience items instead of well-bred tools.

As for which winch brand is best, there isn't a lot to choose between the majors—Andersen, Harken, and Lewmar—as they all feature good-quality gearing and consistently high tech support. But I just have to recommend Andersen as being a standout in fit and finish, as well as having a drum that makes line-handling significantly easier.

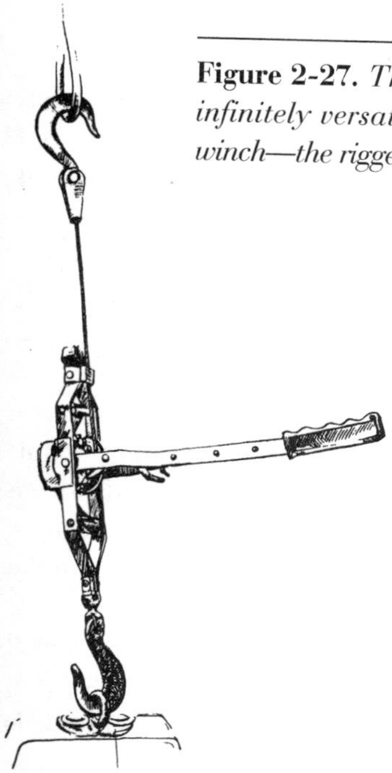

THE COME-ALONG

Figure 2-27. *The come-along, that infinitely versatile industrial-grade winch—the rigger's friend.*

Not exactly part of the rigging, the come-along (Figure 2-27) is an indispensable shop tool and is good to have aboard for installing, shifting, and setting up gear, and for emergencies. It's another winch, but with a wire or rope tackle anchored to the barrel instead of wrapped around it. A ratchet mechanism, not friction, is used to sustain tension, and a relatively small-diameter barrel means a leverage ratio between 20 to 1 and 40 to 1, comparable to the ratios of typical running-rigging winches. With some come-alongs, power is compounded by the use of a block added to the load end of the tackle.

Come-alongs are powerful, but they're very, very slow. Some models ease this problem with a take-up wheel on the side. Nice feature.

Because it's fairly easy to put more strain on these tools than they are meant to take, their handles are usually designed to bend under excess load. Better that than have the wire break with you standing there, cranking resolutely away.

Figure 2-29A. *The Inclined Plane, another form of mechanical advantage. In this case, 125 pounds applied by the truck's driving wheels can lift the (very small) 2,000-pound truck.*

Figure 2-28. *Sweating up. A handy technique to know, especially, as here, if you've lost a winch handle.*

Figure 2-29B. *The threads of a turnbuckle are simply a spiral version of an Inclined Plane.*

SWEATING UP

This is a remarkably simple, effective way to get a little extra tension on a purchase. Hauling sharply outward or sideways on an already taut line exerts leverage on the line; if the line is tailed at the belay point, the load is forced to shift, giving you a little slack. Your outward motion must segue smoothly and quickly into a downward pull, to feed that slack to the belay point, where the tailer takes it up (Figure 2-28). The same principle makes frapping turns effective; the lever is a versatile tool.

TURNBUCKLES (THE INCLINED PLANE)

While we're talking about means of tightening things, let's look at the principal means of inducing tension in the standing rigging. So, step right

up folks, and watch as a mere puny 125 pounds picks up a solid ton! Figure 2-29A,B shows that this feat is accomplished through the miracle of the Inclined Plane. Once force-resisting friction has been reduced to a minimum, it's easy to shift the ton up the slight grade, since only a tiny fraction of its weight is directed against the force. Give me a shallow enough ramp and I'll move the world.

Turnbuckles (and bolts and screws) make use of inclined planes that have been bent into a spiral, thereby packing tremendous mechanical advantage into a very small space (Figure 2-30). Force can be applied by hand or compounded with a lever in the form of spike or wrench. Since the upper and lower threads are oppositely pitched, turning the barrel shortens the turnbuckle, putting tension on the wire.

Because rigs flex and turnbuckles don't, it is extremely important to provide a universal joint in

Figure 2-30. *Here a twisting force of 125 pounds could easily put 2,000 pounds of tension on standing rigging. The device is so efficient that it's very easy to put too much tension into a rig, so tune carefully.*

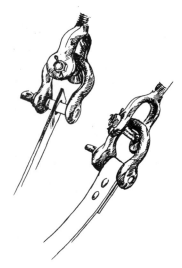

Figure 2-31. *Galvanized shackles are commonly used as toggles with galvanized turnbuckles, but a standard chainplate (left) provides relatively little bearing surface for the long shackle pin. It would be better in this case to have a chainplate shaped as at right, to prevent an excessive unsupported length.*

the form of a toggle on each turnbuckle. When using 1 x 19 wire, rod rigging, or mechanical terminals on any material, it's a good idea to have a one at the upper terminal, too. On stays that carry sails, a toggle at the upper end is mandatory. One often sees galvanized turnbuckles with shackles used as toggles. This doesn't seem like a good idea to me, since shackle pins are designed for broader bearing surfaces than chainplates ordinarily provide (Figure 2-31). It would be better to fabricate a broad-bearing chainplate, go with bronze turnbuckles and toggles, or have galvanized toggles cast.

A GENERAL ADMONITION TO KEEP THINGS TAUT (OR AT LEAST NOT SLACK)

Rope, a creature of tension, does not fare well if it is not kept set up while in use. How firmly set up is determined by vessel, materials, and circumstances, but slack is always to be avoided. Slack allows the large, heavy objects that rope must contain to

shift and bang around, inducing "shock loading."

A shock load occurs when a weight fetches up short on a line, as with a dog running out of leash. As the gauge in Figure 2-32 shows, the force exerted at the fetch-up point is considerably higher than the weight of the object imposing the load. Anyone who has seen pile drivers or draft horses at work knows that shock-loading can be turned to useful employment, but it is hell on running and standing rigging, the fittings they make up to, and the masts and hull that they make up to. Pretty soon you're shock-loading your bank account.

So take up slack smartly, ease it out smoothly, and minimize sail flog with efficient tacks. Keep standing rigging properly tuned (even if you're not concerned with high-level performance) and always be ready to let the sheets run if you're hit by a sudden squall (even if you are interested in high-level performance). Shock load when under tow can be avoided by paying out tow rope until the two vessels rise and fall on the waves simultaneously. Just keep that dog in mind.

Figure 2-32. *Analysis of a cartoon classic. Shock loading is at work with a vengeance in slackly-tuned rigs.*

SORTING

We are now possessed of an assortment of highly evolved tightening tools; it remains for us to employ them to greatest advantage, so to speak. They are each suited to one sort of job or another, but it's easy to go wrong, considering the near-infinite range of boat sizes and types, sailing conditions, and owners' preferences, all of this compounded by the range of variations on a theme for each of the basic tension-ing tools. Confronted with the dazzling gear displays at large chandleries, people have been known to go glassy-eyed, emerging from their trance many dollars poorer and with a chestful of pulleys and winches that are hopelessly inappropriate for their boat.

Do not let this befall you! Scale your gear to the job, check out other boats, and shop around.

CHAPTER 3

Friction, Part 1: Knotting

"If you can't tie a knot, tie a lot."

—Anonymous

Every knot is an exercise in friction; bends, belays, splices, and seizings all are secure to the extent that they make a line stick against itself when under strain.

If this were all there were to knotting, there'd be no art to it, but rope in use needs to be untied nearly as frequently as it is tied, and we are faced with the conflicting needs of maximum friction when tension is on, for security, and minimum friction when tension is off, so that we can untie. There are exceptions—and there are other desirable qualities—but it is this selective friction which best characterizes good knots.

Many different knots have evolved to meet many different situations and rope types. For example, several of the knots in this chapter are relatively new, invented to deal with modern synthetic rope, which is slicker than manila or hemp. Rope flexibility also varies widely, as do the sizes, shapes, and consistencies of the objects to which it is attached. And a knot that is good for one situation might prove inappropriate when used in another; use of a Bowline where hitches or an Eyesplice are better choices is a classic example. Given this range of requirements, it is in the rigger's best interest to have a healthy tying vocabulary. In this chapter I have listed several basic types of knots (bends, end

of rope, loops, etc.) and detailed the best examples of those types that I know.

Some cautionary words: Since hundreds or even thousands of pounds of pressure might come to bear on the knots you tie, it is well to be sure of the finished product. As Clifford Ashley put it, "A knot is never nearly right; it is either exactly right or it is hopelessly wrong, one or the other; there is nothing in between. This is not the impossibly high standard of the idealist, it is a mere fact for the realist to face. In a knot of eight crossings, which is about the average-size knot, there are 256 'over-and-under' arrangements possible. Make only one change in this 'over-and-under' sequence and either an entirely different knot is made or no knot at all may result."

I might add that some seemingly fussy details can make a significant difference; drawing up in a certain way, or stopping to fair a knot while in the process of tying it, can mean the difference between security and failure. Furthermore, today's sailors need to understand that HM fibers (Spectra, Vectran, etc.) are very, very slick; most knots will just crawl right out of them, at loads as low as 10 percent of breaking strength. The few knots that won't slip will usually weaken the rope by at least 60 percent. Splice HM rope. "High Modulus" (HM) is a fairly arbitrary term. Mushy even. But fibers regarded as

HM are typically at least 3 times stronger than conventional synthetics of the same diameter, and are much less elastic, to boot. This includes fibers like Spectra/Dyneema, Technora, Vectran, Kevlar, PBO, and others

A TURN AROUND THE COOK'S LEG

I was at a boat show once that was held in a huge circus tent. The entire structure was bucking and vibrating in a September gale, and the only thing that kept me from fleeing in a panic was the calm presence of Spike Africa, widely heralded "President of the Pacific Ocean." He was sitting in the bow of a skiff, chewing tobacco and covering an increasingly empty whiskey bottle with thousands of teensy knots.

"Spike," I said nervously, "this tent can't be reefed, and there are no cleats to belay to. What are we going to do if it starts to blow away?"

"Do!?" he replied in a conversational bellow. "Why, we'll take a reef in the roof! We'll take a turn

around the cook's leg! Do you think they invented belaying just so's they'd have something to do with *cleats*? Besides," he growled, returning to his hitching, "this thing was put up by pros. Why don't you take a look at their work?"

As it happened, he had every reason to be calm; the tent riggers had sunk plenty of rod anchors deep into the ground and had attached them to the stoutly built tent with heavy rope. And they knew enough about knots to use a Clove Hitch and Rolling Hitch for a secure belay (Figure 3-1).

Seeing all this, and thinking about what Spike had said, I realized that the cleats, bitts, and winches I was accustomed to were no guarantee of security in themselves. With or without them, ultimate responsibility has always lain with the sailor (or roustabout), whose job it is to analyze the circumstances and strains involved, take stock of available materials and fittings, and then secure things accordingly. This doesn't mean that you have to learn a special technique for every situation; a few basic elements are present in every good belay, and many of the techniques are interchangeable. All you need to

Figure 3-1. *Belaying with a Clove Hitch backed up by a Rolling Hitch.*

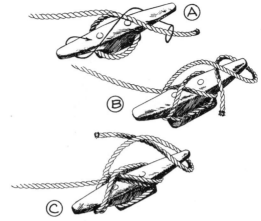

Figure 3-2. *A belay to a horn cleat starts with a full turn around the base (A) and ends with a Half Hitch (B). Avoid turning the finished loop in the wrong direction (C). Note that the cleat is angled to the lead of the standing part. Note that, with a slicker line and/or cleat, more figure-eight turns might be needed, to prevent the line from slipping, and to prevent the locking hitch from jamming.*

keep in mind are: Control, Security, Ease of Casting Off, and Ability to Surge.

To illustrate, let's look again at those tent guys. The Clove Hitch creates friction, so that only a fraction of the strain comes on the rope end, and it's easier to control the load while making the Rolling Hitch, which provides security and a means to take up slack when the line is tightened. This hitch never jams, so the tent will be easy to strike. And the friction of the Clove Hitch makes surging (gradually paying out slack to a line under strain) an easy and safe operation.

All of this is even easier on a cleat, that most highly evolved belaying tool. In Figure 3-2, the line takes a turn for control around the base of the cleat before beginning the two or three figure-eight turns that provide security. Note that the cleat is angled away from the lead of the line. This makes it easier to get a turn started, prevents the line from jamming against its own standing part, and more evenly distributes the strain on the bolts that hold the cleat to the deck. When making fast to a bollard (Figure 3-3), take a turn first around the *nearer* post before commencing figure-eight turns around both. This minimizes the tendency of the farther post to "lever up" under extreme loads.

To keep the turns of a belay from coming loose, make a Half Hitch to finish. Just pretend you're going to make another figure-eight, then slip a loop under the line and over the horn of the cleat

Figure 3-3. *The first turn on a bollard in line with the lead should be around the near post (A). When the lead is perpendicular to the bollard (B) either post will do.*

Figure 3-4A. *Belaying to an anchor bitt. Finish with a Half Hitch around the pin.*

(Figure 3-2). A hitch made in the opposite direction is perversely inclined either to slip or jam, and looks awful besides.

Note: many rigging practitioners inveigh against the use of this finishing hitch, claiming that it can result in a jammed belay. And it can … if it is a bad belay. Without sufficient figure-eight turns on the cleat, a heavy load can cause the rope to "crawl," and eventually pull the hitch so tight you might need an axe to clear it away. If the hitch isn't there, the belay won't jam, but it will keep crawling, with potentially disastrous results. Therefore, the operator's assessment of the number of figure-eight turns needed is an integral part of the belay; small, slick

Figure 3-4B. *When belaying to a pin, as when belaying to a cleat or bitt, take a turn around before starting the figure-eights (left). A turning block can improve the lead to the pin and allows for an upward pull, in which one can exert much more force than with a downward pull (center). Make a Half Hitch to finish the belay (right).*

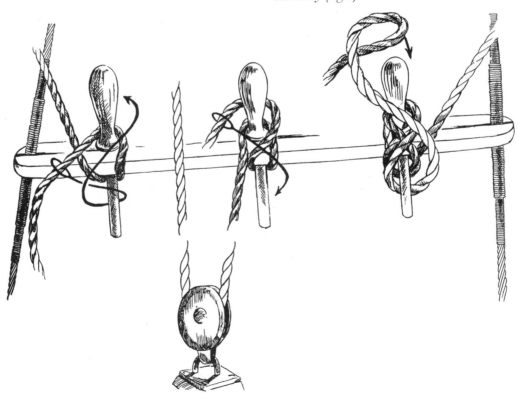

line on a large, slick cleat, for instance, will need more turns than large, gritty line on a small cleat.

A related note: few lines, in any area of rigging, are likely to see extreme loads. That's why people can make truly awful belays, and not have problems until an extreme load comes along. But good belays are, by definition, ready for worst-case scenarios. So if you always belay properly, even when it doesn't matter, you will automatically belay properly when it does.

Cleating procedures also work on bitts, Samson posts, and belaying pins, though at different orientations (Figure 3-4). The belaying-pin rail is mounted so as to follow the line of the sheer. This has the lead advantages mentioned above for cleats and also presents a more pleasing appearance than would a horizontal rail. A fife rail is mounted horizontally at the base of the mast, but the leads themselves come in at an angle whenever possible, often with the aid of turning blocks bolted below the rail. Angled cleats and pins are usually positioned to make things easier for right-handers, but sometimes the angle that a line comes in at gives us left-handers a turn at convenience.

The Capstan Hitch (Figure 3-5) is the best method for belaying to a winch, capstan, rail, or post. It's an elegant, ingenious technique that provides absolute control and security around a cylinder without the need to use the end. To tie it, pass a bight of the tail under the standing part, double back over the standing part, then turn the bight over and drop it over the winch. Then pass a bight from the opposite direction, double back, and drop it over. Repeat from both sides and finish with two Half Hitches made with a bight around the standing part.

When there's no way to drop a bight over, as when belaying to a rail, make the hitch using a long bight as though it were an end or, when convenient, use the end itself. With either method, extra tension can be gained by hauling on the tail after each pass.

When slacking away on a taut line, whether belayed with this hitch or by any other means, don't just flip the turns off willy-nilly; the force of the load might surprise you and get out of control. Keep a

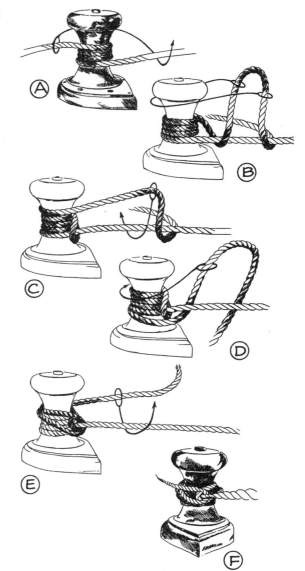

Figure 3-5. *A Capstan Hitch turns a winch into a handy belaying post.*

little tension on the tail as you undo the turns. Keep your hands well clear of the belay. When you get down to the last turns, the line will start sliding and you'll be able to feel how much tension there is. Then you can surge (pay out the slack under load), still keeping your hands well clear of the belay, until you can handle the tension with hands only. When the load is off, you can remove the last turns. To surge on a winch or capstan, hold the standing

53

Figure 3-6. *Surging a line on a winch.*

Figure 3-7. *When there doesn't appear to be anything to belay to, twisting the tackle or just pinching the parts of the tackle together can "belay" a load (A). Belaying the line to the load itself works, too (B).*

part with one hand, and place the palm of the other hand on the same side of the barrel that the standing parts lead to. Ease on the end and press and push away from you with the other hand. For very heavy loads, have someone tail the end while you place your hands on either side of the barrel. Have the tailer give you a little slack, then squeeze your hands against the turns and slide your right hand away from you and your left hand toward you to roll the turns counterclockwise, easing slack into the standing part (Figure 3-6). Be extremely careful not to get your fingers between the turns and the drum; there are some short-fingered sailors around who can tell you about the consequences.

The time might come when there is no post, pin, cleat, or seemingly anything else to belay to. Here resourcefulness must take over, even if it means employing procedures that are harder on your gear

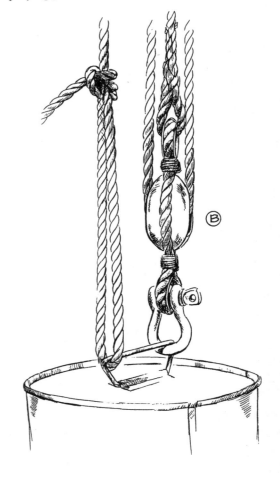

than you might prefer. Jamming a bight of the fall into the upper block of a tackle is an ancient and effective expedient, as is rotating the load to twist the parts of the tackle together. Just be sure things don't unwind until you're ready. Even pinching the parts together with your hands will keep things from moving if the load isn't too great, and sometimes you can belay to the load itself (Figure 3-7).

In an emergency, don't be shy about how you gain the friction needed for a belay, just so long as you don't slice the rope on a sharp corner. Tension is what makes rigging work, so do what you must to maintain it. . . .

Hey, Cookie! Come on over here!

SIX HITCHES

There's a fine line, so to speak, between a belaying hitch and an ordinary one: The former, as we have just seen, is designed to be applied made and released *around* an object while the line is under tension; the latter is most easily applied and released while the line is slack. Belaying techniques are plenty secure for all purposes, but they're more time- and material-consuming to tie, since they must generate sufficient friction for dynamic control. So it makes sense also to have a few simpler hitches in one's repertoire.

A Round Turn and Two Half Hitches

The old salts say that "a round turn and two Half Hitches never fail," and it's pretty nearly true. This basic hitch is ideal for starting or finishing off lashings, since it can be tied under load. It's also useful for tying small craft to mooring rings, tethering

Figure 3-8A–D. *A Round Turn and Two Half Hitches make a secure belay (A). The Clove Hitch is handy but not as secure (B). Reversed Half Hitches just don't "look right" (C). The Round Turn and Two Half Hitches can be tied under load. Here it's Double-Constrictored to the standing part for greater security. Though shown here in side view for clarity, the overhand part of the Constrictor should in practice fall on one of the two round surfaces (D).*

anything but a camel (see below), making off tool lanyards, etc. The round turn distributes strain and chafe across a greater number of rope fibers than a single turn would, while the two Half Hitches provide jam-resistant security (Figure 3-8). But this is an old workhorse, set in its ways, and it doesn't get along well with modern cordage; even under load, the hitches can untie themselves. To make them stay put, seize the end to the standing part with a Double Constrictor. This is easily cut away when you want to untie the knot.

It is widely held that reversed Half Hitches are the mark of a lubber, but there doesn't seem to be any structural justification for this belief. Perhaps the scorn stems from the can't-make-up-my-mind-which-way-to-hitch appearance of the reversed version. Or perhaps it's because reversing the turns takes a little more time and manipulation to tie. In any event, I recommend same-direction hitches, if only for the sake of confusion-reducing uniformity.

The Buntline Hitch

On a square-rigger the buntlines run from the mast to blocks on the yards, down the face of the sail, and are tied with this knot to the foot of the sail. In furling, the buntlines contain the middle, or "bunt" of the sail. Why this particular knot to secure that particular line? Because the job calls for a knot that

is absolutely secure, uncommonly compact (so the foot of the sail will get as close as possible to the yard), and simple enough that one can tie and untie it while hanging head-down 100 or so feet above the water. The same virtues make it ideal for tying a halyard to a bosun's chair—it and the Butterfly are the only knots I go up on—or to hang fenders, or a hammock, or to attach staysail sheets. Its one drawback is that it can jam under heavy loads, so you want to be selective about its use, applying it to lines that are either under moderate loads, or don't have to be untied often.

The Anchor Hitch

This one's a little more involved in the making, but worth the effort. The end is passed over the standing part and under a round turn to form a sort of compound Half Hitch, and all is drawn up well (Figure 3-10). A Half Hitch and seizing are usually added to secure the end.

This knot's primary virtue is that it holds well on lines that are alternately slack and taut, such as anchor rodes; it doesn't work loose, and it doesn't jam either. I didn't fully appreciate this knot until one summer when I met crews from two boats that had both lost anchors from Bowline-secured rodes. When you want insurance and can take the time, use an Anchor Hitch. Make an extra tuck and the

Figure 3-9. *The Buntline Hitch. Make a turn around the standing part, then reenter with the end for a Half Hitch around the standing part. Draw up.*

Figure 3-10. *The Anchor Hitch also begins with a round turn, then the end is passed behind the standing part and under the turns. Half Hitches or a Round Seizing are frequently added for long-term security.*

Anchor Hitch becomes the even more secure Stunsail Halyard Hitch. This knot can also be more compact, as it doesn't require a seizing.

The Rolling Hitch and Variations

This knot can be made under tension, which suits it for cleatless belays, but it is by no means limited to that function; of all hitches, it has the widest range of usefulness.

It can be made up close to an object instead of Half Hitches, or it can be made around rails, rings, spars, or other ropes for slinging or for hanging tackle from. It is adjustable, so tension can be maintained in tidal areas, or in rope that comes and goes when wet, or for temporary staying, when guys must be adjusted relative to one other. It is a ridiculously simple knot, suited either to perpendicular or lengthwise pull, but nevertheless ridiculously underused. To form: Make two turns in the direction of the strain, then a hitch on the side of the turns away from the strain (Figure 3-11). Turns and hitch all travel in the same direction.

If the material is inclined to slip, the Rigger's Hitch, a variation made by jamming the second turn over the first, has a more tenacious grip, though it's also difficult to adjust.

For very slick work, such as hanging a hammock from 1 × 9 wire, try another variation, the Camel Hitch. This is a circus knot, developed specifically for mooring camels, whose copious slobber and head-jerking truculence jam lesser hitches.

For all Rolling Hitch variations, draw up well so that all turns take a strain, and don't push their security by overburdening them; get the right rope at the right length, or use the next knot, which though new is rapidly replacing any form of Rolling Hitch for slick surfaces and extreme loads.

The Icicle Hitch

There is an ancient rigging challenge: devise a hitch that will hold for a lengthwise pull toward the thin end of a smooth, tapering spar. This knot meets that challenge. It is the brainchild of one John Smith, a true knotting genius (see also "The Mobius Bowline" in Chapter 11). Of course, a knot that will hold on a tapering spar will hold on anything. That's why I now use the Icicle Hitch exclusively for things like setting up rigging, stretching wire for serving, and any number of utility and emergency procedures. And as if its astonishing security weren't enough, it is also extremely easy to tie (see Figure 3-12). Thank you, Mr. Smith.

To tie the Icicle Hitch on most objects, take three to five turns around the hitchee as shown in Figure 3-12A with a Stropsicle (see Figure 4-13) or other short length of line. For very slick objects, take ten or so turns.

Figure 3-11. *The Rolling Hitch (A, B) is an adjustable knot for lengthwise pull. The Rigger's Hitch (C) is one variation. The Camel Hitch (D) has three round turns and two Half Hitches.*

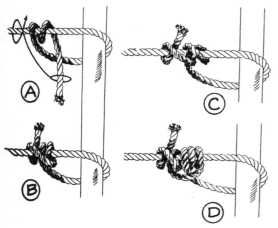

Figure 3-12A. *The Icicle Hitch. Take three to five turns around the hitchee (for slick surfaces, make up to 10 turns).*

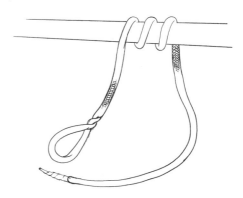

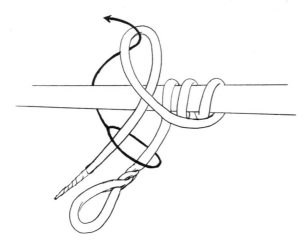

Figure 3-12B. *Form a loop and pull both ends of the strop through the loop.*

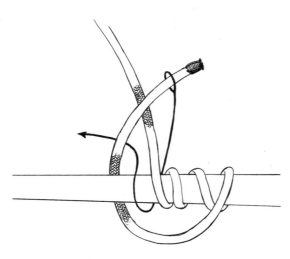

Figure 3-12C. *The Icicle Hitch with halyard (see text).*

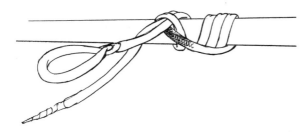

Figure 3-12D. *The finished hitch.*

Pick up the end. Twist it around so the end is under the standing part and next to the beginning of the turns. Reach through the loop thus formed and pull both ends of the strop up through the loop (Figure 3-12B). To draw up, work all the slack out of the turns, then pull on each end in turn.

To tie the Icicle Hitch with a halyard (Figure 3-12C), make three to five turns with the end, then cross back toward the beginning of the turns. Pass the end down behind the hitchee, then over the standing part. Pass it up behind the hitchee, then down alongside the standing part, under itself.

Figure 3-12D shows the finished knot.

The Axle Hitch

Scene: The hold of a ship or the underside of a car or some other god-awful, inaccessible spot. It's hard enough just to crawl or climb in there, and you don't have the time, inclination, or free hand to make a hitch while you're there. Fine—just pass a bight around and bring it back to a more comfortable location (Figure 3-13). Ah, that's better. Now pass the end around a couple of times as shown, add a Bowline or Rolling Hitch to secure the end, and hoist or tow away.

Figure 3-13. *The Axle Hitch comes to your aid in cramped quarters.*

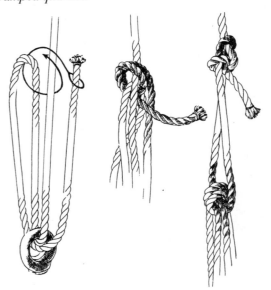

Because hitching is so basic to the use of rope, and because there are so many sizes and shapes of things to hitch onto, the foregoing must be considered a basic sampler of the class; the six knots shown will cover most situations, but be prepared to improvise. Any hitch that is meant to be more or less permanent will benefit from having its end seized to the standing part (Chapter 1). On the other hand, most hitching jobs suffer from an excess of security; people can't trust a good knot, so they keep adding convolutions that invite jamming and take time to do and undo. Always use the simplest knot—hitch or otherwise—that will do the job properly. William of Occam should have been a rigger.

SIX IN THE BIGHT

Lines don't always end where you want them to. When you need a loop to tail onto, reeve through, or hang something from, but there's no end available to make a knot with, then it's time to do some work in the bight.

There are some elementary examples of this class in the "Lashing" section of Chapter 1, specialized knots that depend on a pulley configuration to keep from spilling. But the following examples maintain their integrity unsupported, creating convenient little blurps in the standing part that can be tied and untied easily. Among other things, loops in

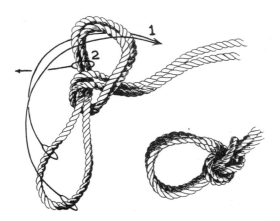

Figure 3-14A. *The Bowline on a Bight begins with an Overhand Knot, tied with a bight. Drop the bight over the Overhand Knot (1) and pull on the uppermost turn of the Overhand (2) to draw in the bight and form the neck of the knot.*

Figure 3-14B. *A Bowline on a Bight with a Bowline on it. Without the Bowline, the main knot can deform or capsize, if the load comes on only one standing part.*

the bight can be used to extend the reach of a come-along, provide handholds for team hauling, make a place to hang a ladder, plank, block, or container from, or make an eye at the top of a makeshift sling. When you have the time, they're more stable, jam-proof lashing loops as well.

The Bowline on a Bight

This is the best-known member of this class, a two-loop beauty that starts out as an Overhand Knot, becomes an amorphous tangle, and finally resolves itself into elegant utility (Figure 3-14A). This knot is the traditional choice for bight work because of its simplicity and double-bearing surface, but it is not entirely dependable when the strain comes on one part only or when the two standing parts are pulled in opposite directions. In the former instance, make a Bowline on a Bight with a Bowline on it (Figure 3-14B). In the latter instance try a different knot such as the Farmer's Loop (Figure 3-15) or the Butterfly Knot (Figure 3-16).

The Farmer's Loop

This is a fine knot for a number of reasons, not the least of which is that it provides sailors with a non-invective use for the word "farmer." Besides that, it is fast to tie, never jams, and has a perfect lead for sidewise pull. And it's fun.

To make it, start with three turns around your hand. Shift the middle turn over the left one, the new middle turn over the right one, the still-newer middle turn over the left one, and pull the newest middle turn straight out while holding on to both standing parts (Figure 3-15). Done. Because it's so handy, you'll sometimes make a Farmer's Loop at the end of a line instead of a Bowline, especially when a shackle, Backsplice, or Figure-Eight Knot make the end difficult to pass.

The Alpine Butterfly Knot

Another important single-loop knot also originated on land: The Alpine Butterfly Knot (also known as the Lineman's Loop) was first used by telegraph company crews, giving each member a comfortable loop to haul on for raising poles and tightening

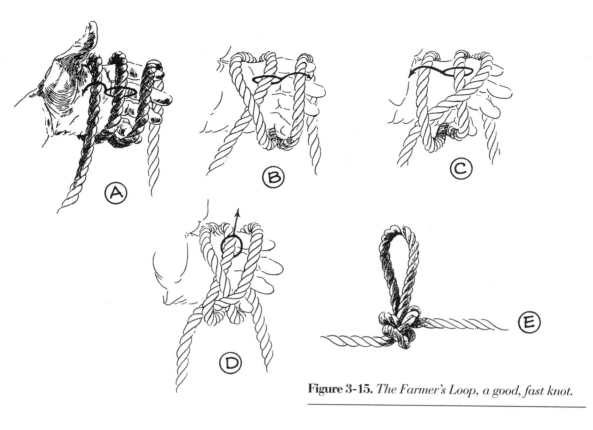

Figure 3-15. *The Farmer's Loop, a good, fast knot.*

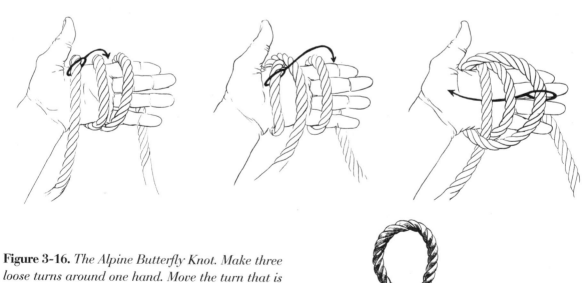

Figure 3-16. *The Alpine Butterfly Knot. Make three loose turns around one hand. Move the turn that is nearest to you over into the middle. Move the turn that is now nearest to you over, then back under, the other two turns. Draw up.*

wires. It is begun with three loose turns around the hand (Figure 3-16). Put the turn that is closest to your wrist over onto your fingertips. Pick up the new closest turn, and put it over, then under the other two turns. Draw up by pulling on the loop and both standing parts. The Alpine Butterfly Knot is strong, secure, compact, and is the foundation of a beautiful double-loop form, the Double Butterfly.

The Double Butterfly

This knot (Figure 3-17) is a little tricky to tie, but its splayed loops make it preferable to the Bowline on a Bight for some slinging applications (ladders, pallets) and for sitting in. Either knot is good as an emergency bosun's chair.

To make a Double Butterfly, start with a loose single one and drop the two "ears" down into

---

Figure 3-17. *The Double Butterfly. Unlike the Bowline on a Bight, this knot will remain stable if the load comes on only one of the standing parts.*

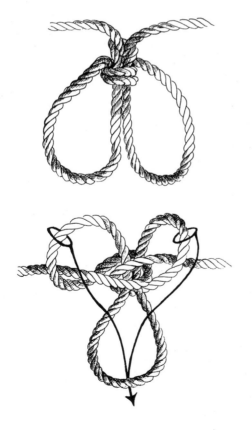

the loop. Pass the loop up to the top of the knot and draw the slack into the ears, which have now become two loops. Note that in the doubled version, the two standing parts can be pulled on together or one at a time, but they must not be pulled *apart*.

The Jug Sling Knot

In a world where plastic and glass containers come with built-in handles, this knot might seem unnecessary and its inclusion here whimsical, but I do have some reasons for showing it. First, it is an excellent example of applied friction. Second, if you've ever had to carry a gallon jug any distance, as from a store to your boat, you know that those convenient little ring handles aren't good for anything but crippling your fingers. Third, this is the best way to secure a wine bottle for a cooling tow astern.

So, clear a space and lay down some line as shown in Figure 3-18. Form an eye by twisting the legs twice. Reach into the eye, palm down. Snag the middle of the bight and pull it out, turning your hand palm up as you do so, to encourage the mess to take the form shown in 3-18D. Pull the leftmost turn back and to the right, turn the knot over, pass one bight under, adjust a bit, and the knot appears. Bend the two ends on one side together through the bight on the other side to form a wrist strap. As long as the line is scaled to the bottle size, this knot will hold on even a hint of a lip with absolute security.

Besides its original purpose, the Jug Sling Knot can be turned to carrying a thermos, slinging a marlingspike, or for emergency shroud attachment. It even makes a decorative button frog.

The Angler's Loop

By way of showing the permutations old knots go through, here is an Angler's Loop history: It started out as the name implies, as a knot for fishing line, back when the line was made of gut. The line was rendered obsolete by the introduction of synthetic line, but the knot adapted, and is still in use for its original purpose. Then someone started using the knot for large line, because although it jammed, it was very quick and easy to tie, whether by the

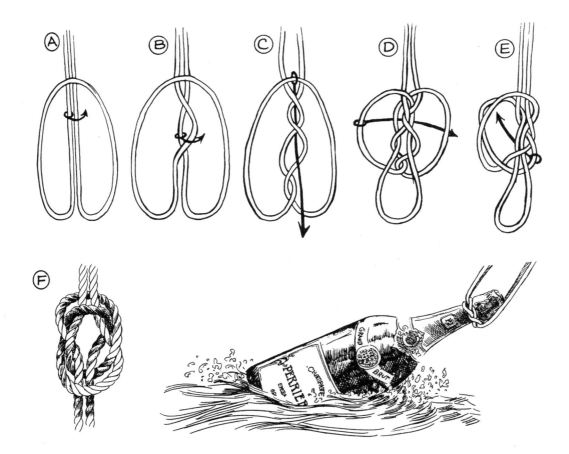

Figure 3-18. *The Jug Sling Knot. Lay a bight back over its standing parts, then twist those parts twice to form an eye. Grasping the knot by its two legs, lift it up slightly, then reach through the eye with the thumb and forefinger to snare the bight between the two legs; pull the bight through the eye (follow the arrow in C), twisting it 180 degrees to arrive at the configuration in D. Now pass the left-hand ear under the knot as in D, then carefully turn the knot over to get the configuration in E. Pass one bight (shown by the arrow in E) under the knot, and arrange the knot to get the configuration in F. Draw up around the neck of your jug.*

method shown here or the showy Tugboat (or Flying) Bowline technique (see the following section, "Seven Bowlines"). So the Angler's Loop survived, used as a speedily produced but little-known alternative to the Bowline. Then along came bungee cord, which is so slick and springy that many common knots will crawl right out of it. Geoffrey Budworth, a past Secretary of the International Guild of Knot Tyers, faced this bungee drawback when he was trying to secure gear on the deck of his kayak. It was he who resurrected the Angler's Loop for this modern material.

This knot is useful elsewhere, of course, but watch out for its tendency to jam. Figure 3-19 shows it being tied near the end of the line, without using the end. This can be done with any bight loop, as alternatives to the Bowline.

There are many other in-the-bight knots, but these are the cream; compare against them any others that you might want to use, to be certain they also possess the virtues of strength, good lead, ease of tying and untying, and especially security. If a bight knot slips, you can get caught in the middle.

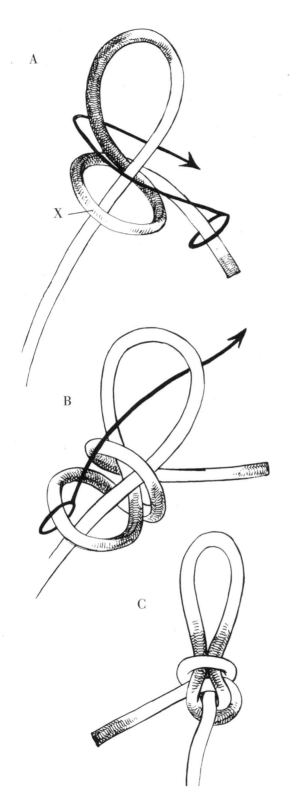

A

X

B

C

Figure 3-19. *An Angler's Loop allows for length adjustment. Begin by making a counterclockwise loop with the end behind the standing part. Make two complete turns with the end around the loop, the second turn to the right of the first. Pass the first turn over the second and through the loop to finish. A hook or snapshackle can be threaded on and kept at point "X" while tying to have it end up on the loop.*

SEVEN BOWLINES

Paul Newman was up there on the silver screen, swaggering his way through a role as a fiercely independent logger. He swaggered as he climbed a tree, he swaggered as he cut one down, and he swaggered as he put a Bowline into a big hawser.

"Wait a minute! Did you see that?" I said to my companion.

"See what?" she said.

"That Bowline. He tied it without letting go of the end! And fast! How did he do it?"

"Calm down, Brion," she said.

"Sshhh!" said people around us. But I was already digging in my pocket for a length of string. The Bowline is the King of Knots because it is strong, secure, and versatile, as kings should be. And simple, as kings generally are. It was rare good fortune to come across a new way to tie it, and I wanted to try to duplicate the movements while they were still fresh in my mind.

"You're a log," I said to my friend.

"I beg your pardon?"

"Quiet, you two!"

"The hawser was around a log," I whispered. "Hold up your arm."

Tidal and Storm Mooring

In strong tidal areas or in storms, set Bowlines around pilings for your mooring lines. The loops can ride up and down, needing no adjustment. If there is an eyesplice in the end of the mooring line, you can make a Mobius Bowline (see page 365) which cannot come untied by accident.

So in the crowded theater, with the aid of my bewildered friend, I practiced the method. Quietly. In years to come, in more appropriate circumstances, it would prove itself as the best technique for putting a Bowline into heavy or stiff line. And I could always say, "Here's one Paul Newman showed me."

Newman Bowline

It's an ingenious knot, even an elegant one (see Figure 3-20). Look how that sweeping judo move throws a turn into the line. True, at one point you do let go, but with a little practice, it doesn't look as though you do.

Compare that one continuous motion with the rabbit-comes-out-of-the-hole-and-runs-around-

the-tree method of tying a Bowline (mercifully not shown here) that many of us learned. Clumsy and slow. How can we call the Bowline the King of Knots and then make it in a manner that can only be described as low-class? And it's not as if there's only one alternative to the rabbit version.

Spilled-Hitch Bowline

When the line is neither bulky nor stiff, its flexibility will make the Newman Bowline difficult to execute. No matter, the Bowline earned its royal sobriquet not only for its strength, security, and ease of untying—other knots possess those virtues—but also for its versatility. So we have a second alternative (Figure 3-21), which starts out as an innocent-looking Half Hitch made with the end around the standing part. A little push and pull spills the hitch into the standing part, the end is tucked, and suddenly you're done. Basically, it is a less flashy version of the Newman method and, like it, is easier in every instance than the usual practice of forming a bight with your hand and threading your way through it.

Fingertip Bowline

Still another variation is used to make a Bowline freehand (Figure 3-22); there's no piling, cleat, or such to brace against, such as the previous knots

---

Figure 3-20. *Newman Bowline. Pass the end of the line around a post and hold the standing part in one hand, the end in the other. Reach across the standing part with your end hand (with the end pointing toward the post), and then pivot your hand under the standing part and back toward you. There should now be a loop around your wrist. Pass the end under the standing part and let go of the end momentarily to reach over and grab it from the other side. Finally, pull it and your hand out of the loop to form the knot.*

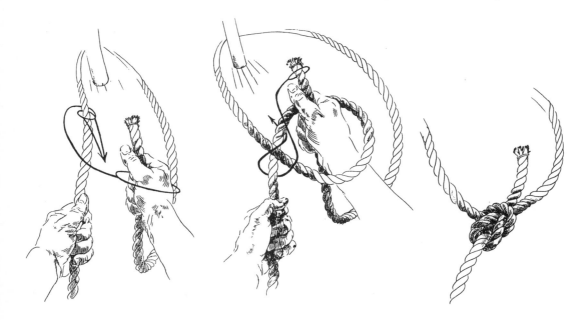

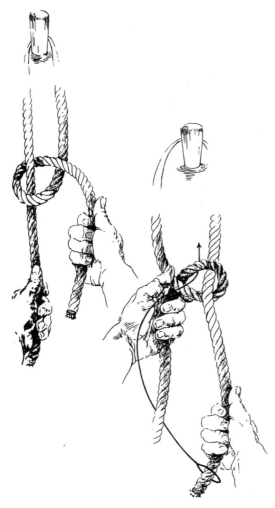

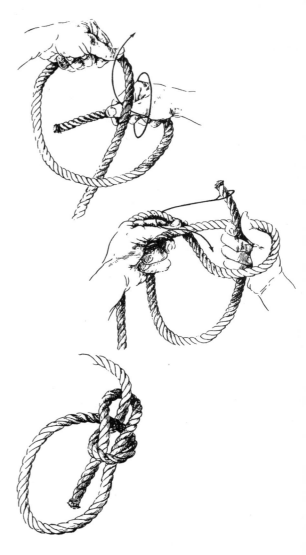

Figure 3-21. *Spilled-Hitch Bowline. With the end around a post, make a Half Hitch with the end around the standing part. Pull the end toward you and ease the standing part away to spill the hitch into the standing part. To finish, pass the end behind the standing part and back whence it came.*

Figure 3-22. *Fingertip Bowline. Hold the line in the position shown first, with the end and standing parts away from you and the bight hanging in front of you. Cross the end behind the standing part, through the loop, and up and away, forming a loop around your fingers. Meanwhile, lift the standing part with the opposite hand, as shown, and pass the end behind the standing part and back through the loop around your fingers. Draw up.*

require. It's all done with the fingertips and a little wrist motion, with the same motion you use to start the Marlingspike Hitch (see page 7).

Once you know these first three knots, you can work with the eye of the Bowline toward or away from you, and with or without a prop. Never again do you have to hang outboard or hunch sideways to get the line in a familiar orientation.

The Fingertip method is the one to use when you want to impress someone by tying a Bowline behind your back.

The Enhanced Bowline

The Bowline is so universally revered that people feel they've done something wrong if it slips or jams. So it's with a sense of bewilderment and guilt that we try to reinforce it with everything from shackles to duct tape, when all along the problem almost certainly lies with the unprecedentedly slick line we use nowadays. But a simple extra tuck, or an extra turn before tucking, is all it takes to restore the King of Knots to its accustomed regal security (Figure 3-23). And this also seems to lessen the Bowline's inclination to jam under extremes of loading.

Slipknot Bowline

And now, for something completely different, a knot startling enough to be performed purely as a trick yet practical enough to save your life. May I introduce the fabulous Slipknot Bowline (Figure 3-24).

The illustrations tell the story, but it's hard to believe the thing actually works until you've tried it yourself. And then it's just about impossible to resist saying "Voilà!" as the knot appears out of nowhere.

I once used this knot to make up to a piling at a cleatless section of dock, in near-dark, in a crowded marina, when a strong tide was running and our engine wasn't. We could have and probably should have anchored out, but we knew the place and the wind was right; so as I stood in the bow with Slipknot ready, we luffed up into the current alongside the dock. I threw the long end around the piling, dropped it through the Slipknot, and the Bowline capsized into being as the boat drifted back. The

Figure 3-23A. *Two-Bight Bowline. Start with the Spilled-Hitch Bowline; after spilling the hitch, add an identical hitch and spill it, too. Then pass the end behind the standing part and through both hitches. This knot is less liable to slip or jam than the regular Bowline.*

Figure 3-23B. *Another Bowline for slick line. Merely tuck the end back through as shown.*

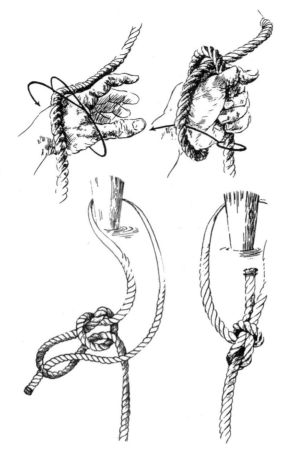

Figure 3-24. *Slipknot Bowline. The tricky part of this knot is making the Slipknot. Lay the line over your wrist as shown, with the standing part nearest you. Reach around behind the end and grab the standing part, thumb uppermost. Hang on and pull your hand out of the loop, and you'll have a Slipknot. Leave it loose. If you haven't already done so, pass or flip the end around the post, and drop the end into the bight of the Slipknot. The Slipknot should be looser than is shown. Haul on the standing part, and a Bowline will spill into existence. (lower left by Margaret Wilson-Briggs)*

only misfortune was that there were no spectators around to witness this neat trick.

Of course, the Slipknot Bowline's usefulness isn't limited to tight situations; some people use it almost exclusively, since it is easy to tie, minimizes opportunities for fumbling, and is very quickly completed. In fact, the only Bowline that takes less time to make isn't really a Bowline at all.

Tugboat (or Flying) Bowline

Call it what you will, this Bowline is really a form of the Angler's Loop (see "Six in the Bight," above), a strong knot with excellent lead but also with a tendency to jam. So, if it's not a Bowline, why is it described here? Because sailors at times need a Bowline faster than a Bowline can be made. So they use this knot instead and think so highly of it, despite its shortcomings, that they call it after the King. Think of it as a royal bastard.

It is an action knot; the odds are that when you use it you will be in a hurry, and I've never seen anyone demonstrate it without the prefatory phrase, "So you're running down the deck, see. . . . " In truth, it can be done in a hot New York nanosecond, at a dead run.

Dragon Bowline

Whew! Exertion. There are so many more Bowlines: made on or with a bight, slipped, from Half Hitches, with round turns, interlocked and running, as well as all the national variations (French, Spanish, Portuguese, Chinese), but six at one sitting is plenty, so let's finish up with an ancient, nasty trick. It's best done after an exchange of unusual knots, like some of those just mentioned. At the proper moment, casually ask, "Ever see a Dragon Bowline?"

If your audience hasn't read this book, they will probably answer, "No, how do you make that one?"

Look at them carefully for a moment, as if uncertain that they are worthy of the knowledge you are about to impart. Then slowly make an ordinary Bowline and place it very gently on the ground, "with the standing part leading straight out, like this." If they've seen the Slipknot or Tugboat (Flying) versions, they'll be staring with rapt attention, waiting for something to happen. Pick up the standing part and walk away, explaining, "Now that's a draggin' Bowline."

Be prepared to duck.

Figure 3-25. *Tugboat Bowline. Start with about 2 feet of end hanging from the thumb side of your right hand, the standing part extending from the thumb side of your left hand, and about 3 feet of line between your hands. By turning your hands inward and toward each other, you form two loops and cause the end to swing over the standing part. As it does so, change its lateral motion to vertical motion by flipping outward with the right wrist and moving your arms sharply away from you (see detail). The idea is to get the end to flip completely around the loop on your left hand and emerge between the two loops. It's a very kinetic knot that requires practice. To finish, reach in through the left loop from the outside with the left hand, and grab the right loop. Grab the standing part with your right hand. Pull your hands apart. Voilà! (This knot takes 30 times as long to describe as it does to make.)*

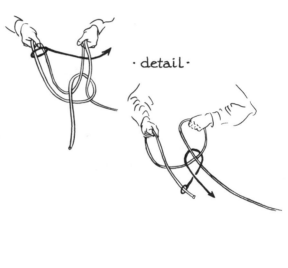

· detail ·

Figure 3-26. Dragon Bowline.

EIGHT BENDS

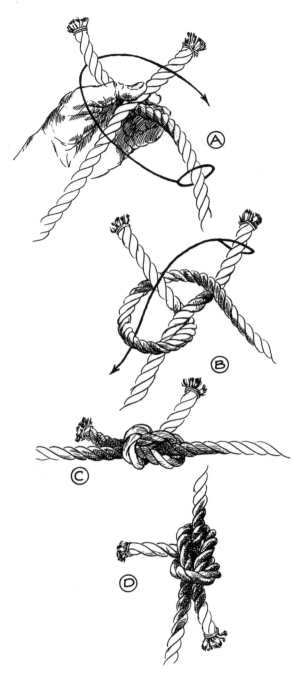

Saying that a bend is a way to tie two ropes together is like saying that Julia Child was a cook; both definitions are true as far as they go, but they leave out a great deal of information about complex and unpredictable subjects.

For instance, there's the matter of style: practiced, easy grace can do wonders, whether one is dealing with a recalcitrant mousse or a frozen hawser.

Then there's the need for appropriate use of ingredients: Ms. Child could fashion a religious experience out of a few simple items which, in the hands of a less talented chef, might yield only indigestion. Similarly, a good bend is an elegant, subtle interweaving of the exact same ingredients from which a lubber will fashion that Spam of knots, the Granny.

Sometimes the worlds of cuisine and ligature overlap, as in the case of the Butcher's Knots used to bind roasts, corned beef, salt pork, etc., but most often the virtues mentioned above are manifested in quite different particulars. Leaving Julia the Chicken Ballantine, let us turn our attention to bends.

The Sheet Bend

This most utilitarian knot, structural cousin to the Bowline, acquires a useful dash of style when made by the Weaver's method (Figure 3-27). Afloat or ashore, ease and speed of tying are among the most important qualities a bend can have. Note that in the finished knot both ends are above the standing part. It is possible to mis-tie and finish with the ends diagonally opposite each other, making a "backwards Sheet Bend"—a form that is much more liable to slip than the proper knot.

But the Sheet Bend is no paragon of virtue, either. It's perfectly adequate for most situations but will jam under very heavy loads, and can slip when made in slick material, as Table 3 (page 73) shows. Much modern synthetic cordage is, of course, very slick. So, although it's a good basic bend and can be tied in a hurry, the Sheet Bend does have its drawbacks.

Figure 3-27. *Sheet Bend tied by the Weaver's method. The arrows detail the method of tying. To draw up, hold left standing part and end together while pulling on right standing part. A backwards Sheet Bend (D), in which the ends are diagonally opposite each other, should be avoided.*

Figure 3-28. *Double Sheet Bend, Weaver's method. Make two round turns with the right-hand standing part, the first turn all the way around and the second finishing between the two ends. Tuck the right-hand end into the turns and draw up carefully.*

The Double Sheet Bend

Enter the Double Sheet Bend, which has an extra turn in it to prevent slipping. This knot can be made by a variation on the Weaver's method (Figure 3-28) unless one is bending an end to an Eyesplice, in which case the end must be rove as in Figure 3-29. By either method, the Double Sheet Bend is the preferred knot for joining lines of different size, consistency, or wetness; the smaller, suppler, or drier line makes the two turns. The Double Sheet Bend is secure but not impervious to jamming, and it needs to be carefully drawn up.

Some texts present these first two knots as the only bends one needs to know, but it is better to think of them as specialized tools, each possessed of important qualities and each afflicted with certain drawbacks. Together they form the foundation of a good bend vocabulary, but we're still only semifluent unless we know some bends that have an additional feature—a good lead.

Both the Sheet Bend and the Double Sheet Bend share the structural defect of poor lead. That is, in each knot an end emerges parallel to the standing part. As you can see from Figure 3-30, the end can snag another object, making the rope hang up in an annoying—perhaps dangerous—fashion. The same

Figure 3-29. *Double Sheet Bend tied with an end. Pass the end through, then twice around the eye, leading it under its own standing part on both turns.*

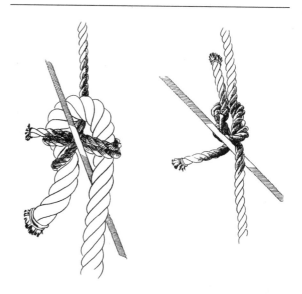

Figure 3-30A. *The poor lead of a Sheet Bend or Double Sheet Bend can cause snags like this.*

Figure 3-30B. *The Square Knot combines poor lead with a tendency to spill and fall apart when snagged. Never use it as a bend.*

illustration shows why the Square Knot is *not* one of our eight bends: weakness and abysmal lead is compounded by the likelihood that a snag will "spill" the knot into two Half Hitches. The same thing can happen even without an end being snagged if the ropes are of different size or consistency, or even if one is wet and the other dry. That is why its use should be restricted to applications where the ends are unlikely to be snagged, the body of the knot is supported, and the loads are low and indirect. Sensible uses include things like shoelaces, reef nettles, and belts for martial arts uniforms.

The Zeppelin Bend

But do use this, one of the very few slip- and jam-proof knots that also has perfect lead (Figure 3-31). It takes a teensy bit of dexterity to tie, but that's a small price to pay for the near-ideal knot that results. The story goes that a Capt. Charles Rosenthal of the airship Los Angeles wouldn't allow his ground crew to use any other bend for his ship's mooring lines. Since the U.S. Navy never called its airships "Zeppelins," it is possible that this knot came from Germany, but that's all I know of its origin.

Figure 3-31. *The Zeppelin Bend. Make a clockwise loop with one end, leaving the end in front of the standing part. Make a clockwise loop with the other end, but with the end behind the standing part. Place the first loop on top of the second. Pass the first loop's end up through the two loops and the second loop's end down through the two loops. Draw up snugly.*

The Ashley Bend

No doubt about the origin of this knot: It was invented by Clifford Ashley on February 3, 1934 (Figure 3-32). It has all the advantages of the Zeppelin Bend and is a little easier to tie (both ends are passed simultaneously to finish). Ashley placed a great deal of emphasis on knot security, so he must have been very pleased to find that this was the only nonjamming bend in his security testing (see Table 3) that did not slip at all after 100 tugs.

In spite of these results, he was too modest to name it after himself and instead simply listed it as #1,452 in his monumental *Ashley Book of Knots.* But so many people found it to be the best bend they'd ever encountered that by 1947, when C. L. Day heartily recommended it in his *Art of Knotting and Splicing,* the inventor's name was firmly linked with his knot.

The Benson Bend

This one needs a preamble: The appearance of a slightly different version of "Eight Bends" in *WoodenBoat* magazine (July/August 1983) resulted in a flurry of letters suggesting variations, new knots,

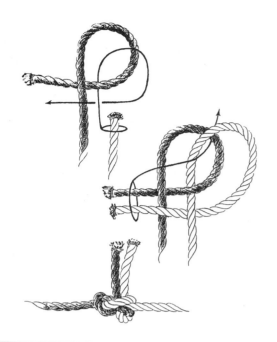

Figure 3-32. *The Ashley Bend. Start with a clockwise loop, end behind the standing part, then weave an identical loop into it, passing the second end in a regular under-and-over sequence. Finish by passing both ends into the eye in the middle.*

and different techniques for tying; bends are still fertile ground for innovation. The Weaver's method for tying the Double Sheet Bend, for example, comes to you courtesy of Fred Kenderdine of Billerica, Massachusetts.

It's only because the scope of this book is not encyclopedic that more suggestions have not been included. But I couldn't leave out the comments of a Mr. John "Fud" Benson who wrote to say, "In tying the Ashley Bend I was struck by its resemblance to a two-strand Wall and Crown Knot. . . ." Indeed, the two knots are analogous, even though they are

---

Table 3. Security

Since experience had shown him that security was one of the most important attributes of a good bend, Clifford Ashley conducted tests on 20 bends to gauge their resistance to slipping. Each knot (tied in mohair—a very slick, springy material) was given a series of as many as 100 sharp, even tugs and rated by the number of tugs needed to pull it apart. The results were presented on page 273 of *The Ashley Book of Knots*, and are reprinted here with permission.

The figures in the table represent relative security and should be considered a guide only, since most bends will fare better in regular cordage. For example, the Sheet Bend is adequate for use in three-strand manila, hemp, and spun Dacron, but should not be used in slicker materials such as filament Dacron, nylon, most polypropylene, or any double-braid rope. In the latter cases, a more slip-resistant bend such as the Ashley or Strait is called for. Of the bends described above, the Sheet Bend fared the worst, coming apart after an average of 22.3 pulls. Next came the Double Sheet Bend at 36.2. The Carrick Bend lasted through 70.8 pulls, and the Ashley Bend endured 100 tugs without slipping at all.

The other three recommended bends were not included in the test, but my own experience leads me to rate the Ashley Hawser Bend in a league

with the Carrick Bend, the Zeppelin, and the Strait Bends on a par with the Ashley Bend.

Note that Spectra is even more slick and springy than mohair. And even if you can get a bend to hold in this stuff, it will likely weaken the rope by at least 60%.

Number of tugs to spill knot*	Name of Knot
1.0	Whatnot
2.6	Single Carrick Bend A
3.	Granny Knot
4.5	Single Carrick Bend B
4.6	Single Carrick Bend C
12.2	Thief Knot
14.6	**Left-Hand Sheet Bend
19.	**Reef Knot
19.6	**Carrick Bend, both ends on same side of knot
22.3	**Sheet Bend
22.8	Overhand Bend in left-twisted yarn
25.8	Whatnot, jammed
30.9	Harness Bend, single
33.1	Overhand Bend, left-handed in left-twisted yarn
36.2	**Double Sheet Bend
42.9	Englishman's or Waterman's Knot
70.8	**Carrick Bend with diagonal pull
100.	Ring Knot (slight slip but did not spill)
100.	Barrel Knot (no slip)
100.	**Ashley Bend (no slip)

Maximum 100.
**Knots mentioned in accompanying text.*

made and drawn up by completely different methods for completely different purposes. Although the Wall and Crown Knot (see Chapter 4, Figure 4-7, and Chapter 10, Figures 10-14 and 10-15) predates this bend by centuries, no one had ever considered using it as anything but a lanyard knot. I'm certain that even Ashley never realized this coincidence of structure, since his knot was the result of trial and error with similar configurations.

In a subsequent conversation, Fud pointed out that this situation was something Ashley stressed: The tendency for dormant or underused knots to find new uses as time goes on. In this case the development of slippery synthetic rope brought the Ashley Bend to the fore.

Not content merely to make incisive comments, Fud set about experimenting with two-strand lanyard knots to see if he might surprise another worthwhile bend. Sure enough, the accompanying knot resulted, which I hereby christen the Benson Bend (Figure 3-33). It is secure, has a perfect lead, and draws up readily; these qualities, combined with its extraordinarily handsome appearance, compensate for a slight tendency to jam—no worse than the Sheet Bend.

The Strait Bend

My own contribution to the world of bends is this one (Figure 3-34), named after the Strait of Juan de Fuca in the Pacific Northwest.

This knot, structurally analogous to the Alpine Butterfly Knot (Figure 3-16), neither slips nor jams. These and other virtues mentioned in connection with the previous knots are hard to find in combination, but they must be part of any reasonable

Figure 3-33. *The Benson Bend. Make an Overhand Knot, then pass each end over the other's standing part and up through the middle of the knot.*

definition of a general-purpose bend. Which knot you might use comes down in part to personal preference; every knot has a friend somewhere.

It doesn't seem reasonable, but here's one more demand: Make a bend in line that is very large or stiff or both, such as the frozen hawser I mentioned at the beginning, without sacrificing any of a good bend's virtues. This is a specialized challenge that none of the previous knots is well suited for. But here are two that are.

The Carrick Bend

This beautiful knot is the traditional big-rope bend (Figure 3-35). It's made with an easily remembered over-and-under sequence, and since there are no sharp curves, wrestling with the subject is minimized.

The Carrick Bend will not jam, but owing to the ornery massiveness of the line it is usually formed

Figure 3-34. *The Strait Bend. Make a counterclockwise loop, end behind standing part. Drop the other end into this loop, then make a clockwise loop with that end, with the end also behind the standing part (A). Pass both ends into the eye (B) to finish (C).*

Figure 3-35. *The Carrick Bend. Make a counterclockwise loop, end in front of standing part. Place the other piece's standing part on the loop, and thread end in regular under-and-over sequence as shown. Drawn up (B), the Carrick Bend is secure but bulky, with a poor lead, and not easily untied. It is usually left loose (C), with ends seized to standing part, for ease of untying.*

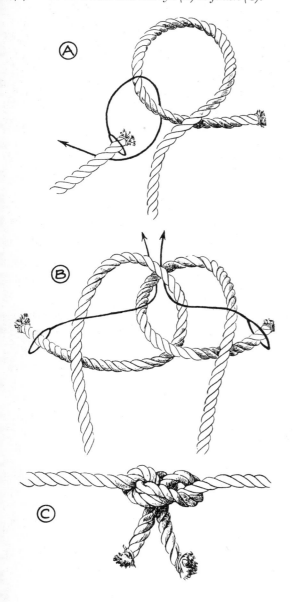

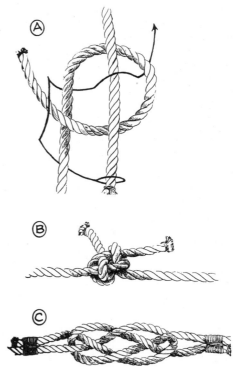

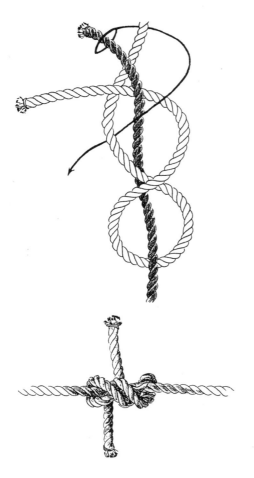

loosen. A seized Carrick is still the preferred knot, but the resourceful big-rope bender will know both.

The Connoisseur's Advantage   Every knot is an exercise in friction, a device to make rope grip itself or another object for a specific purpose and circumstance. As we've seen, even the ostensibly simple task of bending two ropes together can be complicated, even redefined, by basic practical considerations. Some people may prefer a more limited menu of bends, but extreme simplicity can only be had at the expense of effectiveness. Better the pleasures of detail, principle, and resourcefulness—the connoisseur's advantage.

Bend Appétit.

A SPECIALIST

The knots considered so far have all had a pretty wide field of usefulness. This is a hallmark of a good knot, and it's the reason why if you only learn good ones, you only have to learn a few.

However, there are some very specialized knots out there that are also worth getting to know. By way of example, how about a knot that will ensure more accurate (read: less embarrassing) heaving-line throws? A heaving line can be any light line, attached to a mooring line at one end and to a weight at the other. Throwing this is a lot easier than throwing the mooring line itself.

But the traditional heaving line has two serious drawbacks, which I believe have limited its use aboard yachts. The first is that the traditional weight has been a metal-cored knot called a Monkey's Fist. When this thing hits something, be it another boat or the skull of someone trying to catch the heaving line, some serious damage can result. As if this actionable quality weren't enough, Monkey's

in, it can be difficult to untie once it is drawn up. Therefore, it is customary to seize the ends to the standing parts with Round Seizings. These keep the knot open, making it much easier to untie. If the seizings slip under extreme loads, the knot can be relied upon to draw up into its secure compact form. As another look at Table 3 will show, there are several Carrick variations. This, number 17 on the list, is the only one worth tying. Beware of imitations.

The Ashley Hawser Bend

Our eighth selection is another hawser bend, one that does not require the use of seizings and is more compact and easily untied than a drawn-up Carrick. It's another Ashley original—with a Zeppelin-like lead—and can always be loosened by nudging the upper bight (Figure 3-36). Well, nudging might mean hitting it with a sledgehammer, but it will

Fists have a sadistic habit of landing at the edge of a dock, then bouncing merrily into the water. This necessitates recoiling and reheaving as your boat drifts toward disaster. And the heaving line is also devilishly tricky to throw accurately. The usual procedure is to coil the line, hold the coil in one hand, and heave it underhand or sidearm. Sounds simple, but it's very easy to snag the coil with a finger or mis-time the release. The result is a lovely arc of rope that goes nowhere near the dock, usually in full view of scornful onlookers.

Well, friends, if you'll examine Figure 3-37 you'll see a tamed heaving line. The weight is a can-vas bag filled with sand. Any canvas shop can whip one up for you in minutes, or you can get one from an arborist's supply house (see your Yellow Pages). The bag won't cripple, doesn't bounce, and has a certain utilitarian grace to it. The coil is ready for throwing, held by a "trigger," made from the line itself, that was invented by Swiss sailor Sam Rogers. To release, you just lift your thumb. Thanks, Sam.

Figure 3-37. *A tamed heaving line. It won't cripple the receiver or mortify the thrower.*

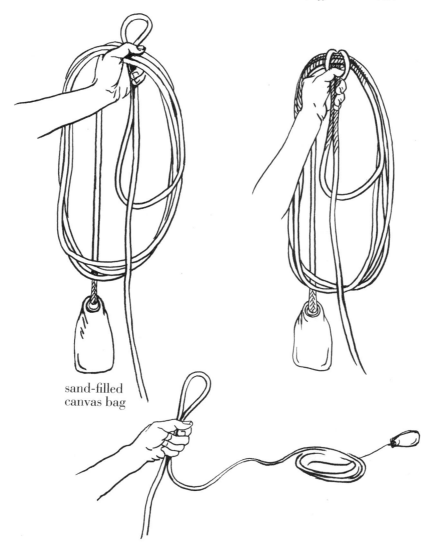

sand-filled
canvas bag

THE END OF YOUR ROPE: STOPPER KNOTS

Some years ago I was sitting next to the helm in a gaff sloop as we ran before a stiff breeze. The sails were set wing-and-wing, and we were all a little too caught up in the beauty of a blustery Puget Sound day. With the boom way out there wasn't enough of the mainsheet to cleat, and the end dangled from the trimmer's hand. Idly, I reached over and put a Figure-Eight Knot in the end of the line, seconds before our inattention resulted in a vicious jibe. The boom sped across, carrying away a running backstay. It probably would have removed the shrouds too, and maybe the mast, if it hadn't been for that knot jamming in the sheet block. It's the standing part of the line that gets the attention—all that hauling and coiling—but from that day forward I've had a particular interest in how lines end.

Basic Bulk

The Figure-Eight Knot is the basic stopper knot, so-called from its function. It is preferred to the simpler Overhand Knot because it is bulkier and a little less prone to jam (Figure 3-38).

When a still bulkier knot is required, as when the block is oversized, tie a Stevedore's Knot or an Oysterman's Stopper (Figures 3-39 and 3-40). For the former, commence making a Figure-Eight Knot, but make an extra turn around the standing part before tucking the end through the bight. For the latter, make a Slipknot as shown and tuck the end

Figure 3-39. *Stevedore's Knot. Start as with the Figure-Eight Knot, but make an extra round turn before passing the end.*

Figure 3-40. *Oysterman's Stopper. Make a Slipknot so that the standing part slides, then pass the end in front of the standing part and up through the loop from behind. Tighten by drawing up the Slipknot, then pulling on the end.*

Figure 3-38. *Figure-Eight Knot.*

into the bight. To draw up, first tighten the Slip-knot, then pull the end snug, and finally haul on the standing part. It takes only a moment.

The Oysterman's Stopper is a handsome knot with an instructive story behind it. Its inventor, Clifford Ashley, assumed like most of us that all possible knots had already been invented. Then one day he saw a knot he did not recognize in the end of the foresail halyard of a passing Delaware Bay oyster boat. Being what I can only describe as obsessed with knots, he promptly got a piece of line and set about trying to reconstruct what he had seen, ending up with the knot you see here. But when he later found that same boat and went aboard, he found that his mysterious knot was simply a Figure-Eight Knot tied in extremely gouty rope! He had invented his first knot, and realizing it could be done he went on to invent many more. I mention this story to illustrate that there is still room for innovation, even in the simplest forms of knotting.

For example, if you make an extra half-turn with the end before tucking it through the bight (à la Stevedore) you will get a different knot, and one less prone to jam. Because it is both secure and removable, I christened it the Sink Stopper (Figure 3-41).

Non-Bulk

Sometimes stoppers are no advantage or even a disadvantage, as on mooring or lashing lines, where they just get in the way. Yet something is needed at the end to keep the line from raveling. Since the advent of synthetic line, the most prevalent technique has been the Butane Backsplice (Figure 3-42), made by fusing the fiber ends with a cigarette lighter. This is fast and convenient, but it does have several drawbacks:

1. When melted, synthetics give off highly toxic fumes and molten sludge.
2. The resulting lump is hard and has sharp edges; in use it will slash away at sails, brightwork, and crew.

Figure 3-41. *Sink Stopper. Start with the Oysterman's Stopper, but make an extra half-turn before passing the end.*

Figure 3-42. *The Butane Backsplice.*

3. Butane Backsplices crack without warning and let the line ravel. On double-braid the core can pull away from the cover, leaving more tension on one than the other and weakening the line.
4. They are ugly.

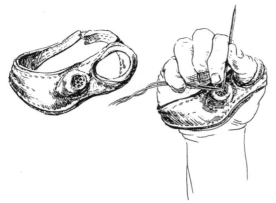

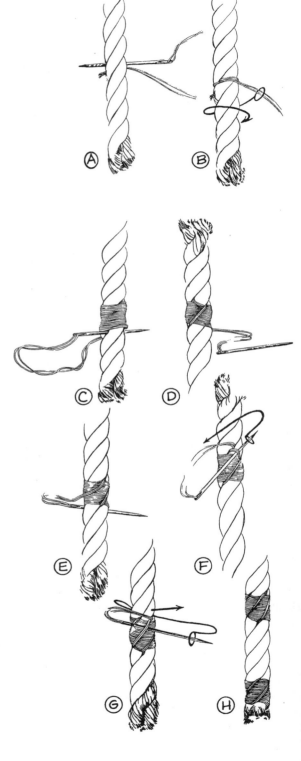

Figure 3-43. *A palm, shown at right on the hand with needle in place.*

Figure 3-44. *The Palm and Needle Whipping. Thread a fathom of twine onto a sail needle, wax the twine, and stick the needle through twice to secure the end. On the second pass, make the needle come out in one of the rope's scores (A). Make a series of tight turns toward the end, against the rope's lay (B). When the turns are about as long as the rope is wide, stick the needle under one strand, with the lay (opposite the direction the turns were made in). The needle should enter into the same score that it exited from at the beginning of the turns (C). End-for-end the rope, lead the twine down the score it emerges from, then stick the needle back into the score and under one strand, with the lay. This makes the first frapping turn (D). End-for-end again, lead the twine down the next score, and stick the needle back into that score, once again under one strand, with the lay. The needle should now emerge in the same space that it went into at the end of the turns (E). Before leading the twine down the last score, pass the needle under the little loop at the end of the turns. This is done so the last frapping turn will hold the loop down and prevent it from working loose. Stick the needle a third time under one strand (F). The needle now emerges at the first frapping turn. Make a hitch around it, pull the hitch snug, stick the needle twice more to bury the end, then cut the twine flush with the surface of the rope (G). Trim the rope close to the whipping, then put on a second "insurance whipping" three diameters up the standing part (H).*

So, throw your lighters overboard. A Constrictor Knot or two (Figures 1-13 through 1-17) is just as handy. The classical method, the Palm and Needle Whipping, is more time consuming but is without doubt the best knot for the job (Figures 3-43 and 3-44). As you can see, the round turns contain the rope strands while the diagonal turns, being pulled down into the scores, tighten the whipping and prevent it from coming undone even if some of the round turns chafe through. One has advance warning of the need for replacement.

Those of you who already know how to make whippings might want to examine the illustrations anyway; there are some particulars of technique that you may not have seen before, which result in a firmer, more symmetrical knot. If you have not been introduced to this knot before, be assured that the hardest thing about it is coming up with the money for a good palm and set of needles.

Notice in the final drawing that there are two whippings on the line, the second about three rope diameters up from the first. This is safety and neatness insurance in case the first whipping chafes through. Otherwise you might find yourself with an Irish Pennant—a raveled rope—something worth taking a little extra effort to avoid, especially with yacht-diameter rope retailing at multiple dollars per foot.

If, as sometimes happens, you are without palm and needle but still want something more permanent than a Constrictor Knot, try this remarkable

barehanded whipping (Figure 3-45) from the British Admiralty's *Manual of Seamanship for Boys' Training Ships* (Vols. I–II, London, 1932). It looks just like the real thing and is at the very least useful to impress your friends.

There are other preparations besides stopper knots and whippings for the end of your rope, of course. They're called splices, but that's a topic for the next chapter.

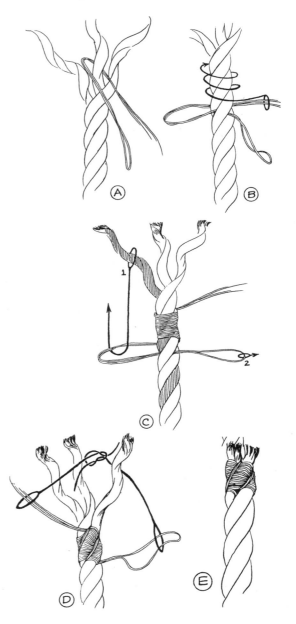

Figure 3-45. *British Admiralty Whipping. Unlay the strands a short distance. Double a fathom of waxed twine and loop it over one strand of the rope. The bight end of the twine need only extend about 4 inches. Lay the rope back up (A). Pull the twine a short distance away from the strand it is looped around and commence making turns against the lay with the long end, as with the Palm and Needle Whipping (B). When the turns are completed, pass the bight over the end of the strand it was looped around. Pull on the bight end to snug it down (C). Reef-Knot the end and bight end together across the middle of the knot. Cut the twine ends off and trim the rope short (D).*

CHAPTER 4

Friction, Part 2: Splicing

"Nothin' don't seem impossible once you've clapped eyes on a whale."
—Elizabeth Goudge

Basic ropework can sometimes seem anything but basic—all those turns and twists, in dizzying variation. But at least you're working with whole line. Now we're going to start taking it apart and reassembling it—it's the only way to get the maximum strength out of a rope. Mysterious at first, and challenging, but wonderfully satisfying.

THE END OF YOUR ROPE REVISITED: MULTISTRAND SPLICES

Splicing is ropework that joins two ropes by interweaving parts of each rope, which forms a semi-permanent joint. Splices can also form a loop, stopper, or eye in the rope. In the following section, you'll learn how to make Backsplices, Eyesplices, Stoppers and Buttons, and Chain Splices with multistrand rope.

Backsplices

The most complex end-of-the-line work is done with the line's component strands. To start with, there's the Backsplice (the real thing, no butane as in Figure 3-42). To make a Backsplice, unlay the strands 8 to 10 inches, make a snug, counterclockwise Crown Knot, then tuck each end in sequence under one and over one, against the lay (Figure 4-1). Make three or four rows of tucks.

The Backsplice is a lousy knot. Oh, it's handy when there's no twine or knife, but basically it's a quick fix for raveling, too narrow to be an effective stopper but too bulky for reeving through chocks or for passing lashings. About the only place it's much good is as a comfortable handhold, say at the end of a deck bucket's lanyard. But there are a couple of very useful variations.

A Tree Surgeon's Backsplice (Figure 4-2) is identical in structure to the above, but after the strands are unlaid and before Crowning, two-thirds of each strand is cut away. When tucked, the one-third-size strands do not greatly increase rope diameter.

The Shackle Splice is a Backsplice with the Crown Knot made through the *eye of a shackle* (Figure 4-3). This can't be beat for compactness and distribution of strain. The same splice can be used to attach an appropriate-sized rode to an anchor chain (see "Chain Splices").

Eyesplices

It's a simple step from a Backsplice to an Eyesplice; the body of the knot is the same, and only the entrance differs (see sidebar on page 87, "Round Eyesplice Entry"). I should mention that my preferred entry is not the standard one—some might even consider it heretical—but it snugs up to a thimble better and is smooth on both sides (see the comparison in Figure 4-4). It is sometimes known as Lever's Eyesplice, but if anyone gives you guff about it, call it by the name towboaters do: the Pro Splice.

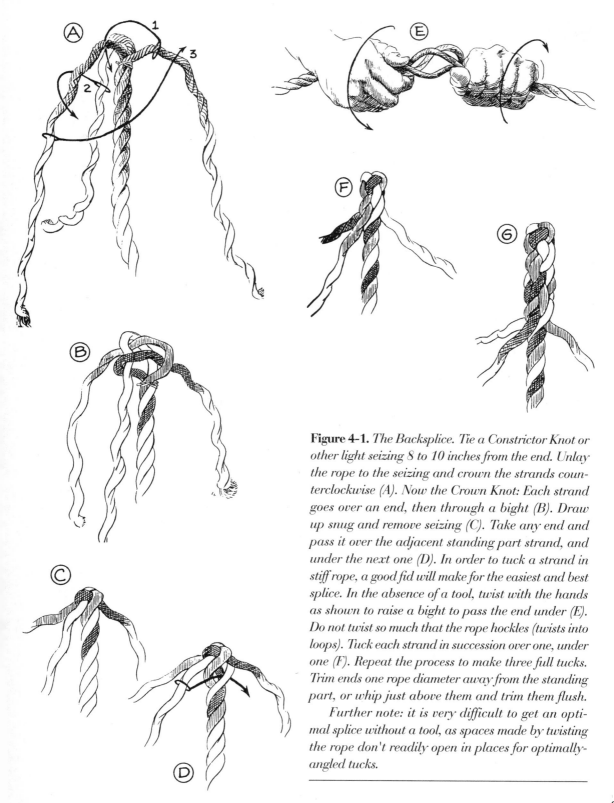

Figure 4-1. *The Backsplice. Tie a Constrictor Knot or other light seizing 8 to 10 inches from the end. Unlay the rope to the seizing and crown the strands counterclockwise (A). Now the Crown Knot: Each strand goes over an end, then through a bight (B). Draw up snug and remove seizing (C). Take any end and pass it over the adjacent standing part strand, and under the next one (D). In order to tuck a strand in stiff rope, a good fid will make for the easiest and best splice. In the absence of a tool, twist with the hands as shown to raise a bight to pass the end under (E). Do not twist so much that the rope hockles (twists into loops). Tuck each strand in succession over one, under one (F). Repeat the process to make three full tucks. Trim ends one rope diameter away from the standing part, or whip just above them and trim them flush.*

Further note: it is very difficult to get an optimal splice without a tool, as spaces made by twisting the rope don't readily open in places for optimally-angled tucks.

Figure 4-2. *Tree Surgeon's Backsplice. Start as with the Backsplice, but lay out two-thirds of each strand before crowning (A). Tuck three full times and trim all ends short (B).*

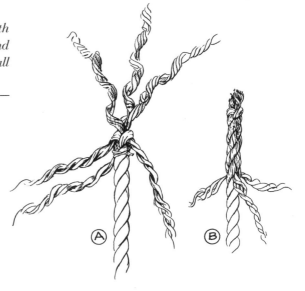

Figure 4-3 (below). *Shackle Splice. Pass one end through shackle (1). On other side lead it to the left of next (white) strand. Pass next (white) strand into eye of shackle from opposite direction over first strand (2). Lead it to the right of next (black) strand. Pass next (black) strand through eye of shackle from same direction as first strand (3). Pass over second (white) strand and under first, forming Crown Knot (A). Fair knot and tuck as before. This splice is compact, handsome, and distributes strain and chafe evenly among all three strands (C).*

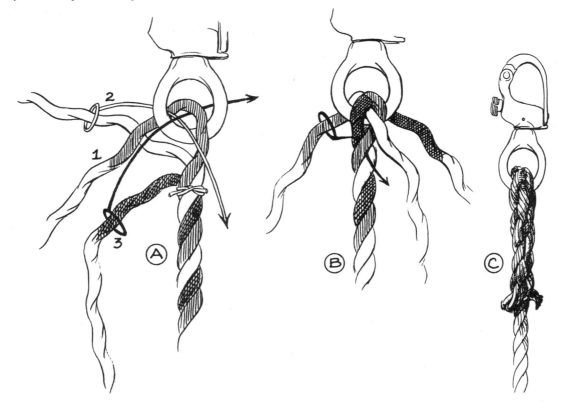

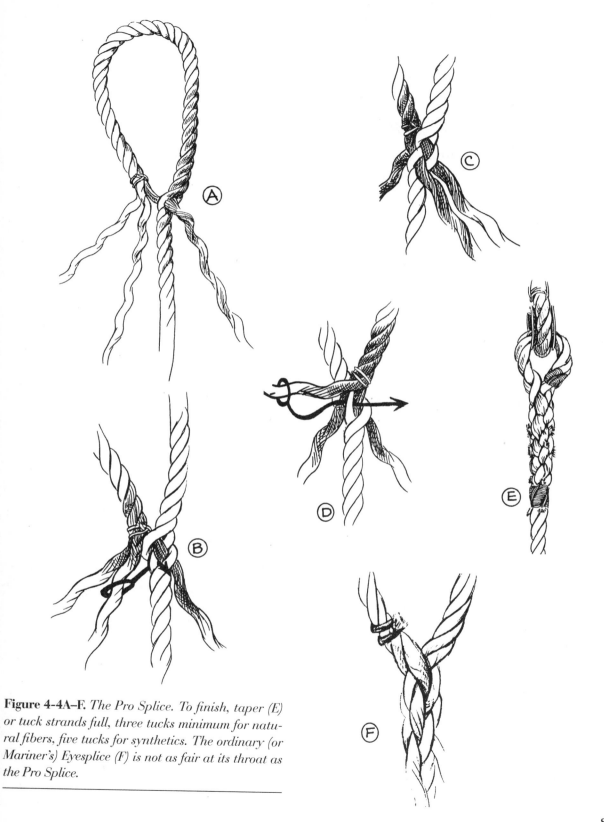

Figure 4-4A–F. *The Pro Splice. To finish, taper (E) or tuck strands full, three tucks minimum for natural fibers, five tucks for synthetics. The ordinary (or Mariner's) Eyesplice (F) is not as fair at its throat as the Pro Splice.*

85

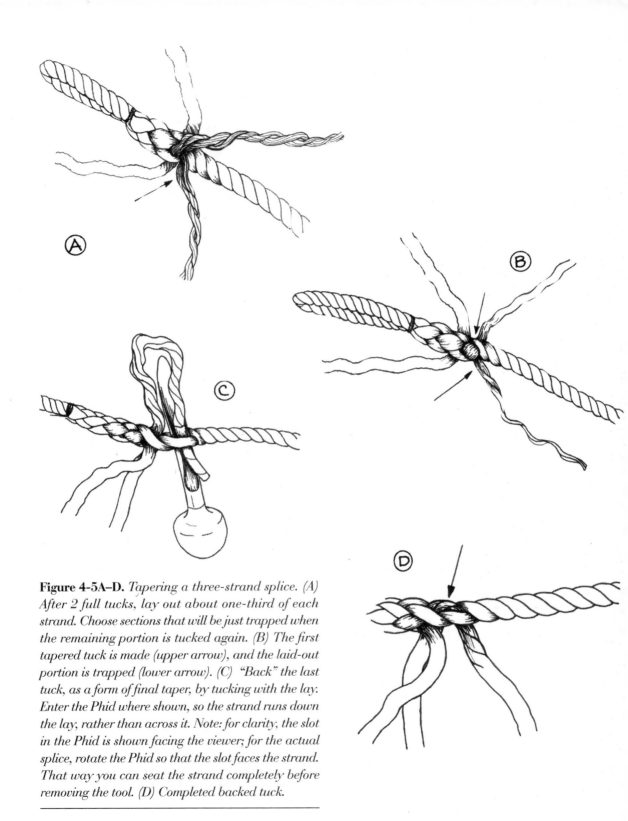

Figure 4-5A–D. *Tapering a three-strand splice. (A)
After 2 full tucks, lay out about one-third of each
strand. Choose sections that will be just trapped when
the remaining portion is tucked again. (B) The first
tapered tuck is made (upper arrow), and the laid-out
portion is trapped (lower arrow). (C) "Back" the last
tuck, as a form of final taper, by tucking with the lay.
Enter the Phid where shown, so the strand runs down
the lay, rather than across it. Note: for clarity, the slot
in the Phid is shown facing the viewer; for the actual
splice, rotate the Phid so that the slot faces the strand.
That way you can seat the strand completely before
removing the tool. (D) Completed backed tuck.*

Start by unlaying the rope a sufficient distance for tucking, preferably to a Double Constrictor Knot, which keeps the three strands evenly aligned while you work. Bend the end around to form the desired-size eye and tuck the leftmost strand under, over, and under again, against the lay. Tuck the middle strand under where the first strand went over, then turn the work over and tuck the third strand under the last remaining uninvolved standing-part strand. It's right there in the middle.

Fair the entry by pulling each strand snug, making sure that they all enter against the lay and come out at the same level; then commence regular under-and-over tucking to finish, as with the Backsplice. Don't try to keep the strands round as you go;

they'll lie fairer and distort the rope less if they're untwisted a little, into a ribbon shape, as you work.

Optional finishes:

1. Taper the splice by laying out one-third of each strand after three sets of tucks (four for nylon). Make another tuck with the remaining parts, then lay out half of each strand, and tuck again. The laid-out parts should be trapped under the tucks.

2. "Back" the last set of tucks. This means to tuck them with the lay. Sailmakers use this method, because it is more compact than tucking against the lay. It is also less secure,

---

Round Eyesplice Entry

The teardrop shape of a regular spliced eye is fine for thimbled eyes, mooring lines, and most anything else. But it won't set fair when made tight around yards or round thimbles. The entry shown here results in a fairer-leading round eye.

To make:

1 Set the eye size, then select the end strand that lies closest to the standing part. Tuck it under the nearest standing-part strand once, against the lay (from right to left when the eye is toward you).

2 Select the middle end strand and tuck it under the first two standing-part strands, against the lay.

3 Turn the eye over. You have one untucked end strand, and there's one standing-part strand waiting for it. Pass the end over, from left to right (with the lay); then tuck back under, from right to left (against the lay).

Finish by tucking as for a regular splice: two more full tucks for manila and hemp; three more for spun Dacron; and four more minimum for nylon and other slick fibers.

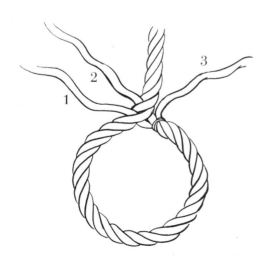

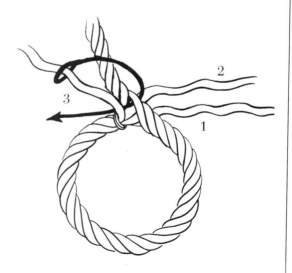

but this doesn't bother sailmakers, because they stitch their splices to their sails. Riggers don't have this luxury, so they tuck against the lay. But once you have enough tucks for security, you can back one more set for a quick taper. Note that backed tucks angle right down the standing part, instead of across it.

Stoppers and Buttons

If it's multistrand bulk you're after, the traditional knot is the Matthew Walker, structurally a series of interlocked Overhand Knots (Figure 4-6). The real challenge comes not in tying it but in drawing it up, a procedure that is for some reason always left out of knot books. The trick is to take out a little bit of slack at a time, first by hand, then with a spike, first pulling down on the bight, then up on the end. For a neat finish, lay the strands up again for a short distance (1 to 1½ inches), whip them, then cut the end flush at the top of the whipping.

Buttons can serve the same function as stopper knots like the Matthew Walker, but differ from them in that the ends are buried in the knot, obviating the laying-up-and-whipping step. But don't think that buttons save labor; they are more intricate and harder to draw up. Their big selling point is that they are not only functional but also stylish and rare. The one shown here (#880 in Ashley) is my favorite for three- and four-strand rope. Like most buttons, it is built up from two basic knots, the Wall and Crown. We've already used the Crown Knot in the Backsplice (Figure 4-1), and the Wall Knot is just an upside-down Crown.

To make this button, tie a Constrictor Knot about a foot from the end, unlay the strands to it, and make a Wall Knot as shown in Figure 4-7. Fair this knot to make it even but not tight, then make a Crown on top of it. Now fair the Crown so that the combined knots look exactly like the drawing. Take a deep breath. Do you see the three bights (scallops or arcs) around the outside of the knot, with an end across the middle of each bight? Take each end and pass it up through the bight to its right, ahead of that bight's end. Looks like a real mess, huh? Fair it into some semblance of order and take a look at

the very center, down inside where the three strands fan out from the Constrictor. There are three spaces there, and you are going to drop each strand into the second space to its right. Got it? Good, that's all there is to it.

Draw up with a blunted spike or awl, making several passes along each strand, until the knot is hard. Carefully trim the ends off flush with the bottom of the knot. This button, the Matthew Walker, and related knots are most often used as stoppers on deadeye and other lanyards (see Chapter 10), as well as hand- and footrope ends, gaskets, beckets, and for decoration. Tied in small enough material, the Ashley #880 makes a lovely, fully functional button for clothing. A two-strand version of this knot is an essential part of my improved Soft Shackle (see pages 388)

Chain Splices

Like a wire-and-rope halyard, a chain-and-rope anchor rode combines two materials in order to gain the virtues of both.

An all-rope rode of appropriate size is plenty strong to make a boat stay put. Made of nylon, it will be elastic, so that staying put will not involve hull- and teeth-jarring shock loads as the hull fetches up in a swell. But an all-rope rode will be subject to chafe; it will chafe away on rocky bottoms, and it will chafe away at the boat's roller or hawse, particularly from storm-induced side loads. An all-chain rode is ultimately chafe-resistant, but it is also ultimately inelastic. It compensates somewhat for this inelasticity because in use its very weight causes it to describe that elegant, shock-absorbing sag we call a catenary. But in heavy wind and swell, the chain goes not quite straight and BAM!, instead of riding over waves, you're colliding with them (as a friend of mine puts it, "There's no catenary at 50 knots"). This is why, with an all-chain rode, a rope snubber is a good idea (see sidebar, "End-of-Bowsprit Anchoring"). You'll find two other snubbers in Chapter 12 (see page 92).

With a snubber in place, you gain the virtues of chain and rope, so who needs a rope rode at all? But there are two other factors to consider. They don't

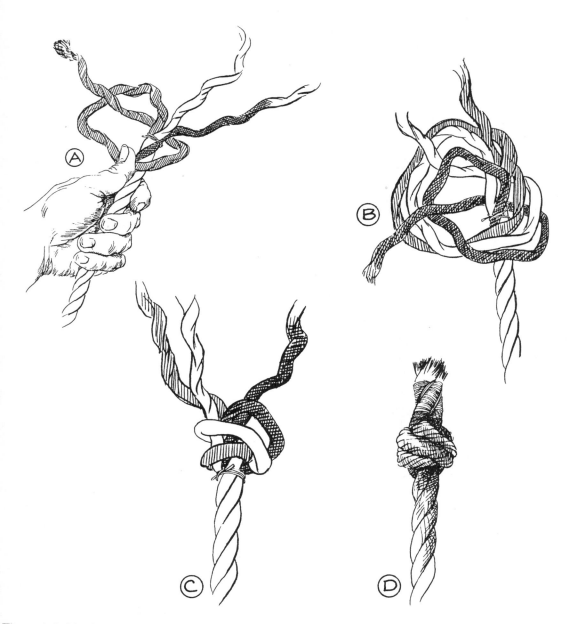

Figure 4-6. *Matthew Walker Knot. Tie a Constrictor about a foot from the end and unlay strands. Take first strand and make an Overhand Knot around the standing part with it (A). Take the next strand to right and make a second Overhand Knot around the standing part on top of the first knot. Pass second end up through bight of first knot, then its own bight (B). Take third end and make another Overhand Knot around standing part, on top of first two knots. Pass end up through all three bights (C). Carefully fair into cylindrical form, then draw up by first pulling a bight down, then pulling up on that bight's end. Do this with each strand in turn, taking out a little slack at a time. Use a small spike to pull bight down as knot gets tighter. Finally, lay up and whip ends to finish (D).*

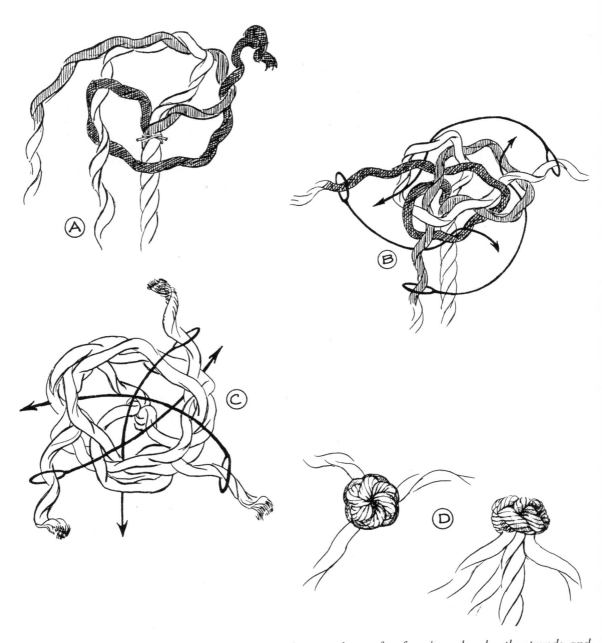

Figure 4-7. *Ashley's Button Knot #880. Constrictor the rope about a foot from its end, unlay the strands, and "Wall" them counterclockwise by passing each strand under its neighbor to the right. A Wall is an upside-down Crown (A). Fair the Wall and make a Crown Knot on top of it, also counterclockwise. Fair the Crown, then pass each end under the bight to its right, ahead of the end to its right (B). Open the middle of the knot up a bit so you can see the three strands where they exit the Constrictor. Drop each end in turn into the second space to its right. Draw up slowly and carefully, working out a little slack at a time (C). Trim the ends off flush with the bottom to get the finished knot (D).*

have anything directly to do with anchoring, but they can nonetheless be crucial to rode selection for your boat. The first is cost: Three-strand nylon is cheap compared to chain. For the yacht-poor sailor, this alone would make rope attractive—if there were a way to prevent chafe.

The second factor is weight. Particularly in light-displacement boats, anchor chain when stowed will trim the hull down at the bow. This cuts speed, exaggerates weather helm, and makes nose-dives more likely. To compound matters, the chain when deployed will leave the bow too buoyant, so that the boat will be inclined to sail around on its anchor.

If your boat is heavy enough and full enough forward that chain doesn't affect your trim, then an all-chain rode with snubber can be a good (if expensive) way to go.

But for the majority of boats afloat, there's a strong argument for combining rope and chain. Put enough chain at the lower end to provide catenary and abrasion resistance down there, and let the rest of the rode be strong, resilient, light, inexpensive rope. To avoid chafe at the upper end, see to it that your hawse or roller has smooth, wide-radiused sides, and that the rope cannot jump free under side loads. You can also cushion the rope with a length of split heavy-duty hose positioned to take the chafe. Finally, always hitch a separate rope snubber onto the rode for insurance, just as with chain.

This brings us at last to the Chain Splice, for we must have a way to join these two materials. The most often-seen way to do this is to Eyesplice the rope around a thimble, then shackle the thimble to the chain. It's an easy method, but it has several drawbacks:

1. The thimble is inclined to chafe the rope, or to pop out, or both. You can seize the thimble to the rope, but seizings can chafe away, too.

2. The shackle can also chafe the rope, despite the presence of the thimble. In any event, it's one more piece that can fail; a primary rule of rigging is to eliminate all possible links.

Nylon Warnings

Nylon warning #1
Nylon is stronger than Dacron, but only when it is dry; unlike Dacron, it becomes 10 to 15 percent weaker when it is wet.

Nylon warning #2
Nylon is significantly more susceptible to chafe than Dacron. Its greater elasticity is considered a plus in preventing shock loads in mooring lines, but it stretches where it passes through chocks. The resulting movement produces chafe. (see "Quick Chafe Gear," in Chapter 12, page 375).

Nylon warning #3
Nylon is also susceptible to UV degradation.

Nylon warning #4
If nylon breaks at maximum strength, it snaps back at approximately 700 feet per second. Yikes.

To recap, nylon is weaker when it is wet, doesn't do well in sunlight, is easily chafed, and can hit you faster than some rifle bullets if it breaks. It is, in short, the worst possible material for mooring and anchor lines. It is also the best, because it can absorb energy by stretching. We just have to deal with its (many) vices, in order to take advantage of its one virtue.

You can improve the chafe resistance of nylon, or of any other material, by getting the smoothest, widest radius chocks you can, and by locating mooring cleats as close as possible to those chocks. You can also, as noted above, make use of snubbers.

3. When hoisting the anchor, you run into trouble when the thimble hits the bow roller or hawse, and again when it reaches the winch—you have to wrestle it past both points.

This is why some authorities recommend a maximum chain length of approximately the draft of the boat plus the freeboard at the bow. With that length of chain, your anchor will have broken out by the time the thimble reaches the hangup points, and it'll be somewhat less of a struggle to wrestle the thimble past them.

But for many boats, this means only 10 feet or so of chain, too little for adequate catenary or chafe protection. I recommend a chain section of about half your average scope. So, if the anchorages in

For boats with bowsprits, rig a stout single-braid three-strand "snubber" line from deck, out to the end of the bowsprit, through a turning block, and back to deck underneath the bowsprit shrouds. After the anchor has been lowered and set, hook or tie the end of the snubber to the rode, then veer more scope so the snubber takes the strain.

If the rode is chain, it is probably best to use nylon for the snubber, as this material will provide significant elasticity to minimize shock loads, assuming adequate length (at least 30 feet, as a rule).

Snubber diameter should be the same as a rope rode would be for a given boat. Single-braid nylon has the best energy-absorbing characteristics.

If the rode is nylon rope, it is probably best to use a Dacron snubber. The idea here is that the rode provides all the elasticity needed, so the snubber can be of a more chafe-resistant material. Again, single-braid is the best construction, but here we like it for its superior handling characteristics and ease of splicing.

In either material, a snubber keeps the bow down and to weather to control yawing and pitching. It also prevents the rode from chafing on the bobstay or hull, and can be quickly and easily slacked or retrieved from deck. End-of-bowsprit anchoring is vastly superior to the practice of rigging a snubber from a fitting on the stem.

Source: *Capable Cruiser*
Lin and Larry Pardey

P.S. *People invariably worry about subjecting the end of their bowsprit to anchoring loads, even though those loads are moderate compared to the ones that a jib puts on that same bowsprit on a normal day of sailing.*

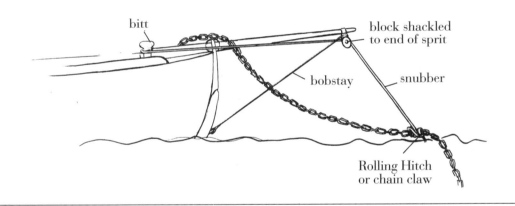

bitt

block shackled to end of sprit

bobstay

snubber

Rolling Hitch or chain claw

your area are typically about 30 feet, you might veer a rode of 150 feet (5:1 ratio), 75 feet of which would be chain. If you're in deeper water, or if the weather picks up when you're in shallow water, the extra rode you'll deploy will be shock-resistant, low-weight rope. And now back to the Chain Splice. This is, after all, a section about the Chain Splice.

The trick is to join the rope directly to the chain, so that there are no hangups when you weigh anchor.

The Crown Splice (used in the Shackle Splice, Figure 4-3) is a good way to join three-strand rope to proof coil of BBB-grade chain. This is signifi-cantly stronger and more chafe-resistant that bending a whole rope through the last link of the chain; with the Crown, each strand has a bigger relative radius, and the load is distributed evenly among all the strands. Be sure to snug the Crown Knot down before cutting away the Constrictor. If the Crown is made snug up against the chain, the rope won't move on the last link, and thus won't chafe there. Instead, articulation happens at the next chain link.

Traditional Irony Chain Splice   In the days before synthetics, rope was so large relative to chain of comparable strength that all three strands wouldn't fit through the last link. The only thimble-free option was the very tidy, very secure, very tricky-to-do-well Chain Splice shown in Figure 4-8. Then along came nylon, which is much stronger than manila or hemp, so it can be much smaller: all three strands fit into the link, making the Crown Splice practicable. But now we have High Test chain, which is too small for all three strands of nylon or Dacron. So the only splice that will work is the previously archaic two-strand splice, now cutting-edge technology. Sweet irony, and it gets even sweeter: destruction tests show that this splice approaches 100 percent efficiency, while Crown splices and the like rarely exceed 80 percent.

Note: this is a high-skill knot, so make at least a couple of practice splices before you put one on an actual rode.

Before we move on to the making of this wonderful splice, I will just mention that there is now yet another skill-intensive rope-chain connection available: the Spectra Soft Shackle (see 388). Using this marvel, you can join the chain's end link to an eyesplice in the rope. The connection is smooth enough to get past chocks and gypsies, but can be disconnected and connected at will, to switch out rodes as needed, depending on anchoring depth, or to replace worn components.

The splice: Prepare the rope by soaking 6 feet of one end in Elmer's Washable School Glue, or similar product. This is a non-toxic gel that will wash right out when the splice is done. Massage it firmly into the rope. When it dries, the individual strands of rope will better hold their spiral shape, or "lay," while you splice. But treat things very gently throughout the splice; unlike most others in this book, this splice requires that you preserve the lay perfectly. If you have no experience at articles like grommets, or the Mending Splice that soon follows, it will be a good idea to practice with one of them,

and work your way up to this more difficult job.

To start the splice, unlay the strands at least 3 feet. Tuck two of the strands through the last link of the chain (Figure 4-8A). Pull the two strands through until the link reaches the odd strand. Be gentle, so you don't disturb the lay of the line. Lay the odd strand out a short way, leaving a groove. Take whichever of the two link strands that leads fairest to the empty space. Bend it down, give it a twist, and lay it firmly into this groove.

Continue laying out the odd strand and laying in the other strand until 6 to 8 inches of the latter remain (Figure 4-8B).

Before proceeding farther, look back the way you came. Can you tell by appearance which strand you just laid in? If you can, that strand is imperfectly tensioned, which means it will bear more or less strain than the other two strands. Either way, the splice is weakened. Put everything in reverse

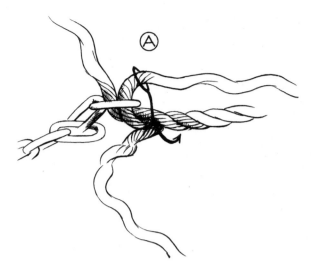

Figure 4-8A. *Beginning the more comely Chain Splice for three-strand. Unlay the strands about 2½ feet and pass two of them through the end link, pulling them through until you reach the junction of the third strand. Now begin unlaying the third strand, leaving a vacant groove to be filled with the nearer of the two other strands (arrow)..*

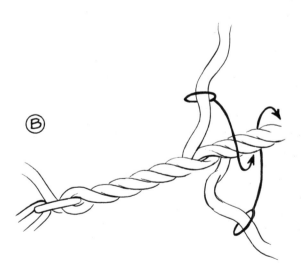

Figure 4-8B. *Continue "laying out and in" until 6 to 8 inches of the "in" strand remain. As you go, give the "in" strand a firm twist and pull at each turn to make it lie fair. It should be indistinguishable from the other two strands.*

and head back to the link. Go back and forth a few times until you can do it right. If the rope loses its lay, make up another practice piece. Remember, this is a high-skill splice; do not practice on your actual rode. The secret is first to twist the strand clockwise while holding a little tension on it, and then to pull it firmly into the groove. This same technique is also used for making rope grommets, long splices, and single-strand repairs, so it's a skill well worth having.

When you're a competent layer-in, return to the position in Figure 4-8B and cut off all but 6 to 8 inches of the laid-out strand.

Here you have options. For the smoothest splice, divide both the laid-in and laid-out strands into two equal bundles of yarns, right down to the rope, then tie an overhand knot with two opposite bundles, left over right. There should be just enough space between the strands for the Overhand Knot to fill (Figure 4-8C). A simpler, slightly bulkier option is to knot the whole strands together (not shown). Note: the bulky option is as strong as the compact version, and is simpler to make.

With either method, the next step is to tuck the knotted ends against the lay, over one and under one, four or five times. If you split the strands, just leave the unknotted ends hanging out. Figure 4-8D shows the left-hand end already tucked and the right-hand end being tucked. (The splicing tool shown is the remarkable Fid-O Awl, a tool no longer available, but which inspired my own Point Hudson Phid (see Supplies).

Figure 4-8C. *Cut off all but 6 to 8 inches of the laid-out strand. An optional step: divide it into two equal bundles. Divide the final 6 to 8 inches of the "in" strand similarly. Overhand-Knot two opposing bundles, left over right. The knot should just fill the space between the strands.*

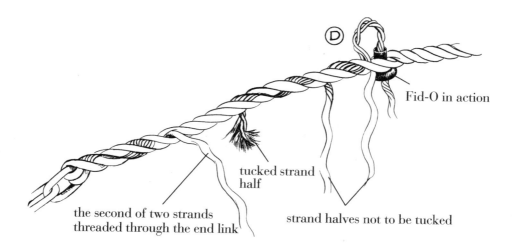

Fid-O in action

tucked strand
half

the second of two strands
threaded through the end link

strand halves not to be tucked

Figure 4-8D. *Tuck each strand (or half strand) against the lay four or five times, just as you would with the strands of an Eyesplice.*

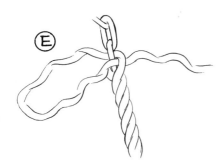

Figure 4-8E. *Return now to the lone untucked strand, which with any luck still hangs forlornly from the end link of the chain. Pass it under its own part to form a Half Hitch . . .*

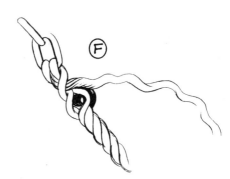

Figure 4-8F. *. . . then tuck it over and under, against the lay, five or six times.*

Figure 4-8G. *Roll the splice underfoot to fair, then trim the ends so they stick out at least one rope diameter. Presto! A finished Chain Splice.*

To finish this part of the splice, roll it under-foot to fair it, then whip or Constrictor over all exposed ends

Almost done now. Go back to the link and that lone, uncommitted strand. Tuck it under itself, against the lay (Figure 4-8E). Pull this first tuck snug, but not so much as to distort (i.e., weaken) the rope. Tuck another four or five times (Figure 4-8F), roll to fair, whip and cut (Figure 4-8G).

Many people wonder how this splice can be strong enough when only two strands pass through the chain. But the load is split four ways, like a line going through a two-sheave block. The link radius is small, but both strands bear fully on it. That's why this splice, done well, is the strongest of all chain splices.

The Shovel Splice Figure 4-9A shows another method: separating the rope into four equal bundles and weaving the bundles into the chain. This is particularly suited to double-braid rope, which cannot otherwise be spliced directly to chain. (For basic procedures on working with double-braid, see "Braided Rope Splices," below.) Two bundles go back and forth through the links in one plane,

and two go up and down through the links in the other plane. For maximum strength, adjust all the rope yarns as you go, so they all bear an even strain. Each pair is tucked six or seven times, then the ends of all four bundles are very securely seized to the chain (Figure 4-9B). Although this splice is easy to do, it is much weaker than any other spliced option. Also, if the rope ever touches the bottom, this splice brings up such prodigious amounts of mud that a friend of mine calls it the "Shovel Splice." I'm including it here because it is the only way to splice double-braid to chain: you put a seizing on the cover; separate core and cover into four bundles; and splice away. However single-braid and three-strand rope are stretchier, absorb energy better, and are cheaper, so either of those constructions is better for rodes.

Figure 4-9A. *The Shovel Splice—Part 1. It is weak, but will work when splicing three-strand rope to chain. But with three-strand a Crown or Irony splice is much better, and with double-braid, if you must use it for your rode, you can get a much stronger connection by putting an Eyesplice in the rope, then connecting that to the chain with an Improved Soft Shackle. To make the Shovel Splice, apply a Double Constrictor or other seizing about 2½ feet from the end of the rope, then separate the three strands (or double-braid core and cover) into four equal bundles of yarns. Weave two bundles back and forth through every other link, and the other two bundles through the intervening links, endeavoring to pull all yarns evenly tight as you go. Don't pull so tight that you put slack in the chain (A).*

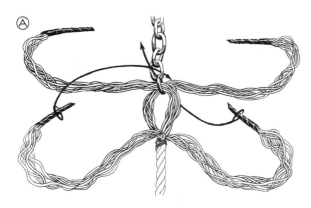

Figure 4-9B. *The Shovel Splice—Part 2. Tuck each bundle of yarns six or seven times, double the ends back on themselves, and seize thoroughly. It ain't elegant, or strong, but is worth including here, if only as an emergency method. (B).*

You might have noticed that only about half of this section's text is devoted to splicing per se. This is because, at this level, any technique is only a reflection of the real business of rigging: understanding the relationships among boat type, strength requirements, sailing efficiency, cost, and convenience. Whether or not your boat can use a Chain Splice, you can, as a way to understand the rest of your rig.

NOT THE END OF YOUR ROPE: MORE SPLICES FOR THREE-STRAND ROPE

A cord of three-strands is not quickly broken. Use this strong rope to make a Short Splice, a Mending Splice, or a Long Splice.

The Short Splice
This book wouldn't be right without a Short Splice (Figure 4-10), the strongest way to lengthen a rope whose end you're not ready to come to.

To make one, unlay two ropes of the same size to Constrictor Knots, as for the Backsplice. "Marry"

them and tuck each strand over one and under one, against the lay. Remove the Constrictors, snug things up, then continue tucking as with the other splices. Carefully done, this knot can't be beat for towlines, pendants, and all sorts of temporary repairs, particularly in emergencies. Its one drawback is that it bulks too much to pass through a block.

Short Splice, short explanation.

The Mending Splice
Every so often a boat will slash away at a piece of running rigging with a burr on a masthead sheave mortise, for example, or an unsuspected sharp porthole corner. You can smooth out the edges that did the damage, but what about the line? You can darn a lightly chafed yacht braid cover with needle and thread, but a deep cut is impractical to mend. So about all you can do is replace it and hope there's

Figure 4-10. *The Short Splice is a very strong multi-strand bend. Unlay the two ropes far enough for three tucks (minimum) in manila, five in synthetics. Marry the two and tuck each set of strands over and under as for the previous splices.*

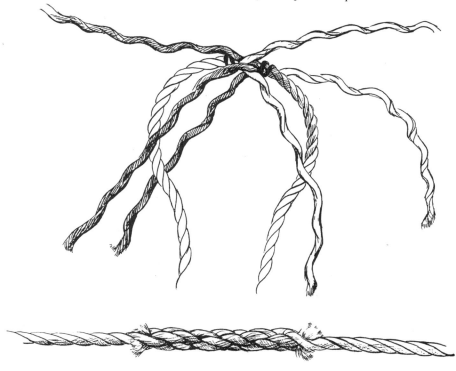

Figure 4-11. *Mending Splice. Cross and finish the ends as for a Chain Splice or Long Splice.*

a long enough piece of whole rope left to use where you need a shorter line.

But if you damage three-strand rope with a sudden slash, it's possible that most or all of the damage will be done to one strand. And if that's the case, the Mending Splice will repair it.

You'll need about 3 feet of the same diameter, construction, and material as the damaged piece. If the damaged piece is plenty long, cut 3 feet off its end. Soak this section in the same gel you'd use for the Traditional Irony Chain Splice; this is to keep the line from losing its spiral shape, or "lay," as you work. Let the line dry, then gently unlay one strand right out of it. This is your mending strand.

Now go to the damaged piece and cut the wounded strand the rest of the way through. Undo, or "lay out," the two resulting ends a full turn each, and set the middle of the mending strand into the space they leave. Lay out one of the wounded ends another turn, and lay in behind it with one end of the mending strand. Twist the mending strand clockwise, with a little tension on it, and pull it firmly into the groove. It should be indistinguishable from the two strands next to it. If it is tighter or looser than they, or has more or less twist, it will take more or less strain than they do, and the rope will be weakened. So, practice until you can lay in smoothly (Figure 4-11).

Lay out and in until there are 6 to 8 inches of the wounded new strand remaining, and split both strands in half down to the standing part, leaving a

small space between the two pairs of strands (as in 4-12B). Tie an Overhand Knot, left over right, with half of each pair. The knot should just exactly fill the space. If it fits poorly, undo it and lay up or unlay the halves until you get two that fit well when knotted. Leave the other two halves hanging out, and tuck each of the knotted ends against the lay four or five times. As a simpler but lumpier option, you may tie the whole strands together and tuck them.

Repeat the procedure with the other two ends, wash the gel out, and you're done.

With a little practice at delicate handling, you will find you can skip starching all but the softest-laid line. This will qualify the splice as not only clever and economical, but also valuable as an emergency procedure.

It's worth noting here that boats are always doing non-emergency damage to rope. They chew on it with fairleads, sheaves, winch drums, and especially with chocks, stoppers, and self-tailing gear. They chew on it gently, but steadily; about the only thing you can do is to try to blunt their teeth. Use bigger fairleads and sheaves. Carefully angle leads to winches so you get no wraps. File gentler curves into the edges of chocks and bow roller side-keepers. Minimize the use of stoppers and self-tailers. And end-for-end lines when wear becomes noticeable, to get the most life out of them.

All of these little details are a lot less dramatic, but in the long run even more valuable than the Mending Splice.

The Long Splice

In all of rigging, there is no knot more often asked about nor less often useful than the Long Splice. There's something undeniably fascinating about it, about the way it leaves a line's appearance and diameter almost unchanged. Perhaps it reminds people of those ever-popular Cut-and-Restored tricks (see Chapter 11)—"And now I will take this severed line and make it whole again!"

Handy as that ability might seem, most of the times I've been called upon to make a Long Splice have been because of mistakes (for instance, a halyard that was made too short), or in emergencies (for instance, a halyard that used to be long enough that suddenly became too short). In either instance, a Short Splice might serve as well, so long as the splice doesn't have to go through a sheave or stopper. And in that case, just having some spare rope as a replacement is the best solution.

Making a Long Splice requires quite a bit of rope and a lot of skill. And unlike the more practical Mending Splice, which only disturbs one-third of the rope, the Long Splice requires that you deal with all three strands of two pieces and that you get them all evenly tensioned to preserve rope strength. As with the Traditional Irony Chain Splice, it's a good idea to practice with a simpler splice, like the Mending Splice, before tackling this one.

Still want to learn it? Okay, here goes:

First, the ropes must be of the same diameter, material, and construction.

Next, it's a good idea to stiffen the ends with washable school glue (see the Traditional Irony Splice), to help the strands to hold their spiral shape, or "lay." This is particularly important with nylon rope. Gel at least 4 feet (1.2 m) of line for every 1 inch (25 mm) of diameter. So, a ½-inch (13-mm)-diameter piece would be starched at least 2 feet (0.6 m) from the end.

When the rope is dry, gently unlay the two lines almost to the untreated section. "Marry" the ends just the way you'd lace your fingers together (Figure 4-12A). Take any convenient strand from the line on the left and "lay it out" of the marriage without disturbing any of the other strands. Hold it off to the

left, leaving a space where it had been. Now adjust the position of the two lines, pushing them slightly closer together or pulling them slightly farther apart so that the corresponding strand from the right side falls neatly into that just-vacated space. This is the most difficult part of the splice; it's tricky getting a good, close marriage while keeping everything together while you make these initial setting-in moves. But just as with a real marriage, you only need to be careful, attentive, and to take your time.

Figure 4-12A–C. *The Long Splice. Marry the two ends and Constrictor four of the six strands together. The other two, which lie in the same groove, are laid "in and out," with the one on the left being removed from the groove and the one on the right taking its place (A). Lay out and in as for the Mending Splice and Chain Splice until the "laid-in" strand is just long enough to make four splice tucks, then halve the two strands (optional), Overhand-Knot, and . . . (B) . . . tuck the ends to finish, again just as for the Chain Splice (C).*

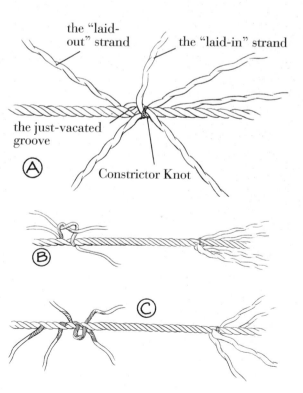

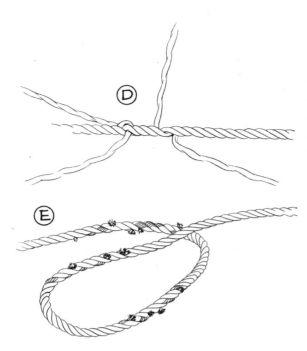

Figure 4-12D–E. *Now return to the other four ends. Cut away the Constrictor and tie two ends together while you lay the other two out and in (in the opposite direction from the first pair). Split and tuck as before. Then untie, adjust, fair, retie, split, and tuck the middle pair right there at the original marriage site (D). A finished Long Splice. Leave all ends a half-inch or so "proud," or whip over all junctures and cut the ends flush (E).*

With that right-hand strand neatly in the groove, seize or Constrictor together the four strands that are still married. This part is easier with an assistant.

Leaving the married strands for the moment, go back to the two working strands and lay them out and in, just as with the Mending Splice. Either knot and tuck whole strands, or, for a more compact splice, split them first (Figure 4-12B,C).

Come back to the married pairs and cast off their seizing. Overhand Knot two whole opposing strands together—with just enough tension to hold them in position for the moment—and lay the other two strands out and in, off to the right (Figure 4-12D). Splice 'em.

Return once more to the original marriage site and undo the Constrictor Knot. Make any adjustments necessary for a fair lead (twisting, untwisting, tightening, slacking). Reknot and splice, splitting the strands first if you prefer. Wash the gel out, and you're done (Figure 4-12E). In an emergency, I'd be inclined to do an eye-to-eye splice or a Short Splice if that part of the line didn't have to get through a sheave or stopper.

BRAIDED ROPE SPLICES

As with basic knots, splices have undergone evolutionary changes in this century due to stronger, slicker materials, and more concentrated rig loads. But whereas contemporary knots are for the most part evolved from old knots, the introduction of single- and double-braided ropes has necessitated the from-scratch invention of splices completely different from any previous ones. Therefore, splicing today involves upgraded traditional skills for three-strand, and a whole new vocabulary for braid.

Many a sailor's response is to say, "Forget that braided stuff. I'll stick to something I can understand." Others say, "I don't understand braid, but I can hire somebody to splice it." These are legitimate attitudes, but I believe that most people stay away from splicing the braid, and particularly double-braid, because of horrible instructions and, to some extent, awkward tools.

Braid is well worth dealing with when low stretch and high strength are important. An extra benefit is that it isn't as weakened by going over a small radius as three-strand is; the fibers on braid can flatten out more, for better bearing. Why is this a "benefit"? Because it means that, for all but the most extreme applications, you don't need a thimble to provide that bearing. Without a thimble, setup is easier. And without a thimble you can make very small eyes for halyards, to give you extra effective hoist length and less bulk to chafe on things up there.

The concept of splicing braid, once you strip it of all the "fid lengths" and assorted marks it is usually obscured by, is very, very simple. What follows are streamlined instructions for several braid splices. Which splice you use is determined by which rope construction you select. And that is determined by the job you want it to do. (For more on this subject, see the "Characteristics" sidebars in Chapter 2, pages 25-26) Double-braid is the most common construction, but I strongly urge you to start with the Stropsicle and the 12-Strand Eyesplice, to become familiar with details and technique.

As with any knot, a splice is secure if it can generate enough friction that no amount of jerking or extreme of load can pull it out. A braid splice accomplishes this by the Chinese Handcuff principle, whereby the exterior of the braid compresses on what's inside as the load is applied. The only trick is to be sure you have buried enough tail for that handcuff effect to work.

As you'll see, tail length varies depending on rope material and construction. Just as with three-strand rope, the stronger and slicker the rope, the more friction you need for security. But instead of making extra tucks, you bury extra length. A good field rule for single- and double-braid Dacron and nylon ropes is to make a splice tail that is 24 times the diameter of the rope. And a brilliantly simple way of calculating it is this: Find the rope diameter in sixteenths of an inch, increase the numerator by half, and bury the result in inches. If, for example, you have $7/16$-inch rope, you'd increase the 7 by half and get $10\frac{1}{2}$, and your splice tail would be $10\frac{1}{2}$ inches long.

If you had $\frac{1}{2}$-inch-diameter rope, that would be $8/16$ inch. Since 8 plus half itself is 12, you'd bury 12 inches. So then, $3/8$ inch is $6/16$ inch, and 6 plus 3 is 9; 9 inches is your tail. With this formula, brought to you by Christian Gruyé, my extremely smart spouse, you'll never have to deal with the pesky fid lengths that confuse standard instructions.

The Stropsicle

The Icicle Hitch (Figure 3-12) will hold better than any other knot, but you can maximize its effectiveness with this first splicing project. The hollow tail grips tenaciously, while the eye stays open and easy

Splicing Wand

The best tool for splicing braided rope is the Splicing Wand, and I'd say that even if I didn't invent it. The Wand is available at some chandleries, and from the author. You'll see it in use in Figures 4-13, 4-16, and 4-18.

The Splicing Wand makes the job less intimidating. Once the tool is in the rope, it slides back to reveal a snare. The snare grabs the tail to be buried and tucks it.

That said, you can do these splices using any tool, including a coat hanger; it just won't be as easy. Regardless of which tool you use, be careful to avoid snagging any interior yarns with the tool.

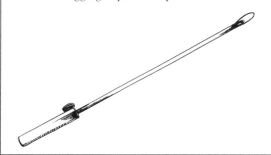

to tie to. The Stropsicle is a short length of rope, configured to take maximum advantage of the Icicle Hitch. Start with a piece of $\frac{3}{8}$-inch double-braid Dacron about 6 feet long. Measure 9 inches for the tail, and form a small eye. Stick a paper clip or safety pin through the rope at the middle of the eye. Pull the core out of the rope at both ends of the eye and cut the core ends. The paper clip will hold the core in the eye in place (Figure 4-13A).

Note: The Stropsicle can be made with any-diameter rope; adjust the splice tail length to suit, using the simple formula described in the introduction to this section for the double-braid splices.

Brummel Splice The Brummel Splice provides extra security for this strop: Tuck the tail through the standing part at the end of the eye. Pull the tail through until the core fetches up in the hole. Tuck the standing part through the tail right below where it emerges. Pull it up snug. Figure 4-13B shows a Splicing Wand (see sidebar) being used for tucking; other fids will also work. (See also the double-sheet

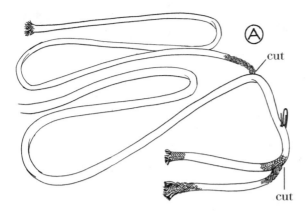

Figure 4-13A. *The Stropsicle. Hold the core in place with a paper clip.*

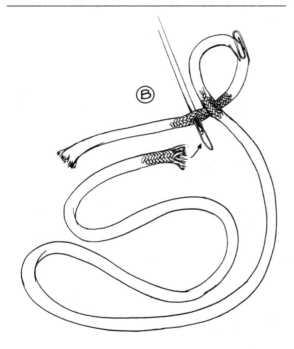

Figure 4-13B. *A Brummel Splice, using a Splicing Wand, provides extra security.*

application of the Brummel Splice in Chapter 5, page 167.)

Finishing   Taper the tail, as in Figure 4-16D (page 109). Bury the tail about 13 inches in the standing part, starting just below the Brummel Splice (Figure 4-13C). Stitch through the rope a few times with a

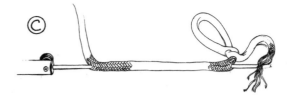

Figure 4-13C. *Bury the tail, starting just below the Brummel Splice.*

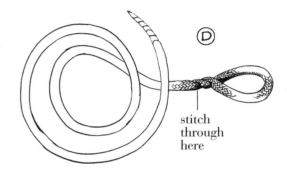

Figure 4-13D. *Tape or seize the end of the standing part.*

thread, to secure the end. Tape or seize the end of the standing part (Figure 4-13D).

12-Strand Single-Braid Eyesplice, Bury Version

A single-braid rope might be made with 4, 6, 8, 12, or some other number of strands. It might be made of a "conventional" synthetic like Nylon or Dacron, a high-modulus fiber like Spectra, or some sort of blend. It would be nice if one splice could be used for all the forms of single-braid, but that is definitely not the case. Some constructions require that the ends be unbraided, so that they can be woven into the standing part. Others have enough room in their centers to allow a (preferably tapered) end to be tucked inside. Consider this splice, which is of the latter type, to be an introduction to the topic. It was developed specifically for New England Rope's Regatta Braid, but it can be adapted to similar constructions made with conventional synthetics.

A single-braid rope has a hollow center, and this splice simply consists of tucking the end of the rope into this hollow, to form an eye.

To start, measure 24 diameters from the rope end, using the simple formula given earlier. Pull a single yarn (not an entire strand) out of the end of the rope to mark this point. Be very careful to avoid disturbing the braid beyond this point.

It will be a lot easier to tuck the end into the rope if you taper the end first. It'll be like driving a wedge in instead of a blunt-ended cylinder. A tapered splice is also stronger, as there is less of a stress riser to weaken the rope where the splice ends. A tapered splice will also last longer, as it has no sharp shoulder to chafe. And if all that isn't enough, a tapered splice just looks a lot better. This is significant, as splices can be as desirable for clean appearance as they are for brute strength.

So, have I convinced you to make a taper? Good. Count about 10 chevrons from the end. Pull out a pair of strands, one leading to the left, the other to the right. Count five more chevrons and pull out the fifth pair. Repeat three more times, pulling out every fifth pair of strands (Figure 4-14A). If you counted right, you will now have eight strands laid out. Finally, go up six more pairs and pull out a single yarn.

Figure 4-14A–C. *12-Strand Single-Braid Eyesplice. The single yarn marks where the eye will begin (A). Bury the tail into the standing part (B). Cut the laid-out ends off flush as they are about to enter the bury (C).*

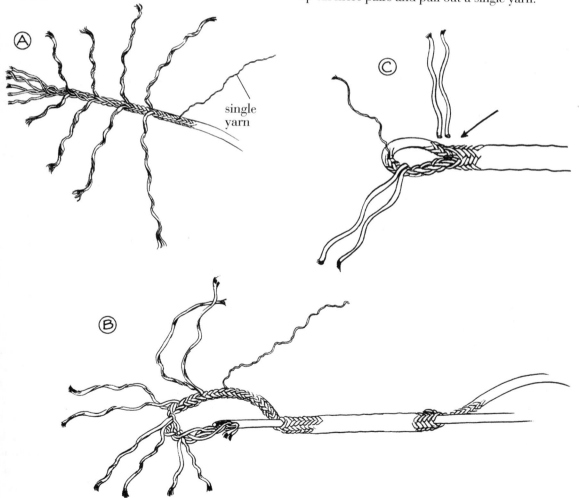

single yarn

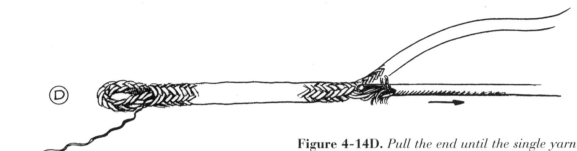

Figure 4-14D. *Pull the end until the single yarn reaches the bury. Smooth and massage the rope out straight.*

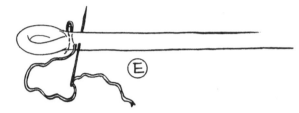

Figure 4-14E. *Stitch the single yarn*

Figure 4-14F. *The finished splice.*

Starting at the single yarn, measure the eye circumference you want. Bury the tail into the standing part, starting at the far side of the eye, for about one-and-a-third times the length of the tail. You bury for the extra tail length because the braid you are tucking into will expand and shorten (as we all do), as it gets filled with the tail. This extra bury is the rule for all braid splices. If you are using the Splicing Wand (see sidebar), enter it at the mark, exit it at the eye, grab the end, and withdraw. Milk and massage your way through, keeping the rope bunched up to make more room (Figure 4-14B).

Cut the laid-out ends off flush as they are about to enter the bury. Waiting to cut them helps keep them from backing out before tucking (Figure 4-14C).

Pull the end down until the lone yarn just reaches the bury; you will then have the eye size you wanted. Remove the tool, then smooth and massage the rope out straight. The tail will disappear inside (Figure 4-14D).

Thread the single yarn onto a large sail needle or darning needle (for an easy needle-threading technique, see sidebar on page 106). Stitch back and forth through the throat of the splice a few times to secure it. Tuck the needle in about ⅛ inch from where it emerged for the previous stitch, so the stitches don't show (Figure 4-14E). Don't pull too tight; just get the slack out. This stitching is very important, because our handcuff effect only kicks in as the load goes up. Under light loads, such as on a sheet in light air, or a mooring line in a quiet

cove, the splice can crawl apart. The stitching holds things for the first few pounds.

Figure 4-14F shows the finished splice.

High-Modulus 12-Strand Splice, with Mobius Brummel

This is a very weird splice, for single-braids made from Spectra, Technora, etc. These ropes are much stronger than either nylon or Dacron, so they need much longer buries to generate enough friction to guarantee high-load security. In addition, they need more low-tension security than a lock stitch can readily provide—and low loads for this stuff can be measured in tons. Therefore, in addition to stitching, make a Brummel Splice. This is the same splice you used for the Stropsicle, and you can make it the same way, if you wish. But because the halyards that the exotics are usually used for are so long, it can take a lo-o-o-ng time to drag the standing part through. So, someone came up with the Brummel shown here, which somehow materializes without passing the standing part. My thanks to Stanley Longstaff and Robbie Young for showing me this version. And yes, there are other versions, including some that allow you to "stack" multiple Brummels. For these and other splicing variants, see my other books in the Sources section.

Instead of 24 diameters, measure 72 diameters from the end. Tuck the end through the rope at this point (Figure 4-15A). Pull the end through, massaging if necessary, until the rope capsizes and smooths out, forming a little hole (Figure 4-15B).

Measure the eye circumference you want, beginning at the hole and working away from the end. Then tuck the end through again at this point,

which is the far side of the eye. Pull the end through to form a second capsized hole (Figure 4-15C).

The eye length lies between the two holes. Using an awl, a piece of string, or your fingers, work the eye length up through the end-side hole. Pull it through until the other hole comes through, too (Figure 4-15D).

The eye length still lies between the two holes. Pull it through the standing-part-side hole this time, until the hole capsizes back. Adjust the splice until it locks together (Figure 4-15E).

Taper the tail before tucking. Count six to eight strands away from the Brummel, and pull out one

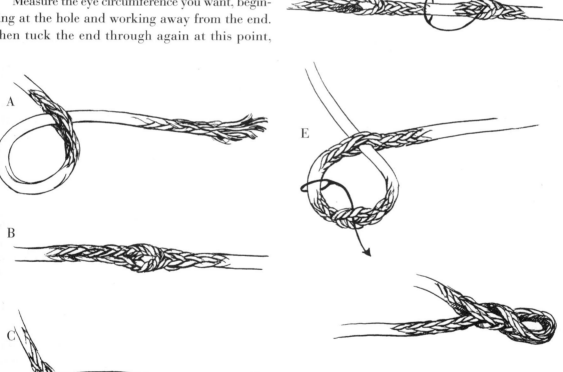

Figures 4-15A–E. *The Mobius Brummel. Measure and tuck (A). Pull, and capsize to form a hole (B). Measure, tuck, pull, and form second hole (C). Work eye length up through end-side hole, pull (D). Adjust splice until it locks together (E).*

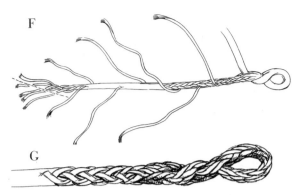

F

G

Figures 4-15F–G. *Finish the taper (F). The finished splice (G).*

strand. Pull out seven or eight more strands at regular intervals, alternating left and right strands. Finish the taper by cutting the end on a long angle (Figure 4-15F).

Finish the splice by tucking it into the standing part about one-and-a-half times the length of the tail, as for the 12-Strand Eyesplice (Figure 4-15G). This is just one taper for this construction of rope. Some ropes are very loosely laid, and won't hold together once you pull all those yarns out to taper them. If this happens to you, check the ropemaker's recommendations for your rope.

The Double-Braid Eyesplice Made Human

Materials needed:
20 feet (6 m) of ½ -inch (or 13-mm)
    double-braided Dacron
heavy-duty scissors
small marlingspike or awl
sail needle
China marker
tape measure
splicing tool

The Rope

To de-alienize the procedure, first picture the rope. It's made of two braided tubes, one inside the other. Why make rope this way? Because you can get more yarns into the same diameter than with three-strand, so the rope is stronger for its size. And

Squint-free Needle Threading

It's tough to get the bulky yarns of rope into even a large needle when stitching a braided rope splice (see text), unless you know this old embroiderer's trick: bend the thread around the needle shaft, and pinch it tight up against the shaft with thumb and forefinger. Slide it off the shaft, and you'll have a flat little nubbin between your fingertips. Just hold those fingertips up against the needle's eye and push. Threaded.

If you can't get the whole yarn in, even with this trick, split out half or less of the yarn. Thread and use that to stitch, and trim the rest flush.

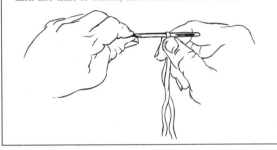

because of the angle of the braids, the yarns travel a shorter distance between the ends, so there's less stretch. The two tubes are not attached to one another, so if the ends are not whipped or (shudder) melted, you can slide back the outer tube (the "cover") to expose the inner tube (the "core"). It's just like sliding the wrapper back to expose a straw. This independence of core and cover is the key to splicing double-braid.

Half the strength of this rope is in the cover, and half is in the core, so it's very important that both take an even strain if the splice is to be maximally strong. All the measurements you'll be doing are there to make things come out so there's no slack in core or cover when you're done.

To make things easier when you're doing practice splices—and please do a few—use new, color-covered Dacron or Nylon rope of good quality. If your rope contains high-modulus fibers, use the Core-to-Core Splice, in the next section.

Setting Up, Part 1   Measure a splice tail whose length is 24 times the diameter of the rope (see formula at the beginning of this section). Pull a lone yarn (not an entire strand) out of the end at this point. This is the Cover Marker Yarn. Be very careful to avoid disturbing the braid beyond this point.

Starting at the yarn, measure an eye of the circumference you want. When you've located the far side of the eye, measure about 8 feet farther and tie a Alpine Butterfly Knot (Figure 3-16) or other jam-proof loop knot.

Go back to the end of the rope, and pull out as much core as you readily can. Just slide it out until the cover is bunched firmly against the knot. Then loop the knot over a good anchor point and smooth the cover back toward the end. Do this with real firmness, squeezing the cover with both hands while you slide them toward the end. You are doing all this in order to balance the core and cover. On a well-made rope, the cover might get right back to where it started, because the whole length of the rope was balanced at the factory. But you have to make sure, because the measurements and marks we are about to make will only work if the rope is balanced.

Return to the far side of the eye. Bend the rope sharply here, and hold it bent while you use the point of an awl (or spike) to nudge the cover yarns aside in all directions, to expose a small portion of the core. Finally, use the awl to bring the core out of the cover. Work it out, easing the cover yarns out of the way. As soon as the core starts to come out, stick

the awl through it, to mark this spot, the Core Exit (Figure 4-16A).

Setting Up, Part 2 Pull the core end right out of the rope. Leave the awl in place, or remove it and make a light mark with your China marker where the awl was. This is the "zero point," which would line up with the cover if you were to smooth the cover out again. Unfortunately it will no longer do so after we distort the cover by tucking extra material into it. So we have to establish a new zero point, to make the splice come out even.

Starting at the awl or mark, measure one-third of the cover tail length (see Table 4) away from the end. Mark the core vividly at this point, or pull out one core yarn there. (Figure 4-16B). This is the second core mark, your new zero point, around which you will orient the splice.

Tucking the Core Let's get back to the cover tail. Measure about two rope diameters toward the end from the Cover Marker Yarn. You can mark

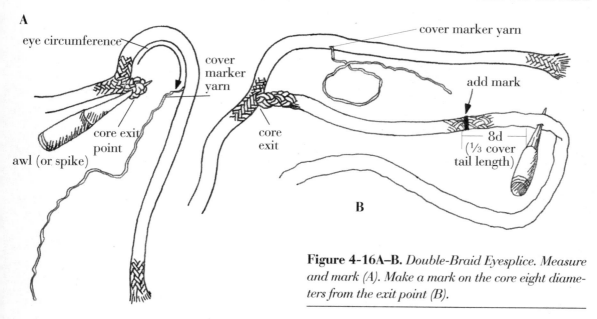

Figure 4-16A–B. *Double-Braid Eyesplice. Measure and mark (A). Make a mark on the core eight diameters from the exit point (B).*

Size(in.]	¼	⁵⁄₁₆	⅜	⁷⁄₁₆	½	⁹⁄₁₆	⅝	¹¹⁄₁₆	¾	1
24 diam. (cover tail)	6	7½	9	10½	12	13½	15	16½	18	24
14 diam. (core bury)	3½	4⅜	5¼	6⅛	7	7⅞	8¾	9⅝	10½	14
8 diam. (core mark for Dacron)	2	2½	3	3½	4	4½	5	5½	6	8
2 diam. (dist. past cover marker yard)	½	⅝	¾	⅞	1	1⅛	1⅜	1⅜	1½	2

Table 4. **Rope Measurements Relative to Size**

this spot if you feel compelled to, but it is enough to make note of where it is (Figure 4-16C). Using a Splicing Wand or other tool, insert the core into the cover, and bring it out at the 14 diameter mark (also Figure 4-16C) The core will travel away from the cover end, refill the now-hollow eye, and dive into the standing part, sliding along between core and cover (Figure 4-16C). (If your rope has tracer marks, this length is about four of them. If your rope does not have tracers, see the accompanying chart for this length. You can see the tracer marks in Figure 4-16D.)

If you want to splice a closed shackle on, you need to do it before making this tuck. Have I ever finished an entire splice, then realized I had forgotten to put the shackle on? Nahh.

Figure 4-16C. *Pull out extra core, to bunch up the cover, then slide the Wand in, starting about 14 rope diameters from the throat of the splice. This is about four tracer lengths. Bring the tool out about two diameters past the cover marker yarn. Pull on the core, to make sure that it wasn't snagged by the tool; if it is free, it will slide in and out*

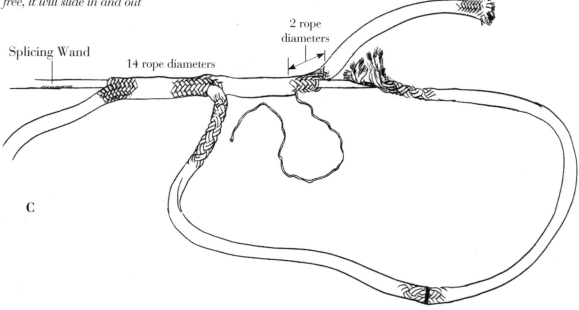

Splicing Wand

14 rope diameters

2 rope diameters

C

Tapering the Cover Bring the core end a short way out of the cover. Measure a tracer length or so toward the end of the cover from where the core goes in, and pull three sets of yarns out. Go down another tracer length and pull another three sets of yarns out. Do this twice more, pulling out three sets of yarns each time. Alternate left- and right-leading sets of yarns. Finish the taper by combing out eight diameters of the end, and cutting it on a long-taper (dotted line, Figure 4-16D).

If you handle the rope gently to keep it from raveling, you can cut the laid-out ends off flush now. Or you can cut them off as you tuck, as in the 12-strand splice.

Some ropes have three yarns in each set, others only two. This taper works for either con- struction.

Tucking the Cover Measure one-and-a-third times the cover tail length, starting at the mark on the core, and continuing away from the cored end. The cover

tail will be buried into this length of core. Again, we show a Splicing Wand doing the tuck (Figure 4-16E).

Tidying Up The spot where the two ends go into each other is called the Crossover. Snug up the Crossover by (a) pulling on the core end while holding the cover just above where the core emerges, then (b) pulling on the cover end while holding the core just above where the cover emerges. Lock the Crossover down tight (Figure 4-16F).

Smoothing The Crossover is tight, but the rope is all bunched up. Smooth it out by (a) holding the core side of the Crossover with one hand, and sliding your other hand firmly down the cover, all the way to where the core end emerges. Repeat, smoothing all the slack out. Then (b) hold the cover side of the Crossover with one hand while sliding your other hand down the core, towards the cover end (Figure 4-16G).

Figure 4-16D. *Using tracer marks, taper the cover. (Note that yarns will be longer than shown here.)*

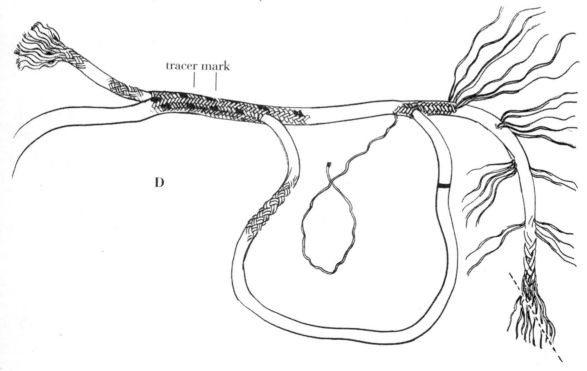

tracer mark

D

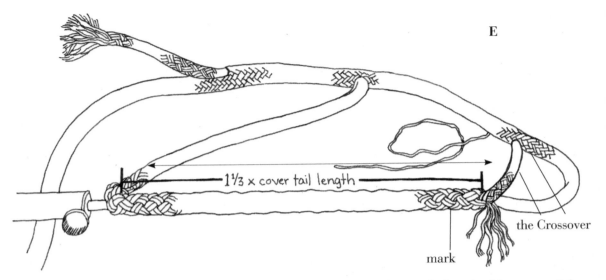

E

1⅓ x cover tail length

the Crossover

mark

Figure 4-16E. *Insert the Wand into the core, about one and one-third times the length of the cover tail from the cover tail's entry point, which is the mark on the core. Tuck the cover.*

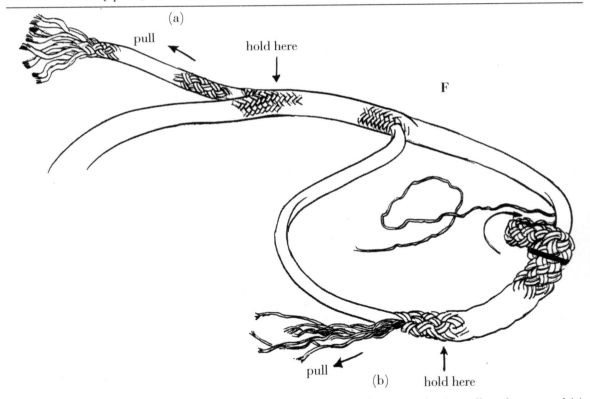

(a)

pull

hold here

F

pull

(b)

hold here

Figure 4-16F. *While holding the cover standing part next to where the core end exits, pull on the core end (a). Hold lightly, so that the core tail can slide inside the rope. This will pull the loose bight of core at the crossover down flat and snug. Then (b) lightly hold the core standing part next to where the cover end exits, and pull on the cover end. This should finish tightening and snugging the crossover point (b).*

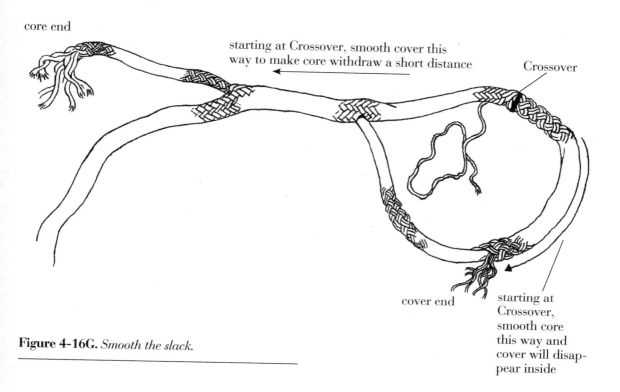

core end

starting at Crossover, smooth cover this way to make core withdraw a short distance

Crossover

cover end

starting at Crossover, smooth core this way and cover will disappear inside

Figure 4-16G. *Smooth the slack.*

The core end will withdraw a short distance, and the cover end will disappear inside. Be careful to hold the Crossover firmly during this operation, so it doesn't pull apart, even a little.

Cutting the Core, Stitching the Crossover　If you pulled a yarn from the core to make the second mark, you have the option of threading it onto a large sail needle or darning needle (see the nifty threading trick shown in the sidebar "Squint-free Needle Threading").

Stitch back and forth through the core side of the Crossover. Use neat stitches, tucking the needle in almost exactly where the previous stitch emerges, so you won't leave lumpy stitches on the surface. The idea is to lock the Crossover together and to make this section, which is the thickest that will have to go into the rope, easier to bury. Snug the first two or three stitches down gently, to anchor the yarn. Pull succeeding stitches firmly. As I say, this is an optional step, and not an important one. And for very small eyes it is a bad idea, as there is not

enough room for the stitches to adjust, so the splice can deform. This is the kind of thing I learn, often after years of doing things a certain way, because patient and knowledgeable people (I'm looking at you, Samson) take the trouble to educate me.

Next, grip the core end right where it emerges from the cover (Figure 4-16H). When all the slack is out of the cover, pinch the core right where it exits, pull it out a few inches, and cut it off right where you're pinching it. Then ravel the end, taper it on a long angle, as in 4-16D. Once more smooth out the cover, starting at the Crossover. This time the core will disappear inside.

Running the Splice Home　In the words of my friend Emiliano, "You now have one more chance to ruin the whole thing." To finish the splice, you need to anchor the Butterfly to something very solid, pull on the eye, and milk all the slack out of the cover, so it swallows the exposed core and the Crossover. This is the place where most people get into trouble, so here are a few tricks to make the process easier:

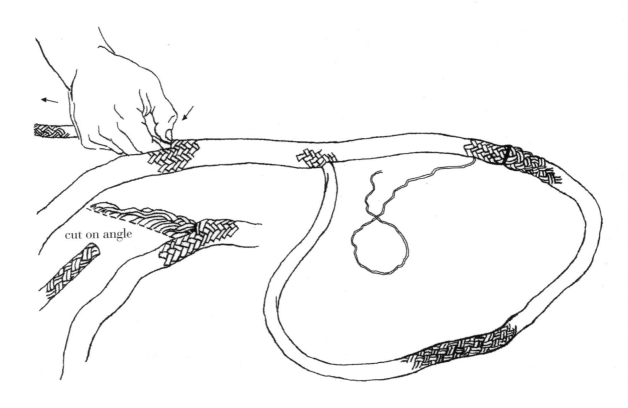

cut on angle

Figure 4-16H. *Grab the core where it emerges from the cover. Pull it out and cut it off right where you grabbed it. Then cut the resulting tail on a big angle.*

1. With the loop knot anchored, start at the knot and milk the cover toward the eye. Stop when you get within a foot or so of the cover tail that's inside the core. As the standing part of the core slides into the cover, it wants to drag the core end into the rope with it. When this happens, the eye cover gets bunched up. To fix this pull back on the cover side of the eye, or put a hammer into the eye and snap the rope sharply against the belay. This will yank the core tail back out and smooth the eye. Repeat this maneuver any time the cover gets bunched up, as soon as you see it happening. If you wait to do this until the splice is mostly home, you will have an extremely hard time budging things. Note that, when snapping with the hammer that it is very important that the handle is always angled away from you. Also

be sure to stand far enough back that you can't hammer yourself in the knee, or have the splice slide up the handle and slam into your hand.

2. Hold the cover side of the Crossover, apply tension, and while keeping the tension on, smooth the core firmly away from the Crossover. This will make the core tight and smooth, so it won't bunch up in front of the advancing cover.

3. By keeping tension on the core while you run the cover home, you remove any slack from the core, so it won't bunch up and make a plug, preventing the Crossover from going into the cover. You also reduce the core's diameter, so the cover can swallow it more easily.

With many ropes, you can maintain tension with one hand and milk the slack toward you with the other. With tougher ropes, get a friend to pull on the eye, to make the core even smaller, while you milk the slack toward the eye. For

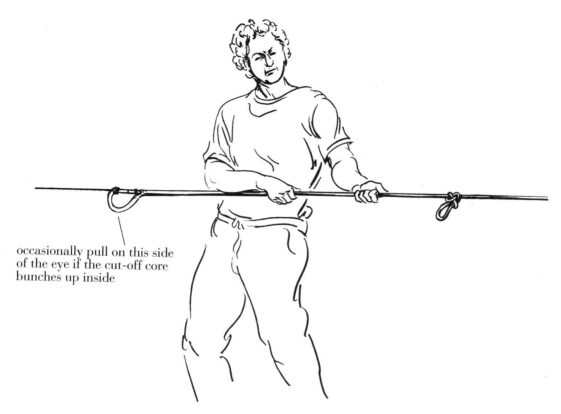

occasionally pull on this side
of the eye if the cut-off core
bunches up inside

Figure 4-16I. *Finishing a Double-Braid Eyesplice in hard-laid rope. A line is Icicle-Hitched to the core side of the eye. A come-along or winch pulls at the other end. The operator works the slack in the cover toward the eye.*

really tough rope, Icicle-Hitch (Figure 3-12) a smaller, separate line to the core side of the eye. Attach this line to a winch or come-along and crank it tight (Figure 4-16I). For absurdly tough or really large rope, you might need to tension with a fork lift. Be certain your anchors can take the strain. Unless something is odd (see problems, page 114) you won't have to revert to this last dodge. Remember to pause occasionally to deal with bunching up in the eye cover.

4. As my friend J. Mark says, "Rope loves to be massaged." So whenever it gets hard to make the cover move, stop and bend the rope, firmly and repeatedly, where it's tight from trying to

swallow all that extra material. This will loosen up the fibers.

5. When forming very small halyard eyes, there will not be room for your hand in the eye as it approaches home; put a marlingspike or screwdriver in and hold on to that.

6. No matter how little or much effort it takes, the splice will be home when you (a) get the Cover Marker Yarn to the edge of the bury; and (b) have no slack in either the eye or the standing part.

If you run out of slack before the yarn is at the bury, if you are positive there's no slack in either the eye or the standing part, and if you're sure that all your measurements are correct, then there's an adjustment you can make for subsequent splices: Let's say you ended up one inch short of your goal. The next time you splice this rope, make the vivid mark on the core one inch farther from the first mark than you did this time.

Given a correct setup, there are only three reasons why you'd need to make this adjustment:

You are splicing lousy rope. Cheap rope is not well tensioned at the factory, so core and cover are not balanced. If you're stuck with splicing this stuff, you have to make up a measurement that works.

You are splicing nylon. For some reason, nylon sometimes reacts differently to splicing than Dacron. Try pulling the core yarn out one-half the length of the cover tail from the spike. As noted elsewhere, double-braided nylon doesn't make a lot of sense, because you use it in situations where you *want* stretch.

You are splicing old, or even slightly used rope. When you know how to splice this stuff quickly and well, people are going to ask you to do their lines for them. It's great work, as a favor or for pay. But sooner or later someone is going to ask you to splice a line that is not new. When they do, you can save yourself a lot of trouble by answering with a firm "no." Old double-braid, broken down by sunlight, salt water, and use, is vicious, unrenderable stuff. If you must try: Wash the line first and use fabric softener; after excising the core, bunch the cover back fiercely against the loop knot to loosen the fibers, then smooth it back out before marking the Core Exit; and pound on the cover with a rubber or wooden mallet before you go to run the splice home. Even all of that might not be enough. There are advanced ways around this, but the one that is most often resorted to—not burying the core into the standing part, so there's more room for the cover—leaves a potentially weak spot on one side of the eye. Reputable manufacturers recommend this, at least for used rope, (I'm looking at you, Samson), but it is a bad idea. Better to get new rope.

Once the splice is completely home, use the Cover Marker Yarn to stitch the throat of the splice a few times, as for the Single-Braid Eyesplice (see 102). Done.

Core-to-Core Splice

The Mobius Brummel (Figure 4-15) is called upon when you are splicing an exotic that has no cover. But you can also get the stuff with a cover, in which case it looks just like regular old double-braid. But it doesn't splice like regular old double-braid; the cover is there only to provide compression for splice security, chafe and UV protection for the standing part, and some extra meat for stoppers, winches, and cleats to grip onto. So the splice, in essence, is a 12-strand splice, with an extra- long bury, that is made inside a cover.

Setting Up   For yacht-diameter ropes, start by tying a Butterfly Knot about 10 feet or so from the rope end. Pull the core out of the end and bunch the cover up, as for the regular double-braid splice. Smooth the cover out firmly and repeatedly. With this rope, all of the strength is in the core. Because the cover isn't structural, it isn't balanced in tension with the core at the factory; balancing is even more important than with normal rope. It is almost a certainty that, after you have finished the balancing,

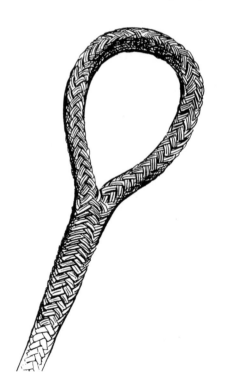

Figure 4-16J. *A finished Double-Braid Eyesplice.*

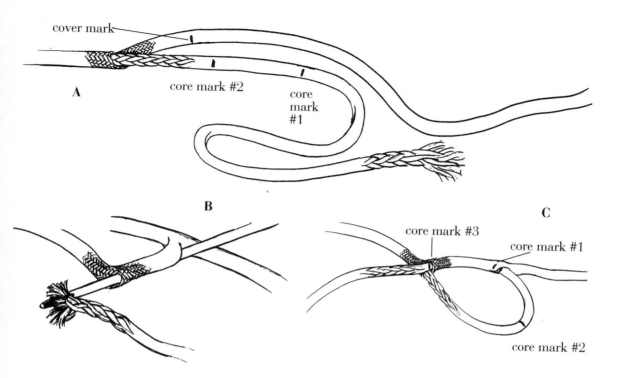

A

B

C

cover mark

core mark #2

core mark #1

core mark #3

core mark #1

core mark #2

Figure 4-17A–C. *Core-to-Core Splice. Mark the core (A). Running the core through the cover of the eye. Thread on the shackle now, if you want one (B). Core Mark #3 (C).*

there will be a significant amount of core sticking out of the cover.

Measure 48 rope diameters from the end of the core, and make a mark on the cover with a marking pen or China marker. Continue on from there to get the eye circumference you want—usually very short, as these lines are used for halyards and sheets. Take the core out at the far side of the eye.

Smooth the cover out one more time, and make a mark right where the core exits (Core Mark #1 in Figure 4-17A). If the core is a light color, use a marking pen or (preferably) a China marker. If it's dark, use a white China marker or white-out. Make a second mark eight diameters up from the first (one-third of a Dacron cover tail length). This is Core Mark #2.

Tucking   Tuck the core in at the cover mark, and out in the same hole it's already coming out of. You just take a trip through the circumference of the eye. If you are splicing a closed-loop shackle on, thread it onto the core now (Figure 4-17B).

More Setting Up   Pull on the core end until the first mark on the core lines up with the mark on the cover. Holding the marks together, smooth out the eye circumference. Then mark the core once more, just where it exits the cover. Call this Core Mark #3 (Figure 4-17C).

Tapering the Core   Pull a yarn out of the core eight diameters or so beyond Core Mark #3. Pull seven to nine more yarns out at regular intervals, working toward the core end. Finish the taper by raveling the end and cutting it on a long angle (Figure 4-17D).

More Tucking   Tuck the core into itself at Core Mark #2. Bury it for about one-and-a-third times

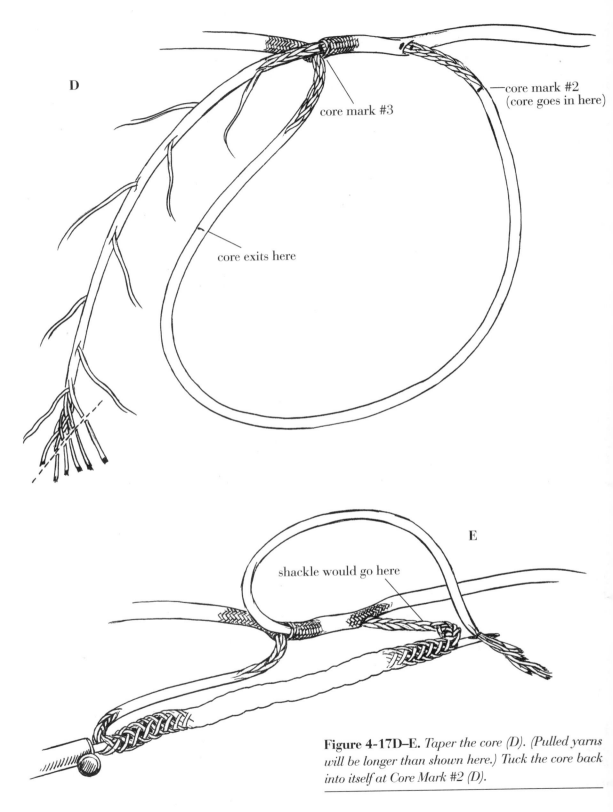

D

core mark #3

core mark #2
(core goes in here)

core exits here

E

shackle would go here

Figure 4-17D–E. *Taper the core (D). (Pulled yarns will be longer than shown here.) Tuck the core back into itself at Core Mark #2 (D).*

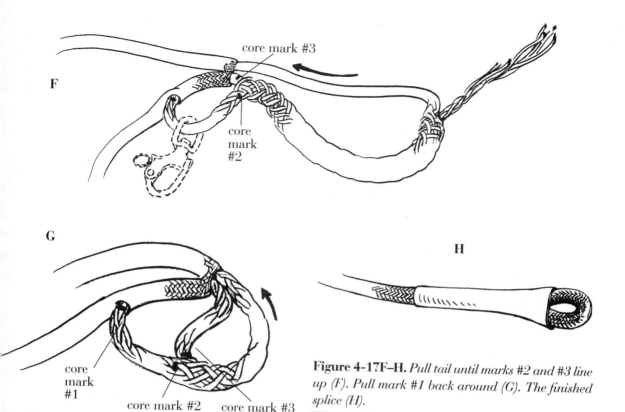

core mark #3

F

core mark #2

G

core mark #1

core mark #2   core mark #3

H

Figure 4-17F–H. *Pull tail until marks #2 and #3 line up (F). Pull mark #1 back around (G). The finished splice (H).*

its length (Figure 4-17E). Cut the laid-out yarns off as they begin to go into the bury. You can cut them off sooner, but at least the first few of them are in a loose enough weave that they can get loose, tangle, bunch up, and generally ruin your splice.

Important Note: Your shackle (not shown) needs to be between the first and second marks on the core at this point.

Running It Toward Home
Yes, it looks very strange now, but it will resolve.

After the core's tail emerges, pull it through until the third mark lines up with the second mark. Don't worry about where the other mark is. Holding these two marks together, smooth the core out. Its tail will disappear inside. In Figure 4-17F the shackle is shown where it should be.

Anchor the Butterfly and begin milking the slack out of the cover. Keep those two marks lined up, and try to keep the core from bunching up.

Walking It All the Way Home
This is the hard part. It's physically difficult to get the cover to swallow all that extra core, and it's conceptually difficult to see where you're going, right up to the moment you get there. Just concentrate on those two marks, keep tension on the core ahead of the marks, and keep the cover coming. Massage. As the paired marks are about to go in, pull the lone mark (#1) back around so it's lined up with the mark on the cover again, as in Figure 4-17G. Massage some more. Snap against the belay. Milk the cover around; it will eventually—just—cover all the exposed core.

The cover is still outside, of course. You just need to whip, tape, serve, or heat-shrink a stub of it to the standing part, and cut off the rest. Figure 4-17H shows the heat-shrink option.

The Finished Splice
Cover the taped-down cover with service, rigger's tape, or, as shown, a layer or two of heat-shrink tubing (Figure 4-17H).

Sta-Set-X Splice

So much for the exotics. Now we come to what used to be my favorite halyard material, Sta-Set-X. As I mentioned in Chapter 2 (page 23), Sta-Set-X stretches less than double braid and costs almost exactly the same. It's also more UV-resistant, as the core takes all the load, shaded by the cover. And it's actually easier to splice, once you get the hang of it. In our shop, it has been eclipsed by VPC, another New England product, which is a blend of Vectran and a polyolefin filler. This rope stretches significantly less than X, and takes a standard core-to-core splice. But it is still hard to beat X as a good value, so here is the splice.

Setting Up   For yacht diameter ropes, make your Butterfly about 8 feet from the end. Balance the rope. As with core-to-core rope, this rope has all the strength in the core, and isn't balanced at the factory, so you need to be sure of the balance now. One thing that is very different about this rope is that the core is wrapped in two helical layers of gauze; try to keep them intact.

Once the rope is balanced, make a mark on the cover 16 diameters from the end of the core. (That length is the rope diameter in sixteenths, expressed in inches. So a $7/16$-inch rope would have a mark 7 inches from the end.) Measure the eye circumference you want. Pull the core out on the far side of the eye. This will be easier to do than with other cored ropes, but be careful not to disturb the gauze. Make sure the cover is smooth. Using a felt-tip pen, mark the core lightly where it exits the cover.

Gauze Removal   Pull extra core out and make a second mark on it eight diameters, or half the cover tail length, farther from the end than the first mark on the core. Make this second mark a heavy one,, to get the ink to penetrate through the gauze.

The next step is to remove the gauze from the length of the core that will form the bury and the eye circumference. The bury length will be naked because the uncovered fibers will grip better than covered ones would. The eye length will be naked because uncovered fibers will flatten out and resist chafe better than covered ones would.

Lay the rope on a firm, flat surface. With a razor knife, slit through the gauze layers for about two inches on either side of the second mark (Figure 4-18B). Don't worry about the fibers inside; as long

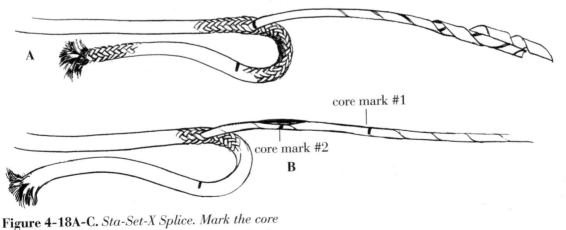

core mark #1

core mark #2

B

A

C

Figure 4-18A-C. *Sta-Set-X Splice. Mark the core (A). Make a second mark on the core and slit the gauze (cutting with, not across, the core fibers, so as not to damage them) one inch either side of the mark. (B) Strip the gauze from the second mark to the core end (C).*

as the slit runs straight down the rope, you won't hurt them.

Gauze Taping   You can now see the fibers inside the cut. If the ink mark did not penetrate, mark the fibers at this spot. Then grasp the gauze at the mark, pull toward the end, and the gauze will strip off. If any gauze projects past the mark, cut it shorter (Figure 4-18C).

To keep the gauze from coming loose past this point, tape it down to the fibers. Start the tape on the gauze, wrap it on smoothly and snugly towards the end, with minimum overlap on the turns of the tape. Stop taping as soon as the gauze is secured, preferably short of the mark on the core. The tape should be on firmly enough that the gauze can't slide on it (see Figure 4-18D). Masking tape works best.

The Shackle   With the gauze taped down, it's time to slide on the shackle (Figure 4-18D).

Tucking   Tuck the core in at the mark on the cover, through the eye, and about one-and-a-half cover tail lengths down the standing part (ten tracer lengths past where the core first came out). Before entering the tool, pull out lots of extra core to bunch up the cover and make more room inside.

If you're using the Splicing Wand (shown), snare only ½ inch or so of the end. The easiest way to do this is to push the taped part through the snare, pull the mass of yarns through, and then back the end up to the position shown in Figure 4-18E. Snare firmly.

No matter what tool you are using, tucking is a

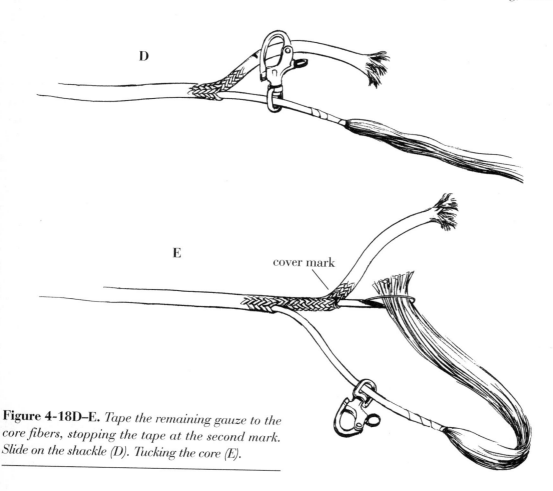

D

E

cover mark

Figure 4-18D–E. *Tape the remaining gauze to the core fibers, stopping the tape at the second mark. Slide on the shackle (D). Tucking the core (E).*

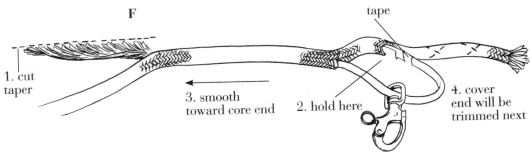

Figure 4-18F. *Tapering the core.*

matter of keeping the cover bunched up while easing the core along.

Bring the core out and remove the tool, then pull more core out until the tape reaches the mark on the cover.

Trimming the Core and the Cover With a pair of scissors, cut the end of the core on a long angle, starting about one-half cover tail length from the end (Figure 4-18F). Then hold the tape at the cover

mark and smooth the cover toward the core end until the core end disappears inside.

Cut off half of the cover tail. Ravel the remainder halfway back to the cover mark. With your scissors, cut the raveled portion on a long angle.

Tape the tapered end neatly and firmly onto the core, starting the tape between the cover mark and the start of the taper. Be sure the original tape is still right at the cover mark (Figure 4-18G).

Running Toward Home Anchor the Butterfly Knot and commence milking the cover toward the eye (Figure 4-18H). When things look like the drawing, stop and pull back on the eye side of the eye, to keep it from bunching up. This splice is initially much easier to get home than double-braid,

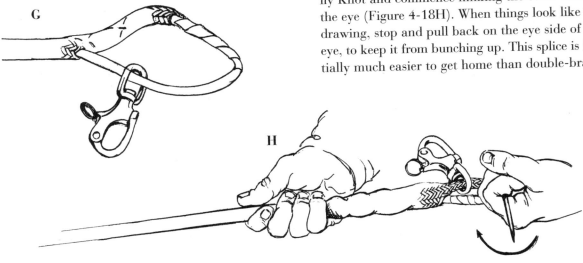

Figure 4-18G–I *Tape the tapered cover end to the core (G). Milk the cover toward eye (H). The finished splice (I).*

but it gets ornery at the end. Get all you can by massaging, milking, and snapping at the belay, as for double-braid. This should get you within an inch or so of the cover mark.

Slamming Home   To get that last inch, hitch a small sledgehammer to the shackle, and snap with that. I am not kidding. Be careful of your back and shoulders. Be sure of the anchor. Keep the hammer handle angled away from you, and stand far enough back that the hammer can't hit you in the knee. Two or three moderate snaps should do it.

With a piece of sail twine, stitch back and forth through the throat a few times, for light load security.

Figure 4-18I shows the finished splice.

BRAIDED ROPE REPAIRS

On behalf of *Practical Sailor* magazine, researcher Drew Frye conducted a series of tests on sewn terminations for rope (October 2014 issue). The results showed that a properly done sewn eye can achieve efficiencies of 85 percent or more. It is important to note that the article shows that not all stitch patterns are equal; I recommend careful study of Drew's methods before you try an eye in earnest.

Note also that the accompanying illustration is not an eye, so the load on the stitching could be twice that for the eye configuration. Add stitches accordingly, and be sure of a generous overlap.

The Stitch Splice
One difficulty with braided rope is that it is very, very difficult to splice after it has been used for a while. This means that this modern line benefits greatly from traditional attentiveness; fairleads, ample-size sheaves, smooth belay surfaces all help to prevent chafe, and thus prevent the need to do another splice.

Figure 4-19A–C. *To begin the Stitch Splice, pull out a foot of core from each rope end and make a rough taper by cutting the marked strands (A). Retract the cores by working the slack out of the covers, and lay the ends alongside each other. Stitch together thoroughly with waxed sail twine (B). The finished Stitch Splice (C).*

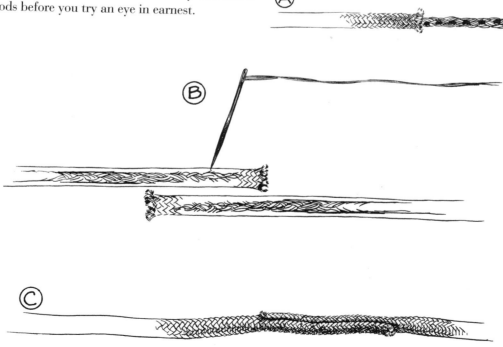

But if you do get serious chafe, say in the run of a halyard, a temporary repair (that will pass through sheaves and stoppers) is possible.

Cut about a foot off the end of each line's core, lay the cover ends alongside one another, and stitch through-and-through like crazy with stout sail twine. If you cut the cores on a long angle to taper them, you can maximize this Stitch Splice's strength without making it too bulky (Figure 4-19). I wouldn't count on this splice for significant loads, but it can definitely be strong enough to get a sail started up. Just be sure the splice is past the winch before you need to start cranking.

A few words of encouragement.

Splicing has always been a high art among sailors, even when the only rope around was three-strand. Marlingspike artists took that simple construction and reconfigured it into beckets, buttons, and variegated bulk, in ways that make the most complex braid seem thud simple. And they came up with these complications, not to show off—or not *just* to show off—but because situations demanded a creative use of cordage.

Nowadays we ask less of three-strand, leaving us more time to deal with the demands of braided rope. But the essential situation is the same: Our vessels need appropriate materials and appropriate splices. Getting to know these new ropes can be difficult, but they're worth the effort.

CHAPTER 5

Standing Rigging Design and Materials

Rig design usually is something the rigger is given. Although we can often suggest modifications, the basic layout and configuration are already established, so that our primary responsibility is proper design execution. But this is not to say that we are excused from technical considerations; we owe it to the vessel and ourselves to understand the characteristics of hull and rig type, the sort of sailing intended, and thus what types and degrees of strain will be imposed on the rig.

There's usually no need to second-guess the designer, just to equip ourselves with the ability to make informed decisions. It would be easier to just do the handwork and let other people worry about design, but getting involved in the abstract side of rigging gives us two very important benefits:

1. Understanding the whole, we see the reasons for using certain materials and procedures; we are not so likely to alter or substitute as we would be if the reasons for each particular were not technically justified. Knowledge keeps us honest and provides motivation for honing our skills.

2. Much of a rigger's work is extemporaneous—replacing failed pieces, inspecting, tuning, shifting leads, lashing, hoisting, lowering,

and jury-rigging. Experience and practice are our greatest allies here, but there's nothing so reassuring as having one's judgment borne out by calculations.

The bias of this book is toward long-proven practices. "We pay attention to tradition," a boatbuilder friend once said, "so we don't have to make two hundred years of mistakes." By studying design, we benefit from the experiences of others. One of the clearest lessons is that good designs always evidence a firm grasp of basic mechanical principles.

DESIGN PRINCIPLES

"The square of the hypotenuse is equal to the sum of the squares on the two sides."

Pythagoras

Angles

Standing rigging is an exercise in leverage, so to explain its mechanics we'll begin with the lever. Figure 5-1 shows a familiar form of lever, the seesaw. The children are seated 9 feet on either side of the support, or fulcrum. Each child weighs 50 pounds, but as far as the seesaw is concerned they each produce a moment of 450 foot-pounds. That is, leverage is a matter of weight (50 pounds) times distance from the fulcrum (9 feet). The children balance not merely because they weigh the same, but because they exert the same number of foot-pounds.

To prove this, let's shift the position of the fulcrum to the right 6 feet (Figure 5-2). Now the child on the left is 15 feet from the fulcrum, which means she produces a moment of 750 foot-pounds (15 feet times 50 pounds). The seesaw now extends only 3 feet on the other side of the fulcrum. As you can see, it takes a 250-pound football player (3 feet times 250 pounds) to balance the seesaw.

Now let's make a lever that takes a 90-degree turn at the fulcrum (Figure 5-3). It's not a seesaw anymore, but the same principles apply. A 50-pound push against the top of the vertical arm, 9 feet from the fulcrum, is balanced by 50 pounds on the horizontal arm, 9 feet from the fulcrum. The same push against the same height vertical arm is balanced by 100 pounds placed 4½ feet from the fulcrum: 9 feet × 50 pounds = 450 foot-pounds, and so does 4½ feet × 100 pounds.

Hang on, we're about to start rigging. If you set up a wire that ran from the end of the horizontal arm to the top of the vertical arm, you would be exerting leverage on that wire (Figure 5-4). This is how stayed masts work. An important change, other

Figure 5-1. *The seesaw, a familiar form of lever.*

Figure 5-2. *Two hundred-fifty pounds placed 3 feet from the fulcrum has the same moment as 50 pounds 15 feet from the fulcrum.*

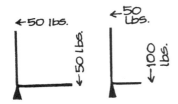

Figure 5-3. *A lever with a right-angle turn.*

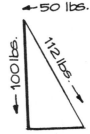

Figure 5-4. *Take away the horizontal arm, replace it with a wire, and you've started rigging. The principle of moments still applies, but now there's also a compression load on the mast.*

than the wire, is that there is now a *compression load* on the vertical member (mast); the wire exerts a downward pull of, in this case, 111.8 pounds. The closer the lower end of the wire is to the mast, the greater the proportion of effort it expends in a downward pull, and the more tension is exerted on it (Figure 5-5). In every instance, the wire must be strong enough to deal with the moment produced by a force exerted at the top of the mast, and the mast must be strong enough not to buckle under the imposed compression load. In addition, the wire now exerts a horizontal compression at its base. On a boat, that base is the deck, so we need to be sure that the deck is strong enough to take that load. A very great thing is that all these forces can be resolved into components having defined direction and magnitude relative to one another—we can figure out how much load is landing where. Using lines of proportionate angles and lengths, or the corre-sponding formulas, we can calculate moments without having to set up a real mast and attach tension gauges.

Figure 5-5 is a graph that represents the results of calculations to determine wire strain at a variety of staying angles (the angle of the wire relative to the mast). As you can see, the amount of tension accelerates as the angle narrows, approaching infinity as it approaches vertical. Since sailboats are usually narrow things with tall masts, and since neither wires nor masts can take loads approaching infinity, the angle-to-load relationship is central to rig design. Notice that the greatest acceleration of tension comes in the range of 0 to 12 degrees. If the shroud angle is 12 degrees or greater, it can more easily resist the pressure of wind on sails without generating undue strain. But can this be done? Rigs are tall and narrow to allow the greatest length of luff and closest headsail sheeting angles.

Figure 5-5. *The curve shows tension on a shroud induced by a 50-pound lateral load at the masthead, given various shroud-to-mast angles*

Figure 5-6. *The closer the lower end of the wire is to the mast, the higher the compression load on the mast and the tension on the wire.*

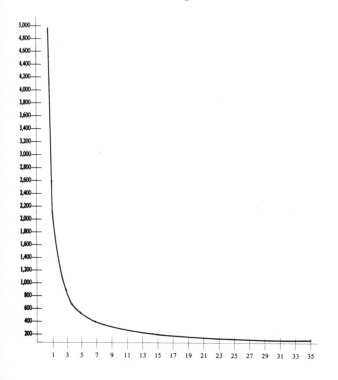

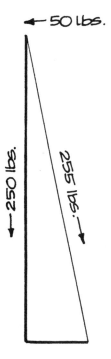

You could say that angles are to rigs as genes are to bodies: They determine the shape, size, and proportions of the finished structure. Rig design involves working out realistic relationships among angles and the loads they produce. The angle a shroud makes relative to its mast, for instance, determines the ratios of compressive and lateral forces that shroud exerts and therefore how strong both mast and shroud need to be. Very steep shrouds can exert compressive loads that could crumple any mast, so in practical terms angles limit rig design options.

With that notion in mind, let's take a break from mast building and look at the effect of angles more closely on a simpler structure.

A Lifeline

Consider a deck lifeline—say, a piece of ⅛-inch (3 mm) 1 x 19 stainless steel wire with a breaking strength rated at 2,100 pounds (955 kg). It is secured at the cockpit at one end and at the foredeck at the other, and is long enough that if you pick it up at the middle, exerting 150 pounds of force, it will deflect about 12 inches (305 mm) over its 30-foot (9.1 m) run (see Figure 5-7). By clipping the shackle of a safety harness around this wire, a crewmember can walk forward and aft, secure from the danger of going overboard. If the lifeline is strong enough.

That chilling "if" might make you receptive to a funny little picture. That is, we can draw what is called a "stress diagram" that will show us just how much load would come on the wire if a hypothetical 150-pound crewmember were to fetch up against it. In Figure 5-8, the load (150 pounds) is represented by a vertical line of arbitrary length. Lines parallel to the two sides of the lifeline are drawn from the top and bottom of this vertical line. Their lengths where they intersect show the relative load on each leg. So if they are five times longer than the vertical line, each leg of the lifeline will experience a load five times greater than the weight of the crewmember, or about 1,125 pounds.

You can get to the same answer by means of a formula. If formulas make your eyes glaze over, skip this part: Load × Length of one leg ÷ Deflection = Tension on both legs combined.

In this case that's 150 pounds × 15.0333 feet ÷ 1 foot = 2,255 pounds. This is the combined tension,

---

Figure 5-7. *A load of 150 pounds applied at the middle of a lifeline run of 30 feet causes a deflection of 12 inches. The tension on the lifeline can be calculated from this observation using the formula in the text or the diagrammatic representation in Figure 5-8.*

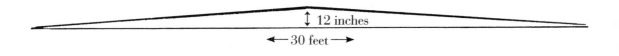

↕ 12 inches

← 30 feet →

Figure 5-8. *To calculate tension on a line or wire graphically, draw a vertical line of any convenient length to represent the deflecting load at the midpoint (in our case, 150 pounds). Now draw in the deflected legs, starting from the top and bottom of the vertical; in our example we get the angles of deflection from Figure 5-7. (We could walk them over to Figure 5-8 with parallel rules if desired.) Line ac or bc divided by line ab and multiplied by 150 pounds yields an approximation of the tension on each end of the lifeline.*

a

150 lbs

b

c

so the load on each leg is 1,127.5 pounds (531.5 kg). You can also say that the total load varies with the sine of the angle. The angle here is about 3.814 degrees. The sine of this angle is .066519, and 150 divided by .066519 is, again, about 2,255.

In practice the formulas are more precise, and the stress diagram is handier for showing the effects of changes in configuration.

But let's come back to that lifeline. Our calculations were based on a static, sustained load of 150 pounds (68 kg), the weight of a lean crewmember. Under those conditions we have a factor of safety of less than 2—marginal at best. Now consider that in real life, that 150-pound (68 kg) load will come on abruptly when the crewmember falls or is washed across the deck. In this "shock load" circumstance, the momentum from the load can easily double or triple the load arrived at by our calculations. It's also worth considering that some members of the crew might weigh more than 150 pounds (68 kg), and that the wire might not be 100 percent efficient, and that the fasteners that anchor the lifeline are mostly subjected to a shearing force, which they cannot withstand as stoutly as they can an upward pull. In other words, the formula or diagram is just a starting point.

Taking this into account, it's clear that this lifeline is ironically named. We need to increase wire strength, reduce tension on the wire, or both.

Let's start by reducing the tension. As shown in Figure 5-9, lengthening the wire until it deflects 18 inches (457 mm) results in a load on each leg of about 750 pounds (341 kg). By increasing the deflection, you reduce the leverage the load exerts on the wire's ends. You can keep on increasing deflection until the two sides are nearly parallel.

Figure 5-9. *Increasing deflection in the lifeline (decreasing the resting tension) reduces the leverage a load exerts on the wire's ends. Expressed more elegantly: the load varies with the sine. In this case the sine is $^1/_{15}$ = .0666. So the load (150 pounds) divided by the sine = approximately 2,250 pounds, or half of that on each leg. With a two-foot deflection, there would be half that. Note that, in the real world of lifelines, it is rare to have an unmoderated impact load, as in someone hurtling through the air and fetching up at maximum velocity, right in the middle of the line. But it's a good idea to design for that eventuality.*

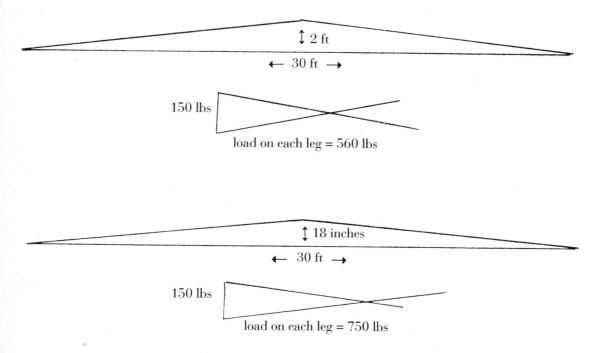

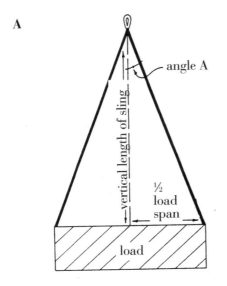

A

angle A

vertical length of sling

½ load span

load

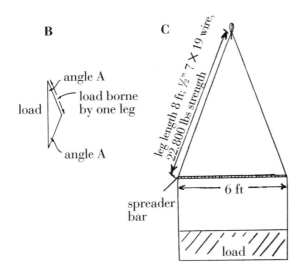

B

angle A

load borne by one leg

load

angle A

C

leg length 8 ft; ½" 7 × 19 wire, 22,800 lbs strength

6 ft

spreader bar

load

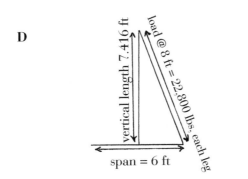

D

vertical length 7.416 ft

load @ 8 ft = 22,800 lbs, each leg

span = 6 ft

Here there's minimal load on the wire, no shear on the deck fastenings—and your crewmember is 200 feet to leeward. So you back up, working out a compromise between minimum tension and minimum deflection. Playing with tether and lifeline configuration can make the compromise less painful.

After you've settled on deflection, choose a wire size that will provide you with a comfortably massive safety factor. In our case, a combination of short tether, 2-foot deflection, and ¼-inch wire (7 x 7 construction, because it resists damage from kinking) gives us a 10:1 safety factor. Now that's a lifeline. But we can do even better. After seeing what a dramatic effect that angles have on loads, we can lead our line through a fairlead secured to an upper shroud, about chest-high. Now we have a much larger angle, thus much lower loads. And that larger angle also results in a very tall lifeline (jackline), so we can use a very short tether. No long tail dragging along behind us. No tether long enough that we can fall into the water.

Slings and Compression

The lifeline gave us a compelling example of the effect of angles on tension; now it's time to see the equally significant effect of angles on compression. The strain on a two-legged sling can be calculated using the same formula or diagram as for the life-

---

Figure 5-10. *A load hangs from a simple sling in Diagram A. If the load is 10,000 pounds, one-half the span of the load is 3 feet, and the vertical measure of the sling is 7.42 feet, then the compression force is 10,000 × 3 ÷ 7.42 = 4,043 pounds, or 2,022 pounds pressing inward at either end of the load. Diagram B shows a pictorial method to solve for the load borne by each leg of the sling—in this case about 56 percent of the supported load, or 5,600 pounds. In Diagram C we've added a 6-foot spreader bar to protect a load from compression. If the load were heavy enough to strain the 7 x 19 wire to its rated strength of 22,800 pounds, the spreader would have to withstand 17,100 pounds of compression. Diagram D shows this graphically.*

line. But neither will tell us the compression load on the object the sling will lift—remember, the ends are being pulled toward each other. This wasn't an issue with the lifeline; the compression load wasn't going to buckle the deck of the boat. But the sling might be picking up a pallet or crate that could be crushed by excessive compression. There's a related diagram (Figure 5-10D) to show the load on each leg and the resulting compression. The wider the angle of the sling legs, the higher the tension and the compression.

Again, we can get to the same place with a formula: Compression = Load × One-half the horizontal span of the load ÷ Vertical length of the sling. Marvelous.

So far we've let the load dictate things. But let's now say that you have an existing two-legged sling of $\frac{1}{2}$-inch (13 mm) 7 x 19 wire, rated strength 22,800 pounds (10,364 kg). You want to put a spreader bar between the legs of the sling (Figure 5-10C). What is the maximum load that can come on this spreader bar before the wire breaks? If you know the answer, you'll know how strong to make the spreader bar. You could take the long way around, first determining what kind of load would put a 22,800-pound (10,364-kg) strain on each leg of the sling, then calculating the compression load. But it's quicker just to juggle the formula again: Total Compression = Tension × Width ÷ Length of one leg. In this example, that's 22,800 pounds × 6 feet ÷ 8 feet = 17,100 pounds (10,364 kg × 1.83 m ÷ 2.44 m = 7,773 kg) that bar has to take, half that amount pushing on it from each side.

And once again, for the graphically minded, a little picture tells the same story.

Use this "prescriptive" method whenever you have some of a system's loads worked out and want to fit other components in.

Edging back toward boat rigging, you might have noticed that widening sling angles produce higher loads, just the opposite of what happens with standing rigging. This is because a sailboat rig

Boom Vang

A boom vang, like a sling, imposes a compression load on the object it's attached to, the load varying with angle.

Older-style boom vangs run from the boom down to deck instead of from boom to base of mast. They impose little or no compression load on the boom, but they must be cast off and reset with each gybe or tack. Worse, they can result in a folded boom, if the boom dips into a wave. This form often doubles as a boom preventer, but it's not so good for that, either; being so far forward, leverage is minimal, so preventing the boom requires a lot of effort. And because the lead is vertical when the boom is right off, the boom can travel aft a bit, even when the preventer/vang is tight. This makes it easier for the wind to catch the sail aback.

The modern vang swings with the boom, but as with so many modern conveniences, it brings with it complications. To start with, it ideally should attach to the boom so that the horizontal distance is about twice the vertical distance from the vang gooseneck to the boom. The resulting angle will give you about 90 percent of the available control for a given height boom (100 percent is achieved at the end of the boom, but that would not exactly be practical).

A high cabintop, low gooseneck, or extra-long boom can conspire to produce a narrow vanging angle, minimizing leverage and maximizing compression. You'll be very lucky to get a 45-degree angle and will probably have to settle for more like 30 degrees. If you can't get even that much, you might be better off either raising the gooseneck or learning to live with a boom-to-deck vang.

No matter what angle you get or what kind of vang you use, bear in mind that vangs are hard on booms, deflecting the midsection by downward pull as well as compression. Therefore, vanged booms need to be appreciably stiffer than vangless ones, particularly when the angle is tight. Before installing a vang, get boom dimensions (depth, width at several points, length, wall thickness, sheet attachment point, and projected vang angle), sail area, and vessel size and displacement figures. Take them to a sparmaker to see if your boom will be up to the loads you want to add to it.

Slings on a Hook

Extremely wide-angle sling legs are bad practice: the load is excessive (see sling formulas), and there is a likelihood that one of the sling legs will jump off the hook. Mousings, whether string or mechanical, are not designed to stop fleeing slings.

is like a sling-and-load turned on its side. I know that's not how Herreshoff might have put it, but forces don't care what they're doing. Explore unfamiliar forces, and you'll get a clearer understanding of familiar ones.

SPREADER LOADS

On a sailboat, the width of the hull limits the shroud angle at the base. Put a tall rig in a narrow boat, and it becomes impossible to get that crucial 12-degree angle, unless we add spreaders. Spreaders widen the angle of the shrouds to the mast, interjecting themselves as compression struts in the process. As Figure 5-11 shows, the longer the spreader, the lower the load on mast and rigging. Long spreaders would seem to be desirable. But there are, as usual, complications.

As the load on the mast and rigging goes down, the load on the spreader goes up. So you have to

make the spreader stronger, and thus fatter and heavier, to compensate.

A longer spreader is more inclined to buckle than a shorter one under the same load. That's because the stiffness of any compression member is relative to its "unsupported length"—the length of the section not braced by shrouds, brackets, or other deflection-preventing devices.

To demonstrate the relationship between unsupported length and stiffness, get out a piece of uncooked spaghetti and brace it between your fingertips. (Figure 5-12). It is very easy to deflect and then break the spaghetti by moving your hands together. Now take one of the resulting shorter pieces and repeat the procedure. This time it takes more force to deflect and break the spaghetti. Finally, have a friend hold the middle of a short piece between thumb and forefinger. This shortens the unsupported length, not the overall length. Push on the ends. Now you're in danger of poking a hole in your hands before the noodle will break.

A mast, by comparison, is usually a moderately stiff item with a long overall length, but it is broken into two or more rela-

Figure 5-11. *The longer the spreader, the lower the load on mast and rigging.*

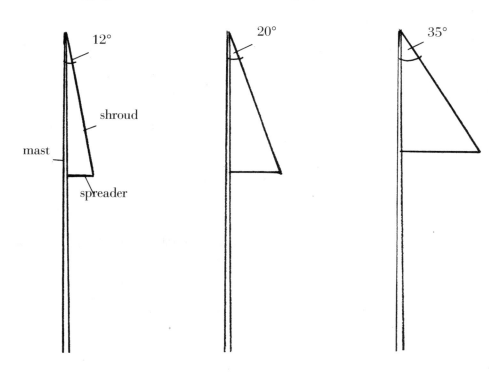

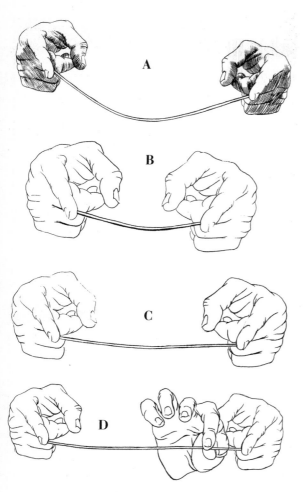

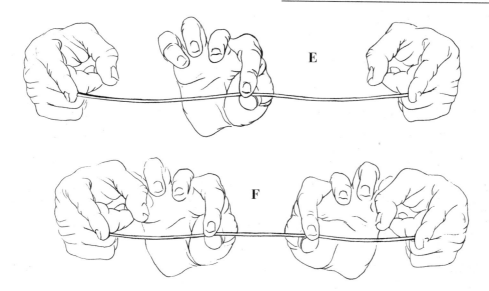

Figure 5-12A–D. It's much easier to buckle A than B because the stiffness of a column under compression varies with the square of the unsupported length. B is about one-half as long as A and thus about four times stiffer. The unsupported lengths of C and D are the same, but D is stiffer because the third hand pinching near one end acts like mast partners, stiffening the section above it and causing it to bend less easily, and higher up.

Figure 5-12E–F. Here the pinching fingers simulate the effect of single and double spreaders. The unsupported lengths are shorter, so a noodle—or mast—of the same overall length is stiffer than it would be with no spreaders.

Spreader Length

A quick way to determine good spreader length for a cruising sailboat is to measure the vertical height—the distance from the base of a spreader to the upper attachment point of its wire—and divide by five. This will give the wire an angle to the mast of approximately 12 degrees. It will actually be just a little less, but it will get you in the neighborhood.

For example, on a 36-foot mast with spreaders attached 19 feet up, the distance from the spreader to the upper shroud throughbolt might be 16 feet. One-fifth of that distance is about 38⅜", and that's the minimum spreader length you should have.

You can also figure spreader length using the trig functions on a calculator. Most often this involves the tangent function, with the mast portion being the adjacent side, and the spreader being the opposite side. The tangent of 12 degrees is about .2125. In the above example we'd multiply 16 feet × .2125 = 40¾". That's a couple of inches less than our quick method gave us. The difference in angle is about .7 degrees, minimally significant in terms of loading. But for the pickily inclined, adding a couple of inches to the quick method result is a good practice.

As a further rule, spreader lengths for a single-spreader rig should be a minimum of 40 percent and a maximum of 50 percent of the vessel's beam at the chainplates (see USSA sidebar, page 148). On a double spreader, they can be 32.5 percent—or .8 times the half-beam for lowers, and .65 for uppers.

A Crane

A simple crane, as shown in the illustration, has compression loads on boom, mast, and the ground or deck beneath the mast. There are also loads on the halyard, topping lift, and guys. And unlike the fixed forces on a sailing vessel's standing rigging, all these loads change as the boom is raised, lowered, and swung side to side. So crane design must take into account a range of possible configurations. It might sound intricate, and the stress diagram does have more pieces to it than for a mast, but the relationships are the same.

No matter what the level of complexity, rigging tends to be invisible to most people's eyes. If they notice it at all, it is to comment on "all those lines," and they seldom see beyond to the relationships that make it work. The next time you play with rope or wire, pay appropriate attention to materials, intended use, and durability. But first and foremost, look to those essential angles.

The compression loads on a crane's mast and boom vary as the boom is raised or lowered.

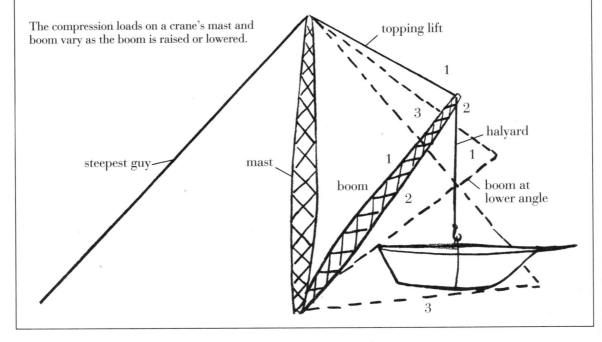

tively short unsupported lengths by shrouds, stays, spreaders, and partners. It can be lighter than if it had a huge unsupported length. And this is good, since a lighter mast can translate into a more efficient sailboat. Spreaders, on the other hand, have a short overall length but no intermediate supports. Overall length, in their case, is the same as unsupported length. Spreaders therefore can only be made to resist deflection by being made stiffer and heavier. And the longer they get, the stiffer they have to be for the same load. So there is a balance between shroud angle and spreader stiffness which tends to limit spreader length (the alternative being massive scantlings of objectionable weight and windage).

In any event, the maximum practical length for spreaders is about half the vessel's beam at the mast. Otherwise you risk snagging docks or other people's spreaders in close quarters. And very few boats have even half-beam spreaders, because spreader length limits how closely you can trim your headsails. Which is why all racers and not a few cruisers sport dinky little spreaders, increased mast and rig loads be damned.

Bear in mind that by putting a few spreaders on a mast, and running a few wires over them, you create a structure much more complex than any sling. The spreaders thrust laterally, and must be checked by still more wires, which in turn load up other spreaders, which . . . well, you can see why rig design is so varied, with each designer trying to juggle the variables to match the demands imposed by a given boat and a given client.

With very tall rigs, the game of long-or-short spreaders becomes even more complex. A big height-to-beam ratio means that even a very long set of spreaders won't produce an acceptable staying angle. And the great unsupported lengths above and below these spreaders would necessitate an extremely heavy mast section to resist deflection. That's why designers go with multiple sets of spreaders. The topmost set gives the upper shrouds a good lead to the masthead, and because they're up high, they can do this and still be stubby enough not to poke a hole in the jib. Lower sets of spreaders are way stations for the upper shrouds on their way to the top, as well as angle-providers for intermediate shrouds. Because all these spreaders break the mast into shorter unsupported lengths, the mast section can be significantly smaller or thinner-walled.

Multiple spreaders are no placebo. On moderate-height rigs, they're just so much extra clutter and expense. And the virtues of multiple spreaders are regularly abused by race-crazy sailors. They want

Figure 5-13. *A double-spreader rig. To calculate the maximum load that would bear on the upper spreader, solve graphically as in Figure 5-10, or use the formula, Total Compression = Tension × Width ÷ Length of one leg. Substituting, we get 6,300 × 4.5 ÷ 8 = 3,544 pounds of compression load, or 1,772 pounds on each spreader.*

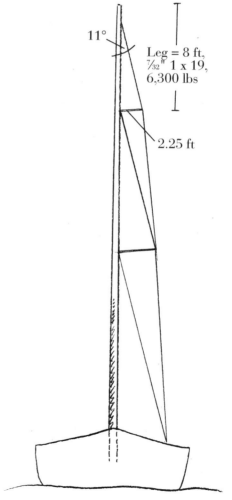

really, really short spreaders for that proverbial close sheeting angle, but they can end up with mast compression and rig tension loads even higher than what they'd get with a single set of moderate-length spreaders.

As an exercise, let's find the load on the upper spreaders in Figure 5-13. They're 2 feet 3 inches (0.69 m) long, and the upper shroud is 7/32-inch (6 mm) 1 x 19 stainless with a rated strength of 6,300 pounds (2,864 kg). The angle of shroud to mast is 11 degrees.

To solve, use the prescriptive diagram detailed under "Slings and Compression," earlier in the chapter. This matches spreader and wire strength, with the assumption that wire strength has been calculated previously to match the loads the hull and sails will impose (see below).

As you can see, once you start playing with angles, you start playing with a lot of other things, too. And all must interrelate, or none will. Where, then, do you start? What factors do you consider first? In sailing vessels rig forces relate directly to the stability characteristics of the hull, but as we'll see in a subsequent chapter, hull characteristics can be largely determined by the design of the rig. Design is a matter of gestalt, arrived at by attentiveness to the interplay of forces. So the double-spreader rig in Figure 5-13 isn't just something to stick on a hull to make it look "modern" (although that has, sadly, happened more than once). Rather, it's a reflection of system awareness.

The 29-foot 6-inch Lyle Hess cutter Syrinx.

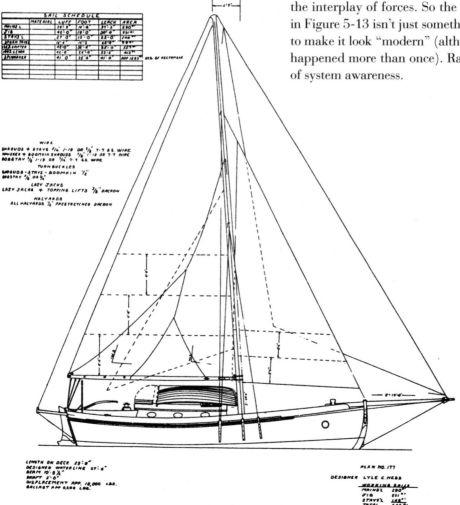

A Lyle Hess Cutter

No designer I know is better at this rig gestalt process than Lyle Hess. Analyzing his rigs is like analyzing a well-written piece of prose: You try to express things differently and discover that the author has already found the best way.

Let's go through a Hess design and see how the principles discussed above can find expression in an actual rig.

When he designed the 30-foot cutter *Syrinx*, Lyle Hess drew in a mast extending 38-plus feet above deck, but the half-beam was only about 5 feet (Figure 5-14). Given those dimensions, a wire

to the top of the mast would describe an angle of less than 7.5 degrees, which is too narrow. Given that he wanted neither to widen the boat nor shorten the mast, the only way to obtain an adequate staying angle was to install a spreader, in this case 20 feet above deck (Figure 5-15). This spreader is 4½ feet long, and the length of the mast above it is about 19 feet. With the aid of a diagram, or of that traditional rigger's tool, the electronic calculator, we can determine that the angle at the top of the mast is now a healthy 13.3 degrees (see Chapter 6 for the how-to of trigonometric functions).

If we now construct a stress diagram that includes the spreader, which functions as a compression member (Figure 5-16), we see that the wire's condition has been eased at the expense of the mast, which now must withstand not only a downward force from the wire without buckling, but also a sideways thrust from the spreader. The solution to

Figure 5-14.

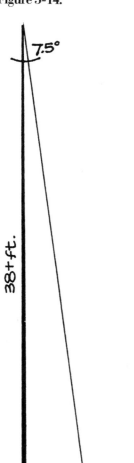

Figure 5-15.

Figure 5-16.

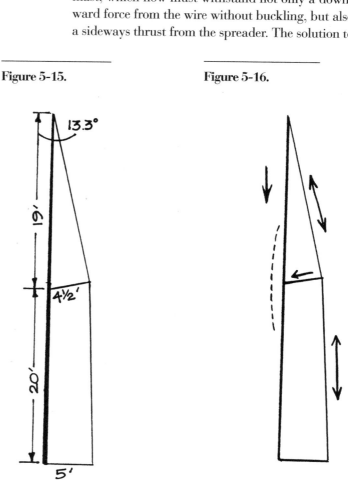

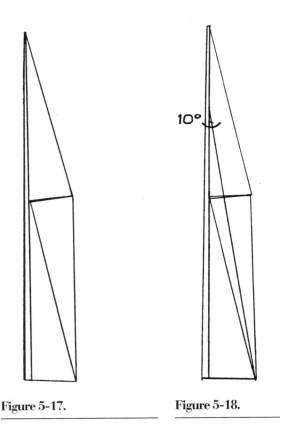

Figure 5-17.   **Figure 5-18.**

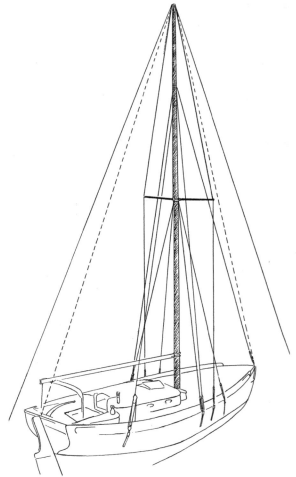

Figure 5-19. *A perfectly balanced rig for* Syrinx— *except that the backstay and jibstay are hanging in midair. Bringing them inboard (dotted lines) would too greatly reduce sail area.*

this problem is the addition of another wire, running from the base of the spreader to the rail, where the first wire is also attached. The new, more equitable diagram that results is Figure 5-17.

Next, since there remains a long length of unsupported mast above the spreaders, we'll add a third, intermediate wire to take the strain there (Figure 5-18). The staying angle without a spreader is only 10 degrees, about as narrow as we can safely go. Have to do something to improve this before we're done.

Meanwhile, things are sufficiently evolved to see that the mast and all the wires have become interdependent, creating a system for delivering strain to the hull: The upper shroud takes a portion of the sail's lateral load at the masthead and delivers some of it to its base, but also "drops" some of it off at the spreader. The lower shroud picks up the spreader's lateral compression load, some of the mast's compression load that was imposed by the uppers,

and the lateral load imposed by the sail, as well as imposing a compression load of its own. At the deck, the mast partners provide one last lateral support before the mast compression load is finally delivered to the keel. Every time you add a wire, you must balance it against all the other wires and the mast so that no one part of the system receives a disproportionate amount of strain.

So far we've assumed that the sail's load will only be imposed laterally, as in the original staying diagram. If this were the case, we could now proceed to calculate actual pounds of strain for a given vessel, choose appropriate materials, and begin construction. But sailing imposes strains from all directions, so the rig must be elaborated to suit.

Starting again at the top, the lateral guying of the upper shroud is complemented by the fore-and-aft guying of the jibstay and backstay. The intermediate shroud can be made to guy both laterally and aft by moving its point of attachment to the hull aft. Happily, this also results in its staying angle increasing from 10 to 10.5 degrees. The forestay leads from the same point on the mast as the intermediate, and since its forward pull is more than the intermediate can handle under some condi-

Aft-led vs. Lateral Intermediates

Intermediate shrouds that are led over the lower spreaders are maximally effective for lateral staying, to oppose lateral pull from the forestay, but they provide no aft staying to oppose the forestay's forward pull. To deal with this problem, designers generally adopt one or more of the following fixes:

1 *Stiffen the Mast.* With a small enough sail on it, the forestay won't generate enough force to deflect a sufficiently stiff mast too much. But since this means a lot of extra mast weight and an ineffective sail, a more careful designer might choose to enlarge the sail, lighten the mast, and add:

2 *Jumper Stays.* These stays project diagonally forward at the height of the forestay (see *Troubador* in the design section). With sufficient mast section, and perhaps a little shaving of staysail size, they suffice to keep the mast in place.

3 *Running Backstays.* These stays make up well aft, so they can oppose the pull of the forestay much more efficiently than jumpers can. They can entirely replace jumpers, as well as allowing for more sail and lighter mast. There is a runner on each side; the weather one takes the load, while the leeward one must be released and taken forward, so it doesn't interfere with the travel of the main.

Racers sometimes take running-back virtues to such extremes that the mast can come down if an inattentive crew "blows a tack," not getting a runner set up in time. More moderate rigs will play mast stiffness off against sail size to get a safe stick. Good designers can dial-in these factors so that cruisers can count on leaving their running backs unused 70 to 80 percent of the time.

The same effect can be achieved by combining runners and jumper stays, once again allowing a lighter and a larger forestaysail than would otherwise be possible.

The drawback to jumpers is that they are expensive to fabricate and install. The trouble with runners is that they require some effort on the part of the crew. While a little careful planning can make runners easier to use (see below), some designers opt for another tactic that is simpler and cheaper than jumpers, and no work at all:

4 *Aft-led Intermediates.* By taking the intermediates off the spreaders and anchoring them a little aft of the mast, you can get them to function for both aft and lateral staying. The drawback to aft-led intermediates is that they don't do either of their jobs very well. They don't lead far enough outboard to provide optimum lateral staying, and they don't lead far enough aft to provide more than trivial aft staying, because with even a minimal aft lead they interfere with boom travel and add to mainsail chafe.

What is worse, their staying angle is so shallow that they add significant extra compression loads to the mast. So, once again, the mast must be heavier and the staysail smaller.

I believe that aft intermediates are attractive partly because people don't realize how ineffective they are, and largely because running backstays can be so very hard to use. As typically configured, tension is supplied by a block-and-tackle, usually 4:1. This configuration must be slacked away and taken up on every tack, a process which involves copious amounts of rope, and has blocks swinging around at head height. And for all this fussing, you get an anemic amount of purchase, not nearly enough to tension the forestay when it matters (i.e., clearing a lee shore in a blow). That is why, in our shop, we run a single-part runner through a single deck block, with a lead to the weather winch. Now you have 40:1 or the like, instead of 4:1, plus runners that set up quickly and slack instantly. No blocks to hit you, no heavy rigging flailing around and chafing the mainsail. The rope is Spectra until just above the block, where a fat piece of Dacron is spliced to it.

The load on the deck block is higher by about 40 percent than with the older arrangement, owing to the angle departing the block, but this can be dealt with when selecting the block and the anchoring hardware.

Figure 5-20. *A bowsprit and boomkin extend outward to pick up the jibstay and backstay. A bobstay and bowsprit shrouds forward and boomkin shrouds aft serve as guys. The bobstay's narrow staying angle can be improved by attaching it lower on the hull or by adding a spreader-like "dolphin striker." Alternatively, we can leave the angle narrow and use larger wire to compensate.*

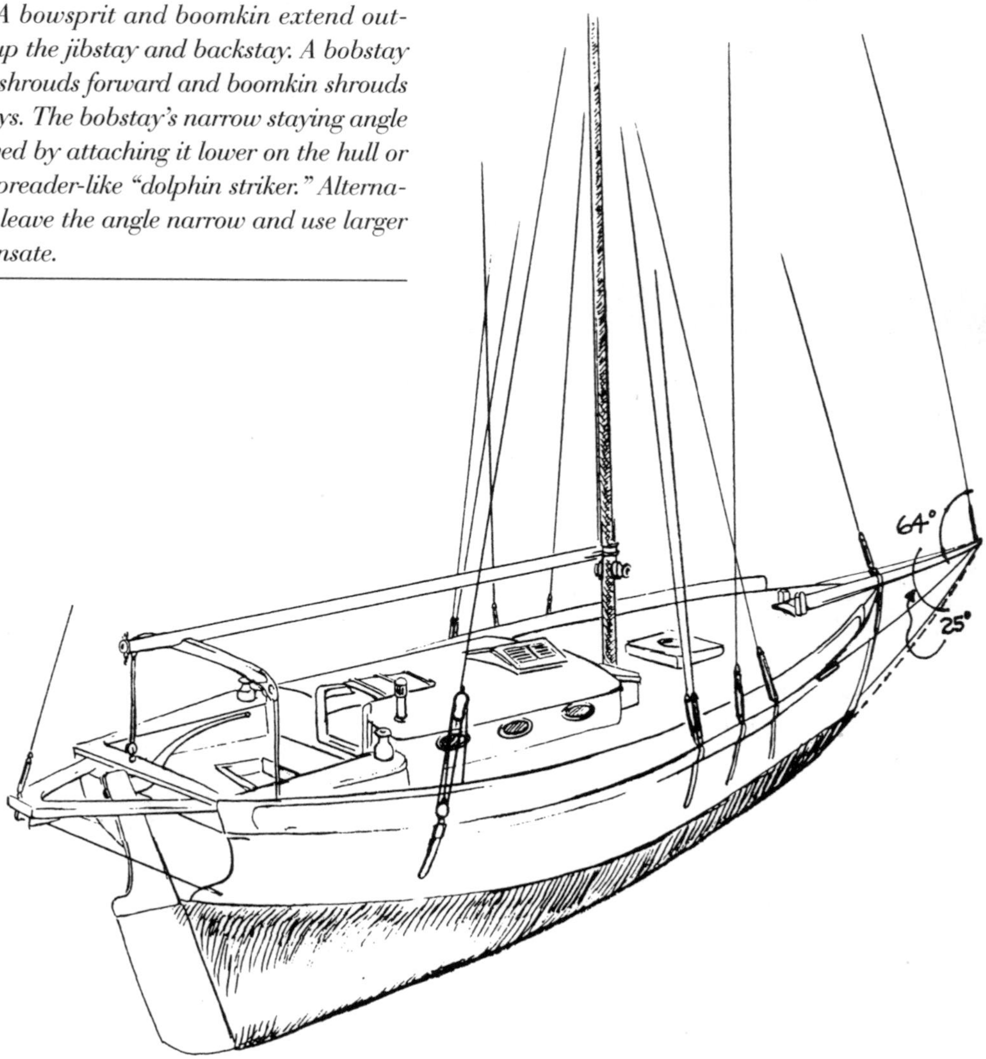

64°

25°

tions, additional aft guying is provided by a running backstay. One could accomplish the same result by angling the intermediate farther aft, but this would interfere with the travel of the boom off the wind. Another configuration would have the intermediate led over the lower spreader. For an analysis of this option, see the accompanying sidebar.

Splitting the lower shroud into two pieces and leading one forward and one aft (Figure 5-18) nicely contains the motion of the middle of the mast, providing both a generous lateral angle and enough fore-and-aft angle (6 degrees is the accepted mini-

mum) to control mast movement fore-and-aft (see the "Tuning" section in Chapter 7).

As you can see from Figure 5-19, we now have a well-formed rig, except for the jibstay and backstay, which are hanging in midair. The boat is too short. We could bring these two stays in (dotted lines) so that they would fit on the hull's 30-foot length, but only at the sacrifice of considerable sail area, and with the addition of mast compression. The alternative is to extend the length forward with a bowsprit and aft with a boomkin (Figure 5-20). These pieces, like the mast and spreaders, are under compression from their standing rigging, but their location near the waterline presents special problems.

First, the bowsprit. The jibstay at its end, with a staying angle of 64 degrees relative to the bowsprit, has an advantage in leverage over the bobstay, which has an angle of only 25 degrees relative to the bowsprit. It's like pitting a long crowbar against a short one. As the dotted line shows, we could increase the bobstay's angle by attaching its lower end at a point just tangent with the hull, but this would make the stay much more vulnerable to corrosion and to damage from striking objects in the water, as well as contributing to drag. Better to keep its lower end above the surface and deal with the leverage inequality with a larger wire and stronger end fittings.

Figure 5-21 shows a diagram for determining just how much more strain the bobstay must endure than the jibstay. By scaling off distances, we find a leverage advantage of 2.8 to 1, so the bobstay needs to be 2.8 times stronger than the jibstay. The bobstay is the most corrosion- and collision-prone wire on a vessel, and much of the rig depends on its integrity.

Lateral staying for the bowsprit is effected by bowsprit shrouds. No asymmetry here, but once again staying angle is at a premium, so we position the chainplates to make the bowsprit shrouds just about tangent to the hull. This has the added benefit of providing a "fender effect;" a glancing blow to a dock, another boat, etc., will be absorbed by the wires, rather than bashing the hull.

At the other end of the boat, the boomkin extends outward to pick up the backstay. The presence of the rudder precludes a staying arrangement like the bowsprit's, so the two boomkin shrouds

Figure 5-21. *Jibstay strain relative to bobstay strain. Measure up the jibstay 1 inch, then draw a line parallel to the bobstay to intersect the bowsprit, and one parallel to the jibstay to intersect the bobstay. The resulting bobstay segment is 2.8 times as long as the jibstay segment, thus the bobstay must be 2.8 times as strong as the jibstay. A dolphin striker will reduce this disparity.*

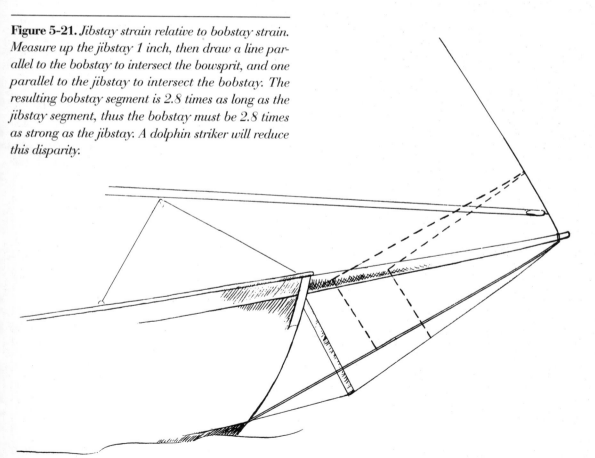

extend diagonally out and down to provide guying in both vertical and lateral planes. Because the stem is relatively beamy, a healthy staying angle isn't hard to come by.

Remember, this is just one possible rig layout for one boat. It is an attempt to make the best use of basic mechanical principles for that particular boat, and might be completely inappropriate. Most multihulls, for instance, have "three-point rigs," with only the jibstay and upper shrouds coming to deck, the latter without benefit of spreaders. Very long unsupported mast lengths result, and this vulnerability is dealt with using jumper struts and stays

SHROUD LOADS

The exact layout of any rig is part mechanical necessity, part intended vessel use, and part designer preference. But no matter what form the design takes, the time comes to translate it into reality, and that means figuring out how much strain comes where. The trouble is, nobody knows with precision. By observing and keeping track of enough successes and failures, designers have developed an empirical data base, and translated that into workable formulas. By conducting strain-gauge and inclining tests while sailing particular boats under a variety of conditions, we can check our general data, more closely determine what happens on those particular boats, and modify the formulas accordingly. But different weather and sea conditions, the habits and skills

---

The Pardey Tie-Rod

Rigging extends past the tangs and chainplates; the entire hull is a member of the rigging system, absorbing the power of the sails and transforming that power into vessel motion. The weather side of the hull is in tension right down to the keel from the upward pull of the shrouds. The shrouds also pull in, because they connect to the hull at an angle. This means that the deck is a set of spreaders. With a keel-stepped mast, even if the vessel's deck is heavily reinforced, it can slowly buckle upward from the pressure of the shrouds. That's why a vertical tie-rod in front of or behind the mast, to hold the deck down in the middle, is a good idea.

Veteran cruisers Lin and Larry Pardey planned to install such a rod on their 30-foot cutter *Taleisin*, but found that it was going to be in the way whether they put it ahead of or behind the mast. Their solution was a mini-rod attached to a tang on the mast face and running diagonally up to a deck beam. The rod is tensioned, like a turnbuckle, by a barrel in its middle (see "Turnbuckles [The Inclined Plane]" in Chapter 2). It's completely out of traffic, provides a convenient handhold or towel hanger, and is easily detached if the mast needs to come out. You'll see variations on this theme on many vessels. Sometimes there is a rod on either side of the mast, sometimes one in front. In every case, the pull is upward on the mast, rather than upward on the keel.

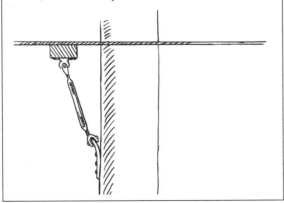

Lucy Belle's Bobstay

For vessels with twin bobstays, the usual procedure is to install a separate fitting for each on the stem. Instead, consider the configuration used on the Friendship sloop *Lucy Belle*: a single piece of wire is seized around a thimble, the two legs measured to suit. Advantages: One fitting instead of two; two splices and a seizing instead of four splices; and a more easily sealed and maintained lower eye, particularly when the bobstay is galvanized wire.

Of course, the seizing must be of excellent quality, since it must hold if either leg fails.

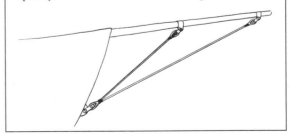

of those on the helm, the quality of rig tune, hull design variations, and many other considerations mean that our figures can only be approximate. So we come as close as possible and try always to err on the safe side.

The process of determining the load that will come on our rig begins by examining the hull.

The wind is always trying to knock the hull over, the hull is always fighting to remain upright, and the rig is caught in the middle. Accordingly, the strength of the rig must be scaled to stand up to the amount of knockover-resisting force the hull generates. Think of the rig as a big lever stuck into the hull; you don't want that lever to break.

The hull also acts as a lever, and it gets its power from ballast and buoyancy. The more ballast it has, and the lower it is mounted, the more the ballast will help lever the boat upright. Likewise, the fuller and more buoyant the hull, the greater amount of leverage buoyancy will exert. Stated in designerese, we are trying to maximize the distance, for a given amount of heel, between the hull's center of gravity and its center of buoyancy. The two forces combine to give a vessel its stability.

Leverage is a matter of force applied over distance—the farther from the fulcrum one exerts a force, the greater the effect it has. So we'll measure our forces in "foot-pounds," to translate our particular forces and distances into measurable effects. The name for the amount of foot-pounds a lever can exert is a "moment." The moment that a hull exerts in trying to stay upright is a "transverse righting moment" (abbreviated RM). This righting moment varies with each degree of heel, depending upon the shape of the hull, the distribution and amount of ballast, the weight of construction materials, etc. You can plot these shifting moments on a stability curve (Figures 5-22 and 5-23). This curve is as distinctive as a fingerprint, and can tell you a lot about the performance and safety of a hull. It's also the fundamental mast and rig design tool, since it tells you the loads the mast and rigging will face.

For some sample fingerprints, see Figure 5-23.

In most monohulls, righting moment (RM) starts at 0 with the hull upright, then climbs in a

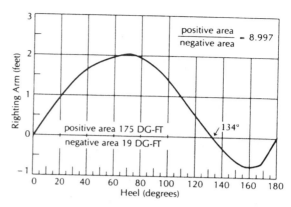

Figure 5-22. *Static stability curve for an Ohlson 38A as calculated under the International Measurement System. The righting arm is simply the righting moment of the boat divided by its displacement. Above the baseline the curve shows positive stability; below the line, negative stability. The larger the negative stability, the more disinclined is the boat to right herself from an inverted position after capsize. The degree of heel at which the curve crosses the baseline from positive to negative righting moment is the angle of heel at which the boat will capsize—134 degrees in this case. The ratio of the positive area of the curve to its negative area—here 8.997—is a measure of seaworthiness. Most boats measured by the IMS will capsize at about 120 degrees and have a ratio of around 4—minimal numbers for medium-size offshore sailing yachts; smaller seagoing boats need higher numbers. (From* Sea Sense, *3rd Edition, by Richard Henderson. International Marine, 1991)*

nearly straight line to at least 30 degrees, sometimes up to 40 degrees. After that, RM increases more slowly, to its maximum (usually at around 60 degrees of heel), and then begins to decrease. Since maximum RM indicates the maximum sustained load the rig will have to bear, designers need to use this figure as the basis for mast scantlings. Nowadays computer programs can spit this number out directly—along with the numbers for load at every angle of heel. But riggers can also find the RM for 30 or 40 degrees, then multiply by a factor to take maximum RM into account. Why do this? For one thing, it's very easy to find RM at a small angle of

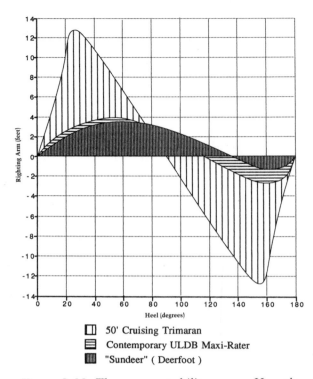

Figure 5-23. *Three more stability curves. Here the righting-arm scale has had to be expanded to accommodate the much higher stabilities, both positive and negative, of a multihull. Note* Sundeer's *exceptionally high capsize angle (135 degrees) and ratio of positive to negative stability; even if it does capsize, it'll right itself immediately. The exceptionally high initial stability of a multihull dictates sturdy rig scantlings. (Courtesy Jeff Van Peski)*

Legend:
- 50' Cruising Trimaran
- Contemporary ULDB Maxi-Rater
- "Sundeer" (Deerfoot)

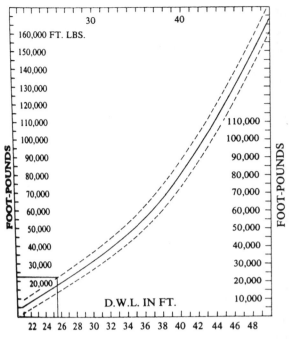

Figure 5-24. *A graph of righting moments at 30 degrees. Note that a small increase in vessel length results in a large increase in righting moment. (From* Skene's Elements of Yacht Design, *Dodd, Mead and Co.)*

heel, then extrapolate along that nearly straight line to find RM_{30} or RM_{40}, then work in the extra factor. You can do this with your own boat at dockside, as a way to get your boat's actual RM_{30}, instead of relying on a generic formula (see sidebar, "Inclining").

For another thing, almost all of a vessel's sailing is done within 30 degrees of heel; you can use that as a benchmark, then safety factor (see below) generously or stingily, depending on how safe and solid for cruising—or skinny and scary for racing—you want your rig to be.

The steepness or flatness of any part of a given vessel's curve will vary depending on hull shape and ballast. But the total load for most monohulls of a given waterline length varies so little that you can get a fairly accurate RM_{30} figure from the graph in Figure 5-24. If you are working on a multihull, brig, or other atypical vessel, consult a designer. Note the dotted lines on either side of the solid line in the chart. These indicate likely limits to extra-solid or extra-flimsy boat RMs. Note also that the RM_{30} for a 32-foot-waterline boat is about 37,000 foot-pounds, while that of a 40-footer is about 80,000 foot-pounds; a little length adds a lot to the moment.

The trick, once you have your RM_{30}, is to convert moment into actual pounds of tension on the standing rigging. Remember, foot-pounds is a convenient way of describing force over distance, whereas when we go to buy the wire, we need to know the load in plain old pounds. To make this

Most rig scantling formulas are based on the vessel's righting moment at 30 degrees (see text). If that information is not available from the vessel's designer, the most convenient way to get that figure is from the chart shown in Figure 5-24.

But that chart is only an approximation for many vessels; if you want a more precise basis for your calculations, you can get it by inclining the vessel yourself. All you need is some form of inclinometer, a bathroom scale, an extra-large pizza or two, and as many of your largest friends as will fit on your side deck. Here's the procedure:

Before everyone shows up, use the inclinometer to see if the boat is relatively plumb athwartships. You can rest it on a hatch top, cabin sole, or other ostensibly level surface that is on the centerline of the vessel. My favorite inclinometer is the Clinometer iPhone app, but you can also go old-school, using a plumb bob, square, and some rudimentary trigonometry skills (see the sidebar to this sidebar).

If the vessel is leaning one way or the other, move things around until it isn't. Once you are set, take the bathroom scale out to the dock, and invite your friends aboard. Weigh each of them as they come aboard, jotting down the figures. Total the result, and set it aside for the moment.

Let's say you have 10 friends, and a 35-foot vessel. Get them to line up, in as straight a line as practicable, along one side deck. Measure the distance from the center of the vessel to their location. Let's say it is 4.5 feet. Note that. Now go to your inclinometer, and see what it says. Make a note of it. Have everyone repeat the heel on the other side of the vessel. If the measurements are a bit different, average them out. Serve the pizza. While everyone is eating, run the numbers.

First, take the total friend poundage and multiply it by the distance they were from the centerline. Let's say that is an even ton (10 friends with an average weight of 200lbs each). This times 4.5 = 9,000 foot-pounds.

Next take a look at how much they heeled the boat. Let's say it is 11 degrees. In other words, 9,000 foot-pounds is needed to heel your vessel 11 degrees.

Since resistance to heeling increases in a straight line at least through 30 degrees of heel, we can calculate how much force will be required to heel the boat to 30 degrees: 30/11 = 2.7273, and this times 9,000 = 24,545.7 foot-pounds. Take your result to 'A Formula,' below, to begin the process of dimensioning the standing rigging. Most often the result will be the same as that derived from the chart in Figure 5-24, but it's always good to verify by other means. If the two methods disagree, recheck everything. If they still disagree, the direct test is likely to be the correct one, though consulting with a naval architect would be a good idea.

---

translation, we divide by the length of the lever arm of the hull, which is to say one-half the vessel's beam at the chainplates. My assistant, Erin Sage, says this is like putting foot-pounds into a colander and straining out the feet.

A Formula

To put what we have so far into numbers, the transverse load on the rigging = RM_{30} (righting moment at 30 degrees of heel) × 1.5, where 1.5 is our extra factor, getting us to maximum righting moment. If our RM_{30} was 50,000 foot-pounds (6,925 meter-kilograms), then RM_{30} × 1.5 would result in 75,000 foot-pounds (10,388 meter-kilograms). Now to strain out the feet. If our sample boat has a one-half beam of 5 feet 6 inches (1.67 m), the formula would read:

$$\text{shroud load} = \frac{RM_{30} \times 1.5}{\frac{1}{2} \text{ beam}}$$

and in our case that's:

$$\frac{50,000 \text{ pounds} \times 1.5}{5.5 \text{ feet}} \quad \overset{\text{or}}{\left(\frac{6,925 \text{ kg} \times 1.5}{1.67 \text{ meters}}\right)}$$

which equals 13,636 pounds (6,220 kg).

At last! We now know how many actual pounds of force will be pulling on the weather shrouds when the boat is heeled to its maximum righting-moment angle.

Selecting Wire—or Rope

But you don't just go out and get a piece of wire with a 13,636-pound (6,220-kg) breaking strength; unless the boat is very small or the mast very short you'll

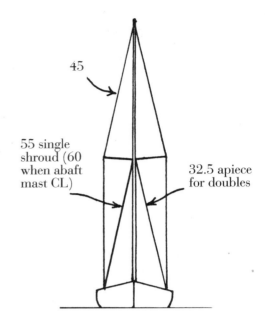

want at least two wires, attached at different heights, to spread the load on the mast. And it is prudent to make these wires stronger than they absolutely have to be—two or three times stronger—as a safety factor.

The safety factor is where our careful calculations meet the real world. It's how we take into account the shock loads that could exceed the calculated maximum RM, how we compensate for the eventual degradation of the wire, or loss of efficiency of terminals, and how we deal with that nagging voice that wonders if we really, really did those calculations right. It also assures us that the wire is strong enough that the load on the wire never exceeds the Elastic Limit (see sidebar).

In theory, you can share the load among any number of wires. In practice, you'd probably choose among a few tried-and-true configurations, depending on the hull, the type of sailing intended, and your own pet theories. Figure 5-25 shows two of

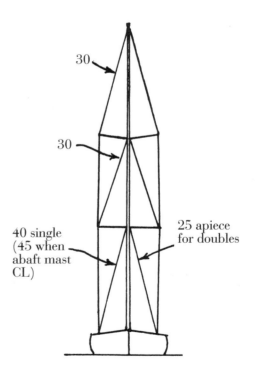

Figure 5-25. *Percentages of the maximum shroud load allotted to each shroud in a single-spreader and a double-spreader rig. (From* Sea Sense, *3rd Edition, by Richard Henderson. International Marine, 1991)*

these configurations, with the percentage of the load each wire will bear. Note that the numbers can add up to more than 100 percent; different combinations of sail and sea condition will put varying loads on each wire.

For our example boat, a cutter with a length on the waterline of 35 feet, we'll use the second configuration shown, a double-spreader rig with a pair of lower shrouds on each side. The lowers share 50 percent of the load, and the uppers and intermediates take 30 percent each. Because the lowers share that 50 percent, many designers make them smaller than the other shrouds, assuming they'll take only about 25 percent each. But because the mast can shift fore and aft significantly under sail, each lower may take a great deal more than it's supposed share at times. It might be prudent to make the lowers as heavy as the uppers.

The jibstay is usually made at least as heavy as the heaviest shroud, to take the big loads from the genoa. When in doubt, make this wire heavier; it will fatigue more slowly and stretch less than a lighter wire.

The backstay can almost always be the next size lighter than the jibstay, since it almost always has a leverage advantage from a wider angle on the mast. In addition, the uppers always pick up a significant portion of the jibstay's load, leaving less load on the backstay.

For our sample, the minimum wire sizes run thus:

	% load	safety factor	1 x 19 load (lbs)	wire diam.
Lowers	25	2.5	3,400	¼"
Intermediates	30	2.5	4,090	⁹⁄₃₂"
Uppers	30	2.5	4,090	⁹⁄₃₂"
Jibstay	30	2.5	4,090	⁹⁄₃₂"
Backstay	25	2.5	3,400	¼"
Forestay	25	2.5	3,400	¼"

Again, it might be better to use stronger wire than noted here for the lowers. Note also that the last-entered wire, the forestay, is a little lighter than the jibstay. Although it will be the sail you'll reef down to, its ultimate loads will be less than that exerted by the most load-inducing sail that the jibstay must endure: a closely trimmed #2 genoa.

Bear in mind that none of these figures is cast in bronze. An extraordinarily tall rig, for example, would have a very steep angle on its jibstay, which means higher loads and the necessity for bigger wire. Also, cruisers often make all their shrouds and stays out of the same size wire so that they only have to carry one size of spare wire, turnbuckle, clevis, etc. An exception is sometimes made for running back-

Elastic Limit

Everything stretches when pulled, and everything recovers its original length when the pull is released—within a limit, the Elastic Limit.

With most steels and steel alloys, the limit is 55 to 65 percent of the metal's ultimate tensile strength. Once past that point the metal is permanently deformed. On a sailboat, a rig tensioned past its elastic limit will become untunable, because tuning is based on full stretch recovery from tack to tack. In addition, overstressed wires suffer from accelerated fatigue, so become untrustworthy.

Therefore, in the design stage one must scale the rig components to be hefty enough that there's no chance of an Elastic Limit–exceeding load.

Furthermore, one must make equally sure that the rig as tuned is not loaded past the Elastic Limit. That is why, in a typical rig, the tightest wires are tuned to at most 25 percent of the wire's strength.

Creep

A related form of permanent deformation to exceeding the Elastic Limit is known as "creep." This involves continuing deformation under a steady load. Spectra is notably vulnerable to creep, so that standing rigging made from it can slowly slacken over time. Not good. To counteract this, Spectra standing rigging should be scaled to keep typical loads low, preferably under 10 percent of breaking strength. This gives you a rope that is still far lighter than wire or rod, and which has a truly massive safety factor.

stay pendants, which can be made of vinyl-coated 7 x 7, or my favorite, Spectra/Technora-blend rope (see page 50). Running backstays can be lighter than the forestay, since the mast itself and the intermediates take up some of the load from the forestay.

These and other considerations will affect what wire you hang on a mast, but it all traces back to that righting-moment curve. As long as your decisions are based on that, you'll at least have an idea of how close to the edge a racing boat will be, or how reassuringly stout a cruising boat will be.

Spectra standing rigging requires higher relative strength than wire. This is because, at loads much over 15 percent of break strength, you get accelerated "creep" (see sidebar).

MAST STRENGTH

Getting to wire size takes time, but it's only a matter of matching expected loads to wire strength. Mast design, however, is a more complex, slippery design challenge. The object is to come up with a column that is stiff enough to take, without buckling, the standing rigging's compression loads, and yet light enough that the boat won't be top-heavy, and small enough in diameter that it won't offer unnecessary drag from wind. Unfortunately, these qualifications call for mutually exclusive responses. Fortunately, it's an old, old challenge; others have faced it in the past, and have left us formulas to plug into. Again, these formulas are meant to be patterns, not straightjackets; to use them creatively, it helps to understand some of the thinking that went into them. For now, let's return to our 35-foot-LWL cutter.

Extra Load
The shrouds put some compression load on the mast, but the fore-and-aft stays impose an additional load—boats also have a fore-and-aft righting moment, and some of that gets transferred to the mast via staysails and stays. Also, stays add compression to the mast simply by trying to keep it in place against boat acceleration and deceleration and the pull of various sails. Engineers Henry and Miller

determined that stays contribute another 85 percent to the compression load on the mast, added to that generated by the transverse stays. So, revising our previous formula, we get:

$$\frac{RM_{30} \times 1.5 \times 1.85}{\frac{1}{2}\ beam} = \text{total mast compression}$$

Condensed, the formula reads:
$$\frac{RM_{30} \times 2.78}{\frac{1}{2}\ beam}$$

In the case of our sample boat, that comes to:

$$\frac{50,000 \times 2.78}{5.5} = 25,272.7 \text{ pounds}$$

or $\quad \dfrac{6,925 \times 2.78}{1.67} = 11,528 \text{ kg}$

Set that number aside for the moment; before we can plug it into one more formula, we need to consider some strength and stiffness variables.

Unsupported Length
Earlier we touched briefly on the significance of unsupported length—how a long column is more likely to buckle under a load than a shorter but otherwise identical column under the same load. Specifically, stiffness varies inversely with the square of the unsupported length; double the length of a mast without adding the intervening support of spreaders, and you have to make it four times as stiff to handle the same load. Remember the uncooked spaghetti?

Spreaders are commonly viewed as a means to widen the angle of shrouds to the mast, but they also serve to shorten unsupported length, allowing designers to make masts adequately buckle-proof without making them massively heavy. Intermediate fore-and-aft rigging (running backstays, forestay) also help with unsupported length, but they, as well as spreaders, add complexity and thus vulnerability to a mast; more things to break. That's why you usually see more than two sets of spreaders only on racing boats, who expect to lose the occasional stick.

End Fixity   But there are other ways to increase stiffness without adding mass. Try another noodle demo to demonstrate one of them: Take two long pieces of spaghetti. Break a couple of inches off one. Press down on this shorter one and notice how much pressure it takes to bend it. Notice also that it bends in the middle. Now take the longer piece and pinch it a couple of inches from the bottom. Press. Even though the unsupported length above the pinch point is the same as the short piece, this piece is stiffer. And instead of bending in the middle of its unsupported length, it bends closer to the upper hand, where spreaders would be on a mast.

What you've just seen is a demonstration of the effects of "End Fixity." The short piece is said to have two "pin ends," while the long piece has "one pin end and one fixed end." A boat's partners do the pinching, so a keel-stepped mast will be stiffer than a deck-stepped mast of the same exposed length. A very stout tabernacle can add some degree of end fixity, but if you're interested in a light mast, keel-stepped is the only way to go.

Why, then, are so many masts deck-stepped? A classic reason is that they're easier to put up and down for traversing canals, passing under bridges, or trailering. The convenience compensates for added weight. (See the discussion on *Sojourner Truth* on page 303.)

But economics are also an issue, since it's cheaper to step a mast on deck than to cut a hole in the deck, and the sole, and install a mast step, mast collar, etc.

And even the arrangement of the interior can be an issue. I once knew some owners who hired an interior designer to redo their boat. The designer came below, took one look at the base of the mast that occupied a large portion of the saloon, and said, "First of all, that has to go." And go it did, to make possible an arrangement of staterooms, sofas, and an entertainment center. For details of the consequences of this simple act, see the description on page 169

Radius

There's one other "weightless" means to mast stiffness: making the mast fatter. Stiffness varies with the square of the distance from the neutral axis of a mast

to the mast wall. With a round or oval mast this neutral axis, around which all the forces are balanced, is in the center of the mast. It can take careful calculation to find this axis with exotic mast cross-sections, but the square-of-the-radius formula holds.

This brings up the reason why most masts are oval instead of round: Because shrouds attach at more points than stays, masts are generally supported better laterally than they are fore-and-aft. You tend to get short, buckle-resistant lengths on the sides, and long, buckle-prone lengths on the front and back. Even on masts with multiple headstays and running backs, induced mast bend can put huge, let's-see-if-we-can-fold-this-thing loads on a stick. Therefore masts need to be stiffer fore-and-aft than they are laterally. The simplest way to accomplish this is to make a mast with the most heavily stressed sides farthest from the neutral axis. This makes the mast stiffer in one plane than the other. A rectangular cross-section works well, but the mass in the corners is pretty much wasted, adding mostly lateral stiffness. An oval offers less wind-resistance and less weight, so that is the most common mast shape. The main exception to this these days is the unstayed mast; it needs to be round, because there are no shrouds to stiffen it laterally. For more on comparisons between stayed and unstayed masts, see the Mast Bend sidebar in Chapter 8.

Wall Thickness

Mast stiffness also varies directly with the thickness of the mast walls. No free ride here; if you want to stiffen by thickening, you pay a price in weight. Some boats have masts that are "sleeved" with double wall sections over heavily stressed areas. This saves making the entire mast thicker-walled. But more often, thick walls are resorted to when other stiffening methods have drawbacks.

For instance, racing sailors will usually select a very narrow mast for low wind resistance. They'll compensate for the loss of square-of-radius stiffness by making the mast very thick and by shortening the unsupported lengths with three, four, or even five sets of spreaders. And they'll accept a low safety factor.

Cruising sailors, though they'll be interested in good performance, will want to minimize the expense, vulnerability, and intricacy of many sets of spreaders, and will be less concerned about an absolute minimum of wind-resistance. A cruising mast section will have moderate radius, moderate wall thickness, and one or two sets of spreaders. And it will be built with a higher safety factor.

In sum, mast design involves juggling various stiffness-inducing factors along with cost, performance, reliability, and even interior design. To get the mast you want, you just have to be able to express those factors with numbers.

Mast Strength Formulas, Part 2

All mast design formulas are variations and refinements on Euler's Formula, an engineering cornerstone which predicts the behavior of columns under compression, with allowances made for all the significant variables. A predigested, easy-to-plug-into form appears in *Skene's Elements of Yacht Design*. I like this version because it's simple and conservative. For another, more race-oriented approach, see the U.S. Sailing Association's recommended scantlings in the accompanying sidebar.

Meanwhile, let's start with the formula for the lateral, or transverse, plane. We're looking for a specific "transverse moment of inertia"—essentially stiffness—which will be expressed, due to multiple squarings hidden in the calculations, in inches to the fourth (in.⁴). I_{tt} (in.⁴) is our symbol.

So:

$$I_{tt} \text{ (in.}^4) = C_{transv} \times \frac{L_t^2 \text{ (in.}^2)}{10,000} \times \frac{\text{Load}}{10,000}$$

Where   C = a transverse constant
              L_t = the length from deck
                    to lower spreader
      Load = RM_{30} compression load.

Stiffness varies inversely with the square of unsupported length, so multiplying the load times the square of the longest unsupported length—deck to spreaders—takes care of that relationship. The constant takes care of end fixity, a safety factor, and

the properties (modulus of elasticity) of the material the mast is made of. The matters of wall thickness and mast radius will be dealt with later, on mast

Scantlings Recommended by USSA Panel

The United States Sailing Association (USSA), formerly the United States Yacht Racing Union (USYRU), developed an alternative to Skene's mast scantling formulas for offshore racing yachts. The two sets of formulas are based on the same elements; the one from the USSA combines them in a different form, uses a lower safety factor, and works with the righting moment at 40 degrees of heel instead of 30 degrees. Resulting masts are considerably lighter than ones designed by the Skene's method, but the USSA formulas do prevent the worst excesses of hold-your-breath spindliness in offshore racing masts.

The formula for longitudinal inertia is:

(Longitudinal Safety Factor × 40 × Righting Moment (ft-lbs) at 1° heel × [Mast Height (inches)]2) ÷ (End Fixity Factor × ½ Beam (at chainplates) π² × Modulus of Elasticity).

More concisely, that's:

$$\frac{FS_L \times 40 \times RMC \times P_L^2}{F \times CP \times \pi^2 \times E}$$

With an inner forestay, the longitudinal safety factor is 1.5, if the forestay is attached to the mast between .651 and .701 of the mast height above the sheer and is backed up with running backstays. Without a forestay, the safety factor is 2.

End fixity is 2 if the mast is keel-stepped, 1.5 if deck-stepped.

For minimum transverse inertia, the formula is:

$$\frac{FS_T \times 40 \times RMC \times P_T^2}{F \times CP \times \pi^2 \times E}$$

Where P_T is the height of the mast to the lower spreaders.

The safety factor is 1.7 for a single-spreader rig, 2 for a double-spreader, assuming the single spreaders are more than halfway up the mast and at least four-fifths of the boat's one-half beam in length, and the lower set of double spreaders is at least .36 of the way up the mast and at least three-fifths of the boat's one-half beam. This spreader placement proviso has the effect of keeping the "P_T^2" measurement high, which results in a heavier, safer mast section.

section charts which take these factors into account without further calculation.

Let's go shopping for a mast section. Assume the stick on this boat is 42 feet above deck, and that the lower spreaders are 17 feet 7 inches above deck. That's about 42 percent of the total exposed length, a number that lends itself to wholesome proportions, so that no part of the rig will take a disproportionate load. If the lower spreaders were higher up, the lowest section of the mast would have to be much stiffer—longer unsupported length. Since the entire mast is scaled to this section, that would make the higher, shorter sections far too stiff and heavy. Conversely, if the lower spreaders were a lot lower, we wouldn't need as heavy a section down low, but the upper and now longer sections would not be heavy enough to support their loads. So somewhere around 40 percent of exposed length is a good location for lower spreaders. For single spreaders, about 55 percent of the way up is a good location, for the same reasons.

In any event, 17 feet 7 inches is 211 inches. Square that, and we have an L_T^2 of 44,521. Our load from the rigging formula at RM_{30} is:

$$\frac{RM_{30} \times 2.78}{\frac{1}{2} \text{ beam}} = 25,272.7 \text{ pounds}$$

Our constant, from the chart in Figure 5-26, is 1.13 for an aluminum mast, keel-stepped.

Plugging into our formula, then,

I_{tt} (in.^{4}) =

$$1.13 \times \frac{44,521}{10,000} \times \frac{25,272.7}{10,000} = 12.71 \text{ in.}^4$$

What the heck is 12.71 in.^{4}? It's just 127,100 reduced to a more compact form by those "10,000" divisors in the formula. In either form, it's our transverse moment of inertia.

The formula for the fore-and-aft or longitudinal moment of inertia is much the same, except for a different, smaller constant. It's smaller because the unsupported length is assumed to be the entire exposed length of the mast. I_{LL} is our symbol for longitudinal inertia. So:

$$I_{LL} \text{ (in.}^4) = C_{f.a.} \times \frac{L^4 \text{ (in.}^2)}{10,000} \times \frac{\text{Load}}{10,000}$$

Where C = fore-and-aft constant
I_{LL} = length, deck to jibstay
Load = RM_{30} compression load.

Accordingly,

I_{LL} (in.^{4}) =

$$.54 \times \frac{254,016}{10,000} \times \frac{25,272.7}{10,000} = 34.67 \text{ in.}^4$$

As you'll note in the constants table (Figure 5-26), there are different figures for wood and aluminum masts, taking into account their different

Figure 5-26. *Values for the constant "C" in the formulas for moments of inertia about the transverse and longitudinal axis of a mast. These values assume a keel-stepped mast. Deck-stepped masts require values for the constant perhaps 50 percent greater, which can be reduced to 20 to 30 percent if a big tabernacle is present to provide partner-like support. (Adapted from* Skene's Elements of Yacht Design, *8th Edition, by Francis Kinney: Dodd, Mead, 1981)*

	C. Transverse		C. Fore and Aft with Double Lowers	
Mast Material	**Single Spreaders**	**2 or more Sets Spreaders**	**Masthead**	**Fractional**
Spruce	6.78	8.11	4.0	3.74
Aluminum	.94	1.13	.54	.52

properties. It should not be thought that because the constants for wood are so much higher the masts will be that much heavier; the constants are scaled to stiffness in a given material, which is not necessarily the same thing as weight or even size. Aluminum masts should work out a little lighter nonetheless, but it is not unusual to find them at least as heavy as wooden ones, perhaps as an anti-lawsuit safety factor, perhaps because someone ran the numbers wrong, or perhaps because that was the section that the spar builder had lying around. Also notice that the constants assume a keel-stepped mast and two lower shrouds per side; if a mast you deal with is deck-stepped or single-shrouded, adjust accordingly.

Mast Charts

Figure 5-27 shows the final step in mast design: choosing a mast cross-section of sufficient stiffness to stand up to our calculated moments of inertia. The cross-hatched graph is a "mast chart," which precalculates for us the effects of radius and wall thickness in determining the desired section. We need only read up from the bottom, which has the transverse scale, to intersect a line drawn across from the side, which has the longitudinal scale. Where the lines meet, we can read off our dimensions—roughly 5 inches on the transverse axis and 8 inches on the longitudinal axis in our example.

A leafing-through-a-catalog-ish alternative is to consult a list of the dimensions and moments of available extrusions, and pick out the one that comes closest to our requirements (Figure 5-28). Either way, we'll usually be faced with two variables:

1. Since calculated moments rarely coincide precisely with those of available mast sections, a choice must often be made between sections that are somewhat stiffer and somewhat more supple than our ideal.

2. Since masts come in varying wall thickness, we have a range of choices, with a very small-diameter, thick-walled mast at one extreme, and a very fat, thin-walled mast at the other.

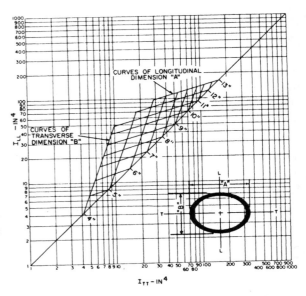

Figure 5-27. *A mast chart for oval sections. (From* Understanding Rigs and Rigging, *by Richard Henderson, International Marine, 1991)*

In practice, these two decisions are settled according to the nature of sailing the boat is intended for. Cruisers will naturally be inclined to go a size up when in doubt, and to opt for a moderately large section, if only because it is less expensive than a very thick one. And likewise, racers are likely to shave away scantlings in the interest of lightness, even as they minimize diameter to minimize windage, and hang the expense.

In the case of our cruising cutter, the catalog mast section that most closely matches our requirements has dimensions of 8.06 inches (205 mm) by 4.88 inches (124 mm) by .180 inch (4.6 mm) thick.

WIRE/ROD OPTIONS

Design is a search for the appropriate. The above bulletproof cruising cutter rig is not the only bulletproof cruising cutter rig; it and any number of other configurations fit the job description. We could have made a single-spreader, deck-stepped, single-shroud design as well. Or we could have made the mast out of wood, which can be custom-made and tapered to

SPAR SECTIONS

6061-T6 ALUMINUM

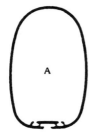 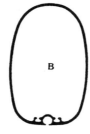 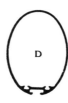

SECTION	SHAPE	DEPTH	WIDTH	WALL	LBS/FT	MOMENTS OF INERTIA I_{xx}	I_{yy}
077	B	2.84 in.	2.125 in.	.085 in.	.917	.60	.34
095	B	3.75	2.75	.085	1.35	1.92	1.15
100	C	3.75	2.25	.100	1.30	1.50	.63
110	C	4.75	2.75	.100	1.50	2.40	1.10
125	B	4.90	3.09	.091	1.48	3.50	1.48
128	B	5.00	3.00	VAR.	1.70	4.80	1.90
130	D	5.00	3.50	.120	2.08	4.22	2.43
150	D	6.00	4.00	.140	2.75	8.91	4.40
152	B	6.00	4.00	.130	2.80	11.50	5.60
165	A	6.52	4.10	.147	3.33	14.41	6.78
166	B	6.50	4.00	VAR.	3.30	16.00	5.70
180	B	7.15	4.50	.148	3.57	18.50	7.44
181	A	7.15	4.50	.148	3.57	18.50	7.44
185	B	7.15	4.50	.170	4.42	19.50	10.00
200	B	7.69	4.86	.180	4.54	27.40	11.45
202	B	8.00	4.25	VAR.	4.46	34.60	8.60
→205	B	8.06	4.88	.180	4.76	32.20	12.00
220	B	8.55	5.40	.188	5.20	39.00	16.60
221	A	8.55	5.40	.188	5.20	39.00	16.60
231	A	9.24	5.82	.188	5.60	49.60	22.20
232	B	9.19	4.86	VAR.	6.19	63.70	15.60
240	A	9.91	6.20	.188	6.30	68.40	27.20
280	B	11.00	5.88	VAR.	10.04	132.91	34.57
305	A	12.00	7.48	.204	8.32	125.90	53.70
061	E	2.25	.61	.070	.38	.13	.01
081	E	3.25	.88	.100	.79	.54	.06
121	E	4.75	1.25	.130	1.50	2.18	.24
171	E	6.75	1.80	.130	2.19	6.51	.77

Figure 5-28. *A page from a Yachttech catalog. For our example boat we choose mast shape B, section 205.*

any needed dimension by a backyard builder. And we could have tapered the top of any of these rigs to reduce weight and windage aloft. The options are endless, and they all make at least some sense. But the time comes when you have to sit down and say, "It's going to look like this"—when the gestalt of everything you know or think you know leads you to what you feel is most appropriate.

You've just been privy to the design of a "classic" rig, one whose form and particulars are the result of long evolution and conservative engineering, and whose physical components are readily available. Most rigs, cruisers and racers alike, come out of this heritage, but designers are always pushing at the envelope. They do this for their own satisfaction, or at the urging of clients for whom "normal" is not enough. In Chapter 8 you'll get a perspective on what's possible when a talented, innovative, and prudent designer goes to work. In this collection the emphasis is on "prudent"; anyone can come up with a novel rig, but only care, skill, and a realistic application of basic design principles will produce a rig that will perform as planned and stay in the boat.

Here are some final considerations, a look at the options we have for translating those numbers into wire we can dress our mast with.

Standing Rigging: The Material Difference

"Nothin' too strong ever broke."

—Maine proverb

In theory, you can make a standing rig out of anything; clothesline of sufficient diameter would do. In practice you are likely to choose from an array of materials and constructions specifically developed for the task. Since the mid-nineteenth century, this array mostly comprised variations on iron and steel for materials, made into various forms of rod and wire rope.

Then, in the late twentieth century, plastic rope made an entry, offering tremendous advantages in weight reduction, increased strength, and sometimes greater durability and reduced cost. Many types and forms of plastic have been tried, and of them, 12-strand Spectra/Dyneema, covered or uncovered, shows the best combination of virtues, and the fewest drawbacks. Making good use of this new material requires new knowledge, and new skills. In the present volume, I won't be going into minutiae of fabrication, but in this chapter we'll see how it stacks up against the metallic competition in general terms.

In some vessels, rigs made from Spectra or some other plastic have completely replaced metal rigging. In others it has made some inroads, and in others still there is not a scrap of plastic to be found. And this is how it should be, given the broad range of rig designs, sailing conditions, and cost constraints, and the varyingly adventurous or conservative inclinations of sailors themselves. Understanding and balancing your rig's specific needs, and your own inclinations, is the key to choosing the most appropriate materials for your vessel.

Windage Figure 5-29 shows, in order of their development, standing-rigging materials that have been in use since the 1850s. The most obvious trend has been an increase of strength relative to diameter. This benefits sailing performance because the smaller a piece of rigging is, the less drag or windage it causes as it passes through the air. With less drag, a boat will go faster and heel less in a given wind speed.

At first, strength-to-size gains were the result of the introduction of different materials: Hemp gave way to iron, and iron, to steel. By the early years of this century, gains based on materials improvements were diminishing, so designers turned their attention to construction. The more cross-sectional area of metal you can cram into a wire of a given diameter, the stronger that stay will be. So 6 x 7 and 7 x 7 constructions were superseded for the most part by the current standard, 1 x 19. Of course, a solid cylinder has the greatest cross-sectional area and thus the greatest strength of all, but until recently, engineering problems made rod rigging too short-lived to be of use to any but the most extreme racing craft. With the

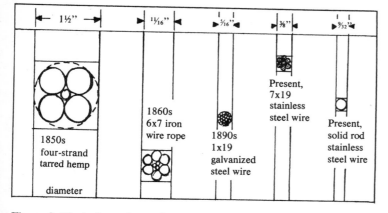

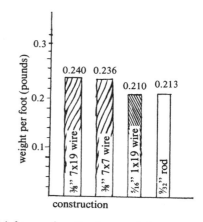

Figure 5-29. *A chronology of materials. All the examples shown are of equal strength, rated for loads of about 12,000 pounds. Over the decades, diameter has shown a downward trend due to better materials and constructions.*

Figure 5-30. *Weight per foot for four stainless steel stay constructions. All are rated for 12,000- to 12,500-pound loads.*

advent of improved alloys and cold-drawing techniques, rod rigging is now at home in the cruising and charter market.

Weight   Another trend has been the reduction of rig weight. One extra pound of weight 30 feet up adds 30 foot-pounds to a vessel's heeling moment, making the vessel that much less stable and putting that much more strain on the mast and rig. Lightness is a virtue. But again, recent developments have produced a diminishing-returns catch: Increasing the cross-sectional area of metal in wire of a given diameter in order to increase wire strength means increasing weight relative to diameter. Faced with this, designers often resort to making the rig lighter by reducing scantlings. According to C. A. Marchaj, rig weights have dropped by an average of 30 percent since the 1960s. (For more on this, see the "Effects of Engineering" section later in this chapter and "Blocks" in Chapter 2.) Figure 5-30 shows in graph form the relationships between weight per foot, diameter, and strength for 7 x 19, 7 x 7, 1 x 19, and rod rigging of comparable materials.

Elasticity   Induced mast bend can alter sail shape to improve performance; unwanted mast bend due to rig elasticity can impair it. It's odd to think of wire rope as something that stretches, and it's true that we're dealing with tiny increments here, even in the most elastic wire, but this is a situation in which tiny increments can make a difference. To the extent that wire stretches more than we want it to, the mast will bend or "go out of column." Stayed masts are designed to function as nearly pure compression members, so it is important that they stay relatively straight. In cases where fore-and-aft bend is induced, in the interests of resistance to flexing, or improved mainsail shape, the mast must be engineered to handle the deflection. Even then, bend must be kept within design parameters. Consult with a rigger or sparbuilder about appropriate bend for your mast.

There are two forms of stretch at rated loads that are of interest to sailors: constructional and elastic. Constructional stretch is a permanent elongation that results from the strands in a new piece of rigging settling into place when it is put to use. This does not affect sailing efficiency unless it is not allowed for when the piece is cut for rig fabrication; with long pieces of the more elastic constructions, one can use up a lot of turnbuckle thread taking out this stretch, and thus have too little adjustment left for tuning.

Although HSR and other standing-rigging-grade forms of Spectra are fabulously

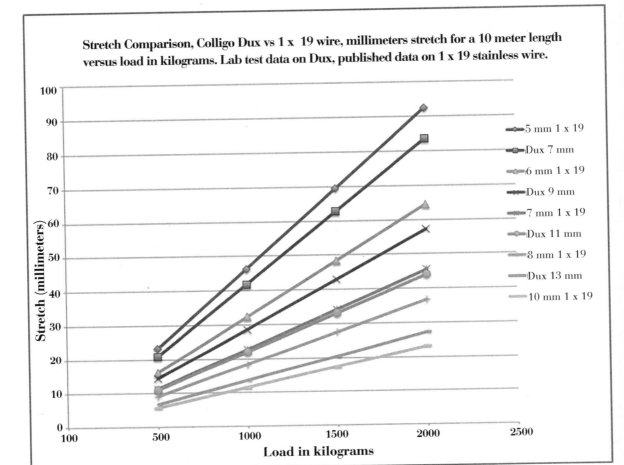

Stretch Comparison, Colligo Dux vs 1 x 19 wire, millimeters stretch for a 10 meter length versus load in kilograms. Lab test data on Dux, published data on 1 x 19 stainless wire.

(Colligo Marine)

Figure 5-31 *Stretch comparison: Colligo Dux versus 1 x 19 wire, millimeters stretch for a 10-meter length versus load in kilograms. Lab test data on Dux, published data on 1 x 19 stainless wire. Results are comparable to those for New England Rope's HSR.*

inelastic once constructional stretch is removed (see sidebar), they tend to have a huge amount of constructional stretch. Even if the manufacturer does everything possible to minimize this at the factory, much of it will return simply from being wound onto a spool, let alone from being handled in the loft when splicing. Addressing this level of constructional stretch is the biggest practical consideration for a rigger working with the stuff. For instance, after you splice one end, it is important to put a temporary eye in the other end and stretch the piece out, with a load of about 10 percent of the line's break strength. This removes the constructional stretch from the standing part, as well as any excess shrinkage you created when splicing. Once the rope is stretched out, you make a

reference mark at your desired finished length. As soon as you release the tension the rope shrinks in length, with the fibers reassuming their original position.

And then there's elastic stretch, a function of load and diameter relative to the inherent elastic properties of the metal used in making the rig. A formula for the approximate percentage of stretch for a given length of rigging is as follows:

$e = [P/D^2] \times F$, where

e = elastic stretch as percentage of length

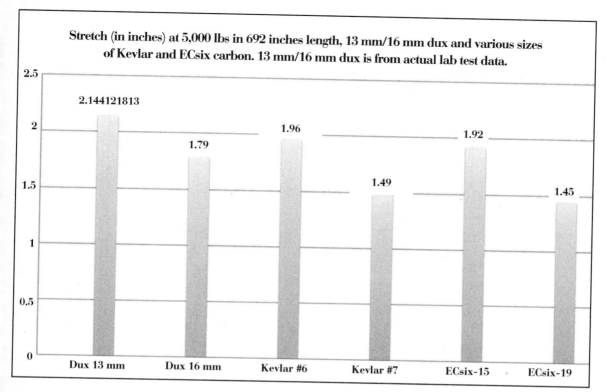

Stretch (in inches) at 5,000 lbs in 692 inches length, 13 mm/16 mm dux and various sizes of Kevlar and ECsix carbon. 13 mm/16 mm dux is from actual lab test data.

Material	Stretch
Dux 13 mm	2.144121813
Dux 16 mm	1.79
Kevlar #6	1.96
Kevlar #7	1.49
ECsix-15	1.92
ECsix-19	1.45

Figure 5-32 *Stretch (in inches) at 5,000 pounds in 692 inches length, 13 mm/16 mm Colligo Dux and various sizes of Kevlar and ECsix carbon. Note that 13 mm/16 mm Dux data is from actual lab test data. Results are comparable to those for New England Rope's HSR.*

(Colligo Marine)

P = load on rope in pounds
D = nominal rope diameter
F = the reciprocal of (A × E × 100)

The factor "F" is the tricky part of the equation because it is the result of a fairly complex equation itself. "A" is the cross-sectional area of metal in a wire rope of given diameter, and "E" stands for the modulus of elasticity, which is to say how much a substance stretches per pound of tension applied. Carbon steel, for example, has a higher modulus of elasticity than stainless steel. Stays with the greatest cross-sectional area, made of materials with the lowest modulus of elasticity will stretch the least. Values of the factor "F" for the materials and constructions commonly used in rigging are as follows:

Construction		F
rod rigging	stainless	4.45×10^{-6}
1 x 19	carbon	6.98×10^{-6}
	stainless	7.79×10^{-6}
7 x 7	carbon	1.07×10^{-5}
	stainless	1.20×10^{-5}
7 x 19	carbon	1.20×10^{-5}
	stainless	1.62×10^{-5}

Don't let those numbers intimidate you; Figure 5-33 renders them into some real-life examples. Theoretical 50-foot lengths subjected to a load of 25 percent of their rated strength would stretch by the amounts shown. A load of 25 percent reflects high rig strain for most vessels. From the 1.05-inch stretch of the rod rigging sample to the 2.07-inch stretch of the stainless 7 x 19 sample, one sees an increase of elasticity with increase of numbers of strands. But once more, the returns diminish as we approach minimum elasticity, with only a 0.44-

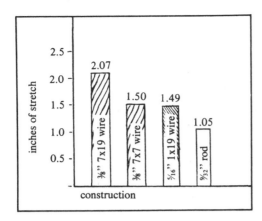

Figure 5-33. *Inches of stretch per 50 feet, at 25 per-cent load, for the stay constructions in Figure 5-30.*

inch difference separating 1 x 19 stainless and rod rigging.

Whether this difference is worth bothering with depends on the boat. The wider spreader angles on cruisers lessen shroud strain and the distance that the masthead travels to leeward for a given amount of stretch. A lower-aspect rig accomplishes the same thing. But the fastest boats have the tallest, narrowest rigs, with shroud chainplates set well inboard so they can sheet in those huge genoas; utter inelasticity is required, so rod rigging can make sense.

Flexibility   The only formula you need to know here is that more strands equal more flexibility. So rod is the least flexible and 7 x 19 wire and HSR are the most flexible of the constructions we're considering. Greatest flexibility is required for halyards, so 7 x 19 is the only construction to use if you want wire halyards. But if you are willing to venture into Spectra territory, you can use a material that is significantly stronger, less elastic, and much lighter, among other virtues. Running back pendants, span wires, straps, and bowsprit shrouds are good in 7 x 7 or 7 x 19, because these constructions are less prone to damage by kinking in these applications than 1 x 19 is. But again, the right forms of Spectra can work even better. And if structural considerations can be satisfied, Spectra is a breeze to splice compared to

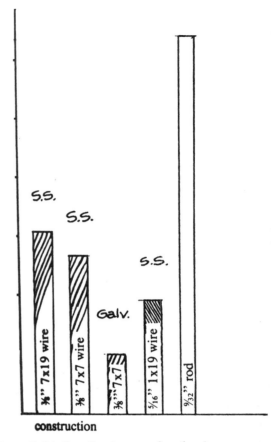

Figure 5-34. *Retail prices per foot for the stay constructions shown in Figure 5-30 change each year. But relative prices, shown above, remain the same.*

any wire. A good choice for spliced standing rigging is 7 x 7 because it is relatively docile and easily worked, while 1 x 19 can be, um, challenging.

Cost   So much for engineering; now we get to the important question, "What's it gonna cost me?" The answers can be found in Figure 5-34, a cost-per-foot chart. Compare this to Figures 5-30 and 5-33, and you can see what you get for your money.

It's easy to see why 1 x 19 wire is the overwhelming first choice for most contemporary craft: the combination of good weight, windage, and elasticity characteristics, and a relatively low price. HSR costs more per foot, but, especially if you splice it yourself, the cheapness of the terminals can bring overall costs

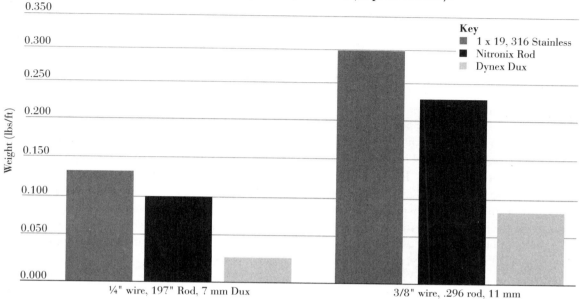

Comparison of weight for stretch equivalent materials, 1 x 19 316 stainless, Nitronic Rod, and Dynex Dux (in pounds/foot).

Key
■ 1 x 19, 316 Stainless
■ Nitronix Rod
■ Dynex Dux

¼" wire, 197" Rod, 7 mm Dux   3/8" wire, .296 rod, 11 mm

Figure 5-35. *Weight comparisons of wire rope and rod rigging.*

into 1 x 19 range. For cruisers,1 x 19, HSR, and 7 x 7 are appealing in that they are more likely than rod to give advance warning of failure. Even if you do spot a flaw in rod rigging ahead of time, where can you safely stow the spare's six-foot-diameter coil? If you want to race, and have the money, it can make sense to indulge in rod rigging, assuming your hull is bred to benefit from the slightly increased efficiency; a cruiser, or even a racer/cruiser, being inherently slower than a pure racer, may not have its performance measurably improved. And some traditional craft that roar along nicely with 7 x 7 wire would be silly with anything else. No doubt there exists somewhere a Norwegian lifeboat with rod rigging and hydraulic backstay, but this sort of design behavior is, as sailing writer David Kasanof once put it, "like paring the hooves of a Clydesdale before entering it in the Kentucky Derby."

Cost-Effectiveness   Now to consider cost over time, a sort of budgetary moment of forces. Aside from proper tuning, scantlings, terminals, and

staying angles, the biggest determinants of rig longevity are what the stays are made of and how well they are maintained. A long-lived rig is a good return on investment, and also provides a sort of insurance: If it's healthy enough to last, it's healthy enough to withstand occasional rough going.

In spite of the obvious advantages of durability, the world of contemporary sailing is filled with tales of spectacular dismastings in moderate conditions. Many of these stories concern racers who shaved a teensy bit too much weight out of their rigging or mast, but many others are about sailors who either started out with poor materials or let good ones degrade. Some unfortunate real-life scenarios:

- Some owners choose good stainless 1 x 19 wire for a corrosive environment, knowing that the small number of strands presents a small total surface area for corrosion to work on. But then they get some not-so-good swages applied, and the small number of strands works against them—if just one strand is broken, or not sharing the load, the wire loses more than five percent of its strength.

- Someone else gets properly applied terminals but accelerates metal fatigue by neglecting to use toggles, and neglecting to tune. If the wire is alloy it will harden up and break if it isn't replaced in time.
- Another party gets a beautifully spliced 7 x 7 rig but uses truly lousy wire because it was available cheap. The mast goes over the side and people blame the splices.
- Some owners get on the Spectra bandwagon, but use Amsteel for their standing rigging rather than HSR, because Amsteel is so much cheaper, and it's all Spectra, right? In short order they encounter vast stretch, alarming mast shape, and rapid fiber creep. Amsteel is an excellent material for many applications, but standing rigging isn't one of them.

Having the right material in the wrong place can also reduce cost-effectiveness. An alloy at home in Maine might not want to spend too much time in Hawaii; charter boat skippers there change rigs every three to five years. Private vessels, sailed less, can expect longer service—maybe 10 years with maintenance. The best thing to do in Hawaii is to invest in a highly corrosion-resistant alloy and take good care of it. The tropics are one place where rod rigging is a sensible choice for non-race-boats. Minimum surface area and excellent metal beat the heat.

Maintenance and regular inspection (more on this in Chapter 7) are crucial even for stainless steel; "stainless" is a relative term, applied to a whole family of alloys with widely differing levels of corrosion and fatigue resistance. Rinsing the rig with fresh water whenever you hose down the deck can greatly prolong rig life, but if the vessel is in a particularly hostile-to-wire environment or if you simply want the rig to last the longest possible time, it's a good idea to give some thought to the alloy it's made of.

For example, Type 302 is a high-carbon alloy with good fatigue and corrosion resistance. This wire has low initial cost, high strength, and will outlast many other alloys. It is best suited to temperate climates, though, because it is vulnerable to corrosion, which is always worse where things are hot and salty.

That's why, if you are planning on a tropical cruise, you will want to consider using Type 316 stainless, which is highly corrosion-resistant. Type 316 is also usually 15 to 20 percent weaker than 302, as well as costing considerably more for a given diameter, so south-bound boats have historically gone up a size in standing rigging, and gone correspondingly down in their bank account balance. But this is not always necessary, because strength and cost are not entirely about materials properties. As of this writing, the wire we use in our shop is a highly polished Type 316, which is cheaper than many brands of Type 302, and which gets consistent independent break tests near–or even exceeding–the rated strength of 302. The point is that it can pay to shop around when selecting standing rigging. In this case, our 316 makes more sense in any climate than 302 does.

Navtec uses another alloy, called Nitronic 50. Extraordinarily strong and corrosion-resistant, it can be drawn with the high uniformity that rod rigging must have.

In times past, it was my practice to urge clients to consider galvanized wire rope. My enthusiasm for it tended to be met with incredulity by most sailors, yet galvanized steel is possessed of virtues that make it ideal for the running or standing rigging of many vessels. Specifically, it is less elastic and more fatigue-resistant than any alloy. It also used to cost far less than stainless. It still does, sort of. The problem is that it is extremely hard to find it, in good quality, in the 7 x 7 and 1 x 19 constructions needed for standing rigging. You can track it down in Europe, but by the time it gets here, freight and duty make it more expensive than stainless. Many traditional vessels, faced with this problem, revert to 7 x 19, which means they get a heavier, stretchier rig that is also corrosion-vulnerable. Much better, I think, to move to HSR or the like.

If you do use galvanized wire, note that while it is strong and resilient, it requires maintenance, which for a boat owner can be like saying that it was a pleasant trip except for the hurricane. But I've seen enough 20-, 40-, and 50-year-old rigs in perfect condition to know that galvanized wire is underrated.

Who Makes It   Officially speaking, all wire sold in the United States must meet federally established standards, notably for breaking strength. These are minimum standards—you meet them, you can sell your wire. In the past, it was my experience that reputable domestic manufacturers made a wire that was stronger and longer-lived than the imported stuff. Production standards had something to do with this, as did America's "no minus tolerance" requirement for domestically produced wire. That is, while importers can sell a wire that is, say, 9 millimeters, plus 4 percent or minus 1 percent, domestic corresponding ⅜-inch size must be ⅜ inch and *no smaller*, but it can be up to 5 percent larger. I think of this standard as a federally provided factor of safety. But times change. The best U.S. wire manufactures, like MacWhyte and Carolina, long ago went out of business, and the few that are left do not, in my experience, seem interested in turning out the best possible product. Which brings us to Korea. Some of the worst wire you can buy comes from Korea. So does some of the best, and at good prices. The wire my shop uses comes from Korea. We get regular metallurgy and destruction test results on this wire, and we've been very happy with it. No matter where you get your wire, I recommend getting similar data on it, as well as making a visual inspection to make sure that all of the yarns are laid in smoothly. If possible, get break test numbers for the specific run that your wire is coming from. In other words, regardless of whom you buy your wire from, learn all you can about it beforehand from manufacturers' reps, riggers, and sailors who've had experience with it, good and bad.

MAST HARDWARE

With running rigging (Chapter 2) and standing rigging settled, we now have a clear idea of what the boat's character, and thus mechanical details, will be. If the standing rigging is fully served galvanized wire spliced around deadeyes, and the running rigging is Roblon, it follows that you'll set soft eyes around the mast rather than installing tangs. Your blocks might be rope-stropped but will definitely be of wood, and chainplates will be hefty, maybe bent outward to clear a high bulwark rail.

On the other hand, you might have opted for rod rigging and gee-whiz cordage that stretches half an inch in a mile of length. Your attendant gear will almost certainly include superlight, super strong plastic-and-alloy blocks, a multitude of two- or three-speed winches, streamlined upper terminals, and chainplates coming out of the deck frighteningly far inboard for close headsail sheeting.

No matter what design choices you make, some things won't change. Tangs and chainplates, for instance, should have a breaking strength at least 33 percent greater than the wire that makes up to them (see sidebars "Tangs" and "Chainplates"), since they must resist fatigue and corrosion far longer than the relatively short-lived standing rigging.

Bolts must be sized to match the gear they hold, whether it's tangs, chainplates, cleats, or the binnacle.

When attaching to wood, concentrate on spreading the load to as many fibers as possible; use compression sleeves, finger tangs, and multiple fasteners.

When attaching to aluminum, drill for bolts and tap for machine screws whenever possible. Avoid pop rivets, using them only when the metal is too thin for machine screws, and then use stainless rivets instead of aluminum ones, unless the load is truly trivial. And always coat any fastener with silicone, anhydrous lanolin (see the "Favorite Goops" sidebar *in the next chapter*), or other goo before putting it into any metal.

Leads must be fair on any boat, to maximize strength and to limit fatigue. Make sure those tangs and chainplates, for instance, are pointing directly at each other.

Regardless of your preferences, it is important to follow through your design decisions. Don't put modern gear on a traditional boat, or vice versa, unless you have excellent reasons for doing so; aesthetics as well as structural qualities might clash. A good example is soft eyes for shrouds—a strong, simple, economical alternative to tangs for many traditional vessels. On tall modern rigs, however, the slight shifting of the eyes around the mast from tack to tack can result in appreciable mast bend that could endanger the mast and will certainly impair sailing performance. Then there is the matter of modern turnbuckles: very nice, very strong. But if you splice your 7 x 7 shrouds around heavy-duty thimbles, you will find that the thimbles will not fit into turnbuckles of

Chainplates

For long-term fatigue resistance chainplates need to be at least 1.5 times stronger than the wires they hold. Chainplates are also as sensitive as tangs to things like hole size, lead, and hole angles.

Chainplates differ from tangs in that they are attached to the hull. They don't need to pivot because the hull doesn't move much. Instead chainplates are locked in place, usually with multiple fasteners, to spread the load to the hull. But this means they must line up precisely with the shrouds, laterally as well as fore and aft. Because chainplates and their fasteners are near the water, crevice corrosion becomes a problem: Poorly-bedded stainless can get wet, and waste away to nothing. Like all corrosion, this problem is worse the farther south you go, but it's a good idea in any climate to pull some chainplates and their fasteners once in a while. If you find water, or any signs of corrosion, rebed, replace, or both.

Highly-polished type 316 stainless has long been the preferred material for chainplates; it is relatively strong, and relatively corrosion-resistant. But aluminum bronze is of comparable strength, and is far more fatigue- and corrosion-resistant. Grade 5 titanium is even stronger than either bronze or stainless, and sneers at fatigue and corrosion. It is also more noble, so is not susceptible to galvanic action.

If you're designing chainplates, the accompanying chart from *Skene's Elements of Yacht Design* is a quick way to the right size. Notice that the offset gives you more "meat" on the load side of the hole. This prevents the hole from deforming into an egg shape over time. You'll find a slightly different chart in Larsson and Eliasson's *Principles of Yacht Design*. Either source will give reassuringly stout chainplate dimensions

If you're designing or checking tangs, each of the two parts should be at least half the strength of the corresponding chainplate.

Note: *This table can be used for titanium. Grade 5 is much stronger than the other materials, but making it thinner will put excess load-per-square-inch on clevis pins.*

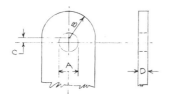

SILICON BRONZE OR STAINLESS STEEL CHAIN PLS
LOAD IS 4/3 BREAKING STRENGTH OF WIRE

WIRE DIAM.	BREAKING STR. IN LBS. 1X19 S.S.	A PIN	B RADIUS	C OFFSET	D* THICK
1/8"	2,100	1/4"	3/8"	1/16"	1/8"
5/32"	3,300	5/16"	7/16"	1/16"	3/16"
3/16"	4,700	3/8"	1/2"	1/8"	3/16"
7/32"	6,300	7/16"	9/16"	1/8"	1/4"
1/4"	8,200	1/2"	9/16"	1/8"	1/4"
9/32"	10,300	1/2"	11/16"	1/8"	5/16"
5/16"	12,500	5/8"	13/16"	3/16"	5/16"
3/8"	17,600	5/8"	7/8"	3/16"	7/16"
7/16"	23,400	3/4"	1"	3/16"	1/2"
1/2"	29,700	7/8"	1 3/16"	1/4"	1/2"
9/16"	37,000	7/8"	1 1/4"	1/4"	5/8"
5/8"	46,800	1"	1 3/8"	1/4"	11/16"
3/4"	59,700	1 1/4"	1 5/8"	1/4"	3/4"
7/8"	76,700	1 1/2"	1 3/4"	5/16"	7/8"

* FOR JIBSTAY & BACKSTAY LUGS ADD 1/16 THICKNESS

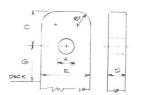

ULTIMATE STRESS

TENSION	40,000 P.S.I.
SHEAR	24,000 P.S.I.
BEARING	78,000 P.S.I.
WELD	21,000 P.S.I.

FACTOR OF SAFETY = 2.5 FOR EACH

ALUMINUM CHAIN PLATES (ALLOY 5086-H32)
(SEE BRONZE OR S.S. CHAIN PLS FOR WIRE STRENGTH)

WIRE 1X19 S.S.	A PIN	B RADIUS	C	D THICK	E WIDTH	LENGTH OF WELD 3/16" 2,780	1/4" 3,780	5/16" 4,640	G
1/8"	1/4"	3/8"	7/16"	5/16"	1/16"	3 3/4"	2 3/4"		1/16"
5/32"	5/16"	1/4"	1/2"	3/8"	1"	6"	4 1/2"	3 1/2"	3/4"
3/16"	3/8"	5/16"	3/4"	7/16"	1 1/16"	8 1/2"	6 1/4"	5"	13/16"
7/32"	7/16"	3/8"	13/16"	1/2"	1/4"	12"	8 1/2"	7"	7/8"
1/4"	1/2"	7/16"	7/8"	5/8"	1 3/8"	15"	11"	9"	1"
9/32"	1/2"	1/2"	1 1/16"	5/8"	1 1/2"	19"	14"	11"	1 1/8"
5/16"	5/8"	1/2"	1 1/8"	3/4"	1 5/8"	23"	17"	14"	1 1/4"
3/8"	5/8"	5/8"	1 1/2"	3/4"	2 1/8"	32"	24"	19"	1 3/8"
7/16"	3/4"	5/8"	1 5/8"	7/8"	2 3/8"	42"	32"	25"	1 1/4"
1/2"	7/8"	3/4"	1 7/8"	1"	2 5/8"	54"	40"	32"	1 1/2"
9/16"	1"	1"	2"	1 1/8"	2 7/8"	66"	50"	40"	1 5/8"
5/8"	1"	1 1/4"	2 3/8"	1 1/4"	3 3/8"	84"	62"	50"	1 5/8"
3/4"	1 1/4"	1 1/4"	2 1/2"	1 1/2"	3 3/4"	108"	81"	65"	1 3/4"
7/8"	1 1/2"	1 3/8"	2 5/8"	1 3/4"	4 1/8"	136"	104"	82"	1 7/8"

* STRENGTH OF WELD IN SHEAR, LBS. PER LIN. INCH.

corresponding strength; turnbuckles are made to fit swaged 1 x 19 these days. Spectra standing rigging is also a little larger in diameter than the 1 x 19 it might replace, but it is possible to get turnbuckles for it nowadays, from the Blue Wave company.

For your mast's standing rigging, there's nothing wrong with using galvanized steel turnbuckles with either stainless or galvanized wire, as long as it's above the water. But don't mix the two metals where galvanic action is likely to be severe, as on the lower ends of boomkin shrouds-and bobstays. For further discussion of galvanic action as it affects rigs, see the accompanying sidebar.

Compatibility is the key to gear selection for a good working rig. Make lists, check catalogs, compare specs, think things through. Do you need to have every line leading to the cockpit? Are there enough of them to make color-coded rope worth the bother? Will the boat look funny with sheer poles with belaying pins in them? Will the boat work well without them? Are you going to regret having a spinnaker, or not having one? Sop up all the data you can, let it slosh around inside for a while, and then solve by association. You probably understand the boat pretty well by now; just pay attention to the engineering and use what suits—the gear that

Tangs

The tang is the intermediary between the mast and the standing rigging. In the tang's short, shiny length a miracle happens: the tension from the wire is absorbed, makes a near-180-degree turn, and is somehow translated into compression on the mast.

A well-made tang will accomplish this miracle through a zillion rig cycles; a poorly made tang will drop the mast in the water. Here are some details that will keep the mast in the boat.

Fair lead
External tangs are angled laterally to point outboard to the chainplate (or to the spreader tip). If your rigging bends as it leaves the tang, you have a foul lead. Tangs are also angled fore or aft, depending whether the chainplate is forward or aft of them. This angle can change according to mast rake, backstay tension, and rig load magnitude. Therefore, the best way to get an appropriate fore-and-aft angle is to hang the tang on a throughbolt, so it can pivot.

Fair loading
The throughbolt can manage the load if you just make it the same size as the clevis pins (or the next size bigger for double tangs). But the concentrated load can be hard on your thin-walled, softer-material mast. That's why it's a good idea to run the through bolt through close-fitting, heavy-walled, flanged bushings, for a fatter bearing surface. Ideally the bushings will run through the tangs as well as the mast. Bushings are superior to full-length compression tubes, in that they are lighter than a comparably thick tube. They also do not require that you cut them to a specific length, as you need to with the tube.

Reinforcing plates on or in the mast will spread the load still further, so they're a valuable option, particularly on wooden masts, or thinner-walled-than-usual aluminum masts. The plates are secured with screws or rivets, and both throughbolt and compression tube run through the plates.

The bolt hole and clevis pin holes in a proper tang are no less than $\frac{1}{100}$ inch, and no more than $\frac{1}{64}$ inch larger than the pin or bolt that goes through them. That is, the hole is big enough that you don't have to hammer the bolt or pin in—and out—yet small enough that you don't get "point loading." If your holes are too big or too small, or if your mast can't take the strain, you have a foul load.

Fair angles
The clevis pin on an external tang bisects the tang at right angles, if the holes are drilled in the right places. Likewise, the throughbolt must bisect the mast at right angles. If pins or bolts don't go through square, you have foul angles, and thus concentrated loads on some points.

True throughbolts
Ideally, both ends of the throughbolt will be threaded to hold nuts, which contain the tang laterally. That way you can remove a tang from either side without removing the entire assembly.

By far the most common tang flaw is bolt threading that extends under the tang; a bolt is weaker where it's threaded, and can invite corrosion, so this is a too-frequent failure point. Get your bolts threaded on a lathe so the threads stop at the tangs. This threading will also assure that there is no danger of buckling the mast wall when tightening the nuts.

fits naturally with all the other gear. If you're less than clear on the nature of the boat, a little study will help inform your selection decisions. For starters, take a look at the Portfolio of Rigs in Chapter 8.

Rigging involves not only the ability to turn up a good splice but to do it in the right materials in the right size, for the right boat. And to understand why.

STAYSAILS

It's called a staysail because it's attached to a stay. This is ironic, since a staysail is inclined to do anything *but* stay. It flaps and flops around when tacking, and is always demanding to be fussed with, even when you've settled on a course. It takes muscling to get it where it needs to go, and even after it's furled it's been known to go racing up the stay on its own if caught by a puff of wind. The time-honored method of reducing a staysail's intractability—lashing a boom to its foot so that it becomes self-tacking—also reduces its efficiency. And that can mean the difference between a daysail and a day-and-a-half sail, or between escaping a lee shore and calling your insurance agent.

The Basic Self-Tending Staysail
In the quest for sailing efficiency without corresponding muscular effort, people have concentrated on improved mechanical advantage (read: larger, more expensive winches) or easier sail handling (read: roller-furling/reefing devices). More on these two approaches later. Right now I'd like to take another look at self-tending staysails, because only a self-tending sail can relieve you of sailing's most arduous burden: tacking. And with intelligent design, loss of efficiency need not be great.

Headsail Prefeeding

With foil-mounted staysails mount two prefeeders at the base of the stay, one just below the foil, one on a short lanyard at the deck. The double prefeeders make for much smoother, quicker sail hoisting.

Galvanic Corrosion

Galvanic corrosion is a side effect of electrical activity. When metals of differing electrical potential are placed against each other, a little moisture and warmth is all it takes to form an electrical current. The metal with the lower potential is eaten away by the current.

So if you have, say, a stainless fastener in an aluminum mast, the aluminum, having the lower potential, will slowly turn into a white powder over time. Fortunately, it's easy to prevent galvanic corrosion in this situation by isolating the two metals. For fasteners, a little Tef-Gel or ECK on the fastener will do. For larger items such as winch bases, make a shim out of Mylar or UHMW tape to put between the fitting and the mast.

Below water, things are tougher, since the water conducts electrical current—the pieces don't even have to touch, and there's no way to isolate them. That's why boatbuilders strive to minimize dissimilar metals below the waterline, and why you put sacrificial zincs (zincs have low potential, so they get eaten instead of something more expensive) below the waterline.

For the rigger, almost everything is above the waterline and easy to isolate. The major exceptions are bobstays, boomkin shrouds, and centerboard pendants, which can spend a bit of time under water.

Bobstays are the worst, particularly on heavily-laden cruising boats. One way to lessen galvanic action is to minimize dissimilar metals. So if, for example, you're working on a wooden boat with bronze fasteners, use a bronze rod bobstay.

Another trick is to install a linkplate at the bottom end of the bobstay. This gets the stay up out of the water, leaving the slower-to-dissolve, cheaper-to-replace linkplate to take the heat.

Skip Green's Hank Rotation Method

Hanks on staysails wear most severely at the lower end of the sail, and the next most severe wear is at the top. To prolong hank life, use extra-large hanks at the top and bottom, and switch these two hanks when the wear on the lower one becomes severe. As an added step, also switch the second-lowest and second-highest hanks; they wear faster than the rest, but not fast enough to warrant oversizing.

First let's look at the traditional design (Figure 5-36). A block-and-tackle sheet slides on a traveler, for trim and some vanging action. The fall of the sheet runs forward under the boom to a turning block, then aft, for a fair sheet lead at any boom angle. You'll frequently see the forward end of the boom attached to the stay the sail is hanked to (Figure 5-36A). This greatly lowers sail efficiency, because the sail has the same shape whether it's sheeted in hard or eased when off the wind.

For more efficiency, try the second arrangement shown, in which the forward end of the boom swivels on a pedestal mounted on deck, aft of the base of the stay. When the sail is sheeted in, the boom stretches the foot of the sail out for a flatter shape. Off the wind, the difference between boom length and sail foot length causes the sail to become fuller for more efficient reaching and running.

Variations Mr. Angleman of Angleman Ketch fame came up with a nifty elaboration on the length-differential theme: attaching the forward end of the boom to a heavy-duty track (Figure 5-37). The turning block at the forward end is so mounted that it pulls the track car aft when the sail is sheeted

Figure 5-36. *Self-tending staysail configurations. A curved traveler provides more vanging action, especially if used in conjunction with adjustable cars on the traveler to control position of traveler sheet lead. Putting a turning block at the forward end of the boom reduces load on the deck block.*

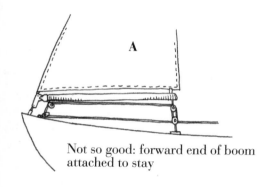

Not so good: forward end of boom attached to stay

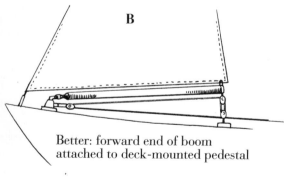

Better: forward end of boom attached to deck-mounted pedestal

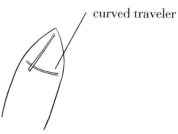

curved traveler

Staysail Tackle

A sheet configuration with a 2:1 advantage. A short pendant, or "lizard," ends in a block. The line rove through it is dead-ended to an eyebolt on the rail and passes aft through a fairlead, also on the rail.

This is the traditional arrangement for gaffers and square-riggers with relatively small staysails and large crews. On shorthanded boats, a small winch back by the belay can be used to set up the sheet when going to weather.

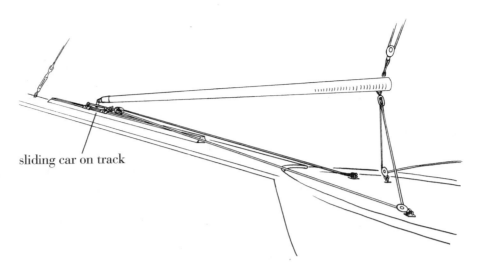

sliding car on track

Figure 5-37. *Mr. Angleman's improvement on the self-tending staysail.*

in and lets it slide forward when the sheet is eased, thus maximizing sail shape variation. As an added feature, the boom slides forward clear to the base of the stay when the sail is lowered, eliminating the need for luff jacklines.

A pedestal, used with or without a track, can help optimize sail shape but still leaves self-tending rigs weak in the efficient sheeting department. As the boom moves outboard when the sheet is eased, it also rises, and most tracks provide no more than a modicum of vanging action, so that sail shape suffers from an excessively open leech. A rising boom and baggy leech also make an accidental jibe much more likely—self-tending staysails are notorious foredeck depopulators.

One intricate and expensive way to deal with this is to install a curved traveler with locator blocks to position the sheet for different points of sailing (Figure 5-36). This works well, and can be used in conjunction with a sort of secondary sheet that varies the distance of the clew from the boom end. But self-tending staysails, a feature of shorthanded vessels, are prized because the sailors of those vessels disdain intricacy and expense every bit as much as inefficiency. Is there no simpler, cheaper way to efficient sheeting?

Some modern self-tending designs are based on the assumption that a small staysail isn't much good off the wind anyway—it's too flat and is often blanketed by the main—so they focus instead to optimize close-reaching and beating efficiency. My favorite self-tending gear for boomless staysails comes from Harken.

The Bierig Cambersail (Figure 5-38) incorporates a pivoting wishbone boom inside the sail, which simultaneously bears the luff/clew compression load and holds the sail in an airfoil shape, one optimized for on-the-wind sailing. The boom automatically flips to the leeward side when you tack. This sail, used with a forward-curving traveler, would have good offwind usefulness, but then again we're getting into intricacy.

So here's one more option: the Semi-Self-Tending Staysail (Figure 5-39). The club is controlled by two separate sheets, in the manner of a regular staysail. The deck blocks for the sheets are mounted well outboard and forward. The sheets can be a multi-part purchase, or get their mechanical advantage from a winch aft. For maximum sailing efficiency, the procedure is to use the weather sheet as a lateral boom locator and the leeward sheet as a vang (vertical locator) and preventer. When you tack,

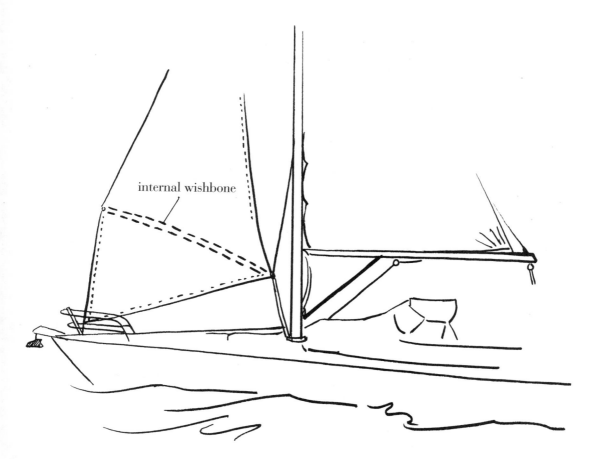

internal wishbone

Figure 5-38. *The Bierig Cambersail.*

ease the vang to let the boom swing across the deck. The vang now becomes a sheet. It's a simple matter to mark the sheets to indicate optimum settings for beating, reaching, or running angles. When the tack is complete, haul in on the old sheet to make it a vang/preventer.

If you're short-tacking or just feeling lazy, leave both sheets slack so each will function on alternate tacks. Not quite as efficient, but completely self-tending.

If your boat is a little slow in stays, leave the vang side belayed as you tack. This automatically "backs" the sail to help you through the wind. You can also back the sail in order to heave-to, and of course, the preventer is a wonderful crew-saver, making the foredeck a safer place when reaching. When you're in port, there's no traveler taking up space on the foredeck. And you can tighten one sheet and detach the other, for maximum lounging space.

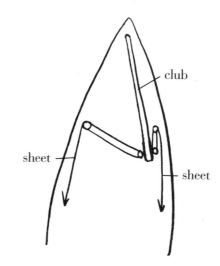

club

sheet

sheet

Figure 5-39. *The Semi-Self-Tending Staysail.*

The Semi-Self-Tending Staysail is a little more work than other systems, but is more efficient, versatile, and safe. There's no traveler to invest in, and no traveler to clutter up the deck.

Tackers

Boomless staysails, the ones you have to tack yourself, are a lot more work than their boomed brethren. Not only are the forces on them higher—no spar to take the load along the foot—but these sails are also usually larger than boomed staysails. Force on the sheets is related to sail area and apparent wind speed, so large sails on fast boats need stronger sheets. That's why you need big winches. This concentration of forces has implications outside the subject of sheets per se (see "Seaworthiness," page 167), but it's sheets we'll deal with here.

First and foremost, you have to attach the sheet to the sail. Most people tie on the sheets with Bowlines, and that's okay except that Bowlines frequently hang up on shrouds and stays in mid-tack. To minimize this, tie the port sheet left-handed and the starboard sheet right-handed (Figure 5-40).

Figure 5-40. *If you attach sheets to headsail clews with Bowlines, tie the port one left-handed and the starboard one right-handed to alleviate snagging when you tack.*

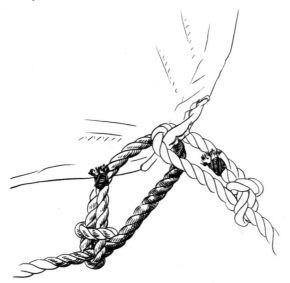

Another problem with Bowlines in these days of slippery, stiff, synthetic lines is that Bowlines can come untied. A locking tuck will fix this.

But even if you take the above measures, Bowlines are by no means the ideal sheet-attachment knot. Though supremely convenient, they weaken the line they're tied in by about 40 percent, in conventional synthetics, and much more than that in HM ropes. And they're just plain bulky and clumsy-looking out there on the corner of your sail. For braid only, the Brummel Splice (Figure 5-41) is a smooth, compact way to make both sheets from a single piece of line in minutes. This splice is removable, with a little work, but you have to unreeve both sheets to do it, so you would only undo this to wash the sheet (see also Figure 4-13).

Eyesplices, the strongest and most compact of all knots, are ideal sheet ends for braided or three-strand line, for sheets that are permanently attached to one sail. Unfortunately, your sailmaker is going to be very unhappy with you if you bring a sail in for inspection or repair with sheets attached. Permanent attachment also means that you can't switch the sheets to other sails. So if you use the same set of sheets for more than one sail, or if you have a reefable staysail, splices are out—you need an easily detachable attachment. One alternative is to splice each sheet to a shackle, or both sheets to one shackle. Expedient, but shackles can come undone, are costly, and are hard—as in hit-you-in-the-face-when-the-sail-is-flogging hard. Fortunately we now have the Grail of sheet attachment: the Spectra soft shackle (see page 388). With one of these, you can put eyesplices into the ends of your sheets, and shackle them to the clew without creating an active hazard (though note that, if the sail is flogging hard enough, even a soft item is hard enough to hurt you if it hits you). You can use lighter, thinner sheets than you ever could with Bowlines, so the sheets won't drag the clew down in light airs. You can change or reef sails, replace each sheet independently, etc. Plus you'll have happy sailmakers.

This chapter began with some nice, safe, linear formulas. But those formulas are put to work in the service of wildly varying human preferences, based

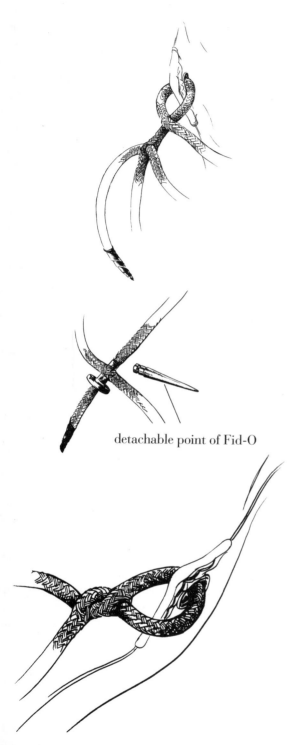

Figure 5-41A. *To make the Brummel Splice, middle the sheet through the clew. Using a Fid-O Awl or similar tool, tuck one end through the opposite standing part just below the clew. Now tuck the other end through the first end's standing part a couple of inches away. Draw up. To make tucking easier, pull out and cut off a few inches of core from the ends, then work all slack out of the covers and tape the ends to a point.*

detachable point of Fid-O

Figure 5-41B. *A finished Brummel Splice—smooth, strong, secure.*

on diverse human assumptions of what will work. The only reason that chaos isn't the rule is that all these formulas and preferences are formed with regard to the ocean, which doesn't care what we like and which will smash us if we don't take it fully, earnestly into account.

"Taking the ocean into account" is as close a definition as I can come to for the term "seaworthy." It's not a term as readily reducible to formula as mast design, but like a lot of other things, you can know it when you see it. In the next section you'll find an utterly subjective view of seaworthiness, with the emphasis on matters affecting rig integrity. Think of it as right-brain design.

SEAWORTHINESS

"There are four kinds of seafarers under sail: dead; retired; novices; and pessimists."
—Tristan Jones

A client once came to me wanting to know how to run his exterior-mounted chainplates around or through the unusually tall bulwarks he had built onto his boat. He was a thoughtful, meticulous man, and I was sure he had a specific reason for his bulwarks' height. So I asked him, and he pointed to his feet and said, "My sneakers."

It turns out what he meant was that if his boat ever approached knockdown, the bulwarks were tall enough that he could stand in them, in relative security, while dealing with getting the boat back up. If I were to give his attitude a name, I would say it was "seaworthy."

Monohull sailors commonly deride provisions, in seagoing multihulls, for living in the hull with the hull upside down. "Why," the complaint goes, "don't they just get a boat that won't capsize?" But well-designed multihulls are very, very difficult to capsize (see "The Transverse Righting Moment Curve," later in this chapter); these provisions are just "sneaker bulwark" prudence. They are seaworthy.

Contrast that with the experience of a friend who'd been foredeck crew in a racing monohull one day. His boat won, and he began jumping up and down for joy. "Stop," shouted the afterguard, "you'll go through the deck!" Obsessive paring away of weight is a hallmark of racing craft, and this vessel's foredeck, where people had to work in often strenuous circumstances, was deemed strong enough if it could just support a cautious sailor. That is not seaworthy.

Seaworthiness is very difficult to define. Seaworthy vessels are strong, but how strong? Easy to steer, but how easy? Have a gentle motion, but how to quantify gentleness? To compound things, the popular perception is that the more "seaworthy" a vessel is, the slower and more sluggish it is. Is this true? To what extent? And why? To answer these questions we must start with:

Effects of Engineering

In terms of rigging, there's essentially just one question: Is it strong enough? That is, regardless of the seaworthiness of the hull, is the rigging likely to hold together under the loads the hull will put on it? But an appropriate rig is intimately wedded to its hull; in order to answer our single question, we must look at many others, like the ones in the preceding paragraph. The formulas earlier in this chapter gave us basic integrity, but now we will be looking for subtler, more elusive harmony.

When engineers design a structure, they must determine not only *whether* it is strong enough, but for *how long* it will be strong enough. They consider a structure overdesigned if it does not break within predicted and/or acceptable time, for a particular use, at a particular intensity. But they do not always, or even usually, know what constitutes perfect design. Thus, structures tend to oscillate in quality

as they are characterized by failure, then lack of failure. As long as no novel parameters or designs are introduced, it should be possible to approach ideal specs. But design is often about novelty, about new scale, new ideas, new materials. And everything is skewed and qualified by human error, neglect, and abuse, by human ingenuity at introducing unexpected factors into the execution of a design, or human inability to predict Nature's introduction of such factors, and of course human obstinacy, preventing quality even when it is available.

In sailing, we seem to have gone from an over-built-but-unimaginative period (traditional) to an underbuilt-but-novel design state. We have found improved performance in some cases, and drastically reduced safety factors in nearly all. In this phase, even seemingly overbuilt items can fail; their novelty mandates that not all consequences have been anticipated. For example, I had a client who, in the interest of "better performance," invested in carbon fiber masts for his ketch. These were excellent masts, built to hefty cruising standards as these things go. He went ocean racing, and all was well until a spinnaker halyard block parted in a breeze. The halyard led from the head of the sail, through the block, then into the mast a few feet below the block. So when the block broke, the load of the sail came on the entry hole in the mast. It was an immensely strong mast, but its fibers were oriented vertically, to take expected loads. The halyard imposed an unexpected load, ripping a 7-foot gash in the face of the mast, right down *between* the fibers. Builders of carbon masts have learned from incidents like this, and as a result their masts have become more seaworthy. Or at least some of them have; remember, the biggest reason to invest in a carbon fiber mast is to improve performance, and this isn't always compatible with durability and safety.

Effects of Attitude

A boat grows, bit by bit, out of the attitude of the designer and builder. The client with the sneaker bulwarks is also likely to pay similar attention to handholds, engine access, navigation—he'll build himself a livable world. And the multihuller who makes careful provision for being upside down will devote even more attention to the far, far likelier state of being upright. And it also follows that the skipper of the thin-decked boat will be edgy not just about the deck, but about the mast, the stability of the vessel, and the stamina of the crew.

Effects of Ignorance

But there's more to seaworthiness than attitude; very careful, well-intentioned people can go very wrong from simple technical ignorance. Take, for example the couple whose interior decorator thought their keel-stepped mast took up too much room below. Here's what resulted:

The couple paid a yard to convert to a deck-stepped rig. No one involved in the project realized that deck-stepped masts have to be stiffer than keel-stepped ones of the same length. So they just put in a skinny little compression post, cut the bottom off of their keel-stepped mast, and didn't realize their mistake until the first time they took the new configuration sailing. Then this mast, which had taken them around the world with no problem, revealed that it was now about 40 percent less stiff, jumping and bouncing around, frighteningly close to folding.

Back to the yard to have a "sleeve" inserted in the mast to stiffen it. Now the mast is okay (if much heavier, but the decorator has wreaked other havoc). In changing around the accommodations, he's eliminated a bulkhead on the port side, amidships, a structural bulkhead where the inboard chainplates used to attach. The starboard shroud chainplates still attach to a corresponding bulkhead, but the port ones now go to a big tie-rod that pierces the cabin sole, attaching to a lug on the hull. Tie-rod and lug are both massively strong, as is the clevis pin that connects them. But the worker who does the installation doesn't bring along the right size cotter pin. The ones he has are a little too big, but he jams one in about halfway, and decides that it is good enough. The sole covers up this arrangement, and it is never noticed by even the very maintenance-conscious owners. Over several years the cotter works its way out; then the clevis gradually wiggles free; then one day in a fine breeze the port shroud chainplate comes up through the deck, and the top of the mast goes over the side.

There was nothing wrong with wanting a comfortable, workable interior. And nothing wrong with properly engineered deck-stepped masts or chainplate tie-rods, or proper-sized cotter pins. What was wrong was the assumption that any of these items could be considered separately, that all of the details of construction would be naturally and inevitably comprehensible. One of the most profound and challenging joys of sailing lies in mastering the intricacies of a little floating world. It's just dangerous to presume mastery.

Effects of Culture

It is difficult to see through the assumptions and norms of one's own society—they're so reflexively there—and yet they shape our craft at least as much as the ocean does.

Consider, for example, the great racing yachts of the turn of the last century. Here was the last gasp of a feudal society, complete with a hierarchy of indolent aristocrats, knight-helmspeople, and forelock-tugging menials. The boats were the size of castles, and the entire ocean was a moat.

Or consider the recently vanished sailing junk of China. Here was a trading vessel which contained a complete merchant community/family. These easily handled boats were designed around a vastly different social and economic order than that of the European yachts, and the result was a correspondingly different design, construction, and handling.

Now look at a typical IOR racer of the past decades. What are we to make of this incredibly expensive, fragile, ill-handling craft? What are we to make of the human ballast that lines its rail, of the vestigial mainsail, of the ludicrously large headsails? If we see these craft as "normal" or "desirable," it might just be because of some unfortunate conditioning.

Effects of Hype

Shortcomings in attitude, education, and culture lead to shortcomings in boats. And that, in our era, has led to vastly profitable "solutions." These are generally based on sound principles, but are hyped to mask the nature of the flaws they are supposed to solve.

For example, we've all seen boats trumpeted as having "all control lines led aft, so you never have to leave the comfort and safety of the cockpit." But the question arises: When did the area outside the cockpit became uncomfortable and dangerous? Similar hype exists for roller-furling headsails, which save us from "venturing onto a heaving, wet foredeck."

It is true that aft-led control lines are a boon for singlehanders and racers, for speed and convenience. And it's true that roller-furling has opened sailing up to a lot of non-acrobats. But that's not the same thing as danger and discomfort being vanquished by these devices. I believe that it's no coincidence that this "comfort and safety" concern arose with the dominance of the IOR. If you have a wet, skittish boat, you'll leap at any gizmo that promises to make life a little less alarming.

And in any event, the "solutions" themselves have downsides: When the roller-furling mechanism breaks, jams, or otherwise goes into a snit, usually in high winds and seas, you have to go onto that foredeck anyway, armed with a crescent wrench and a lifejacket; and aft-led lines can overflow a cockpit in a hurry, making it a crowded, confusing place. It can be enough to make you want to escape to the comfort and safety of an office building.

To compound things, hype has obscured a host of simpler, more dependable, and invariably cheaper alternatives. One dramatic example is the "trapdoor" for staysails aboard Linda and Steve Dashew's *Sundeer* (see Chapter 8). Instead of being fixed on deck, the forestays and jibstays run right through trapdoors to the keel. Lowering the stay-

sails is a matter of opening the doors and slacking away the halyards. The entire sail inventory is stowed in the room below the doors, where they can be hanked on or off in a cockpit-surpassing level of comfort and security.

The *Sundeer* approach would be hard to retrofit to most boats, but how about this one: bear off. That is, when it's time to deal with headsails, change your heading to bring the wind abeam. The boat's motion will be much gentler, the mainsail will blanket the headsail, and the apparent wind will be much less. It's amazing how few sailors think of this, but then we've all been overly influenced by the press-on-regardless acrobatics of racing.

There are many other ways to respond to boat handling challenges, rig-related and otherwise. But no matter how effective these responses may be they are only Band-Aids, things we do after the damage has been done, unless we employ them as part of a conscious design sensibility. I do not want to, and in any event am not equipped to, write a comprehensive treatise on yacht design. What I do want, as a rigger, is to understand how details of rig and hull can be optimally interrelated, and I have found that a few design considerations can help illuminate this question.

The Transverse Righting Moment Curve

Earlier in this chapter (see "Shroud Loads") the transverse righting moment (RM) curve (Figures 5-22, 5-23, 5-24) revealed the maximum load that the rig would have to bear. But this curve can also reveal a lot about how a given hull will behave in varying conditions, and thus what kind of rig design details are appropriate.

Figure 5-23 shows the RM curves of three vessels: a cruising trimaran, a racing monohull, and the Dashews' Deerfoot design.

The tri's curve rises very steeply until about 25 degrees, then plummets abruptly. From 90 degrees to 180 degrees the hull is in "negative stability"; that is, it wants to remain upside down. The racing monohull's curve rises less sharply, peaking at about 55 degrees, then drops—also less sharply, entering negative stability at about 115 degrees. Note that the monohull's maximum negative stability is considerably less than that of the trimaran; the monohull will be easier to right. The stability curve for this boat as sailed will have a much steeper initial section, since such boats invariably carry large crews, most of whose members spend much of their time perched on the weather rail to provide ballast. Thus the boat can stand up to breezes without being slowed down by extra in-keel lead ballast.

The curve of the Deerfoot, also a monohull, rises most gradually of all, but enjoys a long plateau, peaking at about 60 degrees. Then it drops slowly, but look! It maintains positive stability right through 135 degrees, and the maximum negative stability is very small. Should this boat ever be capsized, she'll be boosted back on her feet almost immediately by any modest passing wave.

None of these curves is "bad" or "good," although they are often interpreted as such. Monohullers, for example, never tire of deriding the spectacular range and intensity of multihull negative stability, but fair consideration is hardly ever given to the equally spectacular range of positive stability.

Multihullers are just as nasty about putting down monohulls. "Lead mines," they call them, in which you are always "sailing on your ear." But this is just a way of saying that, with a combination of pendulum stability (the "lead mine" in the keel) and form stability (the buoyancy of the hull), a monohull bends before the wind, spilling gusts instead of taking them full on. For a given displacement, a multihull's sails, rigging, and hulls must be much more strictly and heavily engineered, since they literally have to stand up to every gust. It is good practice to make multihull rigging at least 50 percent heavier than rigging for a monohull of the same displacement.

Multihullers and racing monohullers do agree on one subject: that cruising monohulls are too slow and too heavy. But although the cruiser won't sail as upright, it has a higher ultimate resistance to knockdown or capsize. And if it ever is capsized, it will tend come back upright. For some people, this can be a compellingly attractive feature.

So there are pluses and minuses to each design

approach, the details of which I've barely touched upon. And there are plenty of boats in each category whose vices far outweigh their virtues. By studying transverse stability curves, we can get an idea of how to maximize the virtues and minimize the vices of each type of craft.

To build a better trimaran, for instance, we'd work to make it still harder to tip over, whether from wave action, "tripping" on the outer hulls, or any other reason. And we'd probably try to make un-capsizing easier, just in case. And this is what good multihull designers try to do.

The cruising monohull can be improved by making the stability curve steeper in the first 30 degrees, if this can be done without sacrificing ultimate stability. This generally involves lowering the vessel's center of gravity and fussing with the amount and location of the ballast. Comparing Figures 5-22 and 5-23, you can see that while the righting arm of the Ohlson 38A—a conservative, wholesome cruising monohull—is 1.5 feet at 30 degrees of heel, the 30-degree righting arm for Steve Dashew's *Sundeer* is over 2 feet. *Sundeer* has almost no form stability, but Steve sweated to get all the weight down low. This low center of gravity, combined with a perfectly balanced hull, made for a very stiff ocean cruiser. It can be done.

Racing monohulls are not so susceptible to improvements in seaworthiness. They could be, but their sailors are inclined to sacrifice everything to going well to weather. That and rating rules (see

---

Stability Attrition

Yacht design since the 1960s has followed a steady downward trend in terms of stability. According to C. A. Marchaj (*Seaworthiness: The Forgotten Factor*, International Marine, 1987; Adlard Coles Nautical, 1986), "The positive area under the righting moment curve has been reduced to less than half, and at the same time the negative area has increased dramatically."

Marchaj also notes that the angle of vanishing stability has been reduced from about 180 degrees to about 120 degrees, and that the righting moment maximum is now "about half of that characteristic of the traditional yacht form."

below) pretty much hamper virtue. But even here, responsible designers and rule-making bodies can prevent the worst excesses of unseaworthiness.

Fore-and-Aft Stability

The transverse righting moment curve is only the simplest, most accessible of many seaworthiness-indicating factors, and it is by no means definitive. C. sA. Marchaj addresses these other factors in his book *Seaworthiness: The Forgotten Factor*. Many of those factors are outside the scope of rigging per se. I'll touch briefly on just one, an item of gratifyingly far-reaching significance, and one we can study without having to decode any of Mr. Marchaj's graphs and formulas.

A hull also describes a curve of fore-and-aft stability, again dependent on hull form and ballast amount and location. A heavy vessel, fat at bow and stern on the waterline, will be very stiff fore-and-aft, but with so much hull dragging through the water it will also be very slow. By making the hull—and particularly the bow—relatively skinny at the waterline, but flaring above it, you get minimum resistance to forward motion in light conditions, but "reserve buoyancy" in heavier conditions, when the hull will tend to dip at the ends. The amount and degree of flare is crucial. Too little too high will not keep the bow from diving, or might result in a "hobbyhorse" motion. Too much down low, and the hull will slap and pound in a sea.

Ultimate fore-and-aft stability must be sufficiently high to discourage the somersaulting action known as "pitchpoling." As with transverse loads, sometimes wind and waves can gang up on the most stable vessel, but good design can minimize a flip in either direction.

To sum up, we've worked out stability in two planes, and seen that this stability must be played off against sailing performance. Different hull types and sailing styles, of course, demand different stability compromises. And if this were all there were to the question of stability, rigging sailboats would be a much simpler subject. But aside from matters of preference like rig configuration and materials,

there's one big monkey wrench deeply lodged in the design works.

Rating Rules

The noble, sensible, sporting idea behind most rating rules, which address hull and rig designs, is to provide a basis for comparison among vessels, so that they might be assigned appropriate handicaps for even competition. In yacht racing, handicaps take the form of time allowances; a favorably rated (ostensibly "slow") yacht can finish a race well behind its competitors and still win if its handicap allowance is great enough. This seems fair enough, but rules have historically had unfortunate effects on the integrity of the vessels built to suit those rules. Designers and sailors naturally want to see their boats finish first, and creative exploitation of rules can give them ways to do this without necessarily making the boats go any faster, let alone be more comfortable, stable, or stout.

So, for example, rules often "tax" the waterline length, since in theory a vessel's maximum non-planing speed is approximately 1.1 times the square root of the waterline length. An easy way to exploit such a rule is to design a vessel very short on the waterline, but with great long overhangs at bow and stern. When the vessel heels under sail, more hull length is submerged. As a result, the boat will sail faster than the rule predicts.

The history of sailing rule-making is essentially an endless exercise in loophole-plugging. So rules have grown ever more Byzantine, and hull shapes have grown ever more bizarre in attempts to exploit the endlessly generated loopholes.

The International Offshore Rule (IOR), which predominated from the 1970s into the late 1980s, was originally intended to be an all-time loophole-plugger. But its creators underestimated the resourcefulness of—and perhaps overestimated the principles of—yacht designers. In a nutshell, boats that most successfully exploited the rule were very fine forward, very beamy aft, high-sided, lightly built (rig weights in the 1980s were typically a third lighter than in the 1960s), and relied heavily on human ballast for something like transverse stability. Fore-and-aft stability was severely compromised, making for very wet (read: submerged) foredecks, and the area and degree of negative stability was very high. Many IOR boats became negatively stable at angles less than 120 degrees. Knockdowns and dismastings became commonplace, and crews suffered from the discomfort of riding in sharp-motioned, skittish, wet boats.

Sounds like pure hell, doesn't it? But to make things even worse, these boats were also incredibly expensive and had huge, hard-to-handle staysails. I'm speaking of them in the past tense, but in fact IOR-style boats continue to have a presence in the marketplace. I mention them here partly as a diatribe against their continued existence, but mostly because they make a great Bad Example, illuminating the relationship between fore-and-aft and transverse stability.

When a vessel is at rest and upright, form and ballast stability make it float on its lines. If it doesn't, and if it's not too far off, moving ballast or gear around will level it. This is extremely important, because the boat will only go where you point it to the extent that it pushes through the water in a balanced fashion. If there's too much hull in the water forward, the force of the water will push the bow to windward, resulting in weather helm. A common response to this is to rake the mast forward, since this moves the sail area forward, reducing weather helm. But it's usually much simpler and more effective to leave the rigging out of it and just trim the hull down aft. Conversely, a hull trimmed too much aft will generate lee helm.

But fore-and-aft trim is a tricky thing; most vessels trim differently when heeled than they do when upright, because the shape of the hull in the water is no longer symmetrical, as it is when the boat is upright. This is hard to avoid, since you want a boat to be fine forward to move easily, yet have a beamy midsection to resist heeling. But when you do heel, that beamy midsection gets submerged, and is a lot more buoyant than the corresponding area on that skinny bow. So most boats nose down as they

Efficiency

Cost and structural vulnerability increase exponentially with sailing efficiency. So a well-built, moderately efficient boat will cost far less and be far more durable than a well-built highly efficient boat.

heel and their weather helm increases, no matter how beautifully balanced they are when upright. To counteract heel-induced weather helm, sailors will (a) reef the main, which moves the center of effort down and forward, or (b) move the draft of the sails forward using mast bend or luff tension, or (c) both.

Here is a place the rigger can shine, using the running and standing rigging not just to deliver power but to balance the helm. That is, unless the hull is so sensitive to heel that no amount of rig adjustment can make it right. A worst-case scenario for riggers was the nose-diving, broach-prone IOR fleet. About all a rigger can do for these boats is to help keep people in the cockpit. And as noted earlier in this chapter, that's what roller-furling, aft-led control lines, and other conveniences have done. But ameliorating the effects of bad design does not constitute seaworthiness. For many boats, adding sail-control conveniences is like putting a muzzle on a rabid dog.

Side Effects

There's an old saying that "if you take care of the molehills, the mountains will take care of themselves." A seaworthy rig is one in which the molehills are taken care of. A vessel shaped by concern for bulwarks, handholds, human comfort, longevity, simplicity, and a zillion other details can be engineered to acceptable standards of Speed, Weatherliness, and Maneuverability. But it is an oft-demonstrated fact that vessels dedicated only to Speed, Weatherliness, and Maneuverability are possessed of precious little else. Take care of the molehills, and the mountains will tend to take care of themselves. Take care of the mountains, and the molehills will just drag you down.

Another effect is lowered cost. Gear for racing rigging is ruinously expensive, with the price rising exponentially for every tenth of a knot gained. Cruising gear may be heavy, but you don't pay for frantic engineering.

A third side effect is peace. Once you get out of obsessive race mode, you enter a world in which dismastings are rare, which means you don't have to sweat bullets worrying about a dismasting all the time. Seaworthy rigs sometimes do go overboard, but when they do, it is usually from gear failure, not scantling failure. That is, while a racing mast will collapse because it's just too flimsy to withstand a little extra load, a sensibly scaled mast will do so because something—a clevis pin, a tang, a bolt—has worn out, and the sailors have just not attended to it.

This brings up one last side effect: Molehill care makes you part of the boat, brings you into its life. There are few enough sane reasons to go sailing; no need to throw out the elegant relationship possible between humans and their vessels.

CHAPTER 6

Loft Procedures

My loft is a factory, library, warehouse, office, laboratory, store, and museum. There I can contemplate and execute in a place made just for making rigs.

To hear me talk, you'd think this was some sort of intricately detailed, gizmo-filled fantasy shop, but it's really just a room in an old Odd Fellows Hall where I've bolted down some tools, filled the shelves with other tools and materials, and gone to work. There isn't anything I do in there that I couldn't and haven't done while up a mast, but I'd much rather work where everything is ready to hand. A rigging loft makes difficult work easy.

This chapter covers some of traditional rigging's most involved procedures: advanced ropework and ways to make a gang of rigging fit. You will find that the most difficult part of mastering these procedures lies not in comprehending their intricacies, but in training your hands and eyes; you must develop skill. Make your loft conducive to this. Make it quiet, uncluttered, orderly, and well lit. See to it that your tools are of appropriate size and good quality. Collect reference books. Leave a space where you can sit and think. Rigging work might take up only a small corner of your life in a small corner of your shop or garage, but it is sufficiently involved, in itself and in its relationship with other arts, that it requires no slight accommodation on your part before you can expect to do it well.

MEASUREMENT

Will it fit? God, what a headache of a question. Will it fit? Completing standing-rigging fabrication in the loft is the most efficient method, but you're in there, the boat's out there, and every time you turn up an end you ask yourself once again, "Will it fit?" Sometimes you can't stand the worry or can't get sufficiently precise measurements for confident cutting. Then you can splice the upper end in the loft, leave lots of extra length, and splice the lower end in place. It sounds convenient but seldom is; your working platform is crowded or moving or both, and it is wet, or cold, or hot, and you can't keep track of your tools, and there are too many people looking over your shoulder, and believe it or not there's still a very good chance you'll make a mistake in measurement. Better to work it all out at the loft, using measurement routines that are sufficiently precise and redundant to muffle that recurrent question, if not silence it.

Replacing an Old Rig

We'll start with a piece of cake, a little sloop whose gang has gone brittle. You want to replace it all with the same diameter and construction of wire. Get a notebook and pen and study the boat while the old gang is still in it, to see whether the last rigger

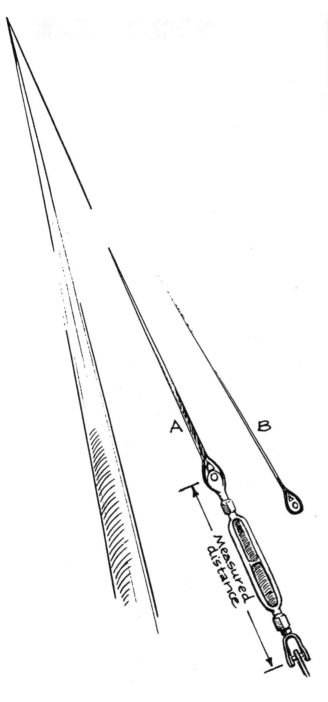

This is the most tradition-intensive chapter in the book, and some topics, like wire splicing and seizing, will apply only to wire rope. But much of what follows can apply wholly or in part to making rigs out of Spectra. Measuring is measuring, and thimbles are thimbles, after all. So even if you never want to pick up a piece of wire in your life, you can find valuable information here. No surprise, really; wire rigging is, after all, the attempt of a previous generation to do with wire what they had previously done with rope. A couple of hundred years later, we are just running things the other way.

measured right; no sense duplicating someone else's mistakes.

First of all, check the turnbuckles:

1. Are they overextended or two-blocked (both threads drawn as close together as possible)? List each piece and note how much longer or shorter the new one will need to be.

2. Are they toggled? Frequently not. Make a note to subtract the length of a toggle from the new piece.

3. Are they the right size? Heavier turnbuckles are longer; lighter ones, shorter. Consult Table 5 to see whether wire and turnbuckle sizes match If not, measure from the existing thimble's clevis-pin centerline to the chainplate's clevis-pin centerline and note the distance (Figure 6-1). Determine whether

Figure 6-1. *Determine the appropriate size turnbuckle for a given wire size and construction, then measure the distance between the chainplate and thimble on the old rig (A). In this instance, the old turnbuckle is too large and two-blocked. If the distance is longer or shorter than the half-extended proper turnbuckle with toggle, add or subtract accordingly for the new wire length (B).*

There's more to measuring a log than seeing how long and wide it is. More often than not it involves fighting your way over difficult terrain while lugging heavy, awkward tools, without even the luxury of a helper to hold the quiet end of the tape for you. And loggers, paid by the board foot, have no time for cranking conventional long tapes up with those silly little handles.

That's why loggers use logger's tapes, often called Spenser Tapes after their original and still preeminent manufacturer. A logger's tape clips to a belt loop, so it's always out of the way but instantly usable. The tape blade is narrow, flexible, reads on both sides, and comes in 50-, 75-, and 100-foot lengths. Repair kits are available, so an errant saw cut won't necessitate buying a new blade. After multiple cuts and kinks, clever little refill kits defang the powerful spring mechanism for safe, easy reloading.

Logger's tapes are a measurement revelation for sailmakers, carpenters, riggers, and any other trade involving large-scale layout, because they leave both hands free to hold tools, pens, or clipboards, and because they can be used without a helper. To accomplish the latter, loggers customarily attach a horseshoe nail or the like to the tape bail. They lightly tap the nail into one end of the log, walk away, letting the tape unspool itself, get the measurement, then retrieve the tape with a light tug. The nail pulls out and the tape winds itself up.

A nail works well for carpenters and sailmakers, but is uncool procedure around varnished wooden spars and impossible around aluminum ones. But an alligator clip and piece of twine make an excellent rigger's alternative. Remove the bit of insulation from the clip, then use the point of an awl to open up the little tube where the wiring is supposed to fit. With a pair of pliers, crimp the tube on around the side of the tape bail. Hitch a two-foot length of twine onto the end of the bail. With some clips, there is a hole near the end into which you can insert an end of the bail at the end of the tape. To get access to this end, push a fat spike into the bail, so its ends get pushed sideways until they pop out of the tape. Warning: use a small clamp to secure the tape end; without the bail it can easily get sucked into the tape body, and merrily unwind. Once you have the bail clear, slip the clip

onto it, return the bail to the tape end, and remove the clamp. You can now measure anything. You can hitch the string onto the standing part of a halyard, above the shackle and splice, for a true deck-to-sheave measurement (always tie the other end of the halyard—or some other line—through the shackle bail as a downhaul).

To measure a shroud, start at the center of the chainplate clevis pin and measure up a short distance, say four inches. Mark the turnbuckle there, with tape or a pen. Tie or clip the tape measure on below this point, and adjust the string until the "0" point is on the mark. Later on you can deduct for an ideal turnbuckle length, terminal, etc. (see text). Then go aloft, both hands free, to the other end. On deck or ashore you can hitch the tape and the item to be measured to the same cleat, post, stanchion, etc. Adjust the string length to your "0" point, and walk away. By clipping the alligator jaws onto just enough of the string to hold securely, you can tug the end loose when you're done, and watch the tape snake its rapid way back to your side.

Of course there is nothing the matter with having help while measuring. If it is available, simply clip the end of the tape to a lifeline or handrail before going up. The person handling this end can get it later. Or you can send the end to the deck if needed: pass a carabiner through the bail, clip the carabiner around a stay or line that goes to the deck uninterrupted, and slide it down.

the new turnbuckle exceeds or falls short of that length, and adjust the new wire length accordingly. If the distance is 1 foot but the current turnbuckle is ridiculously heavy, the new turnbuckle might be, say, 8 inches long.

The new wire will be 4 inches longer than the old one.

Next, check to see whether shackles have been added aloft or alow to extend the wire; note their length. See that chainplate, tang, and stem fittings

When laying out a new rig, pay close attention to hardware compatibility. Do the thimbles fit into the turnbuckles, tangs, and shackles? Are all clevis pin holes the same size, and do they line up? If you're installing a jib foil or other rollerish fitting, is the wire size compatible? Are all components of comparable strength? Rigging layout involves a lot more than length.

are in good condition and lead properly, and find out whether the owner (if you are not the owner) intends to alter or replace any of them. If the upper terminals are spliced or seized soft eyes, see if they are of sufficiently large circumference to lead fairly from the mast (Figure 6-2). Try to think of any other variables peculiar to the particular boat and rig. When you can't think of anything else to note, remove the mast, tag all the pieces, and bring them back to your shop.

On a stretch of floor longer than the longest piece of the rig, lay out a tape measure; drive all but 2 or 3 inches of a large nail in at point "0," making sure "0" is not in the middle of a doorway or other traveled area. For long-term convenience, you might want to mark and number 1-foot intervals on the floor and use a short tape or measuring stick to measure smaller increments from these marks for each piece.

Now go off to the stationer, get an accounting pad, and fill it in as in Figure 6-3. In this case we have a pair of lower shrouds and one upper shroud on each side, plus forestay and jibstay. The "Diameter/Construction" is a uniform $3/16$-inch 7 x 7. "Configuration" is thimbled splice ("Th.") at both ends, and the combined turnbuckle and toggle length for all pieces is 11 inches.

Skipping over to "Notes," we might enter something like:

"All shroud turnbuckles correct diameter ($5/16$ inch) and at consistent $1/2$ extension [ideal] but lack toggles. Subtract $1^1/2$ inches from all shroud lengths to fit toggles.

"Forestay has overextended $3/8$-inch turnbuckle and two shackles. Stay too short. Space between

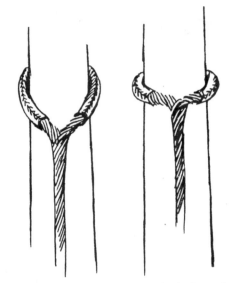

Figure 6-2. *Soft eyes should lead fairly from the mast (left); avoid a soft eye so small that considerable lateral strain comes on it (right).*

thimble head and stem fitting: 16 inches. Add 5 inches to new forestay length, to leave 11 inches space for $5/16$-inch turnbuckle and toggle.

"The $5/16$-inch jibstay turnbuckle two-blocked, no toggle. Space between thimble bottom and stem fitting: $7^3/4$ inches. No slack in jibstay w/ two-blocked turnbuckle, so subtract $3^1/2$ inches from length to fit extended turnbuckle and toggle."

Get out the starboard after lower shroud, set one thimble over the nail, stretch the wire, and check its length to the bottom of the other thimble. According

Table 5. Matching Wire and Turnbuckle Sizes				
Turnbuckle Size Thread diameter (in.)	Tensile Strength (lbs.)		Jaw Width (in.)	
	Bronze	Galv. steel	Bronze (wire size 1x19)	Galv. steel (wire size 7x7 or 7x19)
$1/4$	2,750	2,500	$1/4$ ($1/8$)	$13/32$ ($3/32$)
$5/16$	4,300	4,000	$5/16$ ($5/32$)	$15/32$ ($3/16$)
$3/8$	6,500	6,000	$3/8$ ($3/16$)	$1/2$ ($3/32$-$1/4$)
$7/16$	9,000	9,300	$7/16$ ($7/32$)	$9/16$ ($5/16$)
$1/2$	10,300	11,000	$1/2$ ($1/4$-$9/32$)	$5/8$ ($3/8$)
$5/8$	17,000	17,500	$5/8$ ($5/16$-$3/8$)	$3/4$ ($7/16$)
$3/4$	29,000	26,000	$3/4$ ($7/16$)	$15/16$ ($1/2$)
$7/8$	43,500	36,000	$7/8$ ($1/2$)	$1^1/8$ ($5/8$)
1	56,500	50,000	1 ($5/8$)	$1^3/16$ ($3/4$)

Piece	Diam/Const.	Conf Top/Bottom	Old Length	Fin. Length	Thimble Circ/Length	Soft Eye Circ/Length	NOTES
1. Std Main lower shroud	7/16 /7x7	Th.Th	29'	23'6"	7"/12"	2'6"	Big Sty eye, has wire throat seizing
2. Pt. Main lower shroud			29'2	23'6		2'6	to form 4'4' eye.
3. Std Main int. shroud			39'6	34'		2'4	
4. Pt. Main int. shroud			40'	34'6		2'4	Marline serve shrouds 2' above thimbles
5. Std Lower R.B. pend.			29'8	24'		2'4	
6. Pt. Lower R.B. pend.			29'8	24'		2'4	Seize ring to each main int shroud
7. Spare strop	5/16 /7x7	Grommet				3'	1' above thimble eye. Seize ring with
8. Triatic strop						2'6	shackle to thimble of port forward
9. Triatic Stay	7/8 /7x7	Th.Th	14'6	11'6	8"/13"		foremast shroud.
10. Fisherman Peak haly strop	5/16 /7x7	Grommet				2'3	
11. Springstay		S.Eye/Th	2'2"	20'6		1'2	Eliminate strain from backstay. Use 1/2"
12. Std Upper R.B. Pend.	5/16 /7x19	Th.Th	51'6	48'3		1'2	turnbuckle instead of 3/8 provided. Use 1/2
13. Pt. Upper R.B. pend.			51'6	48'3		1'2	std thimble with marline service under.
14. Std Main upper shr.	3/8 /7x7	S.Eye/Th	58'1	48'		1'4	
15. Pt. Main upper shr.			58'1	49'		1'4	Eliminate turnbuckle on springstay?
16. Main topping lift strop	1/4 /7x7	Grommet				2'3	
17. Std Forward foremast shroud	3/8 /7x7	S.Eye/Th	36'2	31'6		1'5	Triatic strop has 22" eye, seized
18. Pt. Forward foremast shroud			36'2	31'6		1'5	around thimble. Use 1/2" shackle.
19. Std Aft foremast shroud			30'	25'6		2'4	
20. Pt. Aft foremast shroud			30'	25'6		2'4	
21. Forestay strop	5/16 /7x7	Grommet				2'4	
22. Forestay		Th.Th	30'7	27'			
23. Throat halyard strop		S.Eye/Th	5'6			2'1	
24. Jib halyard strop			4'6			1'5	
25. Jibstay	7/16 /7x7		40'5	34'6	8"/12 1/2"	1'8	

Figure 6-3. *To expedite layout organization, list rigging pieces, their pertinent dimensions, and any notes on an accounting pad.*

Table 6. Wire Rope Constructional Stretch as Percentage of Length *(Courtesy MacWhyte Co.)*

	7x19	7x7	1x19
Galv. steel	0.25	0.06	0.018
Stainless steel	0.33	0.07	0.021

to our notes we want to subtract 1½ inches from this length to add a toggle. If the old piece is 12 feet, enter 11 feet 10½ inches under "Finished Length" opposite "starboard after lower shroud."

Now stretch out the port after lower shroud, which is not necessarily the same length as its starboard-side counterpart. Slight irregularities in mast or hull can easily make a significant difference. In this case the lengths match, and 11 feet 10½ inches is entered for this wire, too.

Repeat this procedure for the starboard and port forward lowers, then lay out the starboard upper. Its length is, say, 20 feet. In wire of this length we begin to worry about "constructional stretch," the initial elongation of new wire as its individual strands settle into place under load. The short length of the lowers would result in negligible stretch, and it wouldn't amount to much in a 20-foot length either; but to be cautious, refer to Table 6 showing approx-

imate constructional stretch in percentage of length for various kinds of wire rope. Our 7 x 7 preformed carbon steel will stretch 0.06 percent of its length. This works out to a little over ⅛ inch, not enough to bother deducting from the length of the new wire, so for both uppers we'll just subtract 1½ inches for the toggle. For long pieces, such as uppers and jibstays, we also need to deduct for "working elasticity" (see sidebar). Because long pieces are tuned tighter, they stretch more than shorter pieces.

If we were instead using 7 x 19 stainless wire for the rig, constructional stretch over the same length would have amounted to over ¾ inch, enough to use up an excessive amount of turnbuckle slack; it would have been better to deduct this plus the toggle

When dimensioning standing rigging, deduct for constructional and for working elasticity. For example, a 60-foot upper shroud of 1 x 19 stainless will gain .021 percent of its length, or ⁵⁄₃₂ inch from constructional stretch. 7 x 7 stainless will gain .07 percent, or about ½ inch. Galvanized 7 x 7 will gain .06 percent, or about ⁷⁄₁₆ inch. Constructional elasticity for Spectra varies widely, but can be two percent or more. Therefore it is extremely important to remove all constructional stretch from this material before measuring it.

The other form of elasticity we need to deal with is working stretch. If our 60-foot shroud is tuned to 20 percent of its strength, it will gain almost another 1½ inches or so from working elasticity, in 1 x 19 stainless. Therefore, deduct about 1⅝ inches inch from the measured length of the wire before cutting. The deductions for the 7 x 7 wires will be a bit higher. For the Spectra, if it is properly sized, stretch will be much less than for 1 x 19. This is because we size Spectra to reduce creep in the material, so it will be much stronger, and therefore will stretch less, relative to a given load. For working elasticity information, see page 153.

length from the original length for the new piece.

Moving to the jib- and forestays, subtract 3½ inches from the former and add 5 inches to the latter, as per notes, to obtain finished lengths.

Thimble Length and Circumference   It is one thing to measure thimble-head-to-thimble-head for a finished length, quite another to cut a piece of wire that, when spliced, will have the required length. There are several complications. First, in order to reach the thimble head the wire must detour around the thimble's contours; there is thus a considerable difference between thimble length and eye circum-

ference. We need to know how much extra wire to add for a given thimble length. Second, as you'll see in the "Comforts of Service" section of this chapter, some thimble eyes are oversize to allow for replacing damaged thimbles. With this configuration, one must allow for thimble circumference minus the length from the throat of the splice to the bearing point of the thimble. Third, since the clevis pin that attaches to the wire will affect length, we deduct for one-half its diameter.

The easiest way to solve these problems is to set up a sample eye using the same size wire and thimble that will be used in the actual rig. With the eye clamped in place, measure the distance from thimble head to splice crotch. Then mark this latter point on both sides, remove the wire from the vise, straighten it, and measure the distance between the two points. This gives you the thimble-eye circumference. In our case, the thimble length is 1¾ inches and the circumference is 4½ inches. (When precise thimble-eye length is not important, as when making slings or pendants, use the technique in Figure 6-4 to find thimble circumference.)

To put this information to work, start again with the starboard after lower shroud (Figure 6-5). Subtracting a thimble length (1¾ inches) from each end leaves 11 feet 7 inches. Proper length is restored by adding a thimble circumference (4½ inches) to each end. Finally, add enough length to splice with, in this case 12 inches to each end (see "The Liverpool Eyesplice Made Difficult," later in this chapter). After these assorted additions and subtractions

---

Figure 6-4. *Rolling a thimble along the wire is one way to determine approximate thimble circumference. Add a bit extra for an oversized eye.*

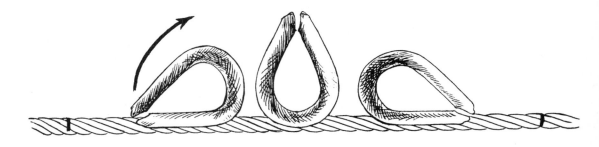

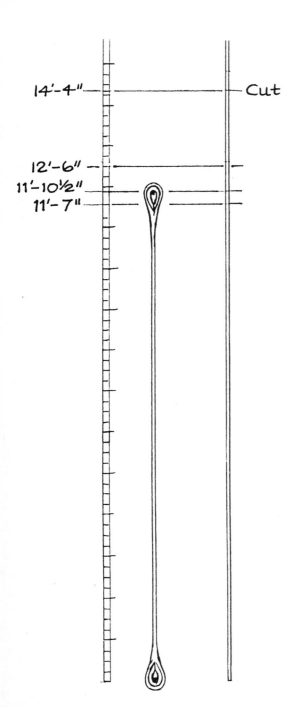

14'-4"

Cut

12'-6"

11'-10½"

11'-7"

Figure 6-5. *In this sample case, a cut length of 14 feet 4 inches is obtained by subtracting two thimble lengths (1¾ inches each), adding two thimble circumferences (4½ inches each), and also adding two splicing lengths (1 foot each) to the finished length.*

we end up with 14 feet 4 inches to enter under "Cut Length." If you take a wire that length and use 2 feet of it to make two splices with 4½-inch-circumference eyes around thimbles, you will most assuredly get a shroud that is 11 feet 10 inches long.

Repeat this procedure with the other wires to obtain the rest of the cut lengths.

Measuring Soft Eyes The above procedure also works for eyes made around deadeyes, lizards, or other thimble-like objects, but a soft eye—an eye made around a mast—poses a couple of extra problems. First, soft eyes might travel at various angles across a mast, ranging from horizontal to a steep diagonal, depending on the rig. How can we determine eye length and circumference for an eye at any angle? Second, what portion of the finished length of the wire does the eye constitute?

For a nearly horizontal lead, the simplest though seldom seen case, the eye rests on a "stop," a shoulder formed by a reduction of mast diameter at the desired height. An obvious and simple procedure is to measure the circumference of the mast above the shoulder and make an eye of this circumference. Unfortunately, this results in an eye that is far too small, since there's no allowance for the thickness of the wire (Figure 6-6). One response is to add wire diameter (including its layers of service and leather) to mast diameter, giving a "working diameter" that extends to the center of the wire on either side (Figure 6-7). Multiply the working diameter by π to find the eye circumference. The eye can still be too tight to be practical, however; the wire has to bend at nearly a right angle where it exits the seizing. Wire rope is reluctant to do this, and the seizing would in

Figure 6-6. *Making an eye exactly the mast circumference doesn't work, because wire thickness isn't allowed for.*

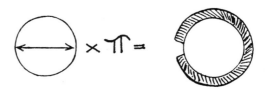

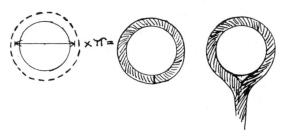

Figure 6-7. *Adding wire diameter to mast diameter and multiplying the sum by π gives a true working circumference, but this would still result in too tight an eye, even for eyes that fit on "stops." Add just enough length so the eye will fit easily on the mast.*

any event be put under extreme lateral strain. Add another 2 inches or so to the eye circumference, and you'll have an eye that goes on more easily and has a better lead out of the seizing, but is still tight enough to stay securely on its shoulder. To determine what the resulting sag adds to the finished length, put a sample eye on the actual mast, or a dummy section, and measure the drop (Figure 6-8).

Eyes sometimes rest not on stops but on "bolsters" affixed to trestletrees at a mast top. These eyes can be considerably larger than those that go to

stops, four times the working diameter being a standard size that provides a good lead and allows the seizing to clear the bolster. Again, sag is measured on the actual or a dummy mast.

When stacking successive eyes on a stop or top, add twice the thickness of each eye to the finished length of the next eye.

The lightest, strongest soft-eye configuration—what you want for a Bermudian or high-efficiency gaff-rigged vessel—features an arrangement in which thumb-cleat-like bolsters are affixed to the side of the mast opposite the strain (Figure 6-9). This allows for the fairest lead and thus the greatest strength of any soft-eye configuration; the wire follows a gradual curve from the bolster to the splice or seizing, the two legs meeting at an angle that, ideally, does not exceed 90 degrees, and can be as low as 60 degrees. The smaller the angle, the less strain each leg bears.

Since Bermudian and efficient gaff rigs are light and precisely designed, approximate measures will result in poor fit, ill appearance, and impaired efficiency. So for a properly engineered soft eye, fire up your traditional electronic calculator with basic trigonometric functions and prepare to lay out the Ideal Soft Eye.

Figure 6-8. *A sample eye on the mast, or on a dummy mast, will show how much an eye will "drop" from a stop or bolster.*

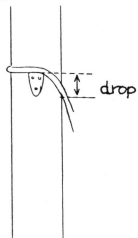

Figure 6-9. *Thumb cleats and long, fair leads characterize soft eyes on Bermudian-rigged craft.*

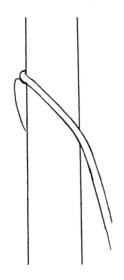

Start by establishing Working Circumference—π x (Mast Diameter + Wire Diameter)—and multiply this by .75. This gives you enough wire to get three-quarters of the way around the mast (Figure 6-10). Now we can decide how much extra wire to allow for a nice, fair lead to the throat of the splice or seizing at, say, an angle of 45 degrees. To do this, measure straight across at three-quarters of the way around. This chord is the hypotenuse of a right triangle (Figure 6-10B), so it's easy to find its length by the good old "sum of the squares of the two sides" method. In this case that's 6 (inches)^2 + 6 (inches)^2 = 72. The square root of this—8½—is the length of our chord. Divide this distance by 2, and then by sin 22.5 degrees. The result will be the length of one of the legs from the three-quarters-circumference point to the throat.

Why does this work? Because each leg of the eye is also part of a right triangle (Figure 6-10C), and half our chord's length for the base for each leg's triangle. That's only one side, and we have to know the length of two sides for the "sum of the square method" to work. That's where that "sin 22.5 degrees" comes in: Long ago mathematicians worked out the proportions of right triangles. Their successors managed to cram all these proportions into the program of any calculator equipped with trig functions. Among other things, these functions enable us to start with the length of just one side and one of the two acute angles in a triangle, and find the length of the other two sides.

In Figure 6-10C we have the length of the base of our triangle: 4 ¼ inches—and we know the angle we'll use is 22.5 degrees—half the desired convergence angle of 45 degrees. What we need is the length of the hypotenuse (the longest side of a right triangle). The sine of any right triangle is the ratio you get by dividing the length of the base by the length of the hypotenuse: B ÷ H = sin T. The sine of 22.5 degrees is .3827. To find "H," transpose a bit to 4 ÷ .3827 = H. This works out to 11⅛ inches.

The two legs together equal 22 ¼ inches. Adding this to our three-quarter circumference of 2 feet 4%₃₂ inches will give us an eye of 4 feet 2⅟₁₆ inches. (Figure 6-10D) Put an eye this size on the mast or

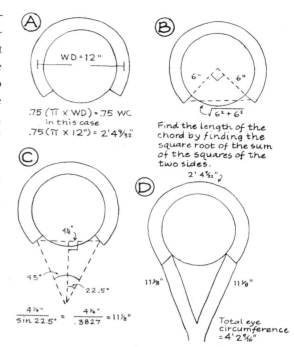

Figure 6-10. *Arriving at the Ideal Soft Eye circumference.*

dummy mast to see how far it drops, and calculate the rest of the shroud length from the point where the seizing or splice touches the mast. If this wire is a shroud, its mate will fit over it, thereby losing a little length. To compensate for this, make the second eye circumference longer than the first by twice the wire diameter, including service and leather.

Measuring for a New Rig

If you skipped over all that trigonometric hoo-haw, figuring you'd just eyeball eye size, you're in big trouble now. That was a way of showing you a useful procedure while introducing some mathematics that are central to what follows. When you don't have an old rig to base measurements on but you still want to turn up both ends in the loft, trigonometry can be a very good friend to know.

The measurements we'll make in this section are for a new gang of rigging for *Katy*, my 16-foot catboat, designed by Sam Crocker in about 1933. The old rig design wasn't quite what I wanted, so sailor

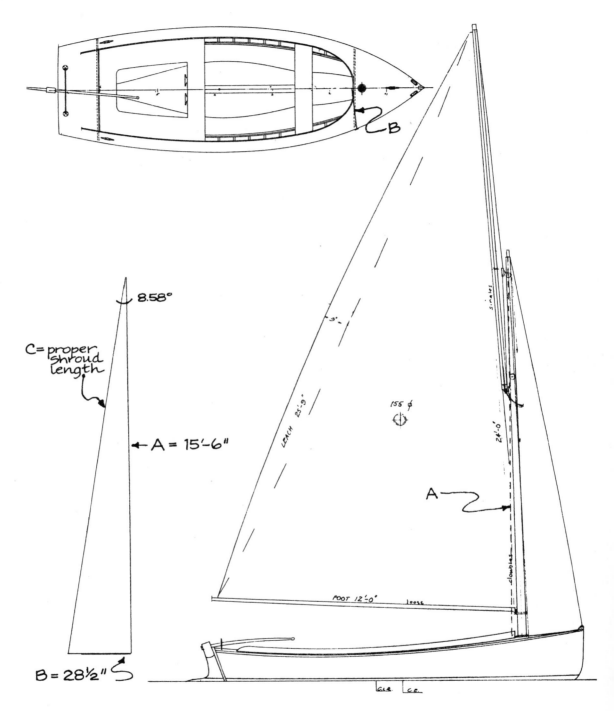

Figure 6-11. *The sail and deck plans of* Katy. *The dotted line in the sail plan represents the vertical leg of a right triangle (A). The line crossing to the chainplate on the deck plan is the base of the triangle (B). The proper shroud length is represented by the hypotenuse of the right triangle (C). To determine the shroud angle relative to the mast, find the arctangent of the ratio between base and height. In this case, the angle is 8.71 degrees.*

and aristocrat David Ryder-Turner came up with the sliding-gunter arrangement shown in Figure 6-11.

The first thing I want to do is check David's work. Ahem. What I mean is that I'm interested in finding out what angles the shrouds and forestay make relative to the mast. For most vessels this angle should be 10 to 12 degrees, but in this case the rig is intended more to check the motion of the mast than to turn it into a compression member, and low stresses are involved. A somewhat lesser staying angle ought to suffice. To find out what the designed angle is, I'll construct a right triangle for the shrouds based on the sail and deck plans shown in Figure 6-11. The base is 28 inches and the length is 15 feet 6 inches. In a right triangle, the ratio of base/height is the "tangent" of the angle opposite the base. (Consult any high school geometry text for a fuller explanation of trigonomic functions; your local library would be a good place to start.) In this case, the tangent is 0.1507936, and a tangent of 0.1507936 means that the angle at the top (represented by the symbol Ø) is 8.58 degrees. How do I know? Because my calculator tells me so. It has a key on it marked "tan-1," a function sometimes written out as "arc- tangent." If 0.1507936 is the tangent of the angle Ø, then Ø is the arctangent of 0.1507936. If you enter 0.1507936 on your calculator and then hit "tan-1," you'll get 8.58 degrees, the angle of the shrouds relative to *Katy*'s mast. A glance at the staying angle-stress curve (Figure 5-5) shows me that this is a very tight angle. This is characteristic of catboat shrouds, as the mast is always well forward, where the boat narrows. I could widen the angle by shortening the mast, but I don't want to lose sail area, but I could lower the upper attachment point of the shrouds instead. This would create a bit of a cantilever above the shrouds, but only a short one. Bringing the attachment down one foot would widen the angle to a bit over 9 degrees. I could also add "channels" for the chainplates (see below) to widen the staying base. With a 2 ½" channel, we'd have almost a 10 degree staying angle. Whether any of this would be worth doing would be a matter of determining cost and benefit. How much would the changes reduce shroud load?

Compression load? Does the old wire or hardware show signs of excess strain? It might turn out that, though we would never stay with 8.58 degrees for a larger, more heavily-loaded boat, it might be okay for this small, light daysailer.

Another example: The right triangle for the forestay has a base of 2 feet 6 inches and a height of 15 feet 6 inches. The tangent of the angle in question is given by Base ÷ Height = 2.5 ÷ 15.5 = 0.1612903, and the Arctangent = 9.162347. The forestay angle relative to the mast is 9.2 degrees. Because staying angles are inversely proportional to standing-rigging loads, the tangent and arctangent functions are of particular value to the rigger.

Hypotenuse and Wire Length   Of all the words of rigger's wit, the saddest are these: "It doesn't fit!"

Thimbles and soft eyes affect finished length, but of course the major determinant of rig fit is length between terminals. Because the sail plan appears to show wire length, many people scale their lengths from it. Their rigs are too short. "Ahh," say others, "but that's why we have the rigging plan" (Figure 6-12), and they scale their lengths from it. Their rigs are too short. The sail plan has no depth, so does not show length-consuming athwartships shroud travel, although it is accurate for fore-and-aft wires, which have no athwartships travel. The rigging plan has no depth, so does not show length-consuming fore-and-aft travel, although it is accurate for the rare shroud that has no fore-and-aft travel. Each plan shows a dimension that the other does not; our problem is how to get the vertical, athwartships, and fore-and-aft dimensions in one place. That's why I used the sail and deck plan to construct the right triangle for *Katy*'s shroud. Height was taken off the sail plan, and fore-and-aft and athwartships travel off the deck plan. We could now measure wire length from our diagram, but for greater precision let's return to trigonometry, which tells us that "the square of the hypotenuse is equal to the sum of the squares of the other two sides." For *Katy*'s forestay, the sum of the squares is 35,496 inches. The square root of this is 15 feet 8 inches, the length of the stay.

Some fine points:

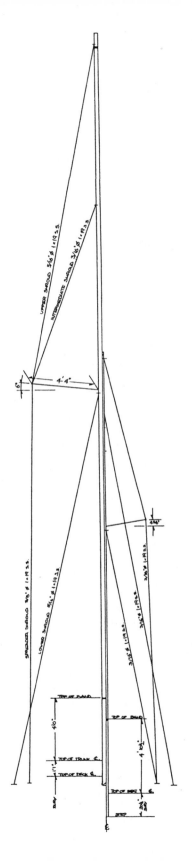

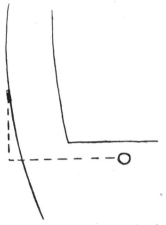

Figure 6-12. *The rigging plan for a Hinckley Bermuda 40 Mark III yawl. Mainmast shrouds are shown on the left, mizzen shrouds, on the right. Because the fore-and-aft angle of a shroud does not show up on a rigging plan, shrouds scaled from one will be too short.*

Figure 6-13. *To obtain a base length when a house or other obstacle intrudes, measure straight out, make a 90-degree turn, and measure straight to the chainplate. The square root of the sum of the squares of these two lengths is the desired base length.*

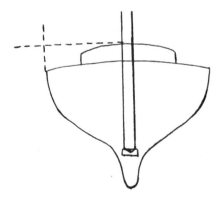

Figure 6-14. *When the mast is stepped through the house, find the height of mast collar above chainplate by measuring horizontally out to a plumb-bob line at the chainplate (assuming the vessel is level in both planes). Proceed as in Figure 6-13.*

If the mast rakes, do not use it for the vertical leg of the triangle. Draw a true vertical line from the upper point of attachment to the deck.

If plans are unavailable, measure directly from the actual mast and deck. Be sure to account for rake. If a house or other obstruction prevents you from measuring a straight line from mast base to chainplate, first measure out to the rail, then aft or forward to the chainplate (Figure 6-13). The squares of these two figures plus the square of the height is also the square of the hypotenuse. If the mast is stepped through a house, or if some other impediment makes a direct horizontal measurement from mast to chainplate impossible, use plumb bobs and level to establish the distance (Figure 6-14). Add the distance from chainplate to intersection "A" to the height of the mast. If the chainplates do not project far above the rail, deck camber alone can necessitate this procedure.

To measure the length of wires that pass over spreaders, proceed in two steps. First, find the point on deck directly below the spreader tip. To do this draw a vertical line on the sail plan from the spreader tip to intersect the deck, then measure how far aft of the stem this intersection is. Turn to the deck plan and measure from the stem aft the same distance, then measure out from the hull centerline the length of the spreader plus one-half the diameter of the mast at spreader height (Figure 6-15). Mea-

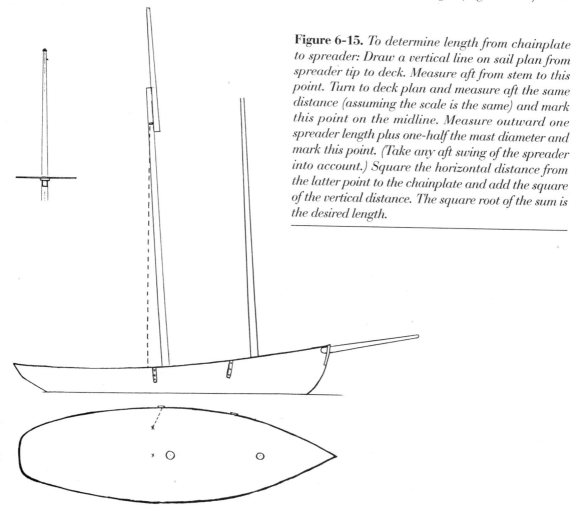

Figure 6-15. *To determine length from chainplate to spreader: Draw a vertical line on sail plan from spreader tip to deck. Measure aft from stem to this point. Turn to deck plan and measure aft the same distance (assuming the scale is the same) and mark this point on the midline. Measure outward one spreader length plus one-half the mast diameter and mark this point. (Take any aft swing of the spreader into account.) Square the horizontal distance from the latter point to the chainplate and add the square of the vertical distance. The square root of the sum is the desired length.*

sure and square the distance from this point to the chainplate on the deck plan, square the height of the spreader above the chainplate on the sail plan, add the two figures, hit the square-root key, and you'll have the distance from chainplate to spreader.

The second step is a lot simpler: Square the spreader length plus one-half the mast diameter at the spreaders, add the square of the vertical distance between the spreader and the shroud's upper end, and find this square root for the length of the shroud above the spreaders. If rake is negligible, you can scale this length directly from the rigging plan. Add the two figures to get the total wire length.

Spreader wires are the most difficult to measure accurately and present the greatest opportunity for error, so don't be tempted by shortcuts. Be picky.

For a tang rig, measure from the mast attachment of the tang down to the chainplate. When you've established total length, subtract tang length from the upper end and turnbuckle-and-toggle or lanyard length from the lower end.

Given that builders do not always build what designers design, first-hand measurements should be made whenever possible, even if you have all the plans. Track down and take into account any discrepancies between the plans and the real thing. If, for instance, you get a measurement of 40 feet from the actual mast but the sail plan says 40 feet 3 inches, don't automatically assume that the mast height is shorter than designed; the boatbuilder might have decided that the mast step was too thin, installed one that was 3 inches thicker, taken 3 inches off the mast to compensate, and forgotten to tell you. But this discrepancy will show up, if no other changes have been made, in the distance from step to partners.

Lofting An alternative method of rig measurement involves making base and height measurements, plotting them on the floor and one wall of a large room, and directly measuring the shroud or stay length with a tape measure. This is full-scale lofting, analogous to the system boatbuilders use to lay out hull shapes. It requires a level floor, a straight wall at right angles to that floor, and the

careful transfer of measurements taken from vessel or plans or both to obtain an accurate result. Trigonometry is quicker.

THE LIVERPOOL EYESPLICE MADE DIFFICULT

"Life is too short to splice wire rope."
—Bernard Moitessier,
circumnavigator and author

"Any idiot can do it."
—Nick Benton, master rigger

Braiding a tremendously strong steel squid into itself is a formidable task. But that is exactly what faces any would-be wire splicer, and it is one reason why there are so few of them. Score one for Moitessier.

On the other hand, a little study, preparation, and care will enable even the most slow-witted and clumsy-fingered among us to produce a sound, relatively painless splice. Score one for Benton, who

Figure 6-16A. *Poured sockets can be used as alternative terminals. This is a forked version, but it is also available with single bails. Both can be used with 7 x 19, 7 x 7, or 1 x 19 wire, stainless or galvanized. (Margaret Wilson-Briggs)*

Figure 6-16B. *Fittings like these (Sta-Lok's and others are similar) are strong, reusable, and inspectable. With the Hi-Mod, made by Hayn, the body of the terminal (bottom section) is placed over the wire rope. The cover yarns are fanned, and the wedge (second from bottom) is placed over the core. The crown ring, which sets wedge depth, as well as providing even spacing for the cover yarns, is placed over the wedge. The terminal end can be an eye, fork, stud, or other configuration. (Margaret Wilson-Briggs)*

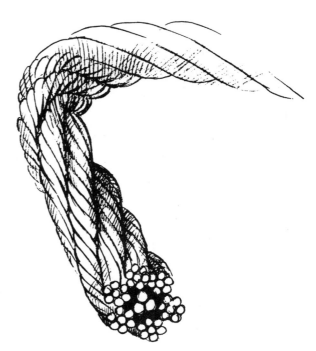

Figure 6-17. *A 6 x 7 wire rope has a three-part rope core surrounded by six strands of seven wire yarns each. A 7 x 7 wire rope would have a seven-yarn wire core. A 6 x 19 wire rope would have the rope core as shown, but each outer strand would be made up of 19 yarns.*

never tired of telling me that I am living proof of this view.

The truth lies somewhere in between: The job is neither easy nor onerous, just difficult. It is up to the individual to decide if learning the Liverpool Eyesplice is worth the effort.

The variation described here is loaded with details that add strength and longevity. And difficulty. But if you practice enough, you should be able to produce a splice that is as good as any the professional lofts can offer. If you are not interested in taking spike in hand yourself, the instructions here will acquaint you with the details of a good splice, so that you can make an informed decision when the time comes to hire a professional.

Tools and Materials

Part of splicing is knowing what to splice: Each job has different requirements. For the job of learning, use an easy-to-splice wire: oil-free $^5/_{16}$-inch galva-

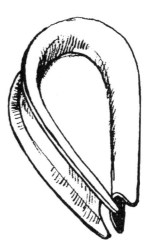

Figure 6-18. *A wire-rope thimble.*

Figure 6-19. *A spike made from a scratch awl.*

nized wire rope with a fiber heart. The construction to ask for is 6 x 7 or 6 x 19 (Figure 6-17); both are readily available at hardware or marine-supply stores. This type of wire is low-cost, supple, and easy to handle.

Speaking of ease, use a rigging vise, shown in Figure 6-21. Manufacturers advertise in the boating-magazine classified sections. As in branding or diaper changing, the trick with wire work is to keep a firm grip on the subject. A vise won't help you with calves and babies, but even the occasional splicer will find it worthwhile for greatly reducing setup time and effort while improving splice quality.

The third basic ingredient is a spike. For this size wire, a Snap-On scratch awl (#7ASA) is perfect, once you file a flat, rounded tip on it (Figure 6-19).

You'll also need some nippers to trim the splice, a mallet (see Figure 6-37)—preferably of hardwood, brass, or lead—to fair it, a bit of seizing wire, and safety goggles. One more item: an unlaying stick (shown in Figure 6-21B). It's a stick with a braided rope tail that is used to untwist the wire slightly, making it easier to enter the spike into the wire.

Setting Up

The first step in making a splice is to put a wire seizing on the wire rope near the rope's end (Figure 6-20). It will keep the wire from unlaying too far and will make it easier for you to put an even strain on all strands. The formula for the seizing position is: 1 foot of splicing length for every inch of wire circumference. The $\frac{5}{16}$-inch wire you are using for practice is about 1 inch in circumference, so put the seizing on 1 foot from the end. Half-inch wire, to use another example, is $1\frac{1}{2}$ inches in circumference, so its seizing would be $1\frac{1}{2}$ feet from the end.

Clamp your vise in place at elbow height, and clamp the wire in the vise around a $\frac{5}{16}$-inch thimble with the seizing at the end of the thimble and just outside the jaws. Be sure that the tail is on the far side of the standing part, as shown in Figure 6-21. Tighten the vise jaws to hold the thimble snugly against the wire, then lead the standing part out

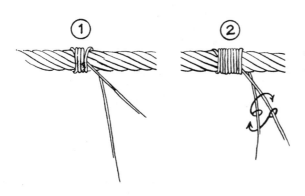

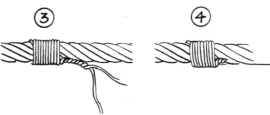

Figure 6-20. *Beginning the Liverpool Eyesplice (continued through Figure 6-38). Put a wire seizing on the wire rope about 1 foot from the end of the wire . . .*

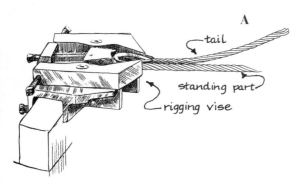

Figure 6-21A–B. . . . *then clamp the wire rope around the thimble in a rigging vise (A). Taking one or two turns out of the wire's lay makes it easier to enter a spike. Wrap a rope tail for unlaying around the standing part of the wire about 3 feet down from the splice (B).*

horizontally. (Splices can be made either horizontally or vertically; which way is better is a subject of frequent and earnest debate among riggers—one of those Ford-versus-Chevy questions that comes down to personal taste. Like any sane, intelligent individual, I always splice horizontally.) Tie or clamp the wire in place with moderate tension on the standing part.

Using the unlaying stick, wrap the tail on tightly, against the wire lay, about 3 feet from the vise. Pass the stick around, against the lay. You want to do this just enough to loosen the area you'll be splicing, but not so much as to make a birdcage out of it. Once or twice around should do. Err on the tight side, and try it out. Be sure to brace the stick so that it can't whip around and smack you. You're ready.

A Little Presplice Theorizing and Practice

The idea in splicing wire, as with cordage, is to lift one or more standing-part strands just enough to pass a strand end underneath. Do this with all strands in succession, several times, and the ends become woven into the standing part very securely and very evenly. Only in splices can the strain be thus distributed among all of a rope's component strands. That is why splices are the strongest knots. When you work wire, capitalize on this virtue by

trying for perfect smoothness. To minimize distortion, use the smallest spike that will make a space big enough to tuck in the strands.

Try a few practice entries now. Face the vise, brace your spike arm against your body, and lay the tip of the spike between two standing-part strands. Using the thumb on your other hand as a fulcrum, lean on the wire, twisting the spike handle counterclockwise just a bit as the tip drops between the strands (Figure 6-22). That's it; you've just picked up a strand. Take the spike out and try it again, but this time go under two strands; then do it again, under three. Outwit the wire, guiding the tip under the strands without snagging the heart.

Remember that wire is too stiff to be tucked directly where you want it to go. It kinks. Therefore you have to tuck it in well down the standing part and then "roll" it home. This is the spike's other duty, to shuttle back and forth, conveying the strands to their destinations. Practice the shuttling motion illustrated in Figure 6-23, keeping the spike parallel with the lay for the least wire distortion. Note that as you move toward the vise you have to push on the handle to keep the tip in. Likewise, traveling away from the vise causes the spike to get swallowed up unless you pull it out a little as you go.

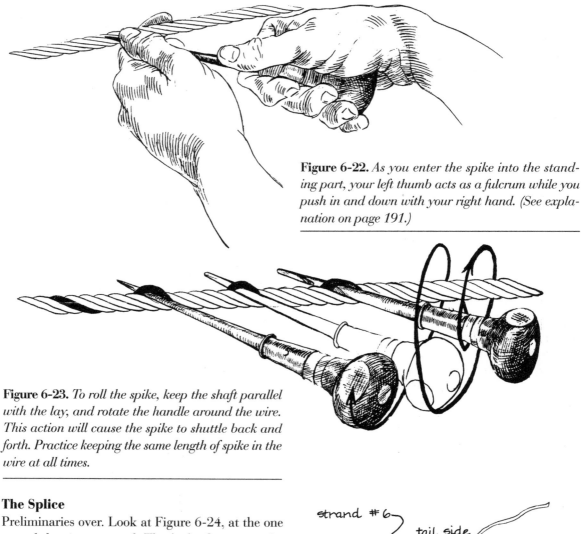

Figure 6-22. *As you enter the spike into the standing part, your left thumb acts as a fulcrum while you push in and down with your right hand. (See explanation on page 191.)*

Figure 6-23. *To roll the spike, keep the shaft parallel with the lay, and rotate the handle around the wire. This action will cause the spike to shuttle back and forth. Practice keeping the same length of spike in the wire at all times.*

The Splice

Preliminaries over. Look at Figure 6-24, at the one strand that is separated. That's the first one to be tucked. It's the innermost tail strand you can see from above at the thimble. By the way, most riggers just unlay the whole bundle immediately, but doing one strand at a time is considerably easier; you'll be dealing with a squid soon enough.

The strands are numbered 1 through 6, and the strand you have just unlaid is #6. I can't explain now why you're starting with the last strand, except to say that how the splice starts is important and that this start is unusually smooth. You'll see why later.

Look again at Figure 6-24, at the two shaded strands on the standing part. Like #6, they intersect

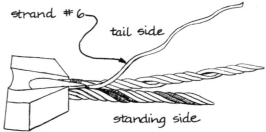

strand #6

tail side

standing side

Figure 6-24. *After separating strand #6, the innermost of the tail strands at the base of the thimble as seen from above, pick out the two strands that correspond to those shaded, and enter the spike under both.*

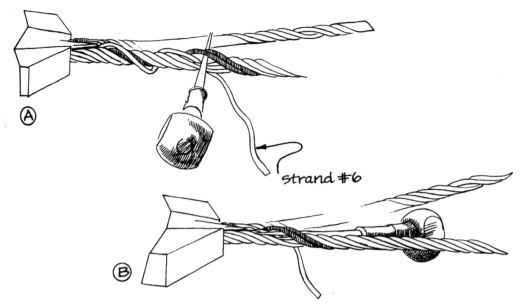

strand #6

Figure 6-25. *Pass the end completely around the standing part, counterclockwise as you are facing the vise (with the lay), and then tuck it against the lay beneath the two strands the spike is under (A), going from the standing-part side (the side nearest you) to the tail side (away from you). Remove the spike, put it back in under the same two strands from the opposite direction (B), and roll it home, rotating the handle as in Figure 6-22.*

the thimble at its base, but the one on the right will not be visible from above the thimble, and the one on the left will barely be visible. Enter your spike under these two and roll it down a full revolution. Take #6 and pass it once counterclockwise around the standing part, and then tuck it under those two strands from the *near side* to the *far side* (against the lay) (Figure 6-25). Turning the spike at right angles to the wire will make a bigger space through which to tuck the end.

Remove the spike, put it back into the same space from the opposite direction, and roll the strand home, toward the vise. Pull on the strand as you roll, to prevent slack and to keep the strand in front of the spike, but do not pull the strand toward the vise; let the spike push the strand ahead of it. The counterclockwise turn you made will come out as you approach the vise, where the strand should snuggle into place naturally. Don't force it.

You will return to #6 soon. For now, enter the spike under the three strands on your wire that cor-

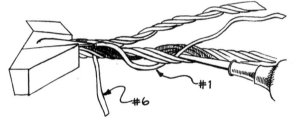

#6 · #1

Figure 6-26. *Separate strand #1; it's the one on the right side of the space vacated by #6. Enter the spike under the three shaded strands. Pass strand #1 around the standing part once, counterclockwise, and pass it under the three strands from the tail side to the standing side. Roll home. All subsequent tucks are also made in this direction.*

respond to the three shaded strands in Figure 6-26. They are the three that are immediately to the left of where #6 went in. It's awkward in this case to make the entry at the vise, so you can trace the strands around with your finger for one revolution, entering the spike where shown. Roll home to make sure you have the correct strands (the point of the spike should come out where #6 went in), and then roll back. Separate strand #1 from the bundle—it's to the right of the space vacated by #6. Pass it once counterclockwise around the standing part as before, but this time tuck from the tail, or *far side*, to the *near side* of the standing part (with the lay). All subsequent strands are also tucked from tail side to standing side. Strand #6 was an oddity in more than one way.

Pull the slack out of #1, and leaving the spike in the way it was entered, roll the strand home as

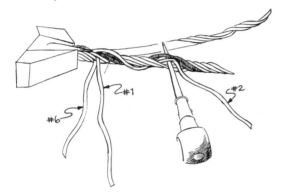

Figure 6-27. *Enter the spike under two strands. The point should come out in the same place as for #1. Separate strand #2, pass it around counterclockwise, tuck from tail side to standing side, and roll home.*

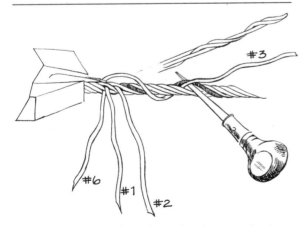

Figure 6-28. *Enter the spike under one strand only, so that the point again comes out in the same space as it did for strands #1 and #2. Separate out strand #3, pass it around, tuck, and roll home.*

in Figure 6-25. Again, keep tension on the strand, keep the strand in front of the spike, and let the spike push the strand ahead.

Now enter the spike under the two strands that correspond to the shaded strands in Figure 6-27. Be sure that the point comes out in the same space that it did for #1. Separate end #2, the next one to the right in the bundle; pass it around once counterclockwise; and tuck it under the two strands from tail side to standing side. Roll it home.

Enter under one strand, as in Figure 6-28. The point still comes out in the same place that it did for strands #1 and #2. Separate strand #3 from the tail, tuck it in, and roll it home. All three strands should now be going cleanly into the same space and coming out under separate, adjacent strands in the standing part.

The Heart

You're probably warming up to the tuck-and-roll procedure, so I hate to interrupt, but we must now deal with the heart. You can see it exposed in the tail and in the middle of the standing part. The common procedure is to cut the heart out of the tail at the outset, but you are going to lay it alongside the heart in the standing part. The idea here is this: When you introduce six strands into a configuration that already has six strands very nicely arranged around a heart, hollow spaces result. By fattening up the interior with an extra heart, you get a firmer splice that won't distort under extremes of loading.

Separate the tail's fiber heart from the remaining two strands and unlay it into its three components. If you're working with a wire heart—not shown—divide it into four or five parts. You are unlaying the heart's tail components to be able to wrap it more easily around the heart in the standing part. Enter the spike into the same space that #6 went into, but put the spike under only one strand (Figure 6-29). Roll the spike ahead as far as it will easily go—and then a little farther. This action will pull the strand the spike is under slightly away from its fellows, leaving a little space. Pull the heart (all its loose parts) down firmly into this space, so

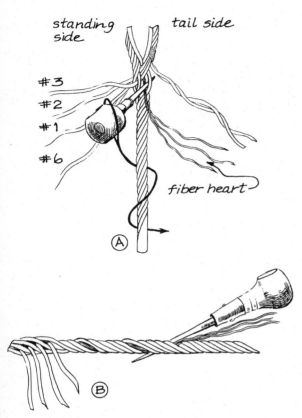

standing side

tail side

#3
#2
#1
#6

fiber heart

Ⓐ

Ⓑ

Figure 6-29. *Enter the spike into the space #6 went into, but under only one strand. This strand is immediately to the right of the one that #3 is under. Roll the spike as far home as it will go easily—and then a little more (A). Pull the unlaid heart down into the space thus formed; then roll the spike back down the wire (B), pushing this extra heart into the middle of the standing part as you go.*

that it is behind the spike. Keep pulling while rolling the spike toward you so the heart will be pushed into the middle of the standing part. Keep the heart behind the spike, keep the spike parallel with the lay, and use as little spike as possible. After being rolled in, the heart will show a little, but a hernia (which happens when the heart completely protrudes from the standing part) will not do—there's too much distortion. If a hernia results, you probably have too much tension on the standing part and/or too much spike.

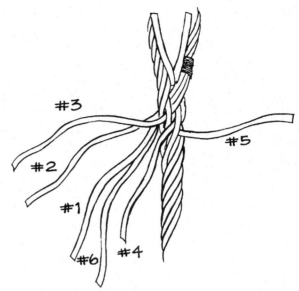

#3
#2
#1
#6   #4
#5

Figure 6-30. *Tuck #4 under the same strand you lifted to roll the heart in. Tuck #5 under the next strand to the right. The splice should now look as shown.*

Back to Roll-and-Tuck

With the two hearts beating as one, you may proceed. Enter the spike under the same strand that you lifted for rolling in the heart. Roll down one revolution, tuck in strand #4, and roll home. Enter under the next strand to the right, tuck in #5, the last untucked strand, and roll home. A light tapping with the mallet will ensure that these two strands are seated well. The splice thus far should look like that in Figure 6-30.

Return now to the mysterious strand #6. Enter the spike under the next strand to the right and prepare to tuck. Ready? Wait.

Breaking the Lay

The strands you've tucked so far have entered almost straight into the wire. But from now on, they'll each describe a tight spiral down the length of the splice. If you allow the strands to keep a round cross section the splice will be bulkier than if they were flat in cross section. The yarns will also grip better if they are flatter. And since a splice relies on even distribution of strain, you need to flatten the strands into a ribbon shape by "breaking the lay."

195

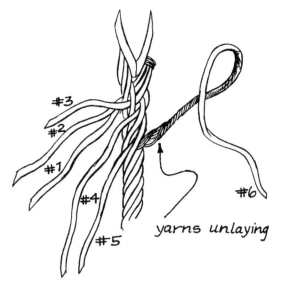

#3
#2
#1
#4
#5
#6
yarns unlaying

Figure 6-31. *Break the lay of #6 before tucking a second time by making a small counterclockwise loop, or bight, and twisting it just enough so that the yarns do not completely spring back when tension is released.*

Make a small bight, close to the splice, by arcing the end of a strand around counterclockwise (Figure 6-31). As the bight tightens, you will see the strand yarns open up. Relax the tension and they spring back. But if you apply a little more tension they will lose some of their elastic memory and stay open when the tension is eased. The trick is to break the lay without completely dissociating the yarns or, worse yet, kinking them, so be very gentle. This is the hardest part of the splice to master. As you proceed with the splice, you will find that the act of passing the strands around to be tucked also helps open up the yarns. I put off describing lay-breaking until I'd gotten the niceties of entry out of the way, but in future splices, start breaking the lay from the very first tuck of #1.

So, to return to the splice, break the lay of #6, tuck it again, and roll it home; it will settle smoothly into place, wrapped flat around its strand.

That Odd First Tuck Finally Explained

Figure 6-32A shows from the underside how the splice would look had you begun in the conventional manner and not made that first tuck under

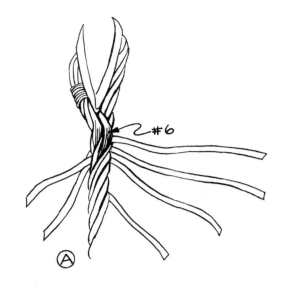

#6
Ⓐ

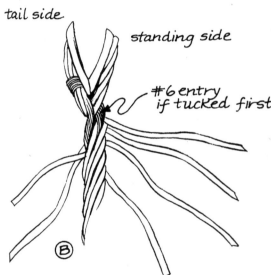

tail side
standing side
#6 entry
if tucked first
Ⓑ

Figure 6-32. *From below, strand #6 would look as in A after the usual entry sequence. Traveling farther before being tucked, it would not lie as fairly as other strands would, so would be less likely to take an even strain. Part B shows how #6 should look after being tucked as in the text.*

two strands with #6 (see Figures 6-24 and 6-25). Without that tuck, the strand would have had to travel a considerable distance from the seizing to its entry point, so far that it would be difficult to make it lie fair and take an even strain. But now it emerges directly to the right of strand #5 (Figure 6-32B), exactly where it needs to be for all consequent normal tucks. (Steven Hyman and Will Gates, fellow riggers of the barque *Elissa*, introduced me to this technique.)

Roll-and-Tuck Again

Now you have tucked strands #1 through #5 once and #6 twice. But pretend you are even and have tucked them all just once. It's easier, because from here on you will be treating them all the same. So, for the second row of tucks, start with #1. It's closest to the vise and comes out from under three strands. Enter the spike where #1 emerges, but pick up only one strand. Roll back (away from the vise), break the lay, tuck, and roll home. Take each of the strands in succession, working away from the vise, always entering the spike under the same strand beneath which each end being tucked emerges (Figure 6-33).

Count the ends aloud as you go so you'll always know where you are in the sequence (for example, "Row two, 3; row two, 4; row two, 5"; and so on). If you get distracted or called away, find your place again by going back to the top of the splice and finding where #4 enters; it's visually distinctive (Figure 6-34). Count strands down from there until you get to the bottom-most (last-tucked) strand. The number you say when you reach it is the number of that strand.

Sooner or later you will probably tuck a strand in the wrong place. Any time things don't look right as you roll home, stop and check. Remember that each strand goes under to the tail side, over to the standing side, then back under to the tail side, always spiraling around its own standing-part strand. To correct a mis-tuck, put everything in reverse, rolling the spike back and pushing on the strand end until it comes out, and then retucking in the proper place.

Keep tucking until you have made four full rows of tucks (not counting the extra one for #6). Five rows of tucks is the standard for a Liverpool Eye—that is, each strand is tucked five times. But since you've done so much work already, you might as well learn the proper finishing touch.

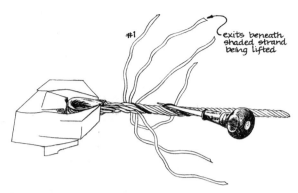

Figure 6-33. *Proceeding with the second row of tucks. Always enter the spike under the strand from which the end to be tucked emerges. Continue in sequence until all strands have been tucked four times.*

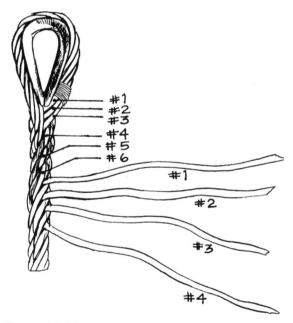

Figure 6-34. *Locating strand #4 gives a point from which to count if you lose track. The other strands lie in relation to #4 as shown.*

The Taper

The taper provides a gradual transition from splice to standing part, blurring the distinction between the two. A tapered splice is more appealing to the eye and less liable to snag running rigging and sails than an untapered one—or a mechanical

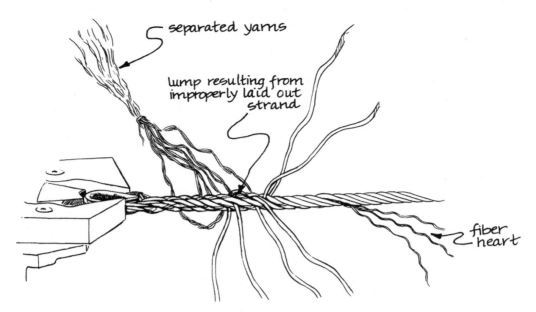

Figure 6-35. *To taper the splice, lay out four yarns of 6 x 19 or 7 x 19 wire or two yarns of 6 x 7 or 7 x 7 wire. Be sure that the yarns will not be caught between the standing part and the strand they are taken from, or a lump will develop on the next tuck. Bundle the separated pieces out of the way, then tuck in the six remaining partial strands once more.*

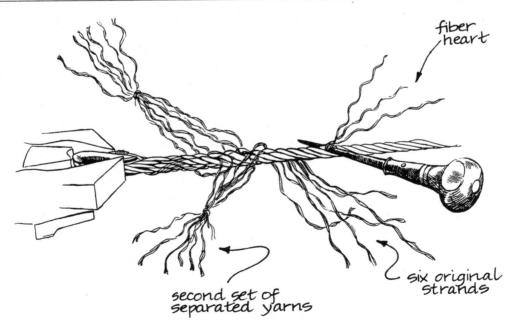

Figure 6-36. *Continuing the taper. Lay the center yarn(s) out of each strand in 6 x 19 or 7 x 19 wire or lay out two more yarns of 6 x 7 or 7 x 7 wire. Tuck each remainder once more. Back out the fiber heart of the wire rope as far as the end of the splice.*

fitting. More important, the taper makes a splice stronger.

After making four full rows of tucks, peel four or five adjacent surface yarns off each strand for 6 x 19 or 7 x 19 wire, or two adjacent surface yarns off each strand for 6 x 7 or 7 x 7 wire. Separate them all the way to the splice; simply make sure they don't stop on the right of the strand they were peeled from—you'll be tucking to the right and don't want separated yarns to be in the way, preventing the tucked strand from lying fair (Figure 6-35). When all the strands have been reduced in size, tuck all six large remainders once more.

Next, separate the center yarn(s) out of each strand for 6 x 19 or 7 x 19 wire or two more adjacent surface yarns out of 6 x 7 or 7 x 7 wire, and then once again tuck the large remainders of all six strands. Those are all the tucks you really need to make, but the taper can be further elongated by tucking once more, with or without splitting the strands again.

Finally, unroll the heart that you rolled in previously back to the splice by entering the spike behind it and rolling the spike toward the vise (Figure 6-36). Just ease it up to strand #4's last tuck and leave it there; then tie all the loose yarns and strands to the standing part.

Note that there are lots of ways to taper a splice. My current preference is to make two full tucks, and then lay out just one yarn for each subsequent tuck (for 7 x 7), until there are three left. All tapers are time-consuming, so people can be inclined to skip them, or to use quickly done ones. If that is your inclination, use #2809 from the *Ashley Book of Knots*. But avoid the "Frisco Taper," in which some strands are given extra tucks, but produce asymmetry in the wire.

Fairing

"Svensken splejser daaligt, men han banker godt."
—*Frank Rosenow, The Ditty Bag Book*

That's a Norwegian saying that means, "The Swedes are lousy splicers, but they're good at pounding."*

---

* No doubt the Swedes have a corresponding proverb.

This bit of slander refers to the temptation to rely heavily on this step, which involves pounding the finished splice with a hardwood or soft metal mallet to smooth out any irregularities (Figure 6-37). You can't beat a poor splice into a good one, but any splice will benefit from a proper fairing. Using a stump or the like as a base, strike glancing blows toward the standing part with the mallet, constantly turning the work, trying to get any slack worked out. It might be useful to think about striking just hard enough to get a tone. That means you have compacted the wire enough to make a difference. Go over the work two or three times.

It is difficult to describe in print exactly how hard one should strike to fair different-sized wires, but the matter is important, so as an aid I will tell you a little story. A sailmaker and I once had a loft on the top floor of City Hall in Anacortes, Washington. Ours was the only unrenovated room in the old building—below, city employees typed and filed away in carpeted, fluorescent-lit comfort. Trying to work quietly, I discovered how little muscle was actually needed to fair a splice. Since gentleness is a good thing for wire, imagine, as you fair, a nest of bureaucrats below. For wire up to $5/16$ inch in diameter, the noise will not bother them at all; pounding $3/8$-inch wire is noticeable but reasonable; $7/16$-inch can be tolerated anytime except first thing Monday morning; $1/2$-inch should be done only during lunch or after hours; and $5/8$-inch and up will drop plaster into the typewriters, so should be done in the parking lot.

Trimming

One more chance to ruin the whole thing. Ends cut too long are "meathooks" that will work their way through service and then through your hide. Ends cut too short will untuck themselves. So hold the work still (you can put it back in the vise with some tension on the standing part) and gently pull the last-tucked bundle toward the thimble, breaking the lay. Nip the wire just above the splice—$1/16$ to $1/8$ inch above—and the ends should fall back until they're nearly flush. If the wire is too thick to cut all at once, take successive bites, working toward the thimble. Be extra careful at the ends of the

After a few thousand feet, your serving mallet will have worn itself into a deeply grooved, organically distorted artifact. Wear is particularly pronounced at the leading edge. So to prolong head life, tack on a tin "shield."

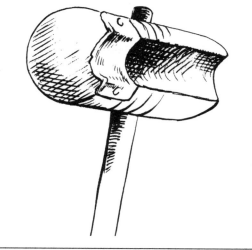

splice, where the strands are most likely to slip out.

With 7 x 7 wire, a very neat finish can be made by completely unlaying each strand and breaking the individual yarns with your bare hands. There's no karate involved—it's more like Aikido, actually. Bend each yarn sharply left and then right, creating a weak point at its base. Then twist the yarn clockwise two or three turns, and the end will break off completely out of the way.

When you trim the heart—fiber or wire—taper it, too, by pulling some of its strands closer to the vise before trimming.

Trimming completed, give the splice a few light taps with the mallet for a final fairing. Your job is done and ready to be cut off and thrown away.

Figure 6-37. *Fairing. Seize all ends down to the standing part. Strike glancing blows away from the thimble, working any slack toward the ends. Be firm but gentle. Trim all strand and heart ends as described in the text.*

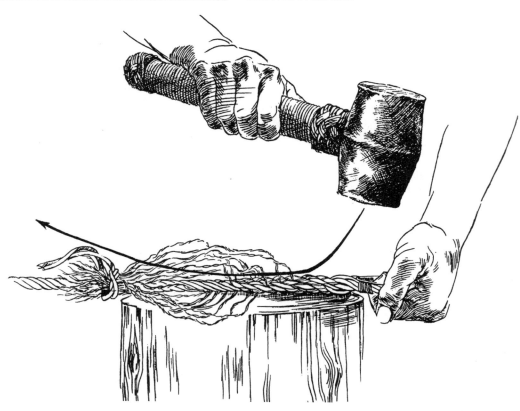

Figure 6-38. *A finished Liverpool Eyesplice.*

"Thrown away! Are you crazy!?"

I know, I know. You've spent hours on your first splice, cursed the wire, probably cursed the instructions; you've finally finished, and you're not about to junk the thing. Well, keep it as a memento if you like; just don't use it. Practice until you develop a *consistent* proficiency, and then take some samples to a testing machine and break them. It's the only way to prove your work.

Splice Strength

Many sailors prefer Eyespliced wire rigging to rigging with mechanical terminals, even though a wide variety of the mechanical terminals is available. Why? Splices are flexible and resilient and thus long-lived. They are also easy to maintain and inspect have no abrupt shoulders to snag other objects or jam in sheaves, and are cost-effective even if you pay someone else to make them for you. Do-it-yourselfers spend nothing but time on their terminals. And if you plan a leisurely cruise across the Pacific, your rigging vise and ditty bag contents are all you need to be a self-sufficient rigger.

But despite these and other virtues, Eyesplices have always faced a major stumbling block: tensile strength. Standard references* list splices as being 10 to 15 percent weaker in sailboat-size wire than swages and fittings such as the Sta-Lok, Norseman, Cast-Lok, and so on. For traditional vessels and some industrial applications, compensating for this deficiency is simply a matter of using slightly oversize wire, thus gaining ample strength along with the splice's other virtues. But on most vessels today, with weight and windage at a premium, this practice is unacceptable. The only alternative is to make a more efficient splice, a knot more nearly as strong as the wire rope in which it is tied.

I've always thought that this was possible given proper technique and a fair level of skill. To prove or disprove it, *SAIL* magazine arranged tests at the Monson, Massachusetts, shop of Daniel O'Connor and Sons, Inc., using wire rope made by the MacWhyte and Carolina companies. O'Connor, a third-generation rigger specializing in ski-lift equipment, is the proud owner of a 200,000-pound-capacity hydraulic testing machine. In January 1983 we fed this device 17 sample wires with Eyesplice terminals. Eleven of the samples were my idea of "proper" splices: smooth, with fair entries and tapers (for the sake of experiment, different tapers were used). Two of the samples were made, after about 40 hours of practice, by a student of mine. The wire used was ⅜-inch diameter in 7 x 7, 7 x 19, and 1 x 19 constructions, both stainless and galvanized, plus one 5/16-inch 7 x 19 galvanized sample. Although the number of pieces tested was small, I believe that the consistency of the results puts well-made splices in a league with any other terminal.

The results, as shown in Table 7, averaged 103.8 percent of the manufacturers' *rated* strength for the rope. None broke at below 100 percent; the highest mark was 118 percent. In case these numbers seem impossible, understand that manufacturers rate their wire rope at a little less than *ultimate* strength, by margins of a few percent to well over 10 percent, depending on the brand. In terms of ultimate strength, the average for the splices was 95 percent for the ⅜-inch samples and 99 percent for the best 5/16-inch sample. The important thing is that the splices were within a few percentage points of the very best mechanical terminals and better than most of them. Compare these results with those obtained by the staff of *Practical Sailor*. In their test, the results of which were presented in the

---

Rossnagel's *Handbook of Rigging*, page 61: MacWhyte Catalog G-18, page 214; Broderick and Bascom's *Rigger's Handbook*, page 163.

	Piece	Diam. (in.)	Rated Str. (lbs.)	Broke at (lbs.)	% of Rated Strength
Table 7. Splice Strength as Percent Rated Strength of Wire Rope					
other taper	7x7 galv.	⅜	13,300	13,350	100.00
	7x7 galv.	⅜	13,300	13,350	100.00
taper described in text	7x7 galv.	⅜	13,300	14,300	107.50
	7x7 galv.	⅜	13,300	13,850	104.00
	7x7 s.s. 302	⅜	12,000	12,150	101.00
	7x19 s.s. 302	⅜	12,000	12,000	100.00
	7x19 galv.	⅜	14,400	14,900	103.50
	7x19 galv.	5⁄16	9,800	11,600	118.00
diff. taper for 1x19 diff. entry too	1x19 s.s. 302	⅜	17,500	17,850	102.00
	1x19 s.s. 302	⅜	17,500	17,950	102.50
Tony's early	7x19 s.s. 316	⅜	11,000	10,100	91.82
Tony's later	7x19 s.s. 316	⅜	11,000	11,350	103.00
untapered, std. thimbles	1x19 s.s. 302	¼	8,200	7,200	88.00
	1x19 s.s. 302	¼	8,200	5,800	70.50
very short	7x19 galv.	5⁄16	9,800	9,400	96.00
old piece (12 yrs.)	7x7 s.s. 302	9⁄32	6,100	5,300	83.00
old piece (12 yrs.)	7x7 s.s. 302	¼	7,600	7,400	97.00

November 1, 1982, issue, fittings were measured against the wire's rated strength. Cast-Lok and Sta-Lok fittings tested at 110 percent and 106 percent, while the swaged wire broke at 95 and 105 percent of rated strength.

The other six samples tested by O'Connor were "improper" splices: an early splice of my student's (made after only a few hours' practice); 1 x 19 splices with standard thimbles instead of the solid or heavy-duty thimbles that should be used with this construction; splices in old wire; and one sample made very short, so that the splices backed into each other at the middle. This group averaged 87.7 percent of the rated wire strength; technique and proper materials do make a difference.

THE 1 x 19 WIRE SPLICE MADE POSSIBLE

In the days of hemp rope, if riggers wanted an eye in the end of a line, they spliced or seized it there. As iron wire rope came to prominence in the latter part of the 19th century, riggers treated it pretty much like hemp, splicing and seizing as they were used to doing. It was more difficult to hold and work the stiffer, tougher material, but they managed—once they had devised some specialized tools such as rigging vises.

With progress, iron gave way to plow steel, and plow steel (at least for yachts) to stainless steel. Wire construction was also changing, with the old 6 x 7 being replaced by 1 x 19 wire (Figure 6-39). These changes were calculated to reduce (even if only slightly) weight, windage, maintenance, and stretch, to aid the performance of twentieth-century

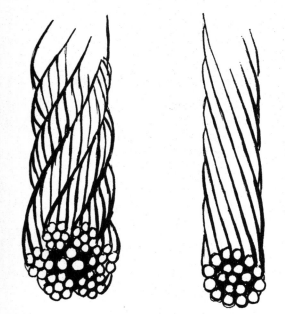

Figure 6-39. *The old 6 x 7 wire rope (left) has given way to 1 x 19 (right).*

sailing craft. Unfortunately for riggers, wire evolution also increased stiffness, intricacy, and the need for precision in measurement and fabrication. With the development of mechanical terminals, particularly swages, a lot of riggers breathed sighs of relief. Today, splices in 1 x 19 wire are rarely seen, and so most sailors, and even many riggers, assume that the stuff is impossible to splice.

Why Splice?

Nevertheless, if you want to use 1 x 19 wire because of its structural advantages of low windage and elasticity, there are some strong, practical arguments for splicing it. First of all, there's cost: True, if you pay a professional to do it, the price of a 1 x 19 splice is going to be higher than that of a good mechanical terminal. But if you do the work yourself, you're only out of time and the cost of a thimble and a few simple tools.

Another advantage is fatigue resistance: Because a splice is flexible along its entire length, there are no fatigue-inducing hard spots, like the point where a flexible wire enters a rigid fitting. North of the tropics, fatigue resulting from cyclic loading is even

more of a problem for stainless steel than atmospheric corrosion. On modern vessels, particularly fin-keelers and multihulls, high initial stability and inelastic sails translate into hard "shock-load" conditions every time a puff of wind hits the sails, so, fatigue-resistance is an even more valuable virtue.

Finally—and this is most important to cruisers—there are the linked virtues of ease of inspection and replacement. By periodically lifting the service from a sample or two, you can see right into the splice to check for evidence of corrosion or fatigue. If something has gone wrong, you don't need a multi-ton press or an expensive screw-on fitting to fix things—just a marlingspike, a rigging vise, and the skill to use them.

It is only fair to warn you that the level of skill required to produce a proper 1 x 19 splice is quite high. Structurally, it is actually simpler than a 6 x 7 wire splice, so figuring out where to tuck the strands will be easier. But 1 x 19 wire is much stiffer, and easier to distort or kink while splicing. So it's up to you to get to know the wire as much with your hands as with your head. Practice until you can turn out consistently smooth, strong splices.

Materials and Tools

Thirty feet (9 m) of ¼-inch (6.5-mm)-diameter 1 x 19 stainless-steel wire rope will be enough for a few practice splices. You'll also need about 15 feet (4.5 m) of ¹⁄₃₂-inch (0.8-mm) annealed stainless seizing wire, either single- or multi-strand construction, and a ¼-inch (6.5 mm) solid-bronze thimble. This last item (Figure 6-40A) is designed to accommodate 1 x 19 wire. The thimble's wide radius suits 1 x 19's bend-resistant nature, and its solid mass will stand up to extremes of loading, yet it is still thin enough to fit into the jaws of the appropriately sized turnbuckle.

A rigging vise clamps the wire around the thimble while the splice is made. In a pinch [the author assures that this gripping phrase is an intentional pun—Ed.], you can cobble one out of Vise Grips and blocks of wood, but a model like the one shown in Figure 6-41B will be faster, surer, and easier, and will enable you to handle a variety of wire sizes.

Figure 6-40A. *A ¼-inch solid bronze thimble works well for the eye.*

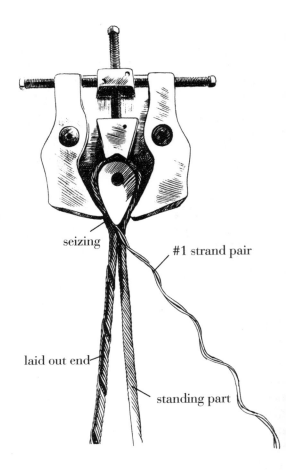

seizing

#1 strand pair

laid out end

standing part

Figure 6-41B. *Wire positioned in rigging vise; #1 strand laid out.*

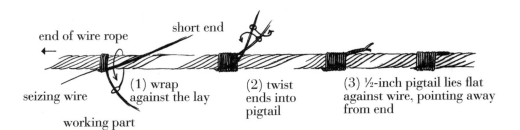

end of wire rope

short end

seizing wire

working part

(1) wrap against the lay

(2) twist ends into pigtail

(3) ½-inch pigtail lies flat against wire, pointing away from end

Figure 6-40B. *A scratch awl makes a good marling-spike for 1 x 19 wire.*

Figure 6-41A. *Beginning the 1 x 19 Wire Splice. Applying a seizing.*

Figure 6-41C. *Rope tail and unlaying stick applied to standing part. Note that the wire has been slightly unlaid. The inset sketch shows a quick-to-make unlaying stick. The setup is for right-laid wire; most 1 x 19 is left-laid.*

Scratch awls (Figure 6-40B) make perfect marlingspikes for wire up to ⁵⁄₁₆ inch (8 mm) in diameter. Snap-On's large scratch awl has a notably superior taper. File the tip flat for easier entry into the lay of the wire.

A rope tail and an unlaying stick (shown in Figure 6-41C), optional for yacht-sized 6 x 7 wire, are essential for working with ornery 1 x 19 wire.

You'll also need nippers, pliers, a hardwood or soft-metal mallet, and—please—a pair of safety glasses.

The Splice

The first step is to put on a wire seizing a short distance from one end to serve as a stop for unlaying strands. The distances for yacht-sized wires are as follows:

⅛" and ³⁄₁₆"	1' (0.30 m)
(3.5 mm and 5 mm)	
¼" (6.5 mm)	1'3" (0.38 m)
⁵⁄₁₆" (8 mm)	1'4" (0.41 m)
⅜" (9.53 mm)	1'6" (0.46 m)
⁷⁄₁₆" (11 mm)	1'8" (0.51 m)
½" (12 mm)	1'11" (0.58 m)

Basically, these tail lengths are about what they'd be for 7 x 7 wire that was ⅛" bigger. These lengths will give you a comfortable length of wire to work with while splicing, although you might find as you gain proficiency that you prefer to work with more or less wire than suggested here.

To apply the seizing, wrap a 1-foot (0.30-m) length of seizing wire onto the 1 x 19 wire, in our case 1 foot 3 inches from the end. Wrap tightly, against the lay, covering the short end with the working part, until the seizing is approximately square. Then twist the two ends around one another to make a "pigtail." Tighten this pigtail with a pair of pliers, nip off all but ½ inch (12 mm) or so, and then press the tail down against the wire as shown in Figure 6-41A. Note that it points away from the end of the wire rope.

Secure the vise at elbow height, and open its jaws as wide as they will go. Measure the circumference of your thimble—not in the score, but around its outer edge—and make a mark on the wire half this distance above the seizing. Bend the wire by hand at this point, so that the tail of the seizing is on the inside of the curve. Bend it just enough so that you can horse it into the vise (end on the left as you're facing the vise). Put the thimble in place, and crank the jaws in until there's no slack around the thimble, with the seizing just outboard of the left hand jaw, and the hollow at the pointed end of the thimble just past the seizing. (Figure 6-41B shows this setup in detail. This setup assumes left-laid wire, which most 1 x 19 is in the U.S. Reverse things if you have right-laid wire).

Tie the standing part of the wire out horizontally under light tension, then wrap on the unlaying stick against the lay (as shown in Figure 6-41C), about 3 feet (0.9 m) from the vise. Take out a single turn. If the stick is not heavy enough to hold the turn with its own weight, brace it securely.

When the stick is set, the lay of the wire should be opened up just a little. If it looks like a loosely woven basket, you've taken out too much lay. The idea is to have it just loose enough for a reasonably easy spike entry.

Now for a little spike practice. Stand on the right side of the wire, brace your spike arm against your body, lay the tip of the spike on the wire parallel with the lay, and with your free hand grip the wire and the spike as shown in Figure 6-41D. Lean on the wire, using your free hand's thumb as a fulcrum to ease the tip down between two surface yarns.

Keeping your spike parallel with the lay, roll it up and down the wire a few times. This is the shuttling motion that will send the strands home as you tuck them. Practice keeping the same length of spike in as you travel—about 1½ inches (38 mm) of the spike's

tip should be showing (see Figure 6-41E). If, as you travel, strands jump over one another or kink, then the spike is at the wrong angle, in too far, or both.

Once you're at home with entry and shuttling, it's time to prepare the strands. Notice that 1 x 19 wire comprises a left-laid outer layer of 12 yarns, a right-laid inner layer of six yarns, and a single, straight heart yarn (Figure 6-39). Nearly all 1 x 19 wire is made this way, though you might stumble across some with opposite lay; if that's what you have, mirror-image these directions.

The trick is to convert this unspliceable mass of yarns into six spliceable strands. This is done by dividing the 12 surface yarns into pairs, and matching each pair with an interior yarn. In the interest of a fair entry, we want particular yarns joined with one another, and tucked into particular points of the standing part.

To find the #1 pair, look at the base of the thimble and find the two end yarns that are just to the right of center where they exit the seizing. That is your #1 pair for the end. Mark or make note of where your #1 end pair should be, then lay out a randomly chosen pair from the end. You just might get the right pair (as shown in Figure 6-41B), but if you don't, count how many yarns it is away from the #1 pair. If it's an even number, proceed to lay

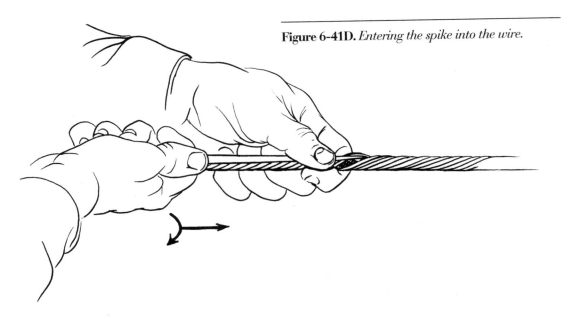

Figure 6-41D. *Entering the spike into the wire.*

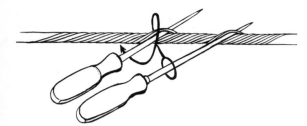

Figure 6-41E. *The "shuttling" motion.*

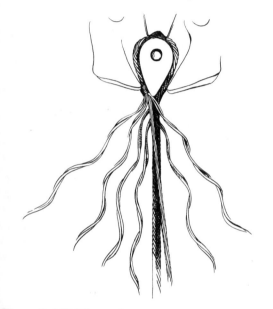

Figure 6-41F. *The surface yarns unlaid in pairs.*

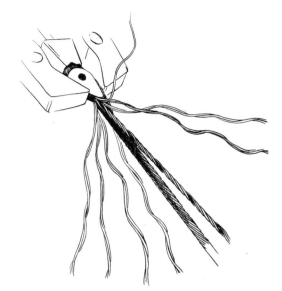

Figure 6-41G. *Laying in the first core yarn with its appropriate surface pair.*

out all the other surface yarns in pairs. If it's an odd number, lay your random pair back up, shift over a half-step, then lay out all the pairs. Bend each pair slightly outward from the seizing, just enough so they won't tangle with one another (see Figure 6-41F). Watch out for sharp ends.

Now lay out a yarn from the interior group. You'll want to match it with the pair of surface yarns to which it will lead most cleanly (see Figure 6-41G). Ideally, the pair of surface yarns will be offset slightly clockwise from the single yarn. Lay the single yarn in with this pair, twisting clockwise. Lay out successive yarns from the bundle and lay them in with succes-

sive surface pairs. If you choose the first match well, and avoid crossing leads, then all will lead fair.

This leaves the heart yarn to deal with: You are going to break it off at the seizing by bending it sharply up and down several times. Find some space between the sets of tucking strands where there's a bit of room. Grasp the heart yarn a few inches from the thimble. Apply some tension, and while maintaining that tension, move the yarn sharply and rapidly up and down. Get as much range of motion as you can. It should break off after a few cycles.

Now it's time for the first tuck. As shown in Figure 6-41H, enter the spike under the standing part's #1 pair (just to the left of center, corresponding to the end's #1 strand) and roll the spike back a full turn. Next, take your #1 strand—remember, it's just to the right of center at the seizing—and bend it to the right and completely around the standing part, following the path of the spike. Pull on the strand as you pass it (Figure 6-41I) so that it lies flat against the standing part, prebending it so it will be fair when rolled home.

To tuck, pass the wire through the space the spike makes, passing from tip to handle (Figure 6-41J).

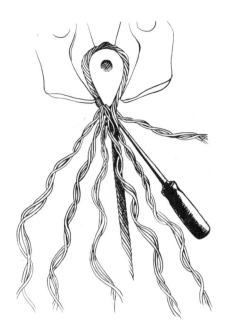

Figure 6-41H. *Entering for first tucks of the #1 strand. Once the spike enters as shown, roll it back a full turn to the position shown in Figure 6-40I.*

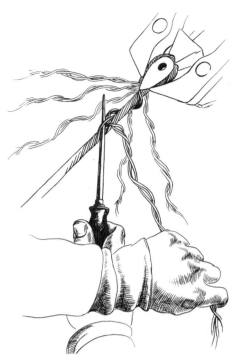

Figure 6-41J. *Tuck the #1 strand through the opening made by the spike as shown, then roll the spike toward the vise one turn to push the tucked strand home.*

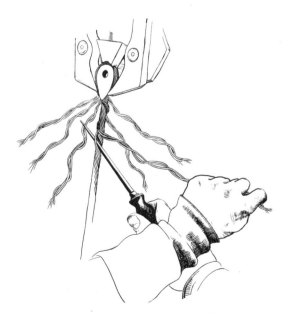

Figure 6-41I. *Prebending the #1 strand.*

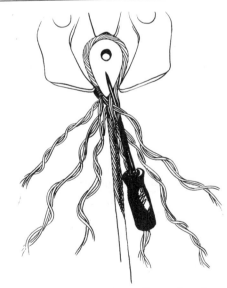

Figure 6-41K. *Enter the spike under the next two standing part yarns to the right, then roll back one turn as before.*

Roll the spike toward the vise, keeping the strand alongside it and under tension. Let the spike push it home, and it will settle into place at the thimble. Be gentle. Holding the strand up toward the thimble, roll the spike back to fair out any distortions you might have caused.

As shown in Figure 6-41K, enter under the next pair of standing-part yarns to the right, and roll back. The #1 strand will now be under four adjacent standing-part yarns (Figure 6-41L). You could have tucked under all four at once, but it's a really tough tuck.

Roll back to fair, then return the spike to the original pair of standing-part yarns. Enter there again, and roll back. Select the #2 strand—it's immediately to the left of #1. Give it a prebending spiral, tuck it, and roll it home. You'll now have the #1 strand going under four yarns, and #2 entering at the same point but emerging after going under only two yarns (see Figure 6-41M).

Roll back to fair, then enter the spike under the next pair of standing-part yarns to the left (Figure 6-41N). Roll back, prebend, and tuck the #3 strand—it's just to the left of #2—and roll home.

Tuck strands #4, #5, and #6 under successive pairs of standing-part yarns. Concentrate on minimizing distortion and prebending the strands so that they lie fair. To aid fairing, give each strand a counterclockwise twist before prebending, to open the lay a little more (see Figure 6-41O).

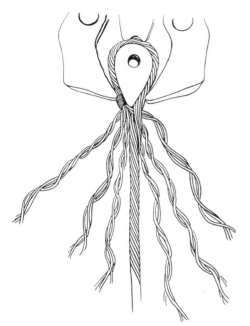

Figure 6-41L. *The #1 strand is now tucked under four standing-part yarns.*

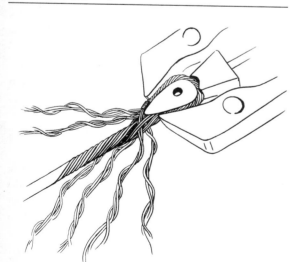

Figure 6-41M. *The #2 strand tucked once.*

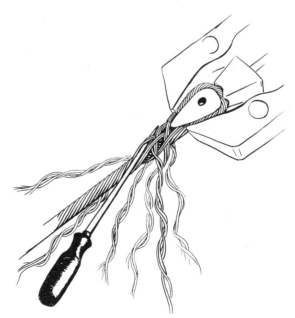

Figure 6-41N. *Here the #3 strand has been tucked, and the spike is entered for #4.*

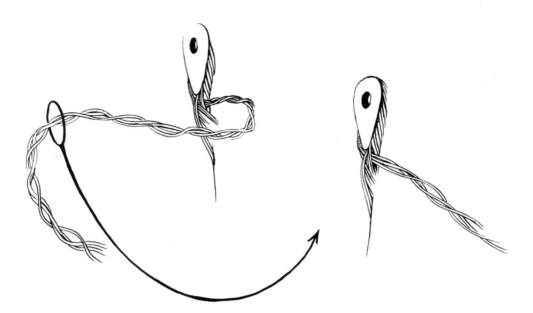

Figure 6-410. *Breaking the lay of a strand to aid fairing.*

A more time-consuming but more easily faired technique involves tucking each yarn separately. Separate the three yarns in each bundle, then prebend and tuck the yarn in each bundle that is nearest the vise. Roll it home, then tuck the middle strand, and finally the strand farthest from the vise. In the first row of tucks, you might want to experiment with changing this order, at least with strands #4, #5, and #6, as the changing angles there can call for different sequences.

The standing-part yarns may tighten up as you work, so pause after each set of six tucks, if necessary, to take out an extra half-turn or so, using the unlaying stick.

As you splice, keep the strands clear of one another and the vise. It will be less confusing visually, and will prevent strands from springing or whipping at you.

To begin the second row of tucks, find the #1 strand. (It will be closest to the vise and coming out from under four yarns.) Enter the spike where the strand emerges, but only under two yarns. Roll back and tuck the #1 strand under these yarns. If you prebend well, the strand will lie down smoothly

when you send it home, wrapped around those two yarns as if it wanted to be there. If it doesn't lie smoothly, work at untwisting and prebending subsequent strands; the knack will come to you.

Now the #2 strand is closest to the vise, emerging—as all strands now will be—from under a pair of yarns. Enter the spike under those yarns, roll back, and tuck.

Proceed with the rest of the strands, moving counterclockwise. It is very easy to mis-tuck, particularly if the wire is distorted by careless spike-work or excessive unlaying. If a strand doesn't look right, trace it back visually. Working from the end toward the vise, it should go under two yarns away from you, back over the same two yarns toward you, then back under them away from you, for as many tucks as you've made.

If you have mis-tucked, put everything in reverse: roll the spike back toward you with the strand alongside it, but push rather than pull on the strand. After a half-turn or so, the strand should spring loose so that you can push and pull it out to untuck. Hunt for the proper location and then re-tuck.

After the second row of tucks is done, taper by laying the third yarn out of each strand, leaving the two surface yarns. Get the third yarn completely clear of the other two at their base, so that it will not be trapped between them and the standing part during the next tuck (Figure 6-41P). If necessary, tug the third yarn toward the vise to get it out from under its pair, then bend it out of the way.

Tuck the remainder of each strand twice more, and you'll be ready to taper again. This time, separate each pair and lay one of them out. If they twist around one another at the standing part, pull them gently apart until they spring clear of each other. Figure 6-410Q shows a splice that is about as rough as it can be and still be acceptable once faired. Your splices must look at least this good at this point before you can consider yourself a splicer. Practice.

Tuck the remaining single wires twice more, and you've finished tucking.

Before fairing, tie all the ends down to the standing part, then take the splice out of the vise and over to a stump. The stump will serve as a soft, organic anvil. To fair, beat the splice with your mallet, work-

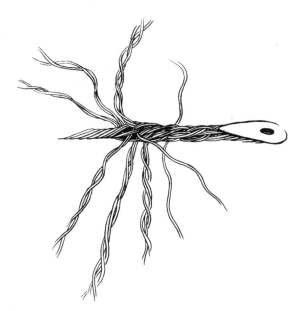

Figure 6-41P. *Second row of tucks done, taper started.*

1 x 19 Oversize Eye Entry

1 x 19 wire is usually spliced up "hard" to a thimble, locking the thimble in place. But occasionally you'll see 1 x 19 splices where the eye is served with annealed stainless steel 1 x 7 seizing wire before being bent around the thimble. In this case the eye is slightly oversized so that the splice service can meet it smoothly. This oversize eye results in a slightly different-looking splice start: Rather than jumping across from one side of the thimble to the other, the ends are right next to the standing part. To get a fair start, choose the pair of standing-part yarns and end yarns that are almost touching each other, as far inboard as you can easily reach.

Served, oversize eyes look real slick—they were often put into the rigs for Concordia yawls—and the wire service helps support the wire yarns as they lay around the thimble.

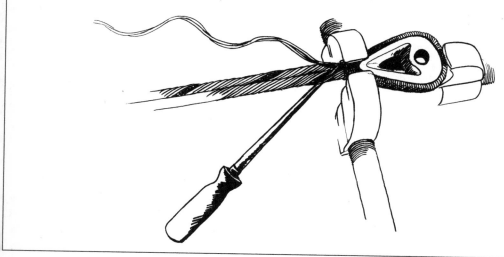

Figure 6-41Q. *Four tucks done, single yarns laid out.*

Figure 6-41R. *Fairing the splice.*

ing away from the thimble, smoothing out any irregularities so that when a load comes on all the yarns will take an even strain. Strike with an L-shaped stroke (Figure 6-41R), coming almost straight down, then ricocheting away from the thimble. Use enough force so that the mallet isn't just bouncing and skidding off the wire; on the other hand, if you're working up a sweat, you're striking way too hard. Be moderate, and go over the work twice. (If that doesn't yield something that resembles the finished splice shown here, there's more wrong with your splice than fairing can cure.)

Put the splice back in the vise, stretch the standing part out again, and pull from the bundle the yarn closest to the vise. Bend it sharply toward the vise, parallel with the lay, then swing it in a low, counterclockwise arc (Figure 6-41S). It should break off after less than a full turn. The part that's left will have a little hook in its end, just at the surface. This keeps the yarn from coming untucked, but it won't protrude far enough to be a "meathook."

Work your way down the splice, breaking off all the yarns. Then, if necessary, you can fair again, very gently, to settle any recalcitrant spots. It's easy here to dislodge ends, so watch how you strike.

The splice (Figure 6-41T) is now complete and ready for tarring, parceling, and service. "Tarring" in this case can be done with a coating of anhydrous lanolin. The lanolin, available at your local pharmacy, will prevent both rust and oxygen starvation under the parceling and service.

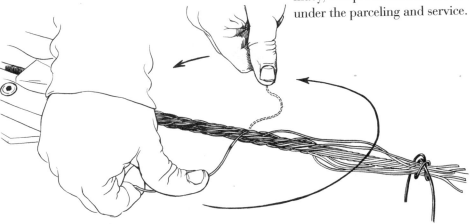

Figure 6-41S. Breaking yarns.

Figure 6-41T. The finished splice.

The parceling can be of friction or adhesive tape, with more lanolin applied to waterproof the splice. If you're going to serve with wire, use parceling made from polyester bed-sheets or soft, light sailcloth instead of, or in addition to, the tape. The cloth parceling won't get chewed up by wire service.

Use wire service of 1/16-inch (1.5-mm) annealed stainless 1 x 7 seizing wire for stays with sail hanks on them, or any other splices that receive a lot of chafe, as from sheets. Chapter 5 shows how to go about it. Otherwise, nylon seine twine of size 30–36 thread makes an excellent, inexpensive, durable service. Paint a finished nylon-served splice with a mixture of one-third black paint, one-third varnish, and one-third net dip (available at fishery supply stores) for a tough, resilient, handsome finish.

Once you get the idea of the splice firmly fixed in your mind, turn out 15 or 20 of them for practice, to get the splice firmly fixed in your hands. When your work consistently looks good, it's probably consistently high in strength. But before you consider using one, send a few of them off to be destruction-tested. Wire rope manufacturers and distributors in your area will know the location of the nearest testing facility.

To test the greatest number of splices with the least work, splice one end of each piece and have the tester swage the other end. They'll pull each piece until it breaks and send you a certificate that says how much strain was on each splice when it broke. By comparing these figures with the wire's ultimate strength, you can determine the strength of your splices.

The actual breaking strength of good domestic wire rope can be 5 to 15 percent more than its rated strength; the specific percentage will vary from batch to batch. The best manufacturers, notably MacWhyte Wire Rope and Carolina Steel and Wire, test every run of their product. When you buy wire, get the production number of the spool it came from, then call the manufacturer's quality-control department for the breaking-strength figures for that production run. That way, you can get precise numbers for your own destruction tests.

Swages and other mechanical terminals are almost universally rated as being stronger than splices, but bear in mind that: (a) a rig's design and safety factors are based on the wire's rated strength; (b) the anti-fatigue splice will degrade more slowly than mechanical terminals will; and (c) mechanical terminals aren't always as strong as their manufacturers claim. You might break a swage or two in your tests.

Possibilities

The 1 x 19 Wire Splice enjoyed an all-too-brief vogue in the first half of the twentieth century, before an expanding yacht population, high labor costs, and a shortage of skilled labor all conspired to make swages and other terminals the preferred alternatives. But this splice just refuses to die. People seek it out for new boats, for born-again classics, and for cruising vessels of all descriptions. It isn't likely to dominate the market ever again. On the other hand, if a splice in 1 x 19 wire is possible, anything is.

Other Terminals

If, after all of the above, you want to pursue other options, there are three main ones: swages, sockets, and mechanical terminals.

Swages   Swages are formed by inserting a wire into a steel cylinder, and then mashing that cylinder down, under tremendous pressure. The steel of the cylinder actually flows into the interstices in the wire, producing a terminal which, if done properly, is 100 percent efficient.

There are two forms of swages: roll and rotary. For roll swages, the cylinder is passed between two rotating cams. These do the mashing. With most machines, the cylinder is removed after the first pass, rotated, and then given a second pass.

In a rotary swage machine, the cylinder is placed inside a close-fitting box, and the box is then hammered on, very quickly and very hard, all the way around. While both roll and rotary swages, in my experience, can claim good efficiency in theory, in practice rotary swages are much more likely actually to achieve it, because the machinery is much more likely to be kept in good shape, and used correctly. They also tend to be more fatigue-resistant.

Sockets   A socket, also called a poured socket, is a funnel-shaped fitting. The wire is inserted into its narrow end, then opened up, or "broomed," and seated into the funnel. Then some form of dam is applied to the narrow end, and a filler of some sort is poured into the wide end. This filler used to be molten metal, but nowadays is a specialized two-part glue. A properly made socket is 100 percent efficient, and unlike a swage, it can be reused; you just melt the glue or metal, clean everything off, and re-apply.

Sockets are a dominant industrial terminal. For instance, every elevator you've ever ridden in was probably hanging from them. But they are bulky, heavy, and require a fair bit of skill to apply, so they aren't seen much in sailboats.

Mechanical Terminals   Mechanical fittings are reusable screw-together items. The wire is inserted into one end, the cover yarns are broomed, a wedge is fitted to the core, and then a top piece is screwed down, compressing the wire against the wedge. Efficiency varies widely with mechanical terminals, with the worst being about as good as cable clamps (80 percent or so), and the best achieving about 95%. Hayn Hi-M0d's are my favorite.

NOTES ON CRIMPED WIRE FITTINGS

There is one more terminal that is worth considering–barely. These fittings, generally known under the proprietary term Nicopress, are commonly used to form eyes on wire rigging, particularly for small ($1/4$ inch and less) wire. The fittings, properly applied, are inexpensive, strong, and quick to make. But they are also ugly, and have hard corners and a little bit of bristly wire end sticking out. To correct these drawbacks, try wrapping some heat-shrink tape over the finished fitting, or thread on some heavy-duty heat-shrink tubing before making the eye, then slide the tubing down over the finished fitting. Apply a little hot air, and you have a suddenly smoother, nearly attractive terminal. Industrial-cute. It's also good practice to slather the fitting, and any wire that will be shrink-wrapped, with anhydrous lanolin.

Some more tips for these fittings:

- Nicopress fittings are wonderfully convenient, but can involve some wrestling during setup. The end is threaded through one side of the fitting, bent to form an eye, then threaded back through on the other side of the fitting. The wrestling comes when you're trying to hold the end so that it projects just slightly beyond the end of the fitting, while you pull on the standing part to snug the eye down around the thimble. Further wrestling ensues when you try to hold the entire spring-load assembly still while you crimp the fitting. To eliminate both problems, lightly crimp the corner of the fitting where the end projects, while the eye is still loose. Use a vise, pliers, Vise Grips, etc. With the end locked in place, it's easy to adjust and hold eye size while pressing.

- When setting up, allow for sleeve lengthening by positioning the sleeve slightly below the thimble, and with the end projecting slightly beyond the sleeve. If this is not done, the sleeve will be distorted as it mashes into the thimble, and the end will slip inside the sleeve, losing bearing surface and thus strength and security.

- When crimping sleeves that require three crimps, crimp the middle first, then the thimble end, then the standing part end. This lets the sleeve expand away from the middle, preventing internal stresses. For sleeves requiring four

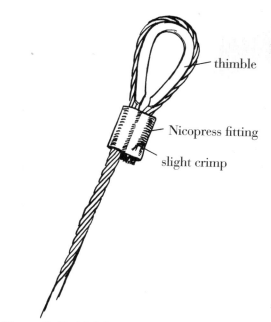

Figure 6-42. *Lightly crimp the end of the fitting to eliminate wrestling.*

crimps, start at the standing-part side of center and work toward the thimble. Finish with the standing- part end.

- Note that Nicopresses are intended for 7 x constructions, and cannot be counted on for 1 x 19 wire. Oh, you'll see them applied to 1 x 19, and they hardly ever fail . . .

GROMMETING

You find them occasionally, littering decks, washed ashore, or hidden away in forepeaks, those pitiful, twisted, lumpy, often bloodstained approximations of rope rings that poor, misguided souls have abandoned in disgust.

And then there are those hapless individuals who curse their way to the last tuck, call the resulting grotesquerie a grommet, put it to use, and so must live daily with the evidence of their failure.

Why do people torture themselves so? Why do they sit there, knot book open on their laps, tangle of line in their hands, desperately trying to come up with something that vaguely resembles the final diagram? Because they are fired up with a notion: Save Money by Replacing Expensive Fittings with Grommets. It's a commendable, reasonable, sensible idea that runs up against two difficulties:

1. It takes skill and patience. This is a big reason why manufacturers can Make Money by Replacing Grommets with Expensive Fittings; most people don't have the time or inclination to master yet another skill. ("Fer cryin' out loud, I learned to navigate, learned to trim the genoa, even learned to varnish the damn brightwork! Why should I go blind and crazy trying to make those stupid little hoops?!") But grommets don't need to be that hard to make. Given time, the inclination, and a good light to work in, it is possible to avoid blindness.

2. Most synthetic ropes don't "hold their lay" when the strands are separated. Each strand in a three-strand rope describes a spiral down the length of the rope. Grommeting relies on the strand retaining that spiral "lay" throughout the process. Manila and hemp do well in this regard,

Figure 6-43. *Making a rope grommet.*

Ⓐ

Ⓑ

Ⓒ

Ⓓ

but most synthetics, the ropes that predominate today, are compulsive lay-losers. To combat this, use a rope "form" equal in length to the circumference of the finished grommet (Figure 6-43A). This form is gradually replaced by the working strand, the length of which is three times the desired circumference plus one foot extra to tuck with. Even lay-holding rope comes out as a smoother grommet when you use a form. For very soft-laid rope, use school glue, as described in the Traditional Irony Splice section.

The Rope Grommet

Begin by laying the working strand into the form while laying one of the form strands out. The middle of the working strand should end up in the middle of the form, with everything nicely adjusted and matched (Figure 6-43B). The working strand

should be laid in so smoothly that it is indistinguishable from the form strands. It needs to be firmly seated at each turn, by a twist-and-pull technique that simultaneously tightens its lay and fits it flush with the other two strands.

Now bring the ends of the form together. Each working strand end will have two form ends next to it. Jump across with either working strand and lay out the form end that is counterclockwise from the

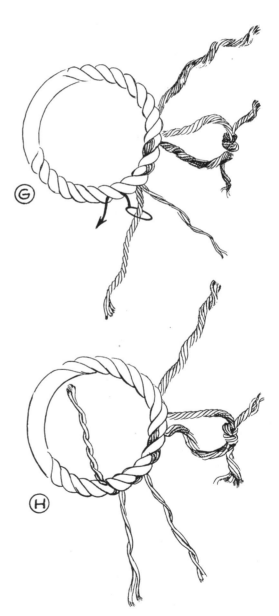

217

other working end. Lay in the working end, being certain that you leave no foul lead at the junction; the rope should maintain a regular spiral all the way around.

Back at the starting point, lay out the last form strand, replacing it with the other end of the working strand (Figure 6-43D). You'll wind up inordinately pleased with yourself, with all three form strands gone and the two ends of the working strand meeting in the same score.

Grommets finish with a type of splice that provides security without bulk—no sense needlessly distorting that perfect circularity. Start by splitting the two strands in half down to where they emerge from the grommet. Make an Overhand Knot, *left over right*, with the two halves that are closest to each other (Figure 6-43E). When you draw this knot down it should look just like a whole strand. If it bulges or flattens, the halves you chose were either too close together or too far apart. Untie the knot and experiment with different ends until you find the two that are just right. With a little practice, it's easy to choose the proper pair.

The other two halves are not employed further; tie them together for now so that you don't confuse them with the others. Then take one of the working halves and tuck it against the lay, over one and under one (Figure 6-43F). As with any splice, flatten each strand by untwisting it a little as you tuck, and be sure to pull any slack out of individual yarns; a fair splice is a strong splice. Tuck both strands whole twice, lay out one-third of each and tuck again, then lay out another third and tuck once more, *with the lay*, to finish (Figure 6-43G, H).

Roll the splice underfoot for a final fairing and trim the ends about ¼ inch from the rope; they will draw back flush or wear off in use. In very slick synthetics it may be necessary to whip or fuse the ends to keep them from pulling out. (For a useful tip on using a rope grommet, see "Grommet and Painter" in Chapter 12, page 373.)

The Wire Grommet

The working-strand-and-form technique can also be used to produce the heavier-duty, longer-lived wire-rope grommet. Here, lay loss is not a problem, since nearly all wire rope these days is "preformed." That is, each strand is permanently set into its spiral shape before the rope is laid up. But here we are dealing not with three but with six strands; if the working strand shifts at all as you are laying up the grommet, it becomes very difficult to make the fifth and sixth passes fit. So again, use a form.

A "perfect grommet" in wire begins with a form the length of the finished grommet's circumference and a working strand a bit over seven times that length. Lay the strand into the form as with rope, but this time start with the middle of the strand at the end of the form. Bring the ends together and jump across with both ends for a firm start. The lay of the wire might not come out exactly at the length you want, in which case you should enlarge the circle a bit until the lays match (Figure 6-44A). If the grommet is small and the wire springy, the remaining form strands might jump apart. Holding them temporarily in place with a bit of electrical tape should cure this, although heavy wire might need the clamping apparatus shown as #2866 in *The Ashley Book of Knots*. In any event, be very careful as you pass the end that it doesn't whip around and smack you. Wear safety glasses.

Every time you cross the gap, be sure you lay in alongside the previous turn—it's easy to get out of sequence. Keep going until all six form strands are on the floor and the working strand is completely laid up around the heart, ends meeting in the same score (Figure 6-44B, C, D).

Now for the hard part. Instead of tucking the ends as with rope, we're going to make them dive into the middle of the wire and run them along until they completely replace the heart. Set things up by clamping the grommet securely in a vise, then pry both ends of the heart a short distance out of the wire. Wrap one end of the working strand around the grommet a few times to keep it from shifting while you deal with the other end (Figure 6-44D).

Enter a spike under the three strands immediately to the right of the end you are going to roll in. Pry the three strands a little to the right and you'll be able to pull the standing part of the end down

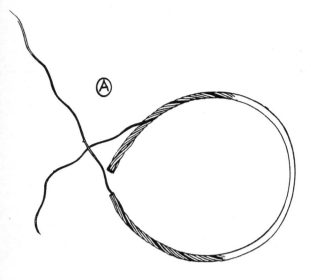

Figure 6-44A. *Making the wire-rope grommet. This grommet also starts with a form equal in length to the circumference of the desired grommet, but has a working strand end measuring exactly seven times that circumference.*

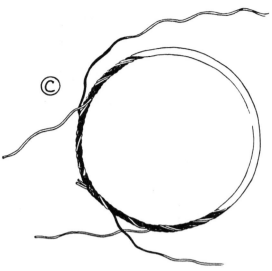

Figure 6-44C. *Keep laying in and out, taking care to remove consecutive form strands each time around; it's easy to get crossed.*

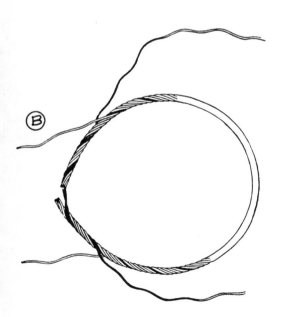

Figure 6-44B. *Jump the gap with both ends and continue to lay out form strands.*

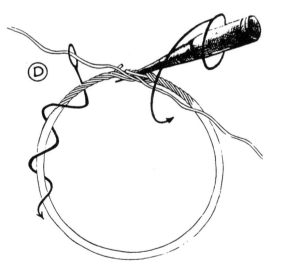

Figure 6-44D. *The working end is completely laid up around the form heart, with the ends meeting. Wrap one working strand end around the grommet several times to keep it from shifting, then enter a spike under three strands, just to the right of the other working strand end and the adjacent heart end. Pull on the working end and use the spike to roll it into the middle of the wire, simultaneously rolling the heart out.*

into the middle of the wire (Figure 6-44E). Rotating the spike counterclockwise will make it travel down one side of the grommet, burying the end and pushing the heart out as it goes (Figure 6-44F). Experiment with the angle at which you hold the spike until you can roll the end in without distorting the strands. When you're halfway around, the taped end will disappear inside. Go back to the start for one last bit of finesse.

The second strand is more difficult to submerge than the first. To get it started I use two spikes, a slightly involved method but one that works every time. Turn the grommet (or yourself) around and insert a spike under the three strands to the right

of where the other end dove in. Insert the other spike, from left to right, under three strands so that it emerges in the same space that the first spike went into. Place the new working end between the spikes and lever it down with the first spike (Figure 6-44G). Then rotate the first spike as before,

Figure 6-44E, F. *Seen from the other side of the grommet, the spike buries the strand end and removes half the length of the heart. Tape the end of the strand.*

Figure 6-44G. *To roll the more stubborn other end in, trap it between two spikes, one going into the wire on its left, the other emerging from the wire on its right. Wedge the strand into the middle, then roll it along as above. When it's well started, remove the righthand spike. Note: The two ends should not cross each other at this juncture, but go into the wire after passing by each other.*

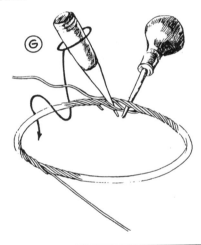

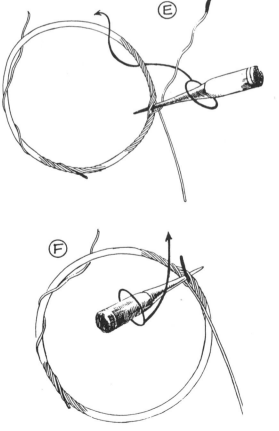

Figure 6-44H. *Roll the second end completely into the wire; the heart will fall free as the end goes in, butted against the other end. Tap lightly with the mallet to fair all turns.*

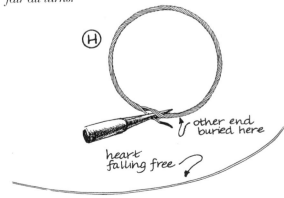

pushing the strand in ahead of it and pushing the heart out. Remove the second spike once you're well started.

As you approach the finish, pause to see how the lengths are going to work out, and to trim one or both ends. You want the two ends almost to meet. If you measure well, the heart will fall out just as you run out of end, and the two ends will nearly meet inside the wire (Figure 6-44H). Ah, perfect. A smooth, steel-strong beauty, and all from a single strand.

Now, getting back to those Expensive Fittings, Figure 6-45 shows a few of the places where your handiwork can be put to use. Wire grommets are usually served and sometimes leathered where they bear on mast or boom, to waterproof and to better distribute strain (see the following section, under "Mending"). Thimbles are held in place with wire Round Seizings. With the softer rope grommets, ser-

vice is optional, and seizings are made with marline or nylon seine twine. Even an ardent Fittingist would have to concede that knowing how to grommet is a useful skill, especially in an emergency. And for those who like to fit out in the traditional manner, the possibilities are endless.

THE COMFORTS OF SERVICE

Service, hah! I can't think of a sillier waste of time than wrapping rope with little-bitty pieces of string. It's an absurd, archaic, ridiculously labor-intensive exercise in drudgery that you, a contemporary sailor, could never conceivably have a use for.

Unless maybe you're looking for a cheap, easy way to hang your boathook from a shroud. A few turns of marline at the appropriate height make a firm base to seize a round sail thimble to, to hold the

Figure 6-45. *Some sample grommet locations, including blocks, yard, painter, sling, bucket, tholepin, and neck, head, and smoke gear.*

Figure 6-46. *To secure a boathook on a shroud, serve two short stretches, 2 feet or so closer together than the length of the handle. Lash sail thimbles in place.*

Figure 6-48. *Worming is set tightly on three-strand rope, filling the spaces where moisture could gather. Parceling of tarred canvas or friction tape provides waterproofing and smooth bedding for service.*

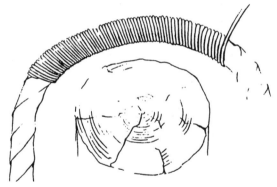

Figure 6-47. *Service applied tightly with the aid of a Marlingspike Hitch provides waterproofing and protects rope from chafe.*

hook. Seize another thimble aloft to slide the handle into (Figure 6-46). A seizing put onto bare wire would be prone to slip.

Start by smearing a little anhydrous lanolin onto the wire—just a bit. A layer of friction-tape or athletic-tape parceling comes next, to keep moisture from settling in the wire's interior (plastic electrical tape grows brittle with age and should be avoided). Put this waterproof "bedding" on from the bot-

tom up, with the lay, so the turns shed water, shingle-like. Next put the service on good and tight with no spaces between the turns. Apply it from the top down so that (a) it disturbs the parceling the least, and (b) the slight untwisting of the wire under load will tighten the service.

Service is traditionally done with tarred marline, but tarred (black) nylon works just as well, is more readily available, and holds up better in tropical climates. Service is usually applied with a specialized tensioning device called a serving board or mallet (Figure 6-49), but a marlingspike will do in a pinch. A serving iron (Figure 6-50) is the tool of choice for seizing wire. Figures 6-47 through 6-49 show the basic setup and procedure.

As turns of service are taken, the hauling part shortens. When it becomes too short, the Marlingspike Hitch (Figures 1-11 and 1-12A, pages 8 and 9) is capsized back into a straight length that in a few more turns becomes part of the service itself. Make the hitch as shown in Figure 1-12A to keep it from jamming.

There are two ways to stop service: If you're using a spike, make the last three or four turns loosely around both it and the wire. Pass the end

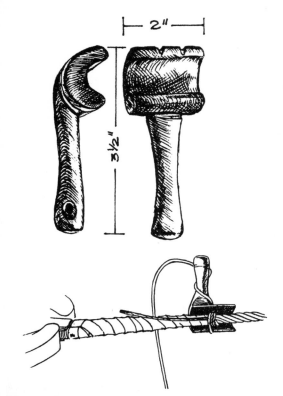

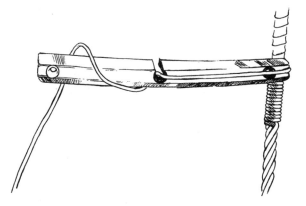

Figure 6-50. A *serving iron can substitute for a board and is the preferred choice for use with seizing wire. This one was cobbled up from the junked bronze stempiece of an old sailboat.*

Figure 6-49. A *typical serving board (top) and the tool in use (bottom).*

under the turns, then tighten the turns by working them around with the spike. Hitch onto the end and pull all slack out, then give a few sharp jerks to snug things completely down before trimming.

If you're using a serving board or iron, stop as in the finish of the Eyesplice service, below (Figure 6-56).

Mending

The oldest rigging afloat is not stainless steel, which has a lifespan limited by fatigue, but parceled and served galvanized wire, which is less susceptible to fatigue and can be completely sealed from rust. Here are instructions for the service mending that chafe occasionally necessitates.

Unwind the service from the affected area and trim the ends to about 2 feet (0.6 m) in length. Inspect the parceling and replace as necessary. Plain old friction or athletic tape makes excellent parcel-

ing, or you can rip up polyester bed sheets (they're no good for sleeping on anyway) into inch-wide (25-mm) strips and tar them. This is a good time to check the condition of the wire under the parceling. Retar as necessary, particularly if the service is over stainless steel, as the tar (or anhydrous lanolin) excludes both air and water, preventing crevice corrosion.

When the parceling is set, make up a hank of twine. If the area to be repaired is a long stretch, calculate how much twine you'll need as follows: Lightly serve a 1-inch (25.4-mm) length, then remove this service and measure how much twine it took. Multiply this by the total number of inches (or mm) to be served, and add a couple of feet (or 0.6 m) for the tails at the finish (see below).

If you are working aloft, thread the end of the twine through the lanyard hole in the end of your serving iron or board. Once you get started, this will trap the iron, so you can't accidentally drop it.

Using a spike, serve over the end of the new twine with the upper tail of the old twine (Figure 6-51A); this anchors the new twine's end. Then twist the two pieces together, lay the old twine's end down on the wire, and begin serving over it with the new twine, using the iron or board. Start carefully, so there's a minimum gap where the two pieces are

Favorite Goops

Most of the things I carry with me are tools, but there are a few substances that I dispense in the course of rigging work. Here are some of my favorites.

One-Drop
This is a lubricant/conditioner specifically formulated for open-race, plastic ball-bearings. If you have a Schaefer or Harken furler, you need to put a drop of this into the bearing races. Do so after every time you rinse the bearings out. You do rinse the bearings out regularly, right?

One-Drop is also perfect for things like traveler car bearings and blocks with open races. It really does only take one drop; the stuff distributes itself wonderfully.

One-Drop is made by the McLube company.

Zero
Another lubricant, this one for metal parts. It is biodegradable, non-toxic (including aquatically), doesn't burn, doesn't smell bad. A wonderful general-purpose oil. Most frequent use: winch pawls.

Eck and Tef-Gel
Galvanic corrosion is one of the banes of contemporary rigging. I've tried many products over the years,

and can say that even low-salt (creamy) peanut butter is probably better than nothing, but that two products stand out. One is called Eck, and the other is Tef-Gel. I cannot overstate the importance of having one of these on any dissimilar metal surfaces that are in contact with each other. Either one will last longer than anything else I know of, even in the tropics. Both can be used very sparingly; a barely visible coating is all you need.

3M 4000UV Sealant
This is the stuff I use inside mechanical wire terminals, and for most hardware bedding jobs (although see below).

Bedit Butyl Tape
Butyl rubber can make an extremely effective hardware bedding material. But it usually doesn't. This is because it comes in a, um, variety of formulations (i.e., most of it is crap). But the good formulation of this stuff is fantastic: suitably adhesive; tremendously elastic, to stay with components as they shift and vibrate; and very, very durable.

twisted together (Figure 6-51B). Serve over the old piece for four or five turns, then trim its end flush. Continue to serve the rest of the bare area.

Simple so far. The tricky part comes when you reach the other end of the service; how do you get a smooth, tight join down there? The best way is to serve right up against the old service, then unthread the iron and stow it carefully away. Now undo

---

Figure 6-51. *Mending service.*

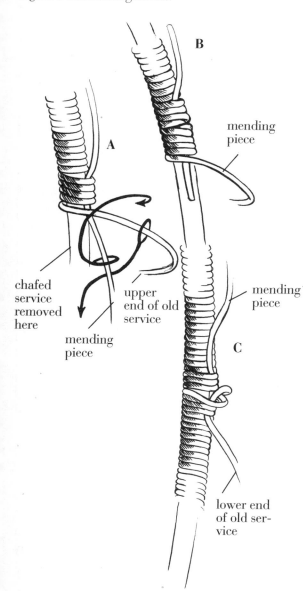

chafed service removed here

mending piece

upper end of old service

A

B

mending piece

mending piece

C

lower end of old service

exactly three turns from the old and new service. Lay the tip of a spike down and lightly wrap three turns back on with one of the ends, around the spike and the wire both. Remove the spike and thread the end under those three turns. Lay the spike back on the wire opposite these three turns, and restore the other end's three turns. Remove the spike, and thread the end under the last turn of the other end, then under its own final three turns (Figure 6-51C).

Begin tightening the turns on one side, slowly and carefully, one turn at a time, with the tip of the spike. When the turns are good and tight, pull the end to draw the last turn down. Tighten the turns on the other side, and pull that end down. Finish by jerking on both ends to tighten the crossover. The two last turns should mesh into one another, leaving a barely discernible join.

Use this same procedure for finishing service on a grommet.

If chafe in an area is a recurring problem, double-serve and/or leather. And check your running rigging leads to see if there's a way to lessen the chafe.

Two-Way Service for Eyes

The best time to serve an eye is before you splice it, so you can work on straight wire. But if you're re-serving an eye, you have no choice but to work within the confines of the eye. And it's very difficult to keep the turns of the twine from separating as you go around the curve of the eye. So start in the middle of the eye, serve down one side, then come back and serve down the other. You'll get fairer service and work with shorter lengths of twine.

Pinned Mallet

Service gets tricky when, as above, you're working in tight spaces. But you can greatly expand a serving board's range of usefulness with a metal pin set into the left-hand shoulder (for right-laid rope) of the board (or mallet). When you approach a constricted area, lead the twine over the pin, as in Figure 6-52. This shifts the body of the mallet away from the obstacle, allowing you to take more turns in clear air.

A Long Splice in wire is analogous to one in rope (see Chapter 4), but instead of three flexible strands, you're dealing with six intractable ones plus a heart that may be wire or fiber. It is much more difficult to get a uniform distribution of load over all six strands, but just as vital as with the rope's three strands; proceed with infinite fussiness.

The wire rope Long Splice is for any 6-strand construction, but is most commonly used on halyard wire (6 x 19, 6 x 19 IWRC, 7 x 19, 7 x 37, and so on).

To start, unlay the strands in pairs to a length indicated in the accompanying table for your-diameter wire rope. Cut off the hearts at the unlay-to point.

"Marry" the two lines. Lay out and lay in two opposing pairs until the laid-in pair is about half used up. For example, if you're splicing with ½-inch wire, you'll have 10-foot tails, and you'll lay the pair in until about 5 feet is still hanging out. The top illustration shows this first step in progress off to the right, with the other four pairs still married in the middle.

Now open up the two pairs of strands you've been working with, leave one member of each pair where it is, and lay in and out with the other two a little farther, until the lay-in strand has about a foot showing. This will give you the bottom illustration, with two pairs of strands meeting at separate points on the wire.

Go back to the marriage and lay out two more opposing sets, this time off to the left, again stopping halfway out and sub-splitting.

This leaves a lone set of strands in the middle. Split them where they lay, and lay each pair away from the middle, in opposite directions, until they're about one-quarter of the way to the farthest pairs.

You should now have six pairs of strands more or less evenly distributed along the wire. To finish, trim all ends about 1 foot long, and bury them as for the wire rope grommet shown in Figures 6-43D, E, F, G, H.

Extra length, each end, for Long Splice:

diam.	length	diam.	length
¼	5'	¾	15'0"
⁵⁄₁₆	6'3"	⅞	17'6"
⅜	7'5"	1	20'0"
⁷⁄₁₆	8'9"	1⅛	22'6"
½	10'0"	1¼	25'0"
⁹⁄₁₆	11'3"	1⅜	27'6"
⅝	12'6"	1½	30'0"

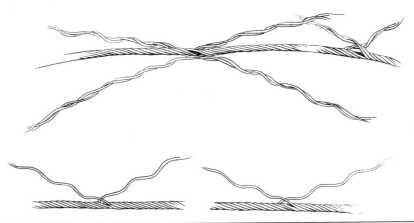

Parceling *sans* Service

Service is a good chafe preventer, but heavy-duty parceling is often as good and much quicker for chafe protection on mooring lines.

The old saying is to "parcel with the lay"—that is, to mimic the rope strands' spiral with the parceling. This lets the parceling lay down smoother under the service, which is put on against the lay. But parceling in the absence of service should go on against the lay (Figure 6-53). That way, when the rope untwists a bit under load, the parceling will tighten and stay put, instead of loosening and slipping out of place.

Birdcage Warning

A serving tool is a form of lever. When it is used with excessive force, this lever can distort the lay of the wire, causing the strands to separate into a strength-destroying "birdcage."

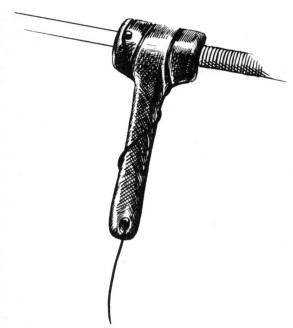

Figure 6-52. *Pinned serving board or mallet. The "pin" (dowel, short nail) set into the mallet head near its leading edge enables you to lift the twine from its usual groove and lead it outside the pin when serving up close to a thimble or other such obstacle.*

Figure 6-53. *When parceling is applied without service, wrap it on against the lay of the rope.*

You can't splice rope lazyjacks into wire topping lifts, and hitching them on just leaves a bulky knot to chafe the sail. So fan out 3 to 5 inches of the lazyjack end, arrange the yarns around the wire, Constrictor them firmly on, then serve over the works. We show three Constrictors; add a couple in the middle.

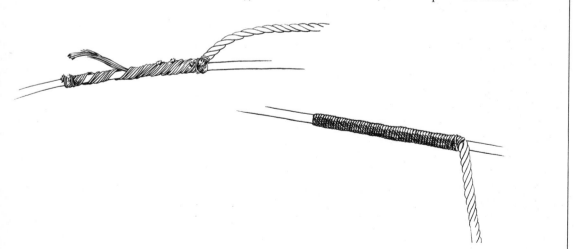

Back when marline was the material of choice, it used to be hard to make a birdcage, simply because the marline would break before sufficient force could be exerted. But nylon, today's service material of choice, is far stronger than hemp. It's also much more decay-resistant and far superior to hemp in every way, except that it allows an inattentive server to destroy the wire.

The question, then, is how tight is tight enough? The answer is that service should feel hard, but not so hard that friction-tape parceling squeezes out between the turns. So take it easy on your parceling, your service, and yourself.

Nylon Slush

Slush is the paint-like substance that goes on service to keep it from drying out. Ideally it is hard enough that it won't rub off on sails or crew, but soft enough that it won't crack and let water in. With marline, slush was traditionally made with a mix of Stockholm tar, boiled linseed oil, and Japan drier, with maybe a little varnish thrown in. This works well with nylon service, too, but there is an even better alternative: equal parts black paint and net dip. Net dip, available from fishery supply stores, is an asphalt-based paint in which twinemakers dip nylon twine to tar it. It's a little too thin and soft to hold up on standing rigging by itself, hence the addition of a good anticorrosive black paint. Test paint a short stretch of service, since some paints dry harder than others. If the slush dries too hard, thin with Cuprinol and varnish to taste. If you can't find net dip in your area, thin some asphalt roofing tar to an almost-watery consistency.

Wire Service

Wire service is rarely needed, but if you have a severe chafe issue, it can be the right thing to do. The serving material of choice is 1 x 7 seizing wire. It might seems logical to serve galvanized wire with galvanized seizing wire, and stainless with stainless. But in practice, annealed stainless seizing wire of 1 x 7 construction is nearly always the better material.

For one thing, galvanized seizing wire, which is made from iron, not steel, is much weaker than stainless. And corrosion is most severe at deck level, where most wire service is needed; stainless seizing wire lasts longer here. Fatigue is not a problem, because the wire is annealed, and is also not structural. Finally, stainless wire is much more widely available, since it has wide commercial use.

Corrosion arising from mixing dissimilar metals is generally not a problem with rigging materials—given the insulation of service, or even just paint—since (if all goes well) rigging is not kept immersed in the electrolytic medium of water. As insurance, it is customary to double-parcel under wire service, mixed metals or no: one layer of friction tape to waterproof, and one layer of lanolined polyester bedsheet to insulate the wire and keep it from chewing up the friction tape.

Wire and twine service are the same in principle, and they can even share tools and techniques. But wire is a bit harder to control, and if a loose end whips around it can do some damage, so be careful. At the start of wire service, you may need to lightly clamp the end down with Vise Grips to get started. Always use a serving iron (Figures 6-54 and 6-55). Alternatively, you can insert the end of the wire under one of the strands of the standing part (Figure 6-55)

To finish wire service, make and undo the turns as with twine (see page 230), pull the slack out

---

Figure 6-54. *"U.P.I.," a serving iron, with suggested dimensions.*

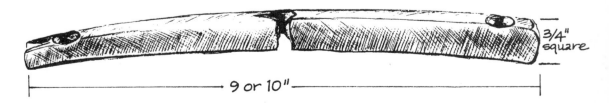

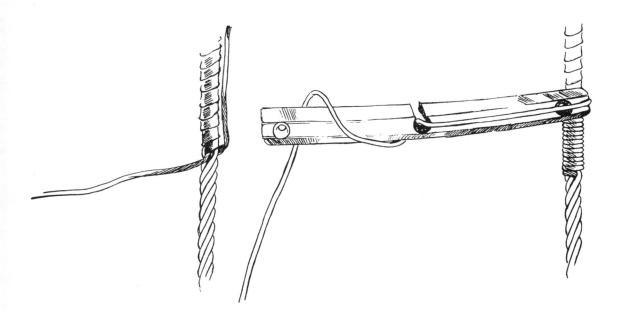

Figure 6-55. *Wire service is begun by putting on safety glasses—on you! Next, insert one end of the seizing wire under a strand of the wire rope, or clamp it lightly in place with Vise Grips. Thread the seizing wire onto the serving iron and serve over the end.*

with a pair of pliers, and get out your heaving mallet. Figure 6-56E shows "Mallet de Mer" with the seizing wire belayed to its head and handle, ready to pull the last turn taut—too much of a job for a marlingspike. Apply just enough tension to bring the turn down snug, then put the mallet over on the other side so that the strand will be pulled to that side, wedging itself permanently between the rope and the turns of service. If the service is very tight the strand will shear off cleanly at its exit point with a good haul on the mallet.

If it won't shear, but you're sure the fit is snug, just bend the seizing wire sharply back and forth repeatedly until it breaks off at the exit point.

The one place you shouldn't mix rigging metals is on splices that do spend a lot of time under water, like the lower ends of bobstays and boomkin shrouds. Also check to see that the wire rope itself is compatible with hull fittings

The best way to stop service is to pause when you are several turns short of your desired stopping place. How many turns short depends on the material and application; elsewhere in the text I've said five, and that is a good default, but with non-slick twine three turns will be sufficient for finishing normal service, while seizing a thimble in with the end of service is usually better off having seven turns, because there will be more lateral loading at the end, with the legs of the eye trying to force the service apart. No matter how many turns you use, the trick is to measure how much length those turns will take up, and pause at that point. To do this, stop when you think you are in the neighborhood, and use a caliper gauge to measure, say, five turns. Then measure how much space there is between you and where you want to stop. If it is farther, add service until the gap is correct. If it is closer, unwind service until the gap is correct.

Tightening the Lay of Seizing Wire

When applied as a seizing, seizing wire sometimes will unlay and flatten under load, preventing it from lying fair. To prevent this, tighten the lay of the wire before using: clamp one end in a vise, the other end in a pair of Vise Grips, and twist the lay tighter.

Figure 6-56A-F. *Elements of Service.*

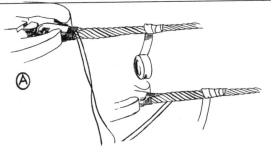

The eye of the splice is served before splicing. The finished splice is tarred, then wormed and parceled. Worming material should be just large enough to provide a smooth surface over which to parcel. Carefully seal the join between eye and splice with parceling.

Holding tension with one hand, use pliers to pull slack out.

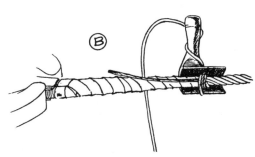

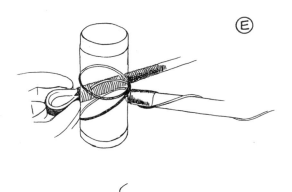

Marline service being applied with another type of serving board—one with a very wide groove suited to splices. Note that marline is threaded through the hole in the handle to gain tension and to prevent accidentally dropping the board overboard.

To finish the seizing, use a heaving mallet or spike to pull first left (facing vise), then right. The wire should snap at the exit point during the pull to the right.

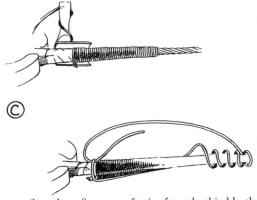

Serve until you have five turns of twine from the thimble, then stop and pass five turns around the standing part of the wire rope. Slip the twine end under its most recent turn of service. Continue serving until all five turns are undone.

A finished oversized eye. Note that the seizing-wire diameter matches the marline. Most often, $3/32$-inch wire will suit.

Now make those turns *on the other side of the board* from the end of the service, quite loosely (Figure 6-56-C). Then tuck the end of the marline under the last turn of service and begin serving over it, thus undoing the turns you made and ending up with a large bight at the end of a smooth, tight service. You'll serve through a loop, and you'll need to clear the end out of your way with each turn. It's confusing at first, but with practice it makes the fastest, neatest finish possible. When you have undone all the turns, you should be at the stopping point you wanted. Remove the serving board and hold onto the service with one hand, hitch onto the end with a spike and pull with the other hand, and guide the slack out, keeping the twine from twisting, with your third hand. Be careful, as you pull, to keep the spike away from face and body; twine has been known to break. This procedure is the same when made with seizing wire, as in Figure 6-56C, D.

Short stretches of service are great for lashing hammocks, lightboards, fairleads, ratlines, or cleats to, or just as a comfortable handhold on backstay or shrouds (see opening illustration for this section). And I don't recall ever seeing a better way of holding spreaders in place than the one L. Francis Herreshoff used to recommend (Figure 6-57, reproduced from construction drawings for *Araminta*). As you can see, the first layer of service fits snugly into the spreader tip, easing the bend and providing a foundation for the little bits of service that go on above and below the spreader, holding it from traveling up or down and making reinstallation easy after a haulout. Leather backing is optional. A metal strap will keep the wire from jumping out, but a light seizing (shown) will do the trick, too.

Splice Service

Figure 6-56F shows a spliced eye that is oversize and served for its entire circumference. The splice and its eye are completely waterproofed, because the join between eye and splice service has been sealed, under the service, by a "diaper" of parceling (unshaded service shows extent of eye service). This diaper is very tidily applied—figure-eight turns taken through the throat of the eye—so as not to

raise a lump in the service that will go on top. An oversize eye also means that you can replace thimble or service should either become damaged. In conventional splices, the thimble service is exactly the circumference of the thimble, so the splice service can't fully overlap it, and there's no secure seal—and no way to repair the eye service or replace the thimble.

To produce this ultimate in Eyesplice protection, serve the circumference of an eye that is big enough to get the thimble in and out of (see Figure 6-4). Splice, then parcel and serve towards the eye (Figure 6-56A, B, C, D, E). Ease up on the tension as you make the transition from splice to eye service, so you don't squash the diaper down and create a

---

Figure 6-57. *Securing a spreader tip to a shroud. The first layer of service fits snugly into the spreader tip; the second layer, applied in two short stretches immediately above and below the spreader tip, contains the up-and-down motion of the spreader. A light lashing keeps the shroud in the spreader groove, or you can use a metal band screwed to the spreader.*

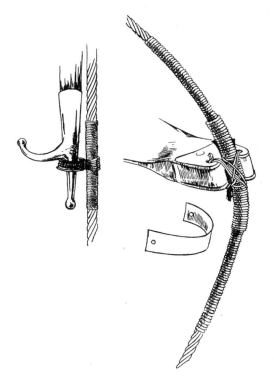

sudden jump in service diameter. Try for a smooth taper. Finish as for normal service, as described in Figure 6-56C.

Full Service

The ultimate in service protection is to wrap your galvanized or Spectra standing rigging (except hanked stays) full length. The rigging is thus indefinitely preserved, assuming an occasional coat of "slush" to keep the service sealed. Although the payoff is ageless rigging as well as less chafe on sails and running rigging, the amount of time and effort that full-length service requires makes low-maintenance stainless–or uncovered Spectra–the choice for all but a few. But for those of us who care to indulge ourselves, here's how it's done.

To start, stretch the spliced wire between two posts, trees, or walls, using a come-along for tension. This will exert extreme strain on the attachment points, so be certain they are very solid. For wire, apply a coat of pine tar or anhydrous lanolin as an anticorrosive—liberally, but not so much that it's going to drip out when warm. Then parcel toward the upper end with friction tape or tarred cloth. Worm both splices; if the wire is $7/8$ inch or larger, you might want to worm the entire length, because water could collect in the large spaces between the strands.

Runaround Sue Sue's a relatively high-tech, spool-fed, self-tensioning, air-cooled, semiautomatic serving board who literally flies through her job. In the old days, service was put on by a rigger and an apprentice, the former passing a spool-less mallet, the latter passing a ball of marline around to match, and both of them inching along with the slo-o-o-wly progressing work. But with Sue, one person just leans back and oscillates the wire to make the mallet move along all by itself, thus bearing witness to the old saying, "They also serve who only stand and wait."

For the best job, start with a not-quite-bar-taut wire, thread the mallet as shown (Figure 6-58), and

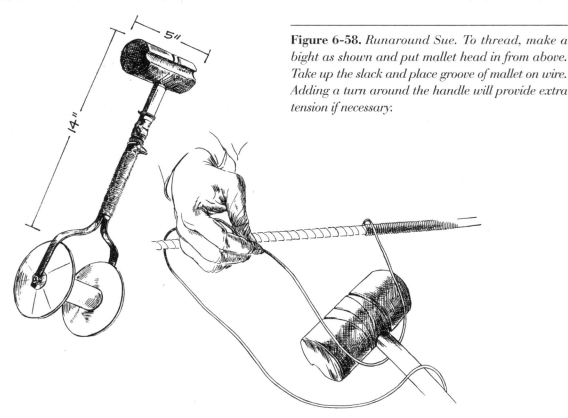

Figure 6-58. *Runaround Sue. To thread, make a bight as shown and put mallet head in from above. Take up the slack and place groove of mallet on wire. Adding a turn around the handle will provide extra tension if necessary.*

Figure 6-59. *Flying Service. Stretch wire rope out taut, but be sure your anchor points can take the strain. Tar and worm the splices, and parcel the wire full length. Thread mallet on and "fly" by oscillating wire with rhythmic pull-and-release motion. If the marline breaks, retrieve mallet and bend in new piece as for service mending.*

use an oscillation technique that swings the mallet around and down on the pull stroke, then eases off to let it swing up and over before the next pull. With a little practice you can time the push-and-pull to maximum effect (that is, minimum effort). Always lean back slightly to dampen jerking motions of the wire (Figure 6-59). Tricing lines can be tied on every 20 feet or so to further control the wire's motion. With this setup, you can parcel and serve 20 to 30 feet an hour. Not exactly a blistering rate by track and field standards, but fast enough to get the job done while you're still young enough to go sailing.

INTO LEATHER

Leather is a cushion, an insulator, that keeps your standing rigging from damaging your mast and sails. A layer of leather over one or two layers of service is standard procedure for soft eyes, and a stretch of leather over service is a tidy alternative to baggywrinkle for chafe-prone stretches of wire

(Figure 6-60). There's nothing terribly complicated about applying leather, so it makes sense to keep a split hide of oiled shoulder or Latigo around for the above uses as well as for oar leathers, gaff jaws, chafing gear on sail eyelets, sheaths, handles, and all the other places you'll find use for it once you have it around and know how to work it.

The traditional stitch for most cylindrical or conical objects is the awkward Baseball Stitch: it's redundant, since it uses two threads; and its criss-cross pattern pulls the edges of the leather together, making a smooth, tight seam (Figure 6-61). But here's a variant that is even better. I call it the Baseball Diamond Stitch. It starts in the middle and works toward both ends, so there's (a) no super-long, tangle-prone lengths of twine to deal with, (b) a tight finish at both ends, and (c) even "shrinkage" in both directions, so you don't get lopsided eyes. And there's this neat little diamond in the middle of the finished piece (Figure 6-63F).

Here's how it's done:

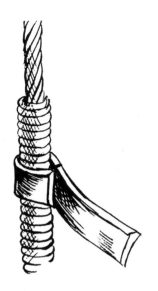

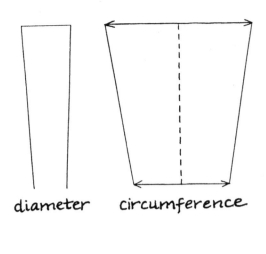

diameter   circumference

Figure 6-60. *Leathering a stretch of wire. To determine circumference, wrap a piece of leather around the wire.*

Figure 6-62A. *To leather a straight taper, such as an oar, measure the circumferences of the oar bole at the positions where the leather top and bottom will lie. Draw a midline of the required length on the leather, and lay out the half-circumference distances on either side of the midline, top and bottom. Connect the top and bottom corners to make the taper.*

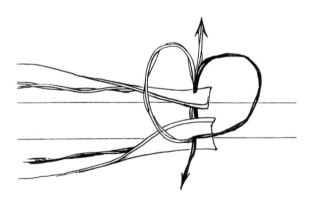

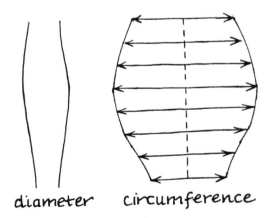

diameter   circumference

Figure 6-61. *The Baseball Stitch, a double-needle technique, requires a fathom of waxed twine per foot of leathering on each needle. The twine is middled on the needle, making a 3-foot working length per foot of leathering an awkward arrangement. In starting the stitch, the needles are passed in opposite directions, in complete round turns, through both end holes in the leather. This tends to distort the corners of the leather. For a much more efficient stitch, see Figure 6-63.*

Figure 6-62B. *To shape a piece of leather for an irregular taper, such as an Eyesplice, measure circumferences at regular intervals along the splice and plot the respective half-circumferences on either side of the leather's midline. In either case, straight or tapered, deduct ¹⁄₁₆ to ⅛ inch for elasticity, depending on the leather.*

First, measure the leather so it fits the leatheree. Figure 6-62 shows how.

Cut a piece of waxed #7 twine 12 times the length of the leather. So, for a 1-foot (.30 m) leather you'd need 12 feet (3.66 m). This assumes stitching holes 3/8 inch (9.5 mm) from each edge and 3/8 inch (9.5 mm) apart.

Fold the twine in half and thread a sail needle—#14 is a handy size—onto each end (Figure 6-63A). If you are pre-punching holes in the leather with a jogging wheel (Figure 6-64C), dull the needles with a fine file; they'll be less likely to snag on the leather or you. Leave the needles hanging a foot or so on either side of the middle for now. Fold the twine in half again, but not quite exactly in half; leave the ends sticking past the bight about 3 inches (76 mm).

Now let go of the ends and fold in half yet again the length that remains in your hands. Move the needles to the middle of this length (Figure 6-63B). The needles are now in position and ready to sew. All that folding rigmarole was just a way of locating them, without tape-measuring, one-quarter of the total length on either side of the middle. With the

needles in this position, you can sew half the length of the job, then come back and use the long ends to sew the other half.

And so to work. Lightly scribe a line 3/8 inch from each long edge. Use the jogging wheel to mark the spaces on one edge. Pre-punch the holes into the leather on that edge with a .00 punch ("double-aught" is what they call it at the leather store). Use a square or bevel gauge or ruler to mark the other edge (you can't use the jogging wheel because it won't jog exactly the same distance between holes). Punch the second set of holes, then rub some neatsfoot oil onto the inside of the piece.

If you do a lot of leatherwork, it can be worthwhile to make a nail board: into a suitable piece of wood, drill a series of holes exactly 3/8 of an inch apart, and 3/8 of an inch from one edge. The holes should be a snug fit for 12-gauge (4 D) nails. Lay out carefully, and use a drill press to make the holes. Use nails that are just an eighth of an inch or so longer than the wood is thick. Drive them all in. Now when you want to mark a line of holes, just position your board on top of the leather, along one edge, points down, and tap the back of the board with a mallet. Shift it over to the other edge and repeat.

Fold the leather in half (crosswise) to locate the middle holes, mark them with a pen, then straighten

---

Figure 6-63A. *Preparing for the Baseball Diamond Stitch.*

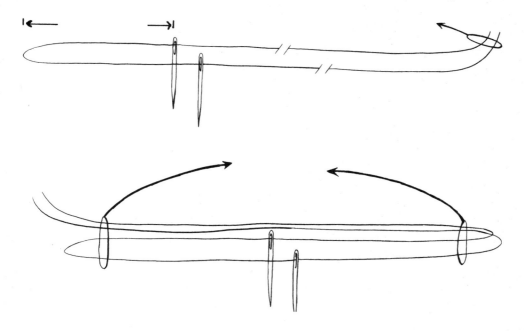

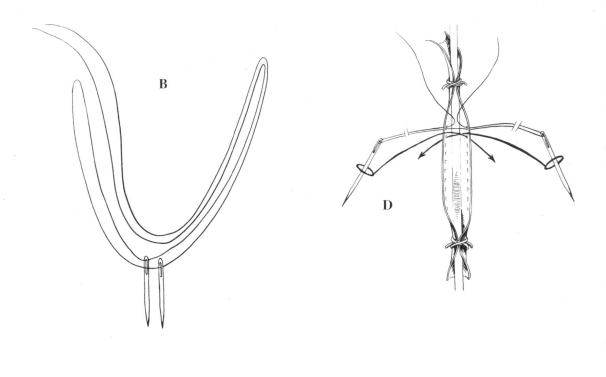

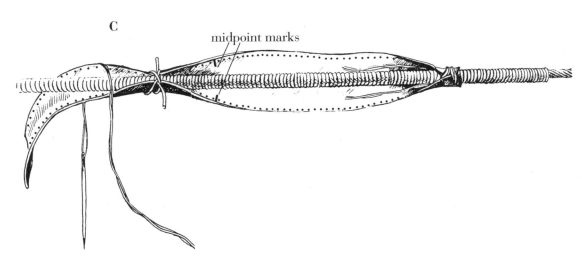

Figure 6-63B–D. *Beginning the Baseball Diamond Stitch. Pass the needles in regular sequence—always the same one first, for a neat appearance. A temporary seizing holds the leather in place for you. For the first couple of passes, haul each just tight enough to bring the two sides of the leather together. Use roping palms or marlingspikes to haul with. After the first passes, haul more firmly, but not to the extent that you are in danger of tearing the leather. You will find that the most recent stitches will be a bit loose, but that your hauling will tighten previous stitches. D shows the first half of the leather being stitched.*

the leather out and Constrictor it lightly to the leath-eree (Figure 6-63C). Thread the needles from the inside out through the center holes (Figure 6-63D). Take up the slack so that the needles are evenly extended. Be careful to avoid letting thread shift in the needle's eyes at this point, as that would leave you short for stitching the second half.

When everything is even, thread one needle diagonally off to one side, then the other needle through the corresponding hole on the other side (Figure 6-63D). Firmly draw all the slack out after each set of stitches, first pulling the threads straight out to the sides to tighten previous stitches, then crossing them over the top of the seam and hauling to the sides again to tighten the current stitch. Wear roping palms or heavy gloves to avoid hand damage.

Keep the seam straight as you go. Always enter the same side first—i.e., if the first stitch you took was with the needle on the right, always begin a set of stitches with the needle on the right. It looks better.

For an idea of what a good seam should look like, get a baseball. You'll see that the leather edges are firmly butted together, with a little ridge of leather bunched up on either side.

Figure 6-63E. *A leather marker jig. Drill holes ³⁄₈-inch apart, centered ³⁄₈-inch from one edge of the jig. The holes should be a tight fit for the nails you will use. Drive in the nails, of a length that just projects above the surface of the jig. To mark the leather, lay it on top of the nails, with the edge of the leather lined up with the edge of the jig. Using a mallet, tap the leather onto the nails, to mark the hole punch locations.*

Avoid, at all costs, pulling so hard that you rip the leather. If the piece is the right size, you shouldn't need to pull that hard.

When you get to the end, make a complete turn through the last set of holes with each needle. They'll come out from under the leather at the end (Figure 6-63F). Haul taut. Reef-Knot the ends together, snapping each half-knot smartly to set it back under the leather. Trim the ends short.

Now remove the leftover thread from the needles and thread them onto the long ends hanging out of the middle of the work. Turn and face toward the unstitched side and begin sewing through the same two holes you started in before (Figure 6-63G). Leave 3 to 4 inches (76 to 102 mm) of thread ends behind, and sew over them to anchor the stitches. For the most pleasing appearance, begin with the opposite needle than you did for the other half. Sew to the end and finish as before.

Some notes on the application of this stitch:

- Latigo is the best material to use where chafe is severe (shrouds, anchor rodes, gaff jaws, oars, etc.). It's the thickest and longest-lived material you can get, and a little boot dressing now and then will keep it healthy.
- "Synthetic leather"—rubber, plastic hose, and the like—can be quite tough to work with and becomes brittle with age.
- For light duty, as where sails chafe on shrouds, the supple, pale-gray leather that sailmakers use

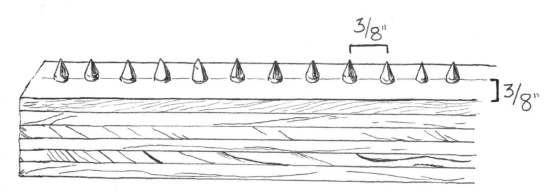

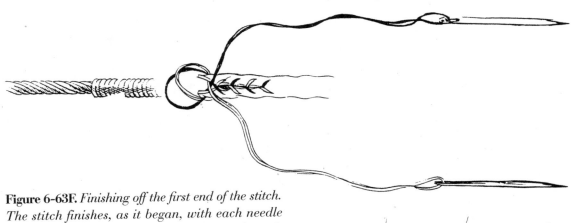

Figure 6-63F. *Finishing off the first end of the stitch. The stitch finishes, as it began, with each needle making a complete round turn. Reef-Knot the ends together and cut off flush with the leather.*

Figure 6-63G. *Stitching the second half of the leather.*

is excellent stuff. It's tough, elastic, and durable, but thin enough that it won't look clunky in place. If you apply it over stainless, rub a generous amount of anhydrous lanolin (available from druggists) into the wire first to minimize oxygen starvation. Tar and serve galvanized wire before leathering.

- Always turn the stitches away from chafe. When leathering nonfeathering oars, run the seam in line with the blade edge. With feathering oars, run it a little aft of the edge so that it won't chafe against the forward side of the oarlock as you feather. Row for a bit before leathering; the chafe marks will show where the middle of the leather should be. If the boat has more than one rowing station or a sculling notch, you'll want an extra-long leather to accommodate the different bearing points. Especially for feathering and sculling oars, it's good to glue the wood and leather together with contact cement before stitching.

- If your twine does chafe through sometime, anchor the repair strand(s) and the original strand(s) under the first several stitches you take. This is far better than tying a knot in the end of the twine, as that knot is liable to pull through under strain.

- Two people with needles can make this stitch go very quickly indeed: Set the work up at waist level, one of you on either side, and commence stitching, hauling tight after each pass. With a bit of practice you'll work into a pleasant little choreography.

- For the neatest job, bevel the meeting edges back from the finished face of the leather and make the piece slightly undersized (1/16 to 1/8 inch, depending on the elasticity of the leather you're using) so that the leather will stretch to fill the gap.

- Rub liberal amounts of neats-foot oil or other conditioner into both sides of the leather before sewing, and renew the coating periodically on the outside, after installation.

- Always leather soft eyes (Figure 6-64) *before* splicing; it is so much easier to leather in a straight line. To leather grommets or to re-leather

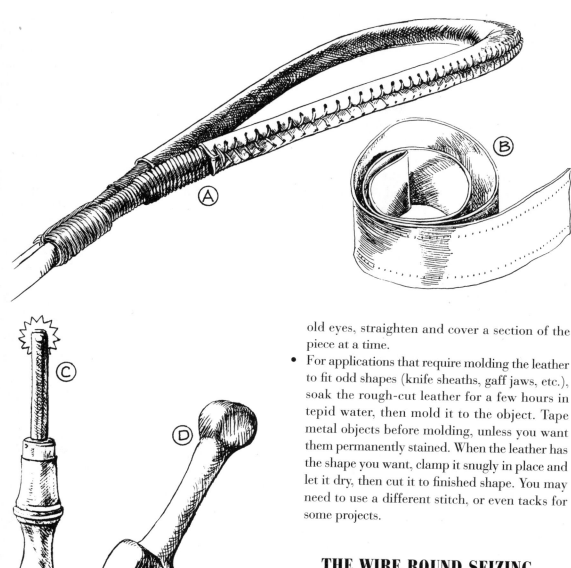

Figure 6-64. *A double-served, leathered soft eye is shown in A. This heavy leather was prepared by pre-punching holes ³/₈ inch apart and ³/₈ inch from the edges (B). The holes were marked with a jogging wheel for regular spacing (C), and the stitches were smoothed down with a seam rubber (D).*

old eyes, straighten and cover a section of the piece at a time.

- For applications that require molding the leather to fit odd shapes (knife sheaths, gaff jaws, etc.), soak the rough-cut leather for a few hours in tepid water, then mold it to the object. Tape metal objects before molding, unless you want them permanently stained. When the leather has the shape you want, clamp it snugly in place and let it dry, then cut it to finished shape. You may need to use a different stitch, or even tacks for some projects.

THE WIRE ROUND SEIZING

There is no more subtle knot than this one. In structure and appearance it is an ordinary Round Seizing, rendered in wire instead of marline. But the stresses it is designed to endure are of a higher order than its twine cousin's, and the technique of making it properly relies so much on fussiness and "feel" that it is the most difficult knot to learn to do well. Because it is intrinsic to many items of traditional rigging, particularly shroud pairs, wire-rope grommets, and deadeyes, I'm going to attempt a description of it here. But understand that practice and something

I can only describe as utilitarian intuition will do you a lot more good than words and pictures will.

Setup

Fully serve an eight-foot length of $5/16$-inch 7 x 7 or 7 x 19 wire rope (seizings should always be applied over a grip-providing layer of service). Clamp this in a vertically mounted rigging vise or, just for this practice, in a machinist's vise (Figure 6-65). Hitch onto the wire ends and haul them up snugly to an overhead block, using block and tackle or come-along to pull the work nearly bar taut. How firmly is your vise secured to the floor?

As with the Liverpool Eyesplice, you can set up to seize either vertically or horizontally. With an upright wire one can walk completely around the work for greater speed and better-controlled "tracking," so a vertical setup is almost universal. But there are times when horizontal is handy, and some people prefer it. For this text, we are going with vertical.

About 6 to 8 inches above the vise jaws, apply a homemade rigger's screw (made from a double-bar clamp with shaped wood jaws screwed to it), and snug it up to pinch the legs firmly together. Hitch a light line to the clamp's handle and lead it out hori-

---

Figure 6-65. *Wire Round Seizing setup. The served wires have been clamped in place at their lower ends, and the upper ends have been pulled taut overhead. The rigger's screw is in position, with a line led from its handle to torque the wire a quarter-turn counterclockwise. This will provide resistance for the clockwise torque that the seizing stick will apply. A strip of canvas and a length of seizing wire have been inserted between the legs at the seizing site, as the text describes. A very compact loop has been formed in the end of the wire as a stopper to prevent the end of the wire from being pulled free when you start the seizing.*

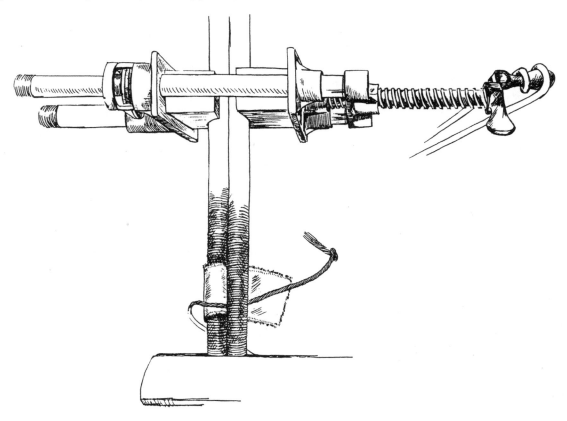

zontally under sufficient strain to put a slight right-hand twist into the wire. This is to counteract the left-hand twist that applying the seizing will cause.

Drive in a small spike below the rigger's screw and insert one end of a 1-inch by 2-inch strip of medium-weight canvas (or nylon webbing) and one end of a 10-foot-long piece of $\frac{1}{16}$-inch galvanized or stainless 1 x 7 seizing wire (Figure 6-65). Work a little stopper crimp into the end of the wire and position the wire down near the bottom of the canvas. Remove the spike. Pull on the seizing wire until the knot fetches up against the wire rope. Wrap the canvas strip tightly around, against the lay, and fix it in place with a layer of friction tape.

Now step over to the bandsaw and cut yourself a seizing stick (Figure 6-66A) out of the toughest, orneriest wood you can find; lignum vitae, some of the oaks, or hickory, among others, will do. Round off the rough edges and get back to the vise.

Round Turns

From here on, an extra pair of hands is a big help, so try to talk someone into reading all this and working with you. I'll assume in the instructions that you were successful. Both you and your helper should don safety glasses before proceeding; the end of the seizing wire can whip around very fast.

Coil and lightly seize the seizing wire, then pull on and bend it at its beginning so that it leads slightly downward from where it emerges between the two parts of the wire rope. Then veer it off horizontally to the left. Thread the wire onto the stick and take up the slack (Figure 6-66A).

Essaying to keep the seizing wire absolutely horizontal, move the stick around, easing up just

a bit on friction as you round the first corner, then clamping down tightly and stre-e-e-tching it across the face. If the end pulls out or if the wire rope starts to twist, stop, redo things more tightly, and then start again. The biggest key to a successful seizing is consistency. You must be consistent in how much and where you slack for the corners, and how much and where you tighten across the faces. Your seizings should look like they were machined out of bar stock.

The first revolution should finish at the level at which it began. At this point, against all instincts of tidiness, you must raise the lead a little so that the wire crosses this face crookedly and lays in directly above its start. In making the turn and wrapping around the other face the lead will be horizontal (Figure 6-66B).

Continue wrapping, moderate tension on the corners, heavy on the faces. Allow no gaps between the turns. Your assistant will pass the coiled wire around for you. Faithfully follow that crooked lead in front. The seizing wire should be sufficiently hard-laid that it won't "flatten out." That is, the strands don't disassociate themselves from one another, but remain round and firm. If you do get flattening, undo everything, clamp one end of the wire in a vise, stretch the wire out, and clamp the other end in a pair of Vise Grips. Then twist the wire against the lay to firm it up. It might take a couple dozen revolutions.

Figure 6-66A. *Bend the seizing wire down slightly where it emerges from the wire, then lead it horizontally clockwise (to the left). Thread it onto the seizing stick as shown and take up the slack.*

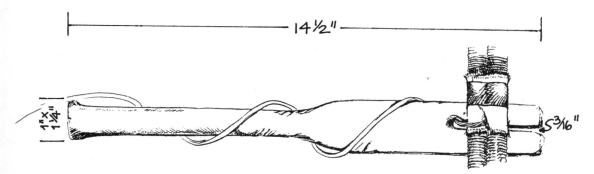

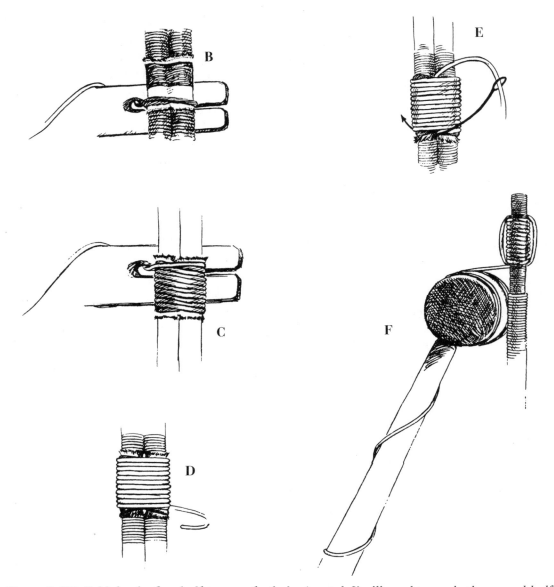

Figure 6-66B–F. *Make the first half turn perfectly horizontal. You'll need to angle the second half turn upward to clear the start, but that's good. Apply tight turns, stretching the wire across the flat faces, easing up a bit at the rounded sides (B). After completing the round turns, angle the lead back down to begin riding turns (C). The last riding turn should cleanly cover the first round turn. Begin frapping turns by poking a hole with an awl or small spike just as close to the bottom of the seizing as you can get. Don't snag anything with the awl. Pass the end through the hole, being careful not to lose any slack, and snap it into place, being careful not to lose any fingers (D). Poke a hole at the top of the seizing and pass the end through this, then back through the first hole. Snap the turn into place (E). Heave the first frapping turn taut with your Mallet de Mer (see Figure 6-56F). A bit of tallow or shortening applied under the turn at its top left and bottom right corners (as seen in the drawing) will help the wire slide around. "Massage" the slack toward the mallet with a marlingspike (F).*

Riding Turns

After you've made enough full turns (12 for this diameter wire) so that the seizing is longer than it is wide, angle the stick down so that the wire eases onto the first layer to begin a series of riding turns (Figure 6-66C). Apply the riding turns snugly too, but not so much that they displace the round turns beneath. As you progress, you will note that the crooked face underneath makes the riding turns lie horizontal on both faces. Elegant.

The wire should continue to feed smoothly right to the bottom of the seizing. When you run out of turns to cover, pinch the bottom turn tightly with one hand to keep it from slipping, and remove the seizing stick with the other while your assistant removes the rigger's screw.

Frapping Turns

Next, one of you hefts a scratch-awl spike and pushes it between the two parts of the wire rope, immediately above then immediately below the seizing (Figure 6-66D). It may be necessary to pound it through with a mallet in order to make holes large enough to pass the seizing wire through. Be sure the flat tip of the spike is vertical so that it will not cut the service as it goes through.

Pull the spike out and thread the end of the wire into the lower hole (Figure 6-66E). When there's just a small bight of wire left on the front face of the seizing, fair carefully and take up the rest of the slack sharply to set the wire. Do this by grabbing onto the wire a couple of feet from the seizing with a pair of pliers. Keeping tension on the standing part, thread the wire end through the upper hole and once more through the lower hole, snapping each time to set the wire. Watch your fingers.

Pinching the seizing so that slack can't work back, bend on your—Mallet de Mer—and take a light strain (Figure 6-66F), just enough to hold things in place. Apply a little tallow or shortening where this first frapping turn goes around the corners of the seizing, then gradually increase the strain on the mallet. The wire will flatten and start to move, and as it does your assistant should lightly tap the last riding turn to work any slack in it toward the

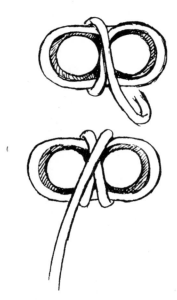

Figure 6-66G. *The second frapping turn crosses over the first at the bottom of the seizing (upper drawing). The end then recrosses its own part at the end of the second frapping turn (the top of the seizing). Haul this turn taut with the mallet also, again massaging slack toward the mallet as you haul.*

mallet, then use a spike handle or other rounded tool to "massage" slack in the frapping turn toward the mallet. Just press down and slide it along the seizing.

How hard do you haul on the mallet? Hard enough to slightly stretch the wire, but not hard enough to be in danger of wasting all your work by breaking the wire. This happens. You just have to get to know your own strength and that of the wire.

Pinch the seizing again with your hand to hold what you've gained, widen the holes a little with the little spike if necessary, and pass the end around again. Cross over the first frapping turn to bind it top and bottom (Figure 6-66G), then apply a bit more tallow and heave and massage this second frapping turn taut.

Finishing

Work the tip of your spike under the frapping turns below the seizing wire end. Remove the spike and thread the wire through the space it made

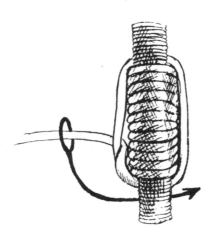

Figure 6-66H. *After two frapping turns, the end will emerge at the point where the seizing started. Make a space with your spike or awl under the frapping turns on that side and pass the end behind those turns, right to left. Pull smartly to set the wire behind the turns. Enlarge the hole between the legs at the bottom of the seizing if necessary, and pass the end back through, creating a hitch in the seizing wire.*

(Figure 6-66H), from right to left. Pull the slack out, being careful not to distort the frapping turns or let any slack escape under them, then thread the end back into the hole from whence it came and snap it tight by hand. Smear a little tallow or lanolin onto the hitch it forms, hook up your Mallet de Mer to the standing part, and pull the hitch gently out of sight, letting up when it is right between the two parts of the wire rope (Figure 6-66I). Note that, from here on, the mallet rests on the seizing, not on the legs of the wire.

Raise another space under the frapping turns on this side and thread the seizing wire through, again from right to left; if this hitch is not made in the same direction as the first one they'll untie each other. Pull out the slack and thread the seizing wire back through as before, snap it down, apply a little more tallow, and haul the hitch in against the first one. Pull square to the seizing until this hitch renders itself around the corner and down into the middle (Figure 6-66J); then set the head of the mallet onto the right-hand leg of the wire rope (Figure

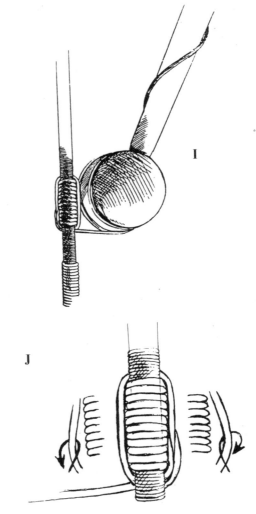

Figure 6-66I–J. *Set the mallet against the side of the seizing opposite the hitch and thread the wire on. Smear a little tallow into the hitch and take a strain. The hitch will slide around the corner and fetch up between the legs of the wire rope. Don't force it, just set it in there firmly. The frapping turns should remain undisturbed (I). Make a second hitch on the side opposite the first one, in the same direction as the first one (see arrows). Set this hitch as before, and pass the end through again (J).*

6-66K) for the coup de grace. If all the turns are in good, snug order, you can just haul tighter and tighter until the seizing wire breaks off cleanly, right where it exits the second hitch. Just the sweetest seizing finish you'll ever see (Figure 6-66L).

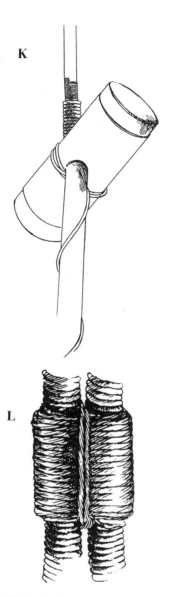

K

L

Figure 6-66K–L. *To finish, move the mallet over to the side of the seizing to sharpen the end's exit from the second hitch, and pull hard. The seizing wire should break cleanly inside (K). A finished wire Round Seizing (L).*

Living with Seizings

As I mentioned at the beginning, wire Throat Seizings are intrinsic to several traditional constructions (for some examples, see Figure 6-67A). They are far neater, cheaper, and easier on wire than cable

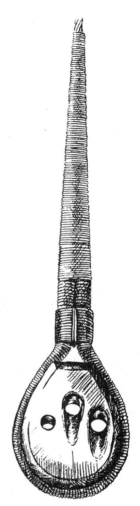

Figure 6-67A. *Deadeyes and Round Seizings. By splicing and then seizing-in a deadeye, one gains a splice with no lateral strain on its legs, a tightly secured deadeye, and the ability to remove the deadeye for repair to it or to the eye's service.*

clamps or Nicopress fittings, the comparable "modern" alternatives. The trouble is—and here I speak as one who has seen the light—if you don't fuss and fume to get seizings just right, you're better off with those alternatives. At boatyards that store old and new traditional craft, one can tour the spar sheds and see Herreshoff and Concordia seizings that are still dependable works of art after 30 years. But next to them you'll find examples that have about as much structural significance as a neckerchief slide.

These are dangerous and unattractive. They give seizings a bad name.

Throat Seizing Details

A spliced-and-seized-in deadeye eliminates lateral strain on the legs of the splice, holds the deadeye most firmly in place, and allows for deadeye removal in the event of damage to it or to the service around the eye.

A series of seizings in place of a splice is a good terminal alternative, especially on large vessels, whose standing rigging is also large and thus difficult to splice. Three seizings are applied for wire up to ⅝-inch diameter, four seizings on wire ¾-inch diameter and up.

When turning up seized ends, leave the bitter end 2 feet or more longer than it will be when finished, in order to be able to take a strain on both parts while seizing. When you're done, trim this end by (1) backing off the service to within ½ inch of the top seizing, (2) driving a thin hardwood wedge between end and standing part, (3) using the edge of an abrasive disc on an electric grinder to cut the end 1 to 1½ inches above the top seizing (the wedge protects the standing part), (4) re-serving to the end of the nub, and (5) capping off with a copper plumbing cap of appropriate diameter. Be sure that it is the end you are cutting—it is frighteningly easy to mistake the standing part for it—and cut in two or three stages, resting a few seconds between each so that the grinder doesn't heat the tar in the wire to the flash point. It is best to start with the seizing that is farthest from the eye. That way, once that one is done you can make sure that the deadeye or thimble is properly oriented, apply a bit more tension to make sure that both legs are under equal tension, and then apply the next seizing. If there is even a little slack in one of the legs, the seizings will not share the load evenly.

When seizing around deadeyes, *always* lead the bitter end of the wire rope so that it is above the lanyard-knot side of the deadeye (Figure 6-67B). This side invariably receives less strain than the other, since when deadeyes are set up one tightens away from the lanyard knot. With the configuration

Figure 6-67B. *An eye turned up with seizings only is a good alternative to splicing and seizing, particularly in larger wire sizes, which are difficult to splice. Note that the lowermost, heaviest-strained seizing is longer than the other two, that the legs of the wire are taking an even strain, and that the end is capped to prevent water from getting in. A bit of adhesive caulk under the cap is a good idea. When turning up with seizings around a deadeye, always position the bitter end over the lanyard-knot hole, as shown; the least strain comes on the knot side of the lanyard so the wire end will not be liable to shift downward, racking the seizings.*

shown, the majority of the lanyard strain will bear on the standing part of the wire, lessening the tendency of the seizings to "rack" (shift) under load.

Since deadeyes, or modern equivalents, are used for Spectra shrouds, seizings might seem to be an attractive option. Unfortunately, the stuff will slip out of the longest, tightest, best seizings you can make, and at rather low loads. You have to splice Spectra.

MYSTERIES OF THE TAIL SPLICE REVEALED

Some knots, like the Bowline or Half Hitch, inspire feelings of familiarity, even friendship. Some, like the Granny, arouse only contempt. But the Tail Splice is considered a mystery; it is treated with awe, spoken of in hushed tones, and is generally considered beyond the capabilities of mere sailors.

This attitude is understandable. In the Tail Splice's finished form a double-braided, many-stranded rope of cordage gradually and elegantly fades into a six-stranded rope of wire. There's something alchemical about this, an aura of magic that has been played up by generations of sailmakers and riggers. But the Sacred Secret is not a mantra, a series of planetary conjunctions, a brew of lengthy formulas, nor even a lot of expensive tools. It's just this: you pretend. That's right; the instructions that follow just offer a way to take two complex, dissimilar pieces of line and connect them by pretending that they are a couple of pieces of ordinary three-strand rope.

Materials

For each practice splice, you'll need 8 feet of ³/₁₆-inch 7 x 19 wire rope and 8 feet of ³/₈-inch double-braided Dacron. Double-braided rope consists of a pair of concentric woven tubes, the inner one

Figure 6-68A. *Double-braided rope. The braided cover contains a braided core.*

Figure 6-68B. *In 7 x 19 wire, standard for halyards, six strands are laid up around a wire core that is the seventh strand. Each strand is composed of 19 "yarns."*

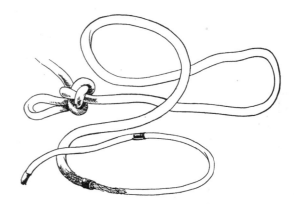

Figure 6-69A. *To prepare the rope for a Tail Splice, make a knot in its standing part, then pull the cover back, exposing the core. Cut about 6 inches of the core end, then tape the core about 10 inches from the new end.*

called the core and the outer one called the cover. The core has fewer strands than the cover, but otherwise the two are structurally the same (Figure 6-68A).

Wire halyard rope, usually stainless steel, is formed of six strands laid up (twisted helically) around a wire core (Figure 6-68B). Each strand comprises 19 yarns. In wire rope nomenclature, this construction is called 7 x 19.

For any Tail Splice, make the rope within ⅛ inch of being twice the diameter of the wire; a larger difference results in distortion and a weaker splice.

Preparation

Make a knot in the double-braid about 5 feet from its end; either a Farmer's Loop (Figure 3-15) or Alpine Butterfly (Figure 3-16) is perfect. Wrap the end of the cover lightly with electrical or masking tape and cut off the whipped or fused end (Figure 6-69A). Slide the cover back, exposing the core; the knot keeps this move from disturbing core-to-cover evenness in the rest of the rope. Cut 1 foot off the core and put a light wrapping of electrical tape on the core 10 inches from its end.

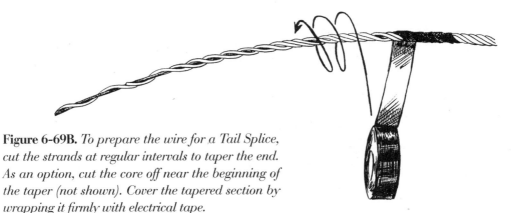

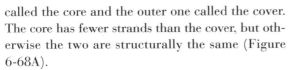

Figure 6-69B. *To prepare the wire for a Tail Splice, cut the strands at regular intervals to taper the end. As an option, cut the core off near the beginning of the taper (not shown). Cover the tapered section by wrapping it firmly with electrical tape.*

With a pair of nippers, unlay and cut the wire strands one at a time to form a tapered end (Figure 6-69B). Cut the core strand short, near the shortest surface strand.

Use a small Swedish Fid or similar tool to make your tucks. It is easiest to use if the handle is clamped in a machinist's vise, so that you can open the lay of the rope a little, and push it down over the fid.

Transformation

Insert the tapered wire end into the core on the end side of the bit of tape on the core. Thread the wire in, being very careful to avoid snagging core yarns,

until the tape on the wire is completely buried in the rope core. Now anchor the wire by taping very firmly over the core at the point where the wire exits. Both wire and core must be made immobile with the tape.

Count the number of yarns in the core. Divide this number by three. Then use an awl to extricate three even groups of adjacent yarns out of the braid—you pry them out back at the tape. If the number of yarns isn't evenly divisible by three, one group will have one more yarn than the others. Wax each bundle thoroughly as you extricate it, running a cake of sailmaker's wax repeatedly over the bundle, always rubbing toward the end, until the bundle feels firm, with all yarns stretched out evenly.

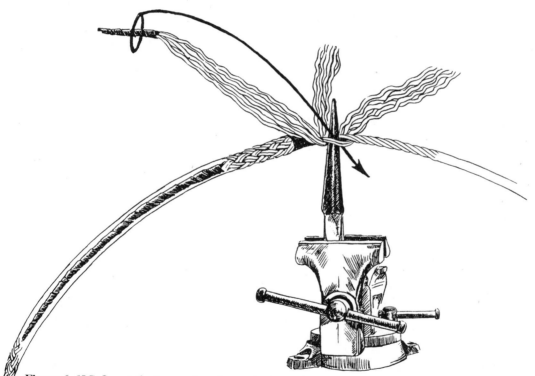

Figure 6-69C. *Insert the tapered-and-taped wire end into the core, then tape the core tightly around the wire in the vicinity of the original piece of tape on the core. Unbraid the core end back to the tape and group the strands into three bundles. Wax each bundle thoroughly by drawing a cake of sailmaker's wax firmly along the bundle several times. Insert the end of a clamped fid under two wire strands, then tuck the most convenient bundle under those strands. Note: the angle of the tuck is important. It should be neither too square to the wire, nor too parallel. At just the right angle, each successive tuck will not be bulky; but will completely cover the pair of strands that each bundle of fiber strands is tucking around. See subsequent illustrations for an idea of what the correct angle is.*

Finally, tape the end of each bundle firmly to a skinny point. There's one of your three-strand ropes.

Splicing the Core

Take your taped-together jumble of line over to the fid, lay the wire on it right next to the tape, and gently push down on the wire to force the fid under a pair of strands (Figure 6-69C, D). Be careful not to pick up any of the wire's heart yarns or to leave any of the pair's yarns behind. Work the wire down over the fid until you have a big enough space to tuck the most convenient rope bundle through, with the lay. If the rope is on your left and the wire on your right, tucking down will be tucking with the lay. Adjust the bundle until all its yarns are snugged down evenly, then pull the wire up off the fid (Figure 6-69C).

Enter the fid under another pair of wire strands and tuck another bundle (Figure 6-69E). You'll probably find it easiest to enter into the same space where the previous bundle entered, but in the opposite direction.

Repeat with the third bundle under the last pair of wires. All bundles should now be exiting at the same level, or "a-tier."

The precise angle that the tucks are made in is important. Too shallow, and wire will show between the tucks, and too steep and the splice will be lumpy. Find that perfect angle, and duplicate it with every tuck you make.

Tuck all three bundles three more times, spiraling each one around and around its own pair of wire

Figure 6-69E. *Preparing to tuck the second bundle. Enter the fid under the two strands above the first bundle.*

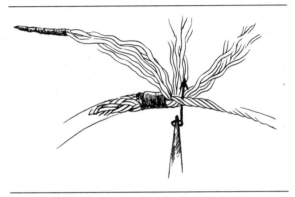

Figure 6-69F. *Tapering the core splice. Make four full tucks with each bundle, then drop one-third of the strands from the wire side of each bundle and tuck again. Drop another one-third, tuck again, and trim the ends close.*

Figure 6-69D. *The first bundle after the first tuck. Be sure to pull all strands down snug and fair for this and all subsequent tucks.*

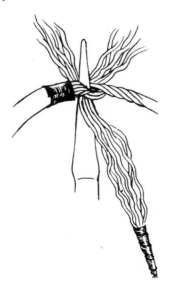

strands. Make each tuck lie as flat and smooth as possible, like a ribbon around the wire. Leave no wire showing. Then taper the last (fifth) tuck by removing about one-third of its yarns from its leading edge before tucking (Figure 6-69F). Remove the tape at the beginning of your tucks. Trim the ends nearly flush with the wire after the last tuck. Finally, wrap a bit of tape around the core right over where the tapered wire ends. This will keep the wire from poking out sideways.

Splicing the Cover

Pull every possible bit of slack out of the cover; when strain comes on the splice, you want core and cover to share the load evenly. It's good practice to belay the rope behind the knot so you can pull on the cover with both hands. When all the slack is out, tightly wrap the cover with electrical tape exactly over the end of the core splice. Comb the strands out, wax and bundle them as before (Figure 6-69G).

The cover splice is a replay of the core splice, except we'll be making more tucks and a longer taper to ensure that the splice will run smoothly through the masthead sheave.

Make four full tucks, then taper by cutting away two yarns at a time (Figure 6-69H). With the greater number of yarns, even more attention must be paid to seeing that the splice is fair. Little if any wire should be visible under the tucks. Stop when you get down to six or eight yarns, trim the ends, and serve over the wire-to-rope juncture with waxed sail twine (Figure 6-69I), to prevent chafe on the strands. Remove the tape on the beginning of the splice, and you're done.

Location

After you've made a few practice splices and feel ready to put one into an actual halyard, you'll need to figure how to position it properly along the length

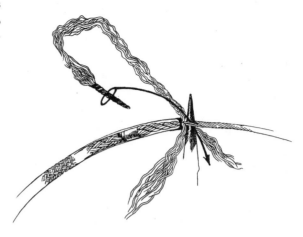

Figure 6-69G. *Beginning the cover splice. Pull the cover over the core, "milking" out all slack. Tape firmly at the point where the core splice ends, then unbraid the cover strands back to the tape and group them in three bundles as with the core. Commence tucking under wire-strand pairs as before.*

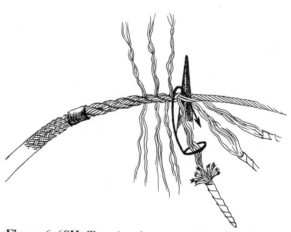

Figure 6-69H. *Tapering the cover splice. After four full tucks, begin dropping two strands with each tuck until just six or eight strands remain. Trim the ends close and serve the splice end with sail twine.*

Figure 6-69I. *Finished Tail Splice.*

of that halyard; the splice should be just above the winch when the sail is fully hoisted.

If you're replacing a properly fitted old halyard, just send it down and reproduce the wire and rope lengths in the new halyard. If the old one doesn't fit right, hoist the sail, measure how far off it is, then send it down and adjust accordingly when you take measurements off it for the new one. If the mast is new, measure while it's out of the boat. For a head-sail halyard on a new mast, be sure to "loft" the angle and length of the stay or you'll come up short. You'll also get a misfit if you cleverly reeve a rope to measure with, marking it "for an exact fit"; when you later stretch it out as a pattern for the new halyard, you'll almost certainly stretch it more or less than you did on the mast. Use a tape measure.

Variations and Aberrations

There are many styles of Tail Splice, as one might expect with such an arcane and complex knot. If the style you use or buy is different from the one described here, just be sure that it, like this one, is thoroughly tested and proven. Avoid those with abrupt shoulders, few tucks, or uneven appearance.

You'll occasionally see a halyard proportioned so that the splice is between cleat and winch when the sail is hoisted (Figure 6-70D). The rationale here is that the splice is the weak link and only the wire should take a full strain. A variation on this involves inserting the wire far enough into the rope at the beginning of the splice that a wire-and-rope "sandwich" will be wrapped around the winch when the sail is fully hoisted (Figure 6-70B). Both of these techniques subject the wire to unnecessary abuse by wrapping it around a winch designed for rope, and the sandwich version, in addition, causes the wire to chafe the rope away from the inside out.

But with either of these techniques the worst moment surely comes when you go to put a reef or two in the sail. The splice that you didn't trust in light air is now exposed, along with the deformed and weakened rope and wire on either side of it, to conditions that can make you uneasy about the stoutest gear. The Tail Splice allows us to combine

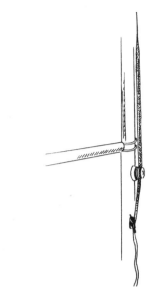

Figure 6-70A. *Having the Tail Splice too far above the winch defeats the purpose of using wire.*

Figure 6-70B. *A rope-and-wire "sandwich" around the winch results in crushed wire and chafed-through rope, shortening halyard life*

a wire halyard's low weight, windage, elasticity, and cost with a rope halyard's speed and ease of handling. Properly made in the right size materials, it's a strong link, not a weak one.

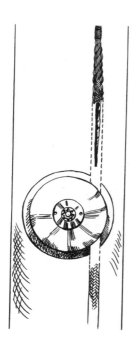

Figure 6-70C. *When the wire portion of the halyard is cut to the right length, the tail of the wire, inside the rope, will be just above the winch drum when the sail is fully hoisted.*

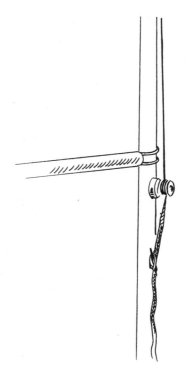

Figure 6-70D. *The splice positioned between winch and cleat: another to-be-avoided variation.*

Splices of the Future: Rope to Rope

We still do wire-to-rope splices in my shop, but more and more we are doing some form of rope-to-rope, with a length of Spectra or Vectran replacing the wire. The resulting halyards can be stronger and less elastic than ones made of wire, as well as much lighter. You won't find instructions for making them here—I'm still refining and testing several forms—but these splices are in your future.

CHAPTER 7

Installation and Maintenance

Installation transforms your work from a series of specialized tasks into an integral part of a sailing entity. When a mast goes in, the boat is changed; it acquires wholeness, intent, life. You, too, must be transformed now, in order to take part in this life. It's a romantic-seeming notion, but one consistent with the complexity and depth of the relationship that begins here.

When everything is at last in its place, your attention naturally shifts to maintenance. This involves a whole new series of tasks, but much more is involved than a "you-take-care-of-it, it-takes-care-of-you" philosophy; ideally, distinctions will blur until the most painstaking labors become a happy matter of course, part of sailing. Writing about this, Joseph Conrad said, "A ship is not a slave. You must make

Toggled Galvanized Turnbuckles

Most turnbuckles are "jaw-and-jaw"—that is, both end fittings are jaws with clevis pins through them. But galvanized turnbuckles are also available in "jaw-and-eye" configurations. A shackle has a better bearing on the eye than it does on the clevis pin of a jaw, so use jaw-and-eye turnbuckles when you use shackles for toggles.

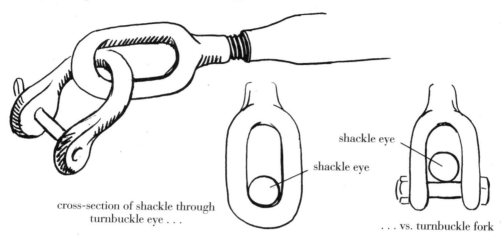

cross-section of shackle through turnbuckle eye . . .

shackle eye

shackle eye

. . . vs. turnbuckle fork

---

her easy in a seaway, you must never forget that you owe her the fullest share of your thoughts, of your skill, of your self love. If you remember that obligation naturally, and without effort, as if it were an instinctive feeling of your inner life, she will sail, stay, run for as long as she is able, or like a seabird going to rest upon the angry waves, she will lay out the heaviest gale that ever made you doubt living long enough to see another sunrise."

This chapter is a run-through of the procedures that put the rigger out of work. The times it is concerned with are always exciting and usually chaotic—thus the emphasis on forethought and preparation. What follows describes preparations for the launching of a good-sized new boat, but the annual outfittings of similar craft, or the launchings of smaller ones, require no less care, even though the operation might be simpler or more familiar. Given the consequences of dropping the stick through the hull, for example, it makes sense always to proceed with studied skill and near-paranoid caution.

Proper Cotters

Unless there is some overwhelming reason to do so, never open cotter pin legs more than about 10 degrees each, so they form a narrow "V." They're no less secure than ones that are open wider, and they're much, much easier to install and remove. If there's some chance of the ends sticking out and gouging passersby, slack the turnbuckle and rotate the clevis pin until the cotter ends are bearing on a flat surface, then squeeze a Hershey's Kiss–size blob of silicone onto the ends. This will cover the ends, so they can't jab anything, and it glues the pin so it can't rotate, but the cotter will still be easy to remove if need be.

The ideal length cotter pin has the shorter leg about 1.5 times the diameter of the clevis pin. This is long enough that it won't be ridiculously hard to open the legs, and short enough that the legs are less likely to stick out past the surface of the fitting.

INSTALLATION: GETTING READY

Set up a workspace out of traffic, and gather together the fewest possible assistants necessary for the job (two or three is usually enough, though you may need some unskilled line-holders later). Improve the chances of an efficient operation by discouraging onlookers and unsolicited help.

TIG Cotters

Turnbuckle-stud cotter pins are tough to install, because you have to bend them back so far to keep them from gouging passersby. And even then you have to tape over the ends. A much cleaner method involves stainless steel TIG (tungsten inert gas) welding rod. It's a flux-free rod. Ask for 3/32-inch (1.6 mm or 2.4 mm) diameter rod for most yacht-size turnbuckles. You can get it in Type 316 if you like shiny objects, but I prefer it in silicon bronze; it's easier to work, and it turns a classy patina green.

To make a TIG cotter, bend one end of a rod to get an "L" shape. The bar of the L needs to be about 1½ inches longer than the diameter of the turnbuckle stud. Insert the bar into the bottom cotter hole, mark where the rod passes the top cotter hole, then take the rod out and bend it just a bit below the mark. If you choose the right spot, the horizontal parts will slide into their respective holes. A very little practice will show you where to make the bend.

Cut the upper leg so it's the same length as the lower, making a "C" shape, then file any sharp corners off.

To install the cotter, insert the "C" into the cotter holes. Using a pair of pliers, bend just the tips of the rods 90 degrees toward each other. Finish by bending the rods together at the studs, so the ends roll inside, out of traffic. No tape needed—and they look sleek.

Source: T. Tracy
Better Boat, Vol. 9, pg. 13

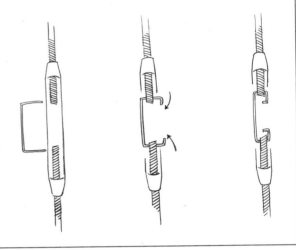

Halyard Reeving

To reeve an internal halyard into a mast in place: Tie one end of a piece of mast-length flag halyard stock to the halyard. Tie the other end to a 2-foot piece of bicycle chain. Lean the boat over to the side the halyard will run on. Go aloft and feed the chain over the sheave. The chain's weight will pull the flag halyard down. When the chain reaches its exit, the deck crew can use a bent piece of TIG welding rod or the like to fish it out. A magnet can also work. The flag halyard then gets tied to the reeving eye to pull the halyard in.

To reeve an internal halyard with the mast down: Turn the mast so the halyard sheave you want is down. Remove the masthead and run a messenger or the halyard into the sheave. Slide a mast-length piece of standing rigging up to the sheave. Attach a messenger or the halyard and pull back. Use the same procedure to reeve lines in booms.

Do you have all the pieces? Check them off your lists, port and starboard, forward and aft. All turnbuckles, toggles, pins, shackles, lanyards, pieces of standing rigging, and spools of cordage for running rigging should be sorted and clearly labeled. Have spare pins, cotters, and shackles on hand.

Is the mast ready? See that all hardware and fittings are in place, their locations checked against the sail plan and common sense. Check all bolts for tightness, cotter pins for security, and in-mast sheaves for smooth running. If there are mast hoops, are they on? Are there enough? Count sail eyelets. Imagine the mast in place, and check the lead and location of everything against that image. Take a few minutes at this; things sometimes get inexplicably out of place, and it's much easier to fix them now than later.

Stand on deck and imagine everything working. Will it work? Cast a critical eye on deck leads, winch locations, and fitting clearances.

Get together tools and items such as marline, seizing wire, and lanolin, to name a few. (More will be mentioned in the section on installing a topmast.) Keep any tools you're not wearing in your rigging bucket or toolbox. If you happen to have a fly-fishing vest, dump all the lures and weights out of it,

Rigging and Tuning for Detachable Forestay and Running Backstays

The cutter is a versatile rig, but in light airs, when you want to fly a big drifter, the forestay can be a serious impediment to tacking. It makes sense to be able to move the forestay out of the way when the wind is light, and secure it aft (made off to a chainplate with a bungee cord is ideal). Racers detach and reattach forestays and babystays frequently, using a compound lever quick-release device. These are efficient but clunky, prohibitively expensive, and the mechanism doesn't tension the stay much. A positive-lock Fas-pin, the kind with a pushbutton and lanyard ring, is much preferable for cruisers. You loosen the turnbuckle, pull the pin, and you're clear. Takes a little longer, but it saves a lot. Johnson Handy-Lock turnbuckles are ideal for this application, since they are secured with fold-down handles instead of cotter pins.

When the breeze comes up or you begin hitting chop, reattaching the forestay helps stabilize the mast. And, of course, the forestaysail can then be used in concert with the jib. In medium airs, tighten the forestay only moderately; too much tension, and you'll slack the jib and flatten the forestaysail and main excessively. If breeze or chop builds more, it's time to set up the running backstays. These further stabilize the mast and tension the forestay, resulting in the flat forestaysail you want in heavy weather. At the same time you can tighten the backstay, to flatten the jib.

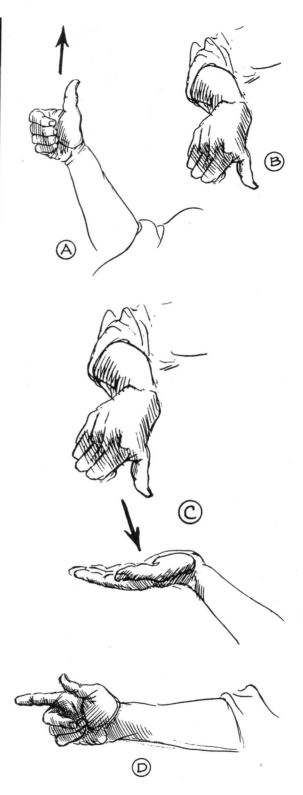

and fill it with all the small items and tools that would otherwise go to the bottom of your rigging bucket. Sharpen your knife.

Go over hoist signals (Figure 7-1) with the crane operator or, if you're using a block and tackle, with the person tailing the fall. Some people use different signals than the ones shown; make sure you're in agreement.

Whenever possible, put all the rigging on the mast now. First get everything over by the boat, and put the mast on sawhorses or oil drums. Bits

Figure 7-1A-D. *Hoist signals. (A) Raise boom. (B) Lower boom. (C) Lower boom slowly. (Palm facing any signal qualifies it as "slowly.") (D) Slew (travel) boom.*

257

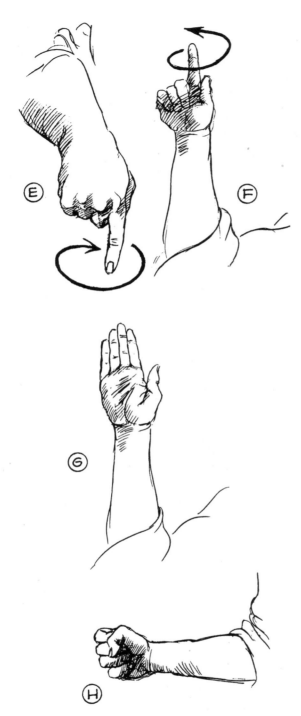

Figure 7-1E-H. *Hoist signals. (E) Lower load. (F) Raise load. (G) Hold that; take a turn. (H) Make fast.*

of carpeting will prevent scratches. If you have an external sail track, lay the mast track-side-up. Otherwise, work out with the crane operator what the best orientation for the pick is.

Running Rigging

Get out the appropriate list along with all the blocks and their shackles. Lay these out in a rigger's smorgasbord, then prepare the rope for reeving by slinging spools on rod or pipe to pay out toilet-paper fashion. If the rope is three-strand, and if it comes in tub coils instead of on spools, place the tubs at convenient points and start them by pulling the end up from the bottom of the coil, to avoid kinks. This trick only works with three-strand.

It's best to step with all halyards rove, but if the work site is notably dirty you might want to reeve temporary lines out of flag halyard stuff, then use these to pull the real thing in later.

If you reeve before stepping, cut the halyards plenty long. As a rule of thumb, they should be twice the height from the water to the top of the mast. If the halyards lead aft, add the horizontal distance traveled to this length. With halyards cut to this rule, they'll be long enough to get something–or someone–out of the water. They'll also be harder to "sky" accidentally.

Check five times or so that all of the halyards are on the proper sheaves, are leading on the correct side as they pass spreaders, and are exiting the mast at the proper spots.

Things can be more complicated if you're setting up a gaffer. Let's say your list starts with a throat halyard. Attach the upper block to the mast and have an assistant hold the lower block close to it. Reeve the blocks and hitch the standing end temporarily to its becket, or, in the case of a double-ended halyard, to the gooseneck or boom saddle. Walk the lower block down to about the level of the boom, pulling rope off the spool or out of the coil as you go. Lead the hauling part down to about the height it will belay, add enough for three turns around a winch, if any, plus 4 to 6 feet for belaying, plus a like amount for shortening up due to chafe. Constrictor the end; cut, hitch the end around the tackle to keep things from fouling; and go to the next line.

Cut gantlines, topsail, and staysail halyards to the get-someone-out-of-the-water rule.

If you're rigging with manila, which shrinks when wet, allow enough length for shrinkage. Lines that see an extraordinary amount of chafe, such as the foresail vang on some gaff schooners, can do with extra length for shortening up. If a line leads to the cockpit or to the end of the bowsprit, pace off the distance away from the mast to get the required length. On a topping lift for a 14-foot boom, for instance, reeve the end through the block on the mast and walk with the end to a point 14 feet out from the gooseneck or boom saddle. Lead the standing part to its belay point and cut.

With any type of rig, keep leads from fouling with other pieces of running rigging. See that the right-diameter rope gets into the right blocks. Leave the sheets and other low lines until the stepping is done. When everything else is rove, it's time to splice or whip all ends. Because this is so time-consuming, it's best done before the launching. Splicing parties are great places to teach and learn different techniques, to socialize, and to become familiar with the gear. Unfortunately, most mast dressings seem to take place with the crane operator fuming at you, the tide cresting, and an expectant crowd looking over your shoulder. And no matter how fast you splice or whip, to others you will look slow and contemplative. So if time is short, have good help on hand, assign them specific tasks, and keep them out of each other's way. The priority is lines that dead-end aloft. If time is very short, just do the ends you won't be able to reach from deck. If there's no time, reconcile yourself to the prospect of some time in the bosun's chair.

With a lashing or lashings, make the running rig off to the mast.

Standing Rigging

The standing rigging goes on second because it has to come loose first, to belay the mast before the crane lets go.

Lay the standing-rigging coils on the ground at appropriate points along the mast, port and star-

board. With a copy of the standing rigging list to hand, begin attaching the pieces starting with the lowers and working up, checking each piece off the list as you go. If the mast is tanged, see that the clevis pins fit cleanly and are the right length. If it's a spliced rig, be sure the thimbles are set well down on the pin or shackle, with no foul leads. Seize and cotter as you go. With a soft-eye rig, remember to put on the starboard eye of any pair first and to seat and lead the eyes as well as you can on the ground. Attach any spreaders or struts and seize-in their wires, lightly, so you can adjust angle and tension later. Uncoil the pieces, either after they're all attached or as you go. Pull them out so they're not sagging too much, and lash them to the mast at gooseneck height. See that all pieces will lead fair; it's easy, for example, to thread a backstay or a halyard between an upper shroud and a spreader, necessitating a trip aloft to clear it before it can be set up. Is everything checked off? Good. Examine all attachments once more, and remove the tags.

You're nearly ready for the pick now, but before everyone gets geared up, take note of the wind: More than 10 to 15 knots of it can make a mast very difficult to handle in transit. If it's blowing, wait.

STEPPING THE KEEL-STEPPED MAST

For anything bigger than a Whitehall, use hoisting gear to step the mast. A raising-of-the-flag-at-Iwo-Jima routine is dramatic and emotionally satisfying when it works, but presents too many opportunities for things to go wrong (picture the butt skidding across your pristine foredeck, or the mast falling onto hapless guests), and in any event is always harder than letting pulleys do the work.

The size of the mast and the availability of equipment and personnel will determine the exact form and size of the gear you use. Block and tackle of three to seven parts can be hung from beams, yards, bridges, docks, etc. Given strong attachment and tailing points, you can pick all but the largest masts without a crane. On the other hand, this system only works if the boat is directly under the gear or can be moved under it after the mast is in the air. Building a derrick on deck or alongside solves this problem, but unless you plan to use it more than once—say, for annual steppings and unsteppings at your own yard—it is more like an emergency fix, something you might lash up if you were dismasted in Faroffistan. Unless you can easily get the boat under the mast, get a crane. This is not as difficult or expensive as you might think. Any boatyard worth the name will have a crane and someone to operate it. If you're launching in some secluded cove, call the phone, power, or cable TV company in your area and make an appointment for one of their boom trucks to come over next time they're in the neighborhood. Schedule your stepping around their schedule, and you'll get the job done quickly, easily, and inexpensively. Finally, you can always call up your local building contractor and arrange to rent a crane and operator. Whomever you get for the job, remember that the better prepared you are, the less time it takes and the less you pay. Before the crane arrives, take a look around the stepping site to see if there are any power lines that you have even a remote chance of fouling. If so, either move the hull or get the power company to come out and temporarily take them down.

The best arrangement I know of for a mast pick is shown in Figure 7-2. A rope collar, preferably padded, is hooked or shackled to the padded lower block of the hoisting gear and belayed to the mast at gooseneck level with a downhaul. The belay can be around a winch and cleat, or mast band, or a lashing below the boom saddle, depending on the type of mast. Just make sure it's very strong. When the mast goes up, the load goes onto the downhaul. If the mast's center of gravity is low enough, you won't have to go aloft to get the gear down after stepping; just slack away on the tackle and pull the collar down to the deck.

Position the collar just above the balance point. This will be just below the spreaders for a keel-stepped, single-spreader mast, and probably just above the spreaders for a deck-stepped mast, either single or double spreader. With the sling at the right

Figure 7-2. *A mast ready for stepping is in the foreground, running rigging omitted for simplicity. The standing rigging is led down and bundled against the mast at the gooseneck. The padded crane pulley and padded mast collar provide mar-free strength. The downhaul on the collar is made off securely to a mast winch and cleat. In the background, the same mast is shown being stepped. Tag lines control movement of the butt as the crane carries it toward the boat. Time to get on deck and guide it home.*

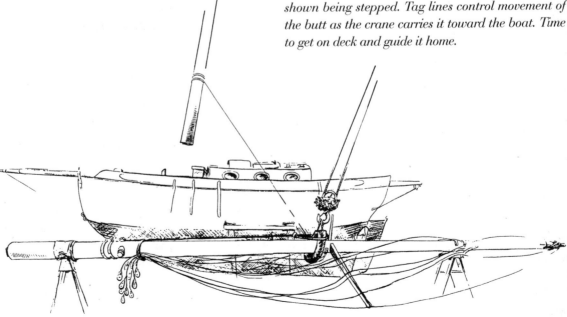

spot, there will be a manageable amount of weight on the butt, and the mast will hang fairly plumb yet be angled enough that it will be easy to move the butt around. Attaching that low also means that the crane doesn't have to lift. Never allow any lifting gear to bear on the spreaders or tangs; they're not designed to take strain from that direction.

It's a good idea at this time to wrap some thin padding around the bury of a keel-stepped mast. This section will be completely exposed below, dominating the cabin, and people will tend to stare at it, clucking over any scratches it might have received on the way down.

As an option, hitch on a tag line and have a volunteer tail it. You will need this if the mast is very large, and/or if it has to travel a long way vertically to reach the deck of the boat. Explain to the tailer that the tag line is just to keep the butt from swinging, and to keep the top of the mast from slamming into the head of the crane, during the intervals that the mast is out of your reach. Easy does it.

Take a look around. Any stray dogs or children nearby? Anything you or the tailer might trip over? Anything likely to snag the mast between where it is and where it's going? Once again, any power lines? Think things through. If necessary, get some help to keep the area clear.

When everyone's ready, position the crane so that the hook is exactly over the lifting collar. If it is off even a little, the mast will want to slide around, which can be dangerous. Signal to hoist and let the top end come off its sawhorse a foot or so. Give the stop signal and check the gear again. All in order? Nothing snagging? Not too much or too little butt weight? Stand from under and continue the pick. Once the mast is clear, signal to lift and travel. Watch the mast, the crane operator, the tailer, and yourself. Keep the mast within easy reach, so that you and your helpers can keep it from spinning or swinging. Take it over to the boat, to the side that is away from the side you will board from. You and a helper or two will have to get aboard before the mast gets to the boat. Just stay out from under. When the mast is over the boat and just above the deck, begin the fine-tuning to steer it to just over the step. It

might want to twist in its gear; stop it. As it moves, look aloft frequently to be sure that nothing is fouling the crane. Jib foils are great at this.

For a keel-stepped mast, send a good hand below to guide the mast into the step, and have one or two other helpers on deck to help you guide it into the hole. On large craft, station a reliable, clear-voiced person in the companionway or next to a porthole to relay information between step and deck.

Make sure the mast is oriented properly (it's amazing how easy it is to put a mast in backward), and signal to lower away, adjusting to center over the hole as you go. It should be plumb laterally, and almost plumb vertically. When it's well in, it is up to the person at the step to begin giving you directions for final adjustments. Properly, these are in terms of the direction of the butt's travel: "Two inches to port" means you signal the crane to move the head to starboard; "Two inches aft" means you signal to move the head forward. When the tenon is right at the step, you and your helpers can help it along by pushing and twisting on the mast. It's almost in the hole now. . . . Wait! Did they put the lucky coin in? Come up a couple of inches, deposit the talisman (after swinging the butt off to one side), and let it down again. Tchunnngk. Stepped.

Is the tenon firmly seated? Are all the wires led properly? Good. Set some temporary wedges, cast off the standing-rigging lashing, and lead the wires out to their homes. What with the relief of tension at this moment, people tend to get a little crazy, grabbing at everything and falling over each other. So send all but one or two helpers away, calm your own giddy heart, and proceed methodically. First the shrouds, then the fore-and-aft stays—just hand tight, enough to stabilize the mast. If the crane is in the way of the fore- or backstay, the shrouds will hold the stick for now. If the rig design does not include shrouds with the necessary lead, rig a temporary stay to a winch or cleat, low enough or at a steep enough angle to clear the crane's boom.

Have the crane operator let some slack into the lift, and see that everything is holding well. Then cast off the heel line and bring the collar down. If the collar is above the spreaders, get your climbing gear on and go cast it off. Detach it and carefully send the lifting gear away; don't let it bash into the stick or your crew. Attach anything that wouldn't lead properly with the crane in the way.

If your meticulous preparations and measurements result in a perfect fit for all pieces, you deserve congratulations—but I know from sad experience that this is not always so. On those unlucky occasions, the riggers may rue the fact that their first opportunity to see a rig in place is often a very public viewing, and any failure will be immediately, glaringly evident to the most untrained observer. I hope that the first time you read this is long before the launching. Go back over your figures, recheck measurements, and reread the layout instructions in Chapter 6. Help your luck.

DECK-STEPPED MASTS

Given a choice, I like to treat a deck-stepped mast like a keel-stepped one, using a crane to set it in place, even if there is a tabernacle designed for raising and lowering. The crane is so much easier and safer. But the reason people have these masts is so they can get them up and down without a crane, so here's the routine.

Carry, parbuckle, hoist, or slide the bare mast aboard and position it longitudinally over the vessel's centerline. These masts are heavier for their size than keel-stepped ones (deck mounting means that the mast must take thrust that the partners would otherwise bear), so proceed carefully, padding points of contact with the hull, tailing hauling parts, and rigging preventer gear to keep the thing from getting away if somebody slips.

Dress as for a keel-stepped mast, but leave one stout line out of the bundle, rove through a masthead sheave. Use a halyard for an aft-hinging mast or the topping lift for a forward-hinging mast. Slide the butt aft or forward, depending on which way the mast hinges, until it can bolt into its tabernacle or plate, and run the line forward to the anchor windlass or aft to a tackle. Since the line is now just about parallel with the mast, cranking in on it will do you no good; you need a strut to widen the angle

between mast and hauling line. There are different ways of doing this, but the most convenient for an aft-hinging mast is to set up a spinnaker pole with its butt locked in place on the mast and its other end attached to the halyard. For a forward-hinger, lead the topping lift to the end of the boom and haul with the mainsheet (Figure 7-3). Failing that, as for junk rigs, make up sheer legs, fastening the butt ends securely on deck. Most trailer-sailers have special upper shroud hardware to keep the mast from swinging laterally as it goes up. If not, attach tag lines near the masthead before hoisting, to prevent it from swinging laterally. Either run these through turning blocks and tail them to cleats or winches, or tail them to secure objects on the ground on either side of the boat.

Take up the slack with the mast end of the halyard or topping lift and belay it on the mast. Clear the area, check all connections, then start cranking away cautiously on the windlass or sheet to raise the mast. The people on the tag lines should take a slight strain against the pull of the halyard or sheet, just enough so there's no slack, and then pay out evenly as the mast goes up. When the butt swings into place, belay the hauling lines and the tag lines as temporary stays, and go about getting the standing rigging secured.

If your vessel is multiple masted, step one mast, then use it to hoist the next one. For example:

The foremast is in place on your junk-rigged schooner and all the standing rigging and tabernacle fittings are secured. You'll be using the foresail halyard to pull the mainmast up, but first you have to get the mainmast into position. The procedure is pretty much as it was for the foremast except that this mast is much heavier, so requires greater care, and is much longer; its balance point might be out over the stem before the butt is at the tabernacle. To prevent having to deal with a 50-foot steel seesaw, make a heavy lashing to arc over the mast, keeping the butt from coming up while still allowing you to slide the mast aft. Tie the ends of the lashing through scuppers, hawseholes, or other structures capable of taking a heavy vertical and aft load. As you approach the tabernacle and friction against the

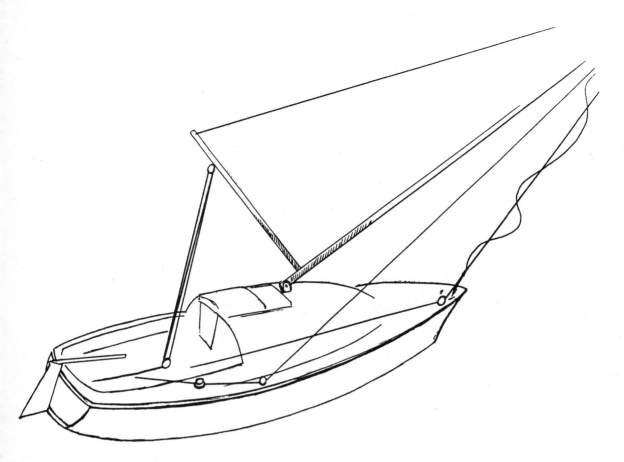

Figure 7-3. *A deck- or tabernacle-stepped mast (forward hinging). Carry the mast on board and secure its butt in the tabernacle. Affix the boom, with sheet and topping lift attached. Belay one end of the jibstay halyard on the mast and lead the other end through a block at the stem and aft to the cockpit. Attach forestay to masthead and stem. Lead two other belayed halyards to turning blocks and thence aft for lateral control. Take up on the sheet, pay out on the jib halyard, and keep tension on the lateral guys as you raise the mast. Attach remaining standing rigging when mast is in fully upright position.*

lashing increases, a come-along or handy-billy can help to move it the last few feet.

Lash the foresail halyard lower block to the main at the point where it rests on the padded taffrail (you did pad the taffrail, didn't you?). If the bulk of the mast is out over the rail, you'll have lashed the halyard on earlier at a point higher up on the mast, to help keep the masthead from dropping. Take up on your tag lines, which lead from the same spot, and hoist away. As the mast gets within 30 degrees of the vertical, carefully lead the tag lines well aft to serve as backstays. Secure all shrouds and fittings and settle down for a nice, cold . . . What? This is a *three*-masted schooner?

LIVING ALOFT

Once I was 100 feet or so aloft, up by the main truck of the bark *Elissa*, installing some gear. Discovering that I hadn't brought enough shackles, I called down to the deck for extras. A new hand ran to get some, ran back with them, then smartly cast off what he thought was an unused gantline (messenger line). The chair dropped out from under me, and only a

primal grab at the backstays kept me from following it down.

And once a friend was doing a routine masthead light replacement on a big sloop. His chair was hanging from the hook of a dockside crane. When he was finished, my friend signaled to the crane operator to bring him down. The boom swung away from the boat and stopped over the dock. Just then someone from the shipyard office called to the driver, who turned to respond, inadvertently releasing the halyard clutch, causing the chair and its occupant to begin an unnoticed freefall. A chance peripheral glance by the driver and a quickly applied brake saved the day, the chair stopping so close to the dock that my friend just stepped out of the chair and walked, unsteadily, away.

When working aloft, gravity is your enemy. But near-death dramas are almost invariably the result of poor planning, poor communication, poor attentiveness. My near fall was a lesson to the deckhand: Look aloft before you let go a line, to be sure you have the one you want. Then take the turns off slowly, so you can feel and control any surprise load before it's too late.

My near fall was a series of lessons for me: Ensure that things on deck are in good, organized hands before you go up; go up on two halyards in case one fails; tie safety tethers to something solid once aloft, for additional backup support; and bring lots of spare shackles.

My friend on the crane had the advantage of being on gear far stronger and more easily adjustable than a sailboat halyard. On the other hand, the operator was the only thing between safety and a Wile E. Coyote–style landing. Redundancy, however primitive, might be preferable to helplessness.

So much for the scary stories and general lessons; now let's get down to the details that can make life aloft a pleasant, relatively safe experience.

First of all, preface any job with an on-deck conference in which you go over the job in detail, including likely material needs. Generate alternative scenarios, in case things go wrong or differently than you expect (for example, what will you do if a tool falls in the water? Do you have a magnet? A spare tool?). You can also take this time to be sure you agree on nomenclature and hand signals, to avoid confusion later. And you definitely want to be sure that you've allowed a generous amount of time to do the job, and that your deck crew can hang around that long. Ever been stuck up a mast at suppertime?

Next, lay out the primary halyard, the one your

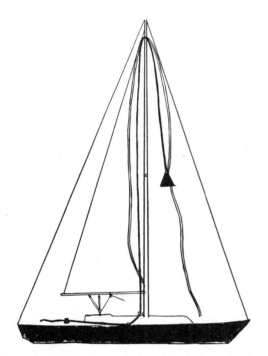

Figure 7-4. *The primary halyard leads from the chair, through the masthead sheave, down to the deck, and aft to a sheet winch. A second halyard belays at the base of the mast and leads through the masthead sheave and down past the chair. The occupant of the chair goes hand over hand up the secondary as the chair is hoisted (better practice would be some form of fall-arrest-rated ascender device on the safety), in case the primary should fail. Once aloft, the secondary can be tied to the chair as a safety line, or used for self-lowering.*

deck crew will be hauling on, in a way that will keep them out from under you, both to protect them from falling gear and so that they can see you clearly at all times. I like to go up on the front side of a mast— the rake assures I'll stay in contact and not swing or spin. If the tail part of the primary halyard is forward of the mast, lead the halyard to the foredeck. The crew can pull by hand or use the anchor windlass. If the tail part is aft of the mast, lead it through deck blocks toward the cockpit (Figure 7-4) for either hand power or one of the sheet winches.

Next, lay out a second, safety halyard. You will be handling this one in case something goes wrong with the primary. One way to arrange a safety halyard is to belay one end of a spare halyard and lead the hauling part to your chair. You just hand-over-hand up this halyard while the deck crew does all the work. Alternatively, you can attach one end of the safety to your chair or harness (see below) and haul on the other end. This is a little more complex to set up, but gives you a 2:1 mechanical advantage, easing the deck crew's job. If you are strong enough to haul yourself aloft with this configuration, then this can be the primary halyard, and the deck crew handles the safety, only needing to keep the slack out and a turn around a belay in case you should tire or slip.

With either safety halyard configuration, lead the hauling part through a carabiner that is clipped to your chair or harness. Then, even if you temporarily lose your grip, the hauling part can't fly out of reach. And with either configuration, belay the safety halyard to yourself once you are in position aloft.

When the halyards are squared away, check all your gear, including blocks, shackles, winches, and chair or harness. Make sure that no snapshackle or self-tailing winch is part of the system; snapshackles sometimes do, and self-tailing mechanisms sometimes don't.

A block and tackle with a very long tackle is one way to make it easier to get you aloft, but it involves a lot of line, and the blocks mean that you can't get very close to the top of the mast. Leading the halyard to a winch is usually preferable when you need mechanical advantage.

Whether the hoisting power is manual or machine, the most important person on deck is the one tailing the line. This individual keeps the line around a belay point and takes up the slack as it comes in. If the people or machinery doing the hauling should slip, it is the tailer who will check your fall. The tailer watches you all the way up, controlling the speed of your ascent and watching for any trouble, while simultaneously keeping everyone out from under the mast and shushing needless noise. If you have a request or a problem, you address it to the tailer, and the tailer is the only one who answers. A prestigious job.

With gear and crew set, all that remains is to test the halyards. The drill is to take up on the safety until it bears most of your weight, then bounce hard on it a few times to make sure it will hold. The shock load you're imposing here will be far heavier than any normal load. So if the halyard and blocks hold for the bounce, they'll probably hold for the haul. Ease off on the safety, have your crew take up on the primary, and bounce on that.

Going Up—In What?

You are about to ascend to dizzying heights; what are you sitting in? The traditional plank-and-rope bosun's chair is a marvel of simplicity, economy, utility, discomfort, and danger. With the addition of the back and crotch straps shown in Figure 7-5, the plank bosun's chair becomes something like safe, and it's certainly the cheapest way aloft provided you know how to splice and seize. But a good canvas chair with wide adjustable back strap and leg straps and with handy built-in pockets is altogether a better way to go.

Figure 7-6 and the accompanying sidebar show a couple of the types of chairs that were available when this book was originally published. You'll find

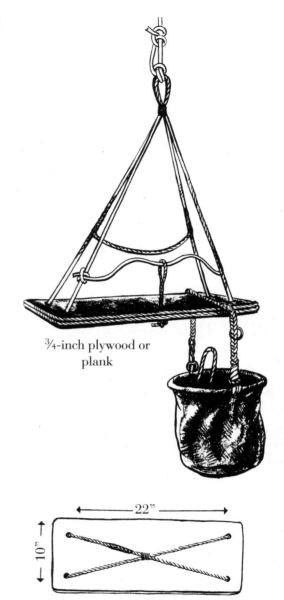

¾-inch plywood or plank

22"

10"

Figure 7-5. *A traditional plank chair with a few new wrinkles: Roped sides are easier on legs and mast; spliced-in back and leg straps provide security. Note in bottom view that the chair legs are crossed and seized so that one broken part will not drop the occupant. The rigging bucket has a shackle on its lanyard for hanging around mast or spreader, with an extra lanyard (bight showing) for intermediate attachment while the main lanyard is being passed.*

Figure 7-6. *Several manufacturers make comfortable canvas chairs, with large pockets, lanyard rings at front lower corners, back and leg straps, and padded seats. The halyard attachment shown here is an Anchor Hitch backed up by two Half Hitches (left loose in drawing for clarity). Shackle pin is moused to prevent unscrewing. Small block on shackle is for gantline.*

comparable chairs at your local chandlery and harnesses at climbing stores. The Hood is a big, padded Cadillac of a chair. Most bosun's chairs fall somewhere between it and the plank. When you go shopping for one, pay attention to fit, just as you would for clothing. Not only should the width and depth be right for your body—tight enough to keep you from sliding around, loose enough that you don't lose circulation—but the chair and its appointments should feel right, with no D-rings in your face, no hard-to-reach pockets, no hard-to-adjust straps. Before you buy it, sit in it long enough to see if it's really comfortable.

If you're satisfied with the cut of the chair, try to tear it apart. I mean, pick it up and haul on all the load-bearing seams really hard. Try to be discreet

Climbing harnesses are secure, and offer unparalleled mobility and hoist height. But most of them are uncomfortable to hang in, and can't hold gear, like the pockets on a bosun's chair can. These and other problems are dealt with by the following features of an ideal bosun's harness:

- Adjustable, heavily padded leg and hip bands, along with good design geometry, to assure maximum hang time.
- A built-in tether with an auto-lock carabiner in the end. The tether can be secured around the mast, to mast hardware, or even tied around stays, to give the climber lateral stability. It can also stand in for a halyard, in case you have to send one to deck.
- Two "D" rings, for uncrowded, independent halyard attachment. One halyard is the primary, the other is a safety.
- Rack loops, from which to hang strops, shackles, and other gear. Since the loops have plastic tubing around them, they stand out from the harness, making them easier to attach to.
- Belt loops, on which to hang sheaths for tools, or as shown here,
- A small rigging bucket, complete with pockets, lanyard loops, and a drawstring closure. You can hold enough tools and materials in here for most jobs aloft.

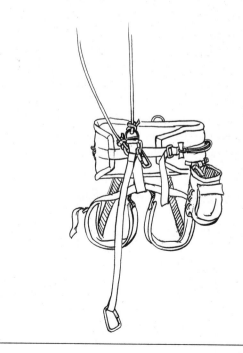

about this, but remember that you will literally be trusting your life to this item.

While not exactly a bosun's chair, a mountaineer's climbing harness is a handy substitute, at least for quick jobs, where you can expect to get back to deck before your legs go numb. A properly adjusted harness is impossible to fall out of, allows unparalleled mobility, and lets you get up higher than any chair, since the halyard attachment point is lower. It's extremely prudent practice to wear a harness even when you're using a chair; attach the safety halyard to the harness so you'll have two independent halyards leading to two independent seats. Reassuring. The best climber's harnesses have broad straps and built-in loops for attaching shackles, bits of spare line, tools, and other gear. The harness that I use is designed with maximum "hang time" in mind. See "Sources and Resources" page 400 for details.

En Route

To ensure good communication, emphasize to your deck crew that you'd very much like it if they would repeat back to you, in a loud, clear voice, any significant words you might utter while aloft. Promise you'll do likewise for them. For examples of this, see "Topmast Installation," below.

Your deck crew's good, your gear is sound, you're ready to travel. Give the command to haul away, and head on up, nice and easy, but concentrating like a diamond cutter. Watch out for mast fittings, wires, spreaders, and anything else you or your gear might snag. Keep an eye out for those inconsiderate souls who motor by too quickly, kick-

ing up a wake; motion is amplified up here, and a wake that is merely annoying on deck can really thrash you around aloft. If you have any problems, let your tailer know, but avoid unnecessary chatter.

If you can't avoid going up while the vessel is heeling or pitching, shackle your chair or harness around a tautly belayed halyard (Figure 7-7). If you only need to go up as far as the spreaders, use the forestaysail halyard for the hoist so that there's less halyard length above you to contribute to pendulum length.

In rough weather or calm, stay completely present mentally as you go up, and don't be shy about implementing extra security precautions, such as having an extra hand tail your safety so that you can hang onto the standing rigging, just in case both

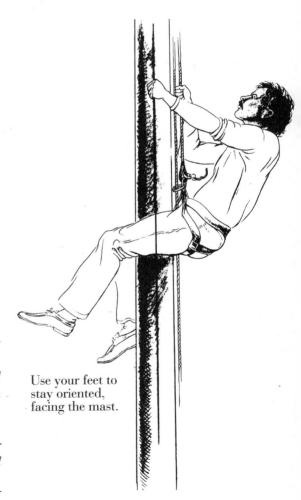

Use your feet to stay oriented, facing the mast.

Figure 7-7. *To avoid becoming a human plumb bob while going aloft on a pitching vessel, shackle your chair or harness around a taut second halyard. Note that the snapshackle on the hoisting halyard in the illustration is not being used; always use a positive-lock shackle for hoisting humans. A suitable locking carabiner or a soft shackle are ideal. Harnesses like the one shown provide great mobility aloft, and are impossible to fall out of when sized and adjusted properly.*

halyards fail, or, more likely, in case you need to stabilize yourself against rough motion. All of these precautions would have seemed excessive to old-time sailors, who thought nothing of single-halyard-and-plank-chair ascents, but bear in mind that they were in big, stable ships, hanging on heavy-duty halyards, with plenty to hang onto aloft and a professional deck crew below. And even then they were taking chances, as the odd fall from aloft attested. Today we have smaller boats with much more severe motion. And one hopes we're smart enough not to scoff at safety procedures.

Procedures Aloft

Once you get to your work station, have the deck crew belay the primary halyard and tell you when it is fast. Then tie or shackle a short tether from your

Figure 7-8. Once aloft, secure yourself to the mast to prevent getting swung about and as insurance against halyard failure. This rigger shouldn't be up there without a safety halyard.

harness or chair to a fitting on the mast, or clear around the mast if you can (Figure 7-8). If you do the latter, be sure that there is some stout barrier, like the spreaders in the illustration, to stop you should the halyard fail; an unsupported turn around the mast won't.

Now you're held in place independent of the halyards. At this point you can have the deck crew belay your safety as well. Or, if you want to be able to lower yourself, Carabiner-Hitch the hauling part of the safety to harness or chair. Then tell the deck crew to ease off slowly on the primary halyard. If

Hugh Lane's Loaded Bat

Conventional-shaped mallets are okay for conventional situations, but try to pull one out of a crowded rigging bucket and you'll likely pull a few other items out with it. If you put it in head-up, it is liable to fall out by itself, after tangling its lanyard on other items.

As an alternative, get a fish bat—available at most any sporting goods store (anglers use them to, uh, subdue fish)—drill its end out, and fill the hole with lead. Melting the lead and pouring it in works best, and lead is easy to melt. Just provide plenty of ventilation for the fumes, and chisel the hole out a bit to make it cone-shaped, so the lead can't come out when it solidifies.

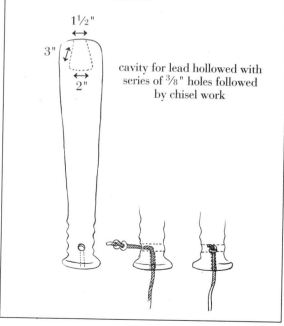

the Carabiner Hitch is secure, they can cast off the primary, which you can now use for a gantline (messenger line) for sending equipment up and down. If you don't need to lower yourself, leave the primary attached and use another halyard as a gantline. If you've run out of halyards, hang a block from your chair or around the mast and reeve a light halyard through it.

Sometimes, as for changing a masthead light or installing instruments, the places you need to get at are just out of reach above you. Because the halyard attaches lower on a climber's harness, you can always get up higher with them than with a chair.

If your legs go to sleep while you're hanging around up there, shift position until they wake up. With a good harness you can slide the leg loops up and down your thighs as needed, for maximum hang time. Leg numbness is a bad sign, health-wise.

Now you're ready for work; all you need are some tools and materials.

Working Aloft

The gear you need will be coming up on a gantline. You could have brought it up with you, but why add all that weight and clutter to the exercise? If you're going to send the primary down as a gantline, stop and tie a Butterfly or other loop knot in the line, about 2 to 3 feet (0.6 to 0.9 m) from the end, before you detach the line from yourself. The knot will prevent the halyard from accidentally slipping out of the block (Figure 7-9). Now tie a Bowline with the end around its own standing part, so that the end won't blow away out of reach as it goes down. It is sometimes convenient to tie the end around a jibstay, backstay, or other piece of rigging instead. In any event, send the line down to deck. If you'll be using another, extra halyard that already has both ends on deck, have your deck crew put the loop knot in.

The first thing to come up will be your rigging bucket. This should be a stout item, preferably of canvas and with a stiff rim, with tool pockets on the inside so the tools can't snag every little thing on the way up. The bucket should be big enough to hold basic tools with enough room for paint or miscellaneous fittings—10–11 inches (250–280 mm) in

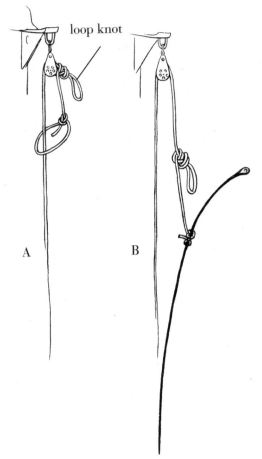

Figure 7-9. *Preparations for sending a line down from aloft are shown in (A). When sending items up, the deck crew ensures that it will not be necessary to untie the line before installing the object. In (B), for example, a stay is coming up with the gantline Rolling-Hitched to its standing part, not its end.*

diameter by a foot (300 mm) tall is a good size—and should have its own tether, so it can be hung from the mast without a halyard.

When the bucket gets up to you, tie its tether on, then detach the halyard and send it back down for the next piece of gear. If everything you need is in the bucket, leave the halyard attached, the other end belayed on deck.

The sure mark of a pro aloft is a profusion of lanyards. Lanyards for all the tools, a lanyard for eyeglasses, a lanyard for each piece of hardware you'll be working with, and two lanyards for heavy objects, plus spare lanyards for any extra requirements that might come up, with each lanyard scaled to the weight of its lanyardee. (That is, the lanyard should have a breaking strength of at least 10 times the weight of the object—cheap insurance.)

There will be times when you say, "I can't deal with all these strings!" But if the lanyards are getting in your way, you're probably trying to work too fast. It's a special world aloft; clearing and stowing tools and lanyards during each step of a job is a necessary ritual, one that will prevent hard, expensive objects from crashing down on crew or deck. Slow down, work on organization, and the strings won't be so intimidating.

Some specific confusion-reducing tips:

1. *Distribution.* Rigging buckets are always overcrowded; relieve the clutter by keeping some items, such as tape, seizing wire, and especially electrical tools, in the pockets of your chair or in a fly-fishing vest. And wear a knife, spike, and pair of Vise Grips on your belt or the belt

of your harness. The gear loops on the harness are also a good place to keep spare shackles and lanyards.

2. *Lanyard Sharing.* Seize small rings to your rigging bucket just below the rim (Figure 7-10). Attach a lanyard to a tool, reeve it through the ring, and attach it to a second tool, one you won't be using at the same time as the first. Likely pairs include a crescent wrench and chisel, hammer and file, hacksaw and screwdriver, etc. You'll be dealing with half as many lanyards, in complete safety. You can seize rings onto your chair, too, or just run lanyards through the halyard-attachment eyes. Or build a sheath

Michelle, Ma Bell

Take this idea aloft with you. The crescent-wrench head is welded to the marlingspike, and both this tool and the knife are secured to the sheath with lanyards. But here's the crowning touch: The "lanyards" are household telephone extension wires, belayed to tools with Knute Hitches. You get plenty of working lanyard scope without trailing long bights of twine through the rigging. You can also use those "corkscrew" shoelaces instead of phone cord.

Figure 7-10. To reduce the number of lanyards you must deal with, thread a single lanyard through a ring seized to the rigging bucket and attach ends to tools that you won't use simultaneously (in this case, adjustable wrench and putty knife).

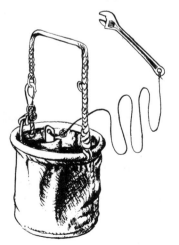

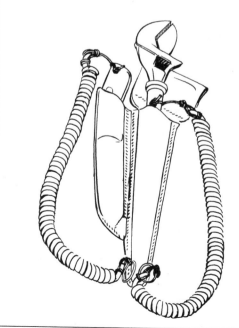

that will hold both knife and spike—so their lanyards can't get tangled between separate sheaths—and seize a ring to the bottom of the spike sheath.

3. *Separating Jobs.* Say you're installing a radar aloft. You need to drill holes, run wiring, mount the bracket, and finally mount the radar. That's four jobs with four partly or entirely different tool requirements. Separate the job into two or more phases before you leave deck, laying out tools and gear in the order you're likely to need them. Then the deck crew can shuttle things up and down in the rigging bucket, instead of overstuffing it and leaving you to struggle with it aloft.

4. *Maximize Versatility.* While job-specific consciousness is important aloft, so is resourcefulness and versatility. Welding the head of a crescent wrench to your marlingspike (Figure 7-11) enhances the worth of that already priceless tool; half-round files are a two-in-one blessing; the positive-lock on Sears ratchet handles prevents dropped sockets; and a cordless electric drill with a variable clutch can work for both making holes and setting screws. Add a keyless chuck to simplify bit changing.

Miscellany

Extremes of motion aside, the single greatest potential for annoyance and hazard aloft comes from how the deck crew attaches the gantline to the gear they send up. Let's say you're replacing a shroud. The hole in the end of the new terminal is the obvious place to tie the halyard. But when the wire gets to you, you must remove the halyard before you can install the wire. This involves either the bother of securing a separate lanyard or the hazard of casting off the halyard and trusting that you won't drop the wire before you get the clevis pin in place. A far better practice is to Icicle-Hitch the gantline onto the wire 2 feet (0.6 m) or so below the terminal. The halyard will be out of your way, and you can get the clevis in before casting the halyard off. If the halyard is too large or stiff to grip the wire securely, hitch on a smaller line and tie the halyard to that.

If you are sending up a tool, don't tie the halyard to its lanyard. Again, the tool must be secure before the halyard is untied.

For sending up sharp-cornered objects, avoid having the line touch the corners. If this is impossible, pad the corners first.

Have a camera handy when you go up, to get a portrait of details aloft that you can examine and analyze before any future work. Hold a ruler or sec-

Figure 7-11. A marlingspike–crescent wrench combination. The lanyard line should be just small enough to fit doubled through the lanyard hole in the tool. The end, with a Figure-Eight Knot, is dropped into the protruding bight, and the bight is withdrawn, jamming in the hole. To release, pull on the end and remove it from the bight. (I call this the "Knute Hitch," Knute being my favorite marlingspike.)

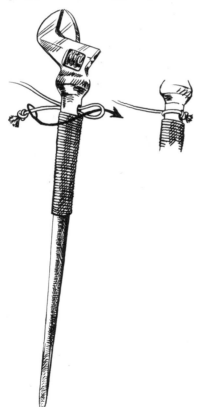

tion of tape measure in the picture for scale. Did you put a lanyard on that camera? I do not know the maximum safe distance for dropping a smart phone to the deck, but I do know that it is less than 55 feet. . . .

Whenever possible, avoid going up in bad weather. Not just because it's uncomfortable and dangerous, but because communications become difficult—it's hard to outshout a storm—and because you just can't do as good a job.

Minimize future trips aloft by making every trip an opportunity to survey the rig (see the "Survey and Maintenance" section later in this chapter). Have handy an assortment of clevis pins, cotter pins, screws, bolts, shackles, tape, etc., so you can deal with small problems immediately.

Wear white-soled or scuff-proof dark-soled shoes to avoid marking masts.

Wear long pants to avoid chafed and bruised legs.

Spinnaker halyard blocks are convenient to work from, since they're up high and they swivel. But like all swivel blocks, they're more fragile than nonswiveling blocks. Use an in-mast safety halyard.

The deck crew will appreciate any help you give them in getting you up, but avoid pulling yourself up so quickly that you put slack into the main halyard; sudden slack can cause the halyard to "wrap" on the winch, or jump off a loose sheave above and jam between sheave and mortise. Slack also means that if you fall, you will have time to accelerate; sharp fetch-ups can damage you.

If a vessel has ratlines, make things easier for everyone by climbing as far as you can on those, then switching to halyards.

With mast steps, it is essential to have a well-tailed safety line on you. Instead of having steps all the way up, consider installing just two, near the top of the mast, for a place to stand when working at the top.

Many vessels today have electric or hydraulic winches and capstans aboard, and it is natural to think of using them to hoist personnel as well as sails and anchors. I will just leave you to imagine how horribly this can go wrong. Any mistake on the

part of the deck crew or malfunction of the machinery can have tragic consequences. This is because the power involved is all out of scale with the work of lifting a human, because the machinery is not designed for this job, and because the deck crew is rarely trained for it, or at least trained well. Besides, you need the exercise. Use ascenders or steps or block-and-tackle or other means to get aloft (see below). Get assistance from a manual winch if you need to, but even then be sure of your deck crew.

Mountaineers and sailors have a long history of information sharing. Two of the most valuable ideas from the mountains are leg-and-hip-encircling safety harnesses and cam-grip rope-climbing devices (Figure 7-12). A good harness is far supe-

Figure 7-12. *A mast climber (taken from an illustration in Lirakis catalog): The "Ropewalker's" cam-grip action gives you a stairway to the spars. Release one side and slide it up, raising the corresponding leg, then engage the cam and straighten that leg while sliding the other side up. Note that one walker is belayed to the safety belt. For a faster, reduntantly secured ascent, use two halyards.*

The carabiner, or 'biner, is a roughly oval, spring-loaded shackle originally developed for mountaineers. In recent times it has found its way aboard boats, primarily for safety tethers. The best models lock shut, and the best of the locking models are easy to operate one-handed. That way you avoid the potentially fatal irony of going overboard because you let go of a secure handhold to deal with your safety tether.

The best models also will stay locked until you unlock them. Ideally, it should take at least three separate actions to open the gate. For example, you might have to slide the locking barrel, then twist it, then hinge the gate open. That way there is no likely circumstance, or even combination of circumstances, that will unlock the carabiner. For instance, screw-lock carabiners can be unscrewed by a rope rubbing the wrong way on the mechanism. If there is no secondary prevention, the gate can open from simple pressure.

If you have no locking carabiners, try the mountaineer's trick of hooking two of them in from oppo-site directions. That way, at least one of them will probably stay closed, no matter how you're washed, dropped, lurched, or bumped around.

As long as you have two carabiners, though, have two locking ones, and put them on separate tethers, one about 18 inches long, the other at whatever maximum length suits your application. Now you can secure yourself with the short tether when you're standing at the helm and don't need to move around much., You can switch to the longer tether when you need greater mobility. Anytime you need to move past an obstruction, clip one tether in before you detach and reattach the other on the far side of the obstruction. Note: very long tethers mean a potential for large shock loads, should you ever fetch up against them after accelerating on a slack tether. Some form of deceleration mechanism built into the tether is a very good idea. There are various forms of this, usually involving an elastic insert and/or tear-away stitching.

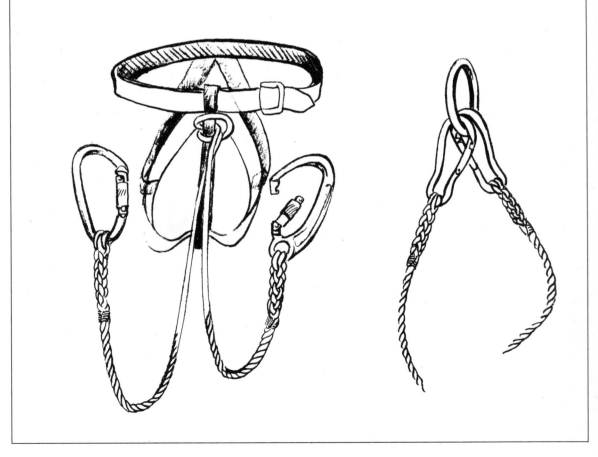

Figure 7-13. *Prusik Knots are an inexpensive equivalent to ropewalkers. Make a 15–18-inch-circumference grommet in line smaller than the halyard. Ring-Hitch the grommet to the halyard, then pass the bight through once more. Draw up securely, and hitch on foot pendants and safety line. Pull outward, then downward before each step to keep knots drawn up.*

rior to an ordinary safety belt in the event of a fall, because it distributes so much better the force of fetching up against the safety line.

Cam-grip devices used in conjunction with one or two belayed halyards allow you to get aloft under your own steam, an invaluable ability in short-handed vessels. Again, climbers' stores are your sources. It is most advisable to practice with these devices at low altitudes before walking up a mast.

A rope or webbing "diaper" and Prusik Knots (Figures 7-13 and 7-14) are low- or no-cost equivalents of harness and cam grips. Like the plank-and-rope bosun's chair, they are not as comfortable, convenient, or foolproof as their manufactured cousins, but they are adequate for some jobs and excellent in an emergency. For a primer on their use, see the excellent booklet, "Ropes, Knots, and Slings for Climbers," by Walt Wheelock (La Siesta Press, 1985; Box 406, Glendale, CA 91209).

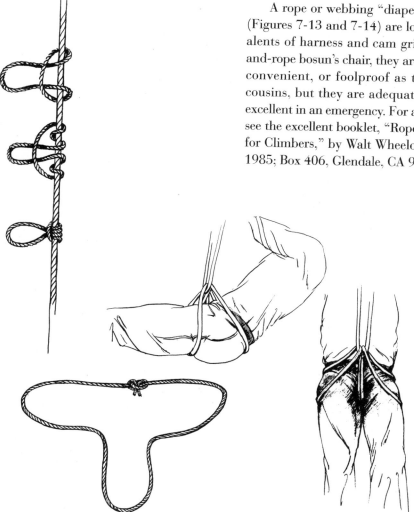

Figure 7-14. *Not quite as uncomfortable as it looks, a rope harness is good for emergencies or limited budgets. To make, tie the ends of a 7–9-foot piece of line together (the thicker and softer, the better), and arrange it in three bights as shown. Bring the middle bight up between the legs and the other two outside the legs. Shackle or tie all three together and to the halyard or safety line. Be sure to use a reliable knot to tie the ends together. Shown here is a Strait Bend (see Figure 3-34).*

Coming Down

When the work is done, the pressure is off, and all that remains is to ease on back to deck. But this is just the time when many accidents happen. Keep caution at a high level until you're past this job-ending transition point. Get to deck first, then relax.

Addendum I wrote most of the above some years ago. At the time I had spent many hours aloft, or tending others aloft. Since then I have spent many, many more hours at this work. My tools and techniques are always undergoing refinement, but the basics have held true; in those same years I have heard of more accidents than I care to think about, and I want to help others to be safer aloft. So in addition to studying the above, I recommend that you take a look the books and videos on the topic in the "Sources and Resources" section. For the time being, please read the next section, even if you are sure you will never need to deal with a topmast. The spar configuration might be different, but the demands of working aloft don't change. In particular, note the importance of communication between aloft and alow. You can never ever be too safe up there.

TOPMAST INSTALLATION

To most sailors these days, a topmast is a hopelessly archaic piece of gear; modern materials and sail plans have obviated its use. But "character boats" and historical reproductions need them, and they can be justified in practical terms since, among other things, they allow you to use one big and one little tree instead of one huge one to set the same amount of sail. Beyond that, they give me an excellent opportunity to present a traditional perspective on working aloft.

So. Your lower is in and well set up, the running rigging is neatly belayed and coiled, and the gear you've been spreading around has been collected and put away; you're ready to send up the topmast. If it's light enough, carry it on deck. Otherwise, set it on sawhorses alongside, abeam of the lower. Because it must pass through the tight confines of the "doubling," the only piece of gear you put on it now is the heel rope, with which the mast will be hoisted. This should be the newest, strongest piece of rope you have that will fit the heel sheave. Reeve this rope through the sheave from starboard to port (if the mast is on the port side of the boat) and pull enough end through so you can hitch it securely to the head of the topmast (Figure 7-15). Take up the

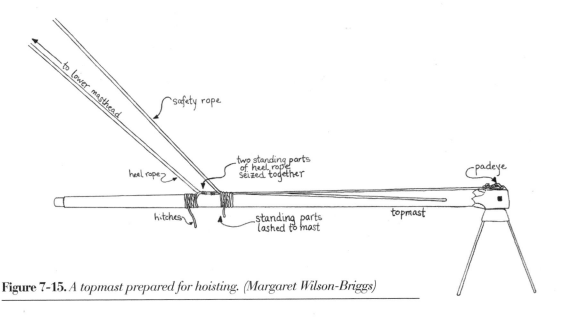

Figure 7-15. *A topmast prepared for hoisting. (Margaret Wilson-Briggs)*

slack with the unsecured standing part, lay it parallel to the part between the sheave and the masthead hitches, then seize the two parts together with two marline Round Seizings. Lash both parts to the topmast about one-third of the way down. Get a good hand to carry the other end of the heel rope aloft and reeve it up through the lower doubling fitting, then from front to back through a block shackled to the starboard side of the lower masthead. The end is carried back to deck and given a fair lead to a turning block and from there to a winch, windlass, or capstan.

It's cheap insurance to hitch a safety line onto the topmast with an Icicle Hitch (Figure 3-12). Take this line up through a second block aloft. Have a reliable hand tail it as the mast goes up.

Lay out the labeled rigging in two piles, port and starboard of the mast, with the pieces that will go on first uppermost in the piles. Labels go near the top ends, so the installer can make one last check before installing. Attach a tag line to the topmast butt, tail the line securely, and haul away on the heel rope. As the strain comes on, the topmast will want to shoot ahead from its horizontal position. Restrain with the tag line, paying out slack gradually until the topmast hangs plumb below the doubling. Time to go aloft.

With complete disregard for the little voice telling you that only fools would voluntarily leave a nice, safe deck, you are about to climb wa-a-ay up in the air and fiddle around with large, heavy objects. No amount of care and skill can make this act absolutely safe, so every precautionary measure is justified. When you climb ratlines, always hold onto the shrouds, not the ratlines, in case a seizing lets go. If you are going up in a bosun's chair, skip back to the "Living Aloft" section.

Wear a safety line when going aloft by either method, and shackle or tie it to something strong at every opportunity. Alternatively, rig a jackline, and clip a fall-arrest device to it.

The moment you're off the deck, very powerful instincts will come to your aid, helping you to move faster and hang on tighter than you've ever believed possible. Combined with some good sense, these instincts will help you to get the job

done and arrive back on deck whole and hearty.

Back to the topmast. Let's say you've made your way to the lower masthead via ratlines, tied yourself off to that mast, and braced your feet securely on spreaders, lugs, ratlines, or whatever else is strong

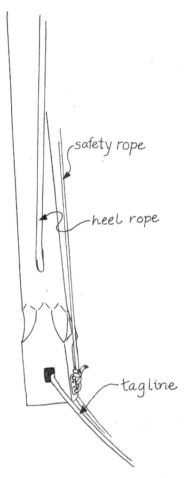

Figure 7-16. *As an option, lash a safety line to the fid hole and masthead hole to back up the heel rope as the mast goes up. Better yet, install a separate padeye or eyebolt at the butt of the mast, where it will end up below the crosstrees. That way you can leave the safety line in place until after the fid is in and secure. In either case, the safety line is led through another masthead block and is tailed on deck. And in either case, lash the safety line to the mast where the heelrope is lashed, so that the mast can't tip over before it reaches the doubling. (Margaret Wilson-Briggs)*

and handy. Look around for hand- and footholds you might need and obstacles you want to avoid. Set them in your mind. Closely scrutinize the condition of the block that the heel rope passes through. Can you trust it beyond all doubt? Good. Get comfortable and give your First Command to the deck crew.

"On deck."

"On deck, aye."

"Send up my rigging bucket on the port gantline."

"Rigging bucket on port gantline, aye."

Now that's a rather formal exchange, maybe too formal for some tastes. Contrast it with a more relaxed version:

"Hey, Lisa! Send up my rigging bucket!"

"Okay!"

Much simpler, true, but it allows too many misunderstandings. By not getting Lisa's attention first, the caller is likely to have to repeat the message. Or Lisa might not have heard the whole thing, and since she didn't repeat it back, you won't know until she starts sending up the topmast rigging. ("Oh, rigging *bucket*. Speak up!") Worse yet, Lisa doesn't know by what means the bucket is supposed to travel. She might come clambering up with it in her hand, spilling tools en route. No, a precise, graceful deck/aloft litany is much to be preferred.

So your rigging bucket is coming up. Brake its ascent slightly with one hand, in case it and the shortening end become outweighed by the standing part. It can easily happen on a long hoist, the bucket zipping upward the last few feet, launching tools when it fetches against the block.

The bucket reaches you and you call, "Hold that!" then, "Belay!"

When the line is belayed, deck calls out "Fast!" (made fast).

In your bucket you should have a spike, hammer, wrench, marline, seizing wire, knife, screwdrivers, nippers, and maybe some tallow—plus whatever else this particular topmast calls for. You packed these items on deck, attaching lanyards to the tools, and mentally went through the procedure you were about to follow to make sure you had everything you needed. It's awful to have to shout down the name

and size of a particular tool that you think is in the cabinet next to the chart table but there might be a spare in the lazarette, etc. For any given job, you can easily forget something crucial, but always taking the items mentioned above will lessen this likelihood.

You and your tools are up and ready, an assistant is perhaps made off on the other side of the mast, and the deck crew is standing by the hoisting gear. The topmast can now come up. Give the signal to haul, and guide the head through the lower doubling. When it's just short of the upper one, give the signal to belay. Now Icicle-Hitch a short, stout piece of line anywhere on the hitched end of the line, below the seizing and above the heelrope sheave; take up all slack and tie the other end of that short line up to the lower doubling. Cast off the hitches holding the end of the heel rope to the topmast head. Even with those stout marline seizings holding, this can be a tense moment, but that short, stout line is insurance in case the seizings slip. Try to ease off slowly to make sure all is well. Wasting no time, take up the slack and make the end off to a lug or other fitting on the port side of the lower doubling. The topmast is now suspended between the two parts of the heel rope, a configuration made necessary by its need to be hoisted well above the tackle's point of attachment. You've also just formed a two-part purchase, something the deck crew will have no objection to.

With the end belayed, carefully cut the seizings, remove the hitched-on insurance line, and give the signal to resume hauling . Guide the masthead through the upper doubling and get it two feet or so through, then again signal to hold and make fast. Time to send the rigging up.

Unless you have a surfeit of gantlines, you'll probably want to tie the bucket onto the mast with its lanyard, then cast off its gantline. In that order. Tie the gantline around its own standing part with a Bowline so it doesn't get tangled on anything on the way down, then have the deck crew slack away and send it to them.

The standing rigging comes up one piece at a time, first starboard, then port. Check each tag as you get it, then drop the eye over the stick. If the eyes are tight you'll need to smear the wood with tallow, then hammer the eyes on with a mallet. When everything's on, check the order once more, then cut the tags off. Give the signal to hoist, and slide the eyes down to their stops as the mast comes up. Pause when the stops are level with you to seat and lead the eyes, then hoist again.

A long score cut on either side of the heel sheave keeps the heel rope from chafing on the lower doubling as it comes through, but check now to make sure the lead is fair in the score. As the sheave passes through the doubling, pause to cast off the tag line, then continue until the fid hole in the mast lines up with the ones in the doubling. Drive the fid in and lock it in place. Done.

As I said before, there's not much call for topmasts these days, but installing one is an operation calling for most of the procedures you're ever likely to need aloft, whether you're re-reeving a parted halyard, inspecting the spreaders, or sending up a new radar. Just remember the need for clear communication, failsafe gear, and personal security. Insofar as possible, keep people away from the area of deck directly below you; if they wander in, call out "Stand from under!" in your most stentorian tone. It's a remarkably effective command.

RATLINES

"Arr, the crew swarmed nimbly up the ratlines as the vessel approached its mooring." The crew, it seems, was forever swarming nimbly up the rungs of these indispensable rope ladders, to set or furl sails, to assist in navigation, or to perform maintenance and repairs. Sadly, ratlines now suffer from the dreaded "Anything-that-salty-must-be-useless-these-days" syndrome.

And that's a pity. Although most contemporary yacht sails are set and furled from deck, ratlines still offer a clear view from aloft for spotting coral heads, windshifts, or land. And since maintenance by no means went out with spritsail topsails, you can still use ratlines to get aloft with varnish and paint. And they're the fastest way up in an emergency. And it just feels so good up there on a warm, breezy day,

with the world spread out beneath you, and the mast tracing gentle arcs in the sky. . . .

Where was I? Oh yes, ratlines. The modern, more expensive equivalent is a system of metal steps affixed to either side of the mast. These are relatively easy to climb when you're in a calm harbor, but have you ever tried going up them while the boat is pitching and heeling? A more versatile, safer arrangement for cruising yachts employs ratlines on the lower shrouds to get you as far as the spreaders, and a good bosun's chair for anything above that (see "Living Aloft," above). With the ratlines, you can ascend unassisted to deal with the jammed sail track, slipping spreaders, and the like. If the problem is at the masthead, you can save your crew half the time and effort they'd ordinarily expend getting you all the way up.

Wood or Rope?

All-wood ratlines make a comfortable, stable ladder. But they're a lot of work to make, a lot of weight and windage in place, and they're often visually clunky. All-rope ratlines are inexpensive, quick to make, and physically and visually unobtrusive. But they're awkward to climb and uncomfortable to stand on. I find that a sequence of two rope ratlines and one wood works best. The wood ones are close enough together that there's always a solid place to stand nearby. And they act as struts to hold the shrouds apart, so the rope rungs don't sag as much when you step on them. So you get an optimal combination of quick production, low cost, and low bulk without sacrificing too much comfort.

Fabrication

Rattling down can be done alone, but it will go much faster if a hand aloft splices and installs rope while a hand alow measures and cuts wood.

Unless your shrouds have sheer poles on them, the lowermost ratline will be of wood. Commonly, this would be an overlong piece lashed outboard of the shrouds. This is easy, but "internal" ratlines—those which fit between the shrouds—are appreciably lighter, more handsome, and have no line-snagging projecting ends.

The first step in layout is to hold a bevel gauge against one of the shrouds, adjusting it so that the blade is level with the horizon (Figure 7-17). Mark this angle on a miter box or other cutting jig. Now get the angle off the other shroud you'll be rattling, and mark this angle on the miter box. Cut these angles on the ends of a wooden ratline of the right length, and it will fit level between the shrouds. Since these angles are constant all the way up, you need only measure them once, and at any convenient height. Shrouds that are served will hold ratline lashings more readily. But sufficiently tight lashings will hold on bare wire. If you do serve, it is easier to do so the full length, as this saves the considerable labor of measuring, starting, and stopping patches of service for each ratline. Full-length service also helps galvanized wire, as well as Spectra, to last forever.

The ratline stock should measure at least 1½ inches (38 mm) from top to bottom edge, and at least 1¼ inches (32 mm) thick. This will be adequate for up to ½-inch (12.7 mm) wire; above that, increase the dimensions proportionately. The grain of the wood must always run parallel with the longer dimension, as this makes a stronger, stiffer rung. Rout the corners for a comfortable-to-stand-on, lighter, smaller-looking rung.

With a drill bit that matches the wire diameter, drill a hole through one end of a piece of stock, at the angle of the forward shrouds. Next drill a ⁵⁄₁₆-inch (7.9-mm) hole parallel to the first one and about 1¼ inches (32 mm) in from it. This is for the lashing line. Finally, drill for and install a rivet right between these two holes and at right angles to them (Figure 7-18). This will keep the end of the wood from splitting.

Cut the first hole you made in half, leaving a deep, angled groove. Round the corners with a file and sandpaper. Fair the lead from the lashing hole with a small gouge or penknife so that the lashing won't have to go over any sharp corners.

Figure 7-17. *Laying out wooden ratlines. To set the angle of wooden rung ends, trim the boat level, then sight parallel to the horizon with a bevel gauge. Rungs cut to the resulting angle will seat level when installed. Note: This technique only works for shrouds in the same plane, as two lower shrouds. If you are rattling between a lower shroud and another at a different angle—say, an intermediate—a spiraling ladder will result. To level these rungs, you'll need to use a builder's level.*

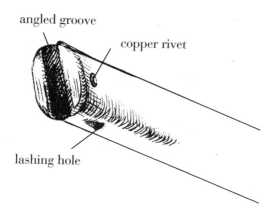

angled groove

copper rivet

lashing hole

Figure 7-18. *Preparing the first end of a ratline rung.*

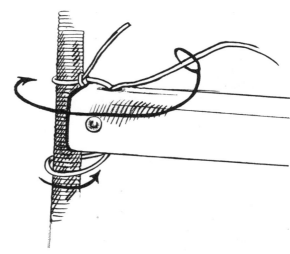

Figure 7-19. *Begin the lashing with a Buntline Hitch (see Figure 3-9), then proceed with a series of Square Lashings as shown. (Figure-eight crossings would leave longer runs of twine to stretch and loosen. Haul taut each turn as you go.)*

With some typist's white correction fluid, mark the height at which you want your first ratline. This will probably be just above the splice or fitting on the forward shroud. (Because of sheer, a start on the after shroud would result in the forward end of the ratline landing on the turnbuckle. The opposite may be true on mizzen shrouds.) Hold the half-done ratline against the shroud, setting the wire firmly into the groove. Level it against the horizon, then mark the top of the after end, exactly where the middle of the shroud touches it. Take the piece back down, drill three more holes at the appropriate angles, install the rivet, and cut the wire hole in half. Smear a little oil, varnish, or other grain-sealer on the ends, go back to the shrouds, and set it in place.

Lashing

You should now have a perfectly fitted ratline, lacking only secure attachment to its new home. Cut 8 feet (2.44 m) of $\frac{1}{16}$-inch (1.5-mm) or so tarred nylon twine and hitch it to one of the wires, right at the top of the ratline. Pass the working end down through the lashing hole, around the wire below, and back up through the hole (Figure 7-19). Continue this Square Lashing until there are four or five turns on either side. Finish with figure-eight turns made over the end, making a Half Hitch with each turn for security (Figure 7-20). Pull each of the square and figure-eight turns very tight as you go, using a Marlingspike Hitch. Secure the end with a couple of Half Hitches made around the wire below the rung.

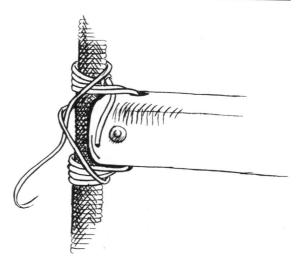

Figure 7-20. *When you can no longer fit turns of Square Lashing through the lashing hole, begin figure-eight turns, finishing each with a Half Hitch. This "fraps" the underlying turns and gives chafe-protection and backup strength.*

Tying a Figure-Eight Knot in the end and working it up very close to the hitches will assure that they never come undone (Figure 7-21).

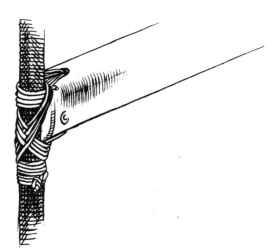

Figure 7-21. *Finished wooden ratline end, with lashing.*

Repeat the lashing procedure at the other end. Don a climbing harness, tether it to a shroud, and step onto the ratline. Jump up and down. Ain't lashings grand?

From where you're standing it is easy to measure up, mark for, and install the second wooden ratline. Space between rungs is a matter of taste and leg length, but 16 inches (406 mm) is standard. With two intervening rope ratlines, the second

wooden one will be 4 feet (1.22 m) above the first. Set the tape measure on top of the first rung and run it up alongside the most nearly vertical of your two shrouds. This will probably be the forward one. Make a mark at 16, 32, and 48 inches (406, 813, and 1,219 mm).

Drill, cut, rivet, and install the second wooden rung. Before moving on to rope, carefully measure the difference in length between these two ratlines. Then simply deduct this length from successive wooden ratlines as you go.

Rope Rungs

To avoid the dreaded "sagging step" syndrome, pre-stretch the rope you'll use. (One-half inch [13-mm] three-strand filament Dacron or Roblon is ideal.) Tie one end to a masthead halyard, belay the other end on deck, and tighten all with a winch. Or stretch it with a come-along ashore. This will remove the "initial elasticity" caused by all the rope yarns settling into place.

Splice a small eye in one end of the rope and lash it in place. Use a Square Lashing as before, but

Figure 7-22. To lash a rope ratline to a shroud, Buntline-Hitch the twine end to the eye, then begin a series of turns of Square Lashing. Be sure turns lie fair and flat on the shroud; none should protrude above its neighbors, or it will suffer chafe. Finish with several frapping turns and two Half Hitches. Work a Figure-Eight Knot into the end up close to the last hitch to prevent the end pulling out.

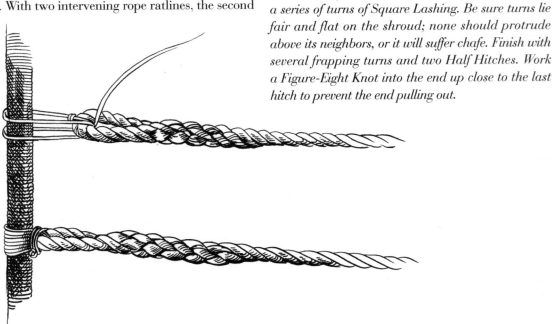

this time finish off with frapping turns between wire and rope (Figure 7-22). Stretch the standing part out level and make a bight to form an eye that just touches the opposite shroud. Mark the middle of the eye, then cut the line, leaving enough to splice with.

Alternatively, make a Crown splice around a half-inch drift punch. Remove the punch, then pass the lashing as for an eyesplice. You might need to use a carpet hooker or the like to get the lashing through the hole easily. This configuration looks remarkably clean, and it also delays the point at which the steps get so short that the splices back into each other.

Speaking of which, if ratlines are big enough to be comfortable, they are very strong for the job of holding up humans, so they don't need as many sets of tucks as regular splices—3½ should be plenty.

When the splices do approach each other too closely, switch to making grommets, of the next smaller-diameter rope.

When you go to lash the second eye in place, you'll find that the splice has "shrunken" the line— it won't quite reach the shroud. Lashing it tightly now will, ideally, result in a snug-fitting ratline, but not so snug that it pulls the shrouds together. Adjust your lengths to suit the shrinking effect of your splices and the rope's own characteristics.

Rope ratlines fit best if you finesse each one as you go, rather than deducting a specific length each time. Be slightly more generous with your initial measurements as you ascend; shorter ratlines aloft stretch less, and splice shrinkage consumes proportionately more of their length. As you proceed, you'll find it easy to fall into a rhythm of splicing and lashing while your partner is drilling and cutting.

A semi-utilitarian historical aside: "Rattling down" originally meant just that—installing ratlines from a bosun's chair, starting at the top and working down. Most or all of the ratlines were rope, and standing on a rope ratline will pull even very tightly set-up shrouds toward one another. "Rattling up" will produce the dreaded "Siamese sine curve" syndrome (Figure 7-23). That problem is prevented here by setting the wooden rungs in place first, then filling between them with rope. But while making your fittings, be very careful to avoid leaning either

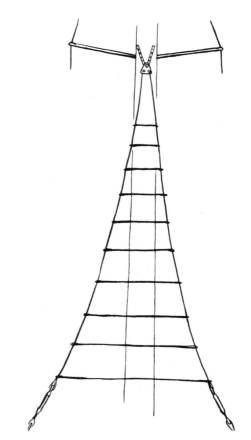

Figure 7-23. *The dreaded Siamese Sine Curve syndrome.*

on the shrouds or the rope ratlines. This requires a good sense of balance, a calm day, and, to repeat, a safety line.

So, you've installed the first two wood and first two rope ratlines. The third wooden one comes next, and you're getting up around 10 feet (3.05 m) off the deck. At this point, have succeeding pieces come up to you on a light gantline. I shackle a small block to my harness for this purpose. Always leave the gantline hitched to the wooden rungs until the first lashing is finished.

Climb up, splicing and lashing as you go, first one wood, then two rope, on and on. Keep everything level; skewed rungs are glaringly obvious to the most casual observer.

As you climb, get firmly in the habit of holding onto the shrouds, not the ratlines; the former are less

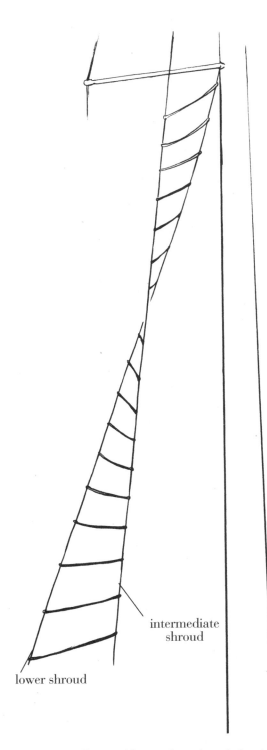

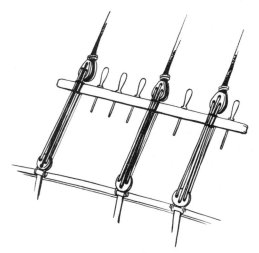

Figure 7-25. *A sheerpole on a traditional rig, lashed under the deadeyes and between the lanyard legs. Lashings must be very secure to prevent the sheerpole from riding up and bearing on the wire eyes. If this happens, the service and even the wire strands can be chafed away.*

intermediate
shroud

lower shroud

Figure 7-24. *Forward lower shroud rattled to intermediate.*

Figure 7-26. *A jack shroud can be wire, lashed to intervening rungs (see text), or, as shown here, a rope hitched to intervening rungs.*

likely to give way than the latter. Ratlines are for feet.

As you near the top and lengths decrease, you'll find that the rope splices will begin to back into one another. When this happens, the sweetest procedure is to switch to rope grommets, making them out of line one-half the size you've been using. Proceed until the space between the wires is narrower than your foot.

Options and Variations

Especially on rigs that have shroud eyes seized in place around the mast, the space between the wires will get baby-foot wide well down from the spreaders. One option to gain a little foot room is to slack the shrouds and lash a grooved triangular block in place just below the seizing. The angle at the apex should be quite shallow to avoid imposing excessive lateral stress on the seizing. Even so, this option should only be used on low-stress rigs, and only with seizings, never with tangs or mechanical terminals.

Another technique is to rattle the forward lower and intermediate shrouds (Figure 7-24), thus escaping the "Narrowing Gap" syndrome altogether. This results in a helical ladder that is quite pleasing in appearance. Unlike mast steps, this ladder is never athwartships, even at the top. The only complication lies in leveling the rungs; your axis shifts as you go up, so you cannot use the horizon as a level reference. This is one place aboard where you can use a builder's level. Get the boat plumb, even if it means shifting gear on deck to balance your weight in the shrouds. And put a lanyard on the level.

A second variation, for vessels with topmasts, is to rattle the lowers until the gap narrows, then to jump over to the topmast backstay for the rest of the distance.

Sometimes the space between the lower shrouds is quite large at the bottom. If you're worried about a wood rung's ability to bear weight over a long span, install a sheer pole at the bottom to double as the first step (Figure 7-25). Or install a "jack shroud," lashed to the middle of the bottom ratline at one end and to the second or third wooden rung at the other (Figure 7-26). The jack shroud can be of ⅛-inch (3.5-mm) plastic-coated wire with a thimble in either end. Make it a little shorter than the space between rungs. Lash to the lower rung first, then pull all snug with the lashing to the upper rung. By Clove-Hitching any intervening rope rungs to the jack shroud, you support their middles, too. Traditionally, this knot is made with the crossing turn outboard, lower end leading aft. If the Clove Hitch slips on the plastic, make a Rolling Hitch instead.

On big, old-style vessels with multiple lower shrouds, rope ratlines are Clove-Hitched to the intervening shrouds, and any wooden ratlines must be lashed outboard. The forwardmost or "swifter" shroud is often left bare, as yards and lines chafe against that shroud. Likewise the aftermost shroud is often left unrattled if the middle shrouds provide a wide enough ladder for proper swarming. A nice touch is to run every fifth ratline to the aftermost or the swifter shroud, so you can get out of the way of traffic while conning or sightseeing.

With a large crew in a large ship, it is prudent to make the first several ratlines heavier than the rest, as there's usually a packed crowd at the bottom.

For vessels of any size, it's safest to climb ratlines when they're on the weather side, so they form a sloping ladder with the wind holding you on instead of a vertical ladder with the wind trying to knock you off.

A final aesthetic/practical note: One frequently sees wooden ratlines secured to shrouds with cable clamps. Lashed ratlines are graceful and tidy. Cable clamps are just a heavy, ugly, wire-damaging, shin-scraping way to avoid doing the job right.

TUNING

The rig exists to distribute strain from the sails in such a way that the boat moves through the water to optimum effect. But without careful tuning, all you've got is a bunch of wires hanging off the mast. This business of bringing the vessel to life involves knitting everything together so that, as nearly as possible, all strains are shared and no single member takes a disproportionate load.

Dockside Tune

For rough tuning at the dock, start by using the shrouds and stays to plumb the mast athwartships, and to induce any desired rake in the fore-and-aft plane. Most riggers accomplish the lateral measurement by running the end of a long tape measure to the masthead on a halyard. Then they triangulate by measuring down to corresponding chainplates on either side. This sounds logical, but there are some problems with it: The halyard is measurably elastic, so pulling the tape tight must be done exactly the same on both sides, or you get skewed readings; the halyard is usually in a sheave that is set off-center, which also skews the results; you have to fight your way around boom and topping lift to get the tape from one side to the other; and even if you get good measurements, the results tell you only where the top of the mast is, when you want to center the whole thing.

Instead, stand in front of the mast and make a mark with a China marker on the center of the front, as high as you can readily reach. If there is a spinnaker track there, choose the center of a fastener at that height. Measure down to the chainplates from there. You are still triangulating, just with a much shorter triangle. No halyard elasticity, no offset, no struggle, and you now know where the bottom of the mast is, so you can use it as a reference point, sighting up the luff to center the mast above. But wait, there's more. What if the mast is not leaning, but actually offset to one side? The step or the partners might be off center, or the chainplates might be asymmetrically placed. If this is so, there will be a different angle of shrouds on one side than the other. So measure from a chest-high point on the center of the face of the mast out to the upper shrouds. If the numbers are different, you have an offset. If it is the partners that are off-center, you might be able to get the mast on center by changing the size of the wedges on either side. If the problem is with the step or the chainplates, things will be harder to fix, but you can at least use the knowledge of the problem when you tune, going a little tighter on the steeper-angled side, to compensate for the difference in lateral pull.

The fore-and-aft rake of the mast is largely an aesthetic consideration. Yes, it can affect the center of effort, and therefore helm balance, but sail and hull trim are usually far more powerful and simple ways to affect this. What is more, significant mast rake throws off things like boom height and staysail shape. In any event, rake is constrained by the size and location of partners on keel-stepped rigs, and the angle of the mast base platform on those that are deck stepped. In general, I find it most effective to set rake according to the designer's intent, and deal with the helm by other means.

When making initial adjustments, take up a little bit at a time on each turnbuckle, and when you think things are about right, take a look from some distance away for perspective.

When you're satisfied, you can begin the actual tuning. What you're after is a mast which is straight laterally, is either straight or has a desired bend fore-and-aft, and which retains its shape under way. Wire stretches under load, and stretches further the longer it is and the more heavily it is loaded. So you have to compensate for that stretch, now, by pretensioning each wire a specific amount, so that it won't stretch too much or too little. That's tuning.

You want the longest wires to be the tightest, because they would otherwise stretch too far. Shorter wire will be less tight, but no wire should ever be slack. In terms of a percentage of maximum wire strength, you'll want 10 to 12 percent load on the lowers, 12 to 15 percent on the intermediates, if any, and 15 to 20 percent on the uppers. You can use any of a variety of tension gauges for measuring these loads, but in the absence of one, start by tightening the lowers, a little bit at a time, until you can strum a low musical note on them. Not just a vibration, a musical note. That's about 10 percent load. Make any intermediates a little tighter, and the uppers tighter still.

Don't go to the next wires until the slack is gone from the ones you're working on and the related section of mast has the desired shape in both planes. Otherwise, it is easy to put assorted bows into the stick without knowing which wires have caused them. Check for this by putting your head right up against the mast and sighting up; you'll be able to see even the tiniest deflections.

Make the forestay about as tight as the intermediates, and the jibstay and backstay about as tight as the uppers.

Bend

Most masts these days, even in cruising boats, can be bent, and the boat will sail better for it. When you bend the mast, you flatten the mainsail; straighten the mast, and you make the mainsail fuller. So, you can suit sail shape to every condition. I can hear some of you out there saying you're not going to race, so why bother? Well, for one thing, flattening the main means you will sail more upright in higher winds, so you'll reef later, less often. Tuning is a labor saver.

There are other benefits to mast bend—for details, see the sidebar "Mast Bend, Stayed and Unstayed" in Chapter 8 and the sailing books in the bibliography—but there are so many rig types that I can't go into much detail about it here. In general, induce a moderate (less than one mast depth) bend with the backstay, then take up on the lowers to control and define that bend, then proceed with the intermediates and uppers.

Dynamic Tune

When things are good at dockside, it's time to go sailing. Wait until there's enough breeze to heel your boat at 15 to 20 degrees, so the rig will really get loaded up. If it's new wire, go out and just thrash around for a while, to get the initial slack out. Then get on a tack to weather, and take a look at your leeward shrouds. They will always be slacker than the weather ones, because the weather ones always stretch some. That's as it should be, but they should never be flopping loose. If they are, take up on them until you feel a slight increase in resistance in the (well-lubricated) turnbuckle. Then tack and do likewise on the other side. Tack back and see how things look. Not bad? Good. Now sight up the mast again, with your cheek right against the luff of the main. Straight? Or does the head fall off to weather?

If it does, it might be because the uppers are too loose, or because the lowers are too tight. Try the lowers first.

Now go and sight up the jibstay. There will always be some sag in it, and your sailmaker should know how much for a given point of sail and wind condition. Is there more than there should be? If so, tighten the backstay.

Get the idea? As I said, there are lots of variations, but they're all variations on the same theme: Keep the stick straight laterally, and bent as much as you want fore-and-aft. With no slack in the wires.

It's definitely a good idea to get a good rigger to tune the boat with you, to get it right on. But it's hard to get in trouble as long as you keep the mast straight and avoid overtightening.

When the tune is set, cotter all the turnbuckle studs.

SURVEY AND MAINTENANCE

A good rig has a designed-in safety factor: a degree of overbuilt toughness that will allow its components to deteriorate to some degree without precipitating a dismasting. A survey is an opportunity to maintain that safety factor, to spot and correct flaws before they're serious. A survey is also an opportunity to minimize expense and labor by assessing lubrication, adjustments, improvements, and other maintenance needs.

The work takes two forms: the formal once- or twice-a-year going-over that leaves nothing unscrutinized; and the reflexive, glance-at-things-as-you-go-about-your-business inspection that is probably more valuable. Rust stains, cracked fittings, and wire with kinks or broken strands or a slight unlaying due to heavy strain are all things that are possible to spot if you habitually look for them but easy to miss if you don't. Cotter pins, shackle mousings, swages, and seizings don't require much effort on your part to examine. If one of these is not healthy and you spot it soon enough, it is easy to fix or replace; if six months' time elapses between looks, serious trouble can develop.

Attitude

Before starting, stand back for a minute and get into "survey mode," a state in which you see and feel the rig as a balanced, integrated whole. Take in the details of running and standing rigging, and feel how they interrelate with mast, sails, and hull. Entering this frame of mind is going to do you at least as much good as the usual procedure—starting with a list of Things to Look For. By envisioning the whole rig, you'll be inclined to notice if something is missing, or could lead better, or is worn.

Next, stir in some general ideas to give your gestalt a little focus. The most succinct survey rules I know of are these four from yacht designer Eva Holman:

1. If it is fastened, it will try to undo itself.

2. If it touches something, it will try to chafe itself or that other something to death.

3. If it is slack, it will try to snag something.

4. If it is metal, it will try to corrode itself or its neighbor.

Details

Armed with an informed attitude, you can now make up a list, enumerating as many details as you can think of. This list will be more complete in the state of mind you're now in than it would be if you'd begun in classic Western analytical mode.

Unfastening For example, things that will try to unfasten themselves can range from the bolts securing chainplates to the pin restraining your windvane, with spreader bolts, link plates, toggles, screws, antenna wiring ties, and sheave pins in between. It can include swages, Sta-Loks, and other wire terminals; sail track, bolts, and lashings; welds and glue joints; and on and on. You can even get compound fastenings: say, a cotter pin holding a clevis pin. Is the cotter secure and in good condition? If it should fall or get pulled out, is the clevis head downward so it, too, will fall out, or head upmost so it will stay

in place for a while, giving you a chance to spot the missing cotter?

As you make your list, feel free to let your categories overlap; you'll get a more complete list and a clearer idea of how rig components inter- relate. For instance, some spreader fastenings secure the spreader to the wire, and some secure the spreader base to the mast. But good fastenings are only as strong as what they're fastened to. In this case, wire sometimes will suffer chafe or accelerated fatigue where it passes over spreader tips; check the wire's condition and the suitability of the tips as well as the condition of the fastenings. Then see if the spreader angles up, as it should, to bisect the angle formed by the shroud. If it doesn't, the wire is always trying to push the tip down..

Chafe For Rule 2, the Certainty of Chafe, look not just for gouges and tears but also for shiny spots—something's been rubbing there. And avoid the trap of looking only where you expect chafe to be. I knew a boat on which the crew always made off the running backstays well forward when not in use, to avoid chafing the mainsail. Instead, the runners chafed on the after edge of the lower spreaders. Moderate pressure combined with the movement of the vessel was all it took for the spreaders and wires to saw into each other.

Sometimes chafe is hidden, so get in the habit of ducking and squinting into unlikely spaces, like the underside of standing rigging terminals. I once saw a rig in which a sheer pole threaded through the upper jaws of the turnbuckles chafed most of the way through the eyesplices on the lower ends of the shrouds. All it took to spot it was a cursory crouched-down look, but for years no one crouched.

Running rigging chafe is usually obvious because the line is always literally passing through your hands. Sheaves, stays, cleats, hawses, and stoppers tend to bear repeatedly at the same point; get in the habit of checking known chafe points so you can end-for-end or adjust the length of the line before chafe becomes too severe. To adjust length, cut off a short length at the working end, then reattach. This moves fresh line onto the chafing area.

But checking and shifting do not lessen chafe. To do that, you need to analyze what is causing it in the first place, and act accordingly. If you have good-quality rope clutches, for example, chafe should not be a serious problem unless the rope size is small compared with the loads exerted on it. Likewise, chafed-through rope or wire strands on a halyard can be caused by a too-small sheave (see "Blocks," in Chapter 2), and mainsail chafe can be caused by the cloth bearing on an after lower shroud. In the latter case, it's not practicable to increase the wire size, so instead pad it with service, leathering, or baggywrinkle, or have a chafe patch sewn onto the sail.

Chafe can also be caused by things being where they don't belong. Staysail sheets delight in bearing on stanchions, shrouds, and anything else between clew and winch. But a little thought and intelligent use of turning blocks will eliminate this problem.

Snags   Rule 3 leads us out of the relatively simple world of fastenings and friction and into the subtler realm of ballistics. An unsecured running backstay, for example, will chafe as it flops around, but is liable to cause even more problems by grabbing at stanchions, turning blocks, gear lashed to cabintops, and you. Surveys are opportunities to take action to prevent snags.

Most often, it is jibsheets that snag, and usually in mid-tack. When doing a survey, flop the sheets around intentionally to see how close they come to snaggable cleats, vents, spinnaker poles, bitts, etc. If a snag seems likely, modify or relocate the potential snagger. A simple strut added to a Dorade vent, for instance, can prevent an inadvertent vent launching (Figure 7-27).

More than running rigging can be slack. If you've attached antenna wire to a shroud with those little electrical ties, watch out for their degrading in sunlight. When they let go, the wiring will start waving around, eager to catch the odd line or sail. Likewise, the tape that secures spreader boots can come undone, exposing a little opening in the boot that halyards just love to crawl into. Worst of all are masthead sheaves that are slack in their mortises,

Figure 7-27. *A strut on a Dorade vent alleviates head-sail sheet snags.*

leaving room for a halyard to wedge itself between the sheave and the mortise wall.

Corrosion   Corrosion is always a problem in a saltwater environment, particularly when you mix antagonistic materials such as aluminum and stainless or stainless and carbon fiber; these materials are on different points on the galvanic scale, and when joined by the conductive medium of water they set up an electrical current. The resulting activity corrodes whichever of the two materials is least noble (lower on the galvanic scale). While not as serious with rigging as with permanently immersed items such as hull fastenings, galvanic corrosion can over time weaken spars, and clog such machinery as winches and blocks.

The first thing to do is to take note of places where dissimilar materials are in contact. Then go about isolating them with some form of nonconductive bedding. This can be as low-tech as parceling and serving to isolate galvanized steel wire from bronze thimbles, or it may involve Tef-Gel, Eck, or other compounds to isolate aluminum or stainless fasteners (see sidebar "Favorite Goops," page 224). When surveying an aluminum spar, pull a few fasteners and examine the screws and the holes they came from. If you see a white powdery substance on either, you've got galvanic corrosion. If the fasteners shear off when you try to pull them, you've got serious galvanic corrosion. Stainless steel, the dominant material in rigging today, is susceptible to its own special form of decay: crevice corrosion, also known as oxygen starvation. Stainless steel contains significant amounts of chromium. When exposed to the atmosphere the surface oxidizes slightly and a thin film of chromium oxide forms, preventing any further oxidation. If exposed to water, salt or fresh, without the presence of air, this film will not form and the metal will corrode. If the water in question is salt water, the process is compounded by chloride corrosion.

You risk oxygen starvation anytime you cover stainless, as when applying spreader boots, shroud rollers, or service. The trick is to exclude both water and air. When serving, some anhydrous lanolin covered with proper parceling and service works fine. Just rinsing stainless with fresh water whenever you can will lessen the corrosive effects of salt water.

When surveying for stainless corrosion, don't be distracted by stains. Contrary to what the name implies, the stuff does stain, often from bits of non-stainless steel scraped off the extruding dies when the wire is formed. But do look closely, preferably with a magnifying glass, for any sign of pitting in the metal—the surface will seem to have teeny-tiny craters in it. Any significant pitting is cause for replacement..

Just how frayed, rusty, or old, or whatever, must a piece be for it to be condemned? There are plenty of people out there who can point to a battered but still-functioning wreck and tell you that it's held up fine and they'd still trust it in a gale. Gear will sometimes hold together far longer than anyone could reasonably expect. But the point is to have, not a long-lived rig, but a *safe* long-lived rig. Why incorporate a safety factor in a rig design, only to erode it away? In view of the possible consequences of gear failure, it seems foolhardy to go out with anything but the strongest, best-conditioned rig that is compatible with performance and your purse. Watch, understand, and respond as if it were an instinctive feeling of your inner life.

Sometimes metal just plain rusts. Stainless steel rusts more slowly, but tropical climates will get to it in just a few years. Galvanized steel left untended can dissolve in a matter of months. Any survey of metal must be a survey for rust.

If served galvanized rigging is slushed whenever it gets to looking dry, it will last a century or more. Very cost-effective. As I write this, the 40-or-more-year-old standing rigging of the Arctic exploration schooner *Bowdoin* is sitting in my loft. The foundation that owns this boat wanted me to replace the gang, but stripping the service off a few splices revealed wire that is as good as new. I had to ace myself out of a big job and talk them into a little renovation instead.

Slush, also known as tar varnish or blacking compound, is a tar-based paint applied periodically to standing rigging to protect it from decay. Recipes vary, but here's a good basic one for served rigging:

6 parts Stockholm tar
3 parts boiled linseed oil
1 part Japan drier
1 part spar varnish

Mix the ingredients together and apply to marline or seizing wire in thin coats until the material is "full" but not overflowing. When dry, slush is hard enough to resist scuffing but resilient and durable enough to maintain a waterproof seal over the wire rope.

The type of tar you use makes a considerable difference; most commercially available pine tars are chemically processed and may contain impurities. Stockholm tar is produced by simple distillation and cooking. It smells sweet, doesn't irritate skin the way other tars do, and holds up much better in the weather.

Be sure the drier you use is fresh and still volatile; it makes the slush "go off" and harden. Mix up small batches and seal containers securely between uses.

When slushing nylon-served rigging, "Net Dip," an asphalt tar available from fishery supply houses, is a good choice for slush.

Using less tar and adding some thinner (Solvex or Xylol is good) makes a good bare-wire slush. Straight boiled linseed oil or mineral oil is less effective but tidier, anhydrous lanolin thinned with mineral oil is also good, and I've recently found that Marvel Mystery Oil applied generously and allowed to soak in is an excellent wire preservative. There are also some extremely expensive wire preservatives developed for industry, which, if you can find them in small amounts at bargain prices, are very effective. Wear gloves and a respirator when working with them. All preservative coatings can be applied with a paintbrush.

It's most convenient, of course, to slush the rigging when the sticks are out; if they're in place and you have to work aloft, you will find on your return that your deck is spattered with hundreds of droplets of slush. To avoid this, bend a springline onto the anchor rode while at anchor and pay out on the rode to form a bridle. This will put you at right angles to the wind, so that as you slush the lee rigging, those spatters will hit the water instead. Turn the boat around to slush the other side. And don't do this bridling procedure in a crowded harbor unless your neighbors to leeward don't mind a tarred bootstripe.

Bare wire is not as long-lived as served wire, but a little attention will keep it from dying prematurely. Any one of the various slush recipes will do for galvanized wire. I recently replaced a couple of 40-year-old shrouds that had been treated exclusively with zinc chromate; they were just about worn out, but a little tar or anhydrous lanolin a few years ago would have gotten them to the half-century mark with ease.

The most-often-unlooked-for place for galvanized wire to rust is at the throat of the splice, at the pointy end of the thimble. Even competent splicers will sometimes neglect to "diaper" this spot adequately. The result will be that salt water will splash up inside and rust the throat, while the rest of the wire stays like new under its service.

A wire seizing made with galvanized seizing wire can rust from the inside out, even though brightly painted on its surface, if the wire isn't rustproofed with thinned tar or other wire preservative first. This is one reason to use stainless steel seizing wire.

Another hidden rust spot is under any item that is lashed to served wire. Unless the service is covered with a chafe-resisting layer of leather or canvas, the lashing can cut through the service and expose the wire.

Swages are much trickier to inspect for corrosion than a served splice; about the only way to tell anything's happening inside a swage is to have it crack from internal pressure or fatigue. Eva Holman recommends tapping swages with a tool handle to determine their condition. With a little practice you can learn to tell the hollow sound of a corroded swage from the live ring of a solid one.

Fatigue   To Holman's four surveying rules I would add a fifth: stainless steel fatigues. No, this is not an all-metal army uniform. It refers to the characteristic of alloyed steels of hardening and becoming brittle with age. The more heavily a piece of alloy is stressed relative to its ultimate strength, the faster it will fatigue. Therefore, you'd survey lightly rigged race boats for fatigue more carefully and sooner than heavily rigged cruisers. Also, the warmer the climate, the faster stainless will fatigue, as the contribution of salt is enlarged.

Fatigue reveals itself with cracks. Sometimes small, "Gee-I'm-glad-I-spotted-that" cracks; sometimes "Oh-my-God-I-could-drive-a-truck-into-that-thing-and-it's-holding-up-the-jibstay" cracks. Sometimes the cracks have a zigzag pattern, caused by what is called stress corrosion. This can come

Fatigue

In his wonderful book, *To Engineer Is Human*, Henry Petroski notes that 50 to 90 percent of failures in engineered objects result from fatigue. There is no certain way, he says, to prove, nondestructively, that a new object is free of internal flaws. So engineers posit the existence of flaws small enough to escape detection when new, then figure how soon use will increase their significance sufficient for detection, and schedule examinations for then.

from a combination of sources, including salt, heat, loading, and from internal, literally built-in stresses like bad tempering or uneven cold-working.

Sometimes the cracks are vertical, or radiate out from a single point. These are usually caused by simple overloading. Vertical cracks on swages are a common example of this; wire rope inside the swage expands with corrosion from moisture, pressing outwards on the walls of the swage until it cracks. Some sailors try to prevent this problem by pouring oil or hot wax down their lower swages. It doesn't seem to make any difference, since water will migrate past anything but an adhesive put in under pressure, as one gets with Sta-Lok-type terminals. But at least the attempt at pouring something in makes more sense than another fix I've seen: tightening a hose clamp around a cracked swage, to hold it together. Obviously it pays to invest in high-quality stainless and to make it plenty heavy, to delay the onset of fatigue. Bronze is nearly impervious to fatigue, which is why it is so often used in toggles, turnbuckles, tangs, and chainplates. Galvanized steel is likewise relatively fatigue-resistant, so if you can keep it from rusting, it will outlast stainless. the size of the stainless wire, but this will also involve increasing the sheave size. Can of worms.

When rigging wire fatigues, its strands will begin breaking. Note that a single broken yarn in 1 x 19 wire reduces strength by more than 5 percent. Wires will usually break first at the lower ends of standing rigging, where corrosion and fatigue work together. But check both ends and all the wire between, just in case. Fatigue can be reduced by increasing wire size, but again this is not always practicable, especially for racers, as it increases weight aloft. It's usually better to use an appropriately sized wire (see "Selecting Wire," Chapter 5) and to employ other fatigue-reducing strategies. The easiest one is the addition of toggles. Put one at either end of each turnbuckle or buy turnbuckles with built-in toggles. Add another toggle at the wire's upper end, particularly on stays with sails hanked to them, as these are most heavily worked. And keep your rigging snugly tuned so that sailing motions won't cause your mast to bang around, shock-loading your wires.

Choosing a Foundry

Have bronze castings done by a foundry specializing in bronze; they'll know which type of bronze is best suited to your application, and will be pickier about ingredients and proportions than a general-purpose foundry.

Minimizing Halyard Fatigue

To avoid accelerated wire fatigue, never let a splice, Nicopress sleeve, or other terminal get within two inches of a sheave or fairlead.

Rigs with swaged terminals are among the most susceptible to failures; frequent inspections are necessary to ensure their integrity. If the strands of a wire rope do not lead fairly into a swaged terminal; if there is evidence of corrosion, especially at the top of the terminal; or if the terminal is cracked or warped, no matter how slightly, it is of uncertain integrity and should be replaced at once. Swages are the overwhelmingly favorite choice for sailboat terminals because of their low cost, neat, compact appearance, and high initial tensile strength. But they are not to be trusted.

When swages fatigue, they'll crack, too. Again, this can also be caused by internal corrosion—the corroded wire expands, trying to split the swage apart (Figure 7-28). Cracked swages can survive for years or days. Replace any wire that has a cracked swage on it immediately, unless you enjoy that sort of gamble. A horizontal crack is always more dangerous than a vertical one. Use a magnifying glass or dye penetrant to spot fine cracks. Check the eye as well as the barrel of the fitting. Some swages are made by a rotary swager, which hammers the fitting rapidly from all angles, making a smooth-finished surface. If you see a lengthwise ridge on the barrel of the swage, it was formed by passing it between the dies of a Kearney swager. Kearney swages are far more likely to crack, and frequently end up with a disquieting banana shape. Don't use them.

Hayn and Sta-Lok fittings are the best mechanical terminals—right up there with splices in terms

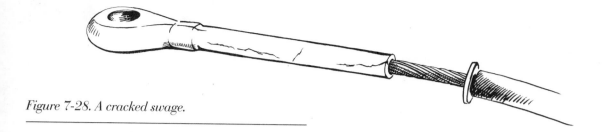

Figure 7-28. A cracked swage.

of trustworthiness. They're screwed onto the wire, which means there are no hammer- or die-induced stresses. And they're reusable, so when you re-rig you only need to buy wire, not terminals.

The above is by no means a complete list of things to look for, but it gives you an idea of how free-ranging and inclusive a survey mentality must be. To give you an idea of how this might translate into reality, a sample survey follows. It's a bit of a flaw collage, excerpted from several vessels. If the number and severity of flaws seem high, bear two points in mind: (1) A moderately run-down rig and one in good condition will have roughly the same number of notations; as you fix big problems, you start noting smaller ones. (2) Assuming the mast is still standing, the list of things that are okay is always longer still.

Hacksawing Wire Rope

The slowest, most frustrating way to cut wire rope is with a hacksaw—unless you tape firmly on either side of the cut mark, then clamp the wire in a vise. Then hacksawing is fast, and leaves a far cleaner edge than shears do. Use bi-metal or carbide blades: 18 teeth per inch (tpi) will make quick work of most wire rope; 24 tpi leaves a significantly smoother edge, and is not much slower.

Be sure to tension the blade moderately firmly; it doesn't need to be twanging tight, but it shouldn't wobble in the cut. Try orienting the blade so that it cuts on the pull stroke. This way the blade tightens, rather than loosens, during the cutting stroke. I find that it is also easier to steer.

A clean edge isn't important if you're splicing, but it makes the wire nice to work with, and it makes a lot of difference when you're assembling Sta-Loks or similar terminals.

Survey of a 34-foot Cutter

Starting at the top:

1. *Topping lift block has unmoused shackle. Shackle pin is upside down.*

Here's one you can fix right away, assuming you brought along some nippers and a length of seizing wire.

2. *Recommend spare halyard at masthead.*

An extra halyard is good as a safety when going aloft (see "Living Aloft" earlier in this chapter) or as a backup in case you lose one of the regular halyards. Ideally, it will be placed so it can substitute for jib, main, or even spinnaker halyard. Affix the block to the side of the mast and reeve it with a length of flag halyard line. This way you avoid weight and windage aloft from a full-size rope, as well as UV degradation of that rope. When the time comes, you can easily seize a real rope to the end of the light stuff and pull it through. Meanwhile, you've got a flag halyard at the masthead.

3. *Jib halyard sheave not turning.*

The sheave sides probably just need a light sanding. If main and jib sheaves share the same axle pin, secure both sheaves with

Surveying a Hook

Hooks are unlikely to break, but they can straighten under heavy loads. The interior curve of a hook should match the radius of a circle. If there's any evidence of distortion, junk that hook.

lanyards before driving the pin out (or see the accompanying sidebar "Tapped Sheave"). Since you're probably hanging from the main or jib halyard at the moment, you'll also want to switch to an alternate means of suspension before driving that pin out. The procedure is to get your deck crew to haul you up just as high as the halyards allow. Then tie two short lengths of stout rope to the chair (or, if you're wearing a harness, one to the chair and one to the harness). Secure these lines to the masthead, hitching around lugs, shackles, or whatever is up there. If there are spare halyards, you can hitch those to the chair instead. When your replacements are tight and secure, have the deck crew slack away on the other halyards. Detach them from the chair and tie them to any convenient shroud or stay. Drive the pin out—constrictoring a lanyard onto it as it comes and pull the sheaves out. Check for wear on the pin, the sheave bushings, and the mast mortise. If they look okay, sand the sides of mortise and sheaves with fine sandpaper. Reassemble. Check for a fair halyard lead, slop in the mortise, proper alignment of the pin, and chafe on the halyard. If there's more wrong with the sheave or pin than the sanding will fix, you'll need to reassemble and come back up when you've got a replacement, unless you already have one aboard.

4. *Clevis pin in port upper shroud tang is too thin or too long.*

At some time in the past, someone needed to replace this clevis and didn't have exactly the right size. So they went with the nearest thing they had to a fit. When a clevis pin is too small, the load from the tang and wire terminal bear at a single point on the pin. This "point loading" causes weakness, accelerated wear, and fatigue. And of course, a too-small-diameter pin is a weak link. If the pin is too long, it provides that much more weight, windage, and cost. It also might jam into the mast, damaging at least the paint.

Tapped Sheave

It's very tricky to remove and replace masthead sheaves without dropping them—they're difficult or impossible to get a lanyard around. Cruiser Steve Dashew has a solution: Drill and tap a small ($1/8$ –$3/16$-inch or 3.2–4.8-mm) hole in the bottom of the sheave groove. A hole this small won't bother the wire or rope halyard. When the time comes for sheave removal, just thread a bolt or machine screw into the hole. Tie a lanyard to the bolt and one to the sheave pin, then remove the sheave.

If you don't have the proper size clevis replacement, make a note on size and fix it on another trip up. If you do have the right size, you're faced with the disquieting task of detaching a shroud from a mast you're sitting at the top of. It is possible to do this, but sufficiently tricky–and dangerous–that I won't go into the procedure here. In general, it is far easier and safer to pull the mast than to replace rigging in situ.

5. *No toggle on upper end of jibstay.*

No toggle with you or aboard, so make a note of the size required and of the space between the sides of the tang, so you will know if the right size toggle will fit. Maybe the space is too small, and that's why there's no toggle here now. If so, you'll have to do something creative, like modifying the tang. Check with a yacht designer first.

6. *Halyard for roller-furling jib is wire with rope tail. Rope tail will not fit through wire-only sheave. Result is that jib cannot be lowered all the way to deck.*

Sheesh. Any more like this, and you'll be thinking of pulling the stick out so you can work on it more quickly and easily on the ground. What happened was that whoever rigged this jib did so on the ground. They made up a halyard of the right length, ran the wire end through the masthead sheave, then Nicopressed an eye in it for the sail, then shackled the eye to the sail, then stepped the mast with the sail hanging in place. Had they tried lowering the sail to check the layout, they would have discovered their mistake. And it was a very dangerous mistake: Picture yourself in a rising wind with a jammed roller-furler mechanism, trying to lower a monstrous, flapping jib and discovering that it only comes halfway down. "Shotgun reefing"— blowing a few holes in the sail—might be your only recourse. Anyway, this is more of a problem than you can solve right now. Measure for an appropriate sheave and halyard and inspect the head of the roller-furling unit. They usually need an occasional rinse with fresh water to get grit off the bearings. Check manufacturer's maintenance recommendations.

7. *Moving down from the masthead, all is well until we get to the spreaders, which are horizontal instead of bisecting the angle formed by shrouds.*

This is the single most common flaw in rigging. If the spreader is angled properly, it functions as a pure compression member. If it is horizontal, the shroud will act to push its outboard end down. This leads at least to an excessive buckling load on the spreader. If the end seizing slips, the spreader could collapse altogether. Dismasting. Besides, horizontal spreaders look dowdy, lifeless.

To fix this, cast off the outboard seizings and tap the ends up to the proper angle. Have one of your deck crew with a good eye get well in front of the boat to help you with this. Aloft or on the ground, use a bevel gauge to get the angles identical. Finish by seizing the spreader end securely to the wires.

8. *Horizontal crack in starboard after lower shroud swage.*

Oops. Measure for a replacement. Then ask yourself: How old is this rig? Is this wire heavy enough? If the wire is new and adequately sized, this might just be a fluke. But it's much more

likely that all the wires are fatigued or badly swaged—you just found the first one to show signs. At least consider a new, good-quality gang.

9. *Spinnaker pole track has machine screw as stop at upper end; screw is bent.*

This stop prevents the car that the butt of the spinnaker pole rides in from coming out of the top end of the track. A machine screw is a quick-and-dirty substitute for a real stop, an item available, cheap, at any chandlery. Get one.

10. *You're back on deck (whew), but not done yet.*

Go to the bow and make sure there's enough thread on the outside of the jibstay turnbuckle barrel that you can add that toggle aloft and still tension the stay. It could be that the turnbuckle is tightened down too far for this to happen, and that's why there's no toggle aloft. You just might be able to shorten the wire by the length of the terminal, apply a new terminal, add the toggle, and have a perfect-length stay. Measure carefully. It might also be that you'll have to replace the entire, expensive stay. But with no toggle aloft, you're going to have to do this relatively soon anyway.

11. *Sticky staysail lead block car.*

Sandpaper and rinsing will probably do it, though cars and tracks sometimes get sufficiently dinged to require some artful filing.

12. *Mainsail halyard cleat angled backward.*

You've had this boat for years and always known there was some reason why this was an awkward belay. The cleat should be angled so that the halyard touches the lower end first.

13. *Nick in mainsheet near standing end. Line badly twisted.*

End-for-end the line. Try to figure out what nicked it. Resolve either to coil by figure-eight or alternate-hitch methods, or to have a halyard bag made up and mounted by the mainsheet winch. Coiling braided line by the conventional clockwise method results in twists that don't come out.

Sailing Is Surveying

The best sailors notice things: wind patterns on the water, how an engine sounds, the shape of a sail, the shape of a cloud. By noticing, they have a greater reference base, and can act quickly and appropriately when they need to. What we call "surveying" is really just a formal exercise in noticing things. So get formal for your surveys, but consider living every day by another of Ms. Holman's maxims: "Feel, rattle, pull, knock, and touch absolutely everything."

CHAPTER 8

A Portfolio of Rigs

If there's one thing that characterizes rig design, it is endless variation. Riggers and designers take the apparently simple task of holding a mast up and accomplish it in more—and weirder—ways than you'd ever think possible. With such a profusion of structures, it can get confusing out there when you're trying to make decisions for your boat.

The good news is that sensible variations are responses to sensible considerations; hull type, climate, sailor's temperament, and other factors inform how a finished rig looks. So if you understand those factors you'll be well along in understanding design. The following portfolio is intended to illuminate design decisions, and to show some (mostly) appropriate results. Soak it up, then turn new eyes on your rig.

MIZZENS

"The elaborations of elegance are at least as fascinating, and more various, more democratic, more healthy, more practical—though less glamorous—than the elaborations of power."

—Wendell Berry

In this sloop-happy world, mizzenmasts don't get a lot of respect. Ketches and yawls generally don't go to weather as well as their single-masted cousins, and so are viewed by many sailors as inefficient—that is, by those whose sole definition of "efficient" is "able to tack through 70 degrees."

But a mizzen can be more than just an extra mast. It can be evidence that the designer and the owner have decided that versatility and comforting redundancy offset a loss of absolute weatherliness. That the expense and complexity of an added mast is offset by reduced size, expense, and labor-intensiveness of the mainmast. That any inconvenience and clutter—the mizzen of a ketch does sit right in the boat's busiest work area—can be more than offset by a center of effort lower than that of a comparable sloop, by less sharply focused hull stresses, by a more versatile sail plan, and by increased power on a reach. This last reason is why so many of the vessels in the old Whitbread Round-the-World Race were ketch-rigged.

Because small (under 35 feet or 11 meters) sloops and cutters already have relatively easily handled sails, mizzens are most appropriate on larger vessels. Crew laziness or non-agility, or a particularly large sail plan might justify a mizzen on smaller vessels.

Regardless of vessel size, a mizzen always presents a challenge in rig design: How do you stay it adequately without interfering with the main? With few exceptions (see "*Sundeer*," below), there isn't room between the mizzenmast and the main boom for a mizzen forestay. There often isn't even room for much of an angle on the forward-leading mizzen shrouds. And because the mizzen is so far aft, there's also rarely room for a backstay. Designers have risen to these and other mizzen challenges with varying degrees of success. What follows is a spectrum of configurations, analyzed for interrelationship.

Cutty Sark

A gaff ketch looks archaic to modern eyes, and it is the least weatherly rig around, but it's also simple, strong, low-cost, and very powerful when reaching. The mizzen on *Cutty Sark*, a 44-foot Angleman design, has a bulletproof simplicity. Because it is so simple, it is easier to see principles that are buried in more complex, latter-day mizzens.

The standing rigging here consists of four shrouds (Figure 8-1), all going to the masthead. Because the mast is relatively short and the vessel relatively beamy aft, the shrouds have a wide staying angle, so there's no need for spreaders (see "Angles"). The shrouds lead well forward and well aft, staying the mast fore-and-aft as well as laterally. When the mizzen staysail is set, particularly if the breeze or chop is up, there is also a pair of running backstays to reinforce the aft-leading shrouds. There's enough space between the runners so that, on the wind, they can both be left set up and still have room to tack the mizzen back and forth.

Note that the chainplates are all the way outboard; there's no need to move them in, since the

only staysail on this mast—the mizzen staysail—is an off-the-wind sail, and, unlike the main staysails, is never sheeted in so far that the shrouds might be in the way. And because the staysail here is never sheeted in tight, it never puts huge compression loads on the mast (see "Mainmasts"), so the mast and its rigging can be lighter than a comparable-size main. Lessened compression load also means that *Cutty Sark*'s mizzen can have a long, unsupported section of mast between tangs and deck. The stick will flex some, but never to the point where lower shrouds are necessary.

Jenny Ives

If *Cutty Sark*'s mizzen were taller, or thinner, or had a narrower staying angle, the compression loads relative to the mast's stiffness would be greater, and that ultra-simple standing rigging wouldn't work; the stick would be inclined to "pump" in its midsection. The Bermudian mizzen on the ketch *Jenny Ives* is taller and lighter, with a narrower staying angle,

Figure 8-1. *The mizzen of the ketch* Cutty Sark.

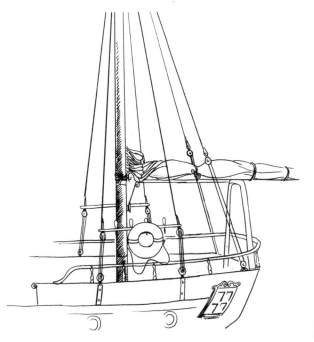

Mizzenmast Scantlings

Because mizzen sails are much smaller in area than mainsails, and because mizzen staysails, set off the wind, do not impose genoa-grade tension or compression loads, and because mizzens are usually furled when the wind picks up to prevent weather helm, mizzenmasts aren't exposed to the level of forces that mains are. Accordingly, the standard formula for mizzenmast scantlings, while still based on RM_{30} (see "Mast Strength" in Chapter 5), uses a much lower constant. The formula is:

$$\frac{RM_{30} \times 0.5}{\frac{1}{2} \text{ beam (at chainplate)}}$$

Because the mizzen staysail is low-load, the same formula is used for both mast and rigging.

A recommended safety factor of only 1.5 to 2 further reflects most mizzens' easy life.

The formula works well for most boats. Even if you lower the main in a storm and sail under forestaysail and reefed mizzen, the latter sail, maybe 20 to 30 percent the size of the main, just isn't big enough to generate a maximum righting moment load. An exception would be vessels like *Sundeer* (see page 303), in which mizzensail area is uncommonly large (around 40 percent of the size of the main).

so it needs a different standing rigging configuration (Figure 8-2).

Since aft-pulling strain is localized at the mast-head, a forward-facing "jumper stay" running over a strut stabilizes the upper section of the mast in this plane, preventing the head from sagging aft under the pull of the sail. To widen the staying angle, the upper shrouds run over spreaders, to handle lateral loads at the same point. To prevent the masthead's whipping forward in a chop, the spreaders are swept aft, so the uppers pull aft as well as laterally, eliminating the need for running backstays.

Figure 8-2. *Jenny Ives's mizzen has a long unsupported length below the spreaders and is deck-stepped. The mast stiffness is adequate, except that as built the mast had no aft-leading lower shrouds; aft staying was provided by the aft-led upper shrouds. The spreaders, along with the pull of the jumper strut, bowed the mast forward in the middle. Aft-led lowers, sharing chainplates with the uppers, solved the problem.*

Unfortunately, the compression load on the spreaders is trying to make the mast buckle forward in the middle. The lower shrouds, which have a slight forward lead, stabilize the lower section of the mast laterally, but exacerbate the spreader-induced forward bow. What to do? We could move those lower shrouds aft, but, oops, this is a deck-stepped mast, with no springstay. It needs forward-leading shrouds to stay up.

To make things even worse, the bottom end of the jumper stay also pulls forward as well as up, adding to the efforts of the upper shroud spreaders and lower shrouds. The grand effect of all this is to make the mizzen frighteningly mobile in any kind of wind or sea.

The lid for this particular can of worms is two-fold: turning those forward-leading lowers into forward-leading intermediates; and adding aft-leading lower shrouds, going to the same (overbuilt) chainplate that the uppers lead to. The intermediates hold the mast stable forward; sufficient tension is applied to the aft legs to keep the mast stable aft. As a bonus, the aft thrust of the jumper strut, which used to be unopposed, causing the upper portion of the mast to bow aft, is now balanced by those intermediates. This is my favorite mizzen staying configuration, the one I start with when designing for a new spar, and the one I usually try to get the client to convert to on an old one.

Cirrus

The N. G. Herreshoff yawl *Cirrus* is from an era—the 1920s—when rigs and hulls were changing from low-aspect designs like *Cutty Sark* and *Jenny Ives* to the sleeker, spindlier rigs of our own era. The mast is relatively tall and set in a skinny boat, so there are higher compression loads on a narrow mast. Accordingly, the mast is supported at more points—with lower shrouds, upper shrouds, and a pair of lateral jumper stays called "diamond stays." The distance between the staying points is called "panel length"; the higher the compression loads and the lighter the mast, the shorter the panel lengths need to be to prevent buckling (see Chapter 5 for mast scantling details).

Short panel lengths are characteristic of modern masts, but *Cirrus* also has some old-timey details (Figure 8-3): Although her lower shrouds go to tangs, her uppers and the upper ends of her diamond stays attach with mast-encircling "soft eyes" set on carved bolsters. Another unusual archaic detail is that the main backstay and aft-leading mizzen lowers are attached by a curved tang; essentially, the mizzen is trapped by a split main backstay. In the interests of easier handling, *Cirrus* was converted from sloop to yawl early in her career, and this novel fitting was one result. It eliminates the problem of the mizzen's being in the way of the main backstay, and simultaneously provides fore-

Figure 8-3. Cirrus's *mizzen is early Bermudian with traditional and contemporary details. The upper shrouds and diamond stays terminate in soft eyes at the mast, while the lowers end in tangs. The main backstay terminates at the mizzen, and a custom fitting takes its load directly to the aft-leading mizzen lower shrouds.*

Figure 8-4. The mizzen of Portunus *has a long unsupported lower section, but avoids* Sojourner's *problems (Figure 8-6) by dint of heavy scantlings, an oval cross section, and being stepped on the keel. In addition, the jumper strut leads to the base of the mast instead of the middle, where it would pull the mast forward. The running backstays can be made off to the quarters in heavy weather to prevent the mast's upper section from "whipping."*

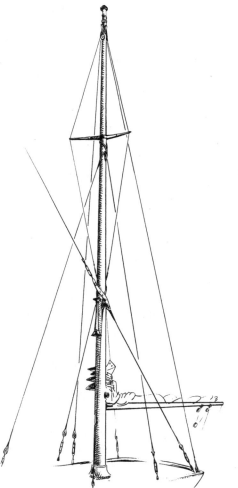

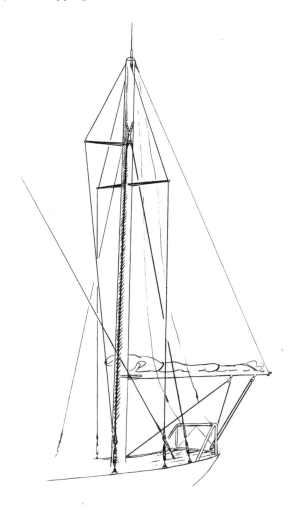

and-aft support for the lower section of the mizzen. This is an effective configuration for a racer like *Cirrus*, but it's a no-no for a cruising vessel, precisely because it ties the two masts firmly together. In the event of a rigging failure, it's "as the main goes, so goes the mizzen."

As a final note, there are running backstays here, because, unlike the *Jenny Ives*'s aft-swept upper shroud spreaders, the diamond stays supporting *Cirrus*'s masthead provide lateral staying only.

Concordia Yawl *Portunus*

If *Cirrus* has an innovative change-of-era rig, the Concordia yawl (Figure 8-4) represents an early mature version of Bermudian mizzen design. The soft eyes are gone, replaced by tangs all around. The main backstay angles off to one side, ju-u-st enough to miss the mizzen, so the two masts are independently stayed. There's a jumper stay, à la the *Jenny Ives*, but here the lower end of the stay comes clear down to the base of the mast, so it doesn't buckle the middle. This has the added advantages of lessening compression on the jumper strut and getting the turnbuckle down where it's easy to adjust.

Mast shape has changed, too. The previous masts in this chapter were round, but *Portunus* has a rectangular mast, with the long side running fore-and-aft. This makes the mast stiffer in this plane, where the strongest buckling forces are. And the mast is big and stiff enough in both planes at the lower end that the long unsupported panel below the spreaders is no problem. Now the lower shrouds can go way up, to stabilize things in the way of the jumper strut. The upper shrouds hold the masthead laterally, while their spreaders stabilize the mast below the lower shrouds. With so much fore-and-aft stiffness, the running backs are practically vestigial, set up far less often than for *Cirrus*.

By playing rig configuration and mast size and construction off against each other, the Concordia's designer, Raymond Hunt, was able to come up with a mast that could take a lot of load, yet be quite simple.

Nabob II

So much for simplicity. *Nabob II*'s mizzen is infested with rigging, radar, baggywrinkle, antennae—it looks like the winner of a design competition for Most Occupied Mast. But once you look at the gear piece by piece, in the context of the vessel it fits, you'll see that it's thoughtfully configured.

Nabob II is a beefy, 55-foot (on deck) Spaulding Dunbar ketch. Her entire purpose in life is to take people to far-off lands in utmost comfort and security. Europe, Africa, the South Pacific, the Far East—*Nabob*'s been there.

So let's start with the upper shrouds (Figure 8-5). They're easiest to find. There are two sets, one going over wide, well-padded spreaders for upper-panel lateral support, and another leading aft as backstays; this second set could have been running backs led right to the stern for a more favorable angle, but that would have meant more strings to tend in a sometimes-shorthanded boat. Instead, the spreader-less uppers angle far enough aft for good support, yet are far enough forward that the mizzen boom can swing out on a broad reach.

Two lower shrouds per side fix the lower panel in all directions. Notice how the wire ends go to different heights; they're independent of each other as redundancy in case one should break, and they spread the load over a wider area of mast than if they both went to the same tang.

The big news on this mast is the jumper stay/radar housing setup. The double jumpers, angled diagonally forward, hold the masthead forward, prevent the middle of the mast from buckling forward, and help stay the masthead laterally.

Just above the radar is a springstay leading to the mainmast. This does tie the masts together, but it's a calculated tradeoff. The compression load from the radar/jumpers wants to push the middle of the mast aft, and those aft-leading uppers don't lead far enough aft to counteract with sufficient compression-bow forward. The springstay takes the excess jumper compression and delivers it to the mainmast. The aft-leading lower shrouds assist the aft-leading uppers in preventing the entire mast being pulled

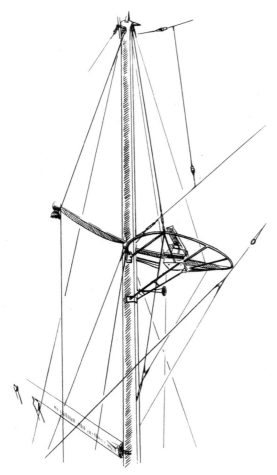

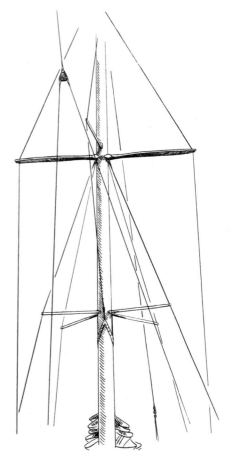

Figure 8-5. Nabob's *mizzen is a heavily and redundantly rigged mast suited for serious cruising. The two sets of lower shrouds are complemented by two sets of uppers, one leading over the spreaders and the other led aft to serve both as backup and backstays. The radar bracket doubles as a strut for the jumper stays. A lower springstay (just above the radar) holds the mast forward, while an upper springstay functions as an antenna. The vertical wire between the springstays is also an antenna leg.*

Figure 8-6. Sojourner Truth's *mizzenmast has a light section, a long unsupported length below the spreaders, and is deck-stepped. The result is an excessively flexible lower section. "X-spreaders" on the lower shrouds are an attempt to shorten the unsupported length. Together with careful tuning, this stabilizes the mast somewhat.*

forward by the springstay. Tricky, but it gets the job done.

There's also an upper springstay at the masthead, but this is solely a place to hang an antenna. Same with the vertical wire connecting upper and lower springstays. The owner is into electronics.

That leaves the main backstay. It has an antenna on it, too (note insulator). But it's of interest to us because it splits into two legs just below the radar. This is the standard contemporary method of getting the main backstay past the mizzenmast. It leaves an uncluttered area directly behind the mizzen, allowing for an aft cabin on this boat, and splits the backstay load between the sides of the hull.

You'll sometimes see two entirely independent backstays in lieu of this arrangement. They make for more weight and windage, are usually an utterly unnecessary redundancy (Why not have four uppers? Eight lowers?), and make tuning a bear, since just getting slack out of the backstays can mean an overtightened jibstay. In addition, twin backstays on a ketch preclude flying a mizzen staysail–a sail that is one of the bonuses of the ketch rig–because you'd chafe the leech on the weather stay.

Sojourner Truth

This beautiful Morgan Giles-designed ketch is plagued by a mizzenmast so limber it makes the one on Jenny Ives look positively docile.

The lower shrouds attach high up (Figure 8-6), à la *Concordia*, but unlike the Concordia, the spreaders for the upper shrouds are also up high, leaving a long unsupported panel to deck. Worse yet, the bottom of the jumper stay attaches to the middle of that unsupported panel, encouraging it to buckle. Even so, these details would not be so much of a problem if the mast were simply stiffer. But it isn't, and being wooden, it can't readily be stiffened, like aluminum, by the addition of an inner sleeve.

It might have helped to relocate those spreaders down below the lower shrouds, but instead this mast has been fitted with "X-spreaders," four struts affixed in the way of the jumper stay's lower end, and braced against the four lower shrouds. It helps some, but since the X's don't deflect the wires, the mast can always move some before the struts stop it.

It's hard to be sure, but I would guess that someone, somewhere along the way, neglected to take into account that this mast is deck-stepped. A keel-stepped mast, because it's supported at deck level by the partners, is stiffer than a deck-stepped mast of the same scantlings. In essence, the partners, acting in concert with the step, form what engineers call a "couple." *Sojourner Truth*'s mizzen acts like a deck-stepped mast designed to keel-stepped specs. For further details on calculating mast loads, see Chapter 5.

Sundeer

Yacht designer and world cruiser Steve Dashew brings mizzens into the New Age. There's a high-aspect, double-spreader, intentionally "bendy" rig on the mizzen of his evolutionary ketch *Sundeer* (Figure 8-7). And there's even a forestay and backstay, details more commonly associated with mainmasts.

Modern details aside, this mizzen has a lot in common with the ones mentioned previously. Like them, it's a place to hang a staysail for reaching power, makes for a lower center of effort than a sloop of comparable sail area, and is part of a versatile, easily handled sail plan. But there are two other important mizzen virtues that *Sundeer* in particular exemplifies. One, mentioned briefly at the beginning of this essay, is the mizzen's helpmate relationship with the main. Sloop proponents talk about a split rig's "inefficiency," then usually go on to how having a mizzen means you have to buy a whole extra mast, sails, and rigging. They admit only grudgingly that a ketch or yawl might be easier to handle or more versatile. And they never mention that the main on a ketch can be much smaller and cheaper than it would be if it had to absorb the mizzen's sail area. Nor do they take into account that the mizzen prolongs the main's life by reducing the intensity of the cyclic loading that contributes to metal fatigue. In *Sundeer* the mizzen is over half the size of the mainsail. This is a big mizzen (20 to 40 percent of main is more typical) for a ketch, but any appreciable mizzen is a lot more than an extra mast stuck in the back of the boat.

The other mizzen virtue has to do with the relationship of the mizzen to the hull. By distributing stress over a wider area, a split rig is kinder to its hull than a monomast. With many boats, this distribution advantage is qualified, since mizzens, at least on ketches, are often reefed or lowered first when the wind comes up, leaving the main to deal with heavy weather. This is sometimes done because main and staysails provide more drive than mizzen and staysails, but most often it's because, on most vessels, weather helm increases sharply with increased heel. Mizzens, being so far aft, only exacerbate weather helm, so down they come. But this is a design flaw in hull, not sail. A balanced hull like *Sundeer*'s does not suffer hull-induced weather helm as it heels.

And on *Sundeer*, Dashew has gone a step further, intentionally matching hull and sail plan so

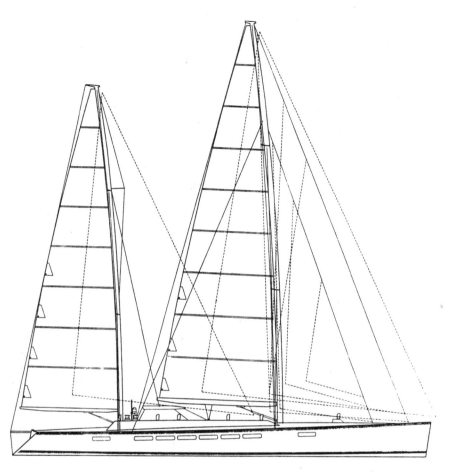

Figure 8-7. *Steve Dashew's* Sundeer.

that there is always a great deal of weather helm, all of it mizzen-induced. On most vessels this would result in a hard-to-steer boat, but *Sundeer* has a large balanced spade rudder, so the helm always feels neutral. Why do this? Because a big, properly shaped balanced rudder can provide lift, just like a keel. If it can provide enough lift, you can make the keel smaller and still go to weather well. So *Sundeer*'s rudder is helping the keel, just as the mizzen is helping the main. The net result is that this 67-foot (20.4-m) LOD ketch draws only 6 feet (1.8 m) loaded, yet will outpoint many sloops, especially in a breeze, when speed gives the rudder more lift. Balanced spade rudders are generally frowned on by cruisers as fragile, vulnerable things, but *Sundeer*'s is built around an

8-inch (203-mm)-diameter rudder shaft (!), and has a sacrificial "crushable" bottom; it's extremely unlikely that even a violent grounding would cause significant damage.

It is unusual to have rig and hull so creatively interlinked, but it's possible to optimize the performance of any split rig relative to the hull it sits in. On some boats this might involve flatter- or fuller-cut sails, adding a bowsprit, changing mast rake, etc. A qualified rigger or yacht designer can help you with particulars. Meanwhile, I hope this section has given you enough information to extrapolate from, whether it's for a configuration that will allow you to disconnect a springstay, or to let you see force relationships more clearly, or just as an introduction to the next section.

MAINMASTS

Mainmasts are more than just great big mizzens. The loads they bear are of a whole other order of intensity and complexity, as described in the "Spreader Loads" section of Chapter 5. Loading from staysails is particularly significant; unlike mizzen staysails, the ones on the main are meant to be trimmed in hard when the boat goes to weather, and this adds tremendously to the compression load on the mast. With more at stake in terms of load, designers can go far afield in search of workable rigs, and work even harder to make those rigs interact with the hull. See, for example, how *Otter's* hull was redesigned to accommodate a single wire: the backstay. Mains demand your attention.

Figure 8-8. *Rig details of* Troubador, *designed by Ted Brewer. Dotted lines show the position of runners referred to in the text. (left by Margaret Wilson-Briggs)*

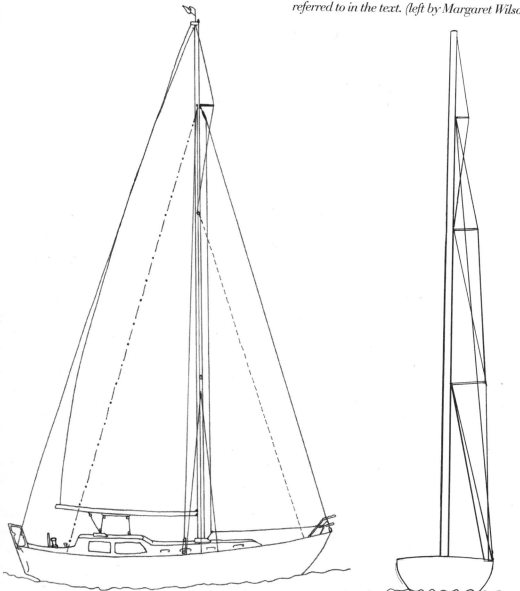

Troubador

Veteran yacht designer Ted Brewer is a direct heir to the people who developed rig scantling formulas. But his designs, for everything from gaff-rigged schooners to BOC racers, have always been characterized as much by freshness and adaptability as by classical conservatism. So when client Dr. Paul Bubak asked for a very easily handled but very efficient fractional rig, Brewer came up with the artful sail plan shown in Figure 8-8.

Traditionally, cruising rigs have minimized the effort expended on staysails by breaking up the single large one of a sloop into two or three smaller ones, to make a cutter. But another method is to shift staysail area into the less truculent mainsail. This results in such a small staysail area that you no longer need to run the jibstay all the way to the masthead in order to have room for the sail. A "fractional rig" results, so named because the stay only comes three-fourths, seven-eighths, or some other fraction of the way up the mast.

Less staysail-wrestling also means less jibstay tension, and thus less mast compression, so fractional rigs can have slightly lighter masts for the same total sail area (see table in Figure 5-26).

It's not all plusses, however. You might not have the chore of changing headsails, but you do have to reef the main sooner and more often. And savings in headsail costs are offset by increased mainsail costs, particularly if it has full battens, lazyjacks, and other options to make the sail more efficient and easier to handle.

Troubador's rig has a very small (non-overlapping) jib and a very large, very tall main. It's a bit radical-looking for a cruising boat, but Brewer simultaneously pushed the envelope and kept his scantlings conservative. The result is a safe rig and low work load for Bubak and crew, without correspondingly low performance.

Rig Details With so little sail area above the jibstay, the masthead needs little lateral staying. Diagonal jumpers are sufficient, and they also act to brace the mast against the forward pull of the jibstay. Running backstays act as backups for the

Sonia Stay

The builders of the 34-foot double-ended yawl *Sonia* were wonderfully creative. The main backstay splits partway down to miss the mizzenmast, and reaches the deck well aft on this fine-sterned vessel. Ordinarily, this would put a lot of upward strain on a delicate part of the hull.

But instead of making the stern heavier (and more expensive) for stiffness, *Sonia*'s builders carried the backstay legs right through the deck, then angled them down and in to attach to the sternpost. Now the only load at deck-level is a moderate compression load between the legs of the backstay. Just as at the main shrouds, the deck functions as a set of spreaders, and the sternpost is itself supported from sagging.

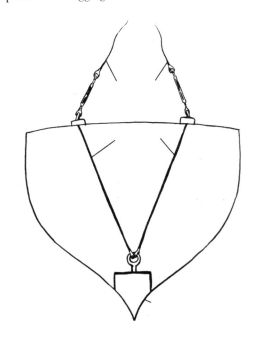

Sonia's through-the-deck backstay configuration.

jumpers for fore-and-aft pull; they can be set up in high winds or choppy water or when the mast is heavily bent by the backstay. Many fractionally rigged race boats dispense with the jumpers and rely solely on running backs. This saves weight and windage but means the runners must be set up promptly with each tack or risk losing the stick. Combining jumpers, runners, and a conservative mast section makes for low labor (you only need the runners about 20 percent of the time) and high safety, and they're still light enough not to cut too much into performance.

A final detail is that Troubador also has a forestay, something rare in a fractional rig. It helps brace this high-aspect mast, leaves enough space for a good-sized working staysail, and is a good wire to hang a storm staysail on—low and well aft. In light airs this stay can be disconnected and made off aft and to one side, for easy tacking of the jib.

Otter

Pump *Troubador*'s mainsail up even further, shrink the staysails down to zero, and move the mast right up into the bows of the boat and you have the rig for *Otter*, a 32-foot Mark Ellis-designed catboat created for Ed Scheu of Hanover, New Hampshire. It's another fractional rig (Figure 8-9), and a requirement for ultimate ease of handling resulted in the complete elimination of staysails. Ordinarily, this would have resulted in reduced efficiency to

Figure 8-9. *Otter's sail and rigging plans. The diagonal jumper stays stabilize the upper end of the mast, primarily fore-and-aft; the forestay and strut stabilize the lower section. The lower ends of the jumpers lead internally through the mast to deck level for adjustment, which is necessary when the backstay is adjusted. The mast's position in the bow of the boat creates a very narrow staying angle. Dotted lines show the initial upper shroud angle, which proved insufficient to prevent lateral bend. This problem was solved by adding a third, upper set of spreaders to take the upper shrouds to the masthead, and lengthening the intermediate spreaders (which had been the uppers). The running backstays are not shown here.*

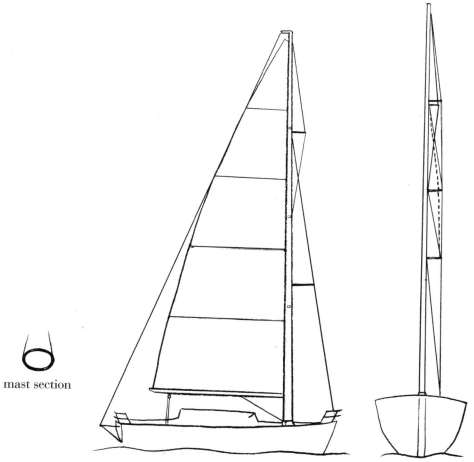

mast section

weather. Many cruisers would have accepted this as the price you pay for ease of handling (and Ellis has designed the line of Nonsuch unstayed catboats for them). But Scheu is a racer. No longer interested in the physical challenge of running the Stars and Concordia yawls of his younger days, he was by no means eager to forgo the joys of passing other boats.

So, just as Bubak had wanted an efficient but low-sweat, heavy-duty cruising boat, Scheu wanted a languorously attended racing catboat. Accordingly, this ultimately simple rig was fitted with a whole raft of sail controls: adjustable jumpers and backstay (the mast can be deflected fore-and-aft 20 inches [508 mm]); high-powered vang and sheet traveler systems; a Cunningham; and single-line reefing. All of this makes *Otter* more work than a Nonsuch but much less work than any comparably efficient staysail-equipped boat.

Two Design Challenges

Good designers seek to mesh rig and hull qualities, but they usually tailor the rig to a given hull or racing rule. In this case, though, the hull was largely molded by a single piece of standing rigging: The backstay.

Otter's main has to compensate, in size and aerodynamic quality, for the missing staysails. But the size of the main is limited by the presence of the standing backstay, a piece of wire crucial not only to rig integrity but also to mast-bending sailing efficiency. The obvious response is to make the mainsail very, very big, and Ellis has done this—note the high aspect ratio, and the generous boomkin length that increases the backstay angle as far as practicable. But even with a heavily roached, full-batten mainsail filling every possible square inch of the resulting space, there's just not enough area to move anything but a notably light hull. And because of the hefty righting arm of such a tall rig, that hull also needs to be stiff. So *Otter* is almost three tons lighter than a cruise-oriented Nonsuch 33, and has a deep keel with all the ballast in a bulb at the bottom.

The first challenge was to modify the hull to accommodate limitations imposed by the rig. The second challenge is the hull's revenge: The mast sit-ting so far forward, where the hull narrows, means adequate staying angle for the shrouds is hard to come by. Moving the mast aft would help this problem, but that would just mean more area cut out of the mainsail by the backstay. The stick's final location was a compromise between staying angle and sail area.

Rig Details   The rig is a three-quarter fractional, with an extra bit of rigging in the area you'd usually expect to find a forestaysail: a removable forestay strut controls mast wobble below the forestay. If a forestaysail were ever installed, this strut would have to be permanently removed and replaced with running backstays. In other words, removing a labor-intensive sail made possible the elimination of a set of labor-intensive running backs. This leaves only one set of runners, at the top of the forestay, to reinforce the diagonal jumper stays.

As originally designed, *Otter* had two sets of shroud spreaders, with the upper shrouds reaching to the height of the forestay, and diamond jumpers for lateral and fore-and-aft staying from there to the masthead. But do you see how long the mast section above the forestay is? It's a lot of mast for skinny-angle jumpers to control (compare with *Troubador*). Too much, in fact, since in initial sailing tests the masthead sagged to leeward.

Returning briefly to the drawing board, the Ellis office moved the upper spreaders to the level of the forestay, added a third set of slightly longer spreaders where the upper spreaders had been, ran the upper shrouds to the masthead for improved lateral staying, and beefed up a bit on the strength of the standing rigging. In other words, having pushed the design envelope as far as they could with this novel configuration, they grudgingly added weight and windage rather than compromise sailing efficiency or rig integrity.

The Freedoms

Because of its standing rigging, *Otter* makes the most efficient use of its one big sail—at the price of a considerable design challenge, focusing on the relationship between standing rigging and hull. A

Figure 8-10. *Sail plan of the Freedom 32.*

free-standing mast, as on Tillotson-Pearson's Freedom line of sailboats (Figure 8-10), removes that design challenge; the hull and sail plan are no longer subject to backstay- and shroud-imposed limitations. But, as is always the case with technology, an entirely different challenge arises from this sweeping solution: how to make an unstayed mast small, light, and inflexible enough to approximate the performance of a well-designed stayed mast.

Unstayed masts are by no means a new idea; they've been characteristic of many traditional craft all around the world since sailing's beginnings. It's just that until relatively recently they had to be made of solid wood, and there was no way to keep them from bending excessively under load, thus compromising sailing efficiency, without making them extremely large and heavy, thus compromising sailing efficiency.

In this century, hollow aluminum and wooden masts have been developed that are sufficiently light, durable, and deflection-resistant to be useful for sailboats, as long as you don't care a great deal about efficiency to windward and have a taste for the fairly tubby hulls you need to hold up a big,

heavy cat rig. Perhaps because sailors tend to like sleek, weatherly boats, unstayed aluminum and wooden rigs have not taken over the market, even though they are usually far simpler and physically easier to sail than their stayed brethren.

Carbon fiber, an even more recent mast material development, is far less elastic than wood or aluminum, so it can be used to make masts, unstayed, that are nearly as deflection-resistant as ones that are stayed. Carbon fiber is spun from, take a deep breath, thermally decomposed polyacrilonitrile, known more familiarly as "PAN." Filaments of PAN are pre-stretched, then stabilized with a relatively mild heat (428 degrees F). Then the filaments are placed in a nitrogen atmosphere and really cooked (at about 2,700 degrees F), a process which essentially burns away everything but tough little strings of carbon.

Sound complicated? Nah, that's just chemistry. The real chore comes in trying to build a mast out of this stuff. First you have to make it into a kind of fabric, just so it can be handled. Then you have to lay it onto a form—usually either an aluminum mandrel or a bladder-filled clamshell mold—under maximally nit-picky levels of heat, pressure, and tension, in a pattern which has been precisely engineered to produce optimal stiffness and durability with minimal weight or size.

Mast Bend, Stayed and Unstayed

A stayed aluminum mast can be bowed in the fore-and-aft plane by tightening the backstay and/or forestay and/or babystay, with hydraulic or manual adjusters. This action flattens the jib by tensioning the jibstay, and flattens the main by pulling the sail's draft forward. This results in improved efficiency when going to windward, and it delays the need to reef because moving the draft of the sails forward lessens heel and weather helm.

Unstayed rigs do not provide the same sail-control options, or at least not in the same way. Full-length battens control sail shape (along with the vang), preventing the draft from moving too far aft. Reefing is delayed not by flattening the sail, but by engineering the mast so that the head sags well to leeward in gusts, effectively depowering the big main.

And when all that's done, you have to convince sailors—a notoriously conservative bunch—that this isn't just some loony engineer's Bright Idea. It doesn't help that other manufacturers, some of whom are not as skilled or careful as the people of Tillotson-Pearson, produce masts which perform poorly and/or break. It doesn't help that the process is very expensive. And it doesn't help that unstayed carbon fiber masts still deflect under load more than a comparably well-designed stayed mast (see the mast bend sidebar, though, for a positive side to mast deflection). In particular, unstayed masts have a hard time dealing with compression loads from big staysails, the ones you trim in to go to weather.

With these drawbacks, carbon fiber unstayed masts might have faded into obscurity but for the evangelical zeal of Garry Hoyt. Early on, Hoyt pitched the advantages of the rig with such force that the public began to focus less on the disadvantages. Hoyt founded Freedom Yachts, convinced that he could do not just a better job, but a revolutionary one. In addition to shrouds, he did away with stays, staysails, vangs, and conventional booms and luffs (he used wishbone booms, which were supposed to be self-vanging, and used mast-encircling luffs).

To make the sail hold an aerodynamic shape on a relatively noodly mast, he installed full-length battens. To make the sail easier to handle he installed lazyjacks and a single-line reefing system he invented. Then he led these and all other control lines to the cockpit. This last detail is important; if you go forward on an unstayed boat, there's nothing to hold on to but the mast.

Hoyt unleashed his early Freedoms on the world of yachting, demonstrated that they were efficient, easily handled, and durable, and waited for sailors to drop stayed rigs like last year's software. He made a dent, but not a big one. Why? For one thing, he'd made a lot of noise about how horrible stayed rigs were supposed to be. To hear Hoyt tell it, going out on a stayed-rig daysail involved an exhausting physical workout, along with a strong chance of suffering a dismasting from "one missing cotter pin or one broken wire." People looked around and saw that it just wasn't so. They also saw that non-rac-

Carbon Fiber and Stayed Racers

Because carbon fiber is vulnerable to impact loads, as well as corrosion from improperly mounted fasteners, and because it is tricky to repair, responsibly made unstayed masts can be relatively heavy for a generous, lifetime-guaranteed safety factor.

But carbon fiber is also extremely light for its strength, and extremely inelastic. So, especially if safety factors aren't a big issue, fiber masts can be much lighter. And if they have standing rigging to support them, they can be far lighter still. This is why, rules allowing, the very hottest race boats have spindly, stayed carbon fiber masts. Expensive like you wouldn't believe, and so, so fragile, but faster.

ing boats didn't require the "deck apes" that Hoyt said were necessary to handle staysails. And they saw that some of his rigging ideas—the wishbone boom, wraparound luff, and lack of staysails—were not only unfamiliar, but also offered no efficiency advantage. It didn't help that his hull designs were less than graceful.

So, over the years, Freedoms have edged closer to the mainstream in terms of overall appearance as well as rig details. This process was accelerated when Tillotson-Pearson bought Freedom Yachts and hired Gary Mull and other naval architects to redesign the boats. The new Freedoms are sleeker, and sport a low-mounted stay with self-tending staysail, along with an ingenious Hoyt-patented "Gun Mount" spinnaker (again, you don't have to go forward to tend it) and a conventional mainsail luff groove, boom, and vang.

The masts themselves are still marvels of engineering (they're guaranteed for the life of the boat), arguably the best production carbon fiber spars made. They are built to extremely high safety factors, partly because that's how Tillotson-Pearson does things and partly because carbon fiber masts are very, very difficult to repair once they've been damaged. An impact shock, for example, can break fibers on the inside of the mast. Carbon fiber can also degrade stainless fasteners, so fasteners must be isolated from the fibers and installed only at places that are specially reinforced during construction.

More recent designs, by Gary Mull and others, have made an impression on the designers of conventional rigs. Seeking to make sailing easier, they've adapted Hoyt-ish details: full-battened mains; smaller, more easily handled running sails; and aft-led control lines.

With the two approaches to mast design moving closer in terms of secondary detail, and roughly equivalent in terms of performance, how is a sailor to decide which is the better rig? As a rigger who works primarily with stayed masts, I might have a heavily biased view, but here it is anyway: Well-designed and well-made unstayed rigs are for people who are disinclined to be involved with their boats. Someone else has done all the work; you just step in and sail. If something goes wrong, you get someone else to fix it. Meanwhile, you just sail.

A well-designed and well-built stayed rig practically invites involvement on the part of the sailor. Sure, you can leave all the work to others, and many sailors do. But a stayed rig allows you to see to the health of your rig, allows you to make repairs and modifications. The rig is built of a series of simple, durable components; if you take care of them, they will take care of you. This turns Hoyt's argument on its head: you can inspect and replace or repair every component, so it won't fail.

Diversity is wealth. Sailors tend to cluster around styles of sailing, and tend to bad-mouth other styles, but diversity in rig and hull design has little to do with superiority and inferiority. It is a reflection of human diversity. Unstayed rigs have had a hard time gaining a toehold in the market,

but they're now sufficiently developed and accepted that they form a strong part of the rigging spectrum.

Tumblehome

Of course, evolution is a tricky thing; lots of rigs less radical-seeming than Freedom's have appeared over the years, been tried briefly or at length, and vanished. It's hard to tell what will be an advance and what will be a dead end. One concept that, after years of halting development, is on its way to the mainstream is the Rotating Wing Mast.

Ordinary masts create a lot of windage and turbulence in front of the mainsail, decreasing its efficiency. But if the mast is made in an airfoil or "wing" shape it provides turbulence-free lift, augmenting or even completely replacing the sail. Of course, wing masts need to be able to rotate, so that the leading edge is always facing into the wind, and they need to be very narrow to function as efficient airfoils. These two factors have created the greatest challenges for designers. If the mast rotates, how can you attach standing rigging to it? And if it's so skinny, how can it keep from buckling under standing rigging–induced compression?

Figure 8-11. *Rig details of Scott Sprague's* Tumblehome.

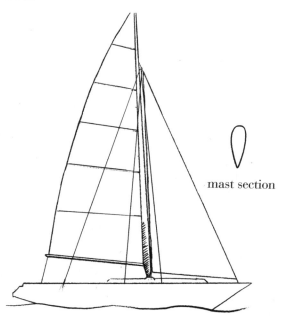

mast section

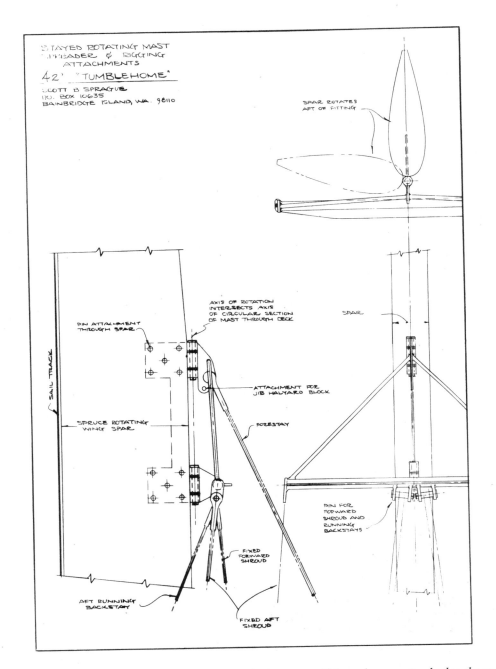

Figure 8-12. *Mast goosenecks are a necessity on stayed wing masts; if shrouds were attached to the mast's sides, the mast could not rotate. Scott Sprague's ingenious gooseneck for* Tumblehome *goes things one better, with the addition of a lower shroud spreader bar. This bar allows him to use aft-leading lower shrouds, which ordinary wing masts cannot carry. The spreader bar is slightly wider than the mast is deep (see top view), so that even when the spar is rotated for running, the wires have a fair lead aft to the chainplates. The running backstays are set up at the base of the spreader bar, along with the forward lower shrouds. When sailing, the leeward runner is slacked, so does not interfere with mast rotation.*

Of all the responses tried so far, the most work-able has involved a sort of glorified gooseneck fitting attached to the face of the mast three-quarters or so of the way up. Shrouds, forestay, and running back-stays attach to this fitting, which remains stationary as the mast pivots behind it. The mast is further rein-forced laterally with diamond stays, which, since they do not attach to the deck, do not inhibit rotation.

This was the configuration chosen for *Tumblehome*, designer Scott Sprague's sleek, fraction-al-rigged sloop (Figures 8-11 and 8-12). (The dia-mond stays are very small and do not show on the drawing.) Sprague is best known as a designer of heavy deep-sea boats like the Hans Christian line, but when he went to design his own boat, he had Puget Sound sailing in mind. He wanted to try something "a little different—lighter, more chal-lenging, and a lot of fun."

Tumblehome's wing mast (4 inches by 14 inches at its largest, with an average wall thickness of ¾ inch) is a vertical-grained Sitka spruce work of art. Here's Sprague on its construction:

"Originally I was going to cold-mold the mast, but after studying the shapes and wall thicknesses, I con-cluded that for this spar solid spruce made the most sense. The mast is really made a lot like a traditional spar. Gluing was a bit of a problem since there was no way to clamp the spar as you would a box mast, so I made a series of female molds out of plywood and set them up on a 50-foot workbench with a transit. The mast was then glued up in two halves and flopped together like a giant submarine sandwich. Blocking, halyard runs, wiring, and internal epoxy sealing were all done prior to putting the two halves together. Let-tuce and mayonnaise are optional."

Stayed wing masts are more popular on multi-hulls than monohulls, since the wide shroud angle of the former makes for less mast compression. Sprague widened his shroud angles by mounting the hinge fitting well down on the mast. This lim-its the size of the staysail, but with no backstay to deal with, there's room for a big, efficient, full-bat-tened main. Note that the section of the mast above the hinge is unstayed; like an unstayed mast, it can deflect to leeward in gusts to depower the main. Call

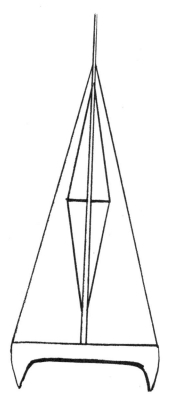

Figure 8-13. *Diamond stays, shown here on a multi-hull, provide lateral support for a mast, preventing buckling without being attached to the deck. This is ideal for masts with long unsupported lengths and narrow lateral cross-sections, notably on multihulls.*

it a semi-stayed mast. Note: In the (many) years since I wrote the above, wing masts have indeed gained wide acceptance, with technical develop-ments, fueled by many miles of all types of sailing, informing the design of masts and hardware. As of this writing, *Tumblehome*'s particulars, while not completely archaic, are by no means cutting edge any more, and should be taken as a primer on rig considerations for rotating masts.

Lyle Hess Gaff Cutter

To many people, the gaff cutter rig is not simply old, it's anti-modern. And yet, for eyes weary of balanc-ing out the high-stress details of the Bermudian rig, the gaff rig is a marvel of engineering.

Just think of it: no standing backstay, so no lim-itation on mainsail area. Sail shape controlled not by bending the entire mast, but just by the height and angle of the little spar at the top of the sail.

You want light-air performance? You get room for a conventional drifter and a gaff topsail, way up there where the light breezes blow. Some gaffers even carry a wardrobe of topsails to suit varying wind conditions. True, you can put a great big main on a Bermudian rig, but when the wind comes up you have to reef that big main. With a gaffer, your first reef consists of dropping the topsail. Much easier.

If the wind continues to rise, reefing a gaff main results in a dramatically lower center of effort compared with a triangular sail of similar area. And since you bring the gaff down at the same time, you also lower the center of gravity appreciably.

A nifty design note relative to reefing: In fully hoisted position the gaff, loaded by the sail and peak halyard, thrusts diagonally down against the mast. Aft lower shrouds take up this thrust, preventing

the mast from bowing. But when reefed, the gaff lies against an unsupported section; you might think the thrust load would burden the mast unfairly. But as you can see in Figure 8-14, the peak halyard is more nearly vertical when the sail is reefed, so that more of the sail load goes into compression on the mast, and less goes into compression on the gaff. The deeper the reef, the less the gaff's thrust.

Stay tension is a bit different on gaffers, too. If the topmast backstays are on aft-swept spreaders, they exert aft pull against the jibstay, and are backed up by, of all things, the mainsheet—via the

Figure 8-14. *Lyle Hess's Falmouth cutter, length on deck 29 feet 9 inches. The reefed gaff position is also shown.*

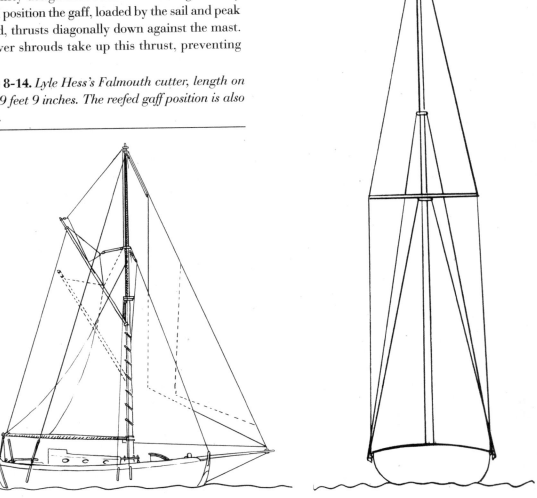

leech and the peak halyard. This won't give you the profound tension you get from a Bermudian backstay, but it's plenty for the light- to medium-air sails you'd hang from a gaffer's jibstay. If the spreaders don't sweep aft, then opposing tension must be provided by running backstays. Some gaffers feature both aft-swept spreaders *and* runners, the idea being that the latter can be activated when the loads are too high for the topmast backstays.

The forestaysail can be set in combination with the jib or by itself, the latter in storm conditions or for shorthanded short tacking. Slightly aft-leading intermediate shrouds can oppose its pull, but not very well, so it almost always makes sense to have runners opposing this stay. Finally, some gaffers feature forked runners, with the upper leg going to the jibstay, the lower one to the forestay, and both converging on a single pendant that is tended on deck. This configuration must be "tuned," usually with a lashing on the upper fork, so that an appropriate share of the load goes to each location.

Gaff running rigging traditionally relies on block and tackle instead of winches for mechanical advantage. This makes sense for the big, heavy mainsail at least; an advantage of two or three is enough for a fit, medium-sized person to raise a yacht-size gaff hand-over-hand. Final tension can be obtained either with a jigger (see the "Jiggers" sidebar in Chapter 2) or with a small winch. It's worth noting here that fully battened Bermudian sails can be as heavy as a gaff sail of comparable area; with no block and tackle they can be slower and harder to hoist than their archaic cousin. That's why you now see so many contemporary boats with 2:1 purchase on their mainsail halyards.

As for staysail sheets, you have a choice: either lead the sheets to conventional winches, or hang blocks on short "lizards" attached to the clew for a 2:1 advantage (see Figure 2-21). The latter is suited to small staysails, but watch out for flogging blocks. If you go with winches, you'll find they needn't be huge, since the staysails are relatively small.

So many advantages. And wait, there's more! Modern sailcloth is far more stable, lightweight, and strong than the canvas of yesteryear, so the gaff rig just about can't help but perform better than it did in the days of cotton. But it helps to have a sailmaker who knows the peculiarities of cutting gaff sails if you want to make the most of the improvement.

Sail design has also evolved. Note, for instance, the high "peak angle" of our example boat: The higher this angle, the smaller the arc the gaff can swing through, and thus the less leech twist you'll get. Combine this with an extra-wide mainsheet traveler, and twist can be minimized to near Bermudian levels (see accompanying sidebar, "Leech Twist").

For even more efficiency, you can give the gaff its own gooseneck and run it up a heavy-duty sail

Leech Twist (The Mother of All Winds Is Apparent)

The direction of apparent wind is determined by vessel velocity and direction relative to wind velocity and direction; but apparent wind always moves forward as vessel speed increases, and aft as wind speed increases. Wind at deck level is slowed by friction with the surface of the water, hence, windspeed is higher at the masthead. Therefore, apparent wind is farther aft at the masthead than at deck level.

Sail efficiency requires that the sail "attack" the wind at a specific angle relative to the boat's fore-and-aft centerline; since apparent wind moves aft as you go up, the sail angle should also change, becoming wider with height. This progressive angle change calls for some degree of "leech twist," in which the sail assumes a shallow spiral shape as the leech gradually twists to leeward. A little twist is a good thing, but too much will leave the sail too tight at the bottom and too loose at the top.

There are a host of ways to control leech twist on Bermudian rigs, including the mainsheet, traveler, mast bend, halyard tension, Cunningham, outhaul, and vang. Advice in sailing books, and telltales on the sail, will let you know what works.

Leech twist is a particularly vexing problem with gaffers, because the gaff sticks out so far, and thus can "fall" so far to leeward. This action can be controlled with vangs on the gaff, but practically speaking only on schooner foresails, with the vang leading from the mainmast. Leech twist can also be minimized, as noted in the accompanying text, by raising the angle of the gaff, and widening the mainsheet traveler, to allow the boom to go to leeward and thus keep under the gaff even when reaching.

track on an aerodynamically shaped wood, aluminum, or carbon fiber mast. And how about making the gaff out of carbon fiber, to save weight? With these and other simple, changes, you can have a gaff rig that goes very well to weather, with none of the high-tension, money-intensive, vulnerable tweaking gear of an only-slightly-higher-pointing Bermudian rig. And when you bear off the wind, you'll find that a gaff rig has infinitely adjustable sail shape for high-powered, low-effort reaches and runs.

So, how come this rig is so rare? Partly because pointing, at any price, is what counts in racing. Partly because handling a big gaff sail can take some skill and, in the absence of winches, physical effort. Partly a lot of other reasons, perhaps the biggest one being that it is no longer available "off the shelf"—you pretty much have to build a gaff rig yourself these days, since the supply and design infrastructure is almost entirely Bermudian-oriented.

Bermudian was the new kid on the block once, too. It grew to dominance because sailors grew to prize its strength—windward ability—above all others. Indeed it might be said that they became blinded to all others, to the point that I can only half-jokingly reintroduce the gaff rig as radical. As further irony, there is now a version of Bermudian rig—the B & R rig, most often seen on Hunter sailboats—that echoes gaff configuration: no standing backstay; aft-swept spreaders; minimum headsails; etc.

CHAPTER 9

Emergency Procedures

Problem: When the 55-foot ketch *Nabob* was off the west coast of Africa, its 14–foot long stainless steel bobstay suddenly parted.

The wind was aft at the time, but the strain on the ½-inch wire was sufficient that the sound of its breaking could be heard and felt back in the cockpit. With a healthy redundancy of shrouds and stays, *Nabob* did not depend on the bobstay for rig integrity to the extent that some craft do, but the accident rendered the jibstay useless and threatened the mainmast above the spreaders. Had the vessel been on the wind this portion of the mast would probably have broken off and fallen aft toward the crew, taking the radio antenna—integral with the backstay—with it.

Response: Even off the wind the situation was serious, since wave action (there was an appreciable sea running) and the aft-directed pull of the mainsail could unduly strain the mast, so the first steps were to lower the main, start the engine, and steer to ease motion. Next, some way had to be found of

317

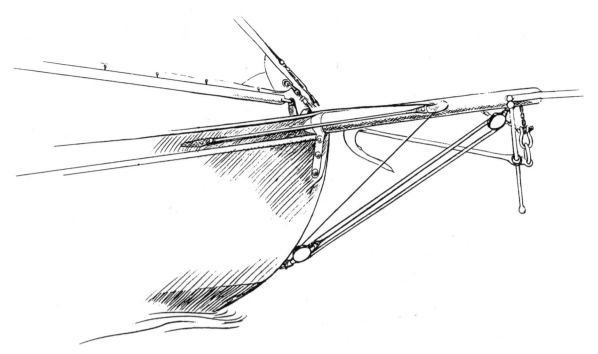

Figure 9-1. *The ketch* Nabob *(or a vessel like it) preparing to anchor after making it to port with a jury-rigged bobstay. A tackle with the fall led through a turning block to the anchor windlass is a bobstay substitute quickly and easily installed under way.*

temporarily replacing the bobstay, bringing the rig back into balance. This was done by attaching a block and tackle to the bobstay fittings, slacking the jibstay turnbuckle, gaining as much tension as possible with the purchase, and then retightening the jibstay. Additional power was gained by leading the hauling part of the tackle through a turning block and aft to the windlass. When conditions moderated, a measured length of chain was shackled to the old turnbuckle to replace the temporary rig.

Good design, the presence of useful gear, the alacrity of the crew, and a bit of luck all contributed to a happy ending when *Nabob*'s bobstay broke. But next we must ask, "How could the accident have been avoided?" It turns out that the lower end of the bobstay had been eaten away by severe galvanic action over the course of years and was just waiting to break. Wire is the best material for a bobstay because, unlike chain or rod, it usually gives

advance warning of failure; not inspecting it throws this advantage away. The galvanic problem was compounded by the bobstay's being slightly undersized relative to the jibstay. This is a common flaw; for some reason many riggers and builders feel that a properly scaled bobstay "looks too big" and opt for a smaller one. So headstay strain, corrosion, and the likelihood of occasionally striking other objects all conspire to abuse a bobstay. I know that I replace a disproportionate number of them.

What happened to *Nabob* was classic rig trauma, the rig-as-strain-distribution system suddenly jeopardized by the failure of one of its parts. But for the rigger and sailor, there's more to the situation than equations involving consequences of strain; people and their skills are part of the sys-

Ingenious Self-Steering

When his Dove *lost its rudder at sea,* Winston Bushnell coiled and stopped 660 feet of spare line into a 6-foot-long bundle, then trailed the bundle about 30 feet behind his boat on two lines, one leading to each quarter. By adjusting the lines, he was able to steer his boat.

Source: *Capable Cruiser*, Lin and Larry Pardey

Pantyhose Fan Belt (Sheer Ingenuity)

If your problem is a broken fan belt, and there's no spare, try knotting a pair of pantyhose to length around the pulleys. It just might get you home.

The pantyhose fan belt.

tem, adding immeasurably to its complexity and strength and giving it the ability to avoid trauma or to respond to it if it does occur. The more prepared and aware we are, the richer the system is.

When people talk about effective responses to emergencies, much is made of preparedness—having the right tools, duplicate parts, and rehearsed procedures. These things are very important, but from a traditional perspective, too much emphasis is placed on specific items and actions. Since things do not always break when and how one expects, specific practices must be complemented by broad knowledge, and by a resilient attitude that fosters the associative thinking that can put broad knowledge to work. When I read or hear accounts of sailors who have pulled the fat out of notably fierce fires, these attributes are usually evident; in accounts of fiascoes they are likely absent. In my own small brushes with misfortune, luck has made a difference more often than I'd care to admit, but basic precautions backed up by odd inspirations usually saved the day.

In an era when pleasure craft have gained aerodynamic efficiency at the expense of systems redundancy, the crew's skills at keeping things working can be severely taxed by incidents that, on "old-fashioned" craft, would be inconveniences,

or at worst easily addressed problems. It's easier to jury-rig a block than a winch, or a shroud than an unstayed carbon fiber mast, or reefing gear than a roll-away mainsail. I'm not saying that the old ways are necessarily better—only that increased efficiency and convenience, with sailboats no less than kitchen appliances, carry with them increased consequences of malfunction; traditional skills can be of *greater* value on a modern boat than on a traditional one.

Problem: The 160-foot barque *Elissa* (shown in this chapter's opening illustration) was on its way in from the last of four daysails celebrating its complete restoration, when the tug that was accompanying it somehow wandered in under the head gear. *Elissa*'s dolphin striker speared the tug's house and was broken off. Jibboom guys carried away, the jibboom cracked, and strain on the foreroyal and topgallant stays pulled the fore topgallant mast forward at a frightening angle, threatening to bring it crashing down, yards and all. It was *Nabob* again only worse, with many more people in much greater jeopardy from a larger, more complex, more heavily damaged rig.

Response: The foredeck was cleared in an instant. Instinct took care of that. As the tug was working clear, the crew lowered staysails and clewed up squaresails; riggers dove into the forepeak to get come-alongs, blocks, and tackle; qualified crew went cautiously aloft to check for mast damage; and passengers were moved well aft. The key was teamwork—skills in concert, with a minimum of noise and motion. There was no opportunity to take stock and plan a formal procedure, and given the crew's familiarity with the boat and each other, none was needed. *Elissa* got home safely with temporary gear guying and supporting its injured jibboom.

Chain Repair

Join a broken chain by bolting a set of linkplates to the chain ends. Use the largest, shortest bolts that will fit.

Problem: The 45-foot triple-spreader racing sloop *Pendragon* was en route to San Francisco, nine days out of Honolulu, when the starboard D-2 shroud broke at its upper terminal. The vessel was close-hauled on the starboard tack in 10 knots of wind, and the suddenly unsupported section of mast bent sharply, obviously close to breaking, until the crew got over onto port tack. The situation wasn't dangerous, at least not immediately, but California was too far to go under engine alone, and part of the course would have to be sailed with the injured starboard side to windward. The crew had to come up with some form of jury rig.

Response: One can imagine them going through a checklist of possible remedies:

Repair the shroud?

No, it was rod rigging, which is extraordinarily difficult to jury-rig. Replace it with a spare?

No spares aboard. Because rod terminals cannot be fabricated aboard ship, the usual practice of carrying a spare length at least as long as the longest piece in the rig would have been no use; rod failure insurance means carrying a complete side of shrouds plus spare stays. This would mean a heavy, 6-foot-diameter coil of vulnerable, expensive metal that would have to find a safe home somewhere aboard a relatively small boat. Carrying a spare piece of Spectra, or 7 x 7, or 1 x 19 wire and some compatible terminals might be a good idea for some boats, but this is not usually done because not just ends but also spreader fittings are highly specialized with some forms of rod rigging; improvising a reliable spreader connection could be a major task. Add to this the exaggerated "failsafe" claims of some rigging salespeople, and it's easy to see why this delivery crew found themselves with no spares aboard.

Emergency Bar Clamp

Join two C-clamps together with rope or seizing wire. Attach to the static ends of the clamp. Adjust the length to fit the span of the project. The static pads will not be in contact with the work. Instead the threaded ends will be facing each other.

Switch rigging pieces?

On a more moderate rig, it would be conceivable in moderate weather to take a shroud from the port side and install it temporarily on the starboard side. But this rig was so fragile that the crew couldn't even lower the mainsail lest the boat's rolling break the mast; they had to stay on port tack, and so couldn't remove a rigging piece from the port side.

It was as though circumstances had conspired with rig design to produce the least repairable problem possible. An innovative solution was called for. Figure 9-2 shows the fix that the crew came up with: a spinnaker pole as spreader, quadrupled halyard above and winched-tight fore and afterguys below, with a spare halyard, assorted blocks, lashings, eyes, and no fewer than five winches called into play before it seemed safe to put the starboard side back to work. The makeshift rig had some elasticity and its components were heavily strained, but everything held together. *Pendragon* was able to make San Francisco in good time (2,600 miles in 16 days, with seven days under jury rig, and three of those days in fresh winds on starboard tack).

Upon first reading an account of this repair in the February 1983 issue of *Sail* magazine, I was impressed with the use of diverse materials in unlikely combination to mimic a shroud. The configuration was of a different order entirely than, say, simply using a halyard to mimic a broken jibstay. I later realized that this configuration was not a repair but a piece of extemporaneous design superimposed on an unrepairable rig. I do not know who else was in the crew, but the skipper was Warwick Tompkins, Jr., who races as well as delivers boats. Tompkins supervised the operation of Jabba the Hut's sailing barge during the filming of the movie *Return of the Jedi*, taught millions of people the mechanical principles of sailing as one of the hosts of Public Broadcasting's "Under Sail" series, and, at the age of nine, rounded Cape Horn aboard his father's 95-foot pilot schooner *Wander Bird*. He personifies the benefits of wildly diverse experience. A deep, intuitive understanding of rigs and rigging is the most valuable component of any emergency procedure.

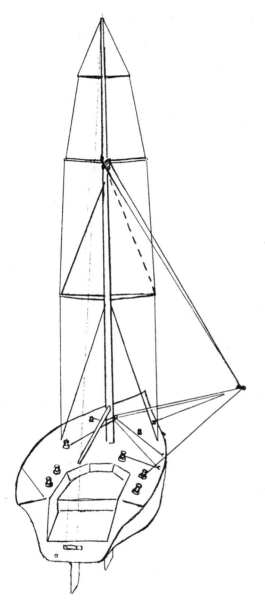

Figure 9-2. *The crew of the racing yacht* Pendragon *used a spinnaker pole, five winches, and assorted blocks, tackle, and lashings to replace the starboard D-2 (second-lowest diagonal) shroud on their rod-rigged mast. The spinnaker pole provided a healthy staying angle and was reinforced with lashings at its base to relieve the heavy compression loads there. The rope and wire rope used as shroud, fore guy, and after guy were far more elastic than rod rigging, but inelastic enough to keep the mast up.*

Some emergencies are even more involved than *Pendragon*'s. What could have been done, for example, had the mast collapsed? But most sudden problems are smaller and simpler though not necessarily any more obvious of solution. Whatever the level of complexity, your road to intuitive understanding begins with a basic idea: restore appropriate tension and compression. As you sail, consider what pieces are under how much tension, and why; study design to see the logical beauty of a resolution of forces; look at and sail many different boats to see how differently and with what varying degrees of success forces can be resolved. Ask yourself, "If that halyard jams now, what could I do? If a crack appears in the mast...there...what could I do? If that roller-furling headsail jams, what could I do?" This line of questioning leads to interesting conversations, encourages design comprehension, occupies the mind, and most important, helps you avoid emergencies by making you aware of potential trouble. The following are a few examples of tension/compression restoration.

Problem: Through inattentive tailing, the turns on a headsail sheet winch become thoroughly, profoundly "wrapped" under a heavy load, so that you cannot cast them off to tack (Figure 9-3). You're in the midst of a closely contested race (not all emergencies are life-threatening), and it's unthinkable that you should create slack in the sheet by bearing off to let the main blanket the headsail. A stiff breeze is blowing, so that even if you were willing to head into the wind, the flogging of the sail would keep you from clearing the line.

Response: Pull the lazy sheet around to the lee side and lead it via snatch block, stanchion, cleat, or what-have-you to another winch. Take a strain to put slack in the jammed sheet. Clear turns and reset properly. Return lazy sheet and prepare to come about. Alternatively, for a quicker, don't-leave-the-cockpit fix, Icicle-Hitch (Figure 3-12) a spare line to the standing part of the fouled sheet and lead this line to a spare winch. Or, for a possibly rope-damaging alternative, take the bitter end

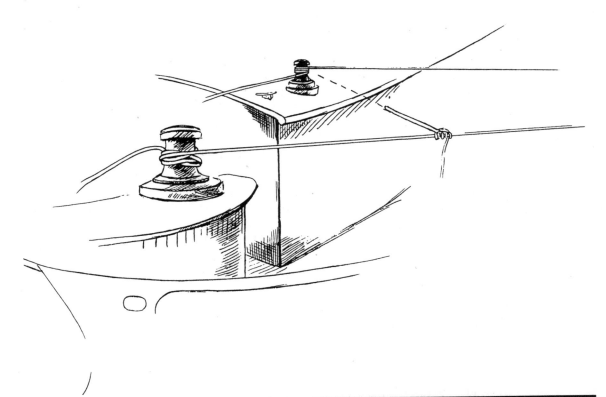

Figure 9-3. *To get rid of a winch wrap in a hurry, without leaving the cockpit, Icicle-Hitch a spare line to the standing part of the wrapped line ahead of the winch. Lead the spare line, via turning block if necessary, to another winch (dashed line) and haul it to put slack in the wrapped line so it can be cleared. Alternatively, bring the lazy jibsheet around and lead it to the other winch (solid line).*

around once, counterclockwise, then lead the tail to another winch. Crank away until the turn tears free. Repeat until the turns are clear. Watch out for a sudden surge as the jam diminishes.

Problem: Preparing to reef, you take up smartly on the main topping lift, not realizing that the pin on the boom-end shackle has been gradually working loose and has chosen this precise moment to fall out. Braced for appreciable tension, you appear to dive for the deck when the pin comes out—a physical gag worthy of Buster Keaton. With the bow of the shackle still hanging in the Eyesplice and giving it carrying weight, the loose end soars up and

Bolt Wrench

If you find yourself wrenchless, thread two nuts onto a large bolt. Adjust the nuts until they just fit on either side of the nut you want to work on. Turn.

out, wrapping itself a few times around the leeward shrouds. You have to dodge in a hurry when the shackle bow finally slips loose and comes hurtling directly at you. Hilarious.

Response: Since you are a prudent sailor and were prepared to reef as soon as you thought of it, there's no reason to panic. Lead a spare halyard aft, set it up as a temporary topping lift, and proceed to reduce sail. Or sheet the main into the gallows, drop the sail, and put in the reef while it's down. Now ask yourself, "Do I really need that loose topping lift?" Sometimes the safest, most appropriate procedure is to do nothing. If it isn't fouling any other lines or sails, let it be. Maybe it'll shake loose and you can at least haul on it until the end fetches up against the block aloft so it stays out of the way. The wind is picking up, so why leave the deck if you don't have to?

But if it's wrapped around not only the shrouds but also vital halyards made off to a sheerpole pinrail, it's a different situation. Sure you can't reach it with the boathook? That it won't come loose by itself? Then get into a safety harness and get out the bosun's chair. No bosun's chair? Put a Bowline on the Bight or Double Butterfly into the halyard end and sit in that. Tie yourself to one or more of the shrouds on a short tether, have the person at the helm steer the course that imparts the least motion to the boat, and go aloft. Just two people aboard, so no one to winch you up? Heave-to to free the other hand. If this isn't possible, reeve a long spare line into a handy-billy, set up some sort of safety (as described in Chapter 7's "Living Aloft"), and haul yourself up. If you have no handy-billy, curse yourself soundly, do a few limbering-up exercises (no kidding), and shinny up a pair of shrouds as shown in Figure 9-4. This little-known technique is strenuous, and on vessels with small-diameter wires it's downright painful. But it's the fastest way aloft and it might be your only alternative.

Get a bosun's chair. Get a handy-billy. And above all, get around to seizing shackles.

It is natural to think immediately of dismastings when we think of rig failures. What if, despite all precautions, your mast does collapse far from help? Here is a scenario based on reports of actual jury rigs, a little disaster sampler for your consideration.

Problem: A weak spot in the mast at the spreaders causes a failure far from land, in 20 to 25 knots of wind. The mast doesn't teeter and fall; it's under tons of compression load, so it comes down Bang! in the blink of an eye and bounces over the leeward side before it fetches up in a tangle of rigging. The boom crumples at its outer end when it hits a corner of the gallows, and shears away at the gooseneck. Some of the shrouds and stays carry away and go whipping through the air, the leeward lifeline stanchions collapse and add to the tangle, and sections of the smashed dinghy fly into the cockpit. Deprived of the rig's stabilizing effect the hull begins pitch-

Figure 9-4. *A ratline-less emergency climbing technique: Wrap feet and hands around adjacent shrouds and monkey your way up. Stretching beforehand to limber knee and ankle joints is a good idea.*

ing and lurching sharply, so footing is none too sure. From belowdecks comes the sound of cascading gear and shouts of alarm. Someone fights their way to the wheel, shoulders the dazed helmer aside, and starts the engine to get the boat under control, only to have a stray piece of running rigging immediately foul the prop.

Then things stop going wrong, and it's time to jury rig.

Response: You attend to any crewmembers who might have been injured, send a distress call if possible, check the condition of the hull, and set a sea anchor to ease the motion. Try clearing that line out of the propeller by taking a strain on the line, then giving little bursts with the starter, with the transmission in reverse. It works more often than not. Then you very carefully begin to clean up the mess in the water, getting everything close and secure alongside. All that tangle is really working against you, so you have at it, with pliers if the cotters are easy to pull, or with a hacksaw or wire cutters if the cotters are overbent. If conditions are calm enough and you have enough time, you can disconnect the wires by unscrewing their turnbuckles. Use spare line to keep things from sinking or slamming around or drifting away as you work.

When things are under enough control that you can remove the sails, cut away or unreeve the running rigging, and even remove the upper ends of most of the standing rigging pieces. All of these salvaged items you stow out of the way for the moment, then take time to do a little housekeeping, clearing the decks of broken gear, splintered wood, and such. Then it's time to return to the two mast sections.

Hmmm. The lower one is buckled badly, with jagged edges at both ends. The spreaders are gone, the tangs are useless, and there are no sheaves in this section. Let it go—just untie it and let it go.

The upper section is longer and fairly straight, but its top is smashed, ruining sheaves and tangs.

Figure 9-5. *Cable clips, properly applied, have the shaped saddles bearing on the standing part.*

No matter, get some hands on the lashing lines at either end, and time the roll of the boat for the best moment to haul the thing aboard. Secure it on deck and set hands to squaring and filing the ends while you work up some shroud attachments. A simple, strong procedure is to unbolt a pair of cleats from the deck and throughbolt them together near the top of the stick. Next you get out four pieces of wire or Spectra rope, each about 6 feet longer than your jury mast, and turn in an eye at either end of each. The upper eye is big enough to slip over the mast, and the lower is maybe 8 inches in circumference. If your wire is 1 x 19, you make the eyes with cable clips properly applied (Figure 9-5). With 7 x 7 wire you can "splice with your bare hands" by turning-in a Molly Hogan at each end (Figure 9-6). This is a very fast and easy method, nearly as strong as cable clips,* and it imposes no chance of dropping tools or nuts overboard.

The four pieces are your forestay, backstay, and two shrouds. Seat them securely on the cleats, and on top of them add some rope grommets for halyard blocks. Seize the assorted eyes and grommets in place. Tie spare lines through the lower eyes so you'll have something to hold onto to stabilize the mast as you raise it. It's going to be a deck-stepped mast, sans tabernacle, so get it up on the cabintop, brace its butt against the stump of the old mast, and lash it down so that it will pivot but not shift. Put a hatch cover, breadboard, or other stout object under-

---

* Tensile strengths (as percent of rated wire strengths): Molly Hogan 70 percent, clips, 80 percent.

neath the butt as a compression pad, and reinforce the cabin beams at this point with heavy bracing salvaged from the boom, whisker pole, or bowsprit. Run the backstay line through a turning block to a winch and horse the mast up by main force until the angle is high enough for the winch to take over. The hands on the shrouds will have a tough time of keeping the mast from falling sideways; go slowly so they can pay out their lines evenly. You'll have to go forward to tend the forestay as the mast goes up, so the backstay, turning block, winch, and winchers

had all better be first-rate. Take a turn around the capstan with the forestay line and snub it to keep the mast from going over backward.

When the mast is plumb, pass the attached ropes through shackles on the chainplates and the lower ends of the shrouds several times to form lanyards, and tighten them moderately. Now get out some more spare lines and a come-along, and lash the base of the mast very tightly to the stump. Take up some more on the shrouds and stays, check all attachment points, and you're ready to hoist a sail or two.

Problem: No matter what jury rig is needed, the crew fails to see it as a design exercise.

Response: Long before such unpleasantness might occur, you get to know your rig on an intellectual level. There are no principles or techniques specific to jury rigging. It is just design and installation, constrained more than usual by time and available materials. One will likely not have the leisure to run

Figure 9-6. *A Molly Hogan splice is made by unlaying three adjacent strands of a 7 x 7 or 7 x 19 wire rope for a distance equal to about two-and-a-quarter times the circumference of the desired eye. Overhand-Knot the resulting two bundles together—left over right—to form the eye (A), then lay the two bundles into each other's vacant spaces, right down to the standing part (B). At this point, cut the heart out of the bundle it's in (C), helix the six strands smoothly down onto the standing part, and tape them down (D).*

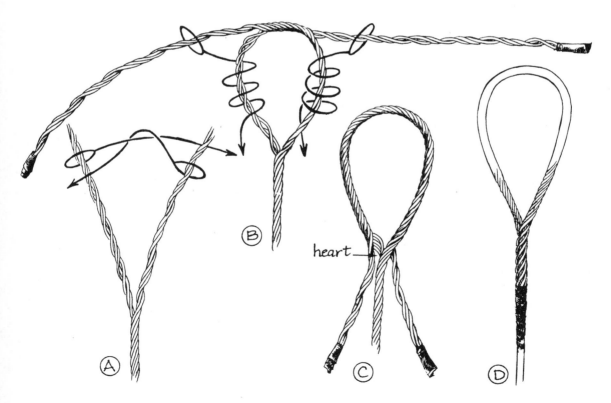

heart

Ⓐ   Ⓑ   Ⓒ   Ⓓ

calculations for an ideal rig, nor install ideal components. But your jury rig can only be as good as what you know, and who you are when the accident happens. Absence of design education is the reason that so many attempted jury rigs fail at the first or second or third attempt: people don't understand the effects of angles, of unsupported lengths, of materials properties, righting moment, and all of the other fundamentals that lie behind the art of rigging.

Most boats do not carry spare rigging, cable clips, wire rope cutters, or much else that might be of use in an emergency. Worse yet, they do not carry crew who can splice barehanded, use cleats as tangs, or raise an impromptu mast. There's no excuse for this; emergency gear costs little and takes up little space, while knowledge is absolutely free and goes with you everywhere. Consider the possibility of accidents, speculate on various courses of action, and stock and learn accordingly. Stress versatility: accidents are never exactly as you imagine, and there are always surprising complications. The result of your wide-ranging preparations will be a greatly reduced chance of ever having to use them. As Stewart Brand's fine-grain philosophy puts it, "Take care of the big problems, and the little problems will defeat you; take care of the little problems, and the big problems will take care of themselves."

Smooth sailing.

CHAPTER 10

Fancy Work

What with the years-long voyages that used to be the rule in olden days, sailors would find themselves with a lot of time on their hands, and lines in them. Given patience, trial and error, and that peculiarly human urge to create semi-useful frippery, hundreds of beautiful, intricate complications came into being: fancy work. It's an art form like scrimshaw or woodcarving, but unlike these pursuits, its artfulness is intrinsic to its use; what's right for a bellrope is wrong for a thump mat.

Today fancy work is too often mere decoration made with no concern for proportion or appropriate intricacy. I know, I know—picky, picky, picky. But as long as we have the fruit of thousands of hours of boredom (the Mother of Invention?), why not take a little time and make good use of it?

HITCHING

For instance, there's decorative hitching, a way to cover cylindrical objects with twine to provide chafing gear or a more comfortable handhold. The simplest form is French Hitching (Figure 10-1), a series

Figure 10-1. *French Hitching is a series of Half Hitches, with each hitch closely succeeding the previous one. Snug the hitches firmly against each other and they'll form a smooth spiral.*

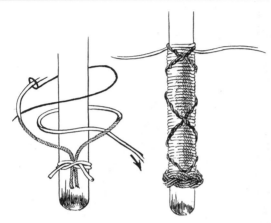

Figure 10-2. *Moku Hitching involves two lines half-hitched alternately in opposite directions. Tighten both spirals with identical, consistent tension. Cover the ends with Turk's Heads.*

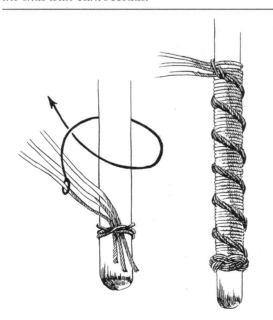

of Half Hitches laid up in mind-numbing sequence. The finished product is functional and nearly attractive, assuming that you "set" each hitch in a consistent fashion against the previous hitch. But use two lines, hitch them alternately in opposite directions, and you have Moku Hitching (Figure 10-2), downright eye-catching and involved enough to keep the mind alive. Again it's important to draw each hitch up snugly and consistently, and to see that the two spirals proceed at the same pace. When the spirals cross, jump by with whichever side is closest for a neat crossing. Many patterns can be made with Moku Hitching by reversing hitch direction at different points in the spirals.

Why the name "Moku Hitching"? Because the first place I saw it was on the gangplank of an old Sacramento River sugar hauler of that name. Who tied the knot or what they called it I do not know, but it hasn't appeared in any other knot book, so it was probably originated by some unknown marlingspike artist. Inspired by that individual I set about developing an original hitch, and came up with the one shown in Figure 10-3, St. Mary's Hitching. As you can see, it is made with three strands, the lowermost one always being hitched in the same direction over the other two. The result looks a lot like a three-strand rope laid over service, a gratifyingly pretty knot to make. If you're feeling particularly energetic, try Moku-izing this hitch, using two sets of three strands, run in opposite directions.

Why "St. Mary's Hitching"? False modesty; I could have called it "Brion's Spiral" or some such, but instead named it after a fine little church building in Anacortes, Washington, where I used to live. Knots should have names.

Both of these knots are new, and there are certainly many more out there waiting to be discovered; play around some, improvise, and you just might find one.

Figure 10-3. *St. Mary's Hitching is made with three strands hitched in succession in the same direction. The result looks like three-strand rope wrapped around a stretch of service.*

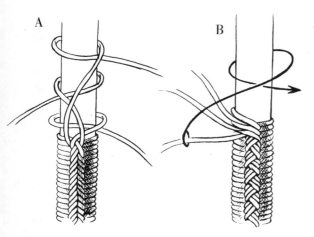

Figure 10-4. *Ringbolt Hitching in its most basic form is made with three strands. The first is hitched to the left, the second to the right, the third to the left, and so on (A). A Ringbolt Hitching variation involves hitching all three strands first left, then right, for a zigzag pattern (B).*

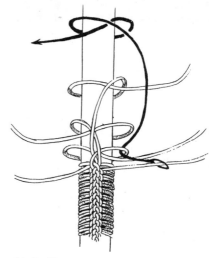

Figure 10-5. *Five-strand Ringbolt Hitching. Pass each end up through the bight above it, then hitch opposite the direction of the top turn. It takes a lot of fussing.*

Next we have Ringbolt Hitching, always involving three or more strands tucked in different directions. In the basic form, the first strand is hitched left, the next right, next left, and so on, so that the hitches form a ridge along one side of the object being covered. Keep the ridge straight (Figure 10-4). A variation involves tucking all three left, then all three right.

For a big jump in complexity, try a five-strand Ringbolt Hitching (Figure 10-5), a lovely, infuriatingly complicated production that is just the thing for a tiller, companionway rail, or other special place. The trick with this is to draw up a little with the lead strand, and a lot two and three stages back.

Ringbolt Hitching, particularly suited to covering arced cylinders such as the rim of a wheel, was developed as chafing gear on the deck ringbolts to which hemp anchor cables were stopped in the days before chain. Nowadays one sees it on chest beckets, lanyards, rail corners, and tire fenders, as well as ship's wheels. And it isn't limited to arcs; by hauling back on the hitches and slightly spreading the underside turns, it works for straight cylinders, too.

Once you've got hitching figured out and have covered the object of your choice, you'll want to hide the hitching ends; they're just hanging out there. This is best done with a Turk's Head at either end (see the "Turk's Head" section later in this chapter), of whatever complexity you feel up to.

Some Practical Details

Whatever form of knot you use, the surface you're covering should be clean and well-sealed. If the surface is slippery, parcel with adhesive tape or, on wood, work over sanded shellac or varnish.

Cord size is important: too large, and you'll get clumsy-looking, lumpy hitches that are uncomfortable to hold; too small, and you'll have a lovely little antimacassar. But by then you'll be old and blind. Linen twine or cotton cod line of of 32 to 60 thread is right for most fancy work. Match the size to the project at hand. Many synthetic twines do not finish well and are unpleasant to work with, but some are rather nice. See the "Sources and Resources" section for where to find the good stuff, both natural and synthetic.

To find how much twine you need to cover a given length and diameter, make a practice run—a good idea anyway—using a known length of twine. Measure how far this length gets, then multiply it to

The Loop-and-Button Becket shown below is inherently lovely as well as practical. The strands that form the Eyesplice are transformed into the button that secures the eye. And the extra bulk of the splice is chafing gear for whatever you're buttoning around. This novel becket, the brainchild of James McGrew, is just the thing for hanging fenders, or for tack pendants or small-craft halyards. In small stuff, this configuration works as a belt lanyard for tools and keys.

To make it, tie a button, such as Ashley's 880 (Chapter 4, page 90) in the same size line you're going to use. Now pick up the line you'll use, and form an eye that's just big enough to slip over the button. Leave a tail long enough for five tucks, plus enough to make another button. Splice in the eye, then seize the ends together and make the button. Done.

There are many traditional button-and-becket variations, and they are the inspiration for today's soft shackles (see page 388).

get enough to cover the whole project. Before you start, make the lengths up into "foxes," figure-eight turns made around the thumb and pinky and seized with a Constrictor Knot. Pull a working length out as you go and draw up the Constrictor occasionally to keep the foxes intact.

ONE HIGH-CLASS KNIFE LANYARD

This next project is a fancy-work sampler, a series of fairly involved knots blended together to form an object of graceful utility. You may never have made any of these knots, but though the diagrams might seem involved, there's nothing going on that can't be handled if you just take things one step at a time. At the end you'll have a useful object plus the ability to use all those knots in any combination for whatever other projects you desire.

To begin, take three 6-foot lengths of number 32 to 40 twine, middle them together, and put on a Constrictor Knot with stout sail twine, 2 to 3 inches to one side of the middle, around all three strands (Figure 10-6). Braid the longer half of the bundle, working away from the Constrictor, until you have a braid about 3 inches long. Is the braid good and tight? Even? Fine, put the whole works down, take the phone off the hook, close the door, and prepare to tie a Star Knot.

Measure off two 18-inch pieces and one 9-inch piece of the same cord you used for the braid. Double the longer pieces, lay the short one alongside them, and Constrictor all together about ¼ inch from the bight end (Figure 10-7). If the twine you're using is inclined to ravel, dip the ends in Krazy Glue before proceeding. I got this idea from my ingenious friend, George Pitkin, who also suggested applying a daub of paint to each end to help keep track of the sequence. George says, "Just remember the old mnemonic for the colors of the spectrum: 'Roy G. Biv.' That's short for Red, Orange, Yellow, Green, Blue, Indigo, Violet."

You only need to go as far as Blue for this knot.

Hold the doubled bights in one hand and open up the ends like the petals of a flower. Start with

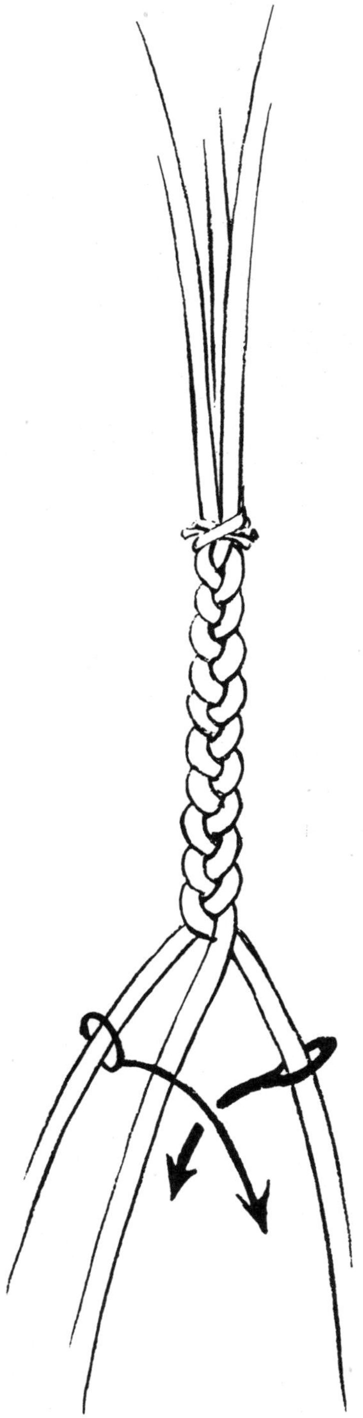

Figure 10-6. *Beginning a knife lanyard. Start by middling three 6-foot pieces of twine and braiding them together at their middles for about 3 inches.*

George Pitkin's Crazy Idea

When doing fancy work with small cordage, the ends ravel easily, making it difficult to tuck them through tight spaces. Taped ends are too bulky, as are Constrictors in all but the finest, most-difficult-to-manipulate twine. But if you dip the ends in Krazy Glue and wait a few seconds, your raveling days are over.

any strand and hitch it around its neighbor to the right (counterclockwise), passing the end over to the right, back under to the left. Now spill the hitch into the other strand by pulling on the one that made the hitch, just as for the Spilled-Hitch Bowline (Figure 3-21), to get Figure 10-7D. Now take the strand into which the hitch was just spilled and hitch it around its neighbor to the right and likewise spill that hitch. Continue with all the strands. Because there's no end hanging down, figuring out where to hitch the fifth strand can be difficult. But if you look close to the stem on the right of #5's beginning, you'll see #1 (Figure 10-7E). Pull a little slack into it to give you room, and hitch around it. Fair everything up so it is compact and symmetrical; fuss with it, or you'll get hopelessly lost later.

Next, Crown all the strands clockwise (Figures 10-7F, G). This is just like Crowning for a Backsplice (Figure 4-1), but in the other direction. Fair the Crown.

Moderately tricky: Take an end, lead it counterclockwise, and follow the course of the strand on the right into the knot (Figure 10-7H), going first under the working strand's own part then down through the loop. Repeat this procedure with the other four strands, taking care that the working strand always stays inside the strand it parallels. Again the fifth strand can be confusing, but since you've kept everything fair you'll see how one of the Crown parts remains undoubled. That's the one you parallel (Figure 10-7I).

Turn the knot over, take a strand, and continue following its neighbor to completely double it, then tuck the working strand directly through the middle of the knot, inboard of everything else (Figure 10-7J). Repeat with each strand, taking care that

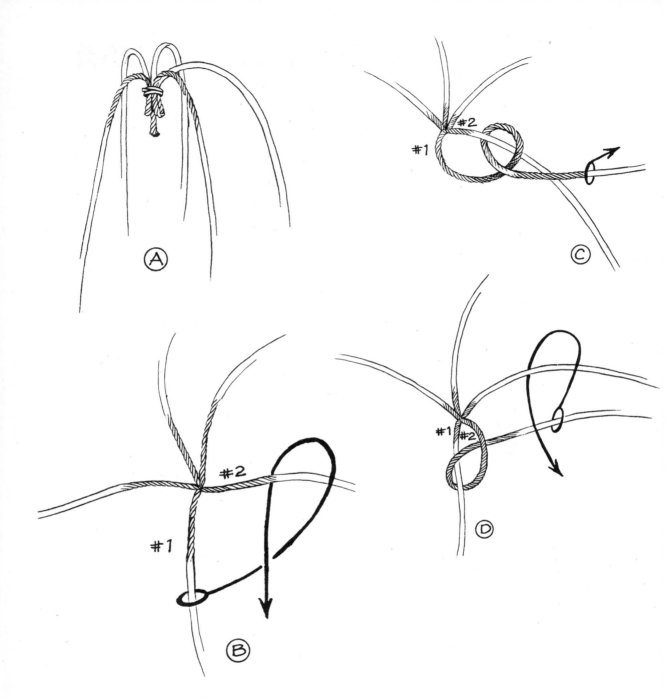

Figure 10-7A–D. *Beginning a Star Knot. Middle two 18-inch pieces of twine, lay alongside a 9-inch piece of twine, and bundle all together with a Constrictor Knot about ¼ inch from the bight end (A). Arrange the ends petal-like and hitch one around its neighbor to the right, passing the end over to the right and back under to the left (B). Spill the hitch just made into the other strand (C), and the result will look like drawing D. Hitch the strand with the hitch in it around its neighbor, and spill this new hitch into the neighbor's strand.*

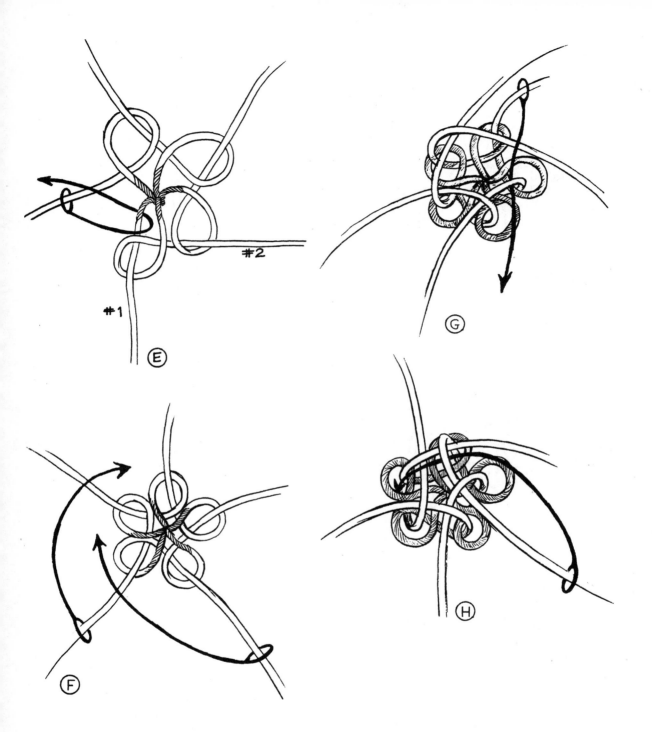

Figure 10-7E–H. *Continue with the other ends. Since there's no end hanging down, it can be difficult to spot strand #1, which strand #5 hitches around. Trace it up from the stem and pull a little slack into it for easier spilling (E). After fairing the interlocking hitches, Crown all strands clockwise (F and G). Then take each strand and lead it counterclockwise, following the course of the strand on its right into the knot (H).*

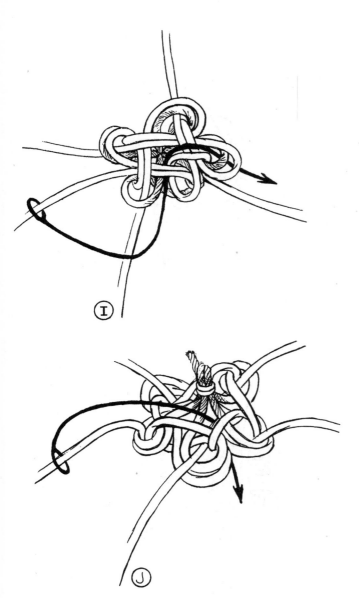

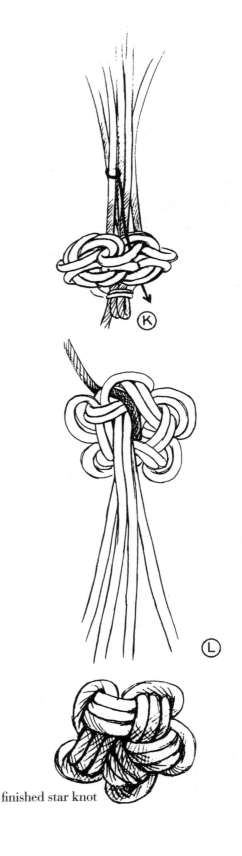

Figure 10-7I–M. *Finishing the Star Knot. Continuing the procedure as in (H) it becomes a bit tricky with the fifth strand (I). Turn the knot over. Each strand continues following its neighbor through the knot, finally emerging in the middle of the knot (J). Turn the knot back over. To finish, tuck each end alongside the second "face" to its right, then down under the four parts at the rim of the knot. Two views of this step are given in K and L. Draw up carefully, working slack away from the stem, one strand at a time. A finished Star Knot Button (M).*

finished star knot

each one goes into a subsequent space at the stem when it is tucked.

Turn the knot back over. The ends should all be coming out of the center. As you can see (Figure 10-7K), the face of the knot is doubled; we'll now use the strands to triple it, finishing the knot. As Figure 10-7L shows, you don't follow the closest face but the one next to it; otherwise you don't get a fair run. So lay each strand alongside the appropriate face and tuck it to the stem, under four parts. A carpet-hooking tool or bent piece of wire is a great help here.

Drawing Up and Trimming

Use your small, blunted spike to draw the knot up. Start with the lower half of a horizontal pair and work your way around, taking out slack as you go. Leave that last, tripling pass standing up a little; pulling it all the way down now will distort things. Tighten each strand in turn, going over them all two or three times until the knot is firm, then pull those last turns down flush. To trim, lay a small, sharp blade at the point where an end emerges, press lightly, and work the end back and forth under the knife; slicing with the knife is liable to result in severed button loops.

Back to the Lanyard

You are the proud owner of a genuine Star Knot Button, which can now be fitted to the button loop of your lanyard. Remember the lanyard? We're making one here. Take that little stretch of three-strand braid and pass it around the circumference of the button. Pinch it down so the fit is tight, then put on a loose Constrictor (Figure 10-8). Check the fit; the button should just fit through the loop. Tighten the Constrictor and lay the button aside for now.

A Six-Strand Double Matthew Walker Knot

Matthew Walker, for a long time "the only man to have a knot named after him," was possibly a master rigger in a British naval dockyard, circa 1800, according to Ashley. Whoever he was, he certainly came up with an elegant, wide-range-of-usefulness knot. I described the three-strand version in Chap-

Figure 10-8. *Continuing the knife lanyard. After fitting the three-strand braid around the Star Knot Button, put a loose Constrictor at the appropriate spot on the legs of the braid.*

ter 4 (see Figure 4-6A, B, C, D); the one we'll do here is tied in the same manner but with twice as many strands, which is to say it's five times more difficult. But this is a fancy-work chapter, so have at it. You can glue and/or paint the strands here as with the Star Knot. The easiest thing is to paint five of them, and count the unpainted one as either "1" or "6." As with the Star Knot, success is largely determined by keeping all the turns compact and fair. Draw up carefully, slowly.

Figure 10-9 shows the finished knot at the base of the button loop braid. Pull that little Constrictor up to the base of the knot when drawing up. You can pry the thread off later.

Before going to the next knot, pound the Matthew Walker into a flattish oval shape, the faces of the oval being perpendicular to the faces of the three-strand braid.

Six-Strand French Sinnet

Hang the braided eye over a nail or peg at chest height and proceed to make some flat sinnet as

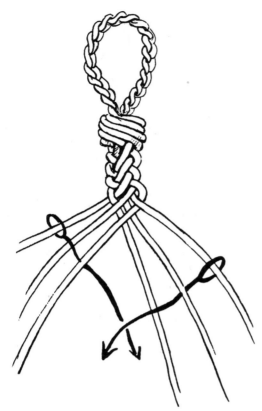

Figure 10-9. *Make a six-strand Matthew Walker at the base of the button loop braid, and add some six-strand French Sinnet as follows: Take three adjacent strands in each hand. Pass the uppermost left strand over one and under one to the right so that it becomes the lowermost strand in the right hand. Pass the uppermost right strand to the left, under one and over two, so that it becomes the lowermost strand in the left hand. Repeat. Experiment to get a fair start out of the Matthew Walker.*

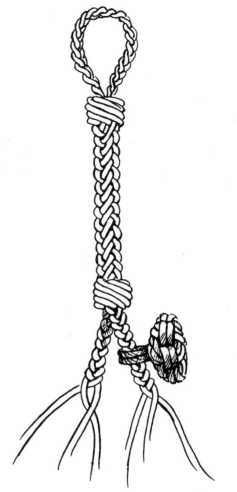

Figure 10-10. *Make another six-strand Matthew Walker at the end of about 2 3/4 inches of French Sinnet, flatten the Matthew Walker with a mallet, and make two three-strand braids below it. Thread the Star Knot onto one of these braids, and make another six-strand Matthew Walker (not shown) below the Star Knot. Which braid you put the button on matters: put it on the one that is opposite the face of the French sinnet that you like best.*

shown in Figure 10-9. It is very important to get a fair start, so experiment with leading different ends first until all six strands travel the shortest possible distance before entering the braid, and the braid is parallel with the faces of the oval. Work the strands up snug and fair.

Make a 2¾-inch length of sinnet and Constrictor it ¼ inch from its end for a fair finish. Unlay the strands back to the Constrictor and put in another six-strand Matthew Walker.

Attaching the Button

Flatten the second Matthew Walker and make up two ¾-inch bits of three-strand braid, one behind the other, as shown in Figure 10-10. Thread the Star Knot onto the front one. Which of these two identical braids is the front one? Take a look at the

6-strand flat sinnet you made. The two sides have a different appearance; put the button on the side that you don't prefer. Later, when you button the lanyard together, the side you do prefer will show.. Once the button is on, Constrictor the two braids together just below it. Make and flatten another six-strand Matthew Walker (Figure 10-11A).

Six-Strand Half-Round Sinnet

This handsome sinnet, which will make up the greater part of the lanyard's length, is begun as in Figure 10-11. Again, experiment to get a fair entry with your braid. This knot proceeds with the upper left strand going behind three strands to the right

and over one strand to the left; then the upper right strand goes behind three strands to the left and over one strand to the right. Keep everything symmetrical with even tension on all strands. Continue braiding until the lanyard thus far will encircle your wrist one-and-a-half times. Custom tailoring.

An alternative Round Sinnet, original as far as I know, goes like this: The upper left strand goes behind four strands to the right, and over one strand to the left. Repeat from opposite side.

A Rather Involved Finish

Constrictor the end of your sinnet and get a small snapshackle; my favorite is the kind shown in Figure 10-12. Take two ends and Ring-Hitch them to the eye of the shackle as shown in the same illustration. Shorten up the hitches until the eye is 1¼ inches from the end of the sinnet, then cut them so that their ends are just shy of the Constrictor (Figure 10-13). With strong, waxed thread, apply

---

Figure 10-11. *Make some six-strand Half-Round Sinnet: With the strands divided three and three, pass the upper left strand behind to the right and out between the lowest and middle righthand strands, then over to the left to become the lower lefthand strand. Repeat from the right. Drawings B through D show how this pattern can be altered for a fair start out of the Matthew Walker.*

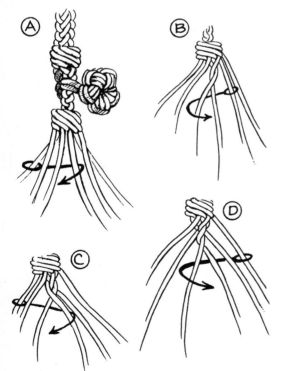

Figure 10-12. *Finishing the knife lanyard. Constrictor the end of the Half-Round Sinnet when the lanyard is long enough to completely encircle your wrist and lead up into your hand. Ring-Hitch a snapshackle to two of the strands about 1¼ inches below the end of the sinnet . . .*

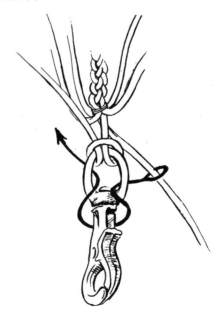

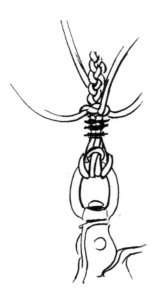

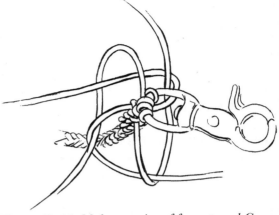

Figure 10-13. . . . *then cut off the Ring Hitch ends and Constrictor them together between the shackle and the end of the sinnet. Wall-Knot the remaining four strands.*

Figure 10-14. *Make a series of four-strand Crown Knots, one on top of the other, to cover the Constrictored ends. Stop when you're just short of the Ring Hitches, and make a Wall Knot as shown.*

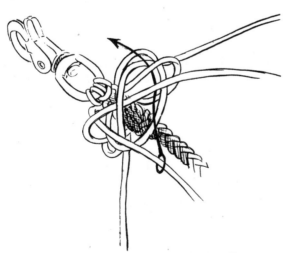

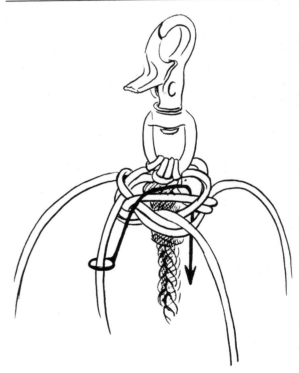

Figure 10-15A. *Finally, make a Crown Knot over the Wall Knot, as shown, to get a Wall and Crown Button. Fair up but do not tighten this arrangement. Double the knot by following above the original lead with each strand (as shown by the arrow) . . .*

Figure 10-15B. . . . *then tuck all four ends down between the knot and the braid, into adjacent spaces.*

Figure 10-16. *A finished high-class knife lanyard.*

several Constrictors to the ends, so that they are securely fastened to each other and their own standing parts.

With the remaining four strands make a Wall Knot as shown, and then a series of Crown Knots, one on top of the other, right over the bound ends (Figure 10-14). Proceed for about an inch, until you're almost at the Ring Hitches, then make a four-strand Wall and Crown Button as shown in Figure 10-15. Draw this knot up as snugly as you can, trim the ends, and you're done.

You should now have a lanyard that is perfect for carrying keys, knife, or other gear in a pocket, and which also can be worn around the hand as a tool lanyard when working aloft (Figure 10-16). If your finished product does not closely resemble mine, do not despair; this is a fairly involved, difficult sampler, and you may have to make several before all the knots come easily.

Once you feel comfortable with this arrangement, try altering proportions or substituting other knots. Remember that it isn't just the intricacy of a knot that makes it valuable, but its appropriateness. Some of the best fancy work is structurally simple, and even makes use of stretches of unknotted line. Always consider proportion, and the job the knots must do.

THE TURK'S HEAD: HARMONIC SEQUENCE AND THE SAILOR

Maybe I'm just easily stupefied, but I've always thought that the Turk's Head's beauty, range of usefulness, and elegant mathematical underpin-

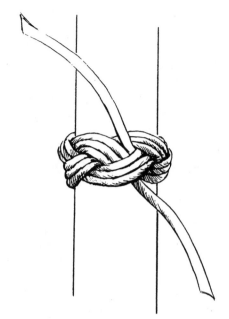

Figure 10-17. *A tripled three-lead-by-five-bight Turk's Head. The ends finish under the same turn and will be trimmed flush.*

nings qualified it as a miraculous knot. I've made different forms of it for ditty bags, bellropes, bottles, wrists, and oars, and when I was almost making a living at fancy work, I used to turn out simple ones by the hundred as candleholders; the knots never failed to fascinate me. In this section, I hope to share this fascination with you by explaining the Turk's Head structure, showing some basic as well as little-known sizes of the knot, and describing a system by which any size knot can be built up into a more complex one.

For starters, take a look at Figure 10-17, which shows a "three-lead-by-five-bight" knot, tripled. "Leads" are the number of parts that make up the width of the braid, and "bights" are the scalloped edges formed when the leads change direction. Because the type of Turk's Head we'll be dealing with here is made with a single strand, only certain combinations of leads and bights will result in a symmetrical knot; the pattern has to match up with itself to form a circular braid with a regular over-and-under sequence. For an example of this,

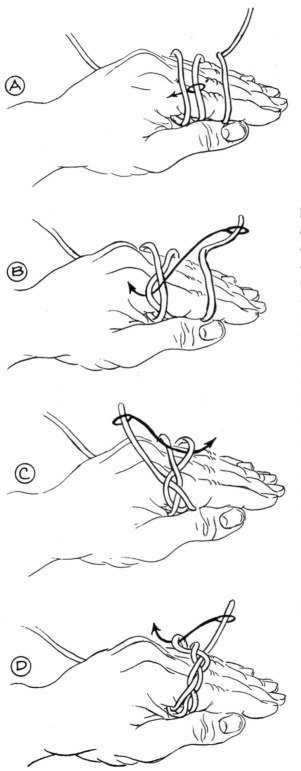

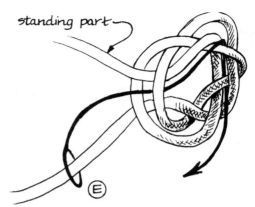

Figure 10-18. *To make a 3L × 5B knot, make three turns around a hand, push the middle turn under the left one (A), pass the end over and under (B), push the middle turn under the right one and pass the end over and under (C), and once more push the middle turn under the left one and pass the end over and under (D). Lead the end back into the knot parallel to the standing part and follow all the way around to double and triple the knot (E).*

look at Figure 10-18, which shows how to make the three-lead-by-five-bight knot. Three turns are taken around the hand and the end and two bights are braided together. Pass the end three times, as shown, and you can lead it alongside the standing part to form an endless braid. But pass the end four times and the braids don't match up. So a harmonic sequence—the end traveling in a certain pattern so that it comes back into sync with itself—is what makes a Turk's Head work. This harmonic sequence will occur whenever the number of leads and the number of bights have no common divisor; a 3L × 4B or 3L × 5B knot is possible; 3L × 6B or 3L × 9B knot isn't. Understanding this mathematical proviso is valuable when you want to make a knot of certain proportions.

But let's return to finish up that 3L × 5B knot. The end lays in alongside the standing part to complete the knot, and if it continues to parallel the standing part, going under where the standing part goes under, over where it goes over, and never crossing it, then the knot will be doubled (Figure 10-18E). Go around once more and the knot is tripled, which is the usual procedure with Turk's Heads. The knot can now be drawn up around a suitable object and the ends trimmed flush after having been led under the same part.

Next trick: Although passing the end four times while forming the knot gave us a mess, passing it five times gives us a 3L × 8B knot; making the braid longer gives us Turk's Heads with more and more bights, the exact size of each finished knot being dictated by the Law of the Common Divisor.

Ah, but wait, you say, we skipped 3L × 7B—that fits the Law. And so it does, which brings up another wrinkle: The Law of You Can't Get There from Here. In order to make a knot of three leads and seven bights, one must have a different "start" than three leads and five bights. In this case it's a knot of three leads and four bights, shown being made in Figure 10-19. As you can see, the technique is a slight variation on the 3L × 5B knot.

So, whenever we want to build up to a knot of a particular size, we must know what the correct starting knot is. There are relatively few starts, and you've already learned two of them, which puts you ahead of most of the world. Learn a couple more and you'll be an expert.

Four Leads by Three Bights

This is a simple knot, but rare. Notice that it is proportionately wider than the previous examples (Figure 10-20), an attribute that looks especially pleas-

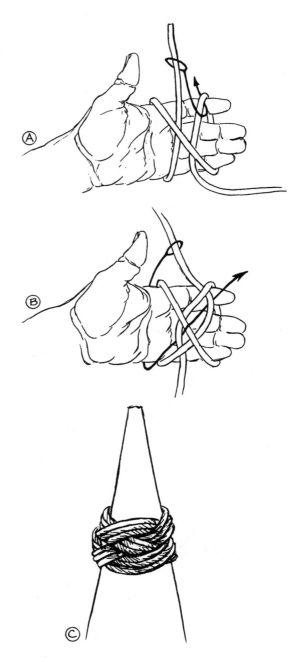

Figure 10-19. *A 3L × 4B knot is made by first moving the end under the left turn, then proceeding as with the 3L × 5B knot by moving the middle turn to the right, passing the end, etc.*

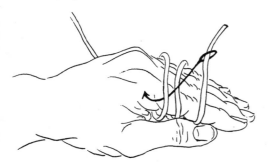

Figure 10-20. *A 4L × 3B knot. Begin with a Clove Hitch and tuck the end under the right-hand turn from right to left (A). Pass the end behind the hand, bring it up on the left side of the standing part, and tuck it under, over, and under as shown (B). Lead the end back into the knot alongside the standing part. Double and triple to finish (C).*

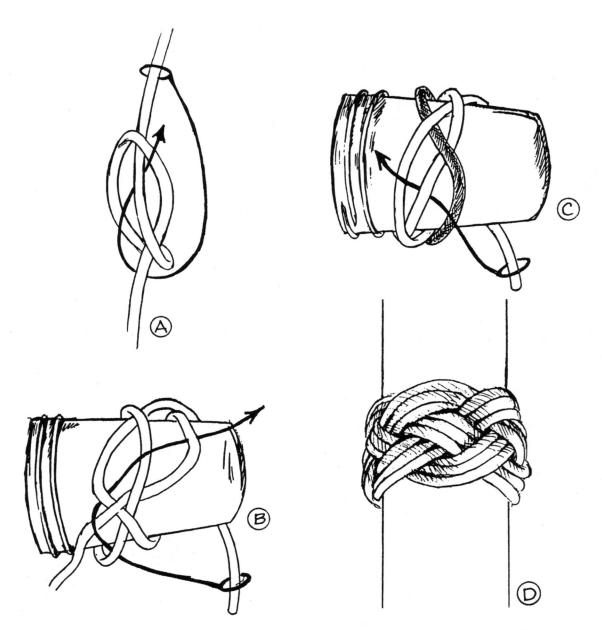

Figure 10-21. *A 4L × 5B Turk's Head. Make an Overhand Knot with the working end leading off to the right. Pass the end down, behind the standing part, then up through the eye of the Overhand Knot and out to the right (A). Slip the evolving knot onto a jar or your hand. Pass the end down behind the jar, back up over the first bight encountered, under the second, and over the standing part to the left. Then pass the end upward to the right, under, over, and under successive sections (B). Important: Note that these sections do not have a regular weave, but pass under or over two parts at a time. By weaving through them as shown you produce a symmetrical weave. Now rotate the knot toward you, and you will find one more series of "bars" (sections that go over and under two at a time). Pass the end over, under, and over as shown (C) to complete the knot. A finished 4L x 5B knot, tripled, is shown in D.*

ing on narrow cylinders such as tool handles and lanyards. It starts with a Constrictor Knot, then the end is passed behind the hand, then under, over, and under, as shown. To finish, take it behind the hand once more, and lead it alongside the standing part, to double and triple.

Four Leads by Five Bights

A handsome knot, and complicated enough to impress the neighbors (Figure 10-21). Start with an Overhand Knot with the end leading off to the right. Pass the end behind the hand, bring it up on the left side of the standing part, and tuck it up to the right, through the center of the Overhand Knot. Rotate the works toward you and tuck the end over and under to the left. Rotate back to where you were, pass the end behind your hand, again on the left side, but this time pass it over the standing part, then under, over, and under as shown. Rotate things toward you again and pass the end over, under, and over to finish.

Building Up

One of the most interesting and least understood features of the Turk's Head is that one can increase the number of leads and bights in a given knot, building it up to make a more complex knot. We've

seen how to increase the number of bights alone, using a 3 × 4 or 3 × 5 knot, but what we're about to do is more involved and results in a much more impressive finished product.

Let's start with a comparison to weaving. Figure 10-22A shows two vertical strands with two horizontal strands woven into them. All the strands follow a regular under-and-over sequence. In Figure 10-22B, a third horizontal strand has been added, but its course duplicates that of the middle strand. As a result, the left vertical strand now follows an under-one-and-over-two sequence, while the right strand goes under two and over one. The symmetry of the weave has been lost. But we can regain it by introducing a fourth horizontal strand (Figure 10-22C) above the third one, in an opposing sequence.

This is essentially the process followed in enlarging Turk's Heads. It's referred to as "splitting the lead"; first you create an asymmetry by leading the end parallel to an existing lead, then you go around again and restore order. The trick is in knowing which lead to parallel, no small matter since the niceties of harmonic sequence must be attended to here as well as in the formation of the knot you enlarge. Typically, writers of knot

Figure 10-22. *A weaving comparison. Four pieces of twine can be arranged in a regular under-and-over weave (A), but introducing a fifth strand between the original horizontal strands makes the weave asymmetrical; the left-hand vertical strand now goes under one and over two, while the right-hand vertical strand goes over one and under two (B). The symmetry of the weave is restored by introducing a sixth strand whose course is opposite that of the fifth strand; once again all strands follow a regular under-and-over sequence (C).*

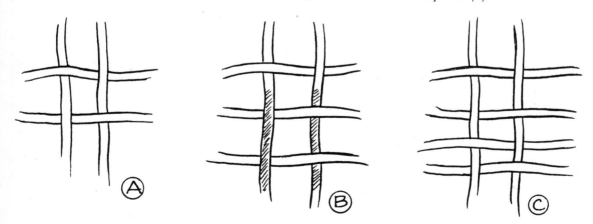

books give specific sets of instructions for enlarging specific starts. This works fine unless they don't describe the one you want to enlarge, or unless you mislay the book. But there is a lead-splitting procedure applicable to any start. To build up any Turk's Head to a larger size:

1. Weave the working end parallel to the previously established lead, but in an opposite over-and-under sequence.

2. Weave parallel to the original lead, with the same over-and-under sequence.

3. Keep the working end either "ahead of" or "behind" (that is, to one side or the other of) the previously established lead. Which one you do depends on the structure of the particular knot and is determined when you begin to split the lead.

For an example, return to the 4L × 3B knot (Figure 10-23). If you trace backward from the working end one full circuit, you will have traced the previously established lead—the last circuit made (shaded line). To split the lead we'll orient to the circuit, going under where it goes over, and vice versa. You'll find that the lead will go under or over two

---

Chinese Good Luck Knot

I have a friend named Joseph Roberts, whose work as a geologist has taken him into the outback, upland, and darkest depths of every continent. Wherever he has gone, he has gained immediate entree to local society by the simple act of approaching the village shaman or equivalent and asking to learn how to tie a knot that brings good luck. And there always is such a knot, and Joseph always picks up another for his collection, and he is always warmly received because he's asking for something simple and nice instead of the shaman's usual diet of requests for love potions, curses on enemies, and relief from colds.

It turns out that just about every basic knot, and quite a few complex ones, are considered good luck by someone, somewhere. Only the Granny and the Hanging Noose stand out as ligaturistically malevolent. It might be argued that most knots are metaphors for luck; that every time you tie a Bowline, or a Butterfly, or a splice, you are engaging in a ritual that speaks to connection, unity, trust.

If that is so, then this particular knot has earned its preeminence as a Good Luck Knot, for it combines an elegant tying procedure, graceful proportions, some utility (it's very secure, but will jam), and a vivid picture of the nature of Good Luck. You'll find front and back views of this knot on this book's frontispiece and endpiece. One side forms a cross, which even in pre-Christian China represented Heaven: linear, yang, to the point. The other side is a square, ancient symbol of Earth: great, broad, enduring. It is in the harmonious interplay of these two profound ideas that good luck arises.

The caption instructions are for a Loop Knot, but the Good Luck Knot can also be made as a bend: Make the round turn with one piece, then weave back and forth with the other piece, under and over, turn, under and under, turn, over and under. Draw up. This bend makes a very handsome knot for a scarf. It is said that the veterans of Trafalgar tied their kerchiefs with it, to let everyone know that they had been there.

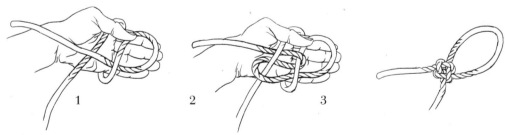

(1) Make a round turn on your hand. Then pick up and form it into a loop on the palm, with the end under its own part and on top of the standing part. (2) Lead the end back under both parts on your palm. Then reverse direction again and lead it over its own part and under the standing part. Remove your hand and draw up carefully, working the square down smaller and smaller (3).

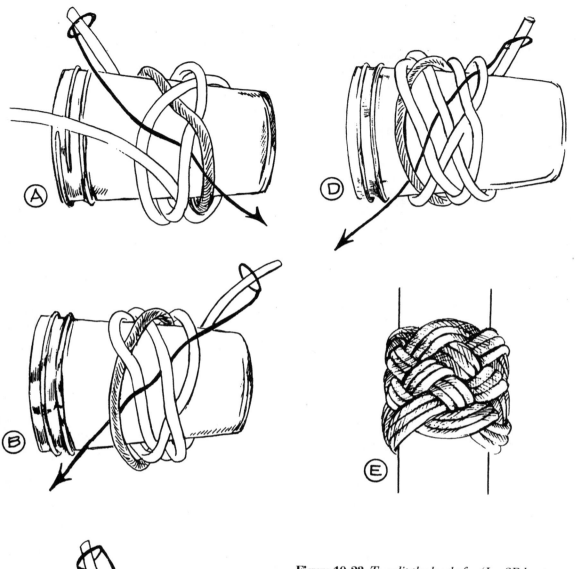

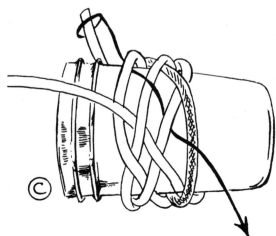

Figure 10-23. *To split the lead of a 4L × 3B knot, pass the working end (arrow) in an opposite pattern to the previous lead (shaded), going over where it goes under and vice versa. Continue following opposite to the previous lead until the end once again meets up with the standing part (C). You'll have a series of "bars"—sections going under two or over two—facing you. Restore symmetry by passing the end under the bars that go under two and over the bars that go over two (C and D). By doing so you're also continuing to travel opposite the previous lead. Double and triple to get the finished knot (E).*

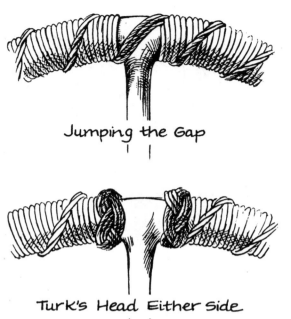

Jumping the Gap

Three-Legged Turk's Head

Turk's Head Either Side

Figure 10-24. *Three answers to the question, "What do you do when you're hitching and reach an intersection of rim and spoke or rail and stanchion?" You can just hitch right by, jumping past the gap, but as Clifford Ashley said, this is "lubberly and not to be countenanced." It looks sloppy, leaves a bare spot, and is an opportunity for slack and snag. Seizing the ends and covering with simple Turk's Heads either side is a satisfactory solution, but for real flair, why not make a Three-Legged Turk's Head? Figure 10-25 shows how.*

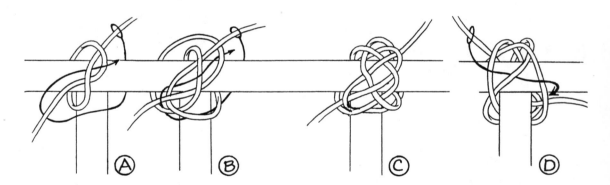

Figure 10-25. *To tie a Three-Legged Turk's Head (4L × 5B), make an Overhand Knot that angles across the T, the end coming out at top right. Pass the end behind the right-hand bar of the T, over the vertical bar from right to left, behind the standing part, then up through the eye of the Overhand Knot (A). Pass the end behind the right-hand bar of the T again, then in front of the upright to the left. Pass it up under, over, under, over, under as shown (B) to arrive at C. To finish, turn the T around and tuck over, under, over (D), and lead the end alongside the standing part for doubling and tripling.*

parts at the edges of the knot in order to continue following opposite to the previous lead. You'll also see that you'll automatically duplicate the weave of the original lead.

When you get back where you started from, you'll see ahead of you a series of "bar" sections that travel either over or under two parts (Figure 10-23C). By continuing to travel as you have, you split these bars, restoring a symmetrical weave. If the bars don't march along in regular sequence, you've distorted the knot while passing the end; fair things up to make the bars appear. If this doesn't work, retie the knot and be more finicky about preserving the pattern.

When you've threaded through all the bars and brought the end in alongside the standing part, you'll have a 6L × 5B knot, ready to be doubled and tripled to finish (Figure 10-23E). Or you can split the lead again and build the knot up even further.

Depending on the dimensions of the Turk's Head, the end can travel on either side of the previous lead, so don't be thrown off by the variation between one knot and another. Just chart your course by the previous lead, keeping to the opposite over-and-under sequence.

The Three-Legged Turk's Head

Here's an odd one to round out your fancy-work vocabulary: a Turk's Head to put at the junction of wheel and spoke (Figure 10-24). It's a 4L × 5B knot made to be three-legged, and it's worth the bother of learning just on the chance that some marling-spike artists will come aboard some day, stare at it in amazement and say, "How did you do that?" That question can gladden the heart, can make you feel as though the eyestrain and tedium were worth the effort.

Come to think of it, there's one question that's even better: Someone looks at a Turk's Head, button, lanyard, or whatever you slaved to finish well, and asks, "But what did you do with the ends?" To which the only reasonable reply is, "I cut them off and threw them away." Never give boring details, however informative, when a smart-ass answer will do just as well.

CHAPTER 11

Tricks and Puzzles

"There ain't no such animal."
—Farmer, on seeing his first giraffe

A good magic trick is about deception on the surface and a sense of wonder at heart. When, after patter and prestidigitation, the magician presents you with an absolute impossibility, you are taken right out of your everyday, everything-has-an-explanation world, if only for a moment.

If you are the magician, and if you're paying any attention to your audience at all, you will find that simply being around delighted, mystified people is far more gratifying than any ego boost you might get from being able to "trick" people. You'll find that the delight is addictive, so you'll practice to make your illusions effortlessly convincing, just to help produce that delight.

Some audiences are kinder than others. If someone is intent on interrupting, trying to expose your technique, they're missing the point; try to see it as their problem. No matter how kind and appreciative an audience is, resist the temptation to repeat these tricks more than once; illusion is a fragile thing.

Yes, I am revealing "how it's done" here, but no, you must not; by some accident of fate you are about to have Great Secrets revealed to you, but I urge you to use them to generate wonder, not deflate it with explanation. As one magician put it, "We do not keep the secrets from you for our sake. We keep them for *your* sake." If someone really wants to know "how it's done," they'll bug you about it for weeks until you give in. But then they'll have earned it, and will be receptive to your admonition "never to share this with another soul."

All of the accompanying string tricks can be performed anytime, anywhere, with no preparation. People expect magic tricks to involve gimmicks, so when you just up and make a miracle, they're doubly delighted. The Professor's Nightmare is the only one of the bunch that requires serious study, but that's only to be expected for a routine that many professional magicians call "the world's greatest string trick." Take your time with it; all by itself, it's worth the price of this book. But only if you do it right.

THE SETUP

You take a piece of line, oh, about 8 feet long. It's ⅛- to ¼-inch three-strand or braided line, not too stiff, a supple, clean tool for magic.

You start talking about the mysteries and profundities of knots, about their vast profusion and universal presence, luring your listeners into a world where knots are so self-evidently magical that you need employ no deceptions to do magic.

As you speak, you casually throw hitches 2 to 3 feet through the air, catching them on your outstretched index finger, hitch after hitch (Figure 11-1). The effect is mesmerizing, surprising.

And then you work into the Grand Theme: We don't understand knots; we use them every day, trust our lives and property to them, know them by reflex, but we do not understand them, no, not even the absurdly simple, elemental Overhand Knot. You tie one, draw it up. It just gets tighter and can't be undone unless you loosen it and pull an end out. You make another, very slowly, explaining in self-evident

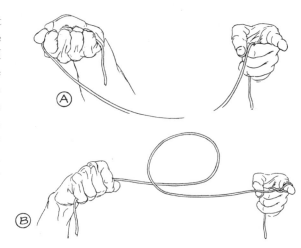

Figure 11-1. *Throwing Hitches. With your right hand grasp one end of a line, standing part emerging between thumb and forefinger. Grasp the standing part about 3 feet away with your left hand, index finger extended. Move your hands apart so the line is just slack, and turn your right hand palm up (A). By flipping your right hand over and moving it slightly to the left, you will form a loop that travels along the standing part (B). Properly aimed, it will land and form a hitch on your extended index finger. Keep throwing hitches until the standing part becomes too short.*

detail that once the end is passed through, that knot is there to stay until it is pulled out. You take this second knot apart and make a third one (Figure 11-2) Those watching will swear it was made just like the others. But this time, after you've drawn it up, you cover it with your hand, apply a little gumption, a dash of mojo, open your hand, and it's *gone*. No, we don't even understand the simplest knots.

Then you lay the line over your hand, and note that the same knot which disappears mysteriously can (flourish of motion) be made to reappear in an instant in the middle of a string. You remove that knot, then with another flourish produce a Slipknot (Figure 11-3). These things can come out of nowhere. With equal facility you produce a Figure-Eight Knot (Figure 11-4), and then a Bowline made out of a Slipknot (see Figure 3-24, in the "Seven Bowlines" section of Chapter 3). That's right, the quintessentially utilitarian must-be-counted-

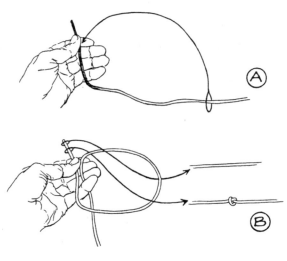

Figure 11-2. *A Vanishing Overhand Knot. Hold the end between your left thumb and forefinger and grasp the standing part a few inches away with your right thumb and forefinger. Both palms face you. Move the hands together, turning the right hand over as you do, and grasp the standing part with your left thumb and forefinger to form a loop (A). If you now reach away from you through the loop with your right hand, grab the end, and pull it out, you'll form an Overhand Knot (B). Keep the two parts pinched in your left hand as you draw up the knot, then display it. If you reach instead through the loop toward you and grasp the end with your right hand, no knot will result, but as you pull the slack out it will look exactly as the Overhand Knot did when it was being drawn up. Cover the "drawn-up" non-knot with your hand and pull theatrically on the end to make it "disappear."*

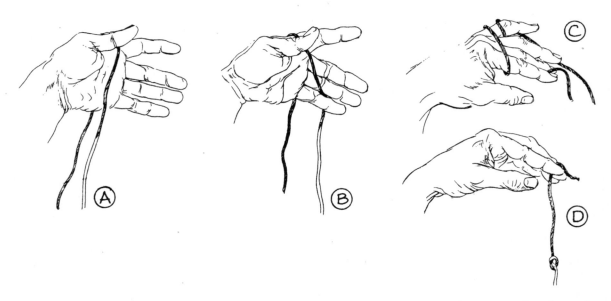

Figure 11-3. *Instant Overhand Knot and Slipknot. Begin with the line draped over your hand, passing between the thumb and forefinger with the end hanging over the back of the hand and extending downward about 1 foot (A). Snag the standing part between pinky and ring finger (B), then reach down sharply and grab as close to the end as you can with your index and middle finger (C). Shake the loop off your hand while holding on to the end and an Overhand Knot will appear (D). The entire maneuver takes less than a second. To produce an instant Slipknot, simply start with the end hanging 2 feet or more below the hand and grasp midway toward it.*

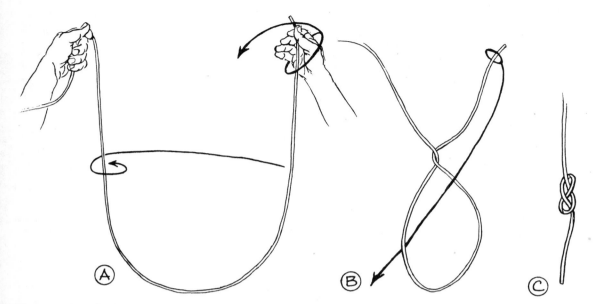

Figure 11-4. *Instant Figure-Eight. Hold the end between the thumb and forefinger of your right hand and grasp the standing part with your left hand so that a long bight hangs between the hands. Drape the rest of the standing part over your left arm or shoulder to keep it out of the way. Move your right hand sharply to the left, causing the bight to twist around into a loop (A). The loop will be held in place by momentum for an instant; throw the end through it with your right hand (B), and a Figure-Eight Knot will appear (C).*

on King of Knots plays tricks with us, too! Or seen another way, the speed and freshness of magic can breathe life and a range of usefulness into the simplest forms of knotting. Ahh, practical magic.

THREADING A RING

But then, lest your audience begin to feel that rope tricks are Logical and Useful, tell them (a) that it is absolutely, positively impossible to thread a solid ring onto a string without passing either end through the ring.

"Impossible? Of course it's impossible," you tell your audience, as you drape your string over your hand.

"The trouble," you continue, picking up a wide, thin ring or bracelet, "is that when you try to put the ring on in the middle, the middle is at the top and the ends are at the bottom. And if I push the middle down to the bottom, the ends just go to the top."

You demonstrate this laying the ring on the string, in the gap between thumb and forefinger, and slowly pushing the ring down (Figure 11-5A). Sure enough, the middle goes down and the ends come up. Repeat this self-evident procedure a couple more times, slowly, with lots of inane, self-evident commentary; you are accustoming your audience to reality.

"So it looks," you say as you begin to press the ring down once more, "as though sometimes the impossible really is impossible, and you'll never get a ring threaded onto the middle of a string. Like this." And with that you take your hand away, and the ring is threaded on to the string (Figure 11-5B).

As you spoke, it turns out, you let the string slip off your thumb, which was hidden by the rest of your hand, which was up near eye level and tilted slightly toward you (Figure 11-5C). Practice in the mirror to get just the right non-suspicion-inducing minimal attitude and amount of tilt. As you passed the ring

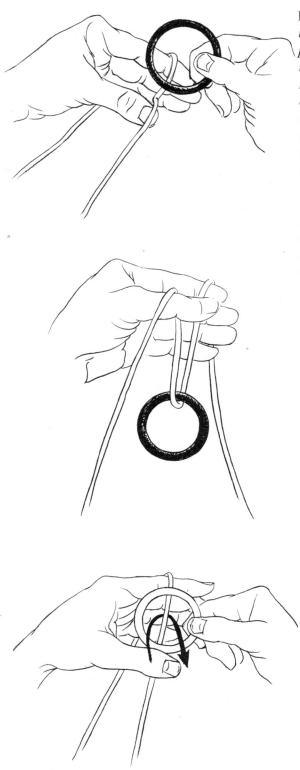

Figure 11-5A–C. *Threading a Ring. Place the ring on the string between thumb and forefinger and begin pushing it down (A). The threaded ring. But how was this accomplished using the hopeless maneuver of Figure 11-5A? The next drawing reveals all (B). Start as in Figure 11-5A, but let the thumb's string fall off, then reach in and re-snag the string from the middle of the slowly descending ring. Practice this move until it's subtle to the point of invisibility when you watch it in a mirror (C).*

down between thumb and index finger, you slipped the tip of the thumb back under the string. A little dexterity is required here so that the ring can continue downward without hesitation. The ends will come up as they have before, but this time one of them will be pulled through the ring on the way up.

THE JUMPING RING

"But some impossible things are possible," you continue. And as you launch into an idiotic monologue on modern physics—Schrodinger's Cat works well here—you tie three Overhand Knots in your 6-foot (1.8-m) string. The first knot is in the middle, the next one a hand's-breadth away, and the third a hand's-breadth beyond that. Slip the ring on, and tie it to the string with the third knot.

"The ring," you announce with exaggerated confidence, "is on the right." Then you pause, appear to consider that statement, then continue with somewhat less confidence. "That is, it's on my right, which is to say it's on your left, right? I mean, well, I'm going to make the ring jump magically to my left, which is stage left, assuming you are the stage. Unless we were both facing the other way, in which case, um. . . ." Confidence is no longer in evidence, but you plunge ahead:

"I'll just put the string behind my back," which you proceed to do, letting go with the hand holding the long end, then reaching behind your back with both hands.

"Now I'll bring the string back out, and—" You stop, hands still behind your back. You fight back panic. You move your arms first one way, then the other, painfully indecisive. "The ring will come out on my, uh, left, which is your right, right?" And you finally bring the string back out and, sure enough, the ring is on your left now because, of course, you switched it while it was hidden, either by turning it over or by simply changing hands.

Before anyone can comment on this obvious, obvious move, you say, "I know, it's amazing, but there's more." You put it behind your back again and say, "Now I'll make it return to your right. No, I mean to my, I'll make, uh. . . ." And while panic returns, you appear to be moving your arms indecisively again and the audience is thinking, "This is funny—is he really that dyslexic?" But while they're laughing, you are quickly and smoothly tying a fourth overhand knot, a hand's-breadth past the third one. It takes only a little practice to be able to do this in the right place without fumbling. The string should need to be out of sight for only four or five seconds.

When you bring the string out again, having once more end-for-ended it, the ring has indeed jumped back to the original side. Your short-end hand covers the new knot—thumb and index finger are all you need. You appear to be very pleased with yourself, and more than a little relieved.

At this point, particularly if your audience contains small children or other snide know-it-alls, someone will proclaim that it's rilly, y'know, a stupid trick, that you just turned the string around when it was hidden.

You are shocked. You are insulted. You are dumbfounded. "How could you think I would do anything so simplistic, so obvious, so easy, so unmagical? You think I just turned it around? Okay then, this time I'll make the ring jump to the middle knot." And with that you whip the string behind your back, grab it by the first-tied knot, and whip it right back out, with no pause at all. This time when you hold it up, the new knot is exposed, and the ring is hanging in the middle.

You have just gone from buffoon to miracle worker. Before your audience can recover, give a wicked smile, stuff string and ring into a pocket,

pick up another piece of string, and prepare to tie an Overhand Knot without letting go of an end, something which is also impossible, so you're going to do it three different ways. One of these is ingenious, the second cheating, and the third is by-God-actual-inexplicable Magic.

OVERHAND KNOT WITHOUT LETTING GO

First, demonstrate that one must indeed let go the end in order to reach around to pass it through the loop; not letting go means, by definition, that no knot will result. But have someone else hold the ends, fold your arms, pick up the ends, then unfold your arms, and an Overhand Knot appears in the middle of the line (Figure 11-6).

That was the ingenious solution. Now explain you're going to use the second method, the one in which you cheat. Be very clear on this point, then immediately explain that you are bound by sacred oath as a member of the FSA (Future Saints of America) to never, ever, cheat, so to preclude any possibility of deception you are going to move very slowly, holding the ends in plain view in your fin-

Figure 11-6. *An Overhand Knot Without Letting Go, First Method. Cross your arms, grasp an end in each hand, and uncross your arms. Presto! An Overhand Knot.*

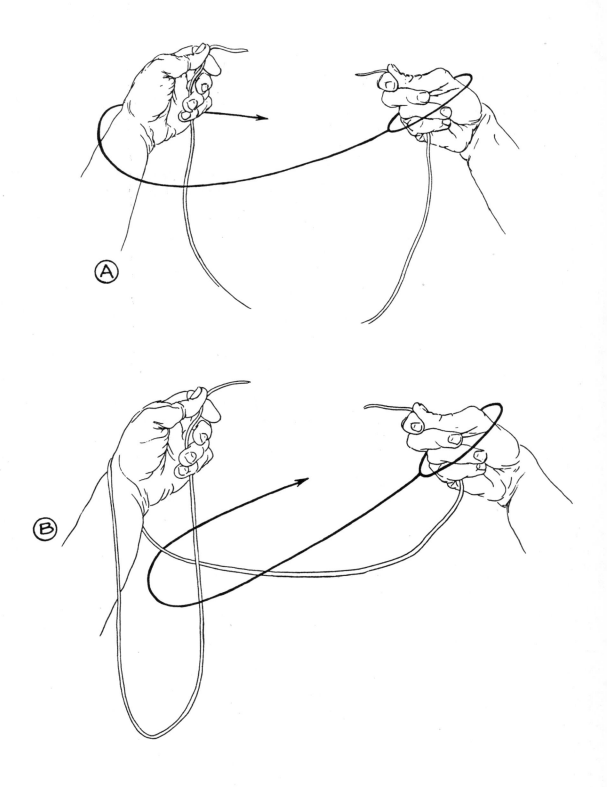

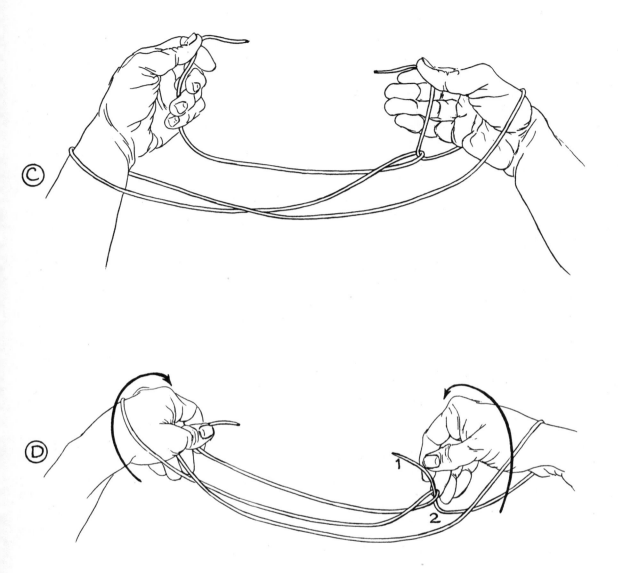

Figure 11-7A–D. An Overhand Knot Without Letting Go, Second Method. Hold an end between the thumb and index fingertips of each hand. A couple of inches of end should be showing, "So you can see the ends," you tell your audience, "at all times." Actually, the arrangement helps you with the trick. Drape the right side of the standing part over your left wrist and move your right hand off to the right side. You'll have a long bight (the longer the better) with a diagonal crossing it (A). Put your right hand in on the left side of the diagonal and bring it out on the right side (B). Move your hands apart and things should look as in C. Drop your hands down while simultaneously turning them inward. As the line falls from your hands the right end (1) will approach the loop at the right side. Let go of the end on one side of the loop and catch it on the other (2). Practice this until the movement is very smooth. An Overhand Knot will appear in the middle of the standing part as you move your hands apart. There'll be a little more end sticking out of your right hand than your left, but since you started with a little end showing, a little extra won't be noticed (D).

gertips at all times. After a simple, easily followed series of moves, during which you reiterate that what you are about to do is impossible, you gently lower your hands, and the knot appears mid-string (Figure 11-7). You repeat, invite volunteers to try, even tie along with them simultaneously. It only works for you. "One of us is cheating, and it certainly isn't me," you note, "so you should just be ashamed of yourself."

While they are apologizing for their dishonest behavior, you prepare for the third method, the Mobius Overhand, getting out a 3-foot by 4-inch piece of paper—newspaper is handy—you twist an end one-and-a-half times, then tape the two ends together to form a circle. You can have someone else do this if you like, so that everyone is sure there is no trickery.

Now produce a pair of scissors and ask rhetorically what would happen if you were to cut length-

Figure 11-8. *The Mobius Overhand. Take a long strip of paper or cloth—about 3 feet by 4 inches. Twist one end one-and-a-half times, then tape the two ends together. If you now cut the resulting loop lengthwise, you will get, contrary to all rational expectation, a single loop with an Overhand Knot tied in its length. Real magic.*

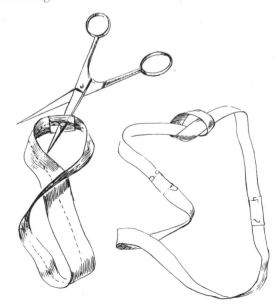

wise along the entire circle; it's obvious that you'll end up with two separate circles. But when you—or someone else—makes the cut, something entirely unexpected and inexplicable happens: you get a single, large circle, with ("Twilight Zone" theme music) an Overhand Knot tied in its length (Figure 11-8). This Mobius-strip variant is real magic, a jolt to the mind and somewhat unnerving, so put it away and return to silliness.

THE CUT-AND-RESTORED STRING

Tell your audience that the best-known rope trick is the cut-and-restored string. This is old hat for you, so you're a little bored as you demonstrate how one can cut a line in the middle and restore it to a single piece (Figure 11-9). It's simple mechanics, you say: Cutting the string in half produces four ends, which necessarily means two pieces, right? So by cutting off one end and throwing the other away, you're back to two ends, thus one piece. It's simple. You, of course, do not do simple cut-and-restored tricks, but you did once learn how to splice with your tongue.

It all started when you were sailing off the coast of (your preference) in company with a wise old salt and a few other friends. You were sitting a little to windward as the old man declaimed upon the necessity for resourcefulness at sea. "Every thumb a marlingspike," he intoned, "and every hair a rope yarn"—a classic saying that, due to the noise of the wind, came to your ears as, "Every tongue a marlingspike to repair a rope yarn." It made no sense, but everyone else was nodding sagely, so you nodded sagely too, suddenly convinced that any real sailor could make a splice using tongue for spike.

People do silly things out of pride, and you were no exception. You began furtively to practice this impossible feat, sitting in darkened closets with string in your mouth. Accidentally discovered, you explained that you were using very large dental floss because your teeth are widely spaced. Your tongue became callused, you grew depressed, certain that you'd never be a real sailor.

And then one day you heard of Swami Seezanahta, the world's leading exponent of Knot

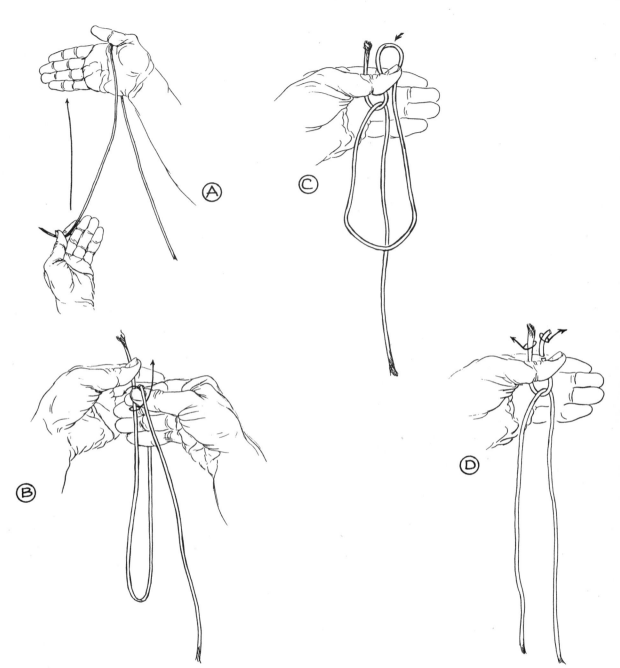

Figure 11-9. *Cut-and-Restored String. Middle a line and hang it over your right hand. Pick up the nearer end with your left hand and move the two hands together (A). Seeming to place the middle bight of the line alongside the end in your left hand, you actually let the bight slip off your right hand as you raise a "false middle"—a bight brought up from the left end (B). Cut this bight at its middle (C), drop the right end down, and you will appear to have two equal-length pieces of line (D). With scissors, cut the right upper end close to your fingers, then "throw the other end away." Before, you had four ends, thus two pieces; now you have only two ends, thus one piece, or so the patter goes as you show the one whole piece.*

Figure 11-10A–D. *Splicing with Your Tongue. Make a circle in string and hold it as shown (A). Bring your hands together and double the circle—but with a twist, which results in a couple of interlocked bights hidden behind your left hand. Hold the doubled line with an unsuspiciously small space between your hands, and have a spectator cut the cord there (B). Put the cut section into your mouth and pretend to work real hard at splicing with your tongue; in fact, work the short bit into one cheek (C). After suitable patter and facial gymnastics, pull out the miraculously restored string (D).*

Yoga. You asked spiritually inclined friends what they thought of him, and were heartened when they said, "What he does is definitely not yoga." You sought him out, gained an audience, and told him of your problem.

"Technique alone is not enough for this difficult thing," he said. "You must have help from the cosmic healing power of the circle." You learned to make a circle and double it to multiply its power, so that when you cut the string and put the two pieces into your mouth, cosmic forces aid you (Figure 11-10). You demonstrate now, making a tapered Long Splice no less, carefully trimming the ends off flush, a real sailor at last.

But enough of mysticism. Now it's time for a little routine that some very good magicians have called "The World's Greatest String Trick."

THE PROFESSOR'S NIGHTMARE

"Sometimes, even when a thing's possible, it's impractical," you begin. "For instance, if I were a very logical, educated person—say, a math professor—and I had to cut this string into three equal pieces, I'd probably measure the overall length, divide by three, make my marks at the appropriate spots, and cut." You pantomime all this with great solemnity.

"But that's so time-consuming, when all you have to do is hold the ends and fold the string in thirds." And here, you hold the string with about 2 inches of end projecting between thumbs and forefingers (Figure 11-11A). Then you reach across with each ring and little finger, snag the line under the opposite hand, and move your hands apart (Figure 11-11B).

"Quick and easy, right? Now you just cut the line where it is bent." And here you let go with your right hand and appear to bring "the line where it's bent" up alongside the end in your left hand. Then you cut it with a sharp pair of scissors. But there's a deception here. What you actually do, with a smoothness born of long practice, is to bring up a bight of line from near the end (Figure 11-11C). The real "bend" is hidden behind your hand (Figure 11-11D). So when you cut, you're only snipping a short piece off the end. There's a bend at the bottom, and you reach down and cut that for real. The original bottom end might be hanging down a little, but you trim it to match the others, saying, "Hey, so what, college professors just don't know how to be expedient."

You now appear to have three equal-length pieces, but you're not through with pedagogues yet: "A professor would probably say something like, 'A' is the same as 'B', and 'B' is the same as 'C', so 'C' is the same as 'A.' Or something ponderous like that. But in the real world, all you gotta know is that all the ends are the same length. The top three here are even, and so are the bottom three. If the ropes are the same length, they stop at the same place. Simple."

Just to emphasize, you bring up the lower three ends, one at a time, and lay them alongside the others in your fingertips (Figure 11-11E).

"See? All even. So we don't need any formulas." And with that, you grab the second, third, and fourth ends from the left with your right hand, yank them out, and present three straightened pieces with a flourish.

"Yessir, three equal-len—whaaa?"

Panic returns. You are holding a long, a medium, and a short piece in your hand (Figure 11-11F). You are as amazed as your audience is.

"But the ends were the same length—I saw

them, they were—did you see them? Well, just wait a minute, let's back up here."

With your left hand you take one piece at a time from your right, with slow, hypnotic movements, "A long, a medium, and a short." With your right hand you take them back again, "short, medium, long." And again.

You point to the pieces now lined up in your left hand. "A professor would say that 'A' is longer than 'B', which is longer than 'C.' It's all very logical. But all the ends were the same length." As you speak, you pick up the bottom end of the longest piece, which should be farthest from your fingertips. You bring it up behind the medium piece and appear to set it in place outside the short piece (Figure 11-11G). But you actually set it to the left of the short piece. It's an easy sleight. It helps to look up and catch your audience's eye as you do it. It also helps to practice the move until you can fool yourself in a mirror.

Now you bring up the medium end and lay it outside the others, then the short end. Note that the short piece passes behind the folded long piece (Figure 11-11H).

Time for another crucial move. You bring your right hand up so that it overlaps your left hand, grasp the three rightmost ends, and move your hands slightly apart (Figure 11-11I). It will look exactly as though the long, medium, and short pieces were draped between your hands. In reality, you'll have both ends of the short piece and one end of the medium piece in your right hand, and both ends of the long piece and one end of the medium piece in your left hand. More mirror time here, so you can bring this off casually without exposing the interlock hidden by your right hand.

"We have a long, a medium, and a short," you continue, "but common sense tells us that if the ends are the same length, the pieces are the same length."

And with that you move your hands smoothly apart, snapping the strings between them smartly as they fetch up. Then you let go with your left hand and hold up the miraculously restored three medium-length pieces (Figure 11-11J).

Resuming your hypnotic examination movements, you reach across with your left hand and

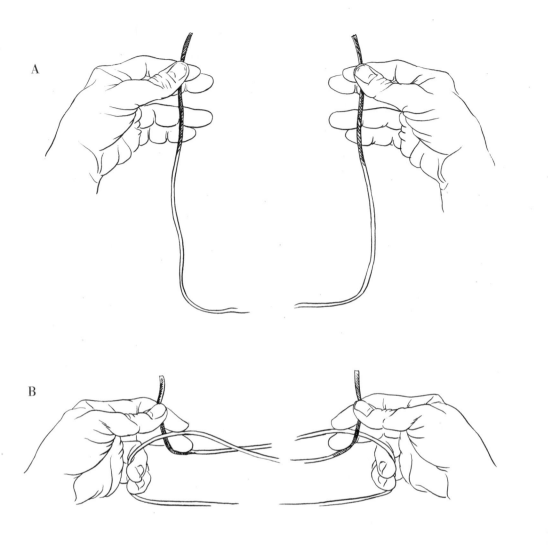

A

B

Figure 11-11A–C. *The Professor's Nightmare. Start with the ends of a 6-foot piece of string held lightly in your fingertips, ends projecting (A). Bring your hands together and snag opposite standing parts with the ring and little fingers of each hand. Move hands apart. As string goes taut, insert middle fingers as shown (B). Let go with one hand and use it to bring up the part that leads from the end on the other hand. Here we show the hands open for clarity; but in performance this move is concealed by the fingers of the left hand (C).*

C

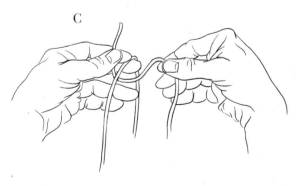

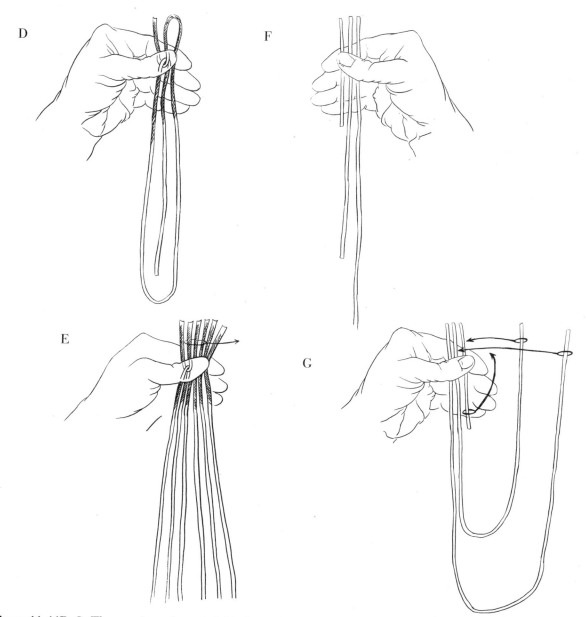

Figure 11-11D–G. *The part brought up is laid alongside the end and pinched between your fingertips. To viewers, it looks like the bight one-third along the length of the string, which is actually hidden (D). Cut the "false" bight, trimming the top ends the same length if necessary. Cut the bottom bight, too, and trim the ends. Then bring up the three bottom ends (to the right in this view) to display alongside the top ends. "All ends are the same length, so the pieces are the same length." Grab the three indicated ends and pull them out of your hand (E). Somehow, the ends are not the same length. Arrange as shown in right hand, "short, medium, and long" (F). After thoroughly displaying the three different lengths, hold them in your left hand in the order shown. Bring up the bottom end of the long piece and lay it between the short and medium pieces. Practice diligently to make this a smoothly deceptive move. Then bring up the other two ends and lay them alongside the short piece (G).*

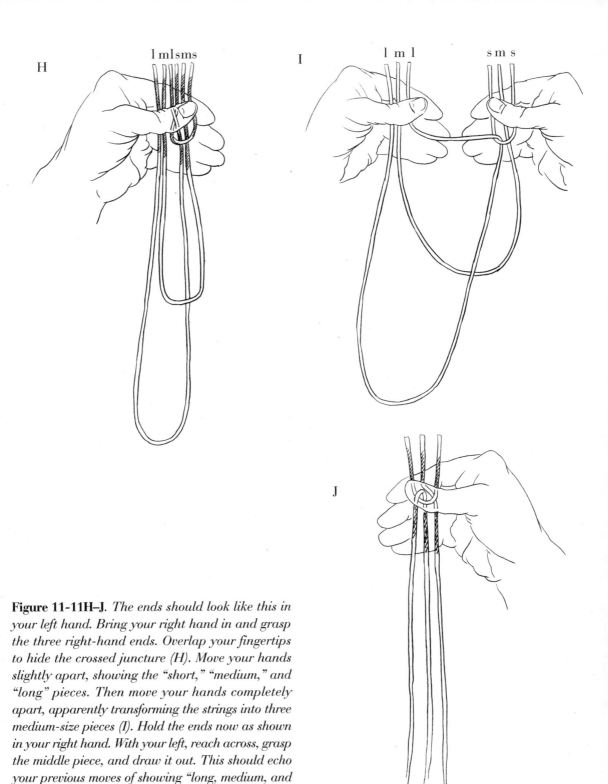

Figure 11-11H–J. *The ends should look like this in your left hand. Bring your right hand in and grasp the three right-hand ends. Overlap your fingertips to hide the crossed juncture (H). Move your hands slightly apart, showing the "short," "medium," and "long" pieces. Then move your hands completely apart, apparently transforming the strings into three medium-size pieces (I). Hold the ends now as shown in your right hand. With your left, reach across, grasp the middle piece, and draw it out. This should echo your previous moves of showing "long, medium, and short" (J).*

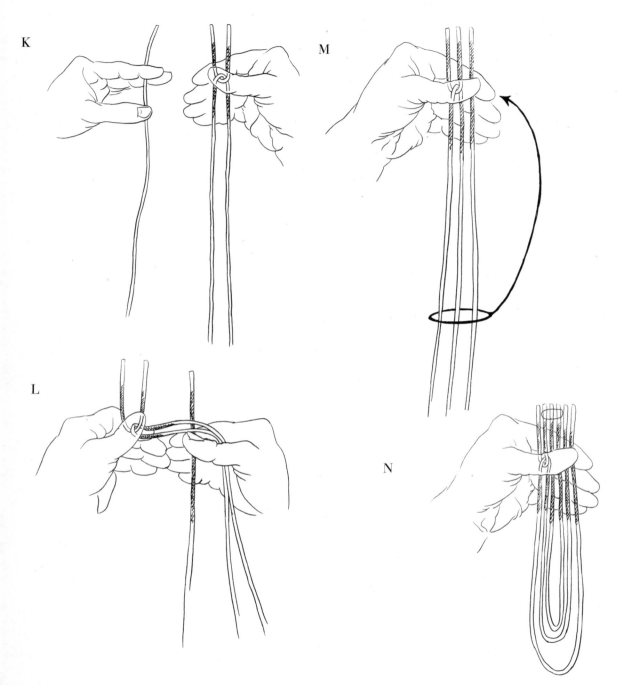

Figure 11-11K–N. *Shifting the real medium piece between the left index and middle fingers, reach across again. Transfer the medium piece to the right hand as you grasp the other two ends with the left thumb and forefinger (K). Draw the other two ends away, leaving the real medium piece behind. "Two medium pieces," you say. Then make a third pass to draw away the real medium piece again. "Three medium pieces (L)." To finish, bring all six ends up into left hand again (M). Finally, grab the indicated ends and yank them out. The pieces will be restored to short, medium, and long (N).*

take the middle end, the actual medium-length piece, and draw it out (Figure 11-11K). Move just fast enough, and the audience will not notice that it isn't one of the end pieces. As you bring it out, you say, "One medium piece."

Now for the final tricky move. As you reach back toward your right hand, you shift the medium piece to pinch it between your left index and middle fingers (Figure 11-11L). It's a very subtle move. When you bring your hands together, your left thumb and index fingers grasp the other two ends and your right thumb and index fingers grasp the medium piece. You draw out the two ends, the interlock hidden behind your left hand, and leave the medium piece behind.

"Two medium pieces," you say, and it looks indeed as though you'd simply pulled out a second medium piece. It's impossible, but the audience sees it happen. Now you reach across, again, and draw away the real medium piece once more, saying, "And three medium pieces."

To finish, you once again bring the bottom ends up one at a time, and lay them alongside the upper ends (Figure 11-11M).

"But because we live in a world where professors have to make a living, too"—you grab the second, third, and fourth ends from the left (Figure 11-11N) and yank them out—"We also have"—once more with the hypnotic moves—"a long, a medium, and a short."

Applause, applause.

TOPOLOGICAL BONDAGE

Get a couple of volunteers to join you to figure out a little puzzle. Ideally they are slightly infatuated, easily embarrassed, and not-quite-comfortable with each other. Tell them that the name of this puzzle is Topological Bondage. Restrain them from leaving. Tie the hands of each together with a 3-foot length of line, the two lines crossing (Figure 11-12). Use loose Bowlines around the wrists so that they can get out if they need or want to. ("Now remember, if at any time this gets to be too much for you, you can slip the loops off, bury your face in your hands, and

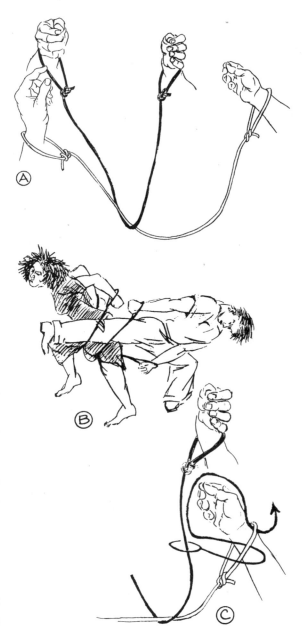

Figure 11-12. *Topological Bondage. Two interlocked ropes bind two volunteers together. The puzzle is to get separated without untying the Bowlines, removing them from wrists, or cutting the cords (or arms). The search for a solution can lead to some creative contortions, but the solution is topological: Pass a bight from one side out through a wrist loop of the other side, over the hand, and back under the wrist loop (C). Sweet.*

run weeping from the room. Fair enough?") Their arms and lines now form two interlocked circles. The challenge is to get separated without untying the knots, removing the loops from their wrists, or severing either the line or their limbs. Anything else is legal, and there is a solution. Explain that if they succeed, everyone watching will be filled with awe and admiration, but if they fail they will be laughed at, not with. Having thus reassured them, you tell them to begin.

If you've chosen your volunteers well, and if those in the audience help by suggesting techniques, you will now be treated to a randy acrobatic spectacle, a series of contortions and intertwinings that look like the Kama Sutra according to Robin Williams. It may be necessary to disentangle the subjects from time to time before you mercifully step in and pass a bight through one of the wrist loops. I call the trick Topological Bondage because it's a perfect example of the main reason knots aren't understood: We assume we understand them, so we limit their range of expression. This particular trick, by the way, has an application in the real world when you want to drop a mooring eye over a piling or bitt that is already occupied by another eye. With yours on too, the other eye, which might belong to another vessel, can't be removed without first removing yours. But if you thread your eye up through the other before putting it over the piling, either one can be removed without disturbing the other. This works for any number of eyes.

But we're sneaking back into practicality here. Time for a less dramatic topological interlude.

THE MOBIUS BOWLINE

The Bowline is such a friendly, familiar knot, but do we really know it? Take out a prepared line, with an eyesplice in one end, in which you've already tied a Mobius Bowline (left, Figure 11-13). Tie the end to a rail or such, and challenge anyone to untie the knot without undoing the end. Potential puzzle-solvers can do anything they want except untie either end. Be prepared to step in, untangle, and retie; people can get carried away.

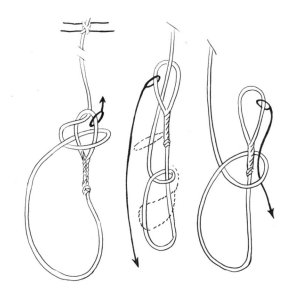

Figure 11-13. *Untying the Mobius Bowline, a topological adventure.*

The solution, as you can see (Figure 11-13), is quite simple: Loosen the turn at the top of the knot, pull it down, pass the body of the knot through it, and you have a Slipknot which can easily be straightened out.

When someone does manage to untie the knot, they will have displayed rare topological ability; be sure to congratulate them. Then invite them to retie it.

By the by, this genetically altered third cousin to a Bowline on a Bight is good for more than giggles; if, as the drawings show, the small eye at the end is spliced, you can make a loop knot that will always stay tied, even in the most slick, springy, jerked-upon line, and yet is easily tied, untied, and adjusted in size just like a regular Bowline.

CIRCLING THE WORLD

And now a brief interlude while you rest your fingers. Regard your bit of string contemplatively, and relate to your audience the following:

Imagine a string tied around the Earth at the equator. Call the Earth's diameter at this point an even 8,000 miles. How much longer would the string need to be in order to be 1 foot above the Earth's surface all the way around?

The amazing answer is: 6 feet 3⅜ inches!

Here's the math: A circle's circumference is its diameter multiplied by π (3.14159. . .). 8,000 miles × π = approximately 25,000 miles. To get the string a foot off the surface all the way around, you just add 2 feet to the diameter (a foot at either end). The diameter is now 8,000 miles plus 2 feet, and π × 2 feet is 6.283 feet or 6 feet 3⅜ inches. If you want to work it out in big numbers, 8,000 miles is 42,240,000 feet (8,000 × 5,280). Eight thousand miles plus 2 feet is 42,240,002 feet. The circumference of the second is 132,700,873.7 feet. The difference between the two, somehow, against all intuitive math, is 6.283 feet, or 6 feet 3⅜ inches. I don't know about you, but no matter how painstakingly and exhaustively I prove it, my brain says, "It just can't be so." Go figure.

THREADING THE NEEDLE

Back into action for you now. Start by talking about the importance of dexterity in pulling these tricks off. Magicians, you note, are fond of saying that the hand is quicker than the eye, but they usually don't explain how to train a hand for such speed. But you can let your audience in on a little exercise called

Threading the Needle, using the long piece from the Professor's Nightmare.

Wrap the string around your thumb, from the base out, making the turns come toward you over the top of the thumb (Figure 11-14A); 4 feet (1.2m or so) of the end hangs down below your hand. After you put on eight to ten turns, bring up a bight, with the end on the inside (away from your fingertips), and pinch it between your thumb and index finger at their very tips.

"Now, this is just a beginner's exercise," you explain. "When you get really good, you can thread a sewing machine while it's running. But this is a good start. See, I'm going to pick up this end here"—and you pick up the end you left hanging down at the beginning of the turns—"and thread it through this little-bitty eye, so it'll look just like this"—and here you slowly thread it through the eye, which is just barely big enough for the line—"only I'm going to do it faster than you can see, so fast that I need all these extra turns here to keep the string from

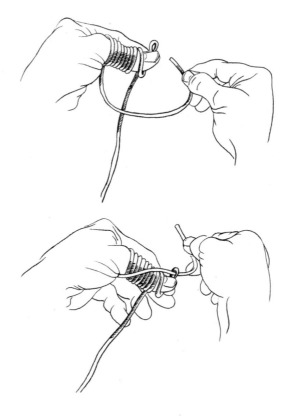

Figure 11-14A–B. *Threading the Needle. Wrap the string onto your thumb starting with the end hanging down 4 or 5 inches. Make the turns with the standing part coming toward you over the top of the thumb. Bring up a little bight of the standing part after you have enough turns, give it a half-turn counterclockwise, and pinch it with the long end innermost from your thumb and forefinger tips. Pick up the short end and make as though to thread it through the small bight with lightning speed . . . (A) . . . but instead simply pull the end taut. This will cause one of the turns to fly off the base of your thumb and emerge in the little bight. It looks exactly as though you've threaded a needle at impossible speed (B).*

flying out of my hands. When I'm through, it'll look just like this"—and after threading it through, you grab the end and pull it taut, so it looks like Figure 11-14B.

The scene set, you take the end back out of the eye, grasp it once more near its end, and commence a squinty-eyed, ludicrously intense warmup-and-taking-aim ritual. Then in a Bruce Lee-like blur of motion (Bruce Lee-like sound effects are a nice touch, too) you shoot your right hand forward. And sure enough, you've threaded the eye at impossible speed.

Or so it appears. What has actually happened is that as the line came taut, the first turn automatically undid itself and was yanked up into the eye. Play with it, and you'll see what I mean. No digital dexterity required. But you don't tell that to your audience. And you don't do this trick anywhere near a sewing machine.

THE GOOD OLD ACTUAL INDIAN ROPE TRICK

"But enough of puzzles and deceptions," you say, "it's time for some real magic. During one of my trips to India" (pause to glare at scoffers, unless you happen to have been to India, in which case they actually might believe what you're about to say), "high up in the Himalayas. . . ." And you go on to some unlikely meeting with a swami who taught you the famous Indian Rope Trick, wherein "an ordinary piece of cordage can be made to stand vertically."

Pick up your much-used big piece of string, hold one end with one hand, and slide your other hand up to the other end, stretching the string out vertically. You do this after having entered a deep trance, of course, and you accompany your moves with a semi-intelligible mantra.

You pause a moment in silence, string held taut, intense concentration etching your features. Then you let go with your upper hand, and the string collapses.

Hmmm. After a moment's puzzlement, you resume your chant, louder and even less intelligi-

bly, and slowly stretch the string taut once more. Another pause, you let go, and . . . it collapses again.

Consternation. Then your face brightens—you have remembered the secret. You repeat your actions and mantra again and then you let go again. With your bottom hand.

"Heh, heh, heh."

THE LOVERS

After that last one, you'd be well-advised to go out with a kinder, gentler trick. This can be a sweet one.

Once upon a time there was a sailor, and a woman who loved him, and he her, and they knew their love would stay. But her father only wished he would stay away. Couldn't see his daughter paired up with someone who couldn't keep his feet on solid ground. The haberdasher's clerk down to the village was the father's sensible choice for a spouse-to-be. The clerk was dull, bony, and his nose tended to drip, but he was steady, moderate, and agreed with the father's political views.

Neither father nor clerk was particularly bright, but synergy plays no favorites, and between them they came up with a clever plan to remove the sailor from the scene: A contest would be held to win the woman's hand. The winner would be the one who could tie the most Overhand Knots while the father counted to 60. The sailor, who like all sailors prided himself to vain excess on proficiency in ropework, would surely accept. But the clerk, whose package-wrapping duties involved a very few simple knots, had been motivated by brisk business and impatient customers to learn to tie those knots very, very fast, and in string, which sailors rarely touch. Sure enough, the sailor promptly accepted the challenge, and the woman, confident in her Jack's ability, agreed to abide by the results.

The day of the contest came, half the town it seemed turned out to watch, the two contestants were each given a length of string, and the father began to count.

The clerk began tying Overhand Knot after Overhand Knot with such celerity that it was

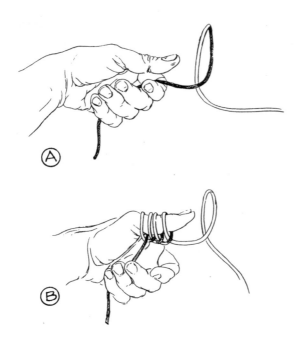

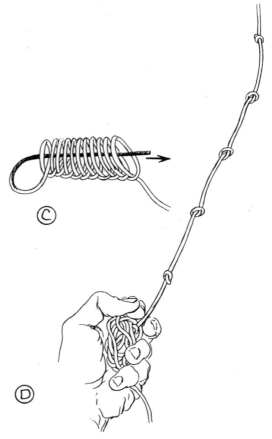

Figure 11-15. *How the Sailor Made Many Knots in Little Time. He made many Half Hitches on his thumb (A,B), passed the left end through all the Half Hitches (C), gently cradled the hitches in one hand, and pulled handsomely on the end with his other hand (D). End of contest.*

thought he might run out of string before the time was up. Flying fingers.

The sailor, meanwhile, began methodically looping Half Hitches around one thumb (Figure 11-15A, B). Now, a half hitch is a fine knot with many uses, but it is not an Overhand Knot and never will be. The count went past 30 and he still hadn't tied anything but a lot of hitches (he had a long piece of string and great large thumbs). The count went past 40 without a single Overhand Knot, and his sweetheart can be forgiven for tearfully wondering if this was a particularly inelegant way of skipping out on her.

There was an exultant tone in the father's voice as the count neared 50, and the clerk had just about given off trying to make any more knots, when the sailor gently removed the hitches from his thumb, threaded the end through them, pulled on it handsomely, which at sea means slowly and carefully, and a plentitude of Overhand Knots emerged like pearls from his hand (Figure 11-15C, D). He tied the string around his true love's throat as a necklace, they tied the archetypal knot the very next day, and they both lived happily ever after.

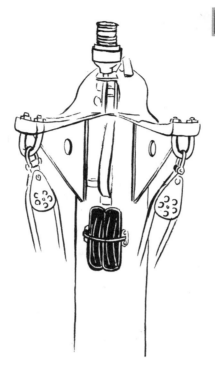

CHAPTER 12

Sheer Ingenuity

"I'd rather make it up than look it up!"

—*Lavinia Jordan*

Nothing brings out creative drive like a length of rope, a bit of hardware, and a pressing need either to move something or keep it from moving. People have been facing the endless permutations of this challenge for thousands of years, and they're still coming up with innovative responses.

Every idea in every preceding chapter is a result of this process, but they were all organized (I hope) into a more-or-less rational order, like a well-laid-down toolbox. But I'd like to close with a chapter that's more like the "unconscious drawer" in your house. It's the one crammed with electrical tape, paper clips, screws, nails, Christmas tree lights, Vise Grips, candles, and bottle openers. Yes, it's a jumble, but odds are you'll find what you need when you go there.

Likewise, I urge you to cultivate an unconscious drawer in your shop, and in your mind, for all those odd bits with no immediately apparent use that might someday come in handy. By all means, strive for order and sensibility, but remember the words of von Clausewitz, "A plan of battle never survives contact with the enemy." Like all arts, rigging is an attempt to finesse coherence out of ornery chaos, and the strangest things can save the day. Fill that drawer; you'll find what you need when you open it.

TIE-DOWNS

Unless you want things to flap, flutter, shred, hum, fall, get lost, or sunburned, you'll need to learn all about tie-downs.

Tarp Tie-down
If you haul your boat for the winter, it is prudent to drape a tarp over it to keep out the elements. But how do you keep the tarp from flapping in the breeze, eventually shredding itself to pieces after beating your topsides to death? Simply cinching the tie-down lines supertight is usually not enough; the rope stretches over time, and in any event can overstrain the tarp grommets.

But if you interject strips of inner tube between the tie-downs and the plank they belay to, you'll have a resilient configuration that can compensate for rope stretch and wind, without creating excess tension.

Wind and Tie-down Straps
Anytime a trailer tie-down strap is over space—as between the gunwales of an open boat—it will flutter and hum in the wind, greatly shortening strap life. To lessen this, give the strap a half twist where it crosses open space.

Figure 12-1. *A resilient tarp tie-down.*

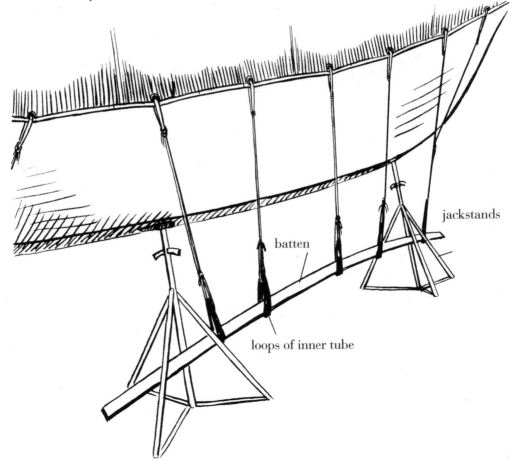

jackstands

batten

loops of inner tube

Moving along to bound feet, we come to what might be the best-known knot of all, the Bowknot, with which most people tie their shoelaces. I say "most" because this relative of the Square Knot is often mis-tied into a relative of the (shudder) Granny Knot. If your shoes have laces, look at them now. Assuming undoubled knots, if the bows sit athwartshoe, they're Square; if fore-and-aft, Granny. Aside from superior appearance, the Square version offers superior security. If you've been tying the Granny, the easiest way to switch is to reverse the way you tie the Overhand Knot that is the first half of the Bowknot, then make the bow part as you always have. The new method will be second nature in no time.

Even a properly made Bowknot is no paragon of security, especially in slick modern laces, or even in new leather ones. The usual way to improve security is to make an extra Overhand Knot with the bights. The result is secure but can be hard to untie when wet and is about as attractive as a hose clamp. The Turquoise Turtle Knot is a handsome alternative—simple, always easy to untie with a pull on the ends, and very easy to remember. Start with the usual Overhand Knot, but pass an end around a second time. Make the loops as usual, but leave a little space between them and the Overhand Knot. Pass the end and loop on one side through this space. Draw up as you usually would, by pulling on the loops. When untying, just be sure that the ends haven't fallen through their loops. If they have, pull them clear, then pull the ends apart as usual to untie.

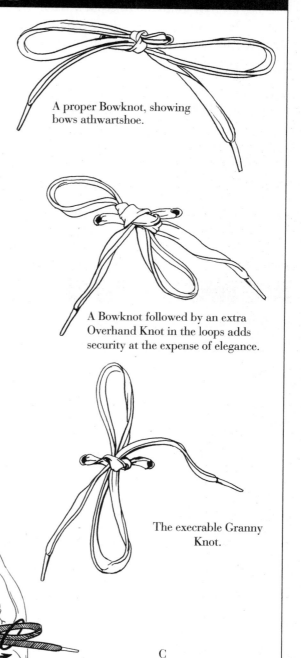

A proper Bowknot, showing bows athwartshoe.

A Bowknot followed by an extra Overhand Knot in the loops adds security at the expense of elegance.

The execrable Granny Knot.

A

B

The Turquoise Turtle Knot.

C

371

Sun and Tie-down Straps

Braided tie-down straps are susceptible to damage from sunlight. As with all regularly exposed plastic items, inspect them regularly for signs of discoloration and brittleness.

Belay Aids

Whether you're pulling a stump, reinforcing mooring lines to prepare for a hurricane, or dragging a boat up the beach on its cradle, this setup will give you a firm anchor when there's no convenient tree and you're fresh out of piledrivers.

To make, drive two long stakes, crowbars, or what-have-yous into the ground, ideally at a right angle to the direction of the pull (Figure 12-2). Set a stout log or beam behind them. If the latter, round the corners so the line won't chafe. Drive two

Figure 12-2. A firm anchor.

Plywood Sling

Ever had to carry a sheet of plywood? It forces you into a wrist-twisting, view-obscuring, back-straining, top-heavy carrying position. If that doesn't appeal to you, make up a sling about 8½ to 9 feet (2.6 m to 2.8 m) long, with an Eyesplice or Bowline at either end. Slip an eye over each bottom corner. Grasp the middle of the sling with one hand and rest the other hand on the top edge of the plywood. *That's* how to do it.

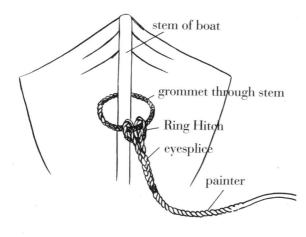

stem of boat

grommet through stem

Ring Hitch

eyesplice

painter

Figure 12-3. A removable painter.

more stakes in right behind, then two more a little farther back.

Lash the back stakes to the middle ones, and then lash the middle ones to the front ones. Working in this order will help assure that the load will be more evenly shared among the stakes.

If you have spare stakes, no harm in driving four or five sets. But beyond that you're probably better off setting up an entirely separate additional anchor.

DINGHIES AND TENDERS

Protect your dinghies and tenders with a removable painter, distribute strain and save your transom.

Painter without Hardware

For a pram painter, bore a hole in the forward transom just large enough to accept the rope. Bore a second hole in the knee that supports the forward transom. Lead the painter through both holes, after fairing the edges so the wood won't cut the rope, then make a Figure-Eight Knot or button knot (Ashley's 880 is perfect, see Chapter 4) in the end of the rope. You now have a painter that is ultimately strong and secure, without buying and installing any hardware. And the painter can be instantly removed, in case you need to use the line for something else.

Grommet and Painter

For painters that go to a ring or a hole in the boat's stem, the usual practice is to splice an eye through the ring or hole. But this means that the painter cannot be removed for other purposes without cutting off the splice. So instead, make a grommet through the hole (see Chapter 6, Figure 6-43), then Ring-Hitch the spliced painter to that (Figure 12-3). Alternatively, install a soft shackle, and secure it to an eyesplice on the end of the painter.

Towing Bridle

When towing large rowing craft, particularly in a chop, the painter can put an excessive strain on the stem. For this situation, make a bridle that runs from a forward oarlock, out through the painter grommet in a bight, then back to an oarlock on the other side (Figure 12-4). This distributes the strain over more of the hull. Seize, knot, or Brummel the eye at the middle of the painter, so it will hold even if one side of the bridle pulls out or chafes through.

Diagonal Towing

In light airs, a dinghy towed astern will often "run up" on its tow and smack it in the transom, due to wave action. To prevent this, lead the painter

Figure 12-4. Strain distribution.

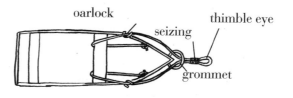

oarlock

seizing

thimble eye

grommet

Figure 12-5. Protect your transom.

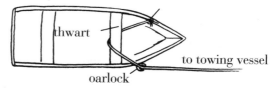

painter belayed to rail

thwart

to towing vessel

oarlock

to a forward thwart (Figure 12-5). This will cause the dinghy to angle out to the side, away from the transom. Adjust the lead forward or aft for the ideal angle at a given rate of travel.

MOORING AND ANCHORING

Don't run aground or drift away—learn proper mooring and anchoring techniques.

Tom Cook's Internal Bungee Snubber

Prudent sailors know the importance of a gentle "snubbing" action on mooring lines, to keep a boat from fetching up with a jerk in wave action. Slamming is hard on deck fittings, on dock fittings, and on the comfort of anyone aboard. It also leads to excess wear on mooring lines You can buy bulky, expensive rubber sausages that the mooring line wraps around to solve this problem, but light- to medium-displacement craft are better off with an Internal Bungee Snubber (Figure 12-6).

The brainchild of Seattle-ite Tom Cook, this snubber is simple, durable, won't foul on chocks and hawses, and can be coiled down with the mooring line. To make it, start with a 2- to 3-foot length of bungee cord that is half the diameter of the three-strand rope. The idea is to insert the bungee cord in the rope at any convenient point along its length. Untwist the strands of the rope enough to work one end of the cord into the middle, and secure the end of the cord with a whipping. Next lay the cord into the rope, twisting the rope strands open as you go. The bungee won't sink all the way in at first—just get it trapped. Fair periodically by stretching the cord out and milking the line down over it. When you've used up almost all the cord, it should be completely and evenly covered except where it exits the rope. Take up moderate tension on the cord—don't overdo it—then, while holding tension, apply a whipping where it exits the line. Trim the excess flush.

When there's no load on, the bungeed section accordions up neatly. As the boat moves, the cord stretches to snub the loads.

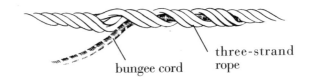

three-strand rope

bungee cord

Figure 12-6A. *The Bungee Snubber. Use a 2- to 3-foot length of bungee cord that is half the diameter of the three-strand rope. The idea is to insert the bungee cord in the rope at any convenient point along its length. Twist the lay of the rope open enough to work one end of the cord into the middle, and stitch with four to six passes of sail twine through first one strand, then the cord, then a second strand. Then lay the cord into the rope, twisting the lay of the rope open a little at a time as you go. Fair periodically by stretching the cord out and milking the line down over it. The cord should be completely covered except where it exits the rope. Work in as much of the cord as you can, then stretch it where it exits the line, using the same stitching as before. Trim the excess.*

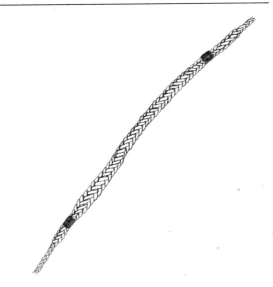

Figure 12-6B. Tom Cook's idea works wonderfully inside single-braid, like this Spectra 12-strand. This can provide a snubbing action for mooring lines, boom preventers, etc. (Margaret Wilson-Briggs)

Addendum

I've been making these snubbers for decades now, with great success. The technique can be adapted to single-braid mooring lines, with the help of a Splicing Wand. I also use it for the Spectra portion of our main boom preventers, where it takes some of the slam out of any sudden loads. The only tricky bit is securing the ends of the bungee without damaging it with the needle; if the cord gets torn up, it will eventually pull free. What I have found works best is a palm-and-needle whipping, made so that the frapping turns barely pierce the surface of the cord. All of the holding power is in the compression from the round turns.

Quick Chafe Gear

A strip of leather with a mooring line–size hole in either end makes tough, adjustable chafing gear. Sewing the leather on is better for staying put, but is not adjustable.

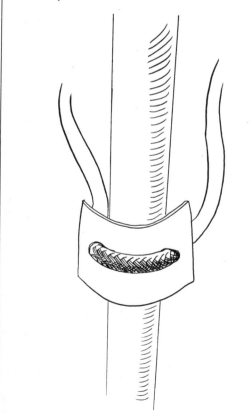

Bag Carry

If you're moored at the end of a long dock, you have to carry your garbage farther than most people to dispose of it. But put it in a bag and hold it as shown, and you won't end up with aching, paralyzed fingers.

Mast Steps

I'm usually not a fan of mast steps—slippery, dangerous things that limit mobility—but it is handy to have a pair opposite one another, about 4.5 feet down from the masthead. There, they provide a good place to stand, to deal with things at the top. The folding variety (shown) won't snag nearby lines.

Two steps, placed opposite each other, about 4.5 feet from the top of the mast, make a dandy place to stand when working aloft. (Margaret Wilson-Briggs)

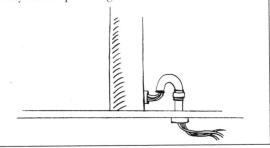
Bill Page's Anchor Tamer

Boatbuilder Bill Page's cutter carries two Fisher-
style anchors, in rollers on either side of his bowsprit. A line seized to the crown of each anchor is led
to a cleat. These lines, hauled taut, keep the anchors
from jumping around under sail.

A small buoy is spliced to the end of each line,
and when an anchor is deployed, line, buoy, and all
go down with it. This provides a convenient, comfortable "handle" if you have to dive on the anchor
to shift it. But Bill also uses it when bringing the
anchor up: When the buoy clears the surface, he
snags it with the boathook. Then he can control the
anchor's ascent to the roller, preventing it from denting the topsides.

HALYARDS

All about halyards . . . blocks, wings, lugsails, hooks,
and sheerpoles.

Masthead Details

The sturdy masthead shown in Figure 12-7 has
two big spinnaker halyard "wings" for the halyard
blocks. The wings extend well forward and to the

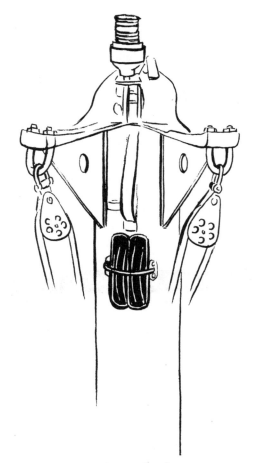

Figure 12-7. *A sturdy masthead.*

side to prevent chafe and fouling on the jibstay. Note
the holes drilled in the wing gussets; these save some
weight, and they can also be used to attach gantlines
and safety tethers when aloft. The bail over the jib
halyard mortise prevents those halyards from jumping off the sheave and jamming between the sheave
and mast mortise.

Lugsail Halyard

A lugsail is a wonderful rig—weatherly, simple,
and easily handled. But sometimes in a chop or
off the wind, the yard swings around and bangs
into the mast. To prevent this, splice the standing
end of the halyard around the mast, then lead it by
way of strap eyes to the usual attachment point
(Figure 12-8).

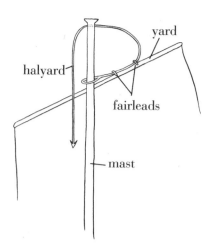

Figure 12-8. *A steady lugsail rig.*

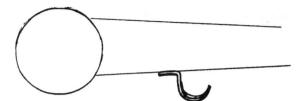

Figure 12-9. *Anti-thwapping halyard hook.*

Note: Selden now makes a very handsome version of this, which they developed as a method for stowing a removable forestay. For this application, the hook goes on the front of the spreader. But it will fit nicely on both sides of many spreaders, and is roomy enough for more than one halyard. So you can install as many as you need.

Anti-Thwapping

To keep halyards from slapping on a mast, most sailors resort to an assemblage of bungee cords hooked around lines and shrouds. A quicker, more elegant solution is to attach "halyard hooks" to the aft side of the spreaders. The hooks can be made from carved wood, or you can cut one leg off a metal strapeye, and screw or rivet this to the spreader, 1 to 2 feet out from the mast. When the sails are down, flip a halyard into one of these hooks, take up, and belay.

Mast Pulpit/Pinrail

Here's a great idea for any boat big enough to accommodate it. A sheerpole is bolted to the mast pulpit legs, and halyard ends are taken to rings on the sheerpole (see Figure 12-10). Hauling parts can be secured to the cam cleat, and the sheerpole is also a handy spot to hang extra lines and coils. Belaying pins and cleats are further options. This is an excellent way to reduce cockpit clutter while adding security for crewmembers forward.

Figure 12-10. *Reduced clutter, added security.*

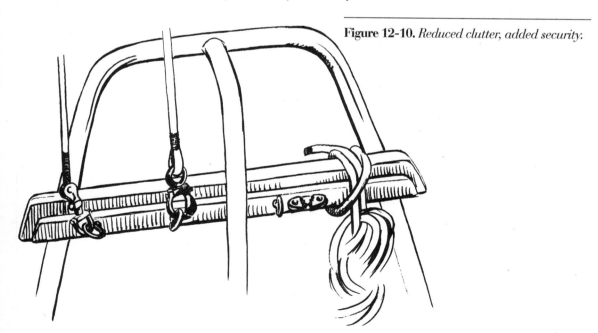

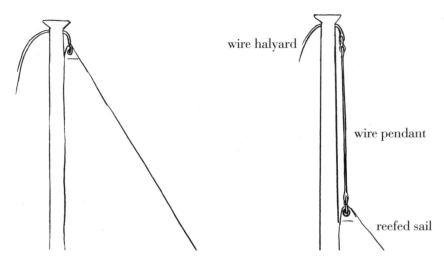

Figure 12-11. *Wire rope pendants for deep reefs and storm trysails.*

Gaff Strips

When a gaff sail is hoisted, gaff jaws can abrade the mast where they bear. The traditional fix is to tack copper or bronze sheet around the mast at bearing height. But the sheet, even when well bedded, invites moisture to gather underneath. Rot follows. And though the sheet does stop chafe, it doesn't keep the jaws from denting and bruising the mast.

As an alternative, screw half-oval bronze or hardwood strips vertically onto the mast. They'll take the load better, drain more readily, and are more easily inspected and repaired.

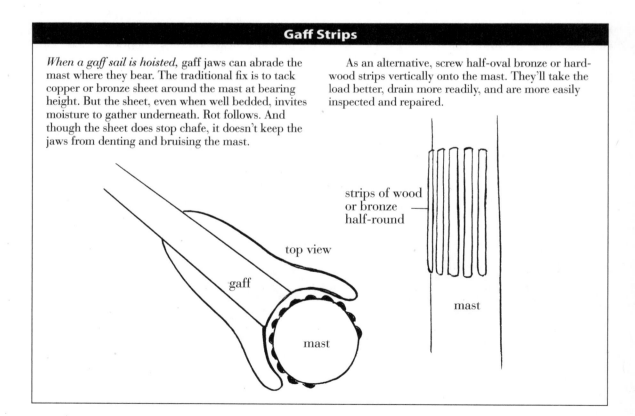

MANAGING SAILS

Wires, ropes, pendants, clewlines, magazines, oh my!

Reefing Pendants

Wire-and-rope halyards are desirable because they are cheaper, lighter, longer-lived, and present less windage than most all-rope alternatives. They are also extremely inelastic, which means they maintain consistent luff tension for optimal sail shape.

Ordinarily, the splice is located just above the winch. But when the sail is reefed, more rope is exposed, and rope is relatively elastic. With a deep reef, halyard tension can be compromised, resulting in a light-air sail shape (baggy, center of effort moved aft) when you least need it.

So, for deep reefs and storm trysails, consider making up a wire rope pendant that will compensate for the loss of luff length when reefed (Figure 12-11). Always shackle the pendant to both sail and halyard before releasing the regular halyard shackle, so you don't risk losing the halyard. A lighter and easier-to-store pendant can be made from one of the "exotics," like Technora or Spectra, if you know how to splice them. Nowadays you might have a "rope-to-rope" halyard, with a length of HM rope instead of wire. With this construction you can still use a pendant, but you can also just make the HM portion long enough that it is still on the winch when the sail is reefed.

Tidy Boom

If a reef clewline belays to a boom, adjust it so that it's a bit slack when the sail is fully hoisted. Then put an

Eyesplice into the end, just big enough to fit over the cleat it belays to, and at a length that will keep this adjustment when the splice is slipped over the cleat. When it's time to reef, just take the eye off and haul.

Hasse's Octopus Magazine

Next to a downhaul, the single greatest low-tech jib-taming tool is an item called a "magazine." It's a piece of wire rope or Spectra with an eye in either end, and with wooden or plastic disks fixed in place near each eye. After lowering the sail, you clip one end of the magazine to a deck eye and the other end either to an eye on the pulpit or to the sail's halyard. You then take the sail hanks off the stay one at a time and hank them to the magazine. No fumbling, no wrestling, no getting two-thirds of the hanks off the stay and losing the whole works to leeward in a malicious gust or wave.

During a Pacific cruise, sailmaker extraordinaire Carol Hasse came up with a magazine refinement called an "Octopus." It's a strip of 1-inch (25-mm) webbing the length of the sail's foot, one end of which is sewn to the top loop of the magazine. Three-quarter-inch (19 mm) strips of webbing, long enough to function as sail ties, are sewn to the long piece at about 2-foot (0.6 m) intervals (see Figure 12-13). You can vary this spacing, making the crosspieces closer together where the sail is bulkiest. If the sail will typically be left on deck for some time, you can also space the ties so that they coincide with stanchions, chocks, or other deck gear you can tie to.

Make a different-colored magazine for each sail, to make sorting easier, and either leave them on deck or in the sailbag while the sail is up. If you always leave the sail on deck, it's a simple step to make an Octopus Magazine House of acrylic cloth.

Figure 12-12. Tidy boom.

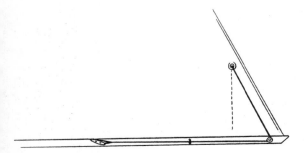

Topping Lift/Outhaul

Here's an excellent small-boat innovation that reduces end-of-boom clutter for a wooden boom. The outhaul sheave is let into the end of the boom, and its axle serves as a bolt for the bail that the topping lift attaches to.

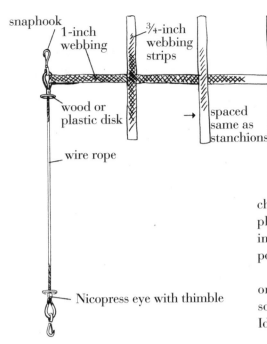

snaphook
1-inch webbing
¾-inch webbing strips
wood or plastic disk
spaced same as stanchions
wire rope
Nicopress eye with thimble

Figure 12-13. Hasse's jib-taming octopus magazine.

CHART STOWAGE

Here's an idea that brings sailboat hardware into a completely unrelated area: chart stowage.

You start by screwing lengths of boltrope track to the underside of the chart table or the top of a designated chart locker. Then you get your friendly local sailmaker to sew lengths of the appropriate-sized rope to the top edges of zipper-opening, clear-plastic chart pouches. You now have the most compact, easily accessed, tidiest method of stowing charts ever known. Keep at least two charts in each pouch (one facing out on either side, others in the middle) and arrange the pouches according to your sailing territory. The pouches can be laid on the

chart table or taken right out on deck, where the plastic cover will keep the wet out. You can even install a strip of track in the cockpit to keep the pouch in place there.

In the, um, decades since this book was originally published, paper charts have become something of a rarity in sailboats, and this Bright Idea might strike some as obsolete. Two thoughts:

1. In the course of the same decades, we've seen numerous instances of complete failure of electronic charts, due to lightning, bad software, mechanical failure, corrosion, etc. Paper charts, kept dry and handy, make for cheap insurance.

2. You can hang moisture-proof Faraday bags on the same sail track setup, to stash at least some of your electronic gear in during a lightning storm, and to keep backups in.

LIFELINES AND TETHERS

Get your tether line off deck so you don't fall.

Flat Tether Lines

Some sailors prefer flat tether straps to rope or wire, because the straps won't roll underfoot. That's true if you want your tether line on deck, but it makes more sense to get the tether line *off* the deck: it's easier to attach to; it's less likely to be in the way as you move fore and aft (it's not, in other words, underfoot); and it is an extra lifeline at the same time. So, how do you get it above deck? First, seize a big

D-ring to the upper shroud on each side, at about chest height. We like to serve a short stretch of the wire as a place for the D-ring to land, and we secure the ring with at least four Double Constrictor knots, pulled tight with two heaving mallets. Numerous vessels have taken this configuration around the world. Attach the lifeline to a strongpoint aft, lead it through the D-ring, and make it off forward, just shy of snug. When you go forward you'll need to detach aft of the ring and re-attach forward. For this and other maneuvers on deck, it's good to have a harness with two tethers.

Rope tether lines made of VPC are nicely inelastic, as well as are more pleasant to work with (and land against) than wire.

Loctite: It's a glue! It's a lubricant! When assembling mechanical terminals like the ones from Hayn and Sta-Lok, apply a generous coat of Loctite when first assembling. It will act as a lubricant, to prevent galling.

Spectra Lazyjacks Use ⅛ " to ³/₁₆" Spectra for any part of your lazyjacks that you don't have to haul on, which is most of any lazyjack setup. The Spectra will be smaller, lighter, and slicker than any comparably strong conventional rope, at about the same price.

Stuck Ring

Try the elegant twine solution to the ancient ring-stuck-on-finger dilemma: Wind thread snugly onto the finger toward the ring. When the thread reaches the ring, slip one end under the ring, then begin unwinding. The ring will walk up. This technique is a favorite among emergency room physicians.

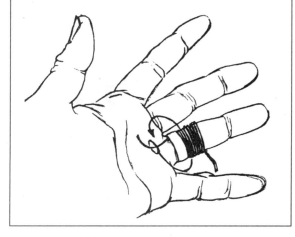

Appendix: Additional Tables and Graphs

NOMINAL SIZE (inches)		MANILA Fed.Spec.TR 605			NYLON (High Tenacity–H.T.)			DUPONT DACRON or H.T. POLYESTER			POLYOLEFINS (H.T.) (Polypropylene and/or Polyethylene)			DOUBLE NYLON BRAID			POLYESTER/ POLYOLEFIN DOUBLE BRAID		
Dia.	Circ.	Net Wt. 100'	Ft. per lb.	Breaking Strength	Net Wt. 100'	Ft. per lb.	Breaking Strength	Net Wt. 100'	Ft. per lb.	Breaking Strength	Net Wt. 100'	Ft. per lb.	Breaking Strength	Net Wt. 100'	Ft. per lb.	Breaking Strength	Net Wt. 100'	Ft. per lb.	Breaking Strength
3/16	5/8	1.47	68.	450	1.	100	1,000	1.3	77.	1,000	.73	137	750	NA	NA	NA	.75	133	900
1/4	3/4	1.96	51.	600	1.5	66.6	1,700	2.1	47.5	1,700	1.24	80.	1,250	1.66	60.3	2,100	1.7	60.2	1,700
5/16	1	2.84	35.	1,000	2.5	40.	2,650	3.3	30.	2,550	1.88	53.	1,850	2.78	36.	3,500	2.6	38.4	2,600
3/8	1 1/8	4.02	24.	1,350	3.6	28.	3,650	4.7	21.3	3,500	2.9	34.5	2,600	3.33	30.	4,200	3.5	28.5	3,500
7/16	1 1/4	5.15	19.4	1,750	5.	20.	5,100	6.3	15.9	4,800	3.9	25.5	3,400	5.	20.	6,000	5.1	20.	5,100
1/2	1 1/2	7.35	13.6	2,650	6.6	15.	6,650	8.2	12.2	6,100	4.9	20.4	4,150	6.67	14.9	7,500	6.8	15.	6,800
9/16	1 3/4	10.2	9.8	3,450	8.4	11.9	8,500	10.2	9.8	7,700	6.2	16.	4,900	8.33	12.	9,500	NA	NA	NA
5/8	2	13.1	7.6	4,400	10.5	9.5	10,300	13.2	7.6	9,500	7.8	12.8	5,900	11.1	9.	12,000	11.	9.	11,000
3/4	2 1/4	16.3	6.1	5,400	14.5	6.9	14,600	17.9	5.6	13,200	11.1	9.	7,900	15.	6.7	17,000	15.	6.7	15,000
7/8	2 3/4	22.	4.55	7,700	20.	5.	19,600	24.9	4.	17,500	15.4	6.5	11,000	20.8	4.8	23,700	20.	5.	20,000
1	3	26.5	3.77	9,000	26.	3.84	25,000	30.4	3.3	22,000	18.6	5.4	13,000	25.	4.	28,500	28.	3.6	28,000
1 1/8	3 1/2	35.2	2.84	12,000	34.	2.94	33,250	40.5	2.5	26,500	24.2	4.1	17,500	35.	2.8	39,000	35.	2.8	35,000
1 1/4	3 3/4	40.8	2.45	13,500	39.	2.56	37,800	46.2	2.16	30,500	27.5	3.6	20,000	40.	2.5	44,000	40.	2.5	40,000
1 5/16	4	46.9	2.13	15,000	45.	2.22	44,500	53.4	1.87	34,500	31.3	3.2	23,000	45.	2.2	49,500	45.	2.2	45,000
1 1/2	4 1/2	58.8	1.7	18,500	55.	1.8	55,000	67.	1.5	43,000	39.5	2.5	29,000	60.	1.6	65,000	60.	1.6	60,000

Table 8. **Fiber Cordage—Typical Weights and Minimum Breaking Strengths in Pounds** (From Chapman, Charles F., et al. *Piloting, Seamanship and Small Boat Handling*, 54th ed. New York: Hearst, 1979)

The figures on synthetics presented here are an average of those available from four large cordage manufacturers. Those for the rope you buy should be available at your dealers. Check them carefully. Also check the rope. In general a soft, sleazy rope may be somewhat stronger and easier to splice, but it will not wear as well and is more apt to hockle or unlay than a firm, well–"locked up" rope. Blended ropes, part polyolefins and part other fibers, may be found. Multifilament (fine filament) polypropylene looks like nylon—don't expect it to be as strong or do the job of nylon. (It floats; nylon doesn't.) Spun or stapled nylon and Dacron are not as strong as ropes made from continuous filaments, but are less slippery and easier to grasp. They are sometimes used for sheets on sailing craft.

	MANILA	NYLON	DACRON	POLY-OLEFINS
Relative Strength	1	4	3	2
Relative Weight	3	2	4	1
Elongation	1	4	2	3
Relative Resistance to Impact or Shock Loads	1	4	2	3
Mildew and Rot Resistance	Poor	Excellent	Excellent	Excellent
Acid Resistance	Poor	Fair	Fair	Excellent
Alkali Resistance	Poor	Excellent	Excellent	Excellent
Sunlight Resistance	Fair	Fair	Good	Fair
Organic Solvent Resistance	Good	Good	Good	Fair
Melting Point	711° F. (Burns)	410° F.	410° F.	about 300° F.
Floatability	Only when new	None	None	Indefinite
*Relative Abrasion Resistance	2	3	4	1

******Depends on many factors—whether wet or dry, etc.*
KEY TO RATINGS: 1=Lowest 4=Highest

Table 9. **Fiber Rope Characteristics.**
(From Chapman's *Piloting, Seamanship and Small Boat Handling*, 54th ed. New York: Hearst, 1979)

Diam.	1x7 galv. iron seizing strand		1x7 annealed s.s. seiz. strand		7x7 galv. improved plow steel		7x19 galv. improved plow steel		7x7 s.s. 302/304		7x19 s.s. 302/304		1x19 s.s. 302/304		Diam.
	strength [lbs]	wt/1000 ft	strength [lbs]	wt/1000 ft	strength [lbs]	wt/1000 ft	strength [lbs]	wt/1000 ft	strength [lbs]	wt/1000 ft	strength [lbs]	wt/1000 ft	strength [lbs]	wt/1000 ft	
1/16	140	10	230	8.5	480	7.5			480	7.5			500	8.5	1/16
3/32	300	20	500	20	920	16	1,000	16	920	16	920	16	1,200	20	3/32
1/8	540	33	900	33	1,700	28.5	2,000	29	1,700	28.5	1,760	29	2,100	35	1/8
5/32	870	50	1,350	50	2,600	43	2,800	45	2,400	43	2,400	45	3,300	55	5/32
3/16	1,150	73			3,700	62	4,200	65	3,700	62	3,700	65	4,700	77	3/16
7/32					4,800	83	5,600	86	4,800	83	5,000	86	6,300	102	7/32
1/4					6,100	106	7,000	110	6,100	106	6,400	110	8,200	135	1/4
9/32					7,400	134	8,000	139	7,600	134	7,800	139	10,300	170	9/32
5/16					9,200	167	9,800	173	9,000	167	9,000	173	12,500	210	5/16
3/8					13,300	236	14,400	243	12,000	236	12,000	243	17,500	300	3/8
7/16*					NA		17,600	356	15,600	342	16,300	356	22,500	410	7/16*
1/2*					NA		22,800	458	21,300	440	22,800	458	30,000	521	1/2*
9/16*									26,600	550	28,500	590	36,200	670	9/16*
5/8*									32,500	680	35,000	715	47,000	855	5/8*

IWRC in 7x19

Table 10. **Weights and Tensile Strengths of Wire Ropes**

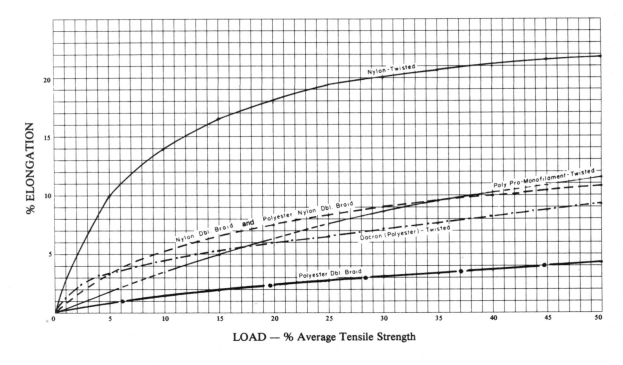

Table 11. **Working Elongation Three-Strand and Braided Ropes**

Data presented in this chart represent percentage working elongation of New England Ropes products under various loads and are results obtained from tests conducted under Cordage Institute Standard Test Methods. (*Courtesy New England Ropes, Inc.*)

DIAMETER		CIRCUMFERENCE		DIAMETER		CIRCUMFERENCE	
Inches	Millimeters	Inches	Millimeters	Inches	Millimeters	Inches	Millimeters
⅛	3.2	⅜	10.0	15⁄16	23.8	3	76.2
5⁄32	4.0	15⁄32	12.0	1	25.4	3⅛	79.4
3⁄16	4.8	9⁄16	15.0	1 1⁄16	27.0	3⅜	85.7
7⁄32	5.6	11⁄16	17.0	1⅛	28.6	3½	88.9
¼	6.3	¾	20.0	1 3⁄16	30.2	3¾	95.2
5⁄16	7.9	1	25.4	1¼	31.7	3⅞	98.4
⅜	9.5	1⅛	28.6	1⅜	34.9	4⅜	111.0
7⁄16	11.1	1⅜	34.9	1 7⁄16	36.5	4½	114.0
½	12.7	1⅝	41.3	1½	38.1	4¾	121.0
9⁄16	14.3	1¾	44.4	1⅝	41.3	5⅛	130.0
⅝	15.9	2	50.8	1 11⁄16	42.9	5¼	133.0
11⁄16	17.5	2¼	57.1	1¾	44.4	5½	140.0
¾	19.0	2⅜	60.3	1 13⁄16	46.0	5¾	146.0
13⁄16	20.6	2½	63.5	1⅞	47.6	5⅞	149.0
⅞	22.2	2¾	69.8	1 15⁄16	49.2	6⅛	156.0
				2	50.8	6¼	159.0

Table 12. **Metric Equivalents of Standard Rope Sizes**

Inches	1	2	3	4	5	6	7	8	9	10	11
Feet	0.0833	0.1667	0.2500	0.3333	0.4167	0.5000	0.5833	0.6667	0.7500	0.8333	0.9167
Inches	⅛	¼	⅜	½	⅝	¾	⅞				
Feet	0.0104	0.0208	0.0313	0.0417	0.0521	0.0625	0.0729				

Example: 5 ft. 7⅜ in. = 5.0 + 0.5833 + 0.0313 = 5.6146 ft.

Table 13. Converting from Inches and Fractions of an Inch to Decimals of a Foot

8ths	16ths	32nds	64ths	Exact decimal values	8ths	16ths	32nds	64ths	Exact decimal values
			1	0.01 5625	4	8	16	32	0.50
		1	2	.03 125				33	.51 5625
			3	.04 6875			17	34	.53 125
	1	2	4	.06 25				35	.54 6875
			5	.07 8125		9	18	36	.56 25
		3	6	.09 375				37	.57 8125
			7	.10 9375			19	38	.59 375
								39	.60 9375
1	2	4	8	.12 5	5	10	20	40	.62 5
			9	.14 0625				41	.64 0625
		5	10	.15 625			21	42	.65 625
			11	.17 1875				43	.67 1875
	3	6	12	.18 75		11	22	44	.68 75
			13	.20 3125				45	.70 3125
		7	14	.21 875			23	46	.71 875
			15	.23 4375				47	.73 4375
2	4	8	16	.25	6	12	24	48	.75
			17	.26 5625				49	.76 5625
		9	18	.28 125			25	50	.78 125
			19	.29 6875				51	.79 6875
	5	10	20	.31 25		13	26	52	.81 25
			21	.32 8125				53	.82 8125
		11	22	.34 375			27	54	.84 375
			23	.35 9375				55	.85 9375
3	6	12	24	.37 5	7	14	28	56	.87 5
			25	.39 0625				57	.89 0625
		13	26	.40 625			29	58	.90 625
			27	.42 1875				59	.92 1875
	7	14	28	.43 75		15	30	60	.93 75
			29	.45 3125				61	.95 3125
		15	30	.46 875			31	62	.96 875
			31	.48 4375				63	.98 4375

Table 14. Decimal Equivalents of Common Fractions

Genoa Sheet Load			
English $SL = SA \times V^2 \times 0.00431$		**Metric** $SL = SA \times V^2 \times 0.02104$	
SL	Sheet load in pounds	SL	Sheet load in kilograms
SA	Sail area in square feet	SA	Sail area in square meters
V	Wind speed in knots	V	Wind speed in knots

LOADING FORMULAS

Here are some additional tables, graphs, and formulas, courtesy of Harken and Lewmar, that I use when calculating loads.

Harken's require calculations, but are an excellent follow-up, for sheet loads at least, because they take apparent wind speed into account.

Lewmar's are easier to access, being entirely visual, and are useful for any ocean-going yacht, not just racers.

HARKEN'S FORMULAS

The following charts and formulas have been compiled by Harken from many catalogs, marine publications, and related resources. Because of the constant developments in hull and rig design, and new materials for sails, lines, and rigging, this information might become dated and is offered only as a general guideline. Consult your rigger or naval architect for your specific requirements.

Boat Type

Most load formulas assume a medium displacement monohull, but you can easily correct for other boat types. Multihulls have great form stability and speed and will often carry sails very high in the apparent wind speed, so calculations must be done with this wind speed in mind. Ultralight Displacement Boats (ULDBs) are typically tender and often change sails or reef quite early, so loading may be done at relatively low wind speeds. For example, a modern trimaran may carry its blade jib in 25 knots of wind at speeds over 15 knots for an apparent wind of nearly 40 knots, where a ULDB will probably remove its #1 genoa at about 15 knots of apparent wind.

Genoa System Loading

Because wind speed is squared, it is the most important variable and can greatly influence loading. Wind is the apparent wind and should be calculated for the specific sail being analyzed. For example, the #1 genoa on a 25-foot (7-meter) boat might only be carried in 15 knots of wind, while the #4 blade on a maxi boat could well be carried in 40 knots.

To calculate loading on a genoa lead car, multiply sheet load by the load factor of the sheet. Most #1 genoas will deflect about 45 degree, while a Kevlar #3 might deflect 75 degree or more.

Lead car adjuster tackle load depends on the angle of deflection of the sheet in the lead car, but is generally assumed to be 0.3 of lead car load when deflection is 45 degree, and 0.5 of lead car load when deflection is 60 degree.

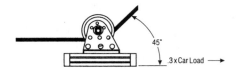

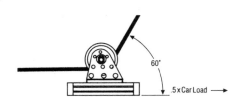

Mainsheet System Loading

The formula for mainsheet loading is not as widely accepted as that for genoa sheet loads, and should be used only as a rough guide for offshore boats from 30 to 60 feet.

Travel car adjuster load is generally considered to be 0.2 times car load.

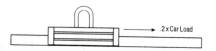

Mainsheet Load			
English		**Metric**	

$$ML = \frac{E^2 \times P^2 \times 0.00431 \times V^2}{(\sqrt{P^2 + E^2}) \times (E - X)}$$

$$ML = \frac{E^2 \times P^2 \times 0.02104 \times V^2}{(\sqrt{P^2 + E^2}) \times (E - X)}$$

ML	Mainsheet load in pounds	ML	Mainsheet load in kilograms
E	Foot length of main in feet	E	Foot length of main in meters
P	Luff length of main in feet	P	Luff length of main in meters
V	Wind speed in knots	V	Wind speed in knots
X	Distance from aft end of boom to mainsheet attachment point in feet	X	Distance from aft end of boom to mainsheet attachment point in meters

LEWMAR'S FORMULAS

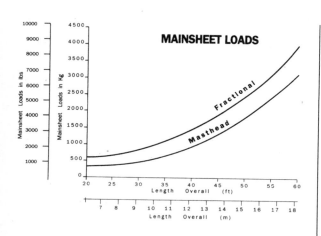

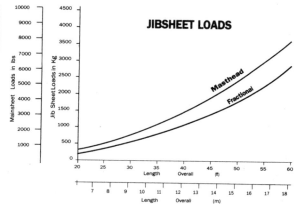

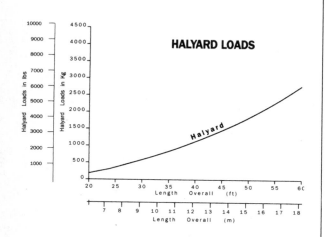

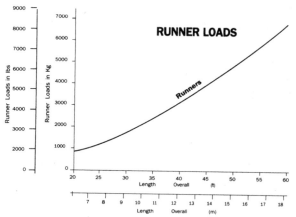

Appendix: Soft Shackle

Illustrations by Margaret Wilson-Briggs

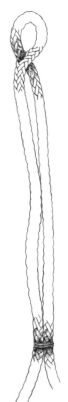

Form a Wall Knot with the strand ends. The diagonal line at the center is the seizing. This and the rest of the instructions for this button are for a two-strand version of Ashley's 880 (see page 90).

Start with a six-foot long piece of ³/₁₆-inch Spectra/Dyneema single-braid rope, like New England's Endura 12. Middle the rope, and pass one end through the rope, to form an eye that fits loosely around two diameters of the rope. Seize the ends together with a Double Constrictor, about 18-inches from their ends.

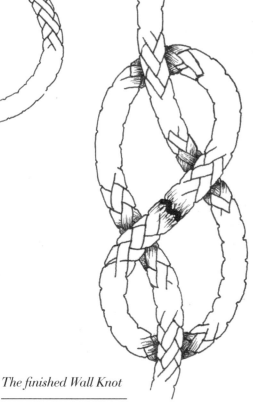

The finished Wall Knot

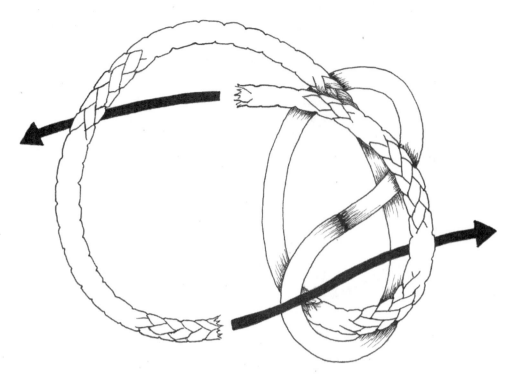

Form a Crown Knot on top of the Wall Knot. In 2 strands, this forms an Overhand Knot.

The finished Crown Knot

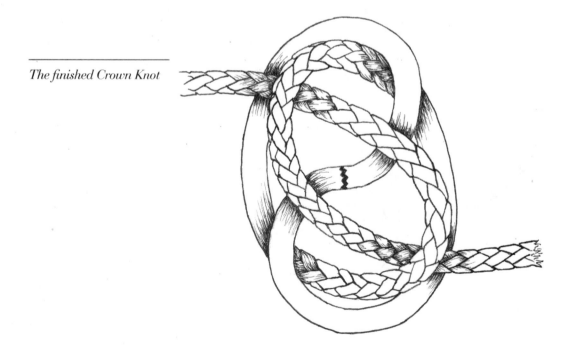

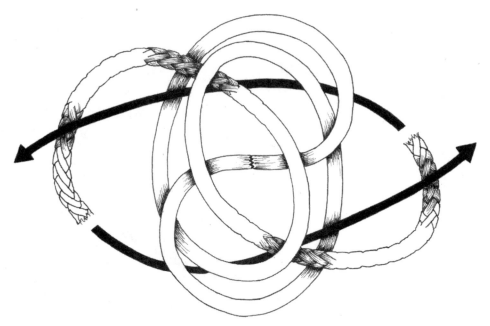

Pass each end up through the opposite Wall chamber, ahead of the other end

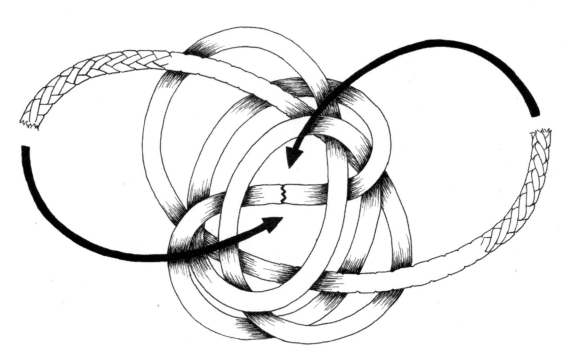

Pass each end down through the center of the knot, into the further of the two openings. Draw up firmly.

Finished shackle

Button Knot. *In the form at lower right, with the ends cut off flush, you will have a decorative soft shackle; just pass the loop end around the objects you want to shackle together, then slide the loop open, slip it over the button, and slide the loop closed.*

But if you want full strength, leave the ends long, and tuck them 10 rope diameters or so down into adjacent standing parts. (Finished shackle, above.)

Cut the ends off at an angle, so that they just barely draw inside when you smooth out the standing parts. Make a few stitches through the rope where the ends enter, under the button, so that they can't crawl out when no load is on.

Congratulations, you have just completed an improved soft shackle, one that is 50% or more stronger than the "conventional" soft shackles that you can commonly find in today's chandleries. Test results on absolute strength vary depending on the quality of fabrication, but it is reasonable to say that you can expect in the neighborhood of twice the rope's strength from the finished shackle. So, for instance, the ³/₁₆-inch rope shackle described here would have a breaking strength of 5 to 6 tons(!)

You can make soft shackles of any length. If for instance you want to hang a block from a boom, you will want a longer shackle than if you wanted to secure a block to a deck padeye or cleat. Soft shackles, improved or otherwise, replace steel shackles for many, many applications, afloat or ashore. They can be made in a few minutes, using scrap lengths of rope, they weigh almost nothing, and they can be easily inspected and replaced. Wonderful.

Finished Button Knot.

Glossary

Abrasion: Chafe or wear on a rope or wire rope. Chafe is most readily found on the surface of rope, but ropes can also abrade internally.

Aircraft cable: Strands, cords, and wire ropes made of very strong wire. Intended originally for aircraft controls, it is now widely used as standing rigging in traditional vessels.

Area, metallic: The sum of the cross-sectional areas of metal. In a wire rope it is the amount of "meat" in the sum of the individual yarns in a wire, which varies with construction.

Back a strand, to:. In a splice, to tuck a strand with, rather than against, the lay.

Backsplice: An end-of-the-rope knot in which the strands are spliced back into their own standing part.

Becket: 1. A rope handle. 2. The eye or hook of a block or block strop where the purchase originates (as opposed to the bail, from which the block hangs). 3. A short rope with an eye at one end and a button at the other, used for securing spars, oars, etc.

Belay, to: To secure a rope with round and figure-eight turns around a belaying pin, cleat, bitts, etc. To make an extemporaneous attachment to any object, especially with the intent of being able to control high loads.

Belaying pin: A wood or metal pin inserted through a hole in a rail, to which running rigging is belayed.

Bend: A knot that ties together the ends of two ropes.

Bight: A slack section in a rope's standing part; a U-shaped bend of a line used in the formation of a knot.

Bitts: Upright timbers, usually in pairs, for making fast mooring and towing lines.

Block: A device with grooved wheels for changing the lead of a line, or for increasing the power of a tackle.

Bollards: Posts, commonly of iron, suitable for mooring. Like bitts, they are usually found in pairs, but they are more often round, while bitts are usually square.

Breaking strength: The measured load required to break a rope in tension. See *Nominal strength*.

Button: A leather stop fitted to the loom of an oar to prevent it from slipping outboard; a firm, compact multi-strand knot in which the ends lead back to the standing part after the knot is formed.

By the run: To let go or cast off instantly instead of slacking gradually.

Cable: A term loosely applied to wire ropes, wire strands, fiber ropes, and electrical conductors.

Capsize: When applied to knots, this means to change the form under stress; to pervert.

Thanks to Doubleday & Company for permission to take many of these definitions from *The Ashley Book of Knots*. Clifford Ashley's precise and painstaking definitions can hardly be improved upon.

Carry away, to: To break and go adrift. Applied to both sails and rigging. "The main topmast *carried away* in the storm."

Chafe, to: To fray, fret, gall, or rub. See *Abrasion*.

Circumference: The perimeter of a cross-section through a rope or wire rope; the girth.

Cleat: A wooden or metal object with two horns, secured to deck, mast, dock, or rigging, to which ropes are belayed.

Clevis pin: A transverse pin in a shackle, tang, turnbuckle, or toggle, to which standing rigging attaches.

Coil: A bundle of rope or wire rope, usually circular, arranged for convenience of handling and storing. See *Reel*.

Come-along: A ratchet winch with wire pendant used to stretch cable for service, to set up lanyards, to effect emergency repairs, etc.

Construction: The design of a rope, including the number of strands, the number of wires or fibers per strand, and the arrangement of wires or fibers in each strand.

Cordage: Fiber rope of any material or size.

Corrosion: Chemical decomposition of a rope by exposure to moisture, acids, alkalines, electrical current, UV, or other destructive agents.

Cotter pin: A split pin used in rigging to prevent clevis pins from backing out of position.

Deadeye: A stout disk of hard wood, strapped with rope or iron, through which holes (usually three) are pierced for the reception of lanyards.

Design factor: See *Safety factor*.

Diameter: The thickness of a strand, a rope, or a wire rope.

Dog-leg: A linear deformation in the run of a wire rope or rod, especially one that is gradual enough that the material can be straightened with no loss of strength. See *Kink*.

Double, to: To continue the lead of a decorative knot around an additional circuit, as in a Turk's Head or button knot.

Ease or ease off: To slacken.

Elastic limit: The limit of stress above which a permanent deformation takes place within the material. This limit is approximately 55 to 65 percent of the breaking strength of steel wire rope.

Entry: The sequence in which strands enter the standing part at the commencement of a splice in multi-strand rope or wire rope.

Eye: A spliced, seized, swaged, or knotted loop, with or without a thimble.

Fair, to: To smooth out or to even a knot, splice, or sinnet, in order to improve its appearance and ensure an even strain on all strands.

Fall: The hauling end of a tackle.

Fast: Secure. "The throat halyard is *fast*."

Fatigue: The progressive fracturing in metal due to a loss of resiliency with age and use; work hardening. Alloyed steels are particularly susceptible to fatigue.

Fiber heart or core: A twisted rope or strand employed as a core in wire rope.

Fid: A tool, usually conical, used in a splice, to open the standing part strands to make room to tuck an end.

Filler wire: Small auxiliary wires in a wire rope strand for spacing and positioning other wires.

Fox: Yarns wound or twisted together to shorten their working length, especially for fancy work.

Frapping turns: A number of crossing turns in a lashing or seizing or in the leads of a tackle, which serve both to tighten and secure the piece.

Galvanized wire: Wire coated with zinc to retard corrosion.

Gang: A set of rigging for a mast or yard.

Grades, wire rope: Classification of wire rope by its breaking strength. In order of their increasing breaking strengths the unalloyed steels are: iron, traction, mild plow steel, plow steel, improved plow steel, and extra improved plow steel. Alloyed steels vary widely in breaking strength depending on their composition, but most of the alloys used in yacht rigging have approximately the strength of improved plow steel.

Grommet: An endless wire or fiber rope, usually made from one continuous strand.

Ground tackle: A general term for all hawsers, chains, cables, buoy ropes, and warps employed in anchoring, mooring, and sometimes in towing a vessel.

Halyard: Rope for hoisting a sail or yard.

Handsomely: Slowly, carefully, gently; as, "to lower away *handsomely.*"

Handy-billy: A small tackle kept handy for small jobs.

Haul, to: To pull by hand on a rope or tackle.

Hitch: A knot that secures a rope to another object, such as a piling, rail, ring, etc., or to its own standing part, or to the standing part of another rope.

Hockle: A capsizing of the strands in a rope or wire rope, resulting from excessive twisting or unbalanced manufacture.

Hoist, to: To lift.

Independent wire rope core (IWRC): A type of wire heart for a wire rope, the heart constructed so that it is itself a miniature wire rope. The IWRC is stronger and more resistant to crushing than fiber hearts and other wire hearts.

Irish pennants: Cordage ends that are frayed or raveled due to neglect.

Jute: A natural-fiber material of low breaking strength, sometimes used for cheap rope and sometimes as a heart for four-stranded fiber ropes and wire ropes.

Kink: A sharp bend in a rope, wire rope, or rod that permanently distorts and thus weakens it.

Knot: Any complication in a rope.

Lanyard: 1. A small rope for making fast the end of a piece of standing rigging. 2. Handles, frequently ornamentally decorated, for tools, bags, watches, or any other small item you don't want to lose overboard.

Lash: To secure or contain an object or objects by binding them with rope.

Lay: 1. The direction of the strand twist or lead in a rope. 2. The firmness or angle of that twist.

Lead: The direction of a rope, or the direction of a strand in a knot.

Leads: The parts of a tackle between the two blocks, as opposed to the standing part and the fall.

Let go, to: To cast off.

Line: In general parlance, a length of rope put to a specific use.

Long-jawed rope: Old rope that has stretched and lost much of its twist.

Loop: A 360-degree turn made in rope, but not around anything. See *Turn, Round Turn.*

Make fast: 1. To secure a rope with a hitch or hitches. 2. To finish off a belay with a single hitch.

Manila: A rope material made from Abaca leaves. Manila is stronger than jute, and is still used for some theatrical and boat rigging.

Marl, to: To secure or contain with a series of Marling Hitches.

Marlingspike: A conical, metal tool employed in just about every procedure of traditional rigging, especially for tightening, loosening, separating, pounding, and toggling.

Marry, to: To intermesh the strands of two rope ends preparatory to splicing.

Meathook: A short stub of broken yard projecting from the surface of a wire rope. Meathooks are usually the result of metal fatigue.

Modulus of elasticity: A mathematical quantity giving the ratio, within the elastic limit, of a defined stress on a rope or wire rope to the corresponding elongation.

Nominal strength: The published or advertised design strength of a rope or wire rope. This is usually though not always less than the actual breaking strength of the rope.

Overhaul: 1. To separate the blocks of a tackle preparatory to another haul. 2. To eliminate kinks in a line by recoiling, stretching, or flaking.

Palm: A narrow leather strap with thumb hole and, affixed next to the thumb hole, a dimpled "iron." The palm is worn around the palm of the hand as an aid to pushing needles through heavy cloth or leather, the blunt end of the needle being braced against the iron.

Parcel: To wrap with canvas or tape the length of a rope or wire rope, in order to produce a waterproof base for service.

Part, to: To break.

Pendant: A standing rope or wire rope to which a tackle is hooked, seized, or shackled.

Pennant: The reward for winning a baseball championship.

Preformed: A wire rope in which the strands are shaped to a permanent helix. The strands of preformed wire will not spring apart when cut.

Prestressing: Stressing a rope or wire rope before use in order to remove constructional stretch.

Purchase: A mechanical advantage gained with block and tackle or winch.

Ravel: To fray, untwist, or unbraid. "Unravel" is a redundant term.

Reel: The flanged spool on which rope or wire rope is wound for storage and shipment.

Reeve: To pass the end of a rope or wire rope through any hole or opening.

Reeve off: To reeve through blocks for running rigging.

Riding turns: In seizings, whippings, and lashings, a second tier of turns over the base of round turns.

Rigging: The art of using knots and lines either to move things or keep them from moving.

Rope: Any cordage one inch or more in circumference.

Round turn: A 360-degree turn made with a rope around an object. See *Loop*, *Turn*.

Running rigging: All rigging that is rove through blocks.

Safety factor: The ratio of breaking strength to maximum expected stress.

Seizing: A means of binding two or more ropes together with cordage or seizing wire.

Seizing strand or wire: A small strand, usually of seven wires, made of soft annealed iron or stainless steel.

Service: Marline, small stuff, or seizing wire wrapped around standing rigging for protection against wear and weather.

Serving board: A small serving mallet.

Serving mallet: A tool for applying marline service.

Set up, to: To tune rigging by tightening lanyards or turnbuckles.

Shears: Two spars lashed together at the top and guyed; used for raising masts and hoisting heavy weights.

Sheave: A grooved pulley that rotates on a pin or bearings and constitutes the moving part of a block. Nonrotating sheaves, as found in topmast heels, are called "dumb sheaves."

Shock loading: The sudden impact that results when a load comes rapidly onto a slack rope. The measured strain of a shock load can far exceed the load that produced it.

Shroud: A standing-rig piece that stays a mast laterally. Classically, a shroud extends from the top of a given mast to the bottom of the same mast. For instance, topmast shrouds start at the top of the topmast, but do not come to deck. Instead they end at the tops. The lateral stays that extend from a topmast or topgallant, and run all the way to the chainplates, however, are called "backstays" rather than shrouds. This remains the case even if they do not angle aft, to avoid confusing them with topmast shrouds.

Sinnet: Braided cordage.

Slack away: To pay out or let out slack.

Sling: Any of numerous configurations of rope or wire rope attached to an object, by means of which that object is to be hoisted.

Slushing: Protecting standing rigging from deterioration by coating it with a waterproofing agent that usually contains pine tar, linseed oil, varnish, or other ingredients in various combinations. Slush applications should congeal to a hard finish that will not scuff off on sails, running rigging, or crew.

Small stuff: Rope that is less than one inch in circumference.

Smartly: Together, with precision and alacrity.

Snarl: An entanglement of cordage.

Soft Shackle: A button-and-becket loop, made from high-modulus single-braid rope, in which the becket fits snugly around the stem of the button, but is formed such that it can be slid open to allow the button to be inserted into or removed from the becket.

Span: A length of rope or wire rope, fast at both ends, to be hauled on at the center; a bridle; a form of sling.

Splice, to: To interweave two ends of ropes or wire ropes so as to make a continuous length. Also, to make a loop or eye in the end of a rope or wire rope by tucking the strand ends into the standing part. Also, to bury the ends into the interior of the rope, for the same purpose.

Stainless steel rope: Wire rope made of alloyed steel, having greater resistance to corrosion than galvanized or untreated steel wire rope.

Stand by, to: To be ready to haul, slacken, or belay.

Standing part: The inactive part, as opposed to the end, bight, or loop.

Standing rigging: All rigging and associated hardware that supports the mast, keeps it straight, or provides means to attach certain sails, and is permanently installed.

Stay: Any piece of standing rigging. More commonly, any piece of fore-and-aft standing rigging.

Strand: A component piece of a rope, itself composed of two or more yarns twisted together.

Strop: A grommet or short pendant seized around a block, mast, or boom, by means of which a purchase is applied, or to which a shroud is attached.

Surge, to: To slack away on a line under strain by allowing it to slide in controlled fashion over the surface of a pin, winch, windlass, etc.

Swage: A fitting into which a wire-rope end is inserted. The rope is secured there by the application of tremendous pressure to all sides of the fitting.

Sweat up, to: To pull on a taut rope at right angles to its length, feeding the slack so gained to the tailer. Sweating up is a dynamic application of frapping.

Tackle: A mechanism of blocks and rope for increasing power. The ancient pronunciation "tay'ckle" is still preferred among riggers and many sailors.

Tag line: A rope used to prevent the rotation or swinging of a load.

Tail: To take up slack in a load-bearing line and subsequently maintain the advantage with the aid of one or more round turns on a pin or winch. The slack is usually fed to the tailer by another crewmember.

Tail on: An order to grasp and haul.

Taper: To diminish the diameter of a rope or a splice in a rope by removing yarns at staggered intervals over a given length.

Tenon: A projection on the end of a structural member, shaped for insertion into a cavity called a mortise, to make a joint. At the butt of a wooden mast, the tenon fits into a mortise in the mast step. (In aluminum masts, the reverse is usually the case.)

Thimble: A grooved metal fitting to protect the eye of a rope or wire rope.

Thoroughfoot: A tangle in a tackle due to a block's upsetting.

Thwapping: The auditory water torture of halyards slapping on masts. A sharp knife is an effective anti-thwapping device.

Toggle: An end fitting to standing or running rigging, providing a universal joint. Toggles are generally attached to a tang or clevis pin, and secured by a cotter ring or cotter pin.

Turn: One round of a rope on a pin, cleat, or rail; one round of a coil.

Turnbuckle: A device attached to a wire rope for applying tension. It consists of a barrel and right- and left-threaded bolts.

Two-blocked: Said of an exhausted purchase, the blocks of which are jammed against one another.

Weed, to: To clear rigging of stops, rope yarns, etc.

Whip, to: To bind the end of a rope to prevent fraying.

Wire rope: A plurality of wire strands helically laid about a longitudinal axis.

With the lay: Ahead and to the right or clockwise with right-laid rope; to the left or counterclockwise with left-laid rope. To go "with the lay" or "against the lay" is to travel both linearly and axially.

Worm, to: To fill the seams of a rope with spun yarns or marline.

Yarn: A number of fibers twisted together.

Bibliography

Ashley, Clifford W. *The Ashley Book of Knots.*
New York: Doubleday, and London: Faber &
Faber, Ltd., 1944. Illustrates, explains, and
analyzes knots, sets them in their historical
context, and encourages their contemporary
application. And it does all this with warmth,
thoroughgoing professionalism, and unfailing
humor. The one indispensable book for the
marlingspike artist.

Calder, Nigel. *Cruising Handbook.* Camden,
Maine: International Marine, 2001. Good rigging
ideas and practices, set in the context of good
sailing and living practices.

Cunliffe, Tom. *Hand, Reef, and Steer.* Dobbs
Ferry, New York: Sheridan House, and London:
Waterline, 1992. Imagine a tour of a big gaff boat,
given by a sweet, quiet, wonderfully competent
sailor. Tom will show you sails, spars, rigging, and
even a bit of maneuvering technique, to help you
feel at home in a proper traditional yacht. Short on
technical detail but long on context.

Dashew, Linda and Steve. *Offshore Cruising
Encyclopedia.* Beowolf, 1989. The Dashews are a
cruising couple like the Pardeys (see *The Capable
Cruiser*), but are polar opposites in many ways:
The Dashews like long, skinny boats instead of
short, beamy ones, and they like all the modern
conveniences (engines, hydraulics, electronics,
etc.). In short, they're like most cruising sailors
today. If you want to know how to select, install,
and maintain all those conveniences, get this
book. And if you'd like seasoned insight into
every conceivable aspect of cruising, convenient
and otherwise, get this book.

Day, Cyrus Lawrence. *The Art of Knotting and
Splicing.* Fourth Edition. Annapolis, Maryland:
United States Naval Institute, 1986. A great
introduction, clear photographs, intelligent
layout, and concise text make this the best basic
ropework text.

Donovan, Harry. *Entertainment Rigging.*
Available from Amazon. Harry Donovan was
one of the great riggers of the twentieth century.
Even if you never deal with the specialized world
of entertainment rigging, this book will provide
you with more technical know-how, elegant
applications, and common-sense approaches than
any other book I know of.

Gerr, Dave. *The Nature of Boats.* Camden,
Maine: International Marine, 1995. The subtitle
is "Insights and Esoterica for the Nautically
Obsessed," but it's much more than that.
Sometimes I just pick it up and start reading
at random, confident that I'll find something
useful. It's a big "unconscious drawer" of a book.
Don't miss his chapter on "Flipper Flapper, the
Ultimate Racer."

Kinney, Francis S. *Skene's Elements of Yacht
Design.* Eighth Edition. New York: Dodd, Mead
& Co., 1981. A compendium of the principles
and procedures of yacht design. Read it to put
your rigging in the context of the entire vessel.

Larsson, Lars, and Rolf E. Eliasson. *Principles
of Yacht Design.* Camden, Maine: International
Marine, and London: Adlard Coles Nautical,
1994. The Danish modern furniture equivalent
of yacht design books: spare, elegant, and more

comfortable than it looks. Gratifyingly detailed rigging section, with some very useful suggestions for things like varying mast sections for specific rig configurations. Great book.

Nares, George S. *Seamanship*. Henley, England: Gresham Press, 1979. A reprint of the 1862 edition of a book first published in 1860 as an instruction manual for naval cadets. The procedures it describes are unquestionably archaic, but its principles can inform the most modern rig. Exceptional illustrations and a helpful question-and-answer format.

Norgrove, Ross. *Cruising Rigs and Rigging*. Camden, Maine: International Marine, 1982. The wisdom distilled from years of paying attention to what makes rigs live longer. Norgrove emphasizes good design and maintenance procedures with stories that are variously amusing and hair-raising.

Pardey, Lin and Larry. *Capable Cruiser*. New York: W. W. Norton & Company, and London: Waterline, 1987. The Pardeys have traveled farther, faster, and safer than almost any other cruisers and they've done it without a lot of gear that most people consider essential (e.g., an engine). There's a lot of distilled information here. My favorite chapter is "Bowsprits for Offshore Voyaging."

Rigging Handbooks. Available from wire rope manufacturers. Every manufacturer prints a list of its products detailing wire materials, constructions, and designed uses. These specifications are supplemented by reference tables, charts, essays on manufacture and use, explanations of inspection procedures, instructions for splicing and seizing, and a few words about slings, lubrication, and sling tolerances. Presto! You've got a little technical manual. Most of the information refers to industrial applications but is easily extrapolated to boat rigging.

Rossnagel, W. E. *Handbook of Rigging: In Construction and Industrial Operations*. Third Edition. New York: McGraw-Hill, 1964. The industrial rigger's bible, and great-granddaddy to the manufacturers' handbooks. Gives safe loads for everything from crane guys to nailed joists, instructions for making a life net, finding the center of gravity of odd-shaped objects, the proper use of steel scaffolding, and just about anything else to know about other-than-strictly-nautical rigging.

Steel, David. *The Elements of Mastmaking, Sailmaking, and Rigging*. New York: Edward W. Sweetman, 1978. A reprint of the 1932 edition of a book first published in 1794 under the title *The Elements and Practice of Rigging and Seamanship*. Helpful in the sense that Nares's *Seamanship* is helpful, but more archaic.

Taylor, Roger C. *The Elements of Seamanship*. Camden, Maine: International Marine, 1986. This little book is to seamanship what Strunk and White's *Elements of Style* is to writing. If you would learn to rig, you must learn to sail.

Sources and Resources

Riggers are part of a practical community, one that includes clients, other artisans, and the people who design and provide tools and materials. Outside of this immediate circle, the community extends to include logistical support like shipping, testing labs, and people who handle payroll, and other vital financial services. Take the community out far enough and you get Civilization. I will limit myself here to a very few recommendations, but I urge you, as a rigger, to cultivate a broad and intricate series of connections.

BRION TOSS YACHT RIGGERS

We still fabricate a limited number of rigs, but nowadays I mostly keep busy as a writer, designer, consultant, expert witness, surveyor, and teacher. If you wish to contact me in any of those capacities, here's how:

Web site: http://briontoss.com/

There you'll find scheduling for workshops and classes, and a catalog of everything from books and DVDs to tools like our Splicing Wand, Rigger's Pliers, Point Hudson Phid, Bosun's Harness, and lots more. You'll also see links to setting up consultations, surveys, and, yes, the actual rigging of boats.

Email: rigging@briontoss.com
Shop phone: 360-385-1080
Address: 313 Jackson Street
Port Townsend, WA 98368

COLLIGO MARINE

As noted in the preceding pages, Spectra/Dyneema standing rigging is a big development in contemporary rigging. The material itself is amazing, but that wouldn't have mattered much without someone to do the arduous, involved work of figuring out how to apply it to actual boats—how to work out optimal terminations and tangs, how to measure it so that the finished pieces were the correct length, and how to address issues like creep, UV, and chafe. The person who did almost all the heavy lifting on the topic was is John Franta, of Colligo Marine. John continues to do far more research and development than seems entirely reasonable, for both running and standing rigging applications, and is one of the most refreshingly forthright, modest people I've ever known. If you are considering the use of Spectra in your rigging, he is the go-to guy.

Web site: http://www.colligomarine.com/

In addition to merchandise, you'll find links to detailed description on materials, characteristics, and uses.

Email: through web site
Shop: 480-703-3675
Address: 1165 Highland Way
Grover Beach, CA 93433

SAILING SERVICES

Of all the rigging suppliers I've dealt with, this one stands out as having the best combination of quality, efficiency, decent pricing, real-world practicality, and what I can only describe as puckish good humor. That last goes for everyone on the staff, it seems, but is particularly true for founder and guiding light Brooks Jones, a canny, rumbling bear of a sailor. Brooks is the U.S. distributor for Sta-Lok, does great in-house swaging and rod heading, carries all the most common running and standing rigging components, and can either get obscure items for you, or direct you to someone who can. Oh, and for all you cruisers, Sailing Services is wise in the ways of shipping to far-off places.

Web site: http://www.sailingservices.com

Bare bones (C'mon, Brooks, flesh that thing out), but it has the essentials. Still, once you have a general idea of what you need, get on the phone to talk with one of the fabulous staff members.

Email: sails@sailingservices.com
305-758-1074

FISHERIES SUPPLY

This Seattle company is right up there with Sailing Services in every respect, and it is a lot closer to my shop. The only thing they really lack is anyone half as colorful as Brooks.

fisheriessupply.com
206-632-4462
1900 N. Northlake Way
Seattle, WA 98103

HASSE AND COMPANY

In my humble estimation, this is the best cruising vessel sail loft in the country, if not the world. Their designs are brilliant, their fabrication techniques result in remarkable sail longevity, and their customer service is otherworldly.

I am tempted to go on for pages about the wonderfulness of the staff, and particularly of owner Carol Hasse, but I will settle for saying that she pos-

sesses an unparalleled level of technical skill, in combination with a spiritual graciousness that makes the Dalai Lama look like a thug. Both attributes, I suspect, are informed by the tens of thousands of sea miles she has covered in the course of her career.

The relationship between sails and rigging is of course intimate; the purpose of rigging is to deal with the energy that the sails deliver, and the two arts have been co-evolving for millennia. So if you hope to be a good rigger, get to know a good sailmaker.

Web site: http://porttownsendsails.com/
Great PDF downloads at that address, on every sail in your inventory. Download them all. Then move over to the "Sources and Resources" section, for articles about sailmaking. Be sure to check out/ memorize the video of Hasse explaining the niceties of sail trim.

Email: info@porttownsendsails.com
360-385-1640

PORT TOWNSEND
MARINE TRADES ASSOCIATION

Here is the result of a self-reinforcing feedback loop. Many years ago, a few manically dedicated woodworking dilettantes moved to a then-moribund Port Townsend. Rents were cheap. Or free. Opportunities were endless. Over time, some of those dilettantes honed their fabrication skills. A smaller percentage also developed some business skills. The latter group was therefore able to stay in business long enough to develop a reputation, assuring an ongoing stream of work. Other artisans showed up, but if they weren't really high quality, they didn't tend to stay, for why would anyone hire a mediocre worker in a town that was rich in maestros?

In time there were so many artisans with sterling reputations that the town started to develop a reputation. And not just for woodworkers; the same feedback loop extended to cover machinists, welders, electricians, sailmakers, and, yes, riggers. Hello Port Townsend Rigging!

Today you can't throw a chisel in Port Townsend without – well you really can't throw a chisel in Port Townsend. It just wouldn't happen. But we must have one of the highest concentrations of demonstrably masterful artisans in the country, and you can see the proof of this by perusing the membership list of the PTMTA:

Port Townsend Marine Trades Association
http://www.ptmta.org/.

HAYN ENTERPRISES

Norseman and Sta-Lok are the established names in the mechanical-wire-terminals market. Over the years there have been numerous attempts to compete with them, but no one made any headway until Hayn introduced their Hi-Mod fittings. It was no easy task, as all the failed brands left riggers skeptical. I remember first hearing about Hi-Mod's and thinking, "Oh, here's another short-lived attempt."

But then I took a look at some independent destruction test and metallurgy reports, and saw that this terminal had a claim to reasonable efficiency (about equal to Sta-Lok, and much better than Norseman). And then I tried one, and saw that it was significantly easier to assemble correctly than the competition. Prettier, too. But what really convinced me was when I ordered a bunch for a large-ish job, and got thrown into a very expensive delay when some of the components did not fit the wire. No, that wasn't a positive experience, but having the owner of the company fly out from the East Coast to apologize, that was a very positive experience indeed. Great design is all well and good; great service is a gift beyond measure.

Hayn Enterprises, LLC
http://hayn.com/
sales@hayn.com
800-346-4296

SCHAEFER AND HARKEN

I am listing these two together because they are both domestic U.S. companies, both providers of blocks and furlers, and both characterized by good, carefully-made gear, and competent, friendly service. They each have their strengths and weaknesses—I tend to prefer Schaefer's furlers and Harken's blocks—but they are alike in being straightforward, glad to take time to explain things, quick to rectify mistakes, and they are even kind when describing the competition's products.

The point here is not just that I am recommending Schaefer and Harken, but that I am holding them up as models of how I think good companies should act. If your supplier bad-mouths the competition, or reflexively blames you if something is not right, or makes excuses about issues, find another brand, one you can trust, and enjoy working with.

Schaefer email: through contact page on web site: schaefermarine.com

Schaefer Marine
http://www.schaefermarine.com/
508-995-9511

Harken
http://www.harken.com/
262-691-3320

NEW ENGLAND ROPES

I have had the pleasure of working with some very, very good ropemakers over the decades. Samson, the biggest, and probably the best-known, is not content to rest on its laurels, and continues to make significant contributions to rope technology. Likewise Yale and Marlow have their own stables of talented rope geeks, who keep coming up with remarkable uses for old as well as new fibers and constructions. But here I would like to single out New England Ropes, for their combination of consistency, meaningful R&D, and what I can only describe as exaggeratedly generous customer service. They recently became part of Teufelberger Fiber Rope, a German company. As near as I can tell, the change has simply added Teutonic obsession with quality control.

Here is an emblematic story about New England Ropes: Early on, I noted that their ropes tended to be harder to splice than the competition's. When I commented on this, their lead technician said something like, "Yeah, we know, and a lot of riggers buy other rope that is easier to splice. But we think somewhat higher splicing effort is a reasonable price to pay for rope that is tougher and/or stronger." That's right, they risked alienating some of the people who buy the most rope, because they want to make a better rope.

New England Ropes
http://www.teufelberger.com/en/products/ marine/new-england-ropes.html
508-678-8200

PORT TOWNSEND FOUNDRY

Even production yachts can involve a lot of custom items. If you have broken a no-longer-produced bit of crucial hardware, or you'd like to make the odd upgrade, or if you'd simply like to have a lovely, well-engineered bit of bronze hardware to replace a piece of stamped-out trash, get in touch with the folks at PTF.

Port Townsend Foundry
http://porttownsendfoundry.com/
360-385-6425

SPARTALK

This is the forum on our web site for consultation questions that are too short to charge for. Most of the posts there concern details of rigging procedures, but if you are looking for an obscure part, or a rigger in your part of the world, or a tool that we don't carry in our catalog, Spartalk is the place for you.

http://www.briontoss.com/spartalk/forumdisplay. php?f=1

The Good Luck Knot (back view): See page 344 for an explanation.

Index